STREE

Wiltshire

and Swindon

www.philips-maps.co.uk

Philip's, a division of
Octopus Publishing Group Ltd
www.octopusbooks.co.uk
2-4 Heron Quays, London E14 4JP
An Hachette Livre UK Company

Second edition 2006
Second impression 2008
WILBA

ISBN-10   0-540-08771-8 (pocket)
ISBN-13   978-0-540-08771-6 (pocket)

© Philip's 2006

Ordnance Survey®

This product includes mapping data licensed from
Ordnance Survey® with the permission of the
Controller of Her Majesty's Stationery Office.
© Crown copyright 2006. All rights reserved.
Licence number 100011710.

Contents

III	**Key to map symbols**
IV	**Key to map pages**
VI	**Route planning**
X	**Administrative and Postcode boundaries**

1	**Street maps** at 2⅔ inches to 1 mile
163	**Street maps** at 1⅓ inches to 1 mile
213	**Street maps** at 2⅔ inches to 1 mile
218	**Town maps** of Andover and Frome

| 219 | **Index** of towns and villages |
| 222 | **Index** of streets, hospitals, industrial estates, railway stations, schools, shopping centres, universities and places of interest |

Digital Data

The exceptionally high-quality mapping found in this atlas is available as digital data in TIFF format, which is easily convertible to other bitmapped (raster) image formats.

The index is also available in digital form as a standard database table. It contains all the details found in the printed index together with the National Grid reference for the map square in which each entry is named.

For further information and to discuss your requirements, please contact james.mann@philips-maps.co.uk

	Motorway with junction number
	Primary route – dual/single carriageway
	A road – dual/single carriageway
	B road – dual/single carriageway
	Minor road – dual/single carriageway
	Other minor road – dual/single carriageway
	Road under construction
	Tunnel, covered road
	Rural track, private road or narrow road in urban area
	Gate or obstruction to traffic (restrictions may not apply at all times or to all vehicles)
	Path, bridleway, byway open to all traffic, road used as a public path
	Pedestrianised area
DY7	Postcode boundaries
	County and unitary authority boundaries
	Railway, tunnel, railway under construction
	Tramway, tramway under construction
	Miniature railway
Walsall	Railway station
	Private railway station
South Shields	Metro station
	Tram stop, tram stop under construction
	Bus, coach station

◆	Ambulance station
◆	Coastguard station
◆	Fire station
◆	Police station
✚	Accident and Emergency entrance to hospital
H	Hospital
+	Place of worship
i	Information Centre (open all year)
🛒	Shopping Centre
P P&R	Parking, Park and Ride
PO	Post Office
Ⅹ	Camping site
🚐	Caravan site
►	Golf course
⋈	Picnic site
Prim Sch	Important buildings, schools, colleges, universities and hospitals
	Built up area
	Woods
River Ouse	Tidal water, water name
	Non-tidal water – lake, river, canal or stream
⟨ ⊢ ∘⊂	Lock, weir, tunnel
Church	Non-Roman antiquity
ROMAN FORT	Roman antiquity
67	Adjoining page indicators and overlap bands
168	The colour of the arrow and the band indicates the scale of the adjoining or overlapping page (see scales below)

Abbr	Full	Abbr	Full	Abbr	Full
Acad	Academy	Inst	Institute	Recn Gd	Recreation
Allot Gdns	Allotments	Ct	Law Court		Ground
Cemy	Cemetery	L Ctr	Leisure Centre	Resr	Reservoir
C Ctr	Civic Centre	LC	Level Crossing	Ret Pk	Retail Park
CH	Club House	Liby	Library	Sch	School
Coll	College	Mkt	Market	Sh Ctr	Shopping Centre
Crem	Crematorium	Meml	Memorial	TH	Town Hall/House
Ent	Enterprise	Mon	Monument	Trad Est	Trading Estate
Ex H	Exhibition Hall	Mus	Museum	Univ	University
Ind Est	Industrial Estate	Obsy	Observatory	W Twr	Water Tower
IRB Sta	Inshore Rescue	Pal	Royal Palace	Wks	Works
	Boat Station	PH	Public House	YH	Youth Hostel

■ The small numbers around the edges of the maps identify the 1 kilometre National Grid lines

■ The dark grey border on the inside edge of some pages indicates that the mapping does not continue onto the adjacent page

The scale of the maps on the pages numbered in blue is 4.2 cm to 1 km • 2⅔ inches to 1 mile • 1: 23810

0 — ¼ — ½ — ¾ — 1 mile
0 — 250m — 500m — 750m — 1 kilometre

The scale of the maps on pages numbered in green is 2.1 cm to 1 km • 1⅓ inches to 1 mile • 1: 47620

0 — ¼ — ½ — ¾ — 1 mile
0 — 250m 500m 750m — 1 kilometre

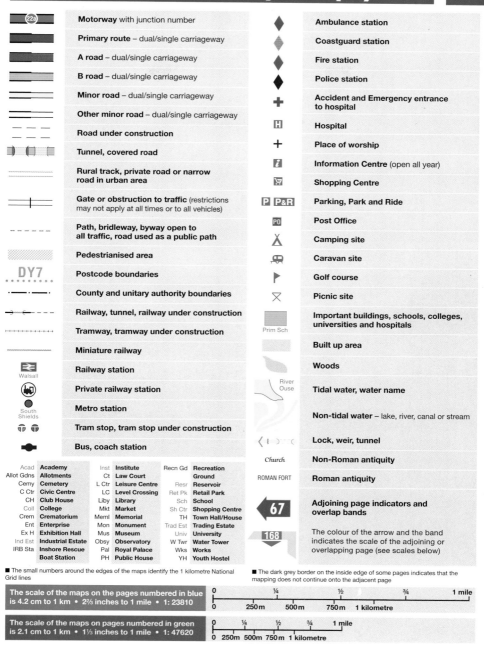

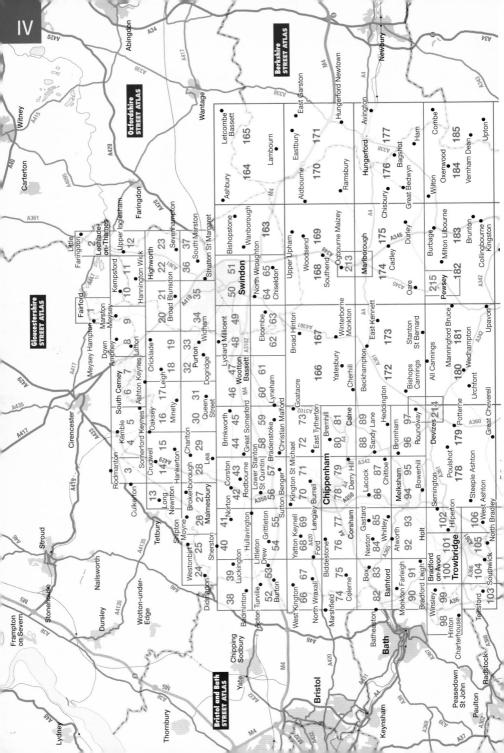

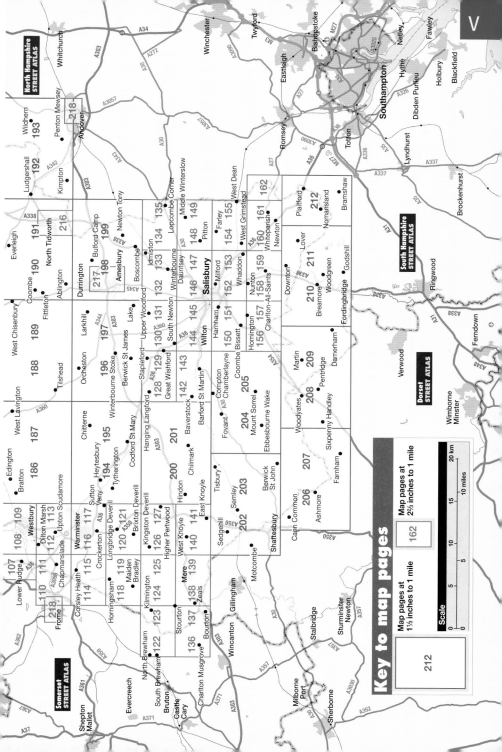

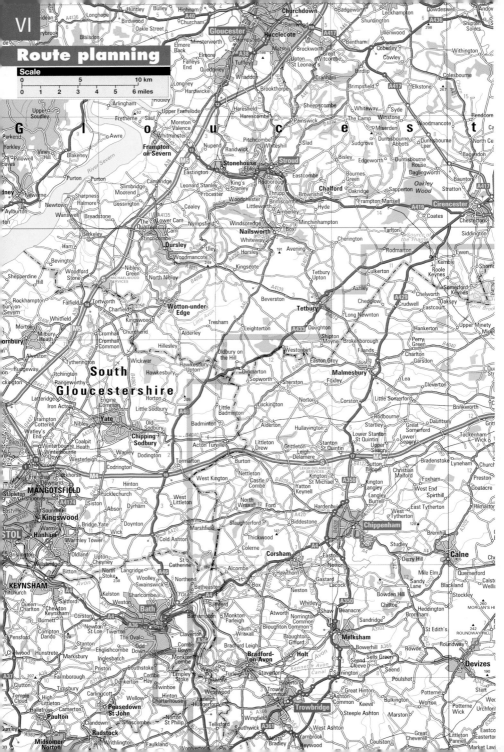

Route planning

Scale

0   5   10 km
0 1 2 3 4 5   6 miles

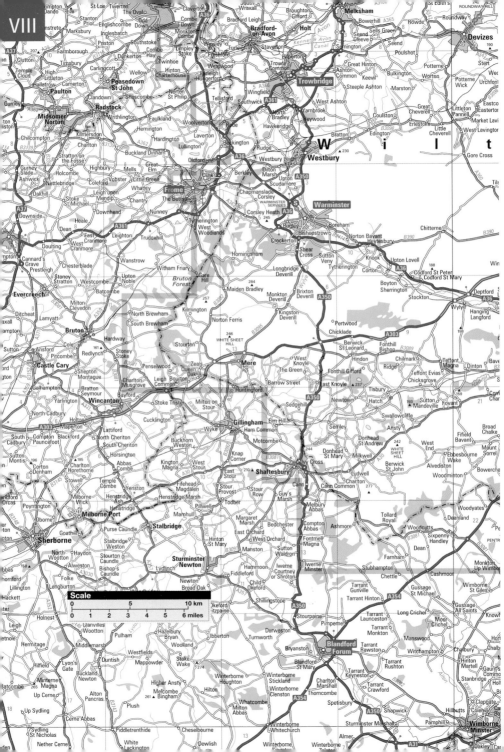

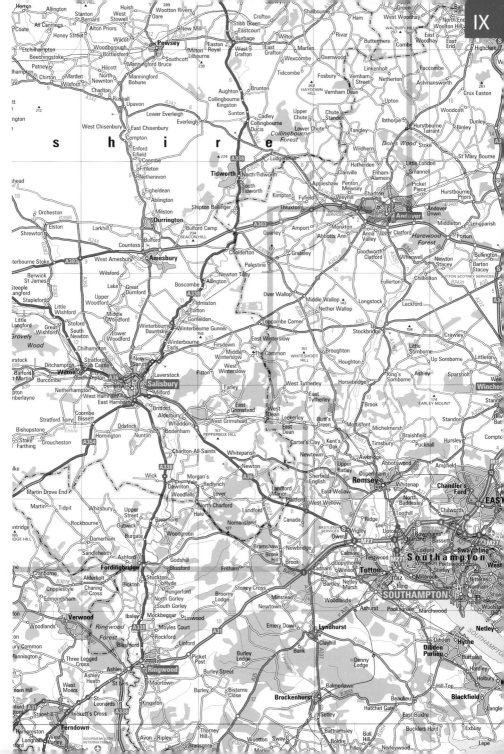

X

Administrative and Postcode boundaries

	County and unitary authority boundaries
	District boundaries
	Postcode boundaries
	Area covered by this atlas

Scale

0 5 10 15 20 25 30km

0 5 10 15 20 miles

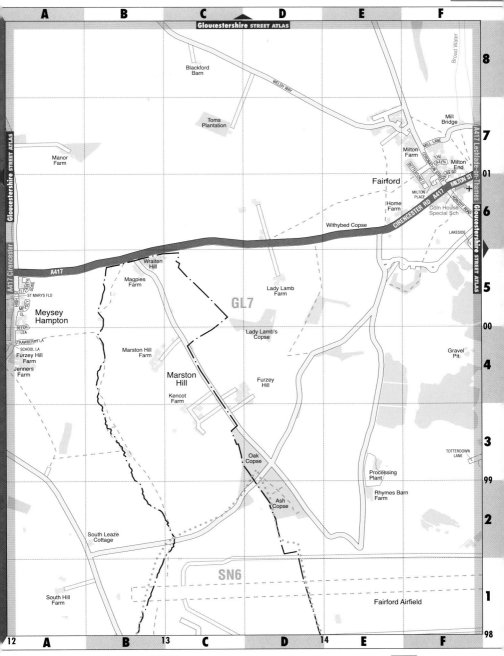

8

Blackford
Barn

WELSH WAY

Toms
Plantation

Mill
Bridge

Milton
Farm

THE
GREEN

Milton
End

7

01

Manor
Farm

Gloucestershire STREET ATLAS

A417 Cirencester

Fairford

Home
Farm

Coln House
Special Sch

CIRENCESTER RD A417

A417 Lechlade-on-Thames

MILTON ST

Gloucestershire STREET ATLAS

Withybed Copse

LAKESIDE

6

A417

Wraiten
Hill

Lady Lamb
Farm

GL7

5

00

ST MARYS FLD

Magpies
Farm

Meysey
Hampton

STRAWBERRY LA

SCHOOL LA

Furzey Hill
Farm

Jenners
Farm

Marston Hill
Farm

Lady Lamb's
Copse

Gravel
Pit

4

Marston
Hill

Kencot
Farm

Furzey
Hill

TOTTERDOWN
LANE

3

Oak
Copse

Processing
Plant

99

Rhymes Barn
Farm

Ash
Copse

2

South Leaze
Cottage

SN6

South Hill
Farm

Fairford Airfield

1

98

12

A

B

13

C

D

14

E

F

9

10

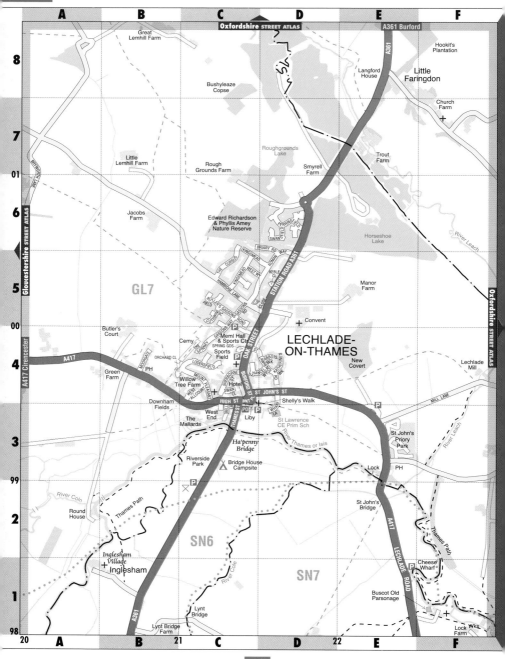

A361 Burford

Great
Lemhill Farm

Hookit's
Plantation

Langford
House

Little
Faringdon

Bushyleaze
Copse

Church
Farm

Roughgrounds
Lake

Little
Lemhill Farm

Rough
Grounds Farm

Smyrell
Farm

Trout
Farm

Jacobs
Farm

Edward Richardson
& Phyllis Amey
Nature Reserve

Horseshoe
Lake

River Leach

GL7

Manor
Farm

Butler's
Court

Convent

LECHLADE-
ON-THAMES

Lechlade
Mill

Meml Hall
& Sports Ctr

Cemy

Green
Farm

Sports
Field

New
Covert

Willow
Tree Farm

Hotel

Downham
Fields

HIGH ST

ST JOHN'S ST

St John's
Priory
Park

River Leach

West
End

The
Mallards

Liby

Shelly's Walk

St Lawrence
CE Prim Sch

Ha'penny
Bridge

River Thames or Isis

Lock

PH

Riverside
Park

Bridge House
Campsite

River Coln

Round
House

Thames Path

St John's
Bridge

Inglesham
Village

Inglesham

SN6

SN7

River Cole

Cheese
Wharf

Buscot Old
Parsonage

Lynt
Bridge

Lynt Bridge
Farm

Lock Wks
Farm

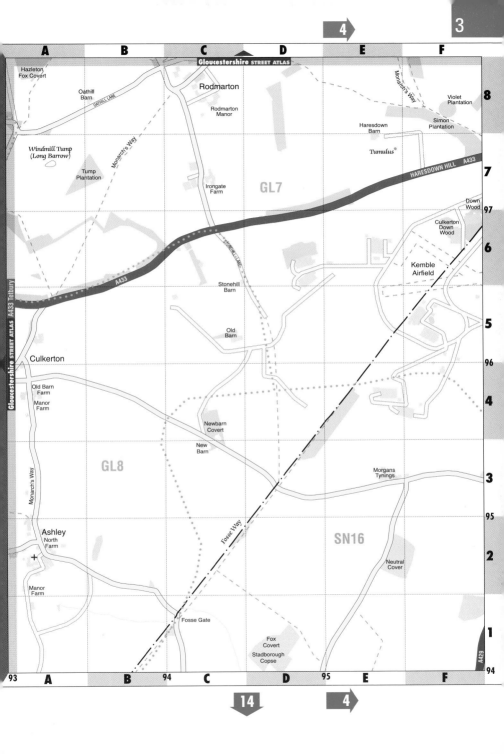

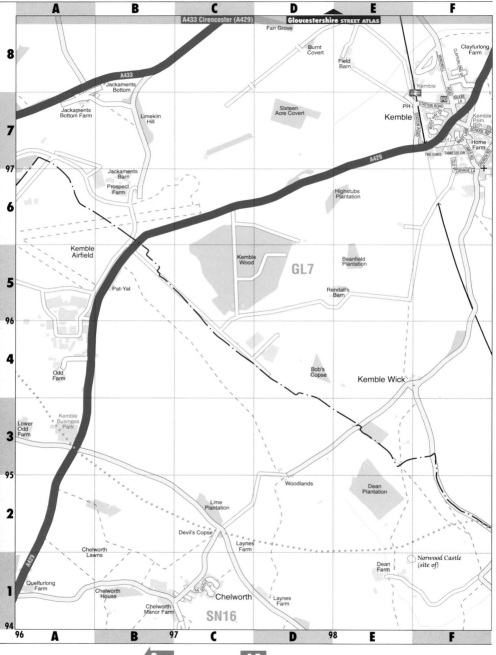

A433 Cirencester (A429)

Fan Grove

Burnt
Covert

Field
Barn

Clayfurlong
Farm

A433

Jackaments
Bottom

Kemble

STATION ROAD

GLEBE
LA

Jackaments
Bottom Farm

Limekiln
Hill

Sixteen
Acre Covert

PH

Kemble

Kemble
Prim
Sch

SCHOOL RD

97

Jackaments
Barn

A429

Home
Farm

Prospect
Farm

Highstubs
Plantation

THE OAKS

TAMESIS DR

OLD RD

LINES RD

GARAGE LA

6

Kemble
Airfield

Kemble
Wood

Beanfield
Plantation

GL7

5

Pat-Yat

Rendall's
Barn

96

Odd
Farm

Bob's
Copse

Kemble Wick

4

Lower
Odd
Farm

Kemble
Business
Park

3

Woodlands

Dean
Plantation

95

Lime
Plantation

2

Devil's Copse

Laynes
Farm

Chelworth
Lawns

Dean
Farm

○ *Norwood Castle
(site of)*

Quelfurlong
Farm

Chelworth
House

Chelworth
Manor Farm

THE BRIDGE

Chelworth

Laynes
Farm

1

SN16

94

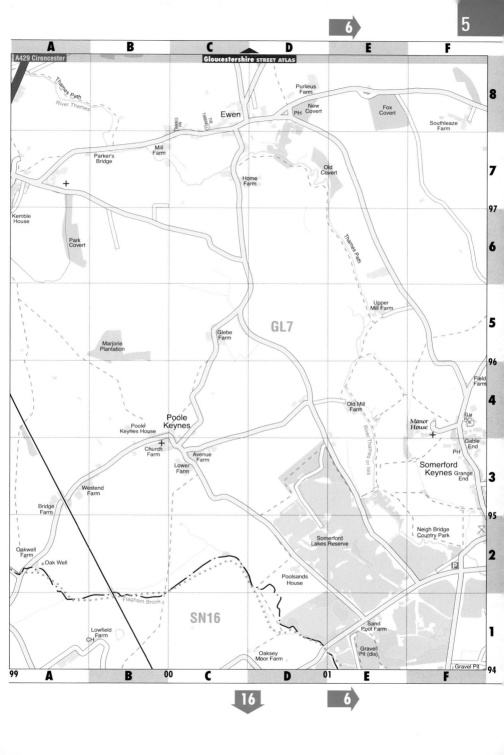

A B C D E F

8

Thames Path
River Thames

Ewen

Purlieus Farm

New Covert

PH

Fox Covert

Southleaze Farm

Mill Farm

Parker's Bridge

Home Farm

Old Covert

7

Kemble House

97

Thames Path

Park Covert

6

Marjorie Plantation

Glebe Farm

GL7

Upper Mill Farm

5

96

Field Farm

4

Old Mill Farm

Poole Keynes

Poole Keynes House

Manor House

ELM VIC

Church Farm

Avenue Farm

Gable End

PH

Lower Farm

River Thames or Isis

Somerford Keynes

Grange End

3

Westend Farm

95

Bridge Farm

Oakwell Farm

Neigh Bridge Country Park

Oak Well

2

P

Flagham Brook

SN16

Poolsands House

Somerford Lakes Reserve

Lowfield Farm

CH

Oaksey Moor Farm

Sand Pool Farm

Gravel Pit (dis)

1

Gravel Pit

Gloucestershire STREET ATLAS

A B C D E F

8

Dryleaze Covert

Hillview Farm
Camperdown
Castle
Berry Farm

Ash Copse

PH
SILVER STREET
SCHOOL LA
CHURCH LA
PO

7

Gravel Pit

Sewage Works

Cross Roads Farm

RIVER WAY
MEADOW WAY
LANGET
LANGET
HIGH STREET

97

Upper Up

Langet End

PH
BERKELEY CL
SUDELEY WY
THE LEAZE

6

Shorncote

Manor Farm
Glebe Farm
Old Manor Farm

GL7

Downs Farm

Ann Edwards
CE Prim Sch

Refuse/Slag Heap

5

P
X

Keynes Country Park

Ashton Down

Sewage Works

96

P
X

Millennium Visitor Centre

Cotswold Community

Cotswold Water Park

Yacht Club

4

Works

WHITEWALLS LANE

SPRATSGATE LANE

3

Bag End

Macks Farm

SPINE ROAD WEST

SPINE ROAD WEST

North End Farm

North End

Clayhill Copse

95

SN6

2

Mill End

Furze Brake

Bell Copse

Manor Farm

Old Manor Farm

B4696
COX'S HILL

Ring and Bailey

Ashton Keynes

PH
BACK STREET
PO

1

Lower Mill Farm

Thames Path

Church Farm

Moat

Manor House

CHURCH WK
HIGH ROAD
RICHMO
PARK
FORE STREET
LASTFIELD

94

Gravel Pit

Freeth's Wood

02 A B 03 C D 04 E F

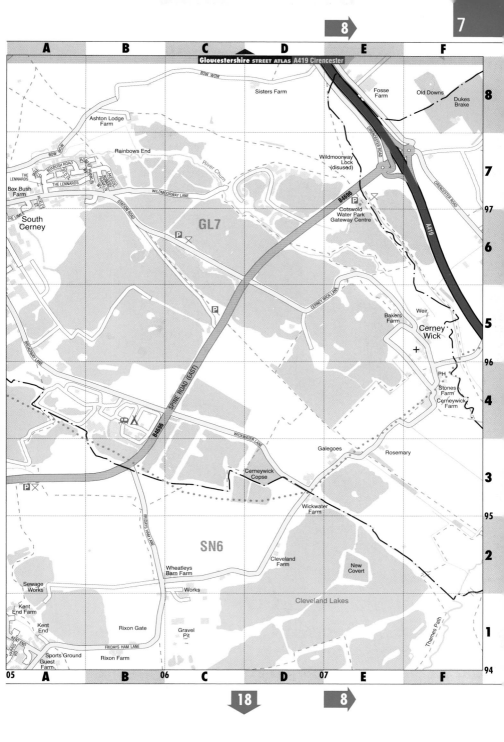

A B C D E F

8
7
97
6
5
96
4
3
95
2
1
94

05 A B 06 C D 07 E F

BOW WOW

Sisters Farm

Fosse Farm

Old Downs

Dukes Brake

Ashton Lodge Farm

Rainbows End

River Churn

Wildmoorway Lock (disused)

CIRENCESTER ROAD

CIRENCESTER ROAD

THE LENNARDS

BOXBUSH ROAD

ROAD OF FRANKLIN

LANGFORD

WILDMOORWAY LANE

THE LENNARDS

Box Bush Farm

THE LIMES

STAITHE ROAD

B4696

Cotswold Water Park Gateway Centre

A419

South Cerney

GL7

P

P

CERNEY WICK LANE

Bakers Farm

Weir

Cerney Wick

P

SPINE ROAD (EAST)

Stones Farm

PH

BROADWAY LANE

B4696

WICKWATER LANE

Cerneywick Farm

Galegoes

Rosemary

P

Cerneywick Copse

Wickwater Farm

SN6

FRIDAYS HAM LANE

Cleveland Farm

New Covert

Sewage Works

Wheatleys Barn Farm

Works

Cleveland Lakes

Kent End Farm

Kent End

Rixon Gate

Gravel Pit

Thames Path

KENT END

HARDS RD

Sports Ground

Guest Farm

Rixon Farm

FRIDAYS HAM LANE

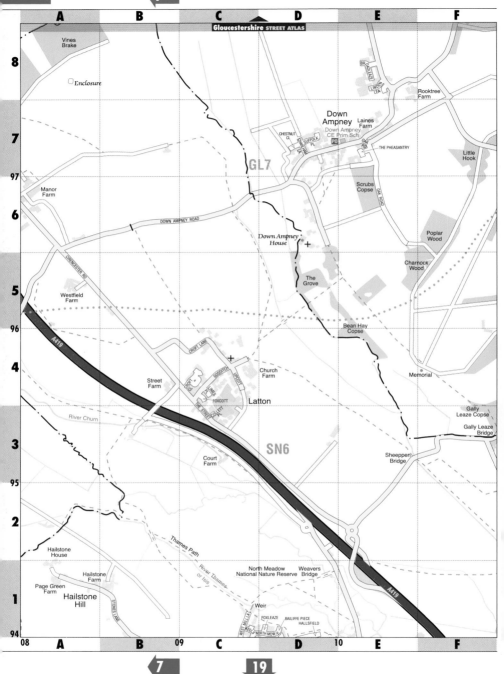

A   B   C   D   E   F

8

Vines
Brake

○ Enclosure

Rooktree
Farm

BRICKLEAZE

LINES
LEA

7

Down
Ampney

Laines
Farm

CHESTNUT

SUFFOLK
PL

Down Ampney
CE Prim Sch

GL7

PO

THE PHEASANTRY

Little
Hook

97

Manor
Farm

Scrubs
Copse

OAK ROAD

6

DOWN AMPNEY ROAD

Poplar
Wood

Down Ampney
House

+

Charnock
Wood

5

CIRENCESTER RD

Westfield
Farm

The
Grove

96

A419

Bean Hay
Copse

Memorial

4

Street
Farm

CROFT LANE

GOSDITCH

Church
Farm

CROFT

+

THE STREET

FOXCOTT

ISIS
MEWS

Latton

Gally
Leaze Copse

Gally Leaze
Bridge

River Churn

Sheeppen
Bridge

3

SN6

Court
Farm

95

2

Hailstone
House

Thames Path

River Thames
or Isis

North Meadow
National Nature Reserve

Weavers
Bridge

A419

Hailstone
Farm

STONES LANE

Page Green
Farm

Hailstone
Hill

1

Weir

FOXLEAZE

BAILIFFE PIECE
HALLSFIELD

WEST MILL LA

NORTH MDW RD

KEEP

94

08   A   B   09   C   D   10   E   F

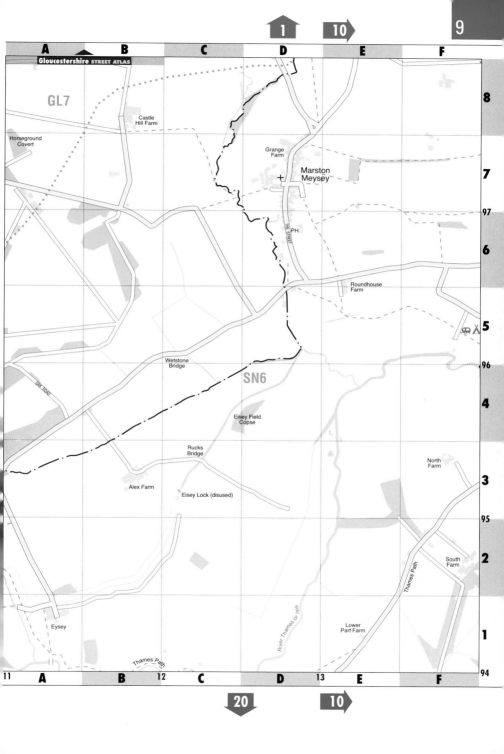

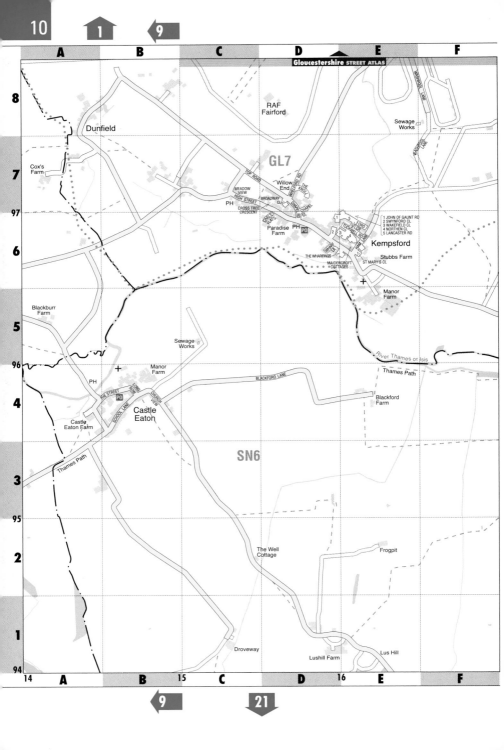

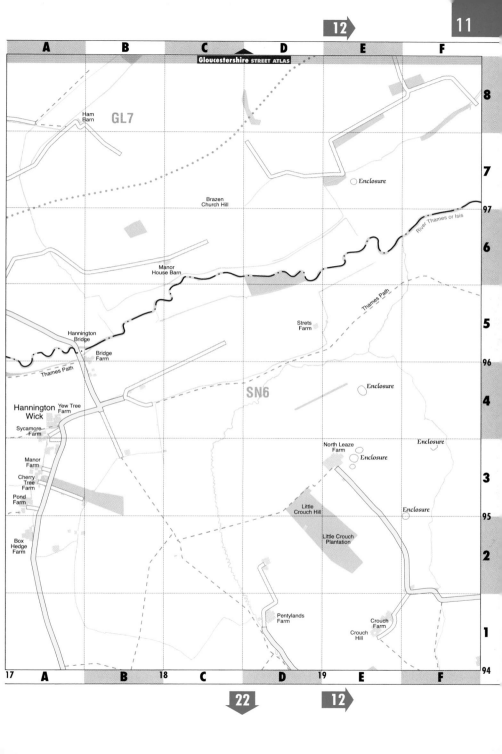

A **B** **C** **D** **E** **F**

Gloucestershire STREET ATLAS

8

GL7

Ham
Barn

7

Enclosure

Brazen
Church Hill

97

River Thames or Isis

6

Manor
House Barn

Thames Path

Strets
Farm

5

Hannington
Bridge

96

Bridge
Farm

Thames Path

SN6

4

Enclosure

Hannington
Wick

Yew Tree
Farm

Sycamore
Farm

Enclosure

Manor
Farm

North Leaze
Farm

Enclosure

3

Cherry
Tree
Farm

Enclosure

Pond
Farm

Little
Crouch Hill

Enclosure

95

Box
Hedge
Farm

Little Crouch
Plantation

2

Pentylands
Farm

Crouch
Farm

1

Crouch
Hill

94

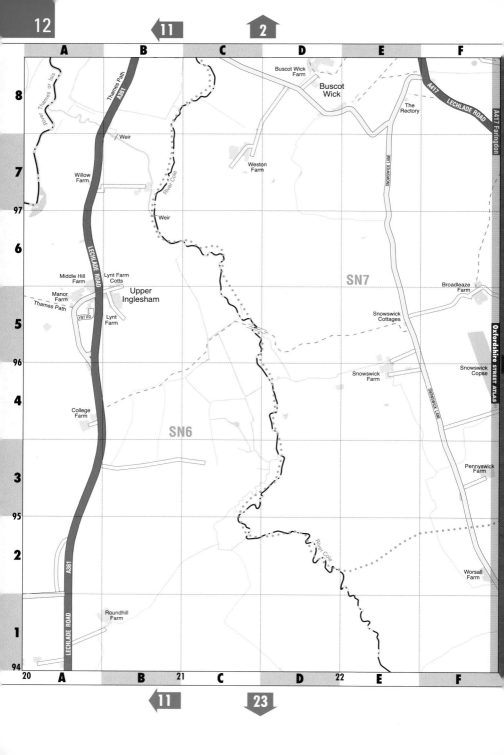

| A | B | C | D | E | F |

8

River Thames or Isis

Thames Path

A361

Weir

Buscot Wick Farm

Buscot Wick

A417 LECHLADE ROAD

A417 Faringdon

The Rectory

7

Willow Farm

River Cole

Weston Farm

97

Weir

SNOWSWICK LANE

6

Weir

SN7

Middle Hill Farm

Lynt Farm Cotts

Upper Inglesham

Broadleaze Farm

Manor Farm

Thames Path

LECHLADE ROAD

Snowswick Cottages

Oxfordshire STREET ATLAS

5

LYNT RD

Lynt Farm

Snowswick Copse

96

Snowswick Farm

SNOWSWICK LANE

4

College Farm

SN6

3

Pennyswick Farm

95

River Cole

2

A361

Worsall Farm

1

Roundhill Farm

LECHLADE ROAD

94

| 20 | A | B | 21 | C | D | 22 | E | F |

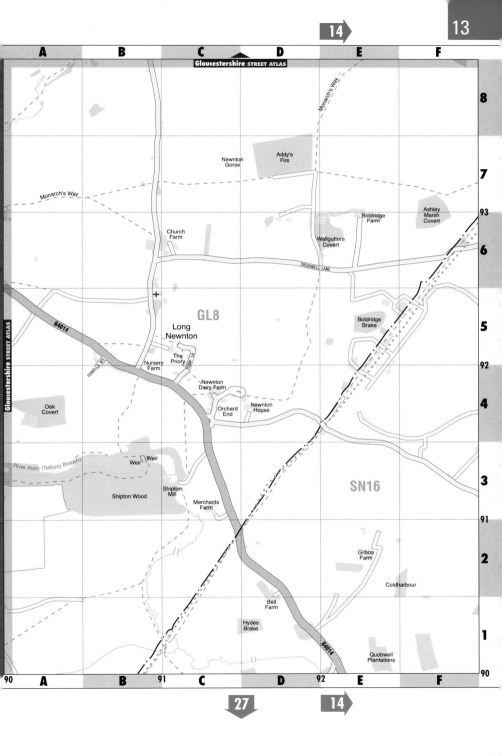

Gloucestershire STREET ATLAS

Gloucestershire STREET ATLAS

Monarch's Way

Monarch's Way

Newnton
Gorse

Addy's
Firs

Boldridge
Farm

Ashley
Marsh
Covert

Church
Farm

Wallgutters
Covert

CRUDWELL LANE

GL8

B4014

Long
Newnton

Boldridge
Brake

POWELLS WY

The
Priory

PRIORY LA

Nursery
Farm

Newnton
Dairy Farm

Orchard
End

Newnton
House

Oak
Covert

River Avon (Tetbury Branch)

Weir Weir

Shipton
Mill

SN16

Shipton Wood

Merchants
Farm

Gilboa
Farm

Coldharbour

Bell
Farm

Hydes
Brake

B4014

Quobwell
Plantations

8
7
93
6
5
92
4
3
91
2
90
1

A   B   C   D   E   F

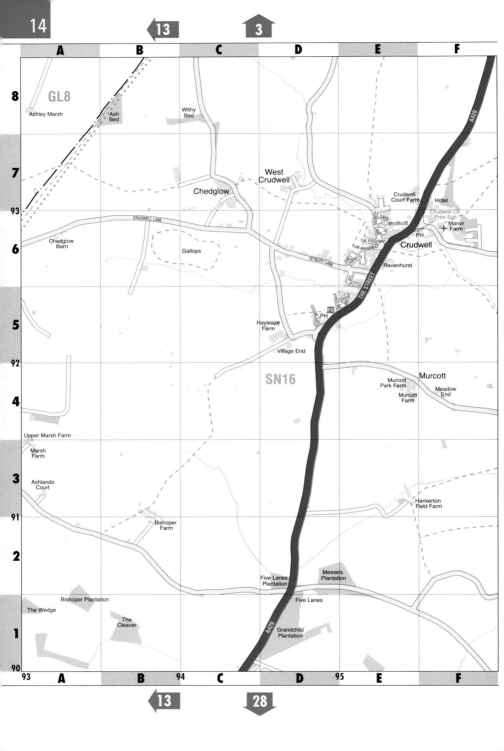

GL8

8

Ashley Marsh

Ash
Bed

Withy
Bed

West
Crudwell

7

Chedglow

Crudwell
Court Farm

Hotel

93

CRUDWELL LANE

TURNERS LANE

DAYS LA

BROOKSIDE

Crudwell CE
Prim Sch

Manor
Farm

Chedglow
Barn

6

Gallops

THE RIDGEWAY

PH

Crudwell

TETBURY LANE

THE RIDGEWAY

DOWNLEYS

Ravenhurst

THE STREET

KINGS MEAD

BUTTS

5

Hayleaze
Farm

GOSS LANES

PO

PH

Village End

92

SN16

Murcott

Murcott
Park Farm

Meadow
End

4

Murcott
Farm

Upper Marsh Farm

Marsh
Farm

3

Ashlands
Court

Hankerton
Field Farm

91

Bishoper
Farm

2

Five Lanes
Plantation

Messels
Plantation

Bishoper Plantation

The Wedge

Five Lanes

The
Cleaver

A429

1

Grandchild
Plantation

90

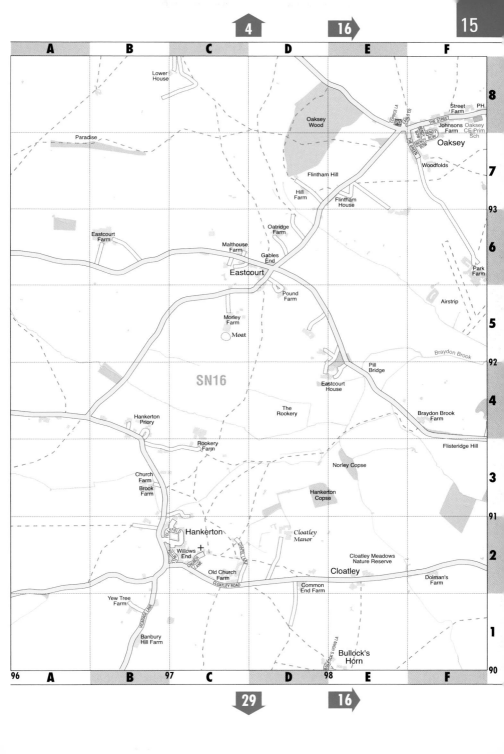

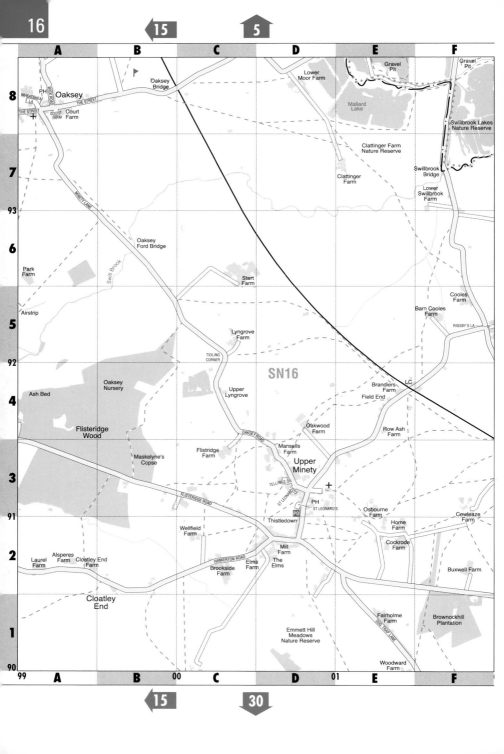

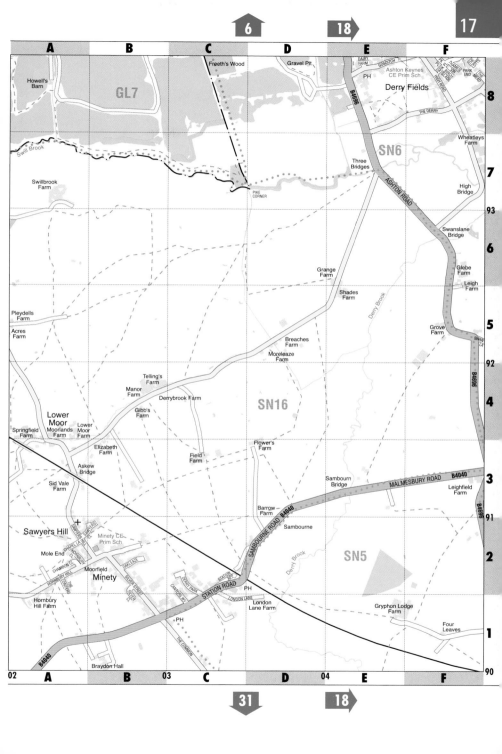

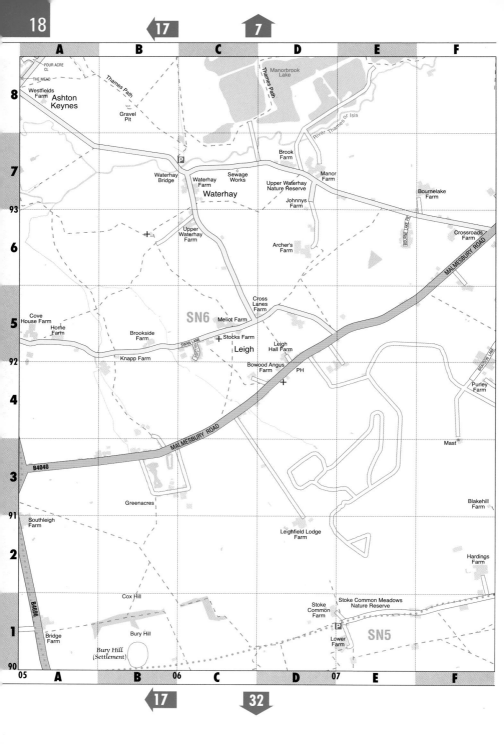

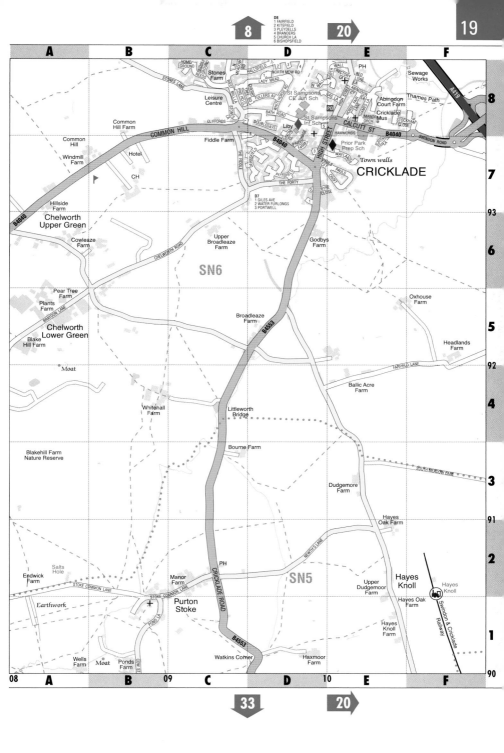

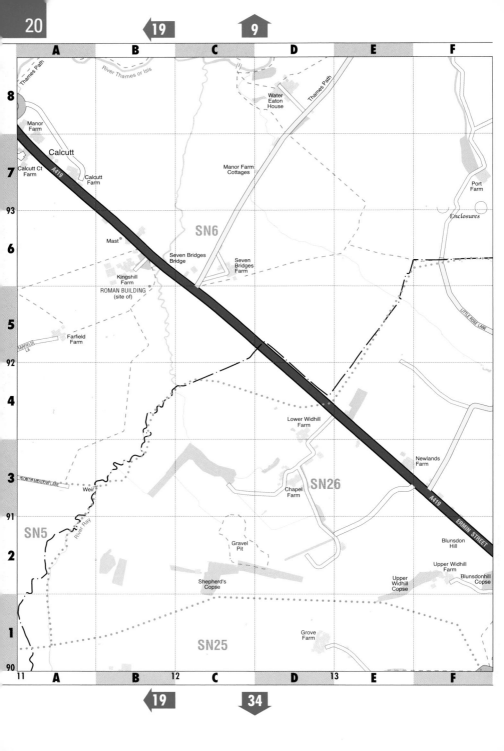

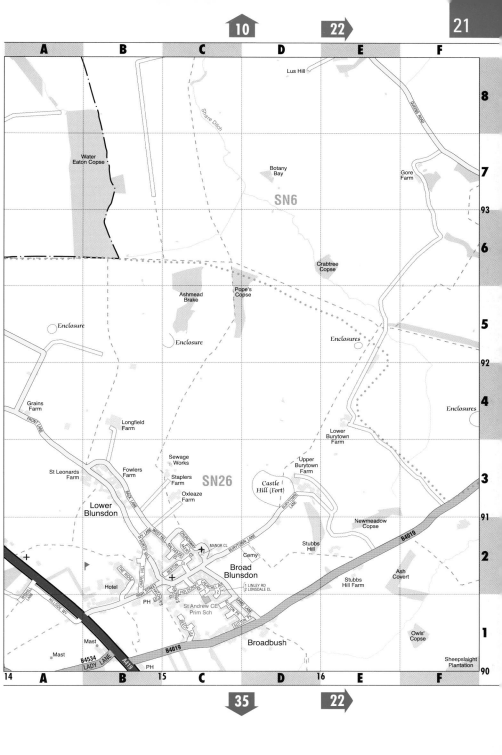

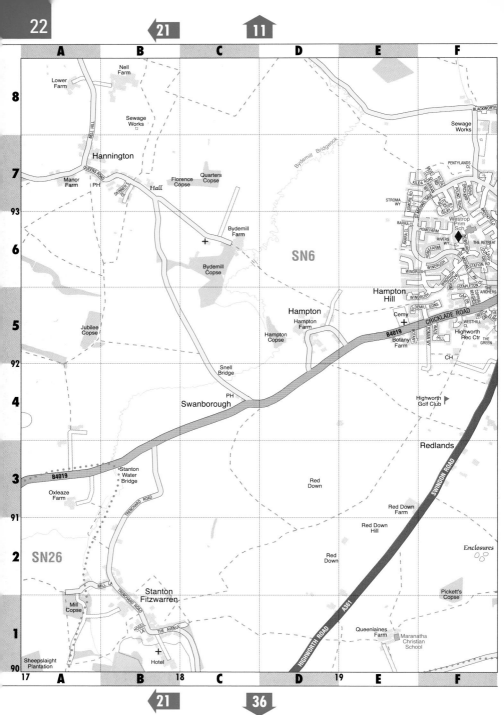

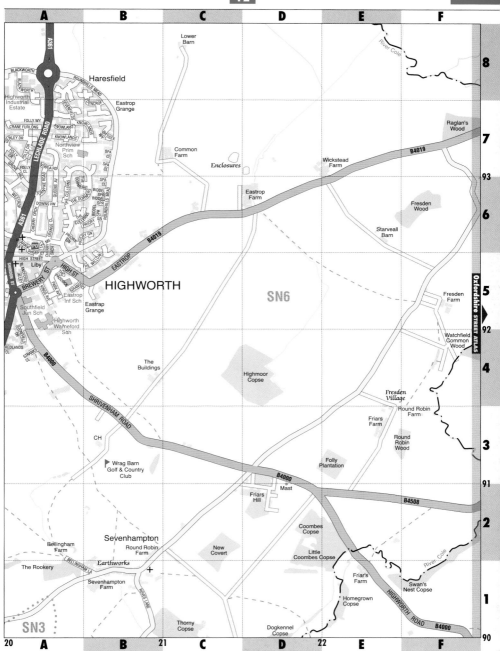

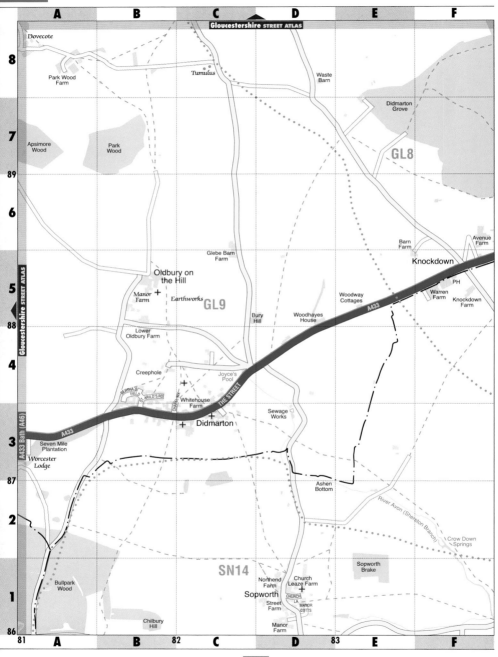

Dovecote

Park Wood Farm

Tumulus

Waste Barn

Didmarton Grove

Apsimore Wood

Park Wood

GL8

Glebe Barn Farm

Barn Farm

Avenue Farm

Oldbury on the Hill

Knockdown

Manor Farm

Earthworks

GL9

Bury Hill

Woodway Cottages

PH

Warren Farm

Knockdown Farm

Lower Oldbury Farm

Woodhayes House

A433

Creephole

Joyce's Pool

THE STREET

BERTHA'S FIELD

ARULD'S RD

CHAPEL WAY

Whitehouse Farm

Sewage Works

Didmarton

A433

Seven Mile Plantation

Worcester Lodge

Ashen Bottom

River Avon (Shereton Branch)

Crow Down Springs

Bullpark Wood

SN14

Northend Farm

Church Leaze Farm

Sopworth Brake

Sopworth

CHURCH

Street Farm

LA

MANOR COTTS

Chilbury Hill

Manor Farm

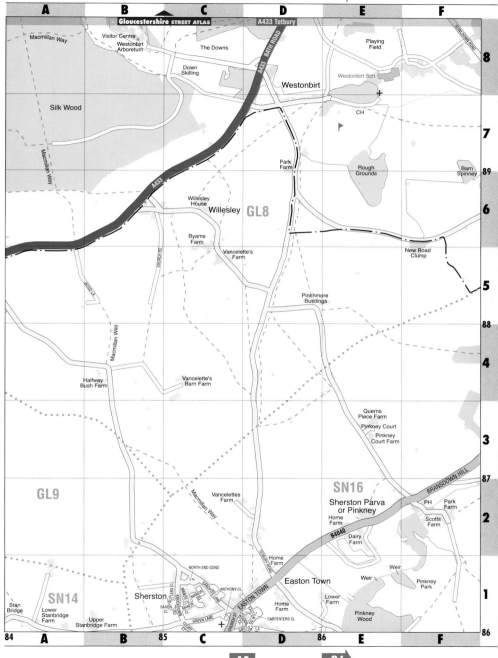

Gloucestershire STREET ATLAS

A433 Tetbury

A	B	C	D	E	F

Macmillan Way

Visitor Centre
Westonbirt
Arboretum

The Downs

Down
Skilling

Playing
Field

Westonbirt Sch

8

Silk Wood

Westonbirt

CH

7

Macmillan Way

A433

Park
Farm

Rough
Grounds

Barn
Spinney

89

Willesley
House

Willesley

GL8

New Road
Clump

6

CHURCH RD

Byams
Farm

Vancelette's
Farm

WOOD LA

Pinchmore
Buildings

5

88

Halfway
Bush Farm

Macmillan Way

Vancelette's
Barn Farm

4

Querns
Piece Farm

Pinkney Court

Pinkney
Court Farm

3

GL9

Macmillan Way

Vancelettes
Farm

SN16

Sherston Parva
or Pinkney

Home
Farm

BRANSDOWN HILL

PH

Park
Farm

Scotts
Farm

87

2

B4040

Dairy
Farm

TENBURY ROAD

Home
Farm

Weir

Weir

Pinkney
Park

Stan
Bridge

SN14

Lower
Stanbridge
Farm

Upper
Stanbridge Farm

NORTH END GDNS

ANTHONY CL

Sherston

SAXON
CL

MANOR
CL

SANDPITS LANE

GREEN LANE

CHURCH ST

EASTON TOWN

Easton Town

Home
Farm

CARPENTERS CL

Lower
Farm

Pinkney
Wood

1

86

A	B	C	D	E	F

84 · 85 · 86

40

26 →

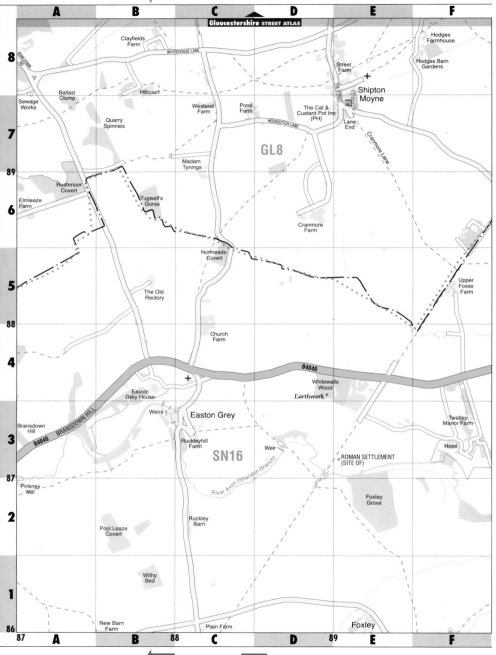

Gloucestershire STREET ATLAS

| | A | B | C | D | E | F |

8

Clayfields Farm

WHITEHOUSE LANE

Hodges Farmhouse

Street Farm

Hodges Barn Gardens

BOWLDOWN RD

Ballast Clump

Hillcourt

Hillcourt

Shipton Moyne

PO

7

Sewage Works

Quarry Spinnies

Westend Farm

Pond Farm

The Cat & Custard Pot Inn (PH)

Lane End

THE STREET

Cranmore Lane

HEDGEDITCH LANE

GL8

89

Madam Tynings

Rushmoor Covert

6

Elmleaze Farm

Tugwell's Gorse

Cranmore Farm

5

The Old Rectory

Normeads Covert

Upper Fosse Farm

88

Church Farm

B4040

4

Whitewalls Wood

Earthwork

Easton Grey House

Weirs

Easton Grey

3

Bransdown Hill

B4040

BRANSDOWN HILL

Ruckleyhill Farm

SN16

Weir

ROMAN SETTLEMENT (SITE OF)

Twatley Manor Farm

Hotel

87

Pinkney Mill

River Avon (Sherston Branch)

Foxley Grove

2

Pool Leaze Covert

Ruckley Barn

1

Withy Bed

86

New Barn Farm

Plain Farm

Foxley

| 87 | A | | B | 88 | C | | D | 89 | E | | F |

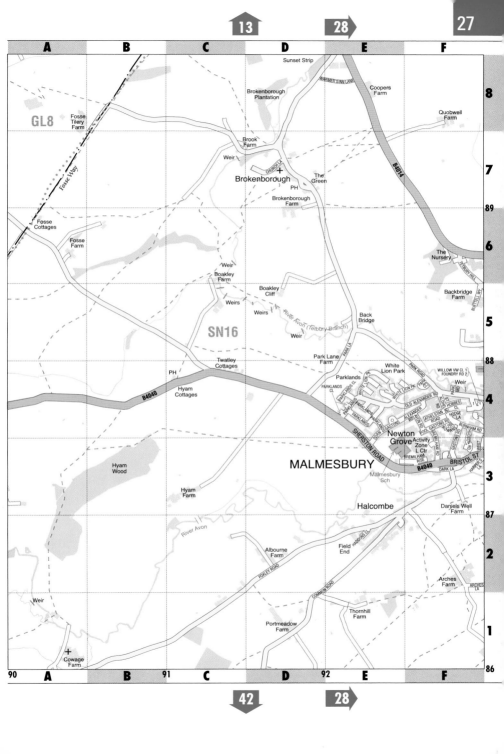

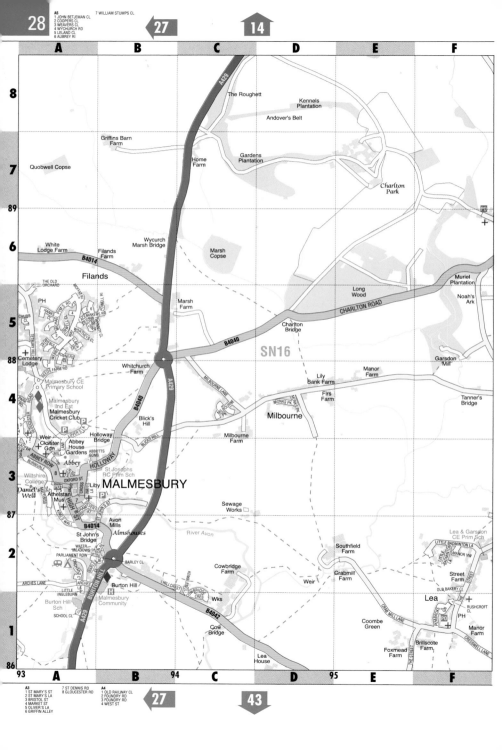

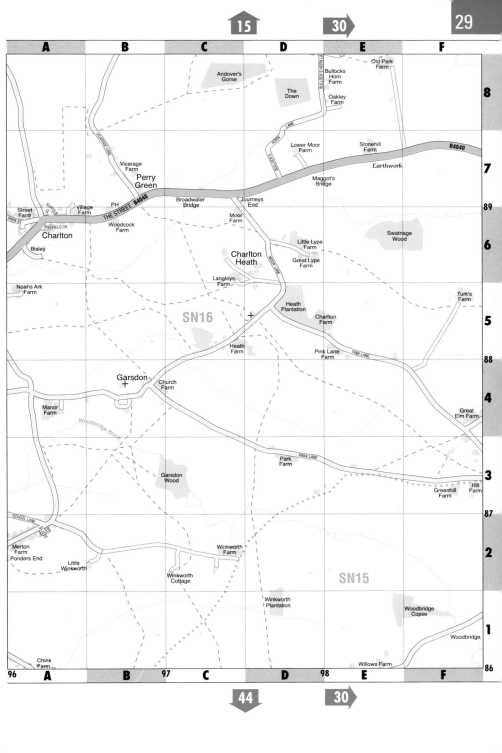

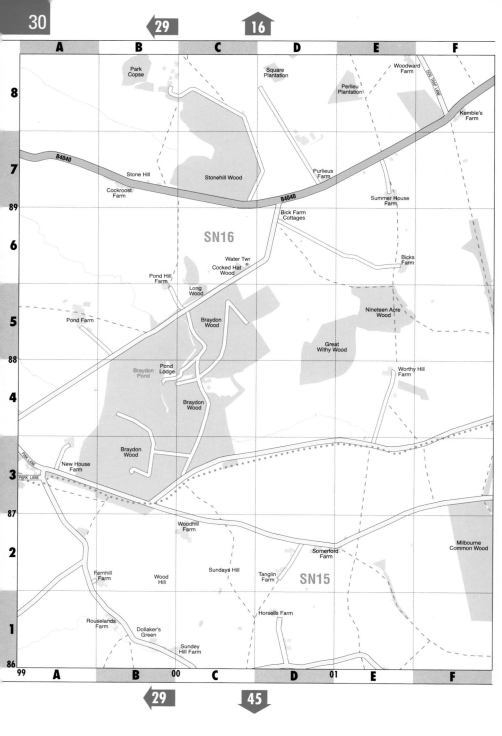

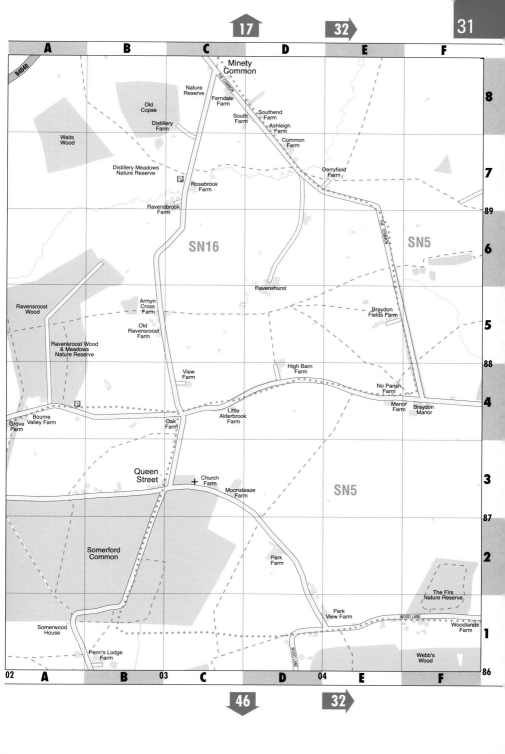

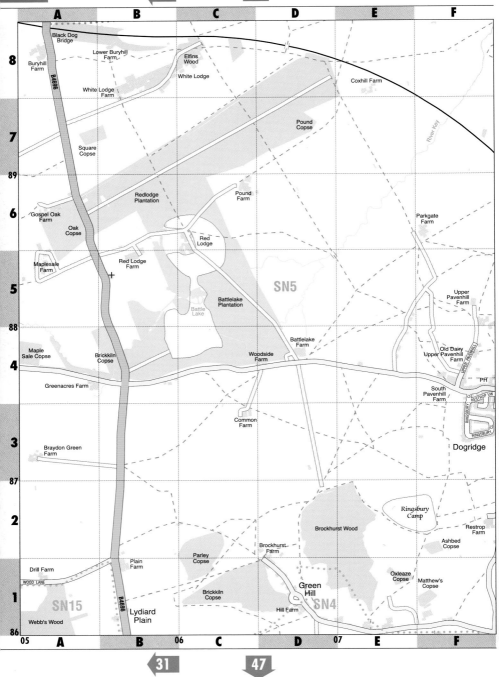

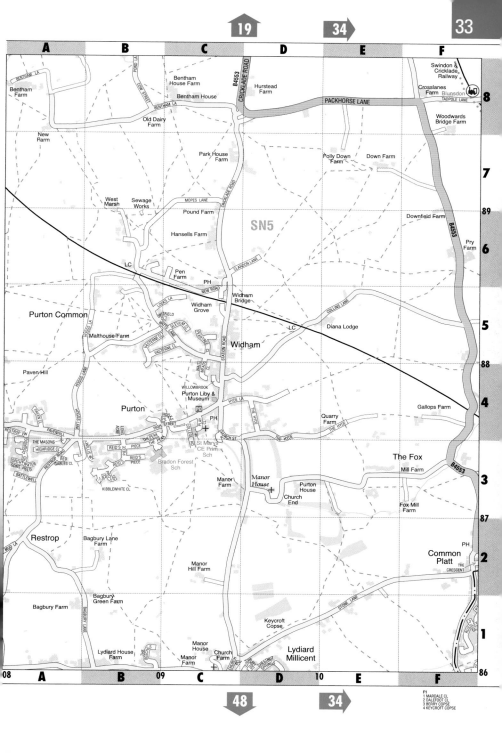

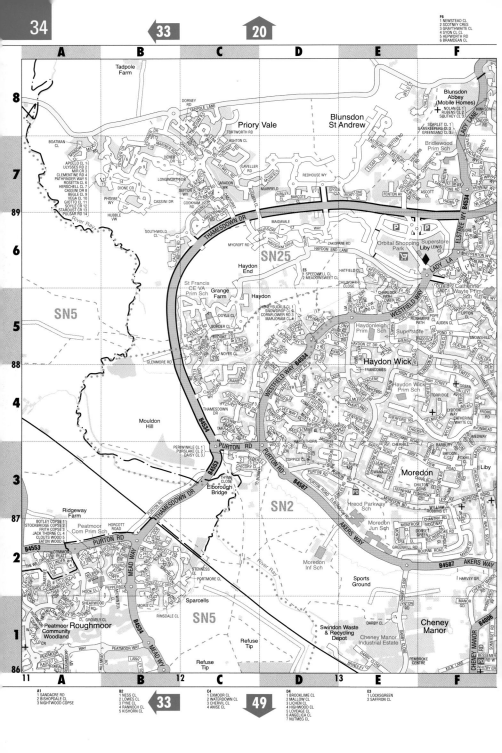

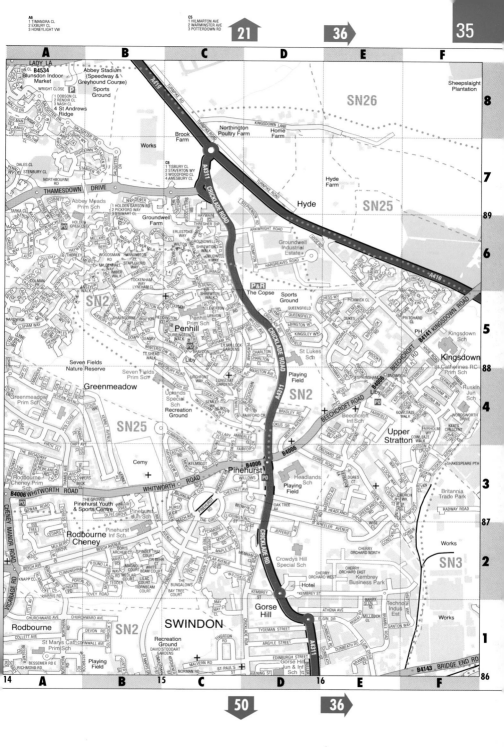

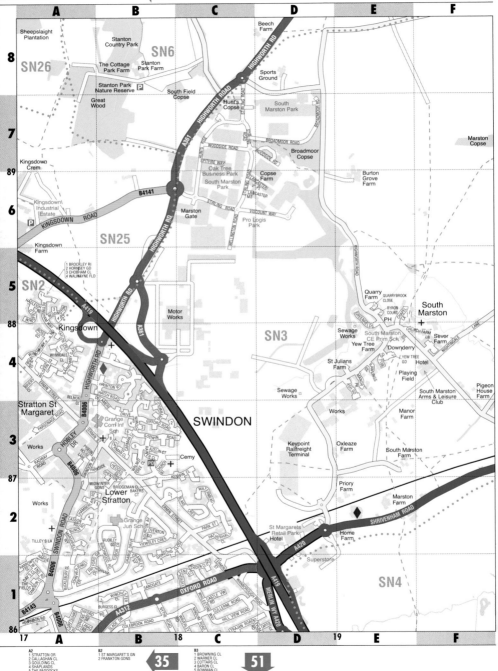

A   B   C   D   E   F

8
SN26
Sheepslaight Plantation
Stanton Country Park
SN6
The Cottage Park Farm
Stanton Park Farm
Stanton Park Nature Reserve
Great Wood
South Field Copse
Beech Farm
HIGHWORTH RD
Sports Ground
Hunt's Copse
South Marston Park

7
A361
Kingsdown Crem
WOODSIDE ROAD
Broadmoor Road
Broadmoor Copse
Marston Copse

89
Kingsdown Industrial Estate
B4141
KINGSDOWN ROAD
SPITFIRE WAY
Oak Tree Business Park
South Marston Park
Copse Farm
Burton Grove Farm

6
SN25
Kingsdown Farm
HIGHWORTH RD
STIRLING ROAD
Marston Gate
LANCASTER MS
VISCOUNT WAY
Pro Logis Park
HIGHWORTH ROAD

5
SN2
1 BROCKLEY RI
2 HORNSEY GD
3 CHOBHAM CL
4 WALWAYNE FLD
HIGHWORTH ROAD
Motor Works
Quarry Farm
QUARRYBROOK CLOSE
BYRON COURT
PH
South Marston

88
A361
Kingsdown
SN3
Sewage Works
South Marston CE Prim Sch
Yew Tree Farm
Downderry
CHURCH FARM
Sever Farm

4
WYNDALE
A419
HATCH ROAD
St Julians Farm
YEW TREE GD
Hotel
Playing Field
Pigeon House Farm

3
Stratton St Margaret
B4006
HOBLEY DR
BELMONT
Grange Corn Inf Sch
GIFFORD ROAD
GODWIN ROAD
SWINDON
Sewage Works
Works
Manor Farm
South Marston Arms & Leisure Club

Works
Cemy
Keypoint Railfreight Terminal
Oxleaze Farm
South Marston Farm

87
B4006
SWINDON ROAD
Lower Stratton
BRIDGEMAN CL
BAKERS CT
WATT END
Priory Farm
Marston Farm
SHRIVENHAM ROAD

2
Works
Grange Jun Sch
PARK ST
HALFMARE
St Margarets Retail Park Hotel
Home Farm
A420
SN4

1
Tilley's La
THE FIELDS
B4006
OXFORD ROAD
SANDGATE
A4312
COLEBROOK CLOSE
Superstore
MERLIN WY A420

86
B4143
SWINDON RD
HILL VIEW ROAD
TRAJAN ROAD

17   A   B2   18   C   B3   D   19   E   F

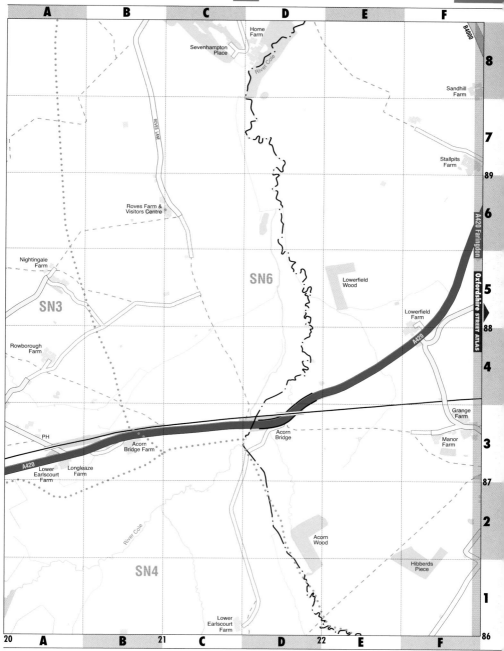

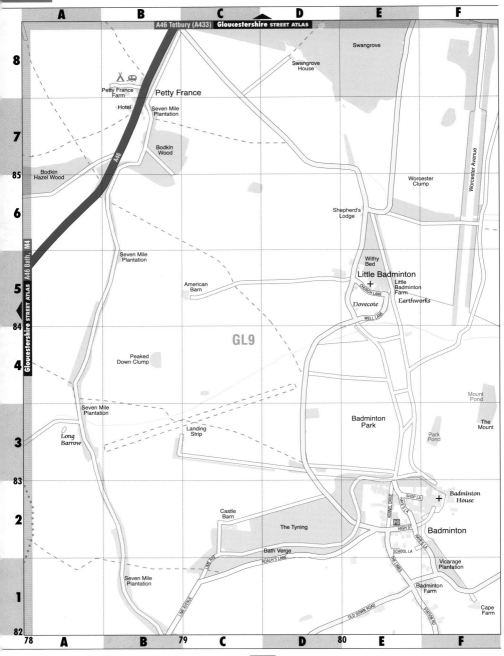

Swangrove

Swangrove
House

Petty France
Farm

Petty France

Hotel

Seven Mile
Plantation

Bodkin
Wood

Worcester
Clump

Bodkin
Hazel Wood

A46

Worcester Avenue

Shepherd's
Lodge

A46 Bath, M4

Gloucestershire STREET ATLAS

Seven Mile
Plantation

Withy
Bed

Little Badminton

American
Barn

Little
Badminton
Farm

CHURCH LANE

Earthworks

Dovecote

WELL LANE

GL9

Peaked
Down Clump

Mount
Pond

Badminton
Park

The
Mount

Seven Mile
Plantation

Landing
Strip

Park
Pond

Long
Barrow

SHOP LA

Badminton
House

KENNEL DRIVE

HAYES LA

Castle
Barn

PO

HIGH ST

The Tyning

Badminton

HAYES LA

SCHOOL LA

Bath Verge

LIME AVE

ROACH'S LANE

THE LIMES

Vicarage
Plantation

Seven Mile
Plantation

LIME AVENUE

Badminton
Farm

Cape
Farm

OLD DOWN ROAD

STECOMB RD

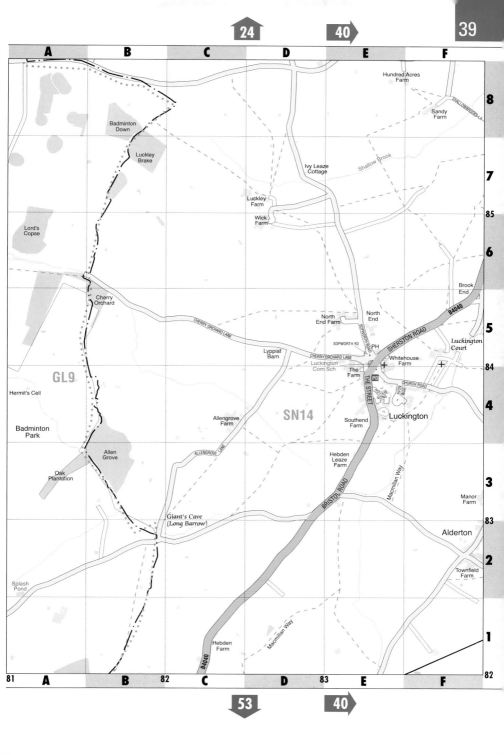

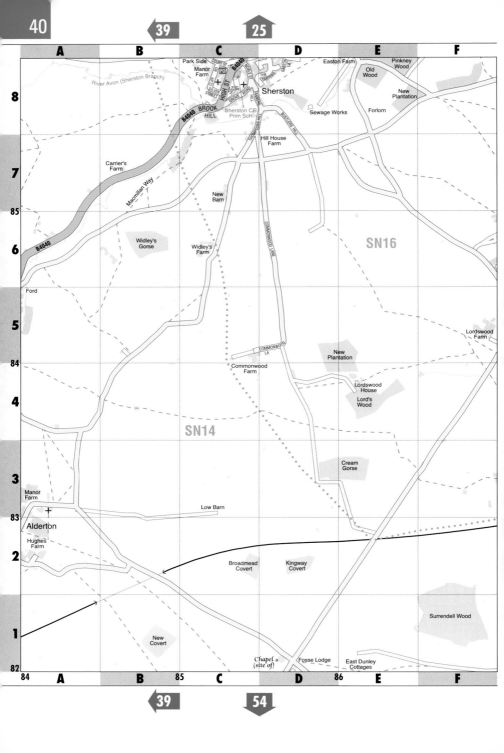

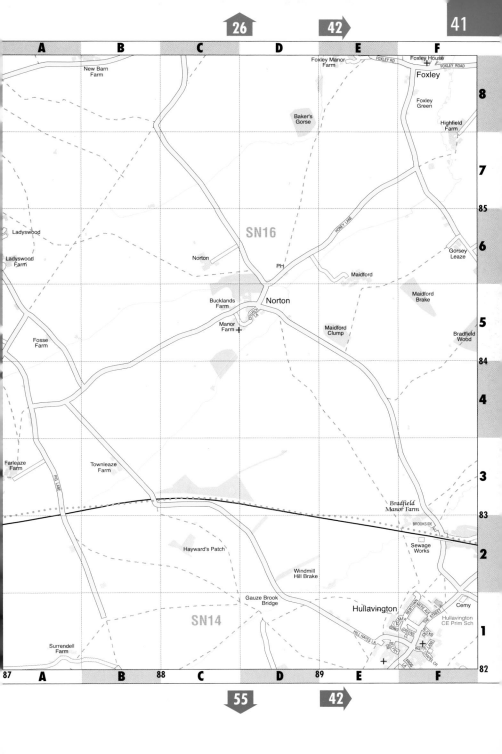

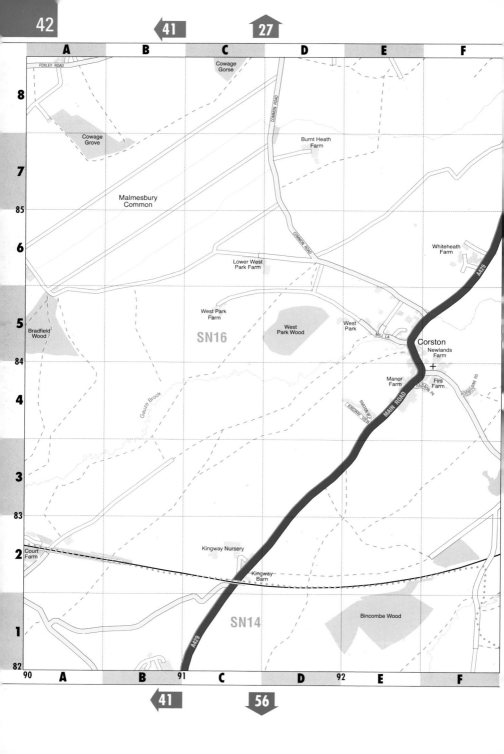

FOXLEY ROAD

Cowage
Gorse

Cowage
Grove

COMMON ROAD

Burnt Heath
Farm

Malmesbury
Common

Whiteheath
Farm

COMMON ROAD

A429

Lower West
Park Farm

West Park
Farm

West
Park Wood

West
Park

Bradfield
Wood

SN16

MILL LA

Corston

Newlands
Farm

Gauze Brook

Manor
Farm

Firs
Farm

ROUNDPONE RD

BRADNOR PK

MAIN ROAD

BARTON PL

KINGWAY VIEW

Kingway Nursery

Court
Farm

Kingway
Barn

Bincombe Wood

SN14

A429

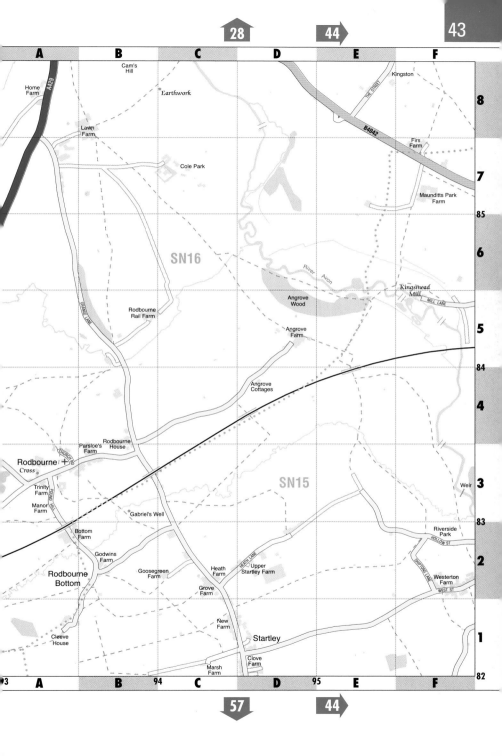

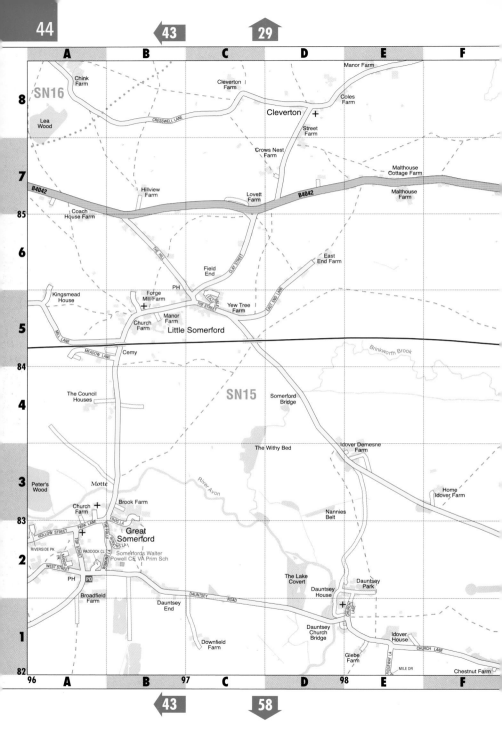

A   B   C   D   E   F

8

SN16

Chink
Farm

Cleverton
Farm

Manor Farm

Coles
Farm

Cleverton

Lea
Wood

CRESSWELL LANE

Street
Farm

Crows Nest
Farm

7

B4042

Hillview
Farm

Lovett
Farm

B4042

Malthouse
Cottage Farm

Malthouse
Farm

85

Coach
House Farm

6

THE HILL

Field
End

CLAY STREET

East
End Farm

PH

Kingsmead
House

Forge
Mill Farm

THE STREET

THE HILL

Yew Tree
Farm

EAST END LANE

5

MILL LANE

Church
Farm

Manor
Farm

Little Somerford

MEADOW LANE

Cemy

84

Brinkworth Brook

4

The Council
Houses

SN15

Somerford
Bridge

3

Peter's
Wood

Motte

River Avon

The Withy Bed

Idover Demesne
Farm

Home
Idover Farm

Church
Farm

Brook Farm

FROG LA

Nannies
Belt

83

HOLLOW STREET

PARK LANE

THE FOLLY

DIP STREET

Great
Somerford

RIVERSIDE PK

PADDOCK CL

PARK LA

WINDMILL LA

Somerfords Walter
Powell CE VA Prim Sch

2

WEST STREET

PH

PO

MANOR RD

The Lake
Covert

Dauntsey
House

Dauntsey
Park

Broadfield
Farm

Dauntsey
End

DAUNTSEY   ROAD

Dauntsey
Church
Bridge

CHURCH LANE

Idover
House

CHURCH LANE

1

Downfield
Farm

Glebe
Farm

RIDGEWAY LA

MILE DR

Chestnut Farm

82

96   A   B   97   C   D   98   E   F

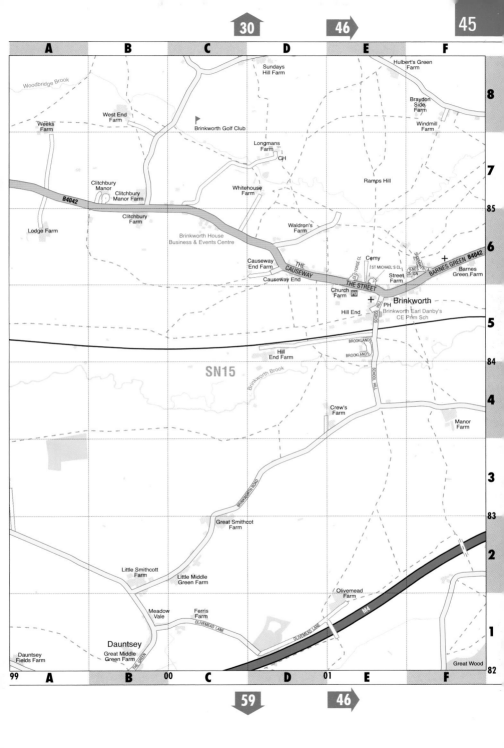

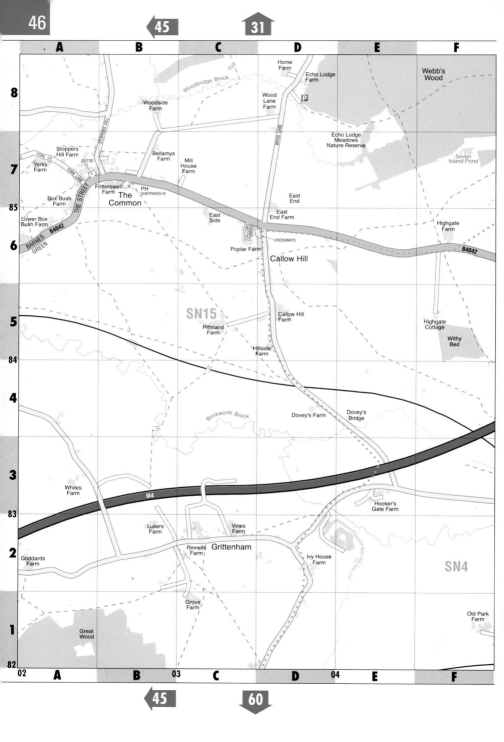

Webb's
Wood

Woodbridge Brook

Home
Farm
Echo Lodge
Farm

Woodside
Farm

Wood
Lane
Farm

P

Echo Lodge
Meadows
Nature Reserve

Seven
Island Pond

Stoppers
Hill Farm

Bellamys
Farm

Mill
House
Farm

CUTTS
CL

Yorks
Farm

YORK LA

YORK LANE

STOPPERS HILL

Fritterswell
Farm

PH
SHEPPARDS RI

The
Common

East
End

Highgate
Farm

Box Bush
Farm

THE STREET

East
Side

East
End Farm

Lower Box
Bush Farm

BARNES

B4042

GREEN

CALLOW1
CALLOW2

CROSSWAYS

B4042

Poplar Farm

Callow Hill

SN15

Callow Hill
Farm

Highgate
Cottage

Pittsland
Farm

Withy
Bed

Hillside
Farm

Brinkworth Brook

Dovey's Farm

Dovey's
Bridge

Whites
Farm

M4

Hooker's
Gate Farm

Lukers
Farm

Vines
Farm

Goddards
Farm

Pinnells
Farm

Grittenham

Ivy House
Farm

SN4

Grove
Farm

Old Park
Farm

Great
Wood

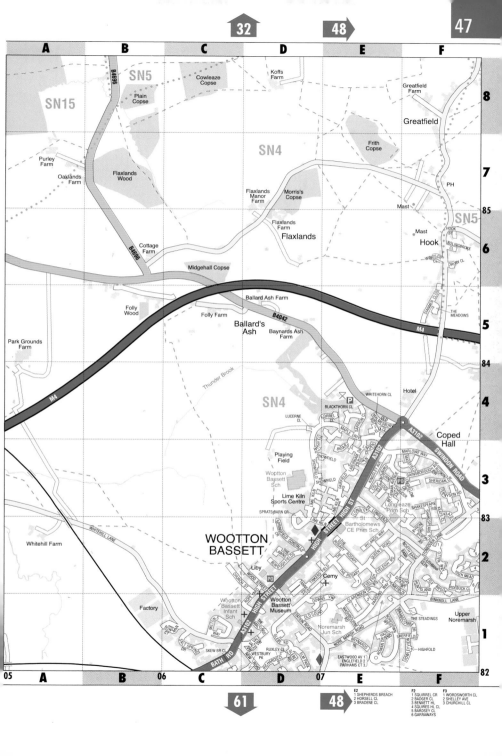

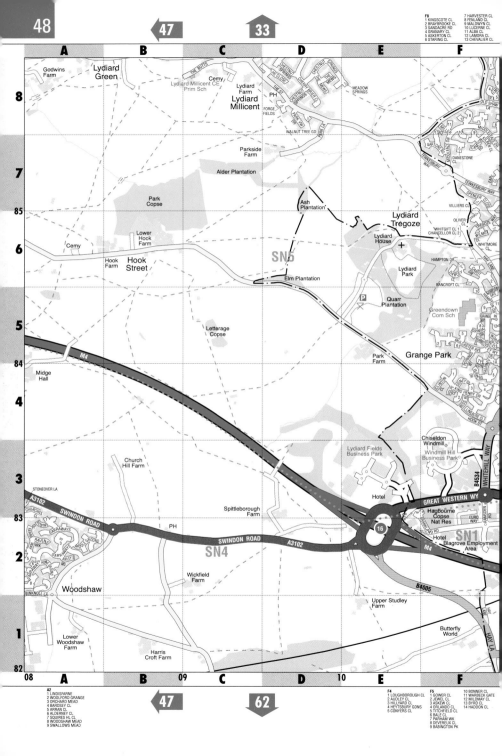

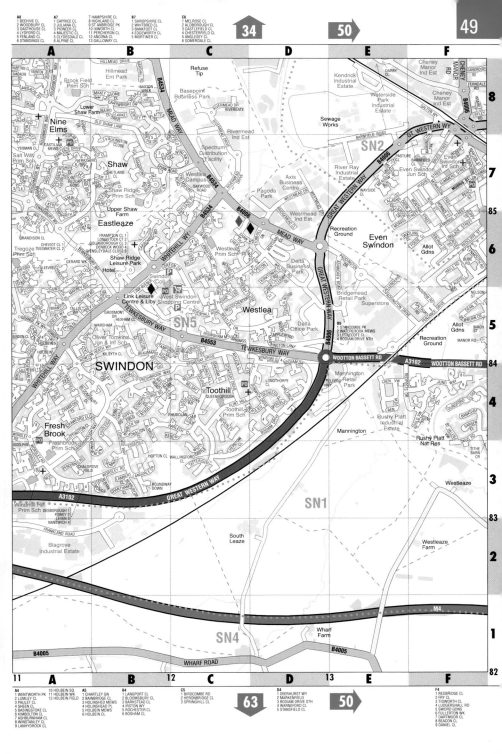

A6
1 BEEHIVE CL
2 WOODBURY CL
3 OASTHOUSE CL
4 LYDFORD CL
5 FENLAND CL
6 STANDINGS CL

A7
1 CAPRICE CL
2 JULIANA CL
3 PIONEER CL
4 MAJESTIC CL
5 CLYDESDALE CL
6 ALPINE CL

7 HAMPSHIRE CL
8 HIGHLAND CL
9 ST ANBRIDGE PK
10 IXWORTH CL
11 PERCHERON CL
12 ANCONA CL
13 GALLOWAY CL

B7
1 SHROPSHIRE CL
2 WHITBRED CL
3 BANKFOOT CL
4 EDGEWORTH CL
5 MORTIMER CL

C6
1 MELROSE CL
2 ALDBOROUGH CL
3 CASTLEFIELD CL
4 CHESTERFIELD CL
5 ANGLESEY CL
6 SOMERDALE CL

34 **50** **49**

8
7
85
6
5
84
4
3
83
2
1
82

A B C D E F

D5
1 STANCOMBE PK
2 WATERCROOK MEWS
3 LITTLECOTE CL
4 BODIAM DRIVE NTH

11 12 13

A4
1 WENTWORTH PK
2 LUMLEY CL
3 PALLET CL
4 SHEEN CL
5 BASINGSTOKE CL
6 KIMBOLTON CL
7 ASHBURNHAM CL
8 WINSTANLEY CL
9 LANHYDROCK CL

10 HOLBEIN SQ
11 HOLBEIN WK
12 HOLBEIN FIELD

A5
1 CHARTLEY GN
2 BAINBRIDGE CL
3 HOLINSHED MEWS
4 HOLINSHEAD PL
5 HOLBEIN MEWS
6 HOLBEIN CL

B4
1 LANGPORT CL
2 BLOOMSBURY CL
3 BARKSTEAD CL
4 IRSTON WY
5 ROCHESTER CL
6 BOSHAM CL

C5
1 BIRDCOMBE RD
2 HERONBRIDGE CL
3 SPRINGHILL CL

D4
1 DEERHURST WY
2 MARKENFIELD
3 BODIAM DRIVE STH
4 WARNEFORD CL
5 STANSFIELD CL

F4
1 REDBRIDGE CL
2 FRY CL
3 TIDWORTH CL
4 LUDGERSHALL RD
5 SWORD GDNS
6 FULLERTON WK
7 DARTMOOR CL
8 BEACON CL
9 DANIEL CL

63 **50**

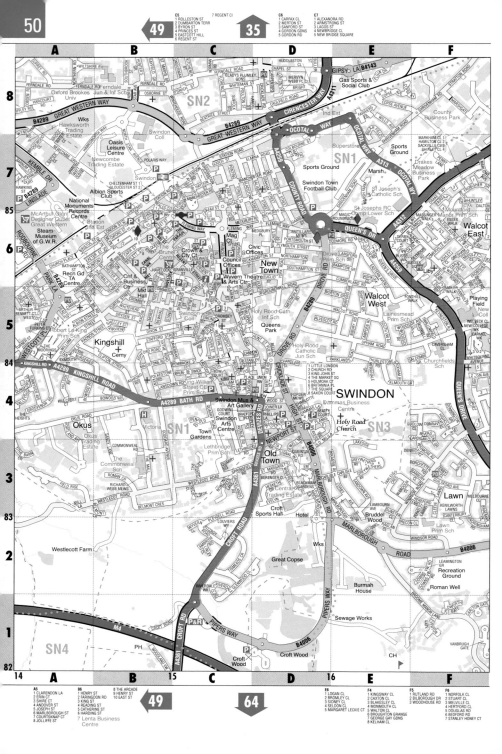

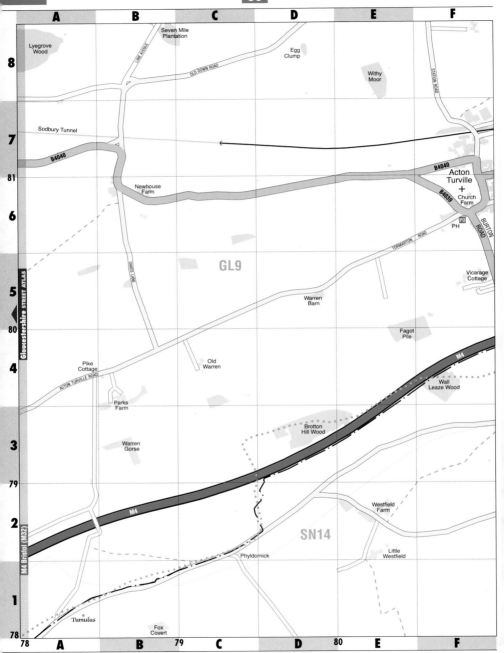

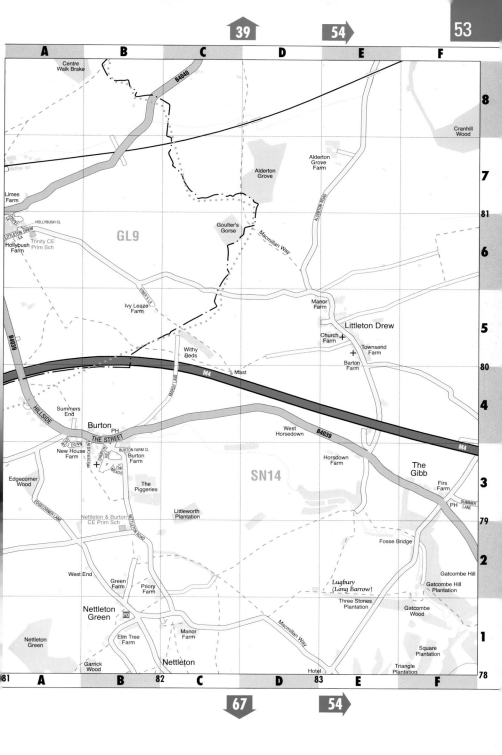

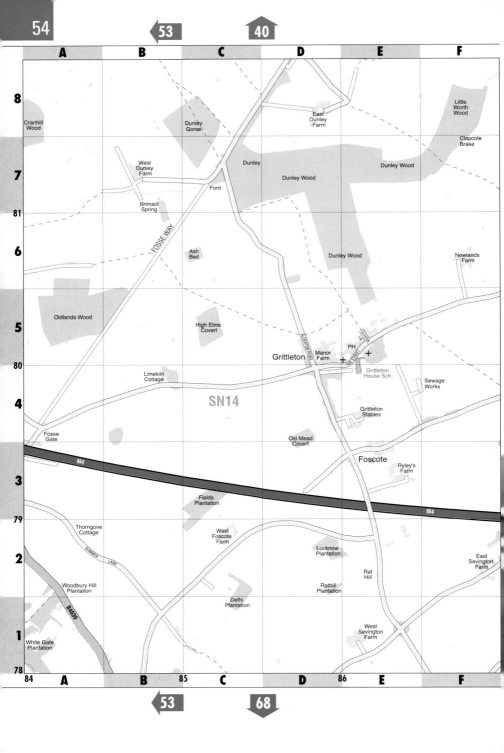

A **B** **C** **D** **E** **F**

8

7

81

6

5

80

4

79

3

2

1

78

84 85 86

Cranhill Wood

Dunley Gorse

East Dunley Farm

Little Worth Wood

Clapcote Brake

West Dunley Farm

Dunley

Dunley Wood

Dunley Wood

FOSSE WAY

Ford

Brimsol Spring

Ash Bed

Dunley Wood

Newlands Farm

Oldlands Wood

High Elms Covert

ALDERTON ROAD

SCHOOL LA

Manor Farm

PH

FORE STREET

Grittleton

Grittleton House Sch

Sewage Works

Limekiln Cottage

SN14

Grittleton Stables

Fosse Gate

M4

Old Mead Covert

Foscote

Ryley's Farm

Fields Plantation

M4

Thorngove Cottage

West Foscote Farm

Lucknow Plantation

East Sevington Farm

SUMMER LANE

Rat Hill

Woodbury Hill Plantation

B4039

Rathill Plantation

Delhi Plantation

White Gate Plantation

West Sevington Farm

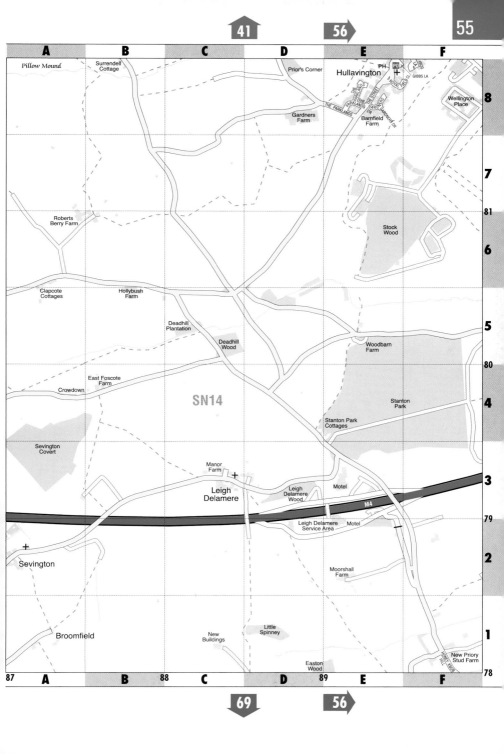

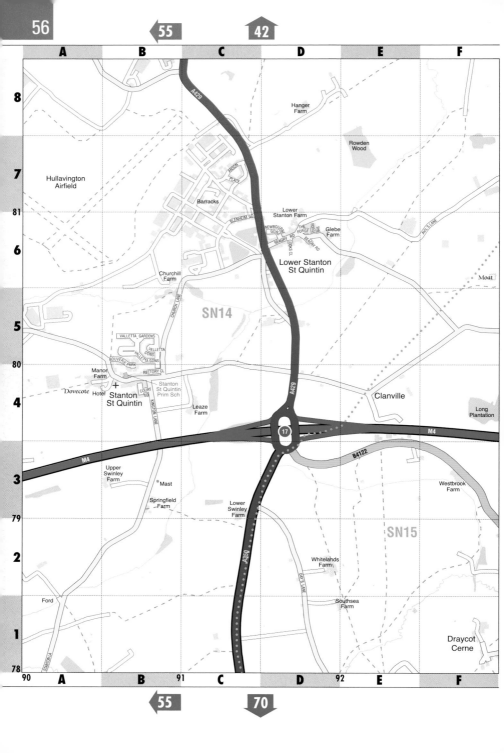

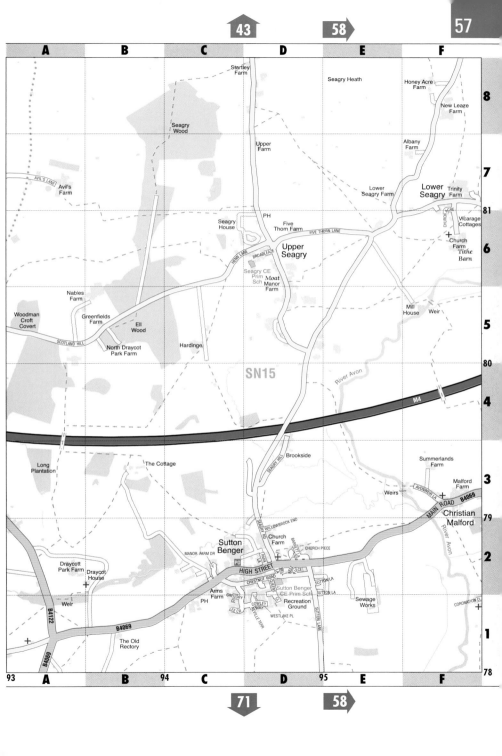

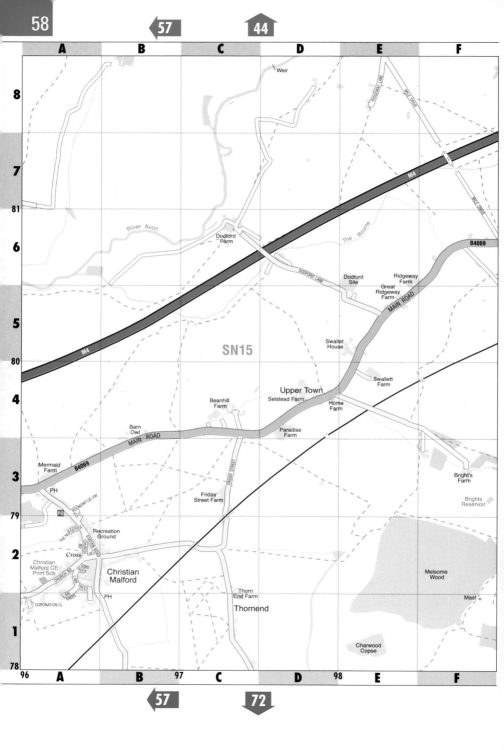

57
44

A   B   C   D   E   F

8

7

81

6

Weir

RIDGEWAY LANE

MILE DRIVE

M4

River Avon

Dodford
Farm

The Bourne

B4069

DODFORD LANE

Dodford
Site

Ridgeway
Farm

Great
Ridgeway
Farm

MAIN ROAD

5

80

SN15

Swallet
House

M4

Swallett
Farm

4

Upper Town

Beanhill
Farm

Selstead Farm

Home
Farm

Barn
Owl

MAIN ROAD

Paradise
Farm

B4069

3

Mermaid
Farm

PH

RINK STREET

Bright's
Farm

Brights
Reservoir

Friday
Street Farm

ROD/WOOD VW

79

PO

THE NURSERIES

Recreation
Ground

CHURCH RD

STATION RD

2

Cross

LIME TREES

Christian
Malford CE
Prim Sch

CHURCH RD

LIME TREES

Christian
Malford

LIME TREES

Melsome
Wood

CORONATION CL

PH

Thorn
End Farm

Mast

Thornend

1

Charwood
Copse

78

96   A   B   97   C   D   98   E   F

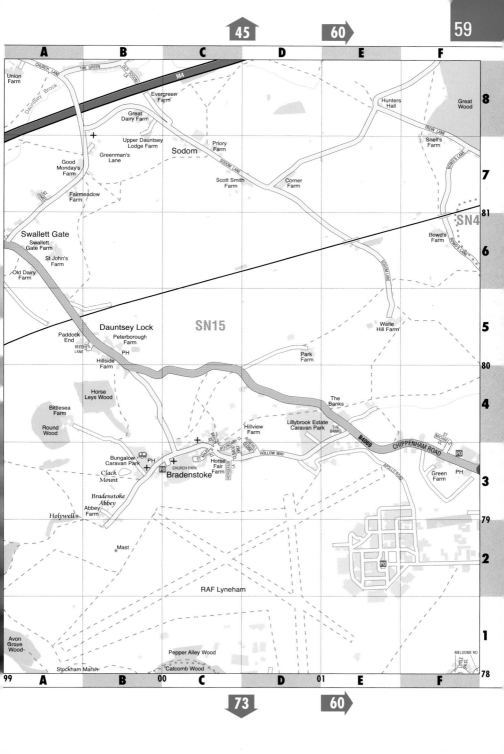

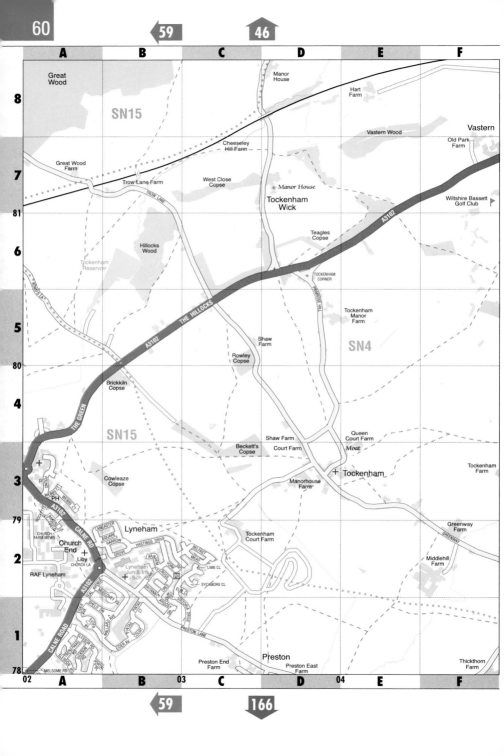

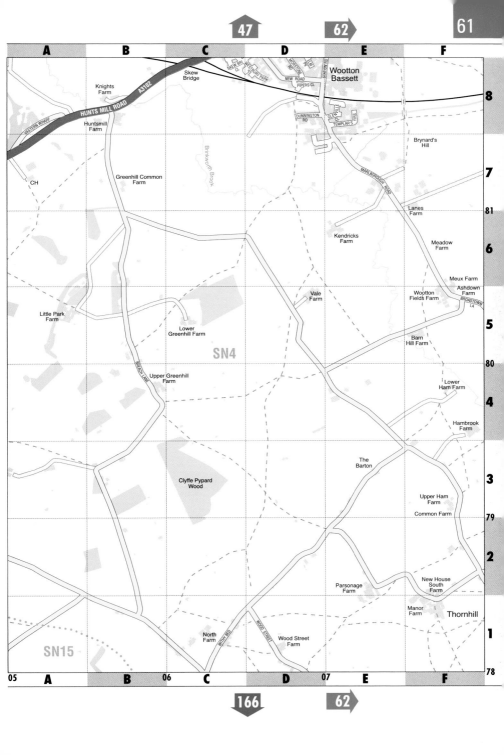

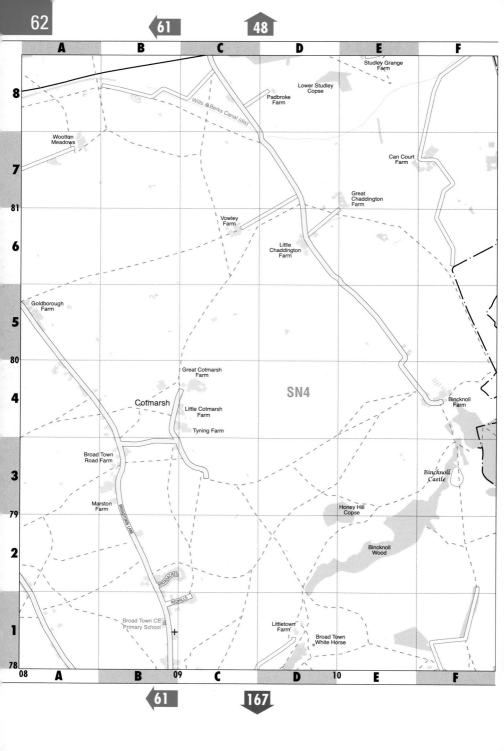

A   B   C   D   E   F

8

Studley Grange
Farm

Lower Studley
Copse

Padbroke
Farm

Wilts & Berks Canal (dis)

Wootton
Meadows

Can Court
Farm

7

Great
Chaddington
Farm

81

Vowley
Farm

6

Little
Chaddington
Farm

Goldborough
Farm

5

80

Great Cotmarsh
Farm

SN4

4

Cotmarsh

Little Cotmarsh
Farm

Bincknoll
Farm

Tyning Farm

Broad Town
Road Farm

Bincknoll
Castle

3

Marston
Farm

Honey Hill
Copse

79

BROADTOWN LANE

2

Bincknoll
Wood

BROADACRES

REDHILLS

Broad Town CE
Primary School

Littletown
Farm

1

Broad Town
White Horse

78

08   A   B   09   C   D   10   E   F

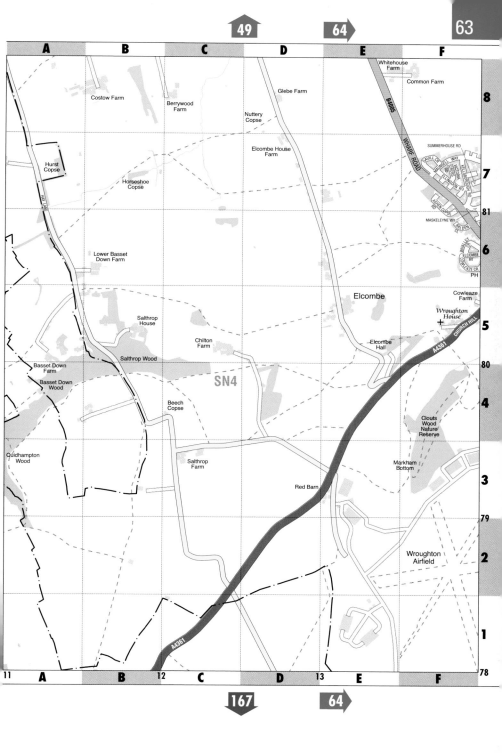

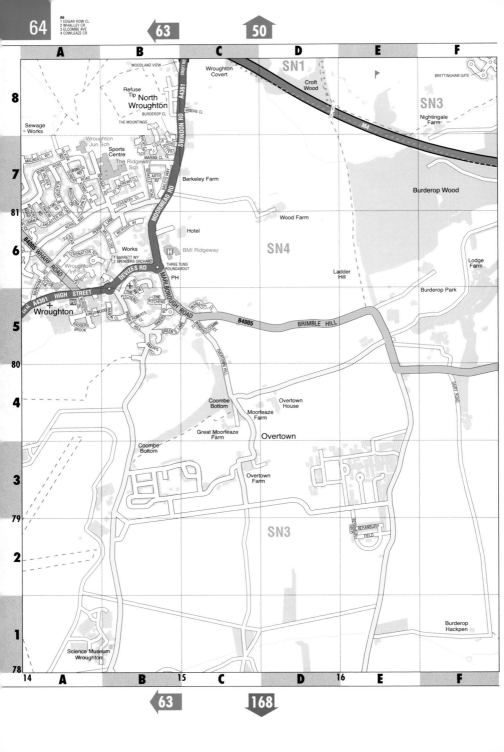

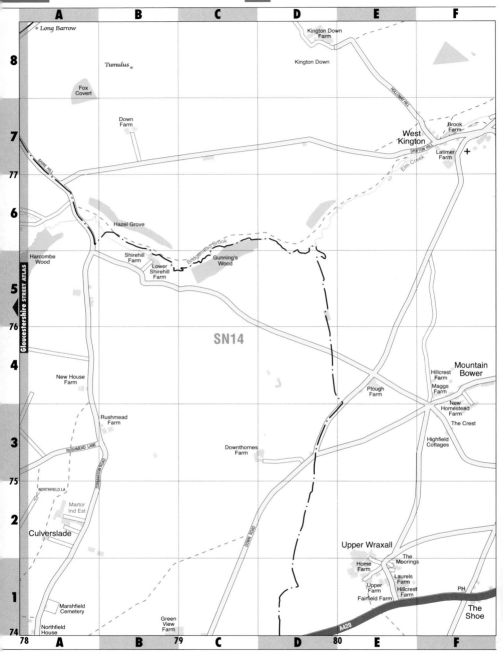

Long Barrow

Tumulus

Fox
Covert

Down
Farm

8

7

77

6

SHIRE HILL

Hazel Grove

Harcombe
Wood

Shirehill
Farm

Lower
Shirehill
Farm

Gunning's
Wood

Bridgemead Brook

5

Gloucestershire STREET ATLAS

76

SN14

4

New House
Farm

Rushmead
Farm

RUSHMEAD LANE

TORMARTON ROAD

3

75

NORTHFIELD LA

Martor
Ind Est

2

Culverslade

1

Marshfield
Cemetery

Northfield
House

74

Downthornes
Farm

DOWN ROAD

Green
View
Farm

Kington Down
Farm

Kington Down

HOLLOW HILL

West
Kington

DRIFTON HILL

Elm Creek

Brook
Farm

Latimer
Farm

Plough
Farm

Mountain
Bower

Hillcrest
Farm

Maggs
Farm

New
Homestead
Farm

The Crest

Highfield
Cottages

Upper Wraxall

Home
Farm

The
Moorings

Laurels
Farm

Upper
Farm

Hillcrest
Farm

Fairfield Farm

PH

The
Shoe

A420

78   79   80

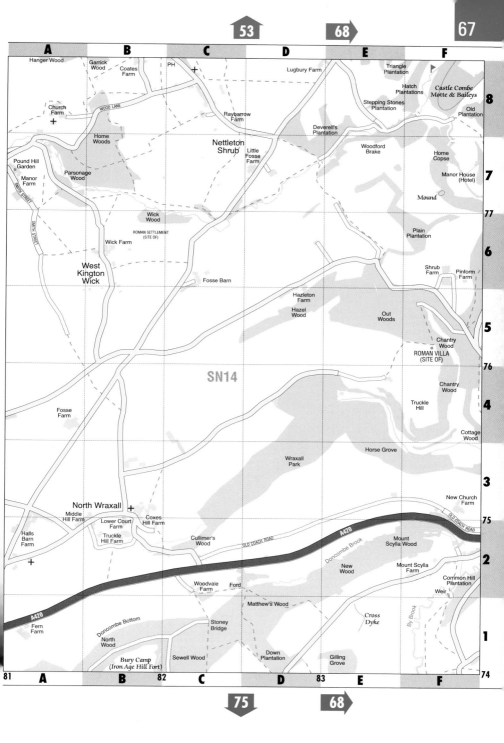

53
68

A   **B**   **C**   **D**   **E**   **F**

Hanger Wood

Garrick Wood

Coates Farm

PH

Lugbury Farm

Triangle Plantation

Hatch Plantations

Castle Combe Motte & Baileys

8

Church Farm

WOOD LANE

Raybarrow Farm

Stepping Stones Plantation

Deverell's Plantation

Old Plantation

Home Woods

Nettleton Shrub

Little Fosse Farm

Woodford Brake

Home Copse

7

Pound Hill Garden

SMITH STREET

Manor Farm

Parsonage Wood

Manor House (Hotel)

Mound

77

Wick Wood

ROMAN SETTLEMENT (SITE OF)

Plain Plantation

6

Wick Farm

West Kington Wick

Fosse Barn

Shrub Farm

Pinform Farm

Hazleton Farm

Hazel Wood

Out Woods

Chantry Wood

5

SN14

ROMAN VILLA (SITE OF)

76

Chantry Wood

Fosse Farm

Truckle Hill

4

Cottage Wood

Horse Grove

Wraxall Park

3

North Wraxall

New Church Farm

OLD COACH ROAD

75

Middle Hill Farm

Lower Court Farm

Coxes Hill Farm

Truckle Hill Farm

Cullimer's Wood

OLD COACH ROAD

A420

Doncombe Brook

Mount Scylla Wood

Halls Barn Farm

New Wood

Mount Scylla Farm

2

Common Hill Plantation

Woodvale Farm

Ford

Weir

By Brook

A420

Matthew's Wood

Cross Dyke

Fern Farm

Doncombe Bottom

Stoney Bridge

North Wood

Sewell Wood

Down Plantation

Gilling Grove

1

Bury Camp (Iron Age Hill Fort)

75
68

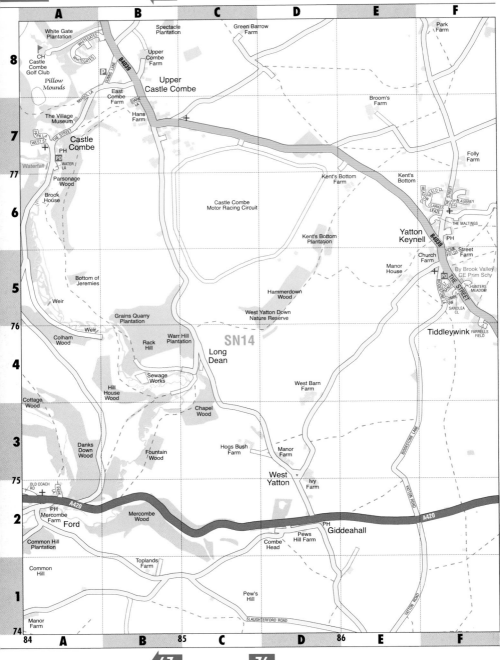

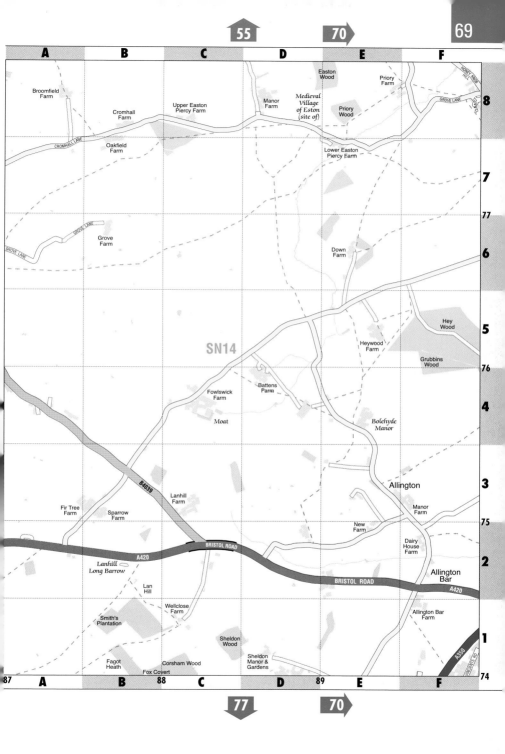

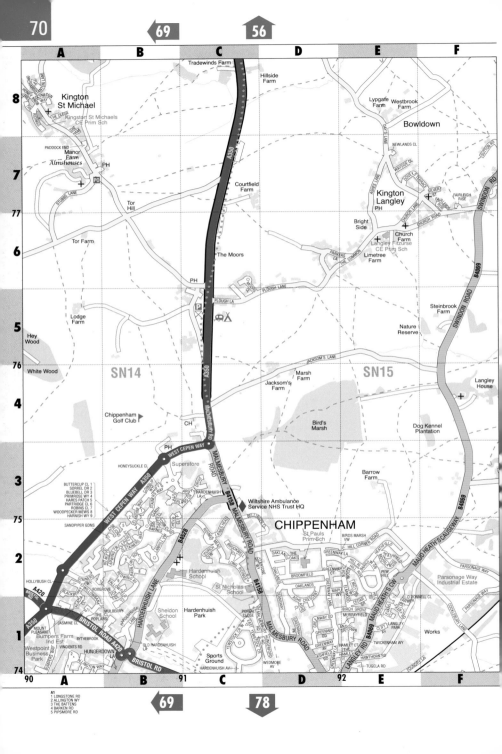

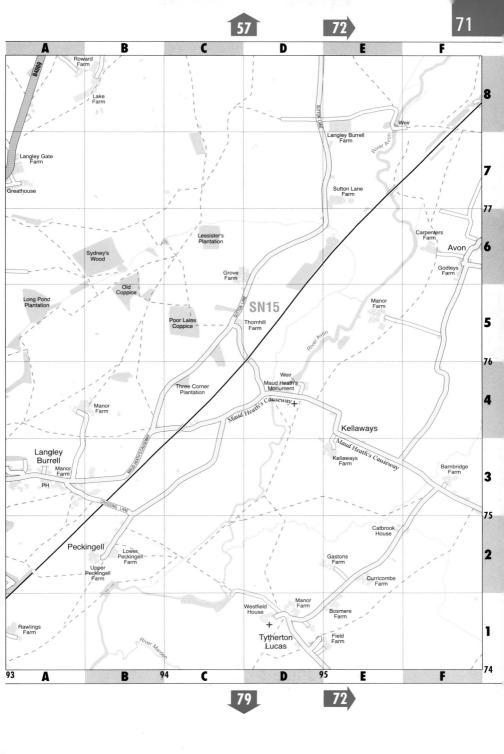

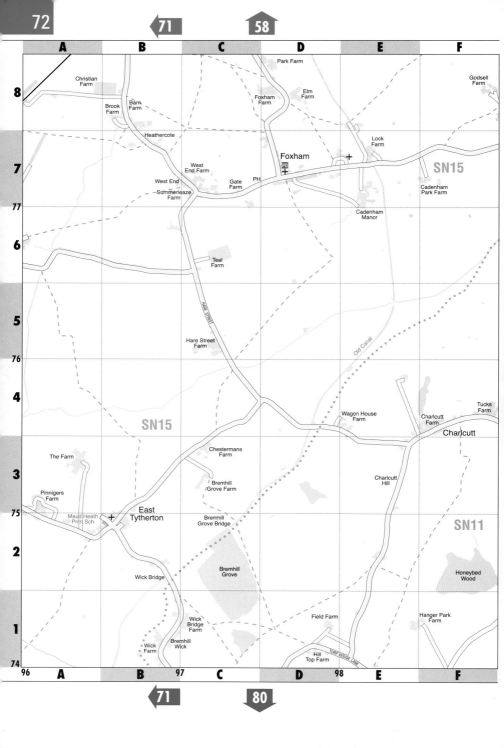

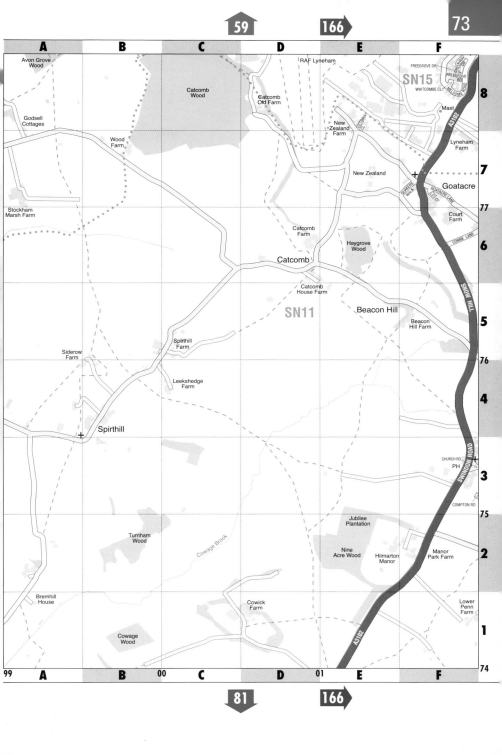

8

Avon Grove Wood

Catcomb Wood

Catcomb Old Farm

RAF Lyneham

FREEGROVE DR
SN15
WHITCOMBE CL

Mast

A3102

Godsell Cottages

Wood Farm

New Zealand Farm

Lyneham Farm

7

New Zealand

Goatacre

QUAKERS WALK

GOATACRE LANE

77

Stockham Marsh Farm

Court Farm

COMBE LANE

Catcomb Farm

Haygrove Wood

6

Catcomb

SNOW HILL

Catcomb House Farm

SN11

Beacon Hill

5

Spirthill Farm

Beacon Hill Farm

Siderow Farm

76

Leekshedge Farm

4

Spirthill

CHURCH RD
PH

SWINDON ROAD

3

COMPTON RD

75

Jubilee Plantation

Turnham Wood

Nine Acre Wood

Hilmarton Manor

Manor Park Farm

2

Cowage Brook

Bremhill House

Cowick Farm

Lower Penn Farm

1

Cowage Wood

A3102

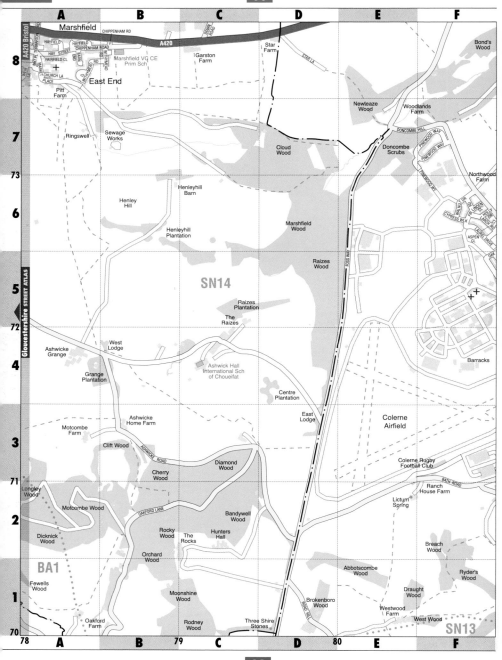

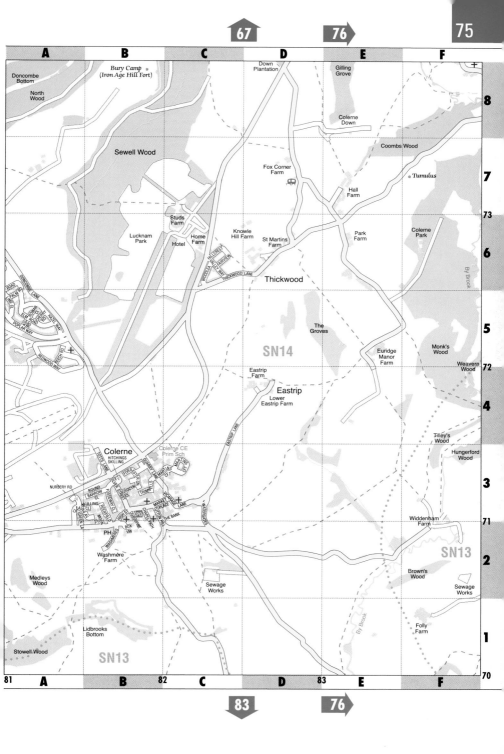

	A	B	C	D	E	F

8

Slaughterford
Backpath Wood
HAM LANE
GERMAINS LANE
Little Glebe
SLAUGHTERFORD RD
YATTON ROAD
COTTLE LANE
Field Farm
Biddestone
Home Farm
THE GREEN
CHURCH ROAD

7

Weir
By Brook
Honeybrook Farm
WEAVERN LANE
WEAVERN LA
White Cliff Wood
SN14
Cemy
THE BUTTS
Field Farm
Mountjoy Farm
BUTTS PL
Pool Farm
PH
Biddestone Manor
Macmillan Way

73

6

Field Barn Farm
WEAVERN LANE
Jubilee Wood
The Grove

5

Husseyhill Wood
Erkwell Wood
Mound
Home Farm
Hartham Farm
Leigh Wood

72

WEAVERN LANE
Square Covert
Tyning Wood
Hartham Park
HARTHAM LANE

4

Weavern Farm
Tyning Wood
Tyning Wood
Prestley Wood

3

Hungerford Wood
The Larches
MIDDLEWICK LANE
Pickwick Lodge Farm
Church Farm
Long Plantation
SN13
Middlewick
CHURCHILL WAY

71

Rudloe Wood
Upper Pickwick
Broad Wood
MIDDLEWICK LANE
Pickwick
DOVECOTE DR
MANOR RD
METHUEN WAY
YORK CL
QUEENS AVENUE

2

RAF Rudloe Manor
QUEENS DRIVE
BATH RD
A4
Corsham Regis Prim Sch
ARNOLDS MEAD

1

Lower Rudloe Farm
BOX HILL
A4
BATH ROAD
Half Way Firs
HALFWAY FIRS
BRADFORD ROAD
CHESTNUT GRANGE
SUMSIONS DR
WEST PARK ROAD
PICKWICK ROAD
BRUNEL CLOSE
Springfield Sports Centre
Sports Ground
The Corsham Sch
B3353

70

Hotel
Rudloe
PINE CLOSE
TOGHILL CR
B3109
Underground Quarry
SAWYERS CL
PICTOR CL
PARTRIDGE CL
Corsham
FIRESTONE WY

84		85		86	
A	B		C	D	E	F

B1
1 SOUTHCROFT RD
2 NORTHCROFT RD
3 PRESTLY WOOD
4 TRENCHARD AV
5 SANDY LEA AV
6 PRIESTLY WOOD RD
7 WEIR HAYES

E1
1 EDRIDGE PL
2 TROPENELL CL
3 BELLOT DR

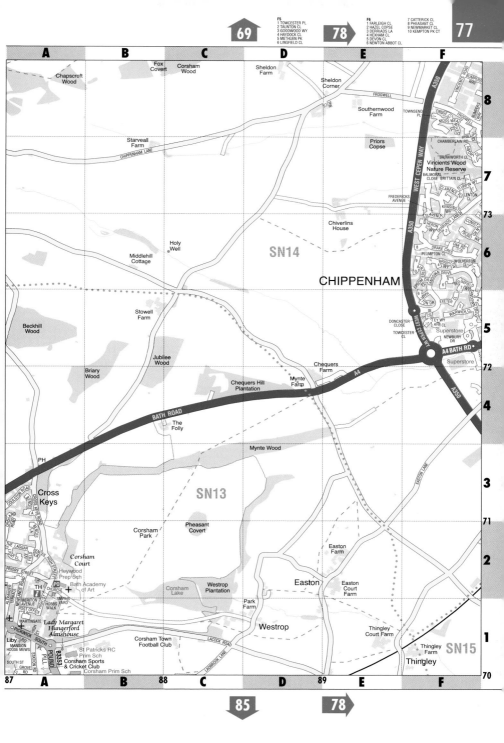

F5
1 TOWCESTER PL
2 TAUNTON CL
3 GOODWOOD WY
4 HAYDOCK CL
5 METHUEN PK
6 LINGFIELD CL

F6
1 FARLEIGH CL
2 HAZEL COPSE
3 DERRIADS LA
4 HEXHAM CL
5 DEVON CL
6 NEWTON ABBOT CL

7 CATTERICK CL
8 PHEASANT CL
9 NEWMARKET CL
10 KEMPTON PK CT

CHIPPENHAM

SN14

SN13

SN15

A B C D E F

8

BARKEN RD
FROGWELL PARK
St Peters CE Prim Sch
WHITTLE CL
Frogwell Prim Sch

BRISTOL ROAD A420 MARSHFIELD ROAD
HARDENHUISH LA
KING ALFRED ST
MALMESBURY RD
PARK LANE
Redland Prim Sch
OAK LODGE
Springfield Buildings
Hathaway Retail Park
MAUD HEATH COURT

7

HONEYBROOK CL
WESSEX RD
APPLEWOOD CL
Chippenham
Council Offices
Olympiad Leisure Centre
MONKTON PARK
Monkton Park Prim Sch
CHIPPENHAM
Chippenham Mus & Heritage Cen
Wiltshire College

73

SN14
Derriads Green
Derriads Prim Sch
ORCHARD CL
LADYFIELD ROAD
LACKHAM CL
St Marys PC Sch
Ivy Road Ind Est
Borough Parade
FOGHAMSHIRE
Monkton Park
1 CAUSEWAY CL
2 CHAPEL MEWS
River Avon

6

Queens Crescent Sch
WESTERLEIGH
Bath Road Ind Est
Rec Gd
St Margarets Gd
St Francis
Chippenham Community
Sports Ground
LITTLE ENGLANDS
WESTMEAD
Magistrates Court
Charter Prim Sch
LONG CLOSE

72

PH
BATH ROAD
Pheasant Business Park
Chiverlins Farm
MELKSHAM ROAD
Rowden Hill
Rowden Manor
AVENUE LA FLECHE A4
BLACKWELLHAMS
MASSEY CL
Englands
PEWSHAM WY

5

Herman Miller Ind Est
HEREFORD CL
EASTON CL
Elm Tree Farm
Patterdown Rifle Range
Moat
STAPLEFORD CL
PEWSHAM WY

4

Hunters Moon Farm
Taffswell Farm
Patterdown Farm
Milbourne Farm
SN15
PEWSHAM WY A4
FARMHOUSE CL
PENNY LA

3

A350
Nursery
Sewage Works
FOREST LANE

71

SALTERSFORD LANE WEST CEPEN WAY
Showell Farm
Lower Lodge Farm

2

Thingley Junction
A350

1

The Barn
Plucking Grove
River Avon
Lackham Country Park
North Wood
Wiltshire College
Lackham Mus

70

90 A 91 B C 92 D E F

A5
1 WETHERBY CL
2 SOUTHWELL CL
3 KELSO CT
4 CHEPSTOW CL

A6
1 SALISBURY CL
2 WINCHESTER CL
3 GLOUCESTER CL
4 WARDOUR RD
5 TRENCHARD CL
6 CRANWELL CL

A7
1 COLLEN CL
2 BERKELY CL

F4
1 KNIGHTS CL
2 MILLARD CL
3 CHANDLER WY
4 ESCOTT CL
5 WILLIS CL
6 SWANBOROUGH CL

F5
1 LOCKSIDE
2 DICKSON WY
3 BRIGHT CL
4 HARFORD CL
5 CARPENTER CL
6 SWAYNE CL

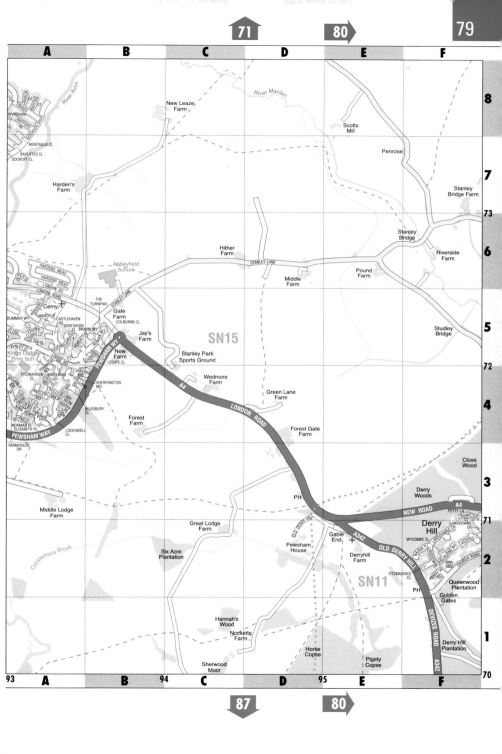

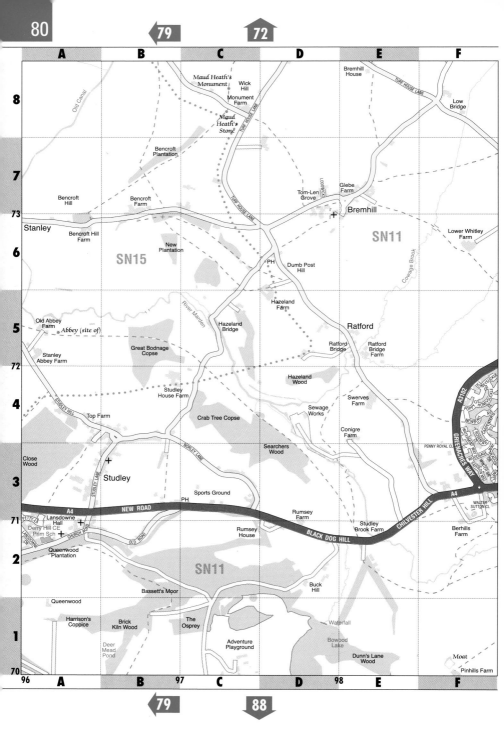

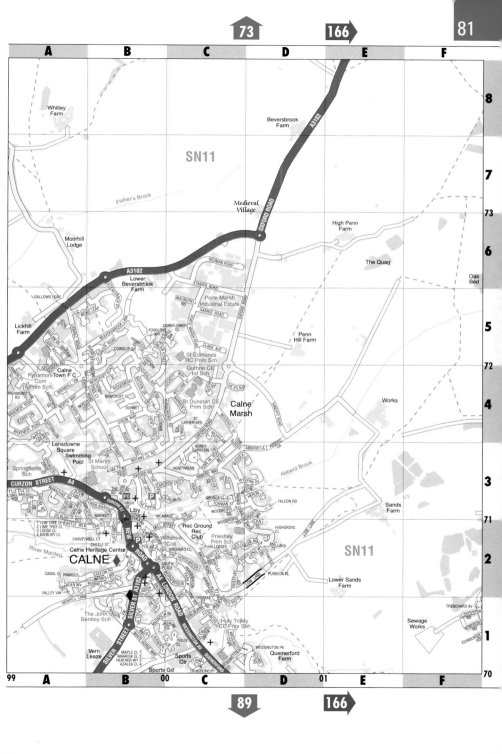

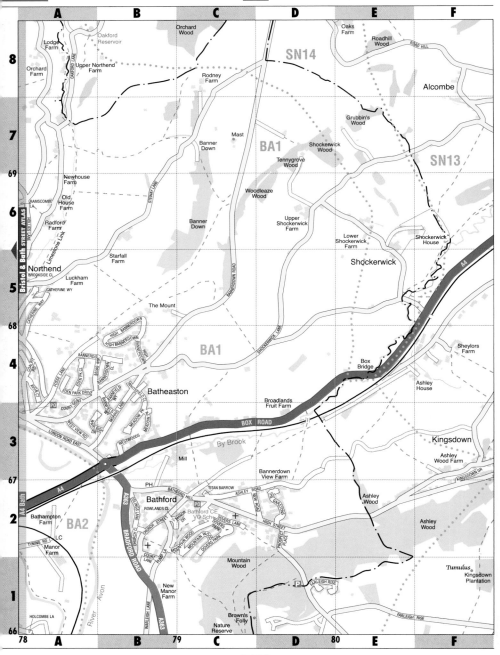

Lodge Farm
Oakford Reservoir
Orchard Wood
Oaks Farm
Roadhill Wood
ROAD HILL

SN14

Upper Northend Farm
Orchard Farm

Alcombe

8

Rodney Farm

Grubbin's Wood

7
Banner Down
Mast
BA1
Tennygrove Wood
Shockerwick Wood

SN13

69
Newhouse Farm

Woodleaze Wood

Old House Farm
Banner Down

Upper Shockerwick Farm

6
Radford Farm
Lower Shockerwick Farm
Shockerwick House

Bristol & Bath STREET ATLAS

Limestone Link
Starfall Farm

Shockerwick

Northend
BROOKSIDE CL
Luckham Farm
CATHERINE WY

5
CATHERINE WAY

BANNERDOWN ROAD
SHOCKERWICK LANE

68
The Mount

HIGH BANNERDOWN

BA1

Sheylors Farm

4
BANNERDO
EDEN PK CL
BANNERDOWN DRIVE
Box Bridge
Ashley House

FIRST LANE
EDEN PK CL
BANFIELD
Batheaston
Broadlands Fruit Farm

3
COURT GDNS
PO
WESTWOODS
LONDON ROAD EAST
BOX ROAD
By Brook
Mill
Kingsdown
Ashley Wood Farm

KINGSDOWN GR

67
A4 Bath
A4
PH
BATHFORD HILL
TITAN BARROW
Bannerdown View Farm
Ashley Wood

2
Bathampton Farm
BA2
Bathford
ROWLANDS CL
CHURCH STREET
MANOR DR
Bathford CE VC Sch
PO
DOVERS LANE
ASHLEY ROAD
NEW ROAD
THE GASTONS
HIGH STREET
PROSPECT PLACE
Ashley Wood

TYNING RD
LC
Manor Farm
COURT LANE
MOUNTAIN WOOD
DOVERS PARK

Tumulus
Kingsdown Plantation

1
New Manor Farm
Mountain Wood

FARLEIGH RISE
P
FARLEIGH RISE

HOLCOMBE LA
WARLEIGH LANE
A363
BRADFORD ROAD
River Avon
Brown's Folly
Nature Reserve
A363

66

78   79   80

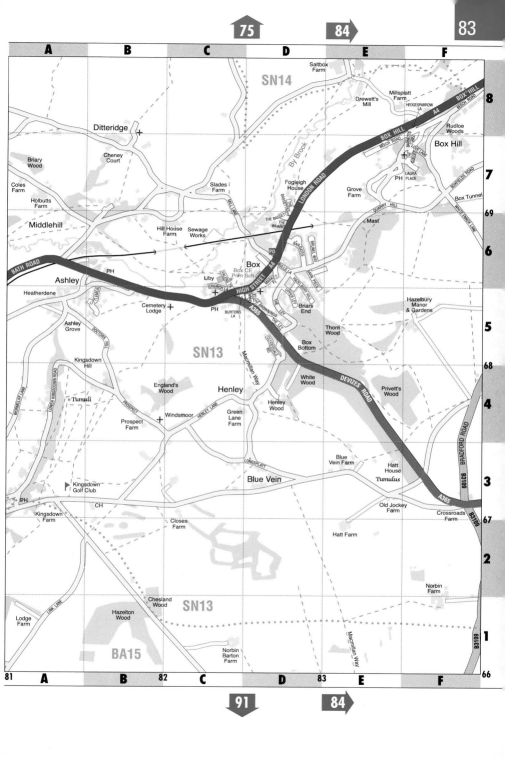

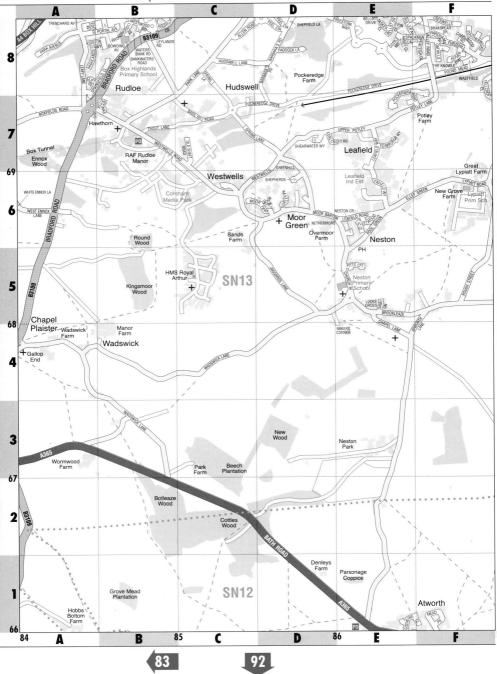

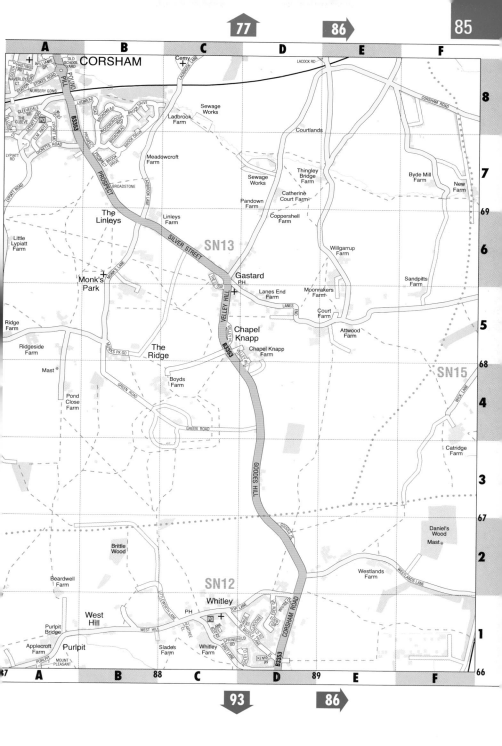

CORSHAM

SN13

SN15

SN12

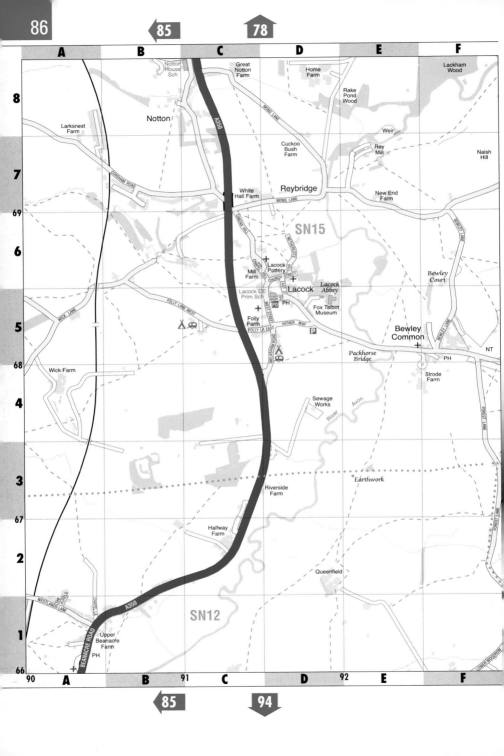

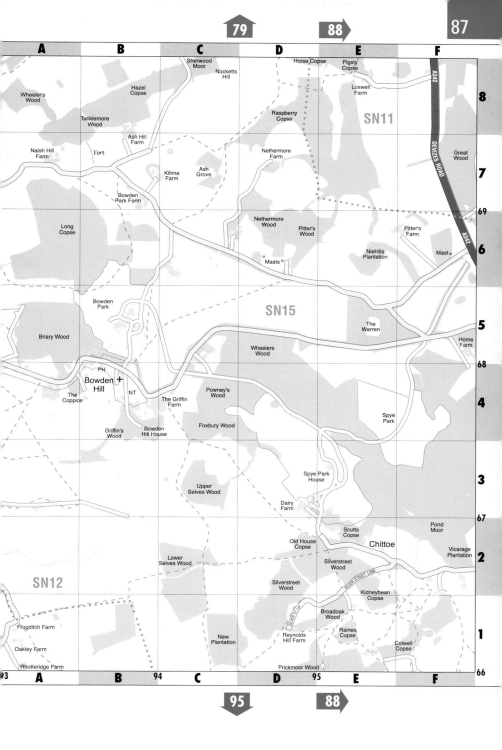

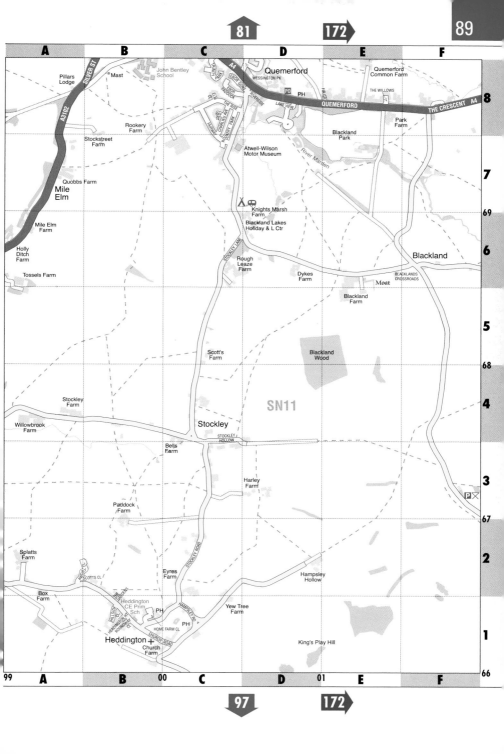

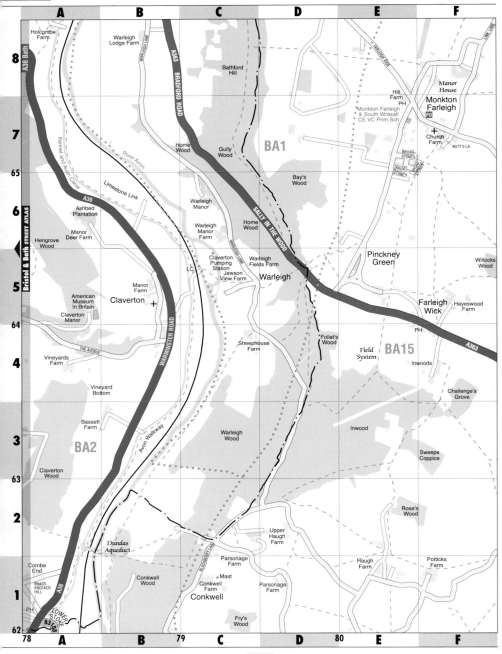

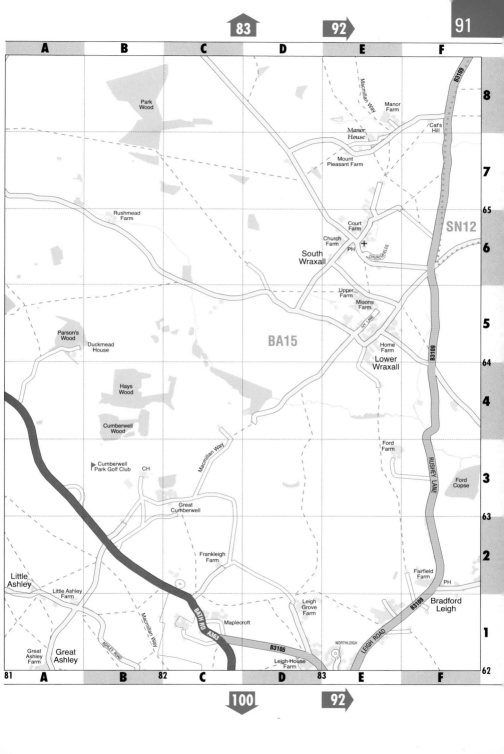

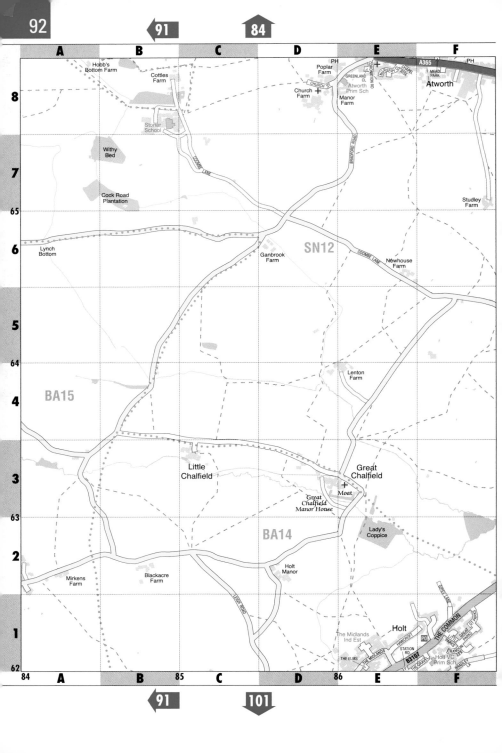

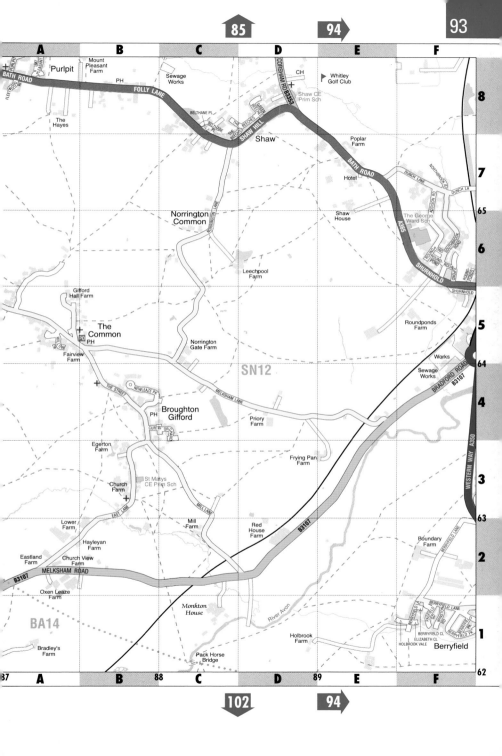

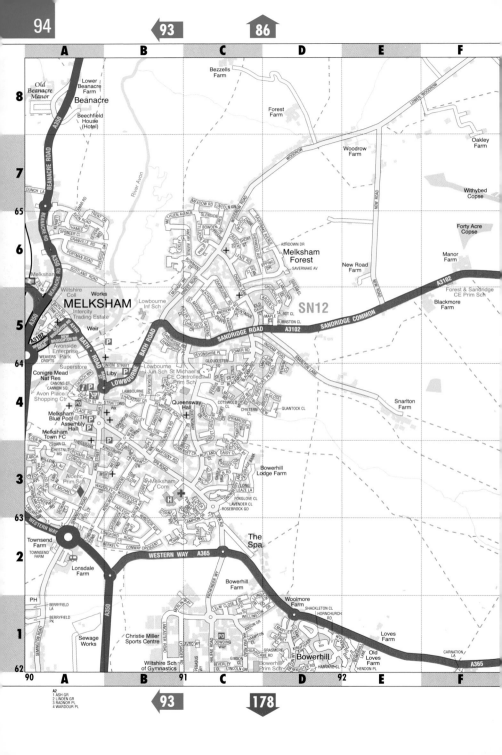

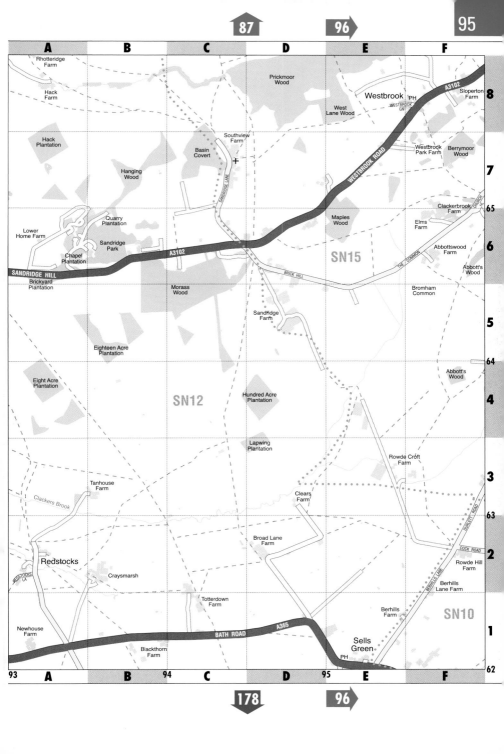

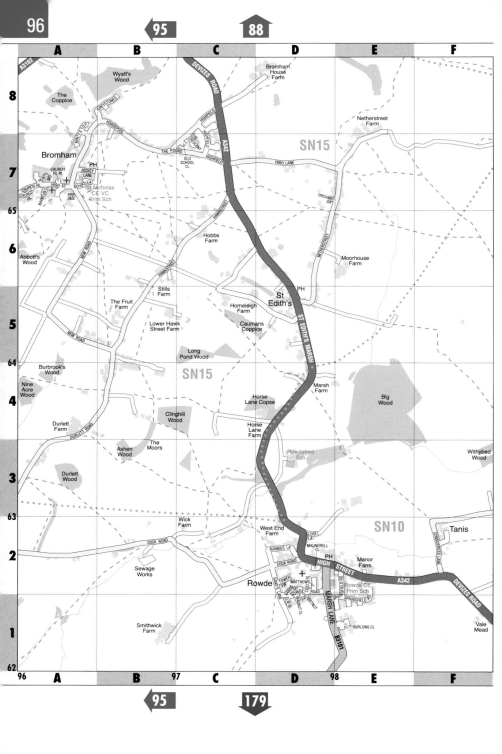

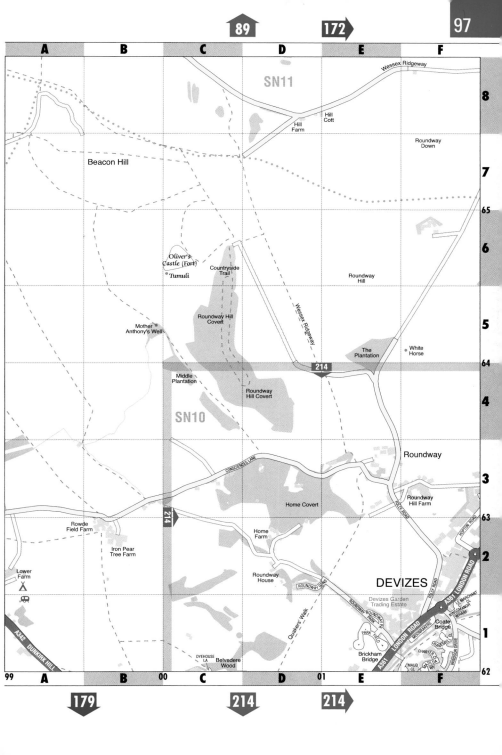

SN11

Wessex Ridgeway

Hill Cott

Hill Farm

Roundway Down

Beacon Hill

Roundway Hill

Oliver's Castle (Fort)

Tumuli

Countryside Trail

Wessex Ridgeway

Roundway Hill Covert

Mother Anthony's Well

The Plantation

White Horse

214

Middle Plantation

Roundway Hill Covert

SN10

Conscience's Lane

Roundway

Roundway Hill Farm

Folly Road

Home Covert

Rowde Field Farm

214

Iron Pear Tree Farm

Home Farm

DEVIZES

Devizes Garden Trading Estate

Folly Road

Nepton Road

A361 London Road

Lower Farm

Roundway House

Roundway Drive

Roundway Roundabout PK

Park Field

Quakers' Walk

Coate Bridge

A361 London Road

Charter

Brickham Bridge

Dyehouse La

Belvedere Wood

Maud Cl

Matilda Wy

A342 Dunkirk Hill

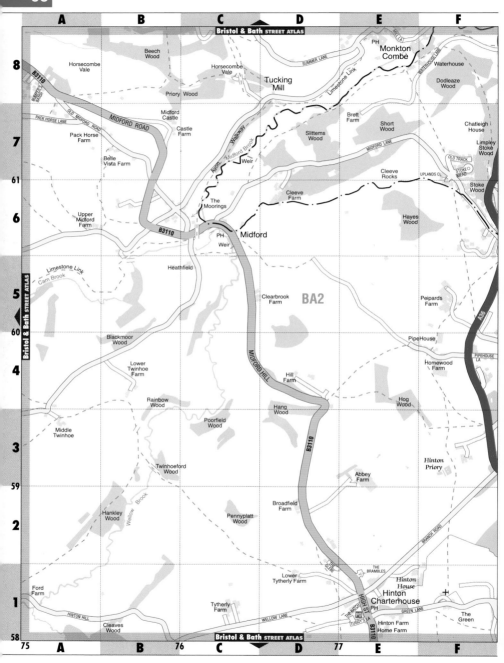

Monkton Combe

Waterhouse

Beech Wood

Horsecombe Vale

Horsecombe Vale

Tucking Mill

Dodleaze Wood

Chatleigh House

B3110

BUNKER'S BATCH

Priory Wood

Midford Castle

Castle Farm

SUMMER LANE

Limestone Link

MILL LA

PH

WATERHOUSE LANE

Brett Farm

Short Wood

Slittems Wood

Midford Lane

Limpley Stoke Wood

OLD TRACK

Pack Horse Lane

OLD MIDFORD ROAD

MIDFORD ROAD

Pack Horse Farm

Belle Vista Farm

Avon

Midford Brook

Walkway

Weir

Cleeve Rocks

UPLANDS CL

STOKE O MEAD

Stoke Wood

Upper Midford Farm

B3110

The Moorings

Cleeve Farm

Hayes Wood

Midford

PH

Weir

Heathfield

Limestone Link

Cam Brook

Clearbrook Farm

BA2

Peipards Farm

A36

Blackmoor Wood

PipeHouse

PIPEHOUSE LA

Lower Twinhoe Farm

MIDFORD HILL

Hill Farm

Homewood Farm

Rainbow Wood

Hog Combe

Middle Twinhoe

Poorfield Wood

Hang Wood

B3110

Hinton Priory

Twinhoeford Wood

Abbey Farm

Hankley Wood

Wellow Brook

Pennyplatt Wood

Broadfield Farm

Ford Farm

THE BATCH

THE BRAMBLES

Lower Tytherly Farm

Hinton House

PH

Hinton Charterhouse

The Green

HINTON HILL

Cleaves Wood

Tytherly Farm

WELLOW LANE

HIGH ST

TUGGY'S LA

B3110

GREEN LANE

Hinton Farm Home Farm

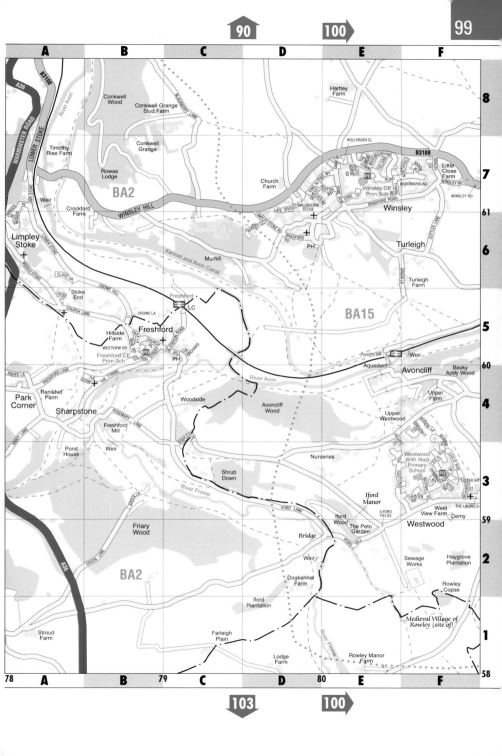

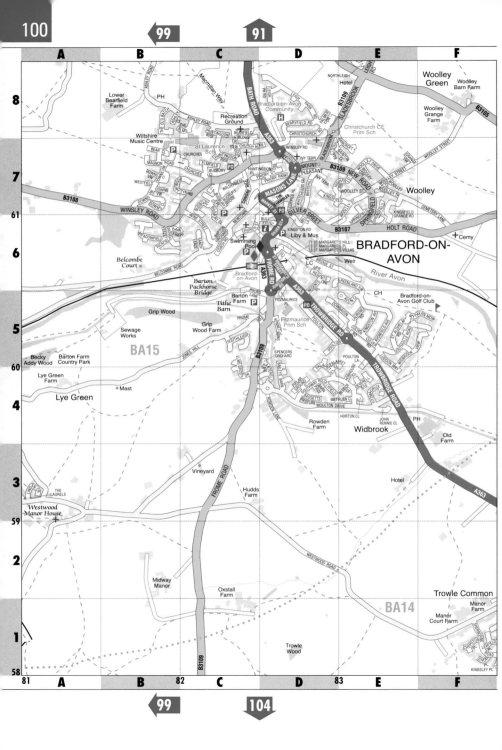

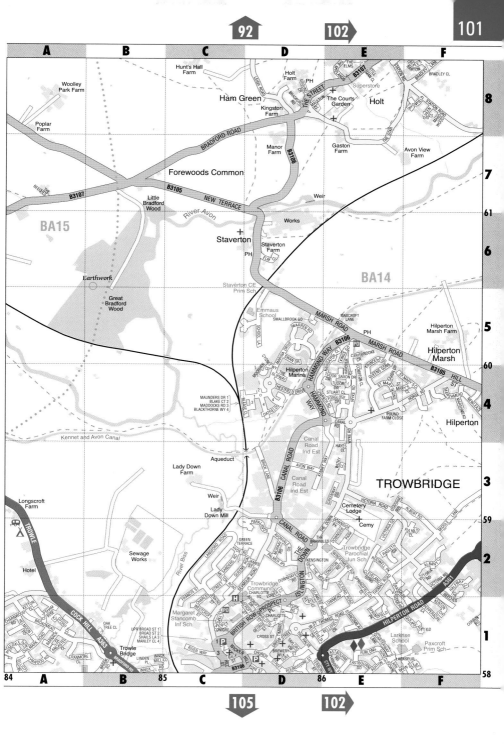

A   B   C   D   E   F

8
7
61
6
BA14
5
60
4
3
59
2
1
58

Woolley Park Farm
Poplar Farm

Hunt's Hall Farm
Holt Farm
PH
THE STREET
B3107
THE ELMS
Superstore
The Courts Garden
Holt
BRADLEY CL

Ham Green
Kingston Farm
BRADFORD ROAD
Manor Farm
Gaston Farm
Avon View Farm

Forewoods Common
B3106
B3107
B3105
New Terrace
Little Bradford Wood
River Avon
Weir
Works

BA15
Staverton
Staverton Farm
PH
ELM

Earthwork
Great Bradford Wood
Staverton CE Prim Sch
Emmaus School
SMALLBROOK GD
WARREN RD
MARSH ROAD
PH
MAXCROFT LANE
Hilperton Marsh Farm

Hilperton Marsh
SCHOOL LA
B3106
MARSH ROAD
B3105
HILL ST

Hilperton Marina
HAMMOND WAY
CARISBROOKE CR
60
Kennet and Avon Canal
MAUNDERS DR 1
BLAKE CT 2
MADDOCKS RD 3
BLACKTHORNE WY 4
THESTFIELD DRIVE
HAMMOND WAY
POUND FARM CLOSE
Hilperton

Aqueduct
Lady Down Farm
Canal Road Ind Est
CANAL ROAD
AVON WAY
HAYES CL

Weir
Lady Down Mill
Canal Road Ind Est
TROWBRIDGE
Cemetery Lodge
Cemy
VICTORIA ROAD
ALBERT RD

Longscroft Farm
Trowle
River Biss
Sewage Works
Green Terrace
PARK
THE BRAMBLES
Trowbridge Parochial Jun Sch
Kensington
ISLINGTON

Hotel
Trowbridge Community
CHARLOTTE
Downsview
HILPERTON ROAD
A361
Larkrise School
Paxcroft Prim Sch

Margaret Stancomb Inf Sch
H
British Row
Prospect
THE DOWN
York Rd
Brewery Wlk
Church St
Cross St
Roundstone
FURLONG
Larkspur
Eastbourne

Cock Hill
A363
Trowle Bridge
OAK TREE CL
UPR BROAD ST 1
BROAD ST 2
SHAILS LA 3
MANLEY CL 4
RIVER WAY
P
P
B3106

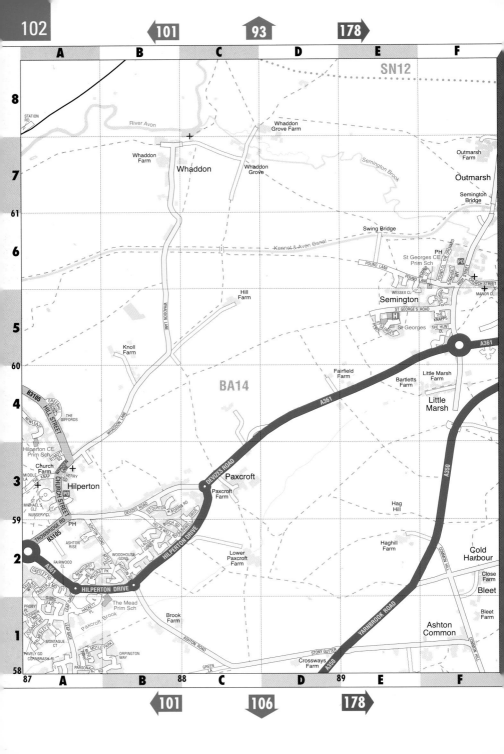

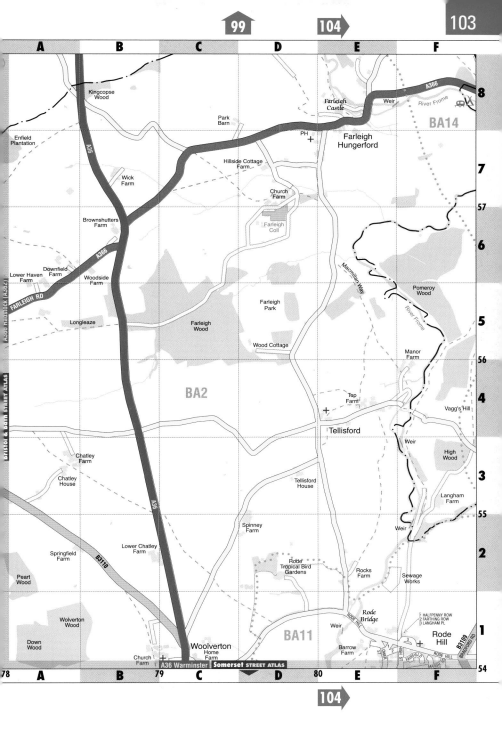

A   B   C   D   E   F

8

A366

Kingcopse Wood

Farleigh Castle

Weir

River Frome

BA14

Enfield Plantation

Park Barn

PH

Farleigh Hungerford

7

A36

Hillside Cottage Farm

Wick Farm

57

Church Farm

Brownshutters Farm

Farleigh Coll

6

A366

Macmillan Way

Downfield Farm

Lower Haven Farm

Woodside Farm

Pomeroy Wood

River Frome

FARLEIGH RD

B3105 PADSTOCK A3017

Longleaze

Farleigh Wood

Farleigh Park

5

Wood Cottage

Manor Farm

56

BA2

Top Farm

4

Vagg's Hill

Tellisford

Weir

High Wood

Chatley Farm

Chatley House

3

Tellisford House

Langham Farm

55

A36

Spinney Farm

Weir

Springfield Farm

B3110

Lower Chatley Farm

2

Peart Wood

Rode Tropical Bird Gardens

Rocks Farm

Sewage Works

Wolverton Wood

RODE HILL

Rode Bridge

1 HALFPENNY ROW
2 FARTHING ROW
3 LANGHAM PL

1

B3109 BRADFORD RD

Down Wood

Woolverton Home Farm

BA11

Weir

Barrow Farm

Rode Hill

HIGH ST

FAIRFIELD

RODE HILL

Church Farm

LOWER ST

MARSH

78   A   B   79   C   D   80   E   F   54

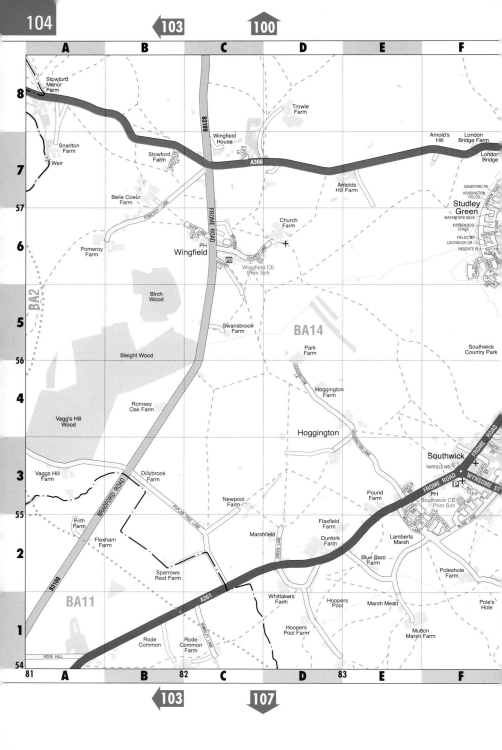

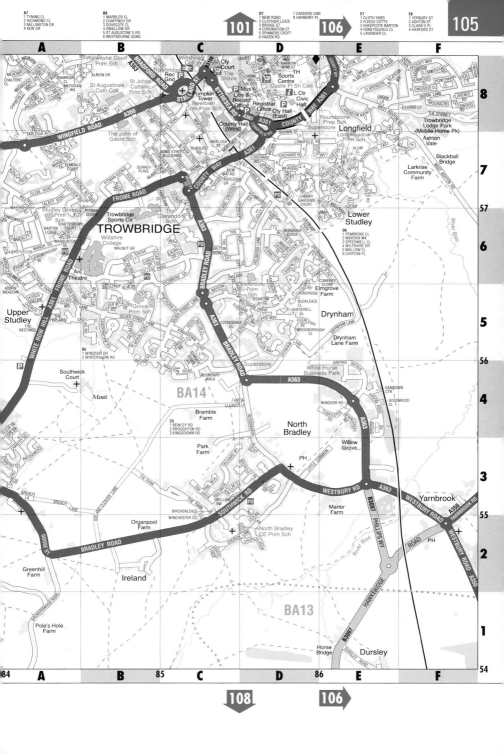

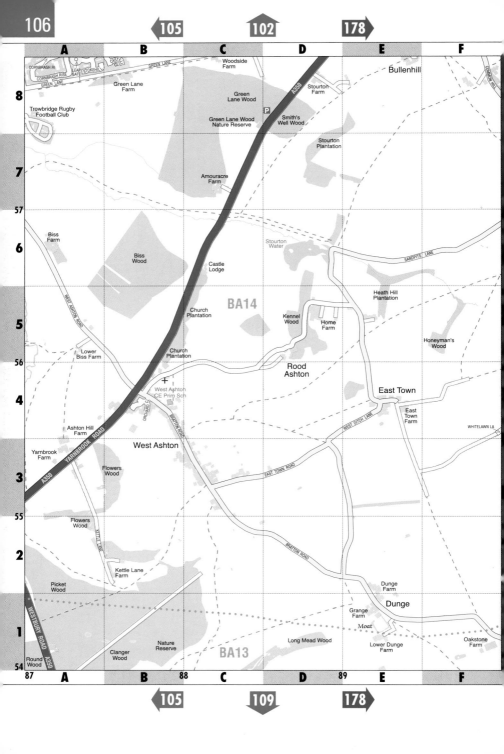

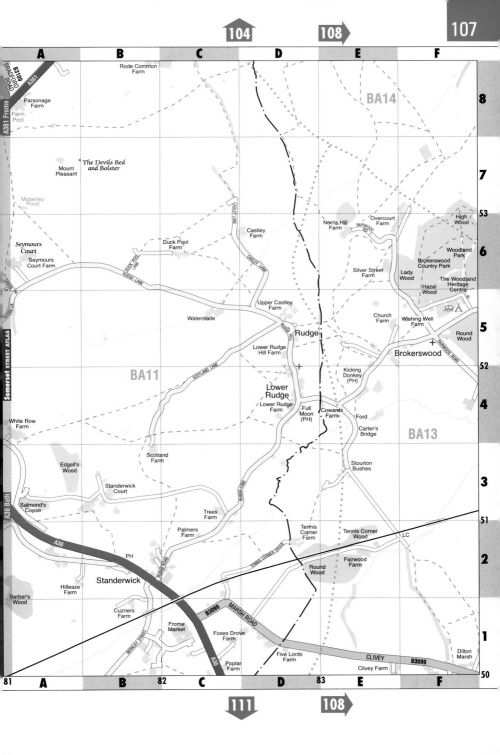

A B C D E F

8
7
53
6
5
52
4
3
51
2
1
50

84 A B 85 C D 86 E F

Druce's Farm
BROKERSWOOD ROAD
Ford
Cutteridge Farm
Conigree Wood
Brook Hall Farm
Court Farm
Norleaze Farm
PH
Hawkeridge
Norleaze
DURSLEY ROAD
CHURCH RD
B3097
HAWKERIDGE ROAD
Lodge Wood Farm
Hawkeridge Farm
LINK ROAD
BA14
BROADWAY NORTH
West Wilts Trading Estate
COURT WAY
Commerce Business Centre
SHAIL LOW STATION RD
VICTORY ROAD
CHEMICAL ROAD
ENGINEER ROAD
WASHINGTON RD
HEADQUARTERS ROAD
Moat
MOAT ROAD
BROADWAY EAST
QUARTERMASTER ROAD
Brokerswood Farm
Ox's Leaze
High Wood
STORRIDGE ROAD
MAIN ST EAST
MAIN ST EAST
Storridge Farm
West Wilts Craft Centre
Glenmore
B3097
HAWKERIDGE ROAD
HAWKERIDGE ROAD
STORRIDGE ROAD
Northacre Ind Park
KINGDOM AVENUE
HAWKERIDGE PK
The Ham
Bass Brook
STEPHENSON ROAD
Sewage Works
Downside
THE HAM
STATION ROAD
ELMS LANE
FROGMORE ROAD
BRAMBLE DR
PHIPPS CL 1
HAYWARD PL 2
INGRAM PL 3
LUDLOW CL 4
Round Wood
Westbury Ind Est
Westbury
STATION APP
HEATHER CL
Westbury United AFC
STATION ROAD
BA13
Brook Farm
BROOK DROVE
BROOK LANE
OLDFIELD ROAD
OLDFIELD PK
OLDFIELD PARK
Fairwood
Fairwood House
Fairwood Junction
Lamberts Farm
FAIRWOOD ROAD
Westbury CE Jun Sch
ABBOTS CL
PHOENIX RI 1
GRYPHON CL 2
GREAT ROC RD 3
WILLOW GR 1
SYCAMORE GR 2
Eden Vale
Little Fairwood
Bremeridge Farm
Penleigh Farm
PENLEIGH ROAD
PERCHERON PL
Moat
Penleigh
Woodland Ind Est
Matravers Sch
SPRINGFIELD RD
SHETLAND CL
BRISKAY GDNS
GREEN LANE
LEIGH ROAD
GOOSELANDS
WILLOUGHBY CL
WARMINSTER RD
Works
Penleigh Mill Farm
District Centre
FAIRHAVEN
A3098
SANDALWOOD RD
Westbury Leigh CE Prim Sch
BECKETT PL
CASPIAN GDNS
LAVERTON ROAD
A350
Sewage Works
ST MARYS LA
Westbury Leigh
FAIRWAYS
Dilton Marsh
BLACK HORSE LANE
LEIGHTON PK N
LEIGHTON PK RD
LEIGHTON PK S

E1
1 SANDALWOOD RD
2 DARTMOOR RD
3 OLDENBURGH RD
4 BRABANT WAY
5 SUFFOLK RD
6 EXMOOR RD

F1
1 PARK VW DR
2 LEIGHTON PK W
3 LAVERTON GN
4 LEIGHTON PK N
5 LEIGHTON PK RD
6 SAND HOLE LA

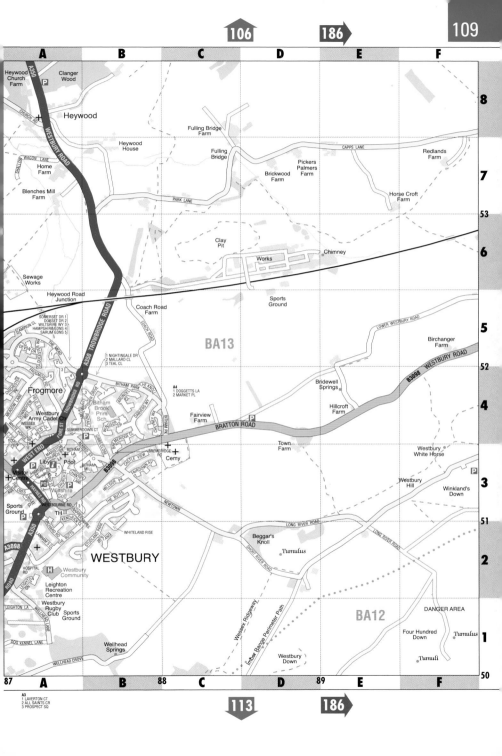

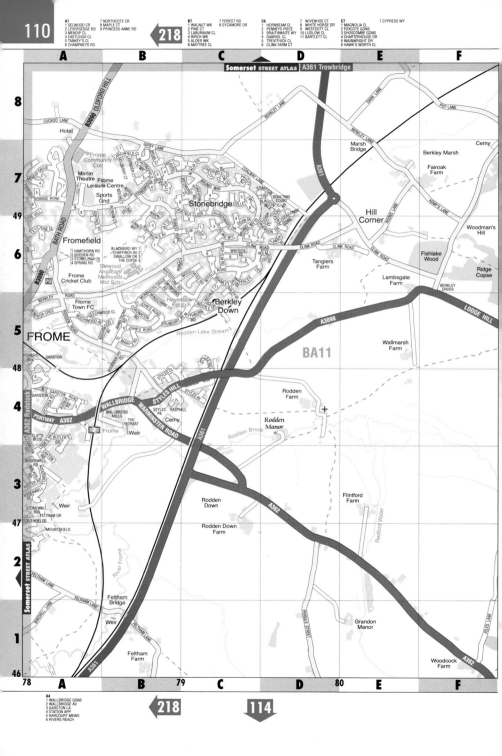

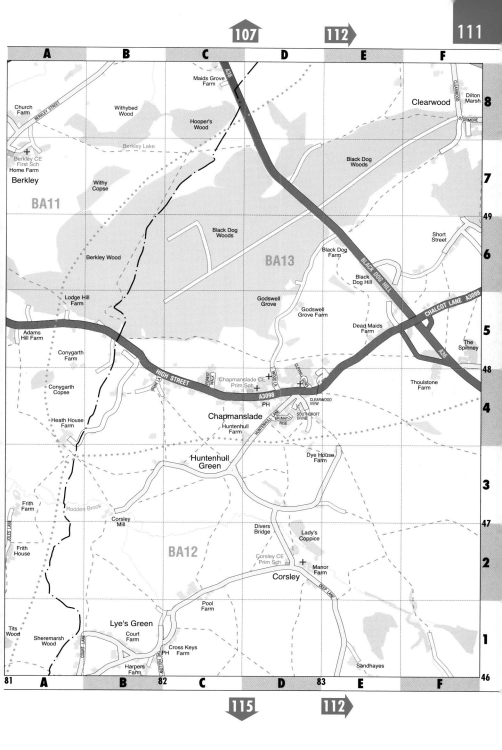

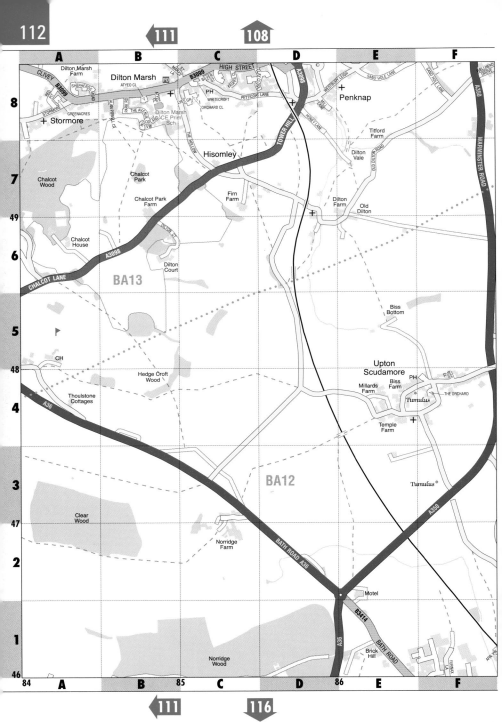

A   B   C   D   E   F

8

Dilton Marsh Farm
Dilton Marsh
ATYEO CL
SHEPHERDS MEAD
CLIVEY B3099
HIGH STREET
B3099
PH
WHITECROFT
ORCHARD CL
Penknap
WESTBURY LEIGH
SAND HOLE LANE
A3098

Stormore
GREENACRES
Dilton Marsh CE Prim Sch
PETTICOT LANE
TOWER HILL
HONEY LANE
MILL LANE
OLD DILTON ROAD
Titford Farm
Dilton Vale

7

Chalcot Wood
Chalcot Park
Hisomley
Firn Farm
Dilton Farm
Old Dilton

49

Chalcot Park Farm

6

Chalcot House
A3098 DILTON CT

CHALCOT LANE

BA13

Dilton Court

Biss Bottom

5

CH
Hedge Croft Wood

48

A36

Thoulstone Cottages

Upton Scudamore
Millards Farm
Biss Farm
PH
THE ORCHARD
Tumulus

4

Temple Farm

3

BA12

Tumulus

47

Clear Wood

A350

2

Norridge Farm
BATH ROAD A36
Motel

1

Norridge Wood
A36
B3414
BATH ROAD
Brick Hill

46

84   A   B   85   C   D   86   E   F

WARMINSTER ROAD A350
SAND HOLE LANE
WELLHEAD DROVE

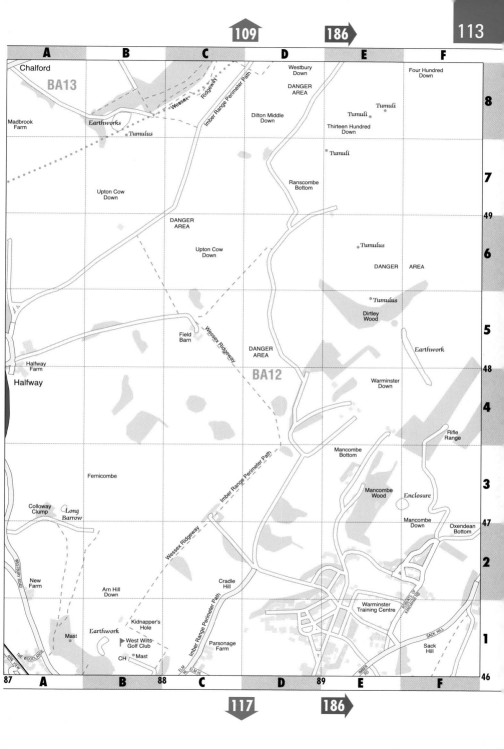

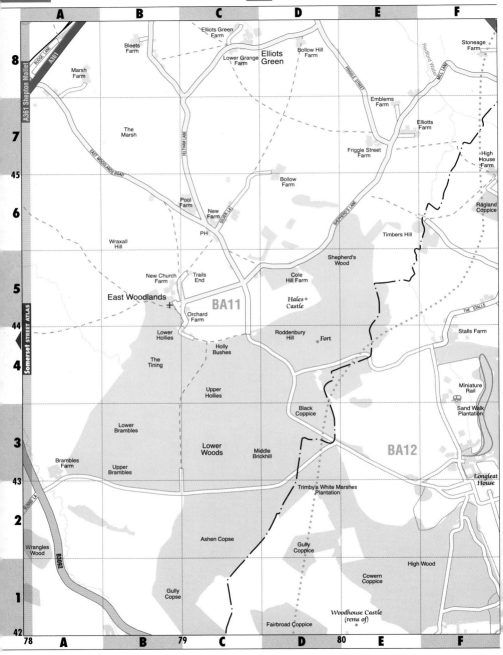

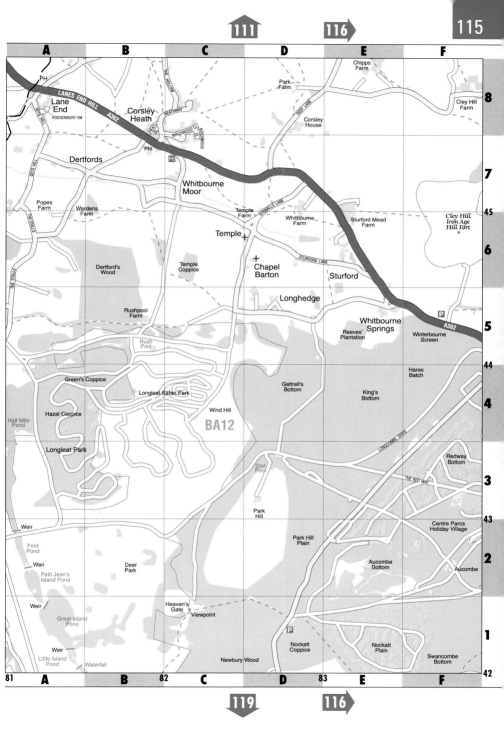

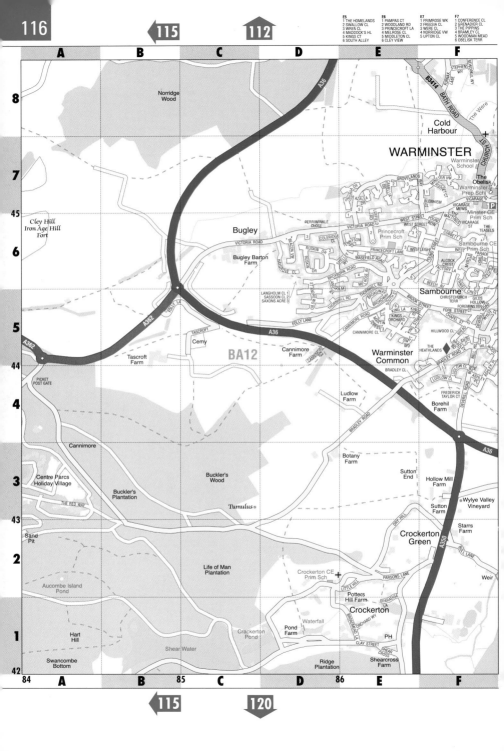

115
112

E5
1 THE HOMELANDS
2 SWALLOW CL
3 WREN CL
4 MADDOCK'S HL
5 KINGS CT
6 SOUTH ALLEY

E6
1 PAMPAS CT
2 WOODLAND RD
3 PRINCECROFT LA
4 MELROSE CL
5 MIDDLETON CL
6 CLEY VIEW

E7
1 PRIMROSE WK
2 FREESIA CL
3 WERE CL
4 NORRIDGE VW
5 UPTON CL

F7
1 CONFERENCE CL
2 GRENADIER CL
3 THE PIPPINS
4 BRAMLEY CL
5 WOODMAN MEAD
6 OBELISK TERR

8

7

45

6

5

44

4

3

43

2

1

42

A   B   C   D   E   F

Norridge
Wood

Cold
Harbour

WARMINSTER

Warminster
School

The
Obelisk

Warminster
Prep Schl

Minster CE
Prim Sch

GROVELANDS

BLENHEIM

VICARAGE
MEWS
THE
TEASELS

Cley Hill
Iron Age Hill
Fort

Bugley

PERRIWINKLE
CLOSE

Princecroft
Prim Sch

WEST STREET

Sambourne CE
Prim Sch

Bugley Barton
Farm

VICTORIA ROAD

COLERIDGE
CL

Victoria Road

PRINCECROFT LANE

WESTLEIGH

ALCOCK
CREST
FACTORY ST

RUSKIN

MASEFIELD ROAD

BROADWAS ROAD

BEECH AV

Sambourne

LANGHOLM CL 1
SASSOON CL 2
SAXONS ACRE 3

ST MARTIN'S RD

CHURNHILL RD

BROADWAY

KINGS
ORCHARD

CHRISTCHURCH
TERR

GILES
HOLLOW

FORE STREET

CHAPEL ST

A362

FOLLY LA

TASCROFT

CANNIMORE ROAD

CANNIMORE CL

FOLLY LANE

A36

HILLWOOD CL

THE
HEATHLANDS

BA12

Cemy

Cannimore
Farm

Warminster
Common

BRADLEY ROAD

BRADLEY CL

LUDLOW CL

Tascroft
Farm

A362

PICKET
POST GATE

Ludlow
Farm

BRADLEY ROAD

Borehil
Farm

FREDERICK
TAYLOR CT

A36

Cannimore

Botany
Farm

Sutton
End

Hollow Mill
Farm

Centre Parcs
Holiday Village

Buckler's
Plantation

Buckler's
Wood

THE RED WAY

Tumulus

Sutton
Farm

Wylye Valley
Vineyard

Sand
Pit

Crockerton
Green

Starrs
Farm

BELL LANE

A350

Life of Man
Plantation

Crockerton CE
Prim Sch

PARSONS LANE

Weir

Aucombe Island
Pond

LITTLE HILL

DRY HILL

Potters
Hill Farm

PARADISE
LA

Waterfall

Crockerton

Hart
Hill

Crackerton
Pond

Pond
Farm

Ridge
Plantation

Shearcross
Farm

PH

CLAY STREET

Swancombe
Bottom

Shear Water

84   A   B   85   C   D   86   E   F

115
120

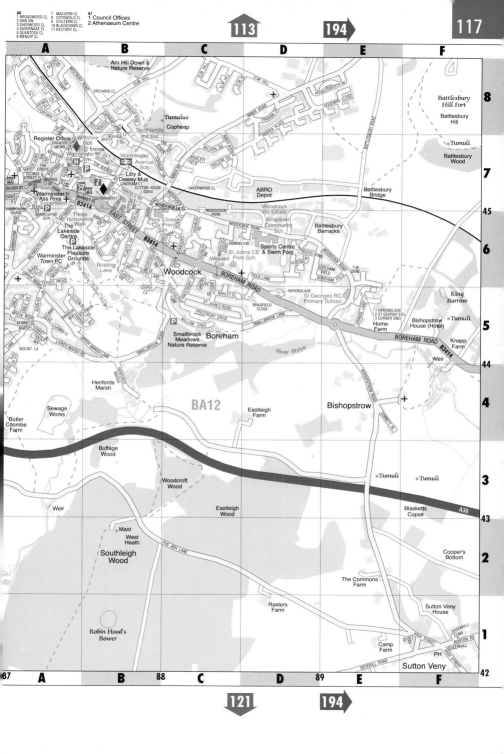

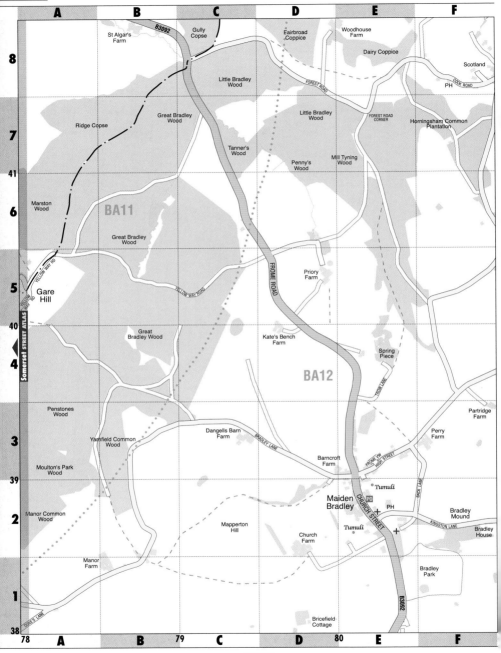

Somerset STREET ATLAS

B3092

A   B   C   D   E   F

St Algar's Farm

Gully Copse

Fairbroad Coppice

Woodhouse Farm

Dairy Coppice

Scotland

COCK ROAD

PH

8

Little Bradley Wood

FOREST ROAD

Ridge Copse

Great Bradley Wood

Little Bradley Wood

FOREST ROAD CORNER

Horningsham Common Plantation

7

41

Tanner's Wood

Penny's Wood

Mill Tyning Wood

Marston Wood

BA11

6

Great Bradley Wood

FROME ROAD

Priory Farm

YELLOW WAY RD

YELLOW WAY ROAD

Gare Hill

5

40

Great Bradley Wood

Kate's Bench Farm

Spring Piece

BA12

TYTON LANE

4

Penstones Wood

Yarnfield Common Wood

Dangells Barn Farm

BRADLEY LANE

Barncroft Farm

FROME VW

HIGH STREET

Perry Farm

Partridge Farm

3

Moulton's Park Wood

39

Maiden Bradley

Tumuli

BACK LANE

Bradley Mound

Manor Common Wood

Mapperton Hill

Tumuli

CHURCH STREET

PH

KINGSTON LANE

Bradley House

2

Church Farm

Manor Farm

Bradley Park

1

FOXLE'S LANE

B3092

Bricefield Cottage

38

78   A   B   79   C   D   80   E   F

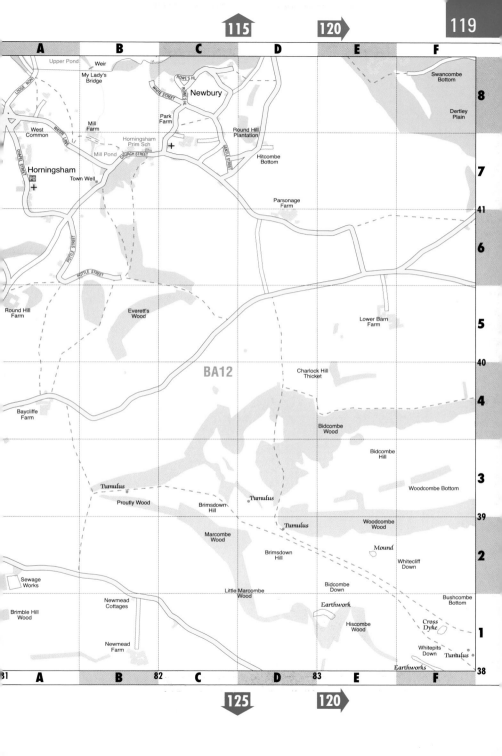

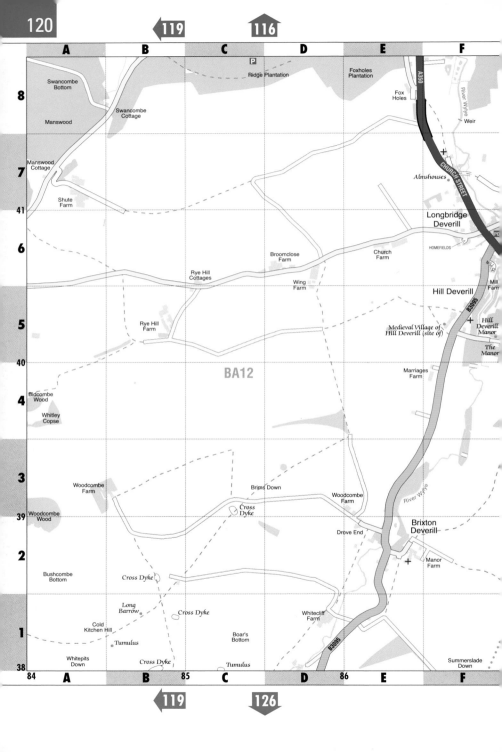

119
116

A   **B**   **C**   **D**   **E**   **F**

P
Ridge Plantation

Swancombe
Bottom

Foxholes
Plantation

8

Fox
Holes

Swancombe
Cottage

River Wylye

Manswood

Weir

7

Manswood
Cottage

Almshouses

Longbridge
Deverill

Shute
Farm

41

CHURCH STREET

A350

6

Broomclose
Farm

Church
Farm

HOMEFIELDS

PO

Rye Hill
Cottages

Wing
Farm

Hill Deverill

5

Rye Hill
Farm

Medieval Village of
Hill Deverill (site of)

Hill
Deverill
Manor

Mill
Farm

B3095

The
Manor

40

BA12

Marriages
Farm

4

Bidcombe
Wood

Whitley
Copse

3

Woodcombe
Farm

Brims Down

Woodcombe
Farm

River Wylye

39

Woodcombe
Wood

Cross
Dyke

Brixton
Deverill

Drove End

2

Bushcombe
Bottom

Cross Dyke

Manor
Farm

1

Long
Barrow

Cross Dyke

Cold
Kitchen Hill

Boar's
Bottom

Whitecliff
Farm

B3095

Tumulus

38

Whitepits
Down

Cross Dyke

Tumulus

Summerslade
Down

84   **A**   **B**   **85**   **C**   **D**   **86**   **E**   **F**

119
126

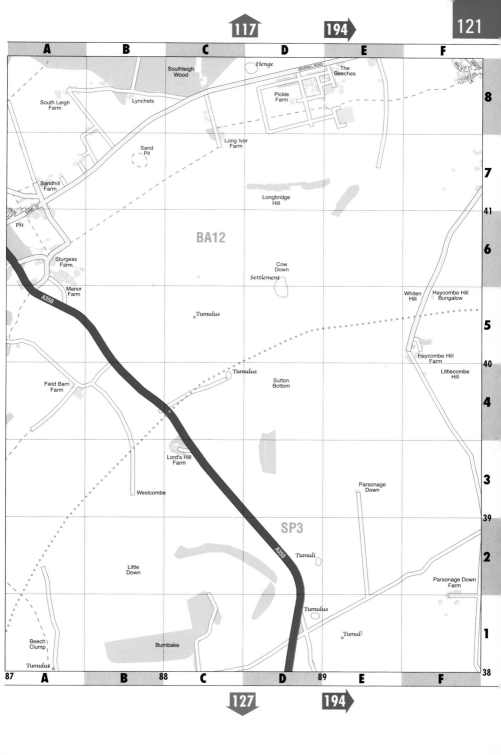

8

7

37

6

5

36

4

3

35

2

1

34

A   B   73   C   D   74   E   F

72

Hick's Park Wood

Hents Hill Farm

CANNWOOD LANE

Canwood Farm

Walters Farm

Forest Gate Farm

Lark Farm

Lipgate Farm

HAMMER STREET

Border Farm

Longfield Farm

Green Acres

JAMES'S HILL

SOCK'S HILL

Horseshoe Farm

Brewham House

Treetops Farm

PH

Jerrards Farm

North Brewham

Brewham Lodge Farm

Cooks Farm

River Brue

Earthwork

TILE HILL

BA10

Bridge Farm

PH

Mill Farm

Street Farm

CHARCROFT HILL

STREET LANE

Haven Farm

King's Wood

South Brewham

Brook Farm

STREET LANE

Jack's Castle Plantation

Charcroft Farm

Holland Farm

Macmillan Way

Tumulus

CHARCROFT HILL

Shave Farm

SHAVE LANE

TOWER ROAD

P

Hookgate Farm

Hilcombe Farm

Alfred's Tower

Convent Bottom

Crawley House Farm

KINGSETTLE HILL

Hilcombe Hanging

Cards Farm

Brewham Brake Farm

Berridge

Tower Road Farm

Leland Trail

Hardway House

Pillinge Farm

Park Farm

Brewham Wood

Beaumont's Wood

Hardway

PH

Picketts Farm

Aaron's Hill

Moss Cottage

Picket's Copse

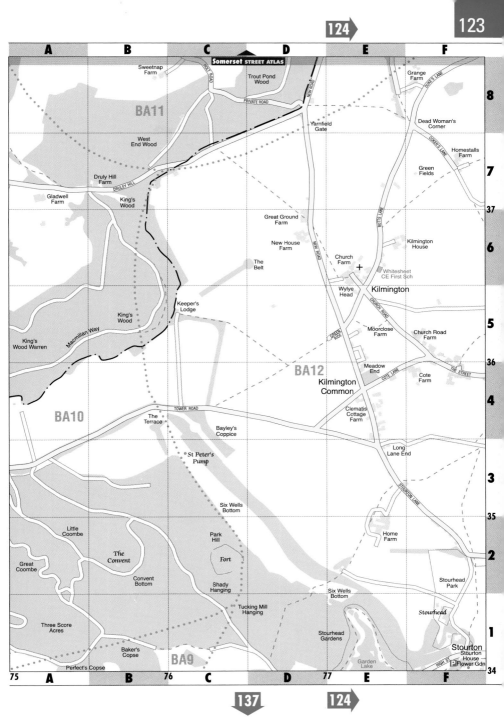

Somerset STREET ATLAS

Sweetnap Farm

Trout Pond Wood

PRIVATE ROAD

NEW ROAD

POOL ROAD

BA11

West End Wood

Yarnfield Gate

Grange Farm

DUKE'S LANE

Dead Woman's Corner

COKER'S LANE

Homestalls Farm

Druly Hill Farm

DRULEY HILL

Green Fields

Gladwell Farm

King's Wood

Great Ground Farm

BUTTS LANE

Kilmington House

New House Farm

NEW ROAD

The Belt

Church Farm

Whitesheet CE First Sch

Kilmington

Keeper's Lodge

Wylye Head

King's Wood

CHURCH ROAD

GREEN RIDE

Moorclose Farm

Church Road Farm

King's Wood

Macmillan Way

King's Wood Warren

BA12

Meadow End

COTE LANE

THE STREET

Cote Farm

Kilmington Common

BA10

TOWER ROAD

The Terrace

Bayley's Coppice

Clematis Cottage Farm

Long Lane End

St Peter's Pump

Six Wells Bottom

STOURTON LANE

Little Coombe

Park Hill

Home Farm

Great Coombe

The Convent

Fort

Convent Bottom

Shady Hanging

Stourhead Park

Stourhead

Tucking Mill Hanging

Three Score Acres

Six Wells Bottom

Stourhead Gardens

Stourton

Stourton House Flower Gdn

Baker's Copse

BA9

Garden Lake

HIGH ST

Perfect's Copse

123
118

A B C D E F

8

Little Knoll Wood

Little Knoll

Rag Wood

B3092

Long Knoll Wood

Tumulus

Long Knoll

7

37

Milbury Coppice

Knoll Farm

6

Manor Farm

Norton Ferris

Elm Farm

COOMBE BARN LANE

Coombe Barn Farm

5

Norton Ferris Farm

COOMBE BARN LA

36

THE STREET

Street Farm

Berkeley Farm

BA12

4

Manor Farm

White Sheet Downs

Earthwork

3

PH

WHITE SHEET LANE

Neolithic Camp

Cross Dyke

Cross Dyke

Coldcot Farm

35

P

Pillow Mounds

Tumuli

2

STOURTON LANE

Beech Clump

White Sheet Hill Nature Reserve

Fort

White Sheet Castle

1

Drove Lodge

B3092

Search Farm

Tumuli

Cross Dykes

34

Stourton

HIGH ST

78 A B 79 C D 80 E F

123
138

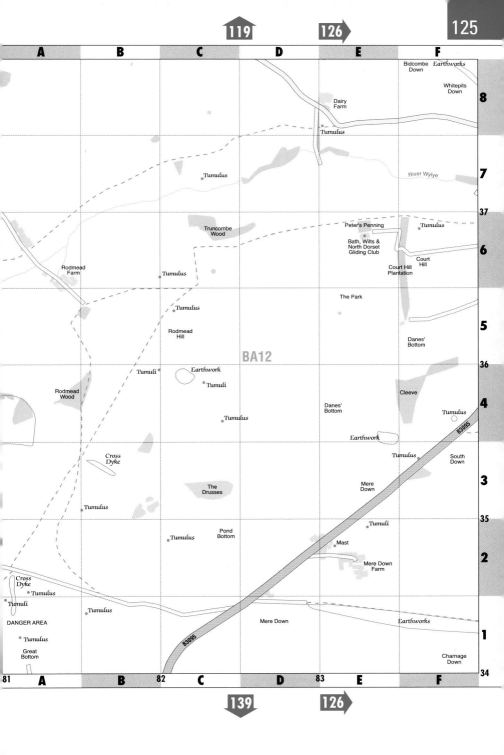

Bidcombe Down
Earthworks
Whitepits Down

8

Dairy Farm

Tumulus

River Wylye

7

37

Tumulus

Truncombe Wood

Peter's Penning

Tumulus

Bath, Wilts & North Dorset Gliding Club

6

Rodmead Farm

Tumulus

Court Hill Plantation

Court Hill

The Park

Danes' Bottom

5

Tumulus

Rodmead Hill

BA12

36

Tumuli

Earthwork

Tumuli

Cleeve

Rodmead Wood

Danes' Bottom

Tumulus

4

Tumulus

Earthwork

B3095

Cross Dyke

Tumulus

South Down

The Drusses

Mere Down

3

Tumulus

35

Tumulus

Pond Bottom

Tumuli

Mast

2

Cross Dyke

Mere Down Farm

Tumulus

Tumulus

Tumulus

DANGER AREA

Mere Down

Earthworks

1

Tumulus

Great Bottom

B3095

Charnage Down

34

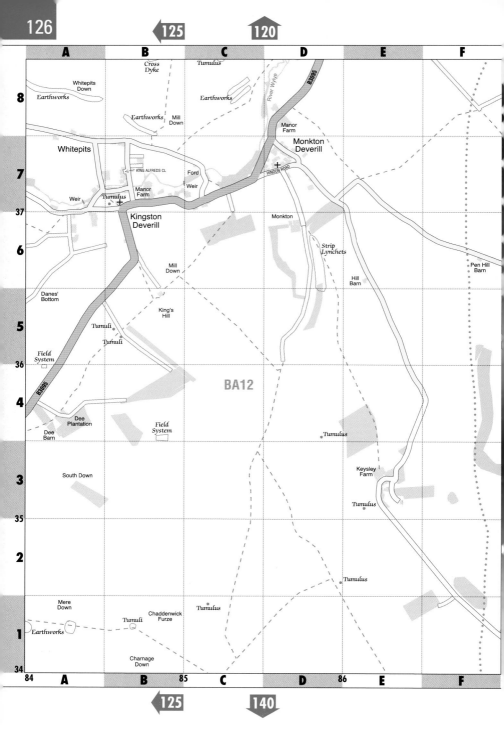

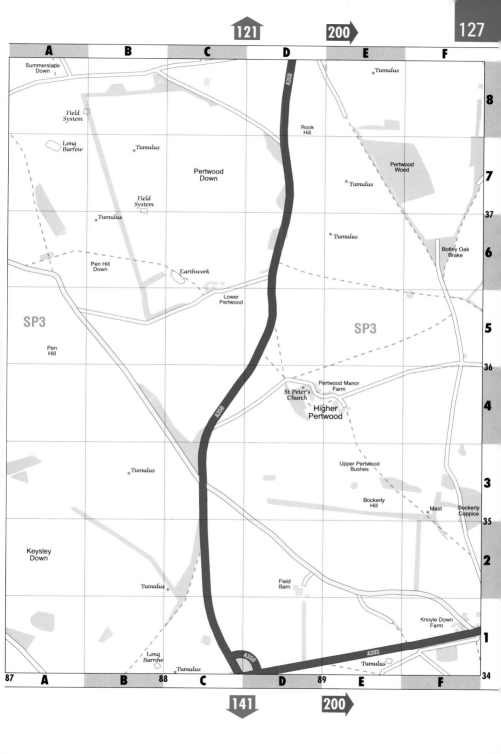

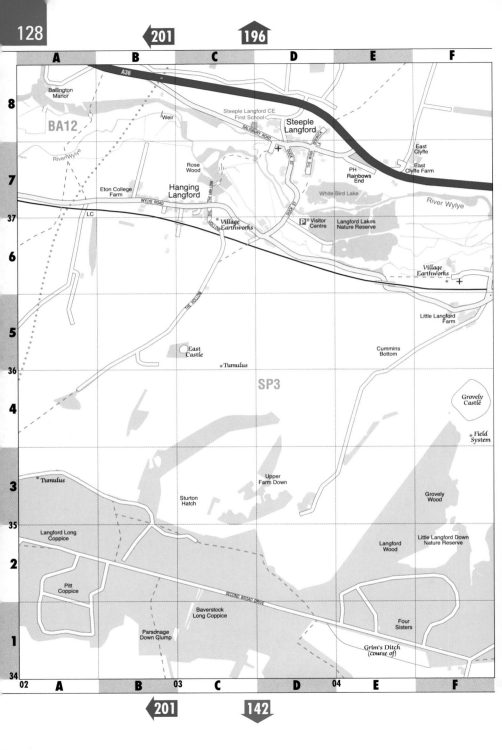

A   B   C   D   E   F

A36

8

Ballington Manor

Steeple Langford CE First School

Weir

SALISBURY ROAD

Steeple Langford

BA12

East Clyffe

7

Rose Wood

THE HOLLOW

BERWICK LA

DUCK ST

THE WARR

East Clyffe Farm

Eton College Farm

Hanging Langford

PH Rainbows End

WYLYE ROAD

River Wylye

White Bird Lake

37

LC

THE HOLLOW

Village Earthworks

P Visitor Centre

Langford Lakes Nature Reserve

River Wylye

6

THE HOLLOW

Village Earthworks

5

East Castle

Little Langford Farm

Tumulus

Cummins Bottom

36

SP3

4

Grovely Castle

Field System

3

Tumulus

Upper Farm Down

Grovely Wood

Sturton Hatch

35

Langford Long Coppice

Langford Wood

Little Langford Down Nature Reserve

2

Pitt Coppice

SECOND BROAD DRIVE

Baverstock Long Coppice

Four Sisters

1

Parsonage Down Glump

Grim's Ditch (course of)

34

02   A   B   03   C   D   04   E   F

A B C D E F

8

7

37

6

5

36

4

3

35

2

1

34

Stapleford Castle
Ring & Bailey

Manor
Farm
Bury
Bridge
UPPINGTON LANE

RIVERSIDE TR
PO

Brooklet
Farm

B3083

CHURCH FURLONG

RIVERSIDE
TERRACE

Staplford

BERWICK ROAD

Mast
Serrington

CHAPEL LA

BUTTS HL

Ford

PH

CHAIN HILL
CHAIN DRIVE

Little
Langford

Hungerford
Lodge Farm

Kingsmead
Bridge

Little
Wishford
Little Wishford
Farm

A36

SP3

River Wylye

36

Strip
Lynchets

Manor
Farm
PH

MANOR

FARM LA

LANGFORD RD

WEST
ST

SP2

Ebsbury

• *Field*
System

Ebsbury
Hill

Great
Wishford

Ebsbury
Copse

• *Settlement*

Monarch's Way

TEYTON ROAD

• *Field*
System

Penning
Bottom

GROVELY ROAD

Penning
Bottom

Grovely
Wood

Hadden
Hill

FIRST BROAD DRIVE

Hadden

Heath
Hill

A36

A 06 B C 07 D E F

129

197

A   B   C   D   E   F

8

Eighteen Acre
Plantation

Stapleford
Down

Camp
Plantation

7

SP3

Chain
Hill

Camp
Cottages

Tumulus

37

Monarch's Way

CHAIN DROVE

Tumulus

6

Stoford Hill
Buildings

SP4

Monarch's Way

5

Stoford
Bottom

36

A36

Enclosure

4

MOUNT PLEASANT
RIVERSIDE CL

Newton
Barrow

PH

Great
Wishford CE
First Sch

Charity
Farm

WEST ST

Masts

PO

Stoford
Bridge

Stoford

Wishford
Farm

Village
Earthworks

SP2

SOUTH ST

Town
End

Stoford
Farm

3

35

KINGSMEAD

River Wylye

2

HIGHLANDS
WEST ST
ASHDELL
ST ANDREWS RD

South
Newton

PH

1

Manor
Farm

A36

SP3

Mill
Farm

34

08   A   B   09   C   D   10   E   F

129

144

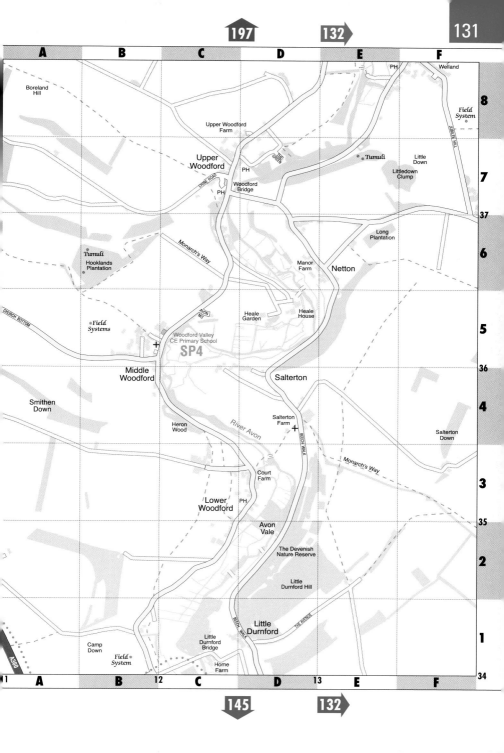

A   B   C   D   E   F

Welland
PH

Field System

8

Boreland Hill

Upper Woodford Farm

Upper Woodford

THE GREEN

PH

Tumuli

Little Down

Littledown Clump

7

CHINE ROAD

PH

Woodford Bridge

37

Long Plantation

Monarch's Way

6

Tumuli

Hooklands Plantation

Manor Farm

Netton

CHURCH BOTTOM

AVON MS

Field Systems

Heale Garden

Heale House

5

Woodford Valley CE Primary School

SP4

Middle Woodford

Salterton

36

Smithen Down

Heron Wood

River Avon

Salterton Farm

4

BEECH WALK

Salterton Down

Lower Woodford

PH

Avon Vale

Monarch's Way

3

Court Farm

35

The Devenish Nature Reserve

Little Durnford Hill

2

BEECH WALK

Little Durnford

THE AVENUE

A360

Camp Down

Field System

Little Durnford Bridge

Home Farm

1

34

A   B   C   D   E   F
12   13

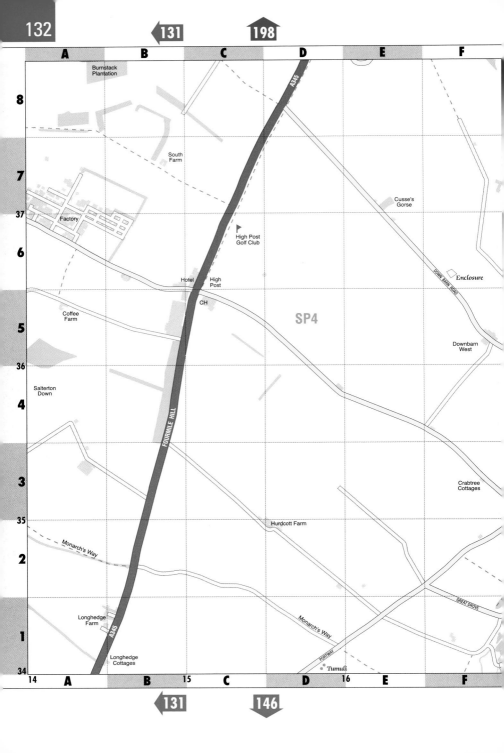

131
198

A   **B**   **C**   **D**   **E**   **F**

Burnstack Plantation

A345

8

South Farm

7

Cusse's Gorse

37

Factory

High Post Golf Club

6

DOWN BARN ROAD

Enclosure

Hotel   High Post

CH

Coffee Farm

SP4

5

Downbarn West

36

Salterton Down

FOURMILE HILL

4

3

Crabtree Cottages

35

Hurdcott Farm

Monarch's Way

2

Monarch's Way

GREAT DROVE

Longhedge Farm

A345

1

Longhedge Cottages

PORTWAY

34

Tumuli

14   **A**   **B**   15   **C**   **D**   16   **E**   **F**

131
146

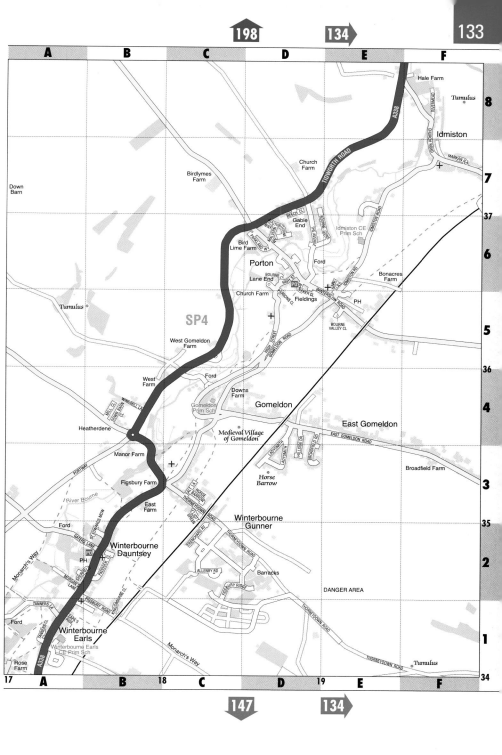

A   B   C   D   E   F

8

Hale Farm

Tumulus

Idmiston

7

Down
Barn

Birdlymes
Farm

Church
Farm

TIDWORTH ROAD

A338

37

Bird
Lime Farm

Gable
End

Idmiston CE
Prim Sch

MARKAN RD

6

Porton

Bourne
Lane End

Ford

Bonacres
Farm

SP4

Church Farm

Fieldings

PH

5

West Gomeldon
Farm

BOURNE
VALLEY CL

36

West
Farm

Ford

Downs
Farm

4

Heatherdene

Gomeldon
Prim Sch

Gomeldon

East Gomeldon

EAST GOMELDON ROAD

Tumulus

Manor Farm

*Medieval Village
of Gomeldon*

Broadfield Farm

3

River Bourne

Figsbury Farm

East
Farm

Horse
Barrow

Winterbourne
Gunner

35

Ford

Winterbourne
Dauntsey

PH

ALLENBY RD

Barracks

DANGER AREA

2

TANNERS LA

Ford

Winterbourne
Earls

Winterbourne Earls
CE Prim Sch

Monarch's Way

A338

THORNEYDOWN ROAD

Tumulus

Rose
Farm

1

17   A   B   18   C   D   19   E   F   34

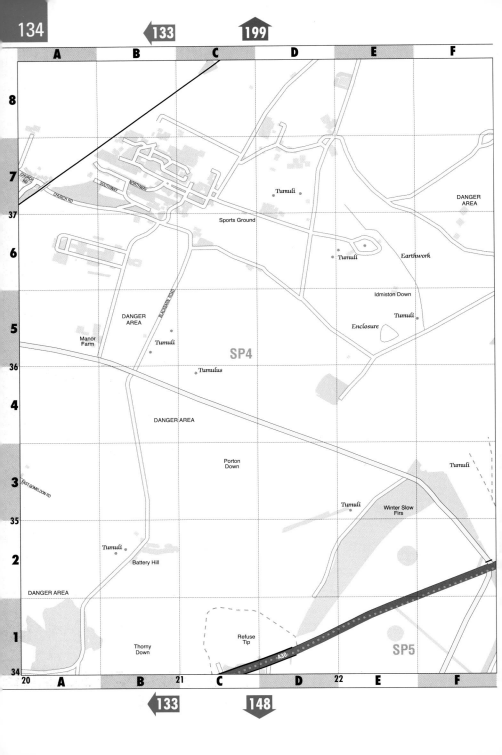

133
199

A   B   C   D   E   F

8

7

CHURCH RD

CHURCH RD   SOUTHWAY   NORTHWAY

37

Tumuli

DANGER
AREA

Sports Ground

6

Tumuli

Earthwork

Idmiston Down

BLACKBARN ROAD

DANGER
AREA

Tumuli

5

Manor
Farm

Tumuli

Enclosure

SP4

36

Tumulus

4

DANGER AREA

Porton
Down

Tumuli

3

EAST GOMELDON RD

Tumuli

Winter Slow
Firs

35

Tumuli

2

Battery Hill

DANGER AREA

1

Refuse
Tip

SP5

Thorny
Down

A30

34

20   A   B   21   C   D   22   E   F

133
148

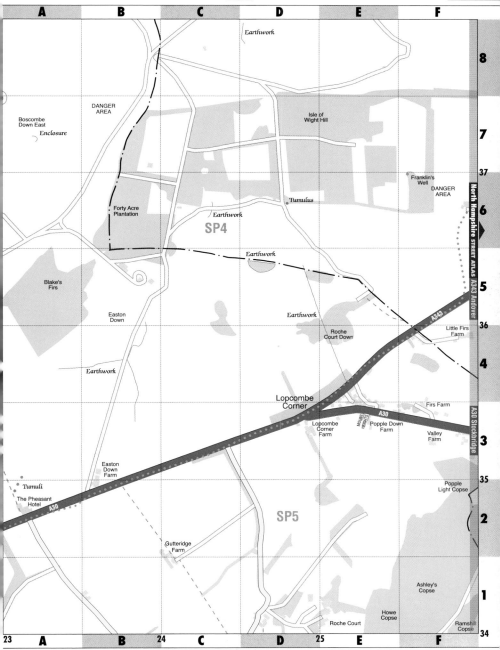

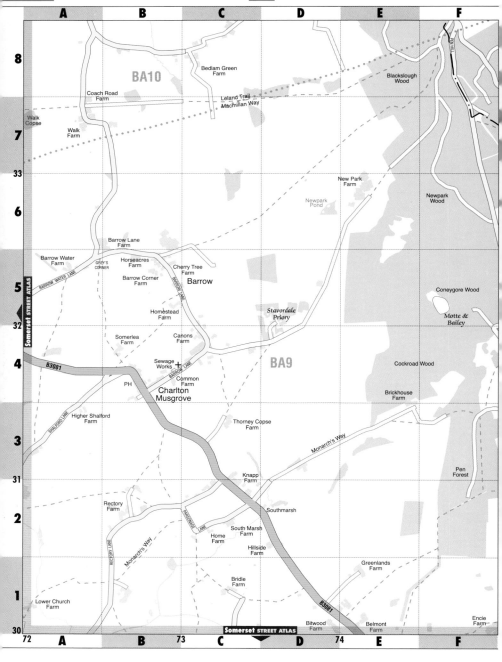

8

BA10

Bedlam Green
Farm

Blackslough
Wood

Coach Road
Farm

Leland Trail
Macmillan Way

Walk
Copse

7

Walk
Farm

33

New Park
Farm

Newpark
Wood

6

Newpark
Pond

Barrow Lane
Farm

Barrow Water
Farm

GREY'S
CORNER

Horseacres
Farm

Cherry Tree
Farm

5

BARROW WATER LANE

Barrow Corner
Farm

Barrow

Coneygore Wood

32

Homestead
Farm

Stavordale
Priory

Motte &
Bailey

Somerlea
Farm

Canons
Farm

4

B3081

Sewage
Works

Common
Farm

BA9

Cockroad Wood

PH

Charlton
Musgrove

Brickhouse
Farm

Higher Shalford
Farm

Thorney Copse
Farm

Monarch's Way

3

SHALFORD LANE

31

Knapp
Farm

Pen
Forest

Rectory
Farm

Southmarsh

2

RECTORY LANE

Monarch's Way

PASSENGER LANE

Home
Farm

South Marsh
Farm

Greenlands
Farm

Hillside
Farm

Lower Church
Farm

Bridle
Farm

B3081

Encie
Farm

1

30

Bitwood
Farm

Belmont
Farm

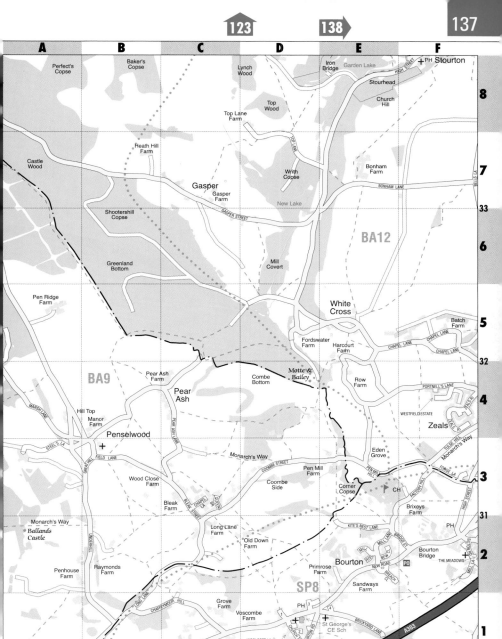

A   B   C   D   E   F

Perfect's Copse

Baker's Copse

Lynch Wood

Iron Bridge   Garden Lake

+ PH Stourton

Stourhead

8

Top Wood

Church Hill

Top Lane Farm

Heath Hill Farm

Castle Wood

Gasper

Writh Copse

Bonham Farm

7

Gasper Farm

BONHAM LANE

33

Shootershill Copse

GASPER STREET

New Lake

BA12

6

Greenland Bottom

Mill Covert

Pen Ridge Farm

White Cross

5

Batch Farm

Fordswater Farm

Harcourt Farm

CHAPEL LANE

CHAPEL LANE

32

BA9

Pear Ash Farm

Combe Bottom

Motte & Bailey

Row Farm

PORTNELL'S LANE

4

Pear Ash

Hill Top Manor Farm

Westfield Estate

Zeals

MARSH LANE

Penselwood

Monarch's Way

COOMBE STREET

Eden Grove

Monarch's Way

STEEL S LA

Pen Mill Farm

3

FIELD LANE

Wood Close Farm

Coombe Side

Corner Copse

CH

Brixeys Farm

GRATTON HILL

Bleak Farm

CHAPEL LA

PEAR ASH LANE

PEN MILL HILL

FACTORY HILL

TONG LA

HIGH STREET

31

Monarch's Way

Ballands Castle

Long Lane Farm

Old Down Farm

KITE S. NEST LANE

PH

UNDERHILL

BRIDGE HILL

MILL LANE

Bourton Bridge

THE MEADOWS

2

Penhouse Farm

Raymonds Farm

Primrose Farm

Bourton

NEW ROAD

+

LONG LANE

CHAFFEYMOOR HILL

Grove Farm

Sandways Farm

SP8

MILL LA

1

Voscombe Farm

PH

St George's CE Sch

A303

Chaffeymoor Farm

WOOLCOTT LA 1
CHURCH CL 2
OLD POUND CT 3
EAST ST 4

Marvins Farm

BRICKYARD LANE

Feltham Farm

30

75   A   B   76   C   D   77   E   F

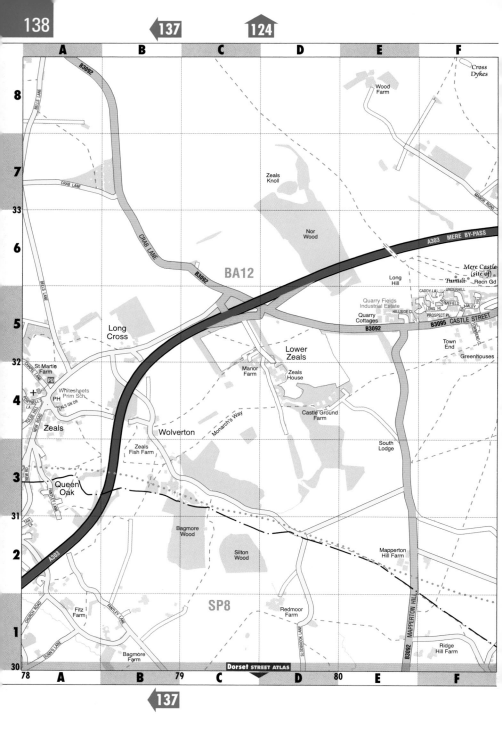

A   B   C   D   E   F

8

7

33

6

BA12

5

32

4

3

31

2

1

30

78   A   B   79   C   D   80   E   F

B3092

Cross
Dykes

Wood
Farm

Zeals
Knoll

CRAB LANE

CRAB LANE

Nor
Wood

A303   MERE BY-PASS

MANOR ROAD

Mere Castle
(site of)
Tumuli   Recn Gd

Long
Hill

CADDY LA

UNDERHILL

MEFIELD

LONG HL

SMILEY

PROSPECT PL

HILLSIDE CL

Quarry Fields
Industrial Estate

B3092

Quarry
Cottages

B3095   CASTLE STREET

TOWNSEND

Town
End

Greenhouses

Long
Cross

St Martin
Farm

PO

CHAPEL LANE

Whitesheets
Prim Sch

PH

FONTHILL LA

NEW ROAD

ZEALS GN DR

Zeals

Manor
Farm

Lower
Zeals

Zeals
House

Castle Ground
Farm

South
Lodge

Wolverton

Monarch's Way

Zeals
Fish Farm

NEW RD

Queen
Oak

HANTEY LANE

31

Bagmore
Wood

Silton
Wood

Mapperton
Hill Farm

TAN LA

A303

SP8

Fitz
Farm

TANTEY LANE

CHURCH ROAD

QUEENS LANE

Bagmore
Farm

Redmoor
Farm

SLODBROOK LANE

MAPPERTON HILL

B3092

Ridge
Hill Farm

BELLS LANE

BELLS LANE

B3092

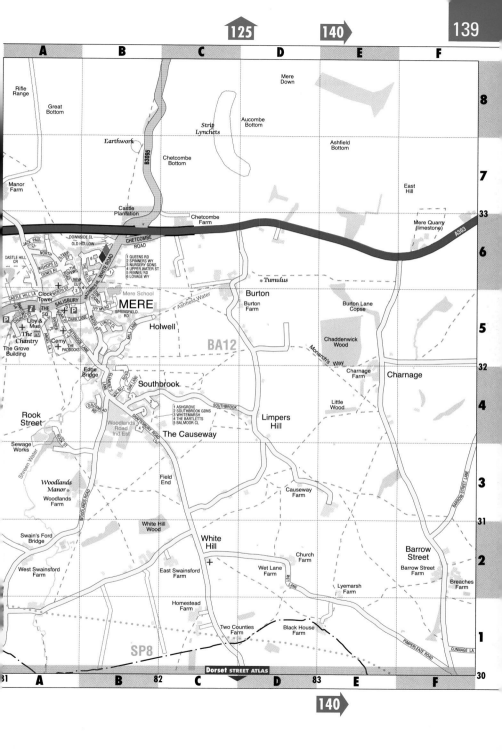

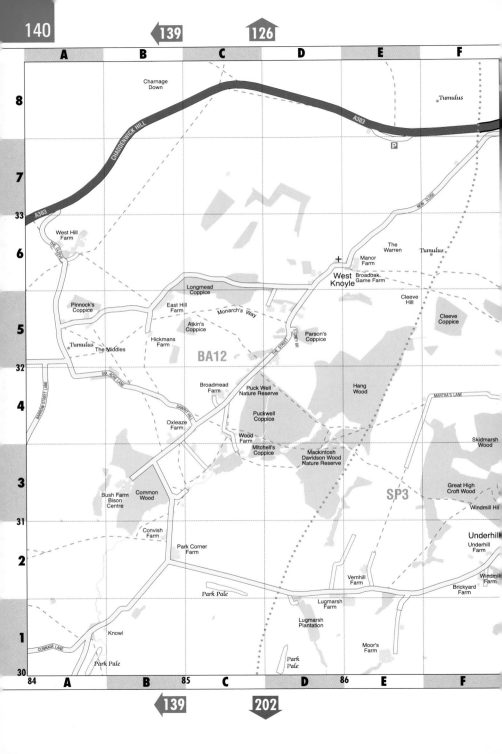

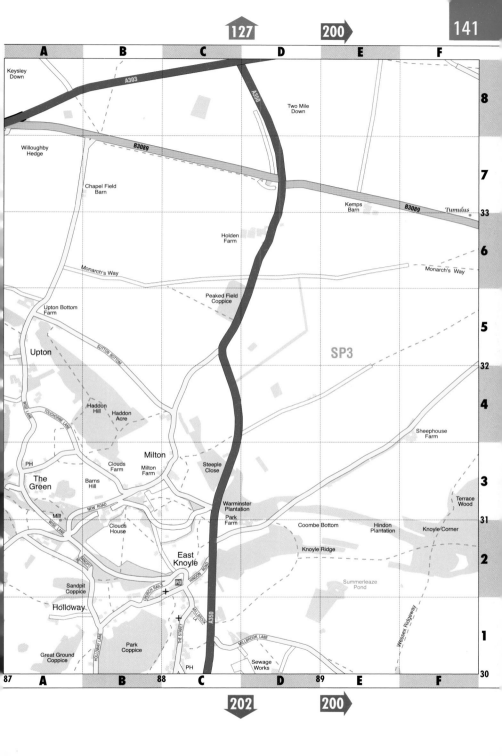

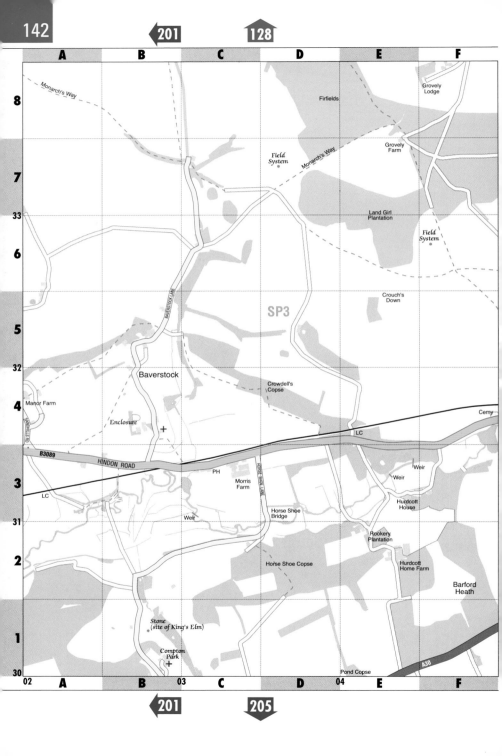

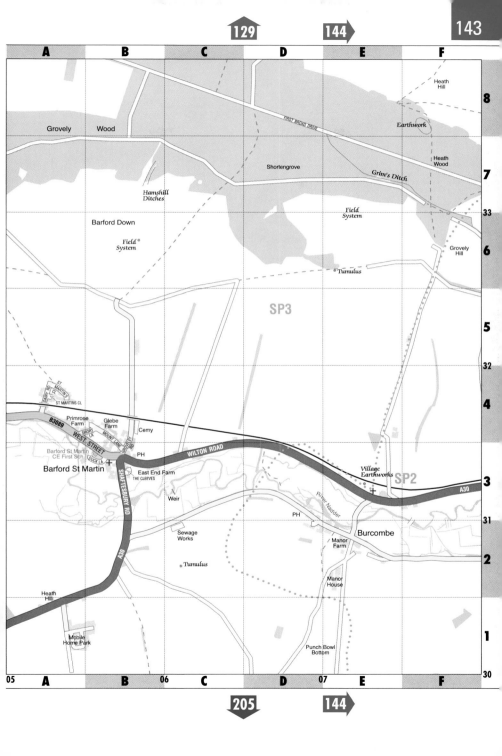

| A | B | C | D | E | F |

8

Grovely Wood

Heath Hill

Earthwork

7

Shortengrove

Grim's Ditch

Heath Wood

Hamshill Ditches

Field System

33

Barford Down

Field System

Grovely Hill

6

Tumulus

SP3

5

32

ST MARTIN'S CL

DAIRY RD

ST MARTINS CL

B3089

Primrose Farm

Glebe Farm

Cemy

4

SHORT

WEST STREET

MOUNT LANE

QUIDS

WILTON ROAD

PH

Barford St Martin CE First Sch

Village Earthworks

SP2

3

Barford St Martin

SHAFTESBURY RD

East End Farm

THE GLEEVES

River Nadder

A30

Weir

PH

Burcombe

31

Sewage Works

Manor Farm

2

Tumulus

Manor House

Heath Hill

1

Mobile Home Park

Punch Bowl Bottom

30

| 05 | A | B | 06 | C | | D | 07 | E | F |

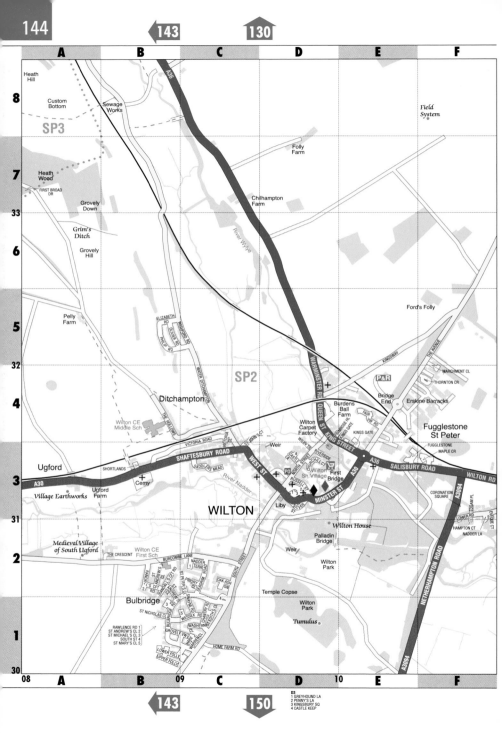

8

Heath
Hill

Custom
Bottom

SP3

Sewage
Works

Field
System

7

Heath
Wood

FIRST BROAD
DR

Grovely
Down

Folly
Farm

33

Grim's
Ditch

Chilhampton
Farm

River Wylye

6

Grovely
Hill

Ford's Folly

5

Pelly
Farm

ELIZABETH
RD

WINGFIELD
RD

OLIVER RD

PHILIP RD

KINGSWAY

THE AVENUE

32

SP2

WATER DITCHAMPTON

P&R

MARCHMENT CL

THORNTON CR

4

Ditchampton

Wilton CE
Middle Sch

THE HOLLOW

VICTORIA
RD

SPIN CT

WARMINSTER RD

QUEEN ST

KING STREET

CROSS KEYS
CROSS GATE

KINGS GATE

FAIR
VW RD

Burdens
Ball
Farm

Bridge
End

Erskine Barracks

Fugglestone
St Peter

FUGGLESTONE

MAPLE CR

Wilton
Carpet
Factory

Weir

VICTORIA ROAD

Weir

WILEY TER

A36

SALISBURY ROAD

WILTON RD

3

Ugford

A30

SHORTLANDS

SHAFTESBURY ROAD

Cemy

SADDLERS MEAD

WEST ST

River Nadder

CASTLE ST

NORTH ST

RIVERSIDE

RUSSELL ST

SOUTH ST

Wilton
Sh Village

First
Bridge

A30

MINSTER ST

CORONATION
SQUARE

A3094

EGDAM CL

LOWER RD

REDLIKE CT

HAMPTON CT

NADDER LA

Ugford
Farm

Village Earthworks

WILTON

Liby

31

Medieval Village
of South Ugford

THE CRESCENT

Wilton CE
First Sch

BURCOMBE LANE

NADDER
TERR

Wilton House

Palladin
Bridge

Wilton
Park

NETHERHAMPTON ROAD

2

Bulbridge

HARNHAM CL

ST PETER'S PL

STEPHENS RD

SOUTH STREET

PRIEST'S RD

SIGISMUND RD

OAK ASH
GM

WESSEX RD

RD

Weir

Temple Copse

Wilton
Park

1

RAWLENCE RD 1
ST ANDREW'S CL 2
ST MICHAEL'S CL 3
SOUTH ST 4
ST MARY'S CL 5

ST NICHOLAS CL

GROVELY VW

WASHERN CL

LOWER FOLLY

UPPER FOLLY

HOME FARM RD

Tumulus

A3094

30

08

09

10

A B C D E F

D3
1 GREYHOUND LA
2 PENNY'S LA
3 KINGSBURY SQ
4 CASTLE KEEP

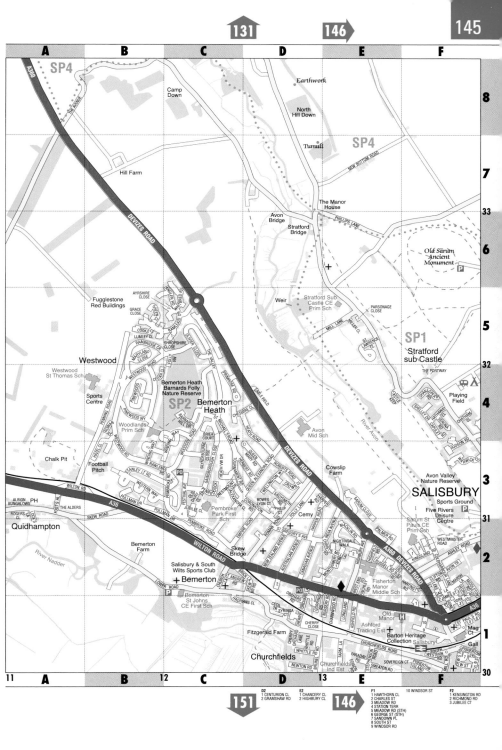

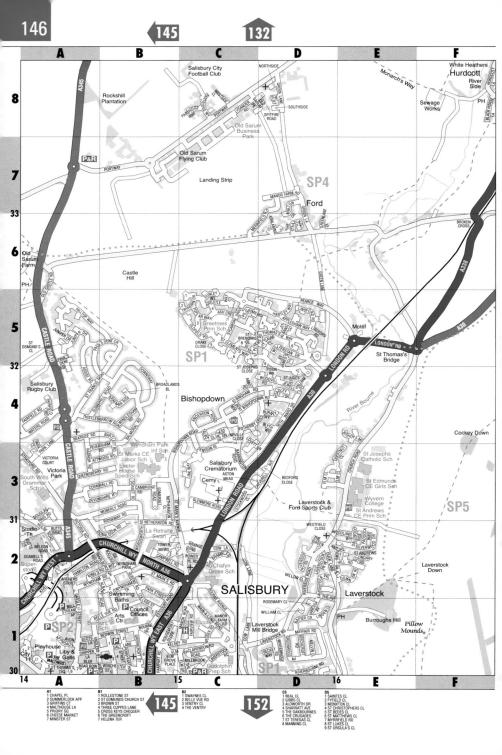

A1
1 CHAPEL PL
2 SUMMERLOCK APP
3 GRIFFINS CT
4 MALTHOUSE LA
5 PRIORY SQ
6 CHEESE MARKET
7 MINSTER ST

B1
1 ROLLESTONE ST
2 ST EDMUNDS CHURCH ST
3 BROWN ST
4 THREE CUPPES LANE
5 CROSS KEYS CHEQUER
6 THE GREENCROFT
7 HELENA TER

B2
1 SWAYNES CL
2 BELLE VUE RD
3 VENTRY CL
4 THE VENTRY

C5
1 NEAL CL
2 GIBBS CL
3 ALDWORTH DR
4 SHARRATT AVE
5 THE OAKBOURNES
6 THE CRUSADES
7 ST TERESAS CL
8 MANNING CL

D5
1 SAINTES CL
2 FYFIELD CL
3 MONXTON CL
4 ST CHRISTOPHERS CL
5 ST BEDES CL
6 ST MATTHEWS CL
7 MYRFIELD RD
8 ST LUKES CL
9 ST URSULA'S CL

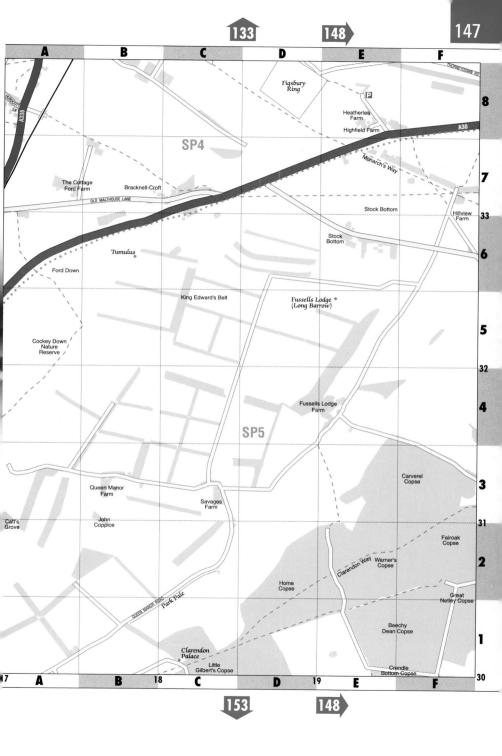

A   **B**   **C**   **D**   **E**   **F**

THORNEYDOWN RD

Figsbury Ring

Heatherlea Farm

Highfield Farm

P

A30

Monarch's Way

SP4

The Cottage
Ford Farm

Bracknell-Croft

OLD MALTHOUSE LANE

Stock Bottom

Hillview Farm

33

Stock Bottom

Tumulus

Ford Down

King Edward's Belt

Fussells Lodge
(Long Barrow)

Cockey Down
Nature
Reserve

Fussells Lodge
Farm

SP5

Carverel
Copse

Queen Manor
Farm

Savages
Farm

Catt's
Grove

John
Copplice

31

Fairoak
Copse

Clarendon Way

Warner's
Copse

Home
Copse

Great
Netley Copse

QUEEN MANOR ROAD   Park Pale

Beechy
Dean Copse

Clarendon
Palace

Little
Gilbert's Copse

Crendle
Bottom Copse

17   **A**   **B**   18   **C**   **D**   19   **E**   **F**   30

8
7
6
5
4
3
2
1

32

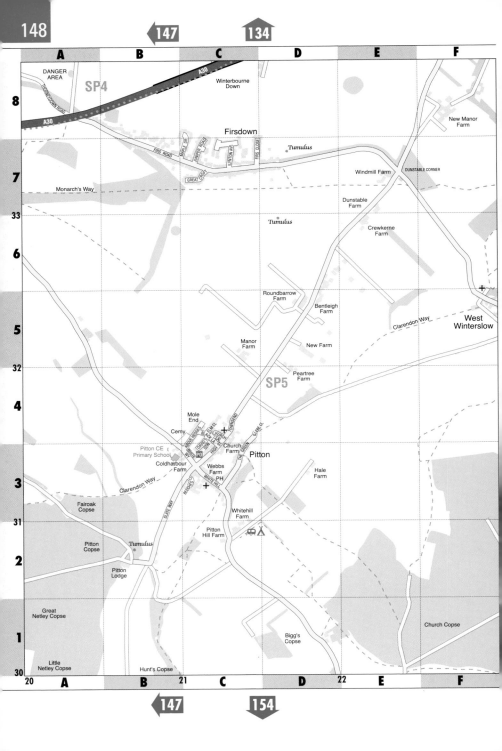

147
134

A   B   C   D   E   F

DANGER
AREA

SP4

THORNDOWN ROAD

A30

Winterbourne
Down

8

A30

Firsdown

New Manor
Farm

FIRS ROAD

MINT DR

JUNIPER ROAD

UPTON AVE

FIRS CLOSE

GREAT CROFT

Tumulus

Windmill Farm

DUNSTABLE CORNER

7

Monarch's Way

Dunstable
Farm

33

Tumulus

Crewkerne
Farm

6

Roundbarrow
Farm

Bentleigh
Farm

Clarendon Way

West
Winterslow

5

Manor
Farm

New Farm

32

Peartree
Farm

SP5

4

Mole
End

Cerny

Pitton CE
Primary School

Coldharbour
Farm

MIDDLE HEDGES

WHITE WAY

BLACK DITCH

SILVER DOWN

HIGH ST

OWENS RD

Church
Farm

GLEBE CL

Pitton

THE GREEN

Hale
Farm

3

Webbs
Farm
PH

BEGGES CL

SLATE WAY

WHITE HILL

Whitehill
Farm

31

Fairoak
Copse

Clarendon Way

Pitton
Hill Farm

2

Pitton
Copse

Tumulus

Pitton
Lodge

1

Great
Netley Copse

Bigg's
Copse

Church Copse

30

Little
Netley Copse

Hunt's Copse

20   A   21   B   C   D   22   E   F

147
154

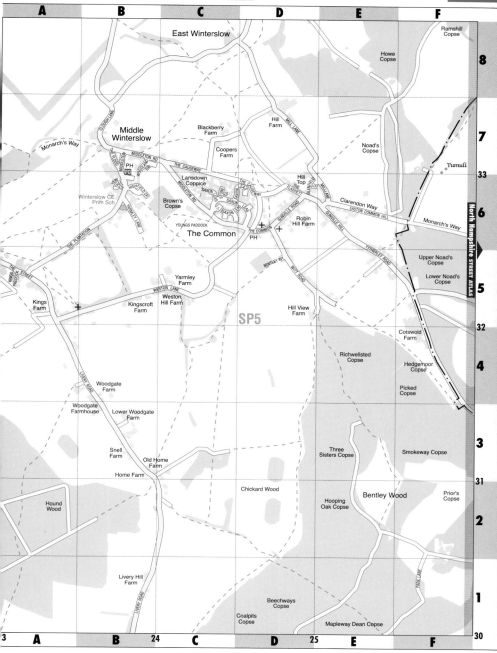

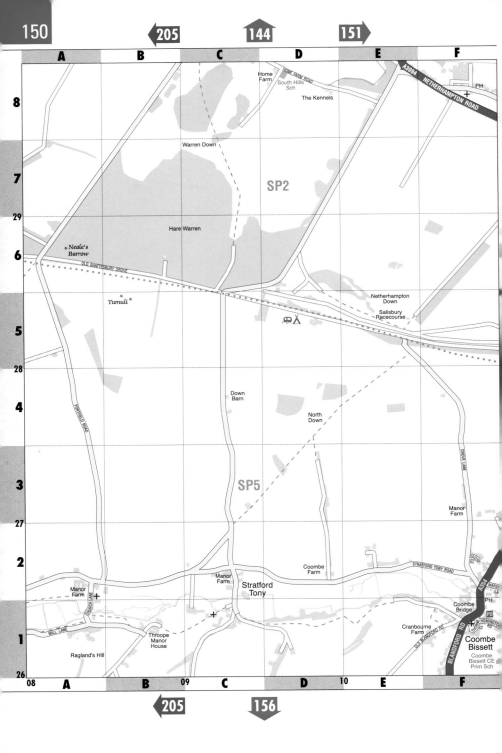

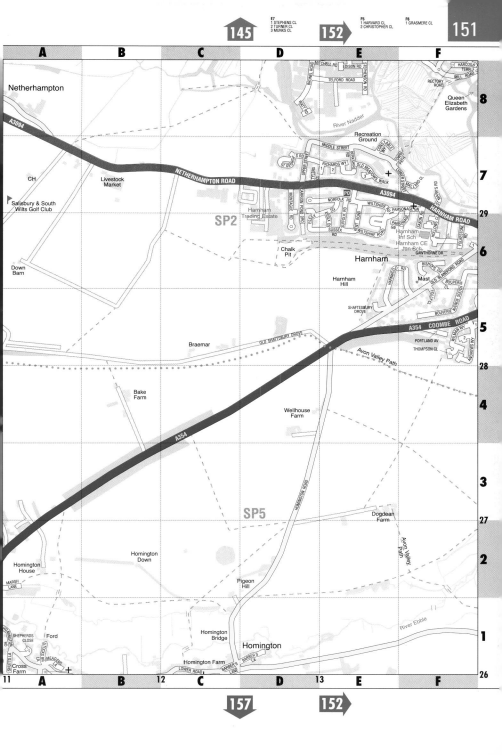

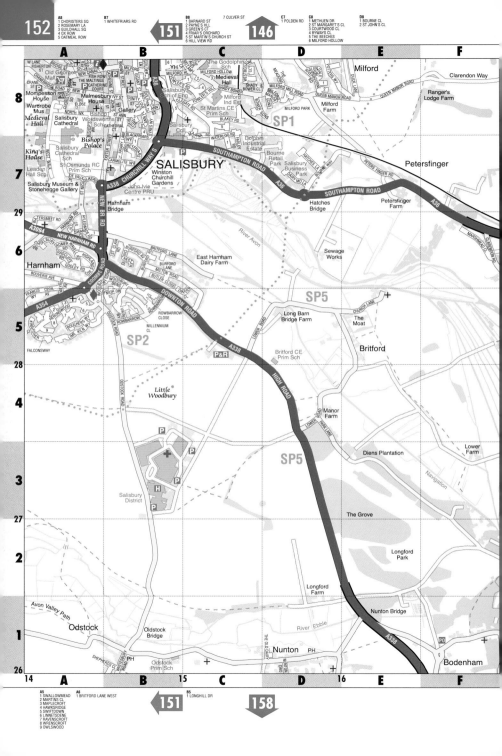

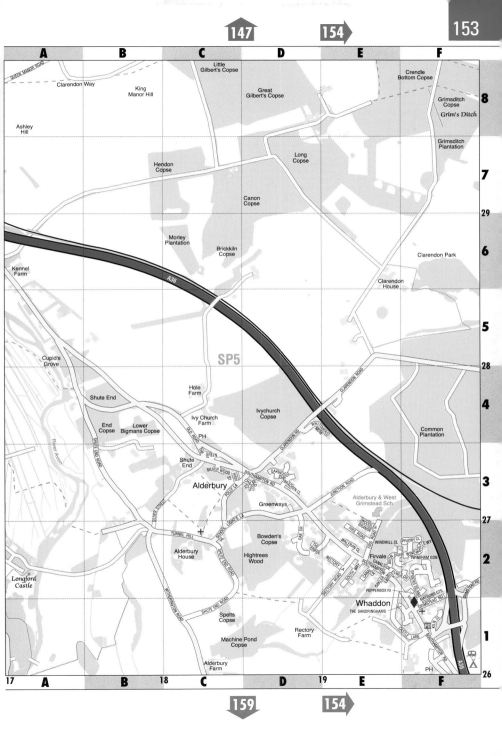

A B C D E F

8

Little Netley Copse
Crendle Bottom
Grimsditch Copse
Hunt's Copse
Farley
All Saints CE Prim Sch
PITTON ROAD
CHURCH ROAD

7

Bests Farm
PARSONAGE HILL
THE STREET
PH
PENNY'S LA
BEN LANE

29

LUGEWOOD LANE
Knightwood Farm
Woodfields Farm
March Farm
Bracken Farm
Farley Copse

6

The Plantation
Nightwood Copse
Adams Mere Farm
GRIMSTEAD ROAD
Brown's Copse

Upper Brickwood Farm
Pitchers Farm
Hazel Hill Wood

5

Old Brickwood Farm
Hazel Hill Farm
Lyvers Farm
Meadow End

Pope's Bottom
CLARENDON ROAD
Furzy Close Copse
SP5

28

Drove End
Whitehouse Farm
Horse Close Copse
Dairy Farm
East Grimstead
Whitehouse Farm

4

LONG DROVE
Pucks Hill Farm

GREEN DROVE
Walden House
BUTTER FURLONG ROAD

3

Walden Farm
Manor Farm

West Common Plantation
Nursery Farm

27

Crockford Copse
GREENFIELDS
CHAPEL HILL
CROCKFORD ROAD

2

Whaddon Common
Emmotts Farm
West Grimstead
Thicket Copse
CHURCH STREET
Redlynch Plantation

GRIMSTEAD ROAD
Hill Top
Hedge End

1

Oakridge Copse
Broadmead Farm
WINDWHISTLE LANE
Gallows Hayes Copse
GRIMSTEAD ROAD

26

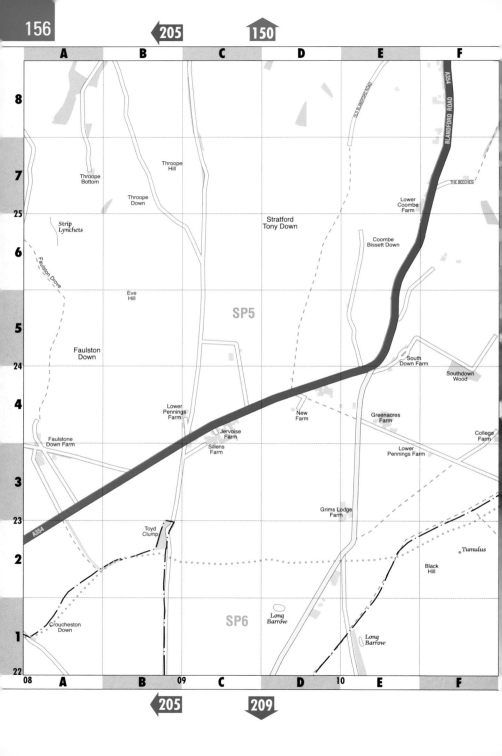

205
150

A B C D E F

8
7
25
6
5
24
4
3
23
2
1
22

Throope
Bottom

Throope
Hill

Throope
Down

Strip
Lynchets

Faulston Drove

Eve
Hill

Faulston
Down

SP5

Stratford
Tony Down

OLD BLANDFORD ROAD

BLANDFORD ROAD

A354

THE BEECHES

Lower
Coombe
Farm

Coombe
Bissett Down

South
Down Farm

Southdown
Wood

Faulstone
Down Farm

Lower
Pennings
Farm

Jervoise
Farm

Sillens
Farm

New
Farm

Greenacres
Farm

Lower
Pennings Farm

College
Farm

A354

Toyd
Clump

Grims Lodge
Farm

SP6

Long
Barrow

Tumulus

Black
Hill

Croucheston
Down

Long
Barrow

08 A B 09 C D 10 E F

205
209

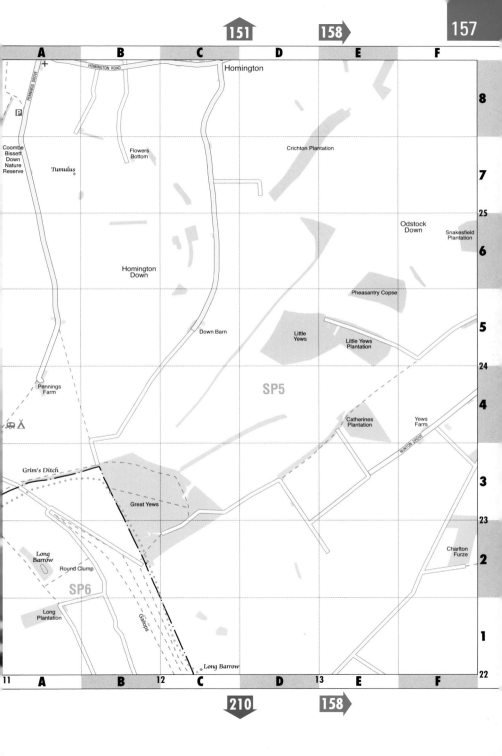

A   **B**   **C**   **D**   **E**   **F**

HOMINGTON ROAD
PENNINGS DRIVE

Homington

8

Coombe Bissett Down Nature Reserve

Flowers Bottom

Crichton Plantation

Tumulus

7

Odstock Down

25

Snakesfield Plantation

6

Homington Down

Pheasantry Copse

Down Barn

Little Yews

Little Yews Plantation

5

24

Pennings Farm

SP5

Catherines Plantation

Yews Farm

4

NUNTON DRIVE

Grim's Ditch

Great Yews

3

23

Long Barrow

Charlton Furze

Round Clump

2

SP6

Long Plantation

Gallops

1

Long Barrow

22

11   **A**   **B**   12   **C**   **D**   13   **E**   **F**

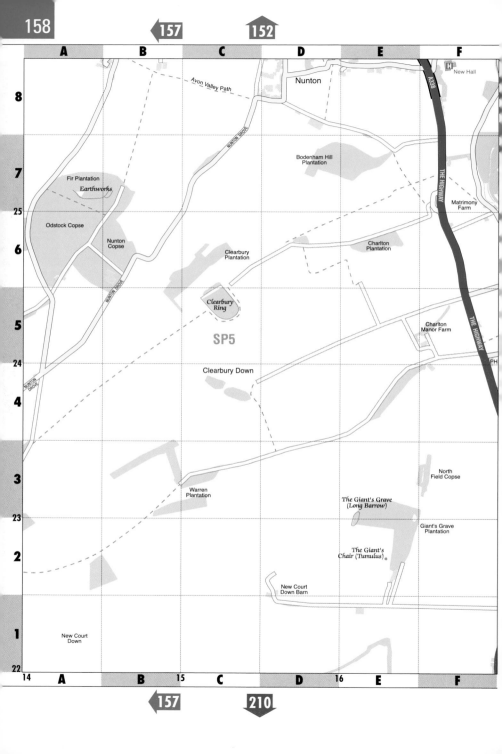

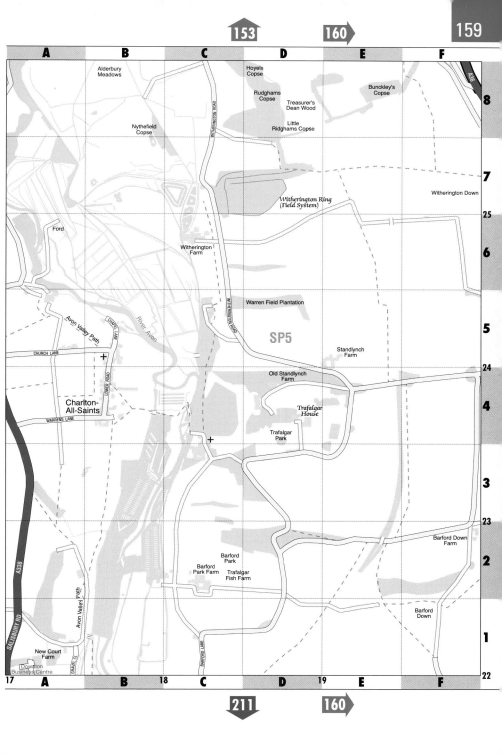

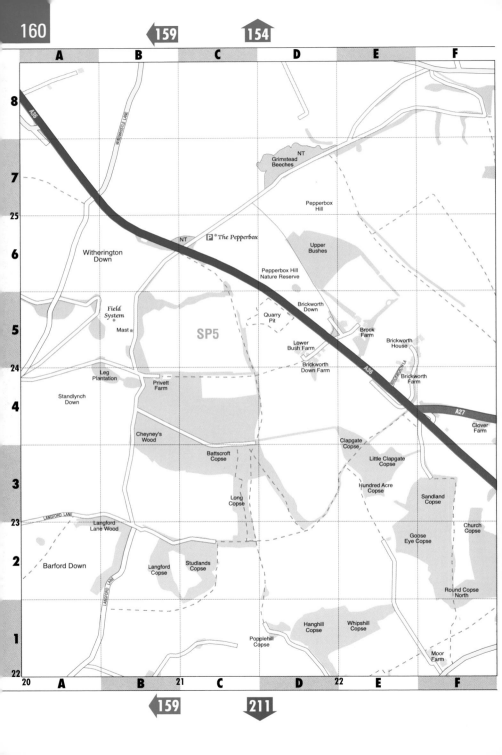

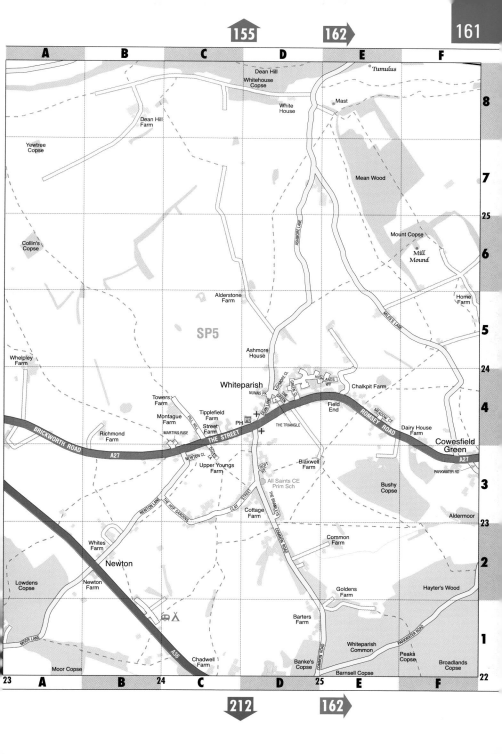

A   B   C   D   E   F

8
7
25
6
5
24
4
23
2
1
22

Dean Hill
Whitehouse Copse
White House
· Mast
Tumulus

Dean Hill Farm

Yewtree Copse

Mean Wood

Collin's Copse

ASHMORE LANE

Mount Copse
· Mill Mound

Alderstone Farm

Home Farm

SP5

MILES'S LANE

Ashmore House

Whelpley Farm

Whiteparish

HIGHLANDS WY

THE GREEN
GREEN CL
DEAN LANE

NUNNS PK
Chalkpit Farm

Towers Farm

Field End

Montague Farm
Tipplefield Farm

PIT HILL
ASHMORE CL

PH
PO

THE TRIANGLE
ROMSEY ROAD
MEADOW CT

Dairy House Farm

Richmond Farm

Street Farm
MARTINS RISE

THE STREET

BRICKWORTH ROAD

A27

NEWTON CL
DODES

Blaxwell Farm

Cowesfield Green
A27

PARKWATER RD

Upper Youngs Farm

All Saints CE Prim Sch

CROFT HT

Bushy Copse

Aldermoor

NEWTON LANE
THE HOP GARDENS

CLAY STREET

Cottage Farm

THE BRAMLEYS

COMMON ROAD

Common Farm

Whites Farm

Newton

Newton Farm

Lowdens Copse

Goldens Farm

Hayter's Wood

PARKWATER ROAD

A36

Barters Farm

COMMON ROAD

Whiteparish Common

Peaks Copse

Chadwell Farm

Banke's Copse

Barnsell Copse

Broadlands Copse

Moor Copse

MOOR LANE

23   A   B   24   C   D   25   E   F   22

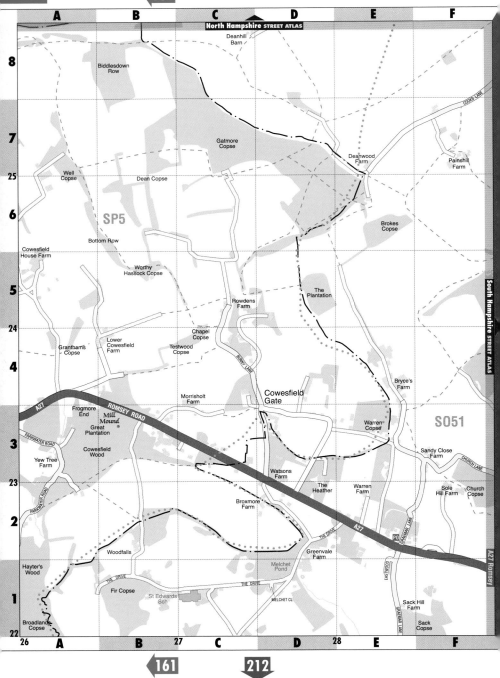

161

North Hampshire STREET ATLAS

South Hampshire STREET ATLAS

A B C D E F

8

7

25

6

SP5

24

5

4

3

23

2

1

22

26 27 28

A B C D E F

Deanhill
Barn

Biddlesdown
Row

Gatmore
Copse

Deanwood
Farm

Painshill
Farm

Well
Copse

Dean Copse

Brokes
Copse

Bottom Row

Cowesfield
House Farm

Worthy
Hassock Copse

The
Plantation

Rowdens
Farm

Chapel
Copse

Granthams
Copse

Lower
Cowesfield
Farm

Testwood
Copse

BUNNY LANE

Bryce's
Farm

Morrisholt
Farm

Cowesfield
Gate

Warren
Copse

SO51

ROMSEY ROAD

A27

PARKWATER ROAD

Frogmore
End

Mill
Mound

Great
Plantation

Cowesfield
Wood

Sandy Close
Farm

CHURCH LANE

Yew Tree
Farm

Watsons
Farm

The
Heather

Warren
Farm

Sole
Hill Farm

Church
Copse

PARKWATER ROAD

Broxmore
Farm

A27

THE DRIVE

GRAEMAR LANE

PO

EASTWOOD

A27 Romsey

Hayter's
Wood

Woodfalls

THE DRIVE

Greenvale
Farm

Melchet
Pond

Fir Copse

St Edwards
Sch

THE DRIVE

MELCHET CL

Sack Hill
Farm

GRAEMAR LANE

Sack
Copse

Broadlands
Copse

COOKS LANE

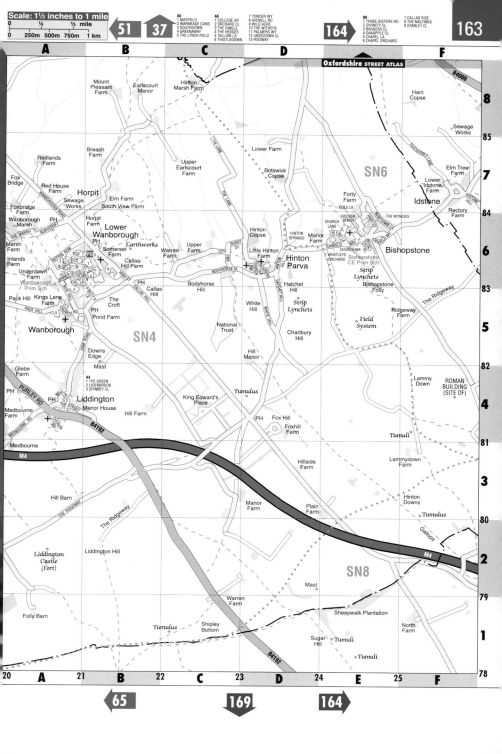

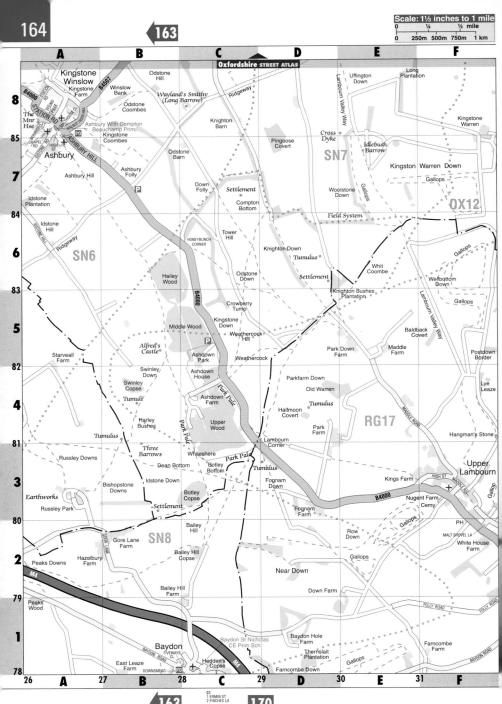

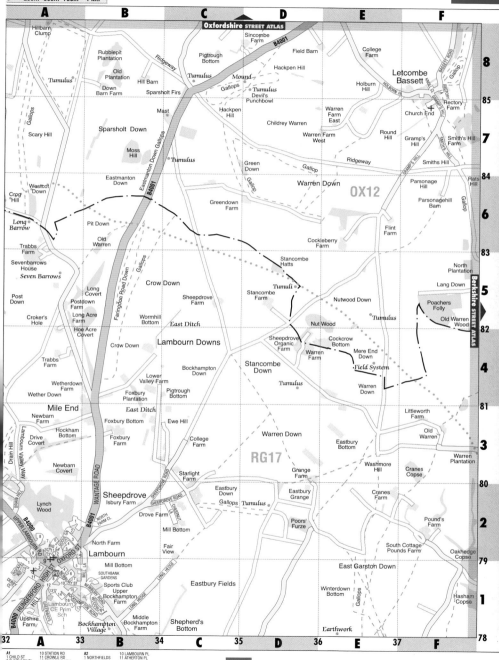

Scale: 1⅓ inches to 1 mile

0   ¼   ½ mile
0   250m 500m 750m 1 km

A1
1 CHILD ST
2 FLINTJACK PL
3 ST MICHAEL'S CL
4 FOXBURY
5 MILLFIELD
6 TUBBS FARM CL
7 AINTREE
8 CLOSE END
9 PARSONAGE LA

10 STATION RD
11 CROWLE RD
12 EDWARD'S HILL
13 SHEEP FAIR WY
14 THE OLD STATION YD
15 BEALES FARM RD
16 THE CLASSICS
17 FRANCOMES FIELD

A2
1 NORTHFIELDS
2 HONEY HILL
3 WALKER'S LA
4 THE GRANTHAMS
5 HARRIS CL
6 LYNCH LA
7 ESSEX PL
8 THE PARK
9 PARSONAGE PL

1 LAMBOURN PL
11 ATHERTON PL
12 CHAPEL LA
13 CHURCH CL
14 GWYNS PIECE

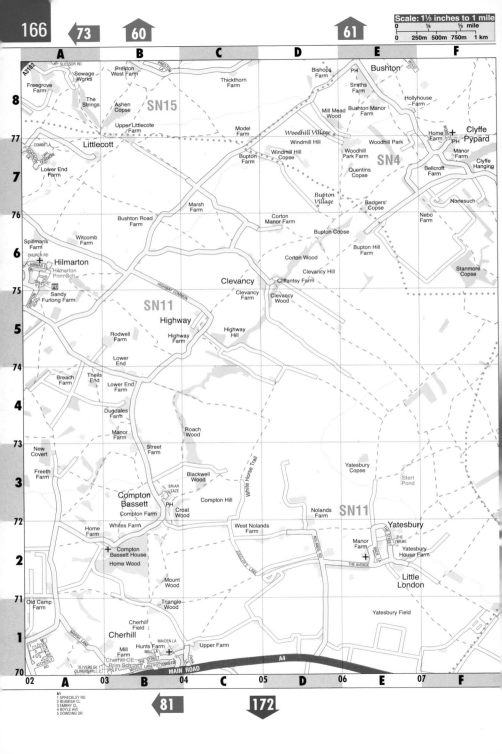

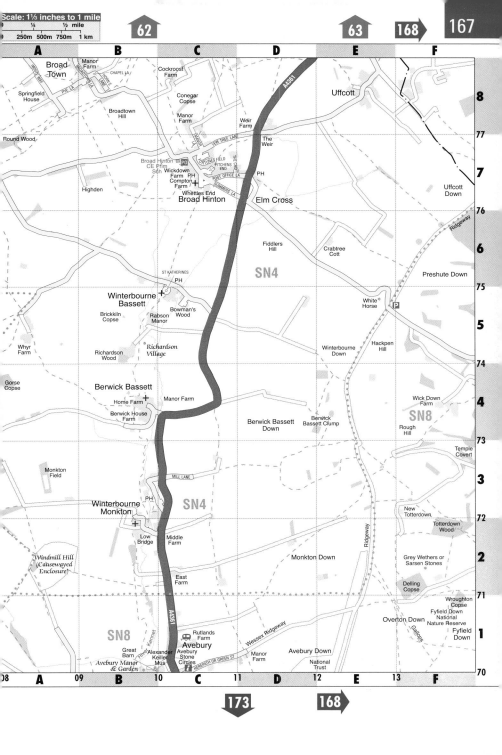

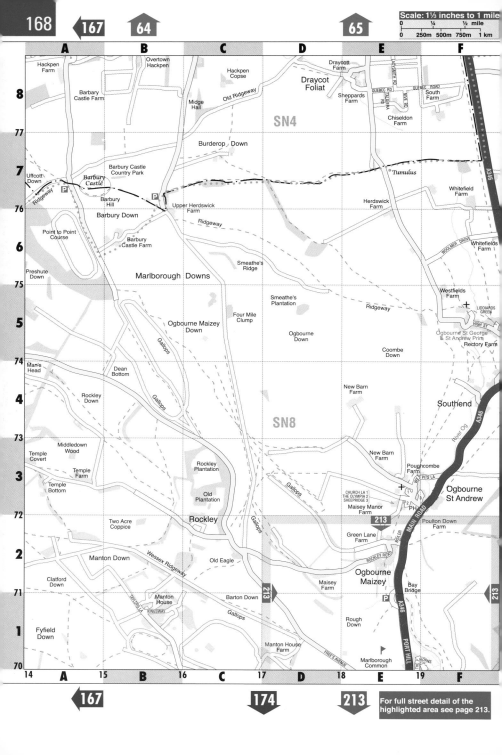

167
64
65

Scale: 1½ inches to 1 mile

0   ¼   ½ mile
0   250m 500m 750m 1 km

A   B   C   D   E   F

Hackpen Farm
Barbary Castle Farm
Overtown Hackpen
Hackpen Copse
Draycott Farm
Draycot Foliat
Sheppards Farm
QUEBEC RD
TALAVERA RD
HYDE RD
ALMA ST
South Park
QUEBEC ROAD
LADYSMITH RD

8

Midge Hall
Old Ridgeway
Chiseldon Farm

SN4

77

Burderop Down

Tumulus
Whitefield Farm

7

Barbury Castle Country Park
Uffcott Down
Barbury Castle
P
P
Upper Herdswick Farm
Herdswick Farm
WOOLMER GROVE
Whitefields Farm

76

Ridgeway
Barbury Hill
Barbury Down
Ridgeway

Point to Point Course
Barbury Castle Farm

Smeathe's Ridge

Westfields Farm

6

Preshute Down

Marlborough Downs

Smeathe's Plantation
Four Mile Clump

Ridgeway
LIDDIARDS GREEN
HIGH ST
Ogbourne St George & St Andrew Prim

75

Ogbourne Maizey Down
Ogbourne Down
Rectory Farm

5

Man's Head
Dean Bottom
Coombe Down

74

Rockley Down
Gallops
New Barn Farm
Southend
River Og
A346

4

SN8

73

Middledown Wood
Temple Covert
New Barn Farm
Poughcombe Farm
PITS LA

3

Temple Farm
Rockley Plantation
Gallops
CHURCH LA 1
THE OLYMPIA 2
SHEEPRIDGE 3
Ogbourne St Andrew
Temple Bottom
Old Plantation
Maisey Manor Farm
PH

72

Two Acre Coppice
Rockley
213
Green Lane Farm
Poulton Down Farm

2

Manton Down
Wessex Ridgeway
Old Eagle
ROCKLEY ROAD
BELL LA
Ogbourne Maizey
MAIN ROAD

71

Clatford Down
Manton House
Barton Down
213
Maisey Farm
Bay Bridge
A346
213

THE OLD KINGSWAY
Gallops
PORT HILL

1

Fyfield Down
Manton House Farm
FREE'S AVENUE
Rough Down
Marlborough Common
HORNS

70

14   A   15   B   16   C   17   D   18   E   19   F

167
174
213

For full street detail of the highlighted area see page 213.

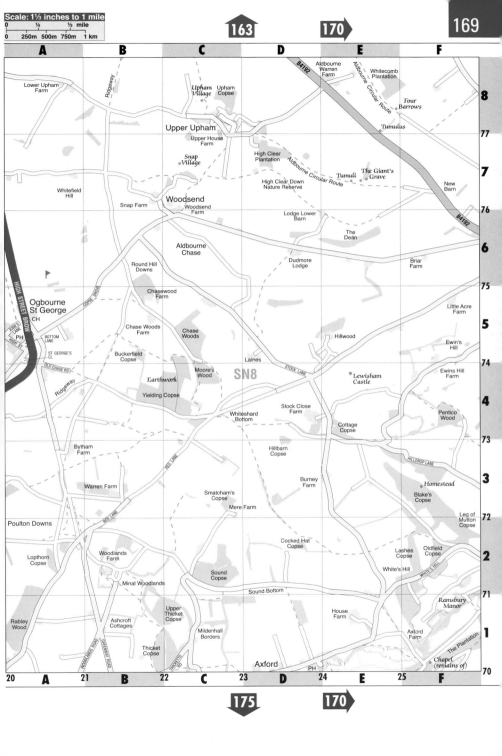

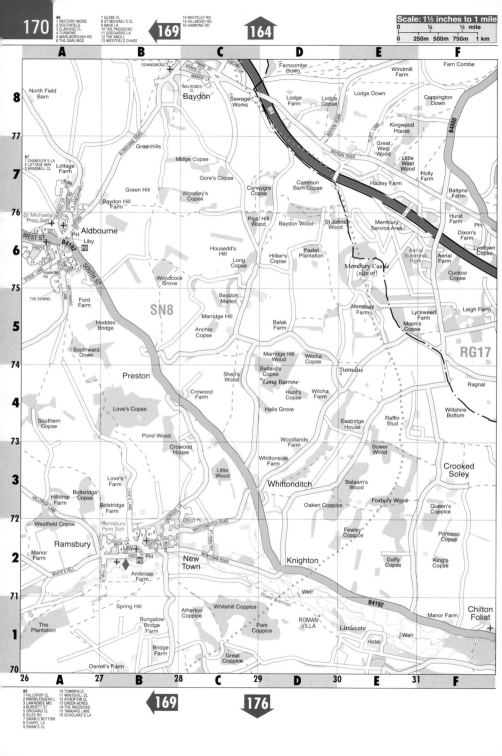

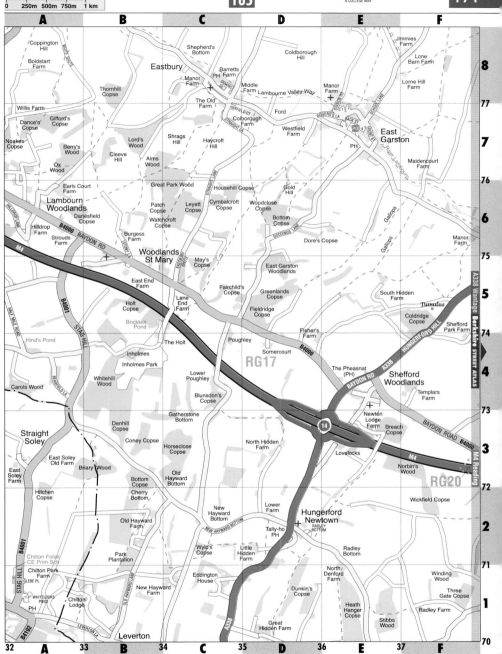

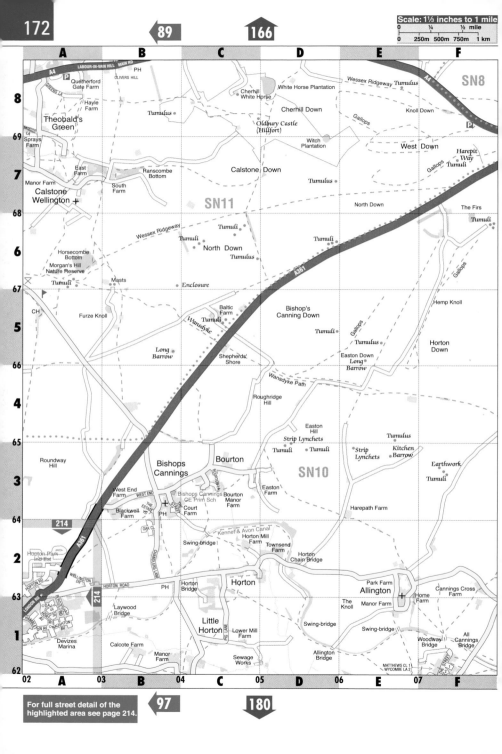

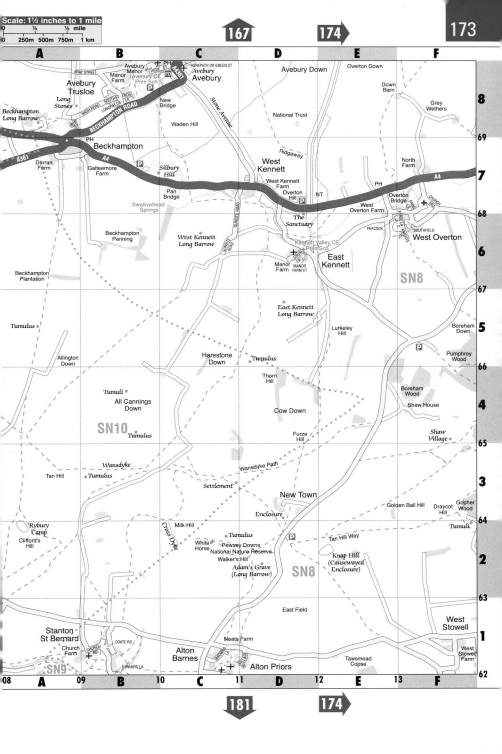

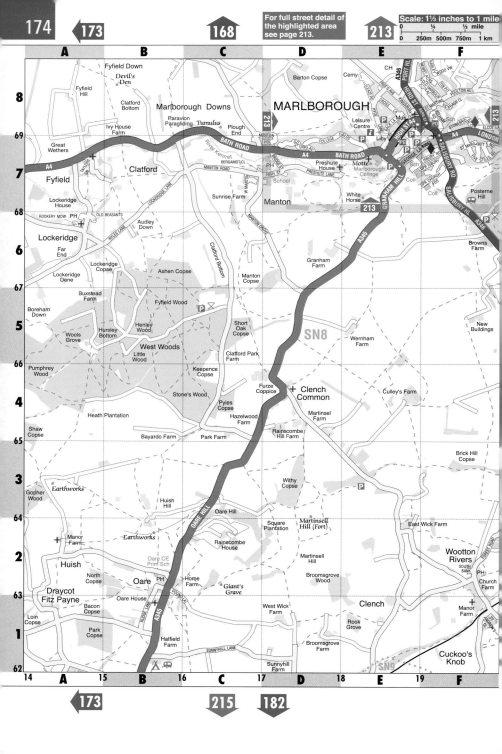

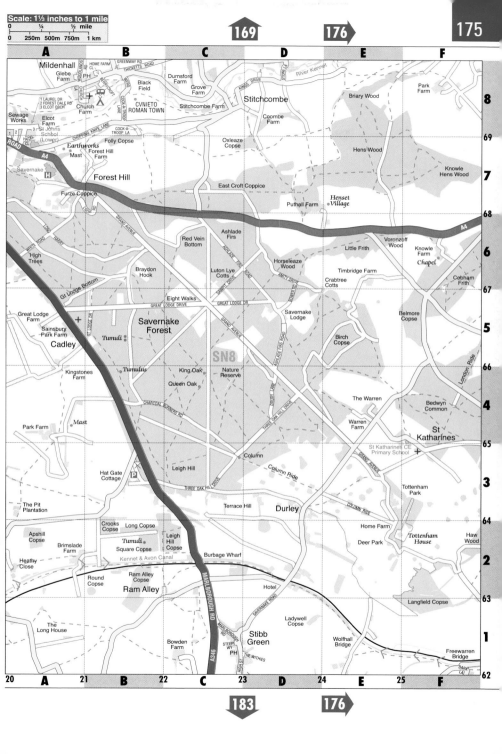

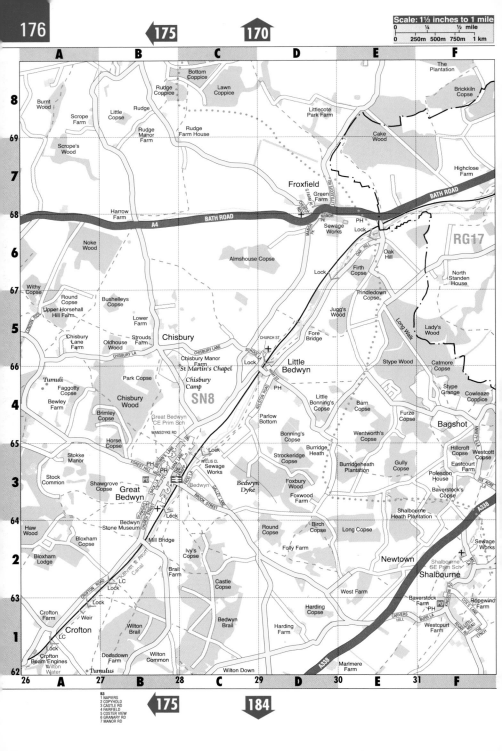

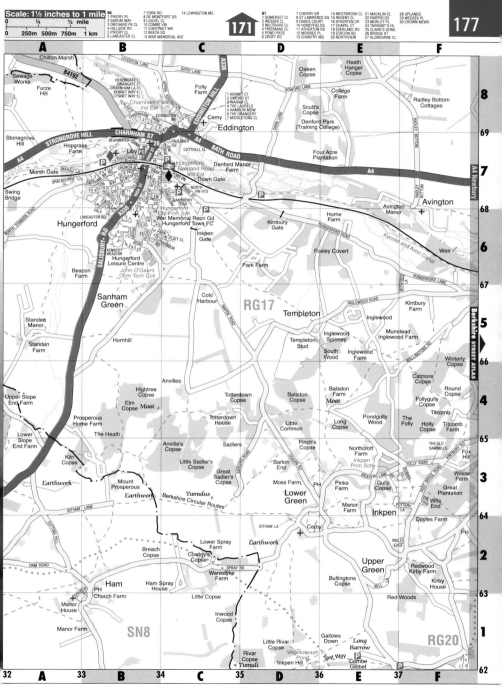

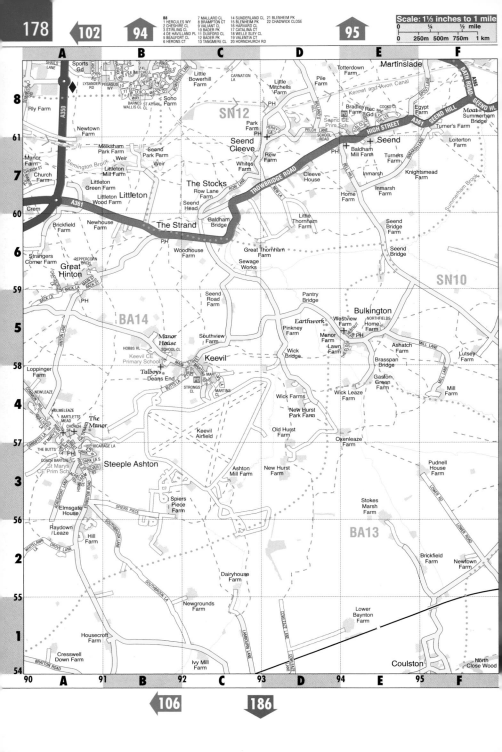

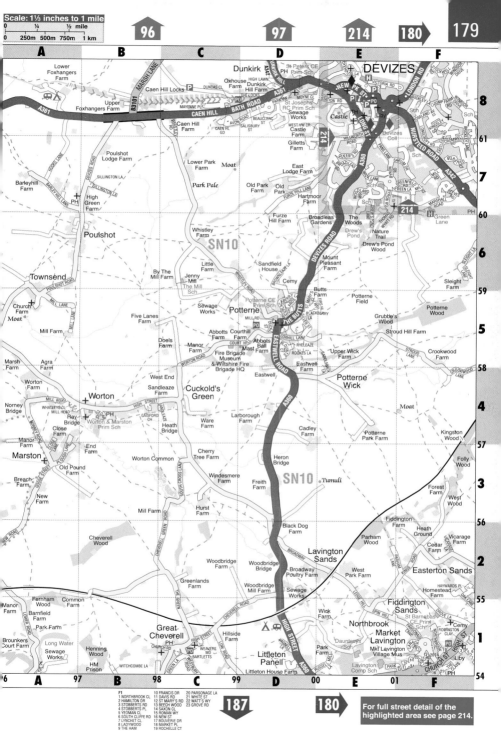

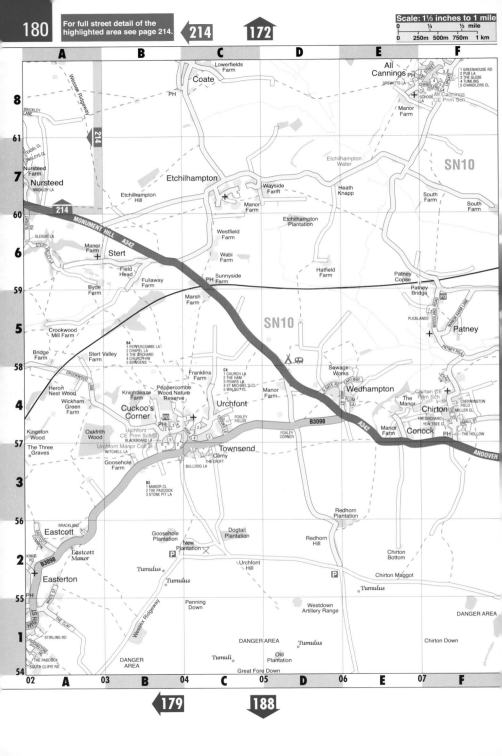

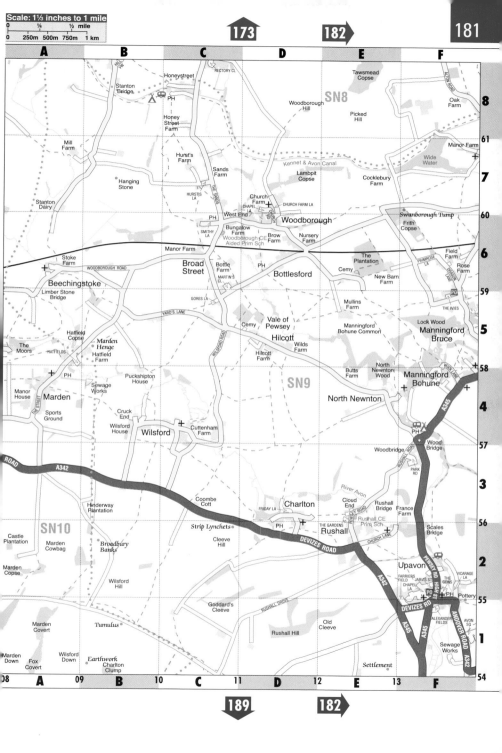

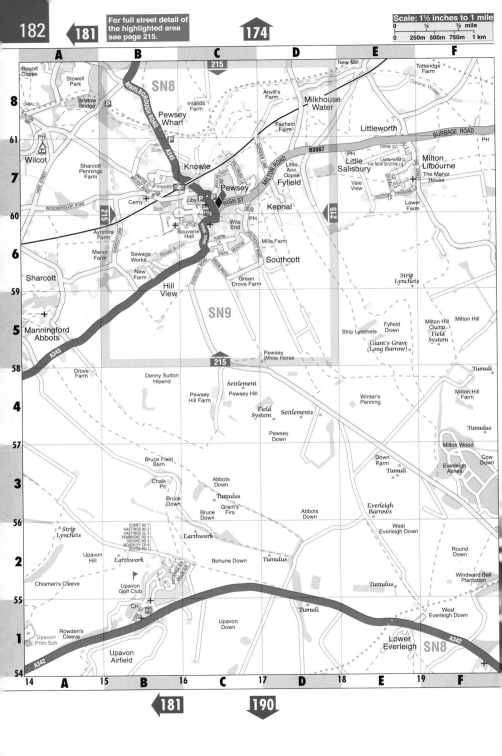

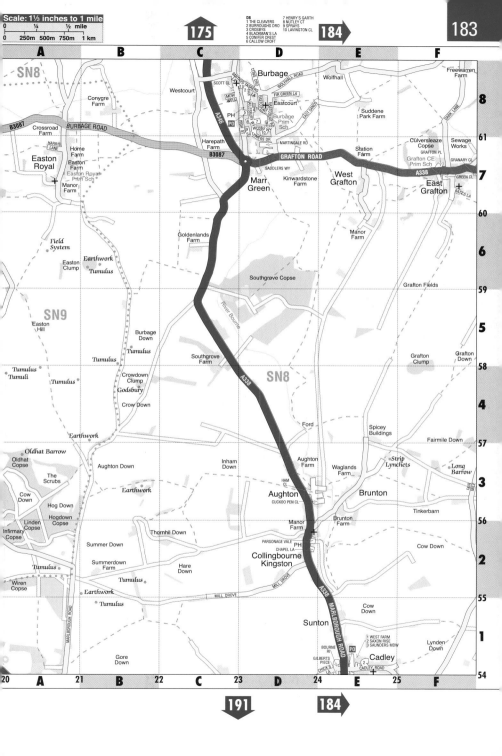

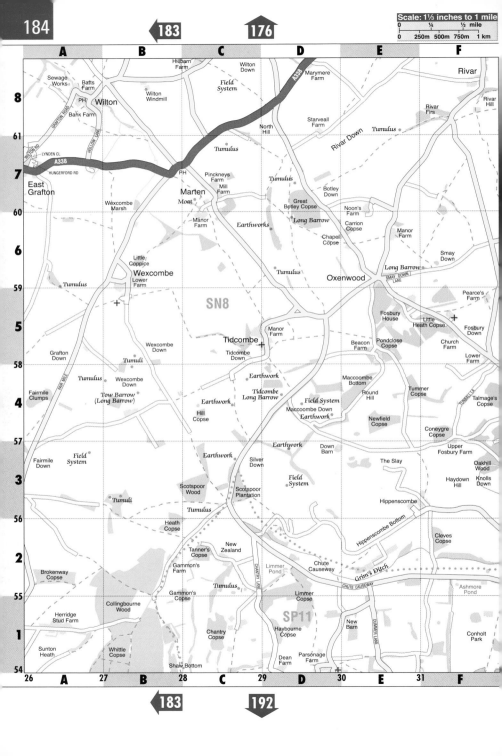

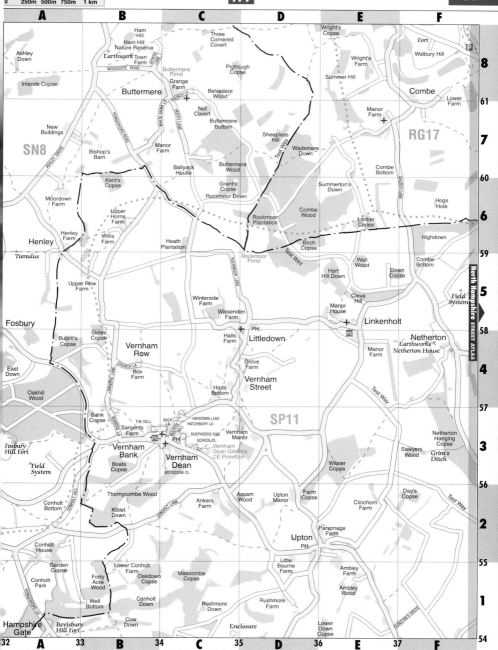

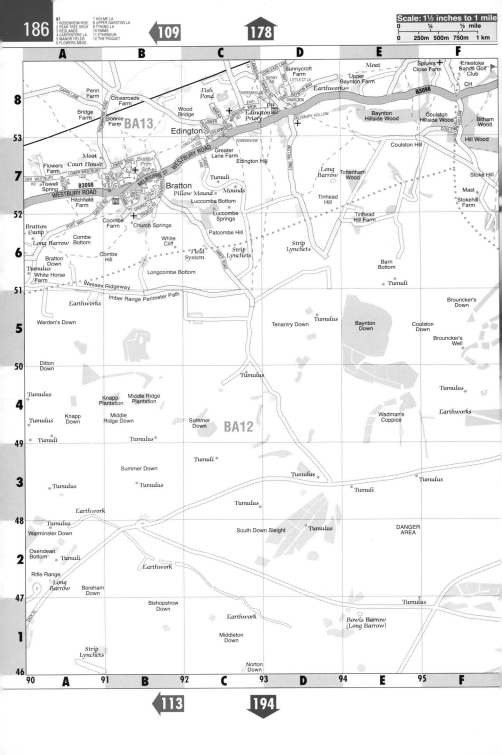

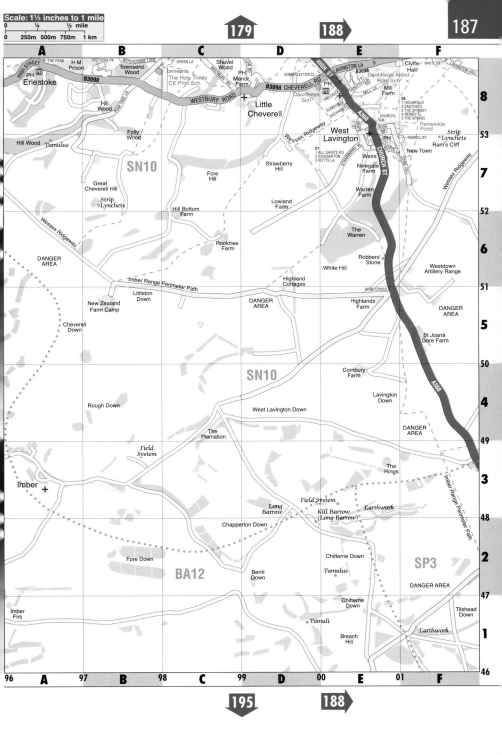

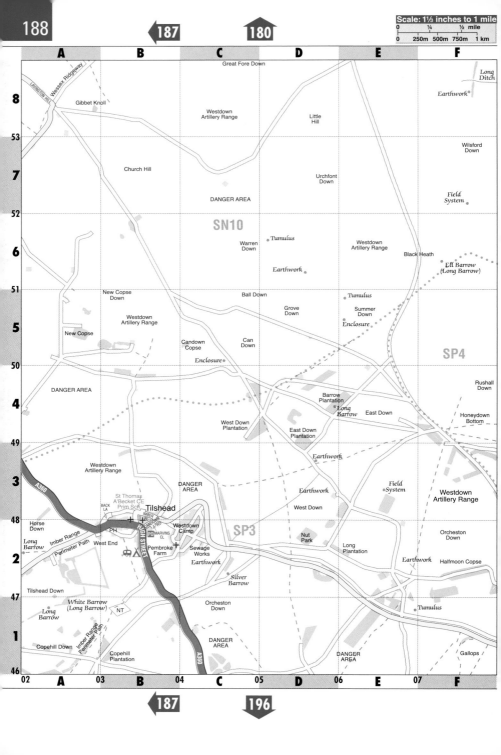

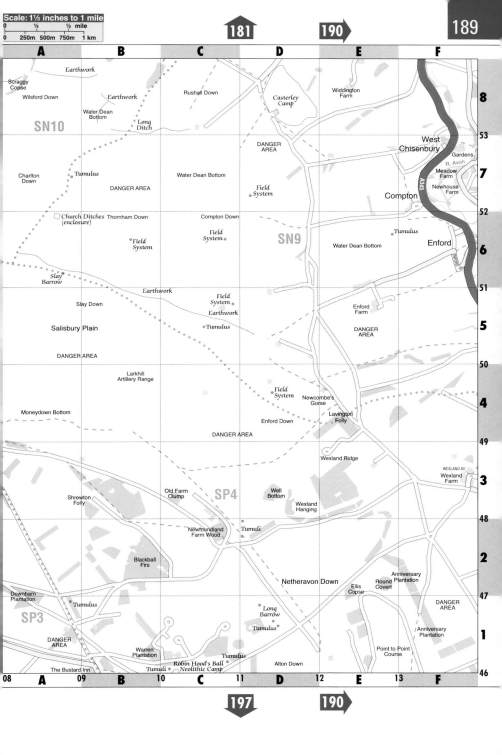

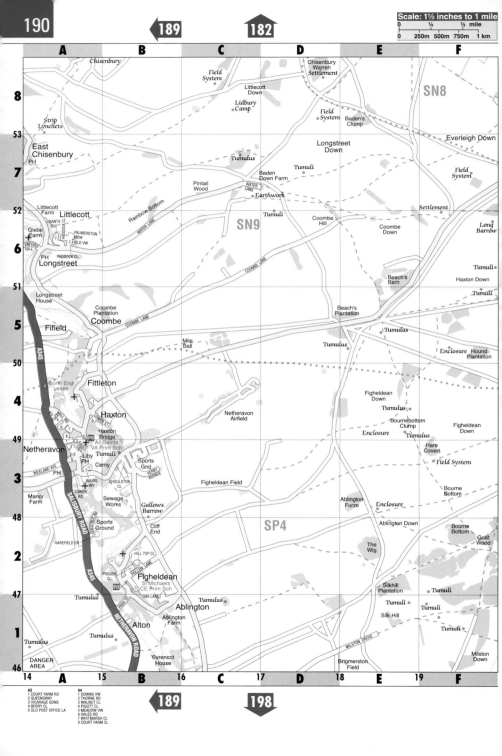

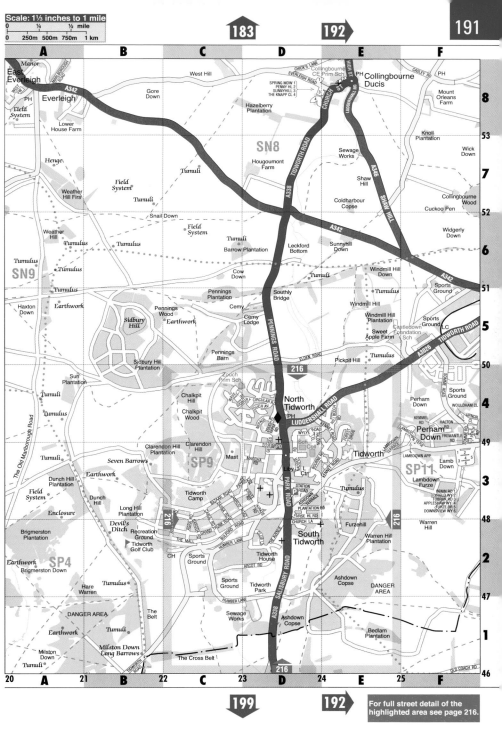

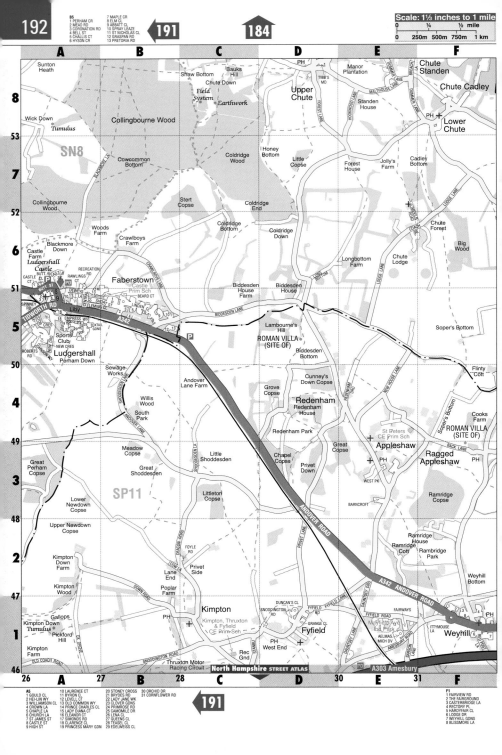

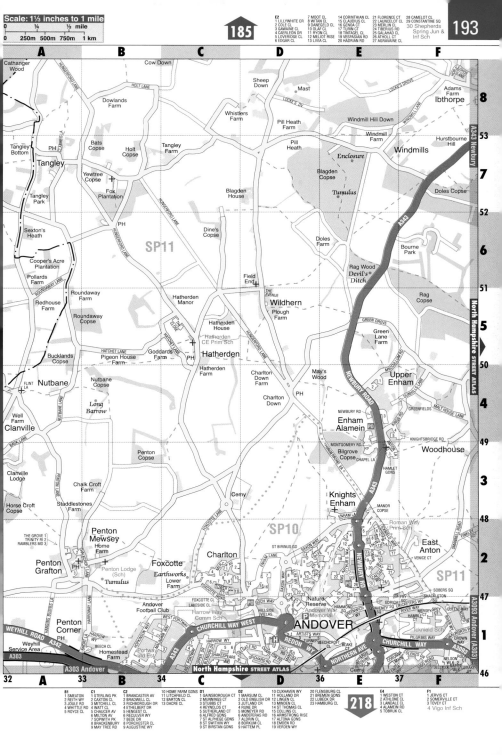

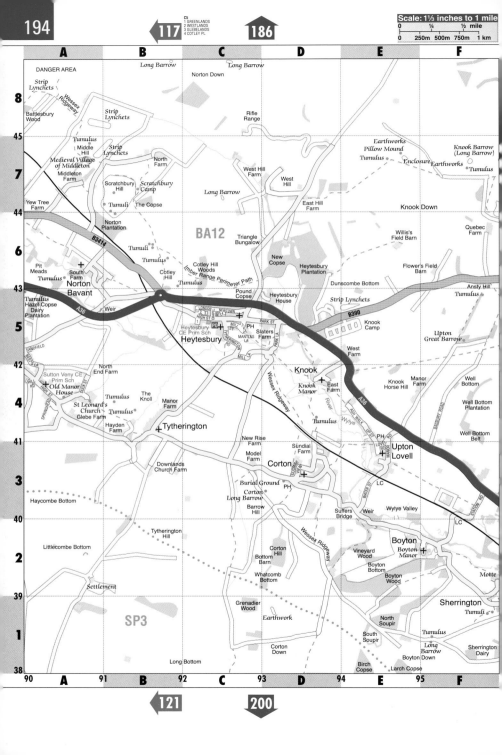

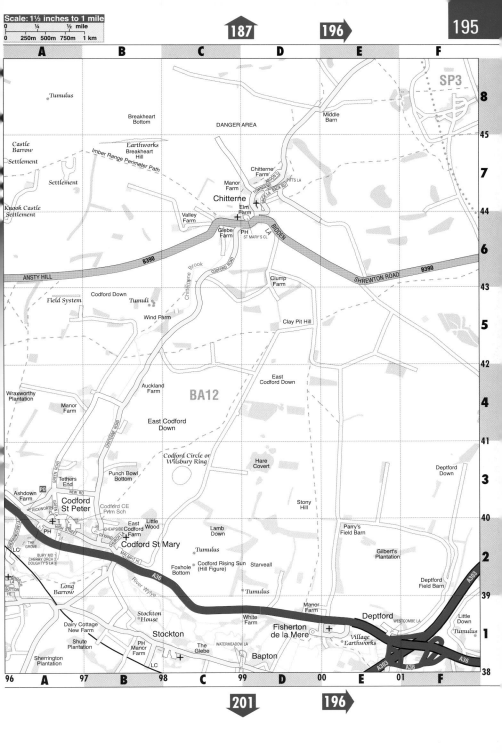

A   B   C   D   E   F

SP3

Tumulus

8

Breakheart Bottom

45

DANGER AREA

Middle Barn

Earthworks
Breakheart Hill

Castle Barrow

Settlement

Imber Range Perimeter Path

7

Chitterne Farm

Settlement

Manor Farm

PITTS LA

TOWNSEND

BACK LA BACK RD

Knook Castle
Settlement

Chitterne

44

Elm Farm

Valley Farm

BIDDEN

6

Glebe Farm

PH
ST MARY'S CL

LA

B390

Chitterne Brook

Codford Road

SHREWTON ROAD

B390

ANSTY HILL

Clump Farm

43

Field System

Codford Down

Tumuli

Wind Farm

Clay Pit Hill

5

42

East Codford Down

Wraxworthy Plantation

Auckland Farm

BA12

4

Manor Farm

East Codford Down

41

CHITTERNE ROAD

Codford Circle or
Wilsbury Ring

Hare Covert

Deptford Down

3

GREEN ROAD

Tethers End

Punch Bowl Bottom

NEW RD

Ashdown Farm

PO

Stony Hill

40

RICKWORTH

Codford
St Peter

Codford CE
Prim Sch

Little Wood

Parry's Field Barn

Gilbert's Plantation

HIGH STREET

East Codford Farm

CHEAPSIDE

Lamb Down

PH

OXYARD

Codford St Mary

Tumulus

2

THE GROVE

BURY MD 1
CHERRY ORCH 2
DOUGHTY'S LA 3

MALMPIT HI

Foxhole Bottom

Codford Rising Sun
(Hill Figure)

Starveall

Deptford
Field Barn

LC

A36

Long Barrow

River Wylye

Tumulus

39

Manor Farm

Little Down

Tumulus

SHERRINGTON LA

SUTTON
HE

Dairy Cottage
New Farm

White Farm

Deptford

WESTCOMBE LA

A303

Stockton
House

Stockton

Fisherton
de la Mere

Village
Earthworks

1

A303

Shute Plantation

PH
Manor Farm

The Glebe

WATERMEADOW LA

Bapton

A36

Sherrington Plantation

LC

A303

A36

38

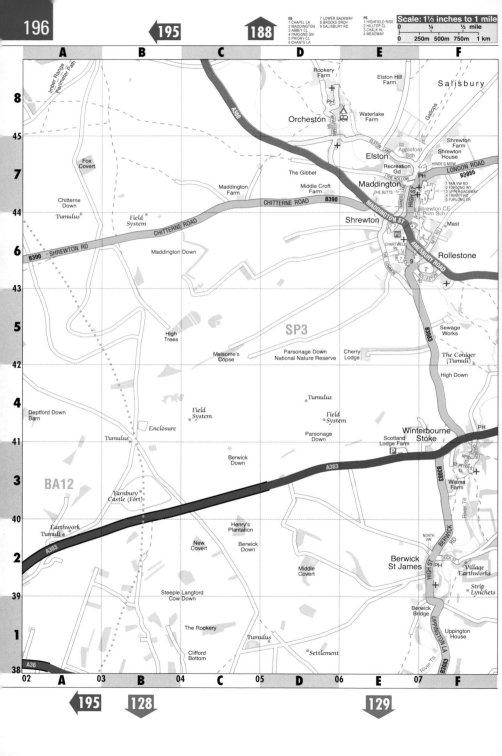

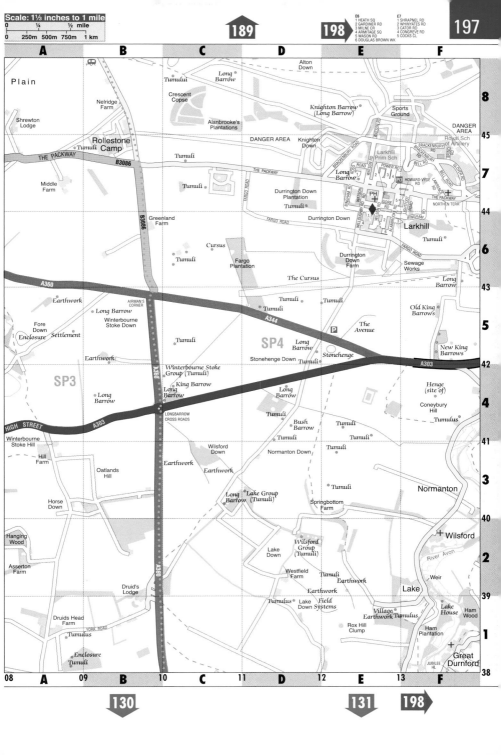

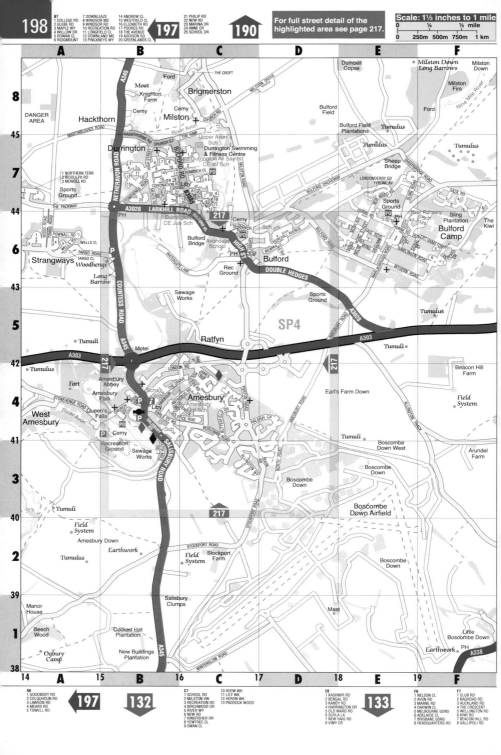

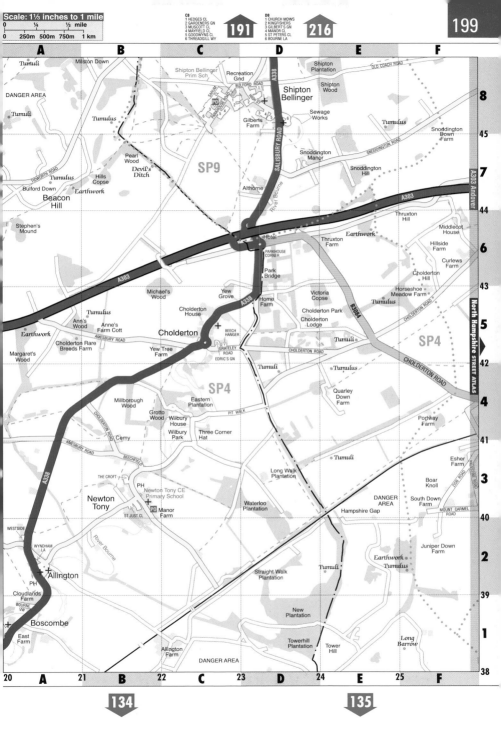

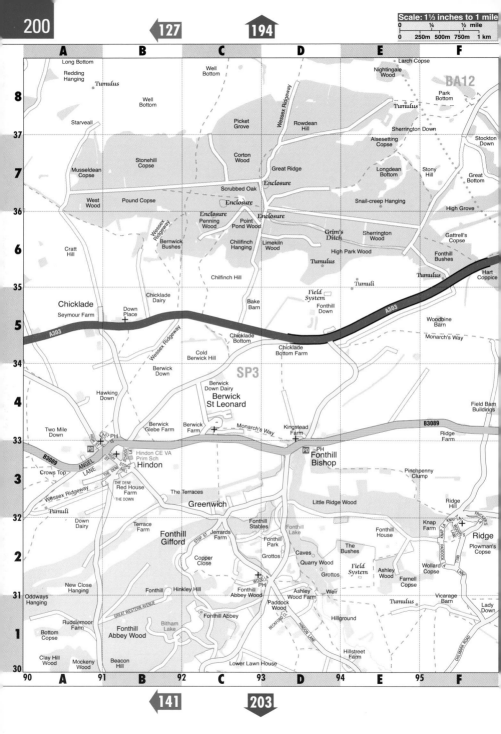

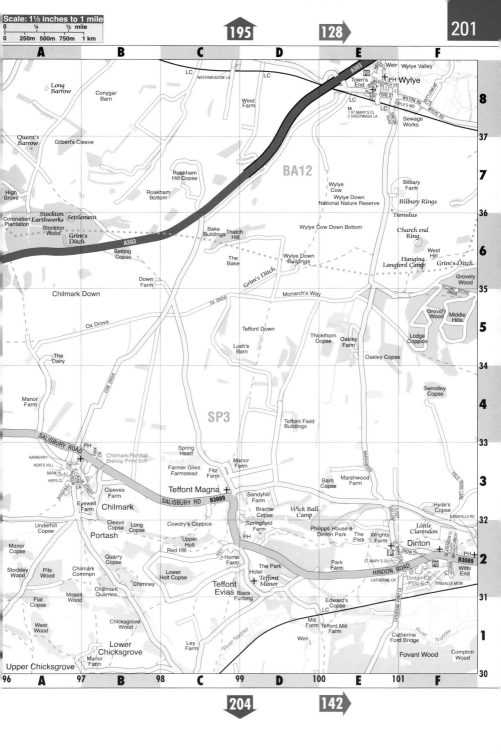

Scale: 1⅓ inches to 1 mile

0 ¼ ½ mile
0 250m 500m 750m 1 km

A B C D E F

8

Park Pale
Higher Mere Park
Snaggs Farm
Parson's Coppice
Leigh La
Sewage Works
Summerleaze Farm

BA12
River Lodden
New Leaze Farm
Friars Hayes Farm

29
Lower Park Farm
Grove Coppice
Corner Farm
Red House Farm
Blackhouse Farm
Upper Leigh Farm
SP3
Kinghay
Linley Farm

Colemans Farm
Lower Leigh Farm
Linley Wood

7
Westmarsh Farm
Pitts Farm
PITTS LANE
Sweetwell Farm
Church Farm
Hayes Farm
Billhay Farm
Priors Farm
Billhay Pond
Billhay Bridge

28
Cowridge Copse
Lower House Farm
Berrybrook Farm
Sedgehill
STREET LANE
Abbey's Wood
TOTES LANE
Weir
Brach Pond
Moat

Withies Farm
Earthwork
Hull Copse
Hayes Copse
Whitebridge Farm
Chaldicotts Farm
Amberleaze Farm
Brown's Wood

6
North End Farm
Sedgehill Manor
Butterstake Lane
Semley Common
Musters Farm
PH
Church Farm

North End
Culver House Farm
Park Farm
Peake's Farm
Sewage Works
Glebe Farm
Semley CE VA Prim Sch

27
Knapp Hill
Stile End
PH
STATION ROAD
SP7
Sem Hill
Semley

PH
Elm Hill
ELM CL
The Corner
CORNER LA
North Hayes Farm
Brock's Plantation
Seniors Farm
South Wood

5
HUNTERS MD
STAINERS MD
Bowmarsh Farm
The Marshes
Marshes Farm
Oyster's Coppice Nature Reserve
Oysters Farm

26
Motcombe Grange Sch
Sewage Works
Shorts Green Farm
SHORTS GN LA
Lyefield's Copse
Westwood Farm
Gutch Common

WILLOW WY 1
THE LIMES 2
GLEBE GDNS 3
GRAYS CL 4
PO
Avenue Farm
Grant's Copse
Nature Reserve
Hart Hill Farm
Kingsettle Wood
Knipes Farm
Hatts Farm
Hilldown Copse
Crates Wood
Tittle Path Hill
Clift Copse

4
Motcombe
CHURCH WK
Motcombe CE VA Prim Sch
Church Farm
Bittles Green
Meaders Farm
Aldermoor Copse
Castle Rings
Donhead Clift

25
Manor Farm
Bittles Green Farm
Ryal's Plantation
Port Regis Sch
Thanes Farm
MOTCOMBE ROAD
The Cliff
Wincombe Business Park
Semley Hill
Lodge Wood
SP7
Wincombe

3
Motcombe House Plantations
Cowherd Shute Farm
TOLLGATE PK
RIDGE WY
Wincombe Park
Ramshill Farm
Lower Wincombe Farm

24
Whitehouse Farm
SHAFTESBURY ROAD
B3081
Hawkers Hill Farm
Lady's Copse
Quoits Copse
HOMEFIELD
Barton Hill House Sch
King Alfred's CE Mid Sch
Great Hanging
WINDWHISTLE CORNER
Step Cross Copse

B1
1 BREACH LA
2 UMBERS HILL
3 LANGFORDS LA
4 LOVE LA
5 LAUNDRY LA
6 TANYARD LA
7 ST JOHN'S HILL
8 RASPBERRY LA
Old Brickyard
Gillingham Adult Ed Ctr
Enmore Green
LONG CROSS
NEW RD
Ivy Cross
Eastleaze Farm
Langdale Farm
Dockham Bottom

2
A30
Grants Farm
CHERRY ORCHARD LA
COLE'S LA
Westminster Meml
Alcester
SHAFTESBURY
St James
Church Farm
Abbey Primary Sch
Mus
SALISBURY ROAD
Shaftesbury Cemy
Prim Sch
Shaftesbury Leisure Centre
Landsley Farm
Long Bottom
St Marys Sch
Knights Barn Farm
Coombe
PH

23
A30 Sherborne
BINPORT
CHRISTY'S LA
Boyne Hollow
Old Cann
A350
B3081
Hillside Farm
CHARLTON LANE
White Close Farm

22
Edwards Farm
ROYAL HILL
Dorset STREET ATLAS

84 85 86 87 88 89

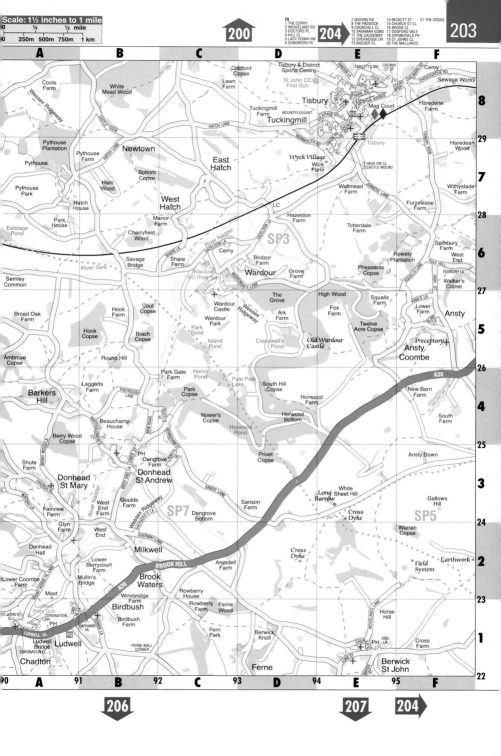

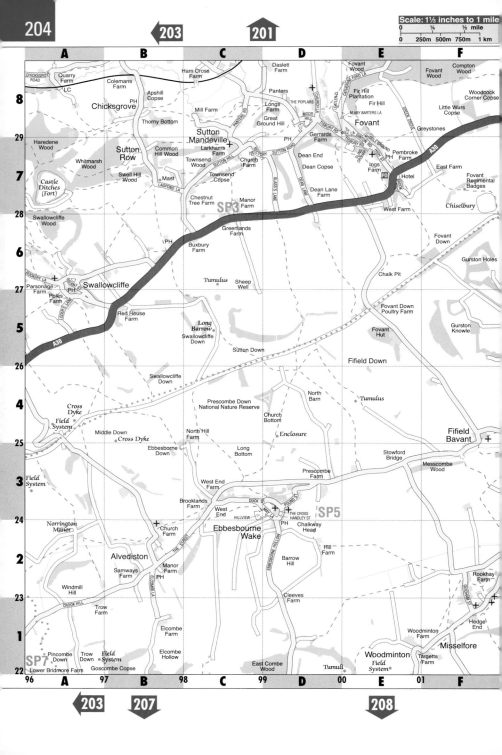

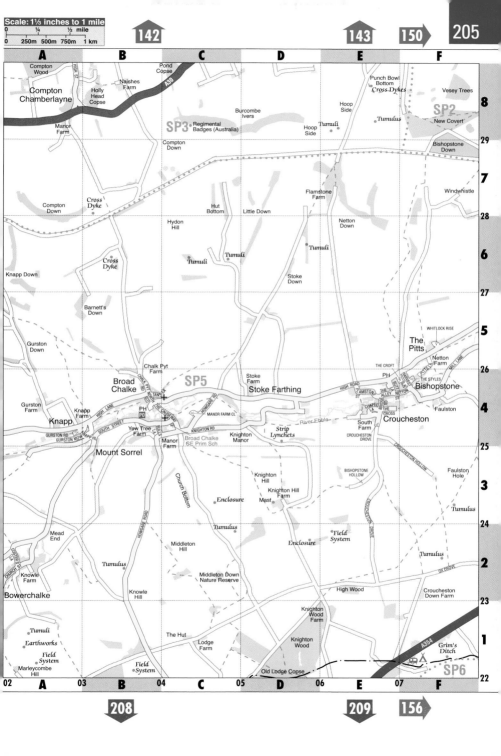

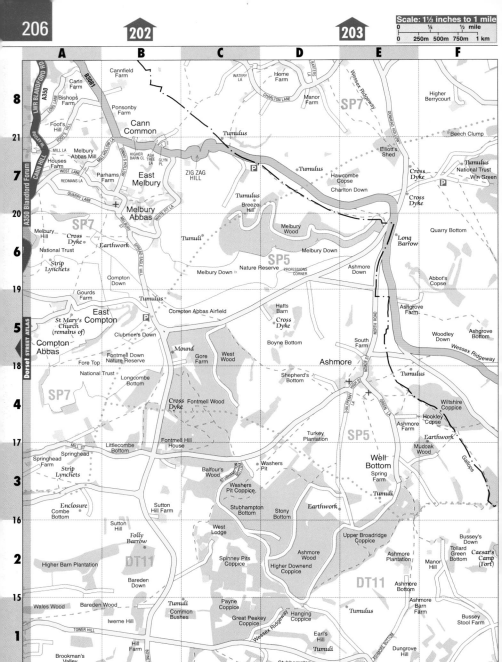

Scale: 1⅓ inches to 1 mile

0   ¼   ½   mile
0   250m   500m   750m   1 km

A   **B**   **C**   **D**   **E**   **F**

8

Cannfield Farm

Carin Farm

Bishops Farm

Foot's Hill

LWR BLANDFORD RD
A350
B3081

Ponsonby Farm

Cann Common

Watery La

Home Farm

Manor Farm

CHARLTON LANE
BARTERS LA

Wessex Ridgeway

SP7

Higher Berrycourt

21

Houses Farm

Melbury Abbas Mill

MILL LA
WEST LANE
FOOT'S LA
CANN HILL

HIGHER BARN CL
ASH TREE LA
GLYN PL

Tumulus

Beech Clump

Elliott's Shed

DONHEAD HOLLOW

7

Parhams Farm

REDMANS LA

East Melbury

ZIG ZAG HILL

Tumulus

P

Hawcombe Copse

Charlton Down

Cross Dyke

Cross Dyke

National Trust

Tumulus

Win Green

P

20

A350 Blandford Forum
Cann Hill
QUARRY LANE

Melbury Abbas

WHITE PIT LA

Tumulus
Breeze Hill

Melbury Wood

Long Barrow

Quarry Bottom

6

Melbury Hill

Cross Dyke

National Trust

Earthwork

SP7

MELBURY
SPREAD EAGLE HILL

Tumuli

Melbury Down

SP5

Melbury Down

Nature Reserve

PROFESSORS CORNER

Ashmore Down

Abbot's Copse

Strip Lynchets

19

Gourds Farm

Compton Down

Tumulus

Compton Abbas Airfield

Hatts Barn

Cross Dyke

Boyne Bottom

NORTH ROAD

Ashgrove Farm

Ashgrove Bottom

Woodley Down

Wessex Ridgeway

5

St Mary's Church (remains of)

East Compton

P

Clubmen's Down

Mound

Gore Farm

West Wood

South Farm

Ashmore

Dorset STREET ATLAS

Compton Abbas

Fontmell Down Nature Reserve

Fore Top

Longcombe Bottom

Shepherd's Bottom

Tumulus

18

National Trust

SP7

Cross Dyke

Fontmell Wood

Fontmell Hill House

HALFPENNY LA
HIGH LA
GREEN LA

Ashmore Farm

Wiltshire Coppice

Hookley Copse

Earthwork

4

17

Springhead Farm

Springhead

MILL ST

Strip Lynchets

Littlecombe Bottom

Balfour's Wood

SUTTON HILL BOTTOM

Washers Pit

Turkey Plantation

SP5

Well Bottom

Mudoak Wood

Gallops

3

Enclosure

Combe Bottom

Sutton Hill Farm

Washers Pit Coppice

Stubhampton Bottom

Stony Bottom

Earthwork

Spring Farm

Tumuli

16

Sutton Hill

Folly Barrow

West Lodge

DT11

Higher Barn Plantation

Bareden Down

Spinney Pits Coppice

Ashmore Wood

Higher Downend Coppice

Upper Broadridge Coppice

Ashmore Plantation

Manor Hill

Bussey's Down

Tollard Green Bottom

Caesar's Camp (Fort)

2

15

Wales Wood

Bareden Wood

Iwerne Hill

TOWER HILL

Tumuli

Common Bushes

Payne Coppice

Great Peakey Coppice

Hanging Coppice

Ashmore Bottom

DT11

Ashmore Barn Farm

Tumulus

Bussey Stool Farm

1

14

Brookman's Valley

Hill Farm

BOYNE LANE

Wessex Ridgeway

Earl's Hill

Tumuli

Stubhampton Down

Dungrove Hill

ASHMORE BOTTOM

Dorset STREET ATLAS

87   **A**   88   **B**   89   **C**   90   **D**   91   **E**   92   **F**

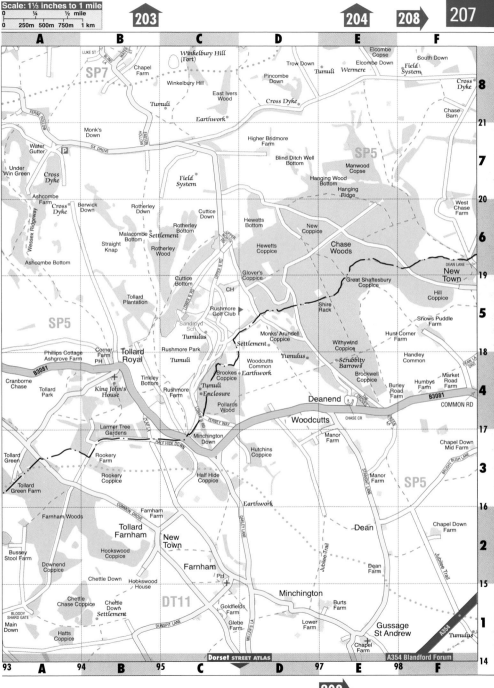

A   B   C   D   E   F

8
Winkelbury Hill (Fort)

SP7

Chapel Farm

LUKE ST

Winkelbury Hill

East Ivers Wood

Trow Down

Tumuli

Elcombe Copse
Elcombe Down
Wermere

South Down
Field System

Tumuli

Cross Dyke

Cross Dyke

Earthwork

21

Monk's Down

Higher Bridmore Farm

SP5

Chase Barn

7

Water Gutter

OX DROVE

Blind Ditch Well Bottom

Manwood Copse

P

Under Win Green

Cross Dyke

FERNE HOLLOW

EASTON HOLLOW

Hanging Wood Bottom

Hanging Ridge

West Chase Farm

20

Ashcombe Farm

Cross Dyke

Berwick Down

Rotherley Down

Cuttice Down

Hewetts Bottom

New Coppice

Chase Woods

DEAN LANE

6

Wessex Ridgeway

Straight Knap

Malacombe Bottom

Settlement

Rotherley Bottom

Rotherley Wood

Hewetts Coppice

Glover's Coppice

Great Shaftesbury Coppice

New Town

19

Ashcombe Bottom

Cuttice Bottom

Tollard Plantation

CH

UPPER IN RD

Shire Rack

Hill Coppice

SP5

Rushmore Golf Club

Snows Puddle Farm

5

Sandroyd Sch

Tumulus

Settlement

Monks' Arundell Coppice

Withywind Coppice

Hunt Corner Farm

Handley Common

18

Phillips Cottage
Ashgrove Farm

Corner Farm
PH

Tollard Royal

Rushmore Park

Tumuli

LOWER IN RD

Woodcutts Common
Earthwork

Tumulus

Scrubbity Barrows

Brockwell Coppice

Burley Road Farm

Humbys Farm

Market Road Farm

DEAN LA DRO

4

Cranborne Chase

B3081

Tollard Park

King John's House

Tinkley Bottom

Rushmore Farm

Brookes Coppice

Tumuli
Enclosure

Pollards Wood

Deanend

CHASE RD

B3081

COMMON RD

17

Larmer Tree Gardens

CHAP LA

HALF HIDE DOWN

Minchington Down

Woodcutts

Manor Farm

Chase Cr

STRAIGHT LANE

Chapel Down Mid Farm

3

Tollard Green

Rookery Farm

COMMON DROVE

Half Hide Coppice

Hutchins Coppice

Manor Farm

SP5

Rookery Coppice

Earthwork

DEAN

Tollard Green Farm

16

Farnham Woods

Farnham Farm

OAKLEY LANE

Chapel Down Farm

2

Bussey Stool Farm

Tollard Farnham

Hookswood Coppice

New Town

Farnham

MILLERS LA

Dean

Dean Farm

Jubilee Trail

BRIGHT BUSH LANE

Downend Coppice

Chettle Down

Hookswood House

PH

Minchington

Burts Farm

15

BLOODY SHARD GATE

Chettle Chase Coppice

Chettle Down
Settlement

DT11

DUNSPIT LANE

Goldfields Farm

Glebe Farm

Lower Farm

Gussage St Andrew

Jubilee Trail

A354

1

Main Down

Hatts Coppice

Chapel Farm

Tumulus

14

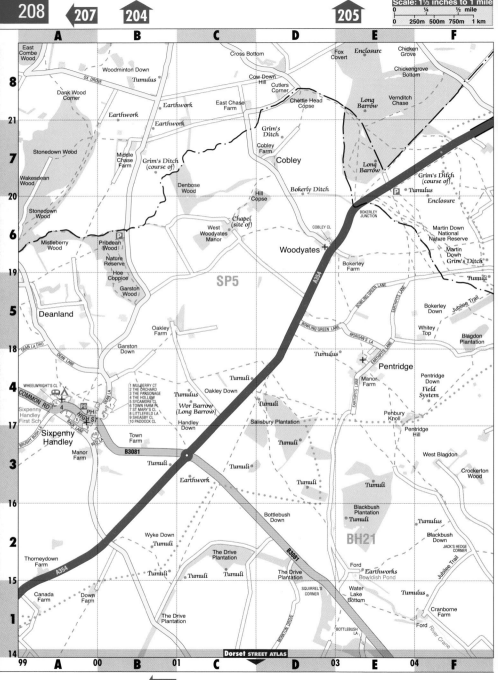

Scale: 1½ inches to 1 mile

| 0 | ¼ | ½ mile |
| 0 | 250m | 500m | 750m | 1 km |

A   **B**   **C**   **D**   **E**   **F**

East Combe Wood

Woodminton Down

Cross Bottom

Fox Covert

Enclosure

Chicken Grove

Chickengrove Bottom

8

OX DROVE

Tumulus

Cow Down Hill

Cutlers Corner

Chettle Head Copse

Long Barrow

Vernditch Chase

Dank Wood Corner

Earthwork

East Chase Farm

21

Earthwork

Earthwork

Grim's Ditch

Stonedown Wood

Middle Chase Farm

Grim's Ditch (course of)

Cobley Farm

Cobley

Long Barrow

Grim's Ditch (course of)

7

Wakesdean Wood

Denbose Wood

Bokerly Ditch

Tumulus

Enclosure

20

Stonedown Wood

Hill Copse

BOKERLEY JUNCTION

Martin Down National Nature Reserve

6

Mistleberry Wood

Pribdean Wood

West Woodyates Manor

Chapel (site of)

COBLEY CL

Woodyates

Bokerley Farm

Martin Down

Grim's Ditch

Nature Reserve

Tumuli

19

Hoe Coppice

Garston Wood

SP5

Bokerley Down

Jubilee Trail

5

Deanland

Oakley Farm

BOWLING GREEN LANE

Whitey Top

Blagdon Plantation

18

DEAN LA DRO

DEAN LANE

Garston Down

MORGAN'S LA

EARTHPITS LANE

Tumulus

Pentridge

Pentridge Down Field System

4

WHEELWRIGHT'S CL

COMMON RD

Sixpenny Handley First Sch

Tumuli

Oakley Down

Manor Farm

1 MULBERRY CT
2 THE ORCHARD
3 THE PARSONAGE
4 THE HOLLOW
5 SYCAMORE CL
6 TOWN FARM PL
7 ST MARY'S CL
8 LITTLEFIELD LA
9 SHEASBY CL
10 PADDOCK CL

Tumulus

Wor Barrow (Long Barrow)

Tumuli

Pehbury Knoll

Pentridge Hill

17

Sixpenny Handley

HIGH ST

BACK LANE

RED LA

Town Farm

Handley Down

Salisbury Plantation

West Blagdon

Manor Farm

B3081

Tumuli

Tumuli

Tumuli

Crockerton Wood

3

Earthwork

Tumuli

Blackbush Plantation

Tumuli

Tumulus

16

Bottlebush Down

Blackbush Down

JACK'S HEDGE CORNER

Wyke Down

Tumuli

The Drive Plantation

B3081

BH21

2

Thorneydown Farm

A354

Tumuli

Tumuli

The Drive Plantation

Ford

Earthworks

Bowldish Pond

Tumulus

Cranborne Farm

Jubilee Trail

15

Canada Farm

Down Farm

SQUIRREL'S CORNER

Water Lake Bottom

Ford

1

The Drive Plantation

MONKTON DRIVE

BOTTLEBUSH LA

River Crane

14

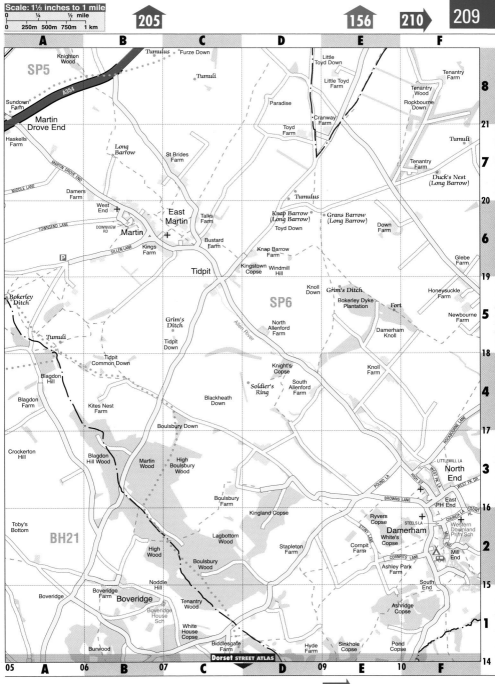

Scale: 1⅓ inches to 1 mile

0 ¼ ½ mile
0 250m 500m 750m 1 km

SP5

Knighton Wood

Tumulus • Furze Down

Tumuli

Little Toyd Down

Little Toyd Farm

Tenantry Farm

8

Sundown Farm

A354

Paradise

Cranway Farm

Tenantry Wood

Rockbourne Down

21

Martin Drove End

Haskells Farm

MARTIN DROVE END

Long Barrow

St Brides Farm

Toyd Farm

Tenantry Farm

Tumuli

7

MIDDLE LANE

Damers Farm

Tumulus

Duck's Nest (Long Barrow)

20

West End

East Martin

Talks Farm

Knap Barrow (Long Barrow)

Grans Barrow (Long Barrow)

Down Farm

DOWNVIEW RD

Martin

Toyd Down

6

TOWNSEND LANE

SILLEN LANE

Kings Farm

Bustard Farm

Knap Barrow Farm

Glebe Farm

P

Tidpit

Kingstown Copse

Windmill Hill

19

Bokerley Ditch

Grim's Ditch

North Allenford Farm

Knoll Down

Grim's Ditch

Bokerley Dyke Plantation

Fort

Honeysuckle Farm

SP6

Newbourne Farm

5

Tumuli

Tidpit Down

Damerham Knoll

Blagdon Hill

Tidpit Common Down

Knight's Copse

Knoll Farm

18

Blagdon Farm

Kites Nest Farm

Allen River

Soldier's Ring

North Allenford Farm

South Allenford Farm

4

Crockerton Hill

Blackheath Down

Boulsbury Down

17

Blagdon Hill Wood

Martin Wood

High Boulsbury Wood

ROCKBOURNE LANE

LITTLEMILL LA

North End

3

WEST PK DR

HIGH ST

WEST PK DR

BH21

Boulsbury Farm

Kingland Copse

POUND LA

BROWNS LANE

East End

EAST PH END

CHURCH LA

Western Downland Prim Sch

16

High Wood

Lagbottom Wood

Stapleton Farm

Ryvers Copse

White's Copse

STONY LANE

STEELS LA

Damerham

COURT HL

2

Boulsbury Wood

Cornpit Farm

CORNPITS LANE

Mill End

Noddle Hill

Ashley Park Farm

South End

15

Toby's Bottom

Boveridge Farm

Boveridge

Boveridge House Sch

Tenantry Wood

White House Copse

Ashridge Copse

Pond Copse

1

Burwood

Biddlesgate Farm

Hyde Farm

Sinkhole Copse

14

A 05 B 06 C 07 D 08 E 09 F 10

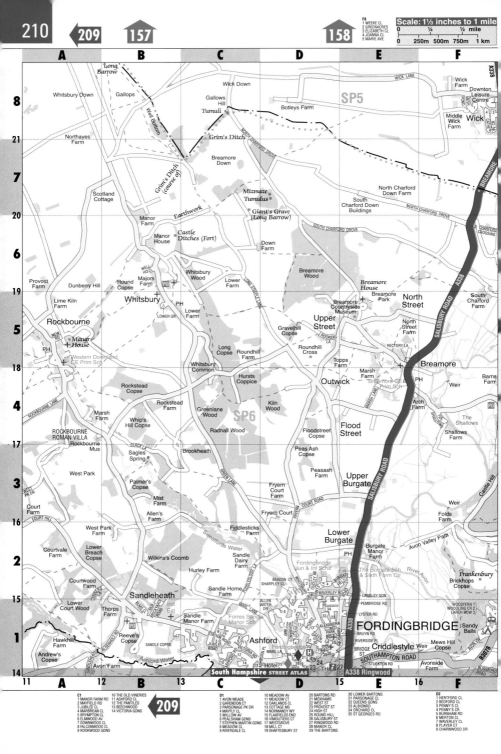

Scale: 1⅓ inches to 1 mile

0   ¼   ½   mile
0 250m 500m 750m 1 km

SP5

Wick

FORDINGBRIDGE

Criddlestyle

Ashford

Sandleheath

Whitsbury

Rockbourne

Breamore

North Street

Upper Street

Outwick

Flood Street

Upper Burgate

Lower Burgate

A338 Ringwood

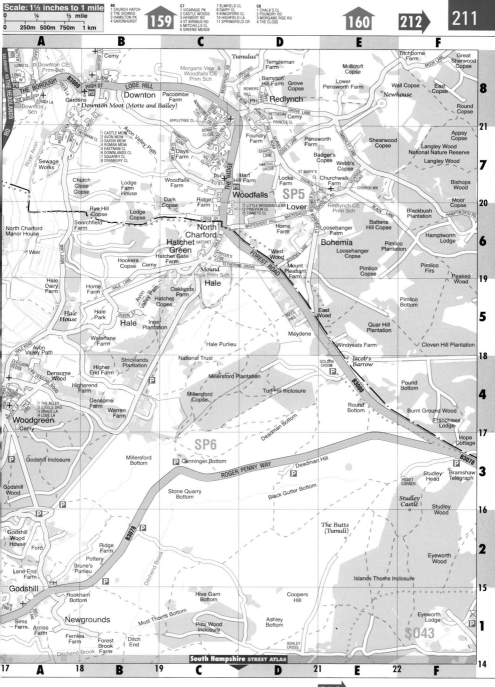

B8
1 CHURCH HATCH
2 THE SIDINGS
3 HAMILTON PK
4 SAXONHURST

C7
1 VICARAGE PK
2 CASTLE WOODS
3 HERBERT RD
4 ST BIRINUS RD
5 MITCHELLS CL
6 GREENS MEADE

7 ELMFIELD CL
8 DAIRY CL
9 KINGSFORD CL
10 HIGHFIELD LA
11 SPRINGFIELD CR

C8
1 CHALK'S CL
2 FOUNDRY RD
3 MORGANS RISE RD
4 THE CLOSE

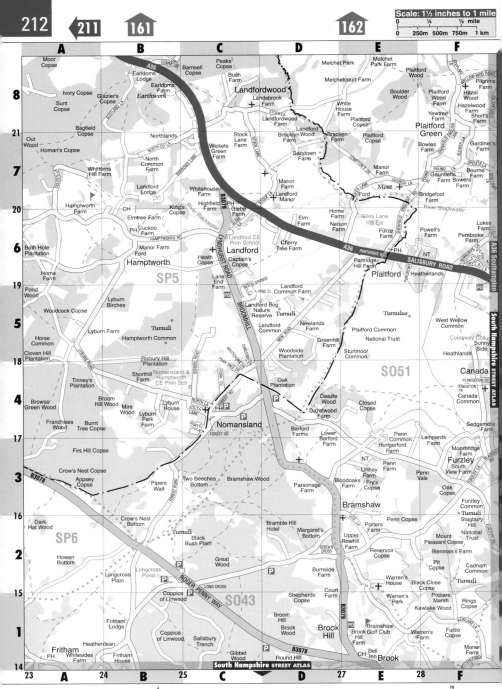

Scale: 1⅓ inches to 1 mile

| 0 | | ¼ | ½ | mile |
| 0 | 250m | 500m | 750m | 1 km |

A B C D E F

8

211

21

7

20

6

19

5

18

4

17

3

16

2

15

1

14

A 23 24 B 25 C D 27 E 28 F

South Hampshire STREET ATLAS

South Hampshire STREET ATLAS

F6
1 BOTTOM LA
2 ITCHEN CL
3 BOURNE CL
4 THE BEECHES
5 STOUR CL
6 ARUN WY
7 PEARTREE CL
8 NIGHTINGALE CL

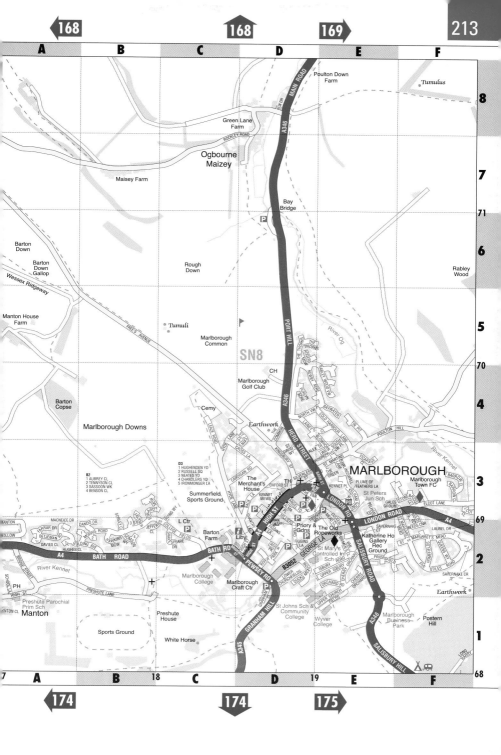

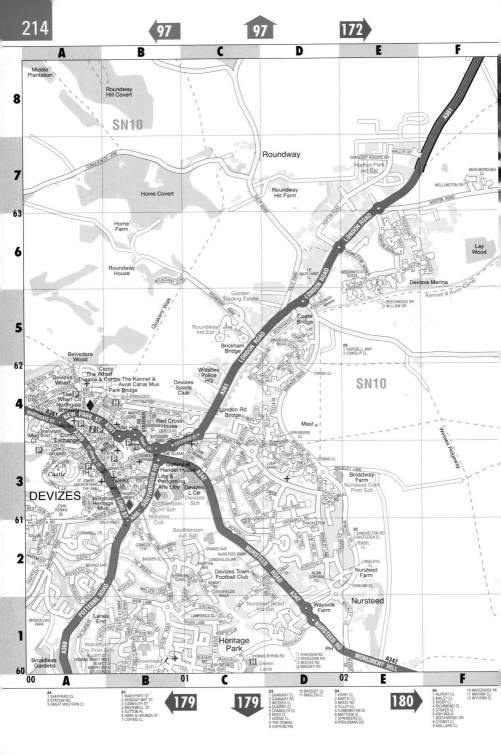

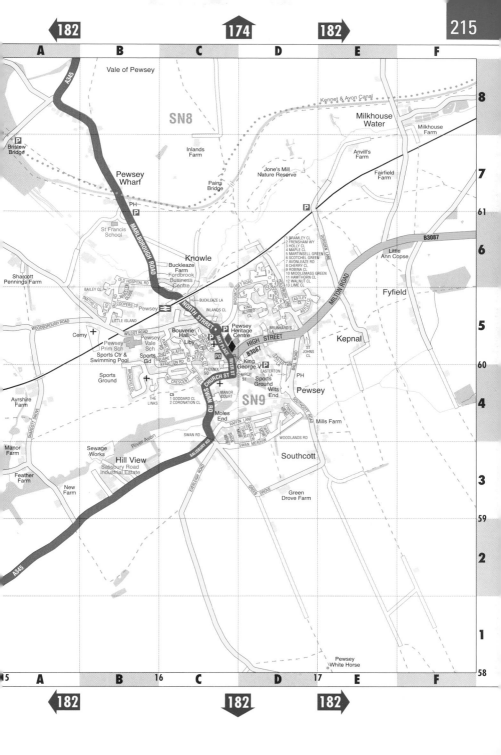

A   B   C   D   E   F

Vale of Pewsey

Kennet & Avon Canal

SN8

Milkhouse
Water

8

Milkhouse
Farm

Bristew
Bridge

Inlands
Farm

Anvill's
Farm

7

Pewsey
Wharf

Pains
Bridge

Jone's Mill
Nature Reserve

Fairfield
Farm

PH

61

MARLBOROUGH ROAD

A345

St Francis
School

P

B3087

6

Knowle

Little
Ann Copse

Sharcott
Pennings Farm

Buckleaze
Farm
Fordbrook
Business
Centre

1 BRAMLEY CL
2 FRENSHAM WY
3 HOLLY CL
4 MAPLE CL
5 MARTINSELL GREEN
6 SCOTCHEL GREEN
7 AVONLEAZE RD
8 CHERRY CL
9 ROBINA CL
10 MIDDLEMASS GREEN
11 HAWTHORN CL
12 WALNUT CL
13 LIME CL

Fyfield

OLD HOSPITAL RD
BAILEY CL

BROADFIELD ROAD

MILTON ROAD

BUCKLEAZE LA

Pewsey
SMITHS CL
COOPERS CT

INLANDS CL

KING
ALFRED
CL

ASTLEY
CL

5

LITTLE ISLAND

WOODBOROUGH ROAD

WILCOT ROAD

Cemy

Bouverie
Hall

Pewsey
Vale
Sch

NORTH STREET

Pewsey
Heritage
Centre

P

BRUNKARD'S
LA

Kepnal

Pewsey
Prim Sch

Liby

LAKE PLACE

ST
JOHNS
CL

Sports Ctr &
Swimming Pool

Sports
Gd

CANING ST

THE SLATER

RIVER ST

HIGH STREET

PO

King
George V

60

Sports
Ground

STRATTON RD

ASTON RD

EASTERTON

Pewsey

THE
SQUARE

PHOENIX
SQ

CHURCH ST

CHURCH

EASTERTON LA

P

PH

4

CRESCENT

BRAUNSTON

CS

1 GODDARD CL
2 CORONATION CL

SWAN RD

MANOR
COURT

Wits
End

SN9

SOUTHGROVE ROAD

Ayrshire
Farm

THE
LINKS

Moles
End

Mills Farm

Manor
Farm

River Avon

BAFFIN LANE

STRATTON RD

SWAN MEADOW

WOODLANDS RD

Southcott

Feather
Farm

Sewage
Works

SALISBURY RD

SWAN RD

3

New
Farm

Hill View

Salisbury Road
Industrial Estate

EVERETT ROAD

GREEN DROVE

Green
Drove Farm

59

A345

2

1

Pewsey
White Horse

58

A   B   16   C   D   17   E   F

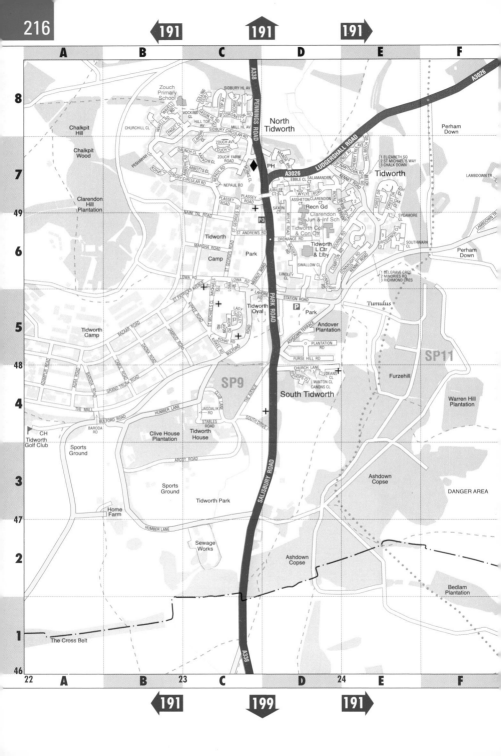

198 ◄   ▲ 198   198 ►

| A | B | C | D | E | F |

PH
Durrington Walls
A345
COUNTESS ROAD
Woodhenge
Long Barrow
Totterdown Clump
Countess
TOLLGATE CL
CLUMP WAY
Motel
A303
AMESBURY LORDS WALK BY-PASS
Ratfyn Barrow
COOPERS CL
LORDS CFT
GAUNTLET RD
HILLVIEW
CARLETON
Amesbury Abbey
EAST
Amesbury CE Jun Sch
THE DROVE
Amesbury Activity Ctr
The Stonehenge Sch
Amesbury City Inf Sch
Mkt
Liby
P
Queen's Falls
AVON BUILDINGS
FLOWER LA
OLD GRANARY LA
CHURCH STREET
River Avon
P
Cemy
Recreation Gd
Sewage Works
Southmill Hill Plantation
A345
SOUTHMILL RD
SALISBURY ROAD
Christ The King RC Prim Sch
SOUTH MILL RD
COACH HOUSE MS
ABBESS CL 1
AVONSTOKE CL 2
SODTH MILL CL 3
Strip Lynchets
ROBBINS RIDGE
EVERGREEN WAY
WINCHESTER CL
BEAULIEU RD
LYNCHURST ROAD

ROBIN HL LA
BULFORD HILL
A3028
Bulford Bridge
Avondale School
Manor Farm
CYGNET DR
WATER ST
HIGH STREET
River Avon
WATERGATE LANE
Long Barrow
Sewage Works
Ratfyn
Folly Bottom
Amesbury Business Park
BEACON
LONDON ROAD
ALANBROOK CL
ARAGON CL
JAMES RD
QUEENSBERRY RD
Amesbury Sports Ctr
ST ANNES CL
LANFEAR CL
ST ANNES CL
CUTSFOOT CL
ORCHARD CL
Amesbury
BRADLEY
SHARMAN WAY
SALICE ROAD
BOSCOMBE ROAD
JAGGARD VIEW
TANNERS FLD
BEAULIEU RD
CHAMBERS AV

LEDGER HL CL 1
CHURCHILL AV 2
Cemy
OLD COACH ROAD
LEONAR
MEADOW
CHURCHILL AVENUE
PERIWINKLE WY
CRESCENT RD
PH
Recreation Ground
Mast
Tumuli
Mast
SALISBURY ROAD
SORTON ROAD
Minton Distribution Park
Solstice Park Business Park
MILLS WY
LANE'S CL
PINE WALK
BUTTERFIELD DR
IPILOTS VW
PORTON ROAD
Beverley Hills Mobile Home Park
BEAUMONT
ROMSEY WY
IMBER
PETERSFIELD
Lark Side
OXFORD
MARTLESHAM RD
BOSCOMBE ROAD
MILTON RD
EARLS CL
IMBER ROAD

BULFORD DROVEWAY
Bulford CE Prim Sch
FRENCH WY
Bulford
1 CLAYTON RD
2 THE LEAZE
3 DUKE'S WY
4 SWATTONS CL
DOUBLE HEDGES
A3028
Mast
Tumuli
Tumuli
SP4
Earl's Farm Down
Tumuli
STOCKPORT ROAD
RALEIGH CRES
MAIN ROAD
NORTH ROAD
ASHLEY WK
Boscombe Down
Mast
Boscombe Down Airfield

WILTSHIRE CL
HAIG RD
DORSET
HAMPSHIRE
Bulford Camp
Tumuli
Sports Ground
A3028
Tumuli
Tumuli

| 8 | 7 | 43 | 6 | 5 | 42 | 4 | 3 | 41 | 2 | 1 | 40 |

| A | B | C | D | E | F |

15 16 17

B3
1 SCHOOL LA
2 SMITHFIELD ST
3 CHAPLINS PL
4 NURSERY CL
5 JOHN GAY RD
6 HAYWAIN
7 LYNCHFIELD RD

C2
1 MILLGREEN RD
2 BEAULIEU RD
3 PAINS WY
4 FLIT CROFT
5 HARVARD WY
6 TUCKER CL
7 WITTENHAM VW
8 DIDDLEDOWN RD

C3
1 FINNIS RD
2 CHERRY TREE WY
3 GENEVILLE RISE
4 LAWRENCE CL
5 RINGWOOD AV

D2
1 LIGHTNING RD
2 HAVARD WY
3 MCKIE RD
4 LEONARD CHESHIRE CL
5 BEYER RD
6 BAWDSEY RD

D3
1 BEAUCHAMP DR
2 CARLTON CL
3 WESTLAND CL
4 FOVELERS BUSHES
5 HURLEY CL
6 JAVELIN CL
7 MOYNE GDNS
8 LUMLEY WK
9 TEMPEST RD

10 CANTERBURY CL

E3
1 VIRGINIA CL
2 VERNON CL
3 CHESTERFIELD CL
4 PURVIS CL
5 CONISTON CL
6 NICOLSON CL
7 BURWOOD CL
8 HEYFORD CL
9 BARNES WALLIS CL

10 THURLOW CL

198 ◄   ▲ 198   198 ►

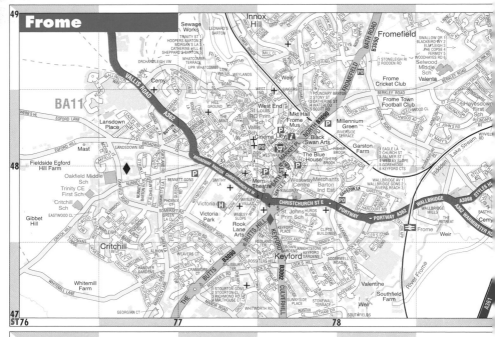

Frome

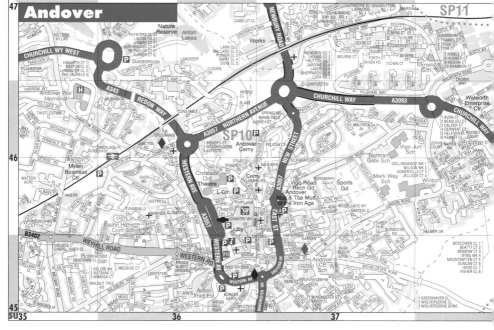

Andover

Place name May be abbreviated on the map

Location number Present when a number indicates the place's position in a crowded area of mapping

Locality, town or village Shown when more than one place has the same name

Postcode district District for the indexed place

Page and grid square Page number and grid reference for the standard mapping

Church Rd 6 Beckenham BR2..........53 C6

Public and commercial buildings are highlighted in magenta. Places of interest are highlighted in blue with a star★

Abbreviations used in the index

Acad	**Academy**	Comm	**Common**	Gd	**Ground**	L	**Leisure**	Prom	**Promenade**
App	**Approach**	Cott	**Cottage**	Gdn	**Garden**	La	**Lane**	Rd	**Road**
Arc	**Arcade**	Cres	**Crescent**	Gn	**Green**	Liby	**Library**	Recn	**Recreation**
Ave	**Avenue**	Cswy	**Causeway**	Gr	**Grove**	Mdw	**Meadow**	Ret	**Retail**
Bglw	**Bungalow**	Ct	**Court**	H	**Hall**	Meml	**Memorial**	Sh	**Shopping**
Bldg	**Building**	Ctr	**Centre**	Ho	**House**	Mkt	**Market**	Sq	**Square**
Bsns, Bus	**Business**	Ctry	**Country**	Hospl	**Hospital**	Mus	**Museum**	St	**Street**
Bvd	**Boulevard**	Cty	**County**	HQ	**Headquarters**	Orch	**Orchard**	Sta	**Station**
Cath	**Cathedral**	Dr	**Drive**	Hts	**Heights**	Pal	**Palace**	Terr	**Terrace**
Cir	**Circus**	Dro	**Drove**	Ind	**Industrial**	Par	**Parade**	TH	**Town Hall**
Cl	**Close**	Ed	**Education**	Inst	**Institute**	Pas	**Passage**	Univ	**University**
Cnr	**Corner**	Emb	**Embankment**	Int	**International**	Pk	**Park**	Wk, Wlk	**Walk**
Coll	**College**	Est	**Estate**	Intc	**Interchange**	Pl	**Place**	Wr	**Water**
Com	**Community**	Ex	**Exhibition**	Junc	**Junction**	Prec	**Precinct**	Yd	**Yard**

Index of localities, towns and villages

A

Ablington 190 B1
Acton Turville 52 F6
Alcester 202 B1
Alcombe 82 F8
Aldbourne 170 A6
Alderbury 153 C3
Alderton 39 F2
All Cannings 180 E8
Allington
Amesbury 199 A2
Chippenham 69 E3
Devizes 172 E2
Allington Bar 69 F2
Alton 190 B1
Alton Barnes 173 C1
Alton Priors 173 D1
Alvediston 204 B2
Amesbury 217 C4
Ansty 203 F5
Ansty Coombe 203 F5
Appleshaw 192 E3
Ashbury 164 A7
Ashford 210 C1
Ashley
Box 83 A6
Tetbury 3 A2
Ashmore 206 D5
Ashton Common 102 F1
Ashton Keynes 6 F1
Atworth 92 F8
Aughton 183 D3
Avebury 173 C8
Avebury Trusloe 173 B8
Avington 177 F7
Avon 71 F6
Avoncliff 99 F4
Axford 169 D1

B

Badbury 65 F5
Badbury Wick 65 D8
Badminton 38 F2
Bagshot 176 F4
Ballard's Ash 47 D5
Bapton 195 D1
Barford St Martin 143 A3
Barkers Hill 203 A4
Barrow 136 C5
Barrow Street 139 F2
Batheaston 82 B4
Bathford 82 B2
Baverstock 142 B4
Baydon 170 C8
Beanacre 94 A8
Beckhampton 173 B7
Beechingstoke 181 A6
Bemerton 145 C2
Bemerton Heath 145 C4
Berkley 111 A7
Berkley Down 110 C5
Berryfield 93 F1
Berwick Bassett 167 B4
Berwick St James 196 E2
Berwick St John 203 E1
Berwick St Leonard 200 C4
Bewley Common 86 E5
Biddestone 76 F8
Birdbush 203 B1
Bishopdown 146 C4
Bishops Cannings 172 B3
Bishopstone
Salisbury 205 F4
Swindon 163 E6
Bishopstrow 117 E4
Bittles Green 202 B4
Blackland 89 F6
Bleet 102 F2
Blue Vein 83 D3
Blunsdon St Andrew 34 E8
Bodenham 152 F1
Bohemia 211 E6
Boreham 117 C5
Boscombe 199 A1
Bottlesford 181 D6
Bourton
Bishops Cannings 172 C3
Gillingham 137 E2
Boveridge 209 B1
Bowden Hill 87 B4
Bowerchalke 205 A2
Bowerhill 94 D1
Bowldown 70 E8
Box 83 D6
Box Hill 83 F7
Boyton 194 E2
Bradenstoke 59 C3
Bradford Leigh 91 F1
Bradford-on-Avon 100 E6
Bramshaw 212 E3
Bratton 186 B7
Breamore 210 F5
Bremhill 80 E7
Brigmerston 198 C8
Brinkworth 45 E5
Britford 152 E5
Brixton Deverill 120 E2
Broad Blunsdon 21 C2
Broadbush 21 D1
Broad Chalke 205 B4
Broad Hinton 167 C7
Broad's Green 88 F3
Broad Street 181 C6
Broad Town 167 A8
Brokenborough 27 D7
Brokerswood 107 F5
Bromham 96 A7
Brook 212 E1
Brook Hill 212 D1
Brook Waters 203 B2
Broomfield 55 A1
Broughton Gifford 93 C4
Brunton 183 E3
Bugley 116 C6
Bulbridge 144 B1
Bulford 217 E8
Bulford Camp 198 F6
Bulkington 178 E5
Bullenhill 106 E8
Bullock's Horn 15 E1
Burbage 183 D8
Burcombe 143 E2
Burton
Acton Turville 53 B4
Mere 139 D5
Buscot Wick 12 D8
Bushton 166 E8
Buttermere 185 B8

C

Cadley 175 A5
Calcutt 20 A7
Callow Hill 46 D6
Calne 81 B2
Calne Marsh 81 C4
Calstone Wellington 172 A7
Canada 212 F4
Cann Common 206 B8
Castle Combe 68 A7
Castle Eaton 10 B4
Catcomb 73 D6
Cerney Wick 7 F5
Chalford 113 A8
Chapel Barton 115 D6
Chapel Knapp 85 D5
Chapel Plaister 84 A5
Chapmanslade 111 C4
Charlcutt 72 F4
Charlton
Andover 193 C2
Malmesbury 29 A6
Pewsey 181 D3
Shaftesbury 203 A1
Charlton-All-Saints 159 A4
Charlton Heath 29 D6
Charlton Musgrove 136 B4
Charnage 139 E4
Chedglow 14 C7
Chelworth 4 C1
Chelworth Lower Green 19 A5
Chelworth Upper Green 19 A6
Cheney Manor 34 F1
Cherhill 166 B1
Chicklade 200 A5
Chicksgrove 204 B8
Chilmark 201 B3
Chilton Foliat 170 F1
Chippenham 78 E7
Chirton 180 F4
Chisbury 176 B5
Chiseldon 65 D3
Chitterne 195 C7
Chittoe 87 E2
Cholderton 199 C5
Christian Malford 58 B2
Churchfields 145 D1
Chute Cadley 192 F8
Chute Standen 192 F8
Clanville
Andover 193 A4
Stanton St Quintin 56 E4
Clatford 174 B7
Claverton 90 B5
Clearwood 111 F8
Clench 174 E1
Clench Common 174 D4
Clevancy 166 C6
Cleverton 44 D8
Cloatley 15 E2
Cloatley End 16 B1
Clyffe Pypard 166 F8
Coate
Devizes 180 C8
Swindon 51 C2
Cobley 208 D7
Codford St Mary 195 B2
Codford St Peter 195 A3
Cold Harbour
Trowbridge 102 F2
Warminster 116 F8
Colerne 75 B3
Collingbourne Ducis 191 E8
Collingbourne
Kingston 183 D2
Combe 185 F8
Common Platt 33 F2
Compton 189 F7
Compton Abbas 206 A5
Compton Bassett 166 B3
Compton
Chamberlayne 205 A8
Conkwell 90 C1
Conock 180 E4
Coombe
Durrington 190 B5
Shaftesbury 202 F1
Coombe Bissett 150 F1
Coped Hall 47 F4
Corsham 85 A8
Corsley 111 D2
Corsley Heath 115 B8
Corston 42 F5
Corton 194 D3
Cotmarsh 62 B4
Cotswold Community 6 D4
Coulston 178 E1
Covingham 51 D7
Cowesfield Green 161 F4
Cricklade 19 E7
Criddlestyle 210 E1
Crockerton 116 E1
Crockerton Green 116 F2
Crofton 176 A1
Crooked Soley 170 F3
Cross Keys 77 A3
Croucheston 205 F4
Crudwell 14 E6
Cuckold's Green 179 C4
Cuckoo's Corner 180 B4
Cuckoo's Knob 174 F1
Culkerton 3 A5
Culverslade 66 A2

D

Damerham 209 F2
Dauntsey 45 B1
Dauntsey Lock 59 B5
Dean 207 E2
Deanend 207 E4
Deanland 208 A5
Deptford 195 E1
Derry Fields 17 F8
Derry Hill 79 F2
Dertfords 115 B7
Devizes 214 A3
Didmarton 24 C3
Dilton Marsh 112 B8
Dinton 201 F2
Ditchampton 144 C4
Ditteridge 83 B8
Dogridge 32 F3
Donhead St Andrew 203 B3
Donhead St Mary 203 A3
Dorcan 51 D5
Down Ampney 8 D7
Downton 211 B8
Draycot Cerne 56 F1
Draycot Fitz Payne 174 A2
Draycot Foliat 168 D8
Drynham 105 E5
Dunfield 10 A8
Dunge 106 E1

Dunkirk 179 D8
Durley 175 D3
Durrington 198 B7
Dursley 105 E1

E

East Anton 193 F2
Eastbury 171 C8
East Chisenbury 190 A7
East Compton 206 A5
Eastcott 180 A2
Eastcourt 15 D6
East End 74 A8
Easterton 180 A2
Easterton Sands 179 F2
East Everleigh 191 A8
East Garston 171 E7
East Gomeldon 133 E4
East Grafton 183 F7
East Grimstead 154 F4
East Hatch 203 C7
East Kennett 173 E6
East Knoyle 141 C2
East Martin 49 B6
East Melbury 206 B7
Easton 77 D2
Easton Grey 26 C3
Easton Royal 183 A7
Easton Town 25 D1
Eastrip 75 D4
East Town 106 E4
East Tytherton 72 B2
East Winterslow 149 C8
East Woodlands 114 B5
Ebbesbourne Wake . . 204 C2
Eddington 177 C8
Eden Vale 112 A1
Edington 186 C8
Elcombe 63 E5
Eldene 51 C5
Elliots Green 114 D8
Elm Cross 167 D7
Elm Hill 202 A5
Elston 196 E7
Enford 189 F6
Englands 78 F5
Enham Alamein 193 E4
Enmore Green 202 B2
Erlestoke 187 A8
Etchilhampton 180 C7
Even Swindon 49 E6
Everleigh 191 A8
Ewen 5 C8

F

Faberstown 192 B6
Fairford 1 E7
Fairwood 108 B4
Farleigh Hungerford . 103 E7
Farleigh Wick 90 F5
Farley 154 D8
Farnham 207 C2
Ferne 203 D1
Fiddington Sands 179 F1
Fifield 190 A5
Fifield Bavant 204 A1
Figheldean 190 B2
Filands 28 A6
Firsdown 148 C8
Fisherton de la Mere . 195 D1
Fittleton 190 A4
Flaxlands 47 D6
Flood Street 210 E4
Fonthill Bishop 200 D3
Fonthill Gifford 200 B2
Ford
  Chippenham 68 A2
  Salisbury 146 D7
Fordingbridge 210 E1
Forest Hill 175 E4
Forewoods Common . 101 C7
Fosbury 185 A5
Foscote 54 E3
Fovant 204 E8
Foxcotte 193 C2
Foxham 72 D7
Foxley 41 F8
Fresh Brook 49 A4
Freshford 99 B5
Fritham 212 A1
Frogmore 109 A4
Frome 110 A5
Fromefield 110 A6
Froxfield 176 D7
Fugglestone St Peter . 144 F4
Furzley 212 F3
Fyfield
  Andover 192 D1
  Pewsey 215 E5

G

Gare Hill 118 A5
Garsdon 29 B4
Gasper 137 C7
Gastard 85 D6
Gideahall 68 D2
Goatacre 73 F7
Godshill 211 A1
Gomeldon 133 D4
Gorse Hill 35 D1
Grange Park 48 F5

Great Ashley 91 A1
Great Bedwyn 176 B3
Great Chalfield 92 E3
Great Cheverell 179 C1
Great Durnford 197 F1
Greatfield 47 F8
Great Hinton 178 A6
Great Somerford 44 B2
Great Wishford 129 F3
Green Hill 32 D1
Greenmeadow 35 B4
Greenwich 200 C3
Grittenham 46 C2
Grittleton 54 D5
Gussage St Andrew . . 207 E1

H

Hackthorn 198 A8
Hailstone Hill 8 A1
Halcombe 27 E3
Hale 211 C5
Halfway 113 A4
Half Way Firs 76 C1
Ham 177 B2
Ham Green 101 C8
Hampshire Gate 185 A1
Hampton 22 D5
Hampton Hill 22 E5
Hamptworth 212 B6
Hanging Langford . . . 128 C2
Hankerton 15 C2
Hannington 22 B7
Hannington Wick 11 A4
Hardway 122 A1
Haresfield 23 B8
Harnham 151 E6
Hatchet Green 211 C6
Hatherden 193 C5
Hawkeridge 108 E8
Haxton 190 B4
Haydon Wick 34 E5
Hayes Knoll 19 E2
Heddington 89 B1
Heddington Wick 88 E2
Henley
  Box 83 C4
  Shalbourne 185 A6
Heritage Park 214 C1
Heytesbury 194 C5
Heywood 109 A8
Higher Pertwood 127 E4
Highway 166 B5
Highworth 23 B5
Hilcott 181 D5
Hill Corner 110 E2
Hill Deverill 120 F5
Hill View 215 B3
Hilmarton 166 A6
Hilperton 102 A3
Hilperton Marsh 101 F5
Hindon 200 B3
Hinton Charterhouse . 98 C1
Hinton Parva 163 D6
Hisomley 112 C7
Hodson 65 A5
Hoggington 104 D4
Holloway 141 A1
Holt 92 E1
Holwell 139 B5
Homington 151 D1
Hook 47 F6
Hook Street 48 B6
Horningsham 119 A7
Horpit 163 B7
Horton 172 C2
Huish 174 A2
Hullavington 41 E1
Hungerford 177 A6
Hungerford Newtown . 171 D2
Huntenhull Green . . . 111 C3
Hurdcott 146 F8
Hyde 35 D7

I

Ibthorpe 193 F8
Idmiston 133 F8
Idstone 163 D8
Imber 187 A3
Inglesham 2 B1
Inkpen 177 E3
Ireland 105 B2
Ivy Cross 202 D2

K

Keevil 178 C5
Kellaways 71 E4
Kemble 4 E7
Kemble Wick 4 E4
Kempsford 10 E6
Kepnal 215 E5
Kilmington 123 E5
Kilmington Common . 123 D4
Kimpton 192 C1
Kinghay 202 F8
Kingsdown
  Box 82 F3
  Stratton St Margaret . 35 F3
Kingshill 50 B5
Kingston Deverill 126 B6
Kingstone Winslow . . 164 A8
Kington Langley 70 E7

Kington St Michael . . . 70 A8
Knapp 205 A4
Knapp Hill 202 A5
Knighton 170 D2
Knights Enham 193 E3
Knockdown 24 F5
Knook 194 D4
Knowle 215 C6

L

Lacock 86 D5
Lake 197 F2
Lambourn 165 B2
Lambourn Woodlands . 171 A6
Landford 212 C6
Landfordwood 212 D8
Lane End 115 A8
Langley Burrell 71 A3
Larkhill 197 F6
Latton 8 C4
Laverstock 146 E2
Lavington Sands 179 E2
Lea 50 F3
Lea 28 F1
Leafield 84 E7
Lechlade-on-Thames . . 2 D4
Leigh 18 C5
Leigh Delamere 55 C3
Letcombe Bassett 165 F8
Leverton 171 B1
Liddington 163 B4
Liden 51 D3
Limpers Hill 139 D4
Limpley Stoke 99 A6
Linkenholt 185 E5
Lipe 91 A2
Little Ashley 91 A2
Little Badminton 38 E5
Little Bedwyn 176 D5
Little Chalfield 92 C3
Little Cheverell 187 D8
Littlecott
  Calne 166 A7
  Durrington 190 A6
Littledown 185 D4
Little Durnford 131 D1
Little Faringdon 2 F8
Little Horton 172 C1
Little Langford 129 A6
Little London 166 E2
Little Marsh 102 F4
Little Salisbury 182 E7
Little Somerford 44 B5
Littleton 178 B7
Littleton Drew 53 E5
Littleton Panell 179 D1
Littleworth 182 E8
Lockeridge 174 A6
Longbridge Deverill . . 120 F6
Long Cross 138 B5
Long Dean 68 C4
Longfield 105 E8
Longhedge 115 D5
Long Newnton 13 E5
Longstreet 190 A6
Lopcombe Corner 135 D3
Lover 211 D6
Lower Blunsdon 21 B3
Lower Burgate 210 D2
Lower Chicksgrove . . . 201 B1
Lower Chute 192 F8
Lower Everleigh 182 E1
Lower Green 177 D3
Lower Moor 17 A4
Lower Rudge 107 D4
Lower Seagry 57 F7
Lower Stanton St
  Quintin 56 D6
Lower Stratton 36 B2
Lower Studley 105 E4
Lower Wanborough . . 163 B6
Lower Woodford 131 C3
Lower Wraxall 91 E5
Lower Zeals 138 D5
Luckington 39 E4
Ludgershall 192 A5
Ludwell 203 A1
Lydiard Green 48 B8
Lydiard Millicent 33 D1
Lydiard Plain 32 B1
Lydiard Tregoze 48 C8
Lye Green 100 A6
Lye's Green 111 B1
Lyneham 60 B2

M

Maddington 196 E7
Maiden Bradley 118 D2
Malmesbury 28 B3
Manningford Abbots . 182 A5
Manningford Bohune . 181 F4
Manningford Bruce . . 181 F4
Manton 213 A1
Marden 181 A4
Market Lavington 179 E1
Marlborough 213 F3
Marr Green 183 D7
Marshfield 74 A8
Marston 179 A8
Marston Hill 1 C4
Marston Meysey 9 D7
Marten 184 C7
Martin 209 B6
Martin Drove End 209 A8
Martinslade 178 E8

Melbury Abbas 206 B7
Melksham 94 A5
Melksham Forest 94 D6
Mere 139 B5
Meysey Hampton 1 A5
Middlehill 83 A6
Middlewick 76 D3
Middle Winterslow . . . 149 B7
Middle Woodford 131 B4
Midford 98 C6
Milbourne 28 D4
Mildenhall 175 A8
Mile Elm 89 A7
Mile End 165 A3
Milford 152 E8
Milkhouse Water 215 E8
Milkwell 203 B2
Milston 198 B8
Milton 141 B3
Milton Lilbourne 182 F7
Minchington 207 D1
Minety 17 B2
Minety Common 31 C8
Misselfore 204 F1
Monk's Park 85 A6
Monkton Combe 98 E8
Monkton Deverill 126 D7
Monkton Farleigh 90 F7
Moor Green 84 D6
Moredon 34 E3
Motcombe 202 A4
Mountain Bower 66 F4
Mount Sorrel 205 B3
Murcott 14 F4

N

Neston 84 E6
Netheravon 190 A3
Netherhampton 151 A8
Netherton 185 F4
Nettleton 53 C1
Nettleton Green 53 B1
Nettleton Shrub 67 C7
Neton 131 E6
Newbury 119 C8
Newgrounds 211 B1
Newton 161 B2
Newton Grove 27 E4
Newton Tony 199 B3
Newtown
  Shalbourne 176 E2
  West Tisbury 203 B7
New Town
  Alton 173 D3
  Farnham 207 C2
  Ramsbury 170 C2
  Sixpenny Handley . 207 F6
  Swindon 50 D6
Nine Elms 49 A8
Nomansland 212 C4
Norleaze 108 F8
Normanton 197 F3
Norrington Common . 93 C6
North Bradley 105 D4
Northbrook 179 E1
North Charford 211 C6
Northend 82 A5
North End 6 E2
North Newnton 181 E4
North Street 210 E5
North Tidworth 216 D8
North Wraxall 67 B3
North Wroughton 64 B8
Norton 41 D5
Norton Bavant 194 A6
Norton Ferris 124 C6
Norton 86 B8
Nunton 152 D1
Nursteed 214 E1
Nutbane 193 A4
Nythe 51 C7

O

Oaksey 15 F7
Oare 174 A2
Odstock 152 A1
Ogbourne Maizey . . . 213 C7
Ogbourne St Andrew . 168 F3
Ogbourne St George . 169 A5
Okus 50 A4
Oldbury on the Hill . . . 24 B5
Old Town 50 D3
Orcheston 196 D8
Outmarsh 102 F7
Outwick 210 D4
Overtown 64 D4
Oxenwood 184 E6

P

Park Corner 99 A4
Park North 51 A5
Park South 51 A4
Patney 180 F5
Paxcroft 102 C3
Pear Ash 137 C8
Peckingell 71 B2
Penhill 35 C5
Penknap 112 E8
Penleigh 108 D2
Penselwood 137 B4
Penton Corner 193 A1

Penton Grafton 193 A2
Penton Mewsey 193 B2
Pentridge 208 E4
Perham Down 191 F4
Perry Green 29 B2
Petersfinger 152 E2
Petty France 38 B8
Pewsey 215 D4
Pewsey Wharf 215 B4
Pickwick 76 E2
Pinckney Green 90 E8
Pinehurst 35 D3
Pitton 148 C3
Plaitford 212 E6
Plaitford Green 212 F6
Poole Keynes 5 C4
Portash 201 B3
Porton 133 D6
Potterne 179 D5
Potterne Wick 179 E4
Poulshot 179 B6
Preston
  Aldbourne 170 B3
  Lyneham 60 D3
Priory Vale 34 C7
Purlpit 93 A4
Purton 33 B5
Purton Common 33 A4
Purton Stoke 19 C8

Q

Queen Oak 138 A4
Queen Street 31 B4
Quemerford 89 D3
Quidhampton 145 A4

R

Ragged Appleshaw . . 192 F6
Ram Alley 175 E8
Ramsbury 170 A2
Ratford 80 E7
Ratfyn 217 C5
Redenham 192 D6
Redlands 22 F7
Redlynch 211 D6
Redstocks 95 A4
Restrop 33 A5
Reybridge 86 D2
Ridge 200 F3
Rivar 184 F1
Rockbourne 210 A4
Rockley 168 C5
Rodbourne
  Malmesbury 43 A4
  Swindon 35 A4
Rodbourne Bottom . . . 43 A4
Rodbourne Cheney . . . 35 B4
Rode Hill 103 F7
Rodmarton 3 C7
Rollestone 196 F8
Rollestone Camp 197 E8
Rood Ashton 106 D2
Rook Street 139 A4
Roughmoor 64 F4
Roundway 214 D3
Rowde 96 D6
Rudge 107 C5
Rudloe 76 B4
Rushall 181 E6

S

St Andrew Ridge 35 A4
St Edith's 96 C6
St James 202 C3
St Katharines 175 F7
Salisbury 152 C5
Salterton 131 D2
Sambourne 116 F4
Sandleheath 210 B3
Sandy Lane 88 C2
Sanham Green 177 B3
Sawyers Hill 17 A7
Sedgehill 202 C5
Seend 178 B1
Seend Cleeve 178 C1
Sells Green 95 F5
Sem Hill 202 B3
Semington 102 B2
Semley 202 B5
Serrington 129 C2
Sevenhampton 23 E4
Sevington 53 E4
Shaftesbury 202 A4
Shalbourne 176 F1
Sharcott 182 A4
Sharpstone 99 A4
Shaw
  Melksham 93 D1
  Swindon 49 E1
Sheepbrow 165 F1
Shefford Woodlands . 171 B4
Sherrington 194 B4
Sherston 25 E1
Sherston Parva or
  Pinkney 25 E1
Shipton Bellinger 199 B5
Shipton Moyne 26 E5
Shockerwick 82 F4
Shorncote 6 F4
Shrewton 196 E7
Sixpenny Handley . . . 208 A3
Slaughterford 68 B3

Sodom 59 C7
Somerford Keynes 5 F3
Sopworth 24 D1
South Brewham 122 A4
Southbrook 139 B4
South Cerney 7 A6
Southcott 215 D3
Southend 168 F4
South Marston 36 F5
South Newton 130 B2
South Tidworth 216 D4
Southwick 104 F3
South Wraxall 91 D6
Spirthill 73 B4
Standerwick 107 B2
Stanley 80 A6
Stanton
  Fitzwarren 22 B1
Stanton St Bernard 173 A1
Stanton St Quintin 56 B4
Stapleford 129 E7
Startley 43 D1
Staverton 101 C6
Steeple Ashton 178 B3
Steeple Langford 128 D8
Stert 180 B6
Stibb Green 175 D1
Stitchcombe 175 D8
Stockley 89 C4
Stockton 195 B1
Stoford 130 A3
Stoke Farthing 205 D4
Stonebridge 110 C7
Stormore 112 A8
Stourton 123 F1
Straight Soley 171 A3
Strangways 198 A6
Stratford sub Castle. . . .145 F5
Stratford Tony 150 C2
Stratton St Margaret . . .36 A3
Studley 80 B3
Studley Green 104 F7
Sturford 115 E6
Sunton 183 E1
Sutton Benger 57 C2
Sutton Mandeville 204 C8
Sutton Row 204 B7
Sutton Veny 117 F1
Swallett Gate 59 A6
Swallowcliffe 204 A6
Swanborough 22 C4
Swindon 50 E4

T

Tangley 193 A7
Tanis 96 F2
Teffont Evias 201 C2
Teffont Magna 201 C3
Tellisford 103 E4
Temple 115 C6
Templeton 177 D5
The Causeway 139 C4
The Common
  Brinkworth 46 B7
  Melksham 93 B5
  Winterslow 149 C6
The Fox 33 F3
The Gibb 53 F3
The Green 141 A3
The Ham 108 E5
The Linleys 85 B6
The Pitts 205 F5
The Ridge 85 B5
The Shoe 66 F1
The Spa 94 C2
The Stocks 178 C7
The Strand 178 B6
Thickwood 75 D6
Thingley 77 F1
Thornend 58 C1
Thornhill 61 F1
Tidcombe 184 C5
Tiddleywink 68 F4
Tidpit 209 C6
Tidworth 216 E7
Tilshead 188 B3
Tisbury 203 D8
Tockenham 60 E3
Tockenham Wick 60 D7
Tollard Farnham 207 B2
Tollard Royal 207 B4
Toothill 49 C4
Townsend
  Poulshot. 179 A6
  Urchfont 180 C3
Trowbridge 101 B3
Trowle Common 100 F2
Tuckingmill 203 D8
Tucking Mill 98 D8
Turleigh 99 F6
Tytherington 194 B4
Tytherton Lucas 71 D1

U

Uffcott 167 E8
Ugford 144 A3
Underhill 140 F2
Upavon 181 F2
Upper Burgate 210 E3
Upper Castle Combe 68 B8
Upper Chicksgrove 201 A1
Upper Chute 192 D8
Upper Enham 193 F4
Upper Green 177 E2
Upper Inglesham 12 B5
Upper Lambourn 164 F3
Upper Minety 16 D3
Upper Pickwick 76 C3
Upper Seagry 57 D6
Upper Stratton 35 E4
Upper Street. 210 D5
Upper Studley 105 A5
Upper Town 58 D4
Upper Up 6 E6
Upper Upham 169 C8
Upper Woodford 131 C7
Upper Wraxall 66 E2
Upton
  Mere 141 A5
  Vernhams Dean 185 D2
Upton Lovell 194 E3
Upton Scudamore 112 E5
Urchfont 180 C4

V

Vastern. 60 F8
Vernham Bank 185 B3
Vernham Dean 185 C3
Vernham Row 185 B4
Vernham Street 185 D4

W

Wadswick 84 B4
Walcot East. 50 F6
Walcot West 50 E5
Wanborough 163 A5
Wardour 203 D6
Warleigh 90 D5
Warminster 116 E7

Warminster Common . . .116 E5
Waterhay 18 C7
Wedhampton 180 E4
Well Bottom 206 E3
West Amesbury 198 A4
West Ashton 106 B3
Westbrook 95 E8
Westbury 109 B2
Westbury Leigh 108 E1
West Chisenbury 189 F7
West Crudwell 14 D7
West Dean. 155 F3
West Grafton 183 E7
West Grimstead. 154 C2
West Hatch 203 C7
West Hill 85 B1
West Kennett 173 D7
West Kington 66 F7
West Kington Wick. 67 B6
West Knoyle 140 E6
West Lavington 187 E8
Westlea 49 D5
Westonbirt 25 D8
West Overton 173 F6
Westrop 77 C1
West Stowell 173 F1
Westwells 84 C6
West Winterslow 148 F5
Westwood
  Bradford-on-Avon 99 F2
  Salisbury 145 B5
West Yatton 68 D3
Wexcombe. 184 B6
Weyhill 192 F1
Whaddon
  Alderbury 153 E1
  Hilperton 102 C7
Whitbourne Moor 115 C7
Whitbourne Springs 115 E5
White Cross 137 E5
White Hill 139 C2
Whiteparish 161 D4
Whitepits 126 A7
Whitley 85 C1
Whittonditch 170 D3
Wick 210 F8
Widbrook 100 E4
Widham 33 C5
Wilcot 182 A7
Wildhern 193 D5
Willesley 25 C6

Wilsford
  Amesbury 197 F2
  Pewsey 181 B4
Wilton
  Burbage. 184 A8
  Salisbury 144 C3
Windmills 193 F7
Wingfield 104 C6
Winsley 99 E7
Winterbourne Bassett . .167 B5
Winterbourne Dauntsey .133 B2
Winterbourne Earls 133 A1
Winterbourne Gunner . .133 D3
Winterbourne Monkton .167 B3
Winterbourne Stoke. . . .196 F4
Wolverton 138 B4
Woodborough 181 D6
Woodcock 117 C6
Woodcutts 207 D4
Woodfalls 211 D7
Woodgreen 211 A4
Woodhouse. 193 F3
Woodlands St Mary 171 B6
Woodminton 204 E1
Woodsend 169 C7
Woodshaw. 48 A2
Woodyates 208 D6
Woolley 100 E7
Woolley Green. 100 F8
Woolverton 103 C1
Wootton Bassett 47 C2
Wootton Rivers 174 F2
Worton 179 B4
Wroughton 64 A5
Wylye 201 F8

Y

Yarnbrook 105 F3
Yatesbury 166 E2
Yatton Keynell 68 E6

Z

Zeals 137 F4

A

Abberd La SN11 ....81 D3
Abbey Way SN11 ....81 C3
Abbess Cl SP4 ....217 B2
Abbey Cl
  Chippenham SN15 ....79 B5
  3 Shrewton SP3 ....196 E6
Abbey House Gdns*
SN16 ....28 A3
Abbey La
  Amesbury SP4 ....217 A4
  Hinton Charterhouse BA2 ....99 A3
Abbey Meads Prim Sch
SN25 ....35 A7
Abbey Prim Sch SP3 ....202 B1
Abbey Rw SN16 ....28 A3
Abbey Stadium SN25 ....35 A8
Abbey View Rd SN25 ....34 E3
Abbey Wlk 6 SP7 ....202 C1
Abbeyfield Sch SN15 ....79 B6
Abbot Rd SP1 ....146 C4
Abbots Wlk GL7 ....2 D4
Abbotsbury Way SN25 ....35 A8
Abbotts Cl SP9 ....216 C7
Abbotts Gdn SN16 ....28 A3
Abbotts Rd SP9 ....216 C7
Abdon Cl BA12 ....195 D7
Abingdon Ct La SN6 ....19 E8
Abingdon Way SN2 ....35 D5
Abney Moor SN3 ....51 E2
Abotts Cl BA13 ....108 F3
Above Hedges SP5 ....148 C3
Acacia Cl SN14 ....70 A1
Acacia Cres BA14 ....105 A8
Acacia Dr BA11 ....110 C7
Acacia Gr SN2 ....35 C2
Academy Dr SN13 ....76 E2
Acorn Cl SN3 ....51 C5
Acorn Meadow BA14 ....105 A5
Acre Cl BA14 ....178 A3
Acres Rd SN10 ....214 C3
Acreshort La BA14 ....178 A3
Activity Zone Leisure Ctr
SN16 ....27 F3
Acton Turville Rd GL9 ....52 A4
Adam's Grave (Long
Barrow)* SN8 ....173 D2
Adampur Rd SP9 ....216 A4
Adcroft Dr BA14 ....101 D1
Adcroft St BA14 ....101 C1
Adderwell BA11 ....110 A3
Adderwell Cl BA11 ....110 A3
Adderwell Rd BA11 ....110 A3
Addison Cl SN10 ....214 C2
Addison Cres SN2 ....35 F3
Addison Rd SN12 ....93 F6
Adelaide Sq 10 SP4 ....198 F6
Adelaide Cl 6 SP4 ....198 F6
Adlam Cl SN10 ....214 A2
Admirston Cl SN5 ....49 F4
Aelmus Mich Dro
SP1 ....192 E1
Aerial Bsns Pk RG17 ....170 E6
Affleck Cl SP4 ....49 C5
Agra Rd SP9 ....216 A4
Agravaine Cl 27 SP10 ....193 E2
Ailesbury Cl SN5 ....33 A4
Ailesbury Way SN8 ....183 D8
Ainsworth Rd SN1 ....51 A4
Aintree 7 RG17 ....165 A1
Aintree Ave SN5 ....105 E4
Aintree Dr SN14 ....77 F6
Airman's Cnr SP3 ....197 B5
Aisne Rd SN4 ....65 D1
Akenfield Cl SN25 ....34 F5
Akers Cl SN26 ....21 C2
Akers Way SN2 ....34 E5
Alamein Rd 4 SP11 ....193 E4
Alan Cobham Rd
SN10 ....214 D2
Alan Powell La BA13 ....112 B8
Alanbrook Cl SN4 ....217 B4
Alanbrooke Cres SN2 ....35 A2
Alanbrooke Rd SP4 ....197 E6
Alba Cl 11 SN5 ....48 F8
Albany Cl BA14 ....101 F2
Albany Rd SP1 ....146 B1
Albert Rd BA14 ....101 F3
Albert St SN1 ....50 D4
Albion Bglws SP2 ....145 A3
Albion Dr BA14 ....105 B8
Albion Rd 33 SP6 ....210 D1
Albion St SN1 ....50 A5
Alcock Crest BA12 ....116 F6
Aldborough Cl 2 SN5 ....49 C5
Aldbourne Cl
  Blunsdon St Andrew SN2 ....35 C6
  27 Hungerford RG17 ....177 B7
Aldbourne Four Barrows*
SN8 ....169 E8
Aldbourne Rd SN8 ....170 B7
Aldeburgh Pl BA14 ....104 F6
Alder Cl Swindon SN2 ....34 D4
  Trowbridge BA14 ....105 B5
Alder Way SN12 ....94 A4
Alder Wlk 5 BA11 ....110 D7
Alderbury & W Grimstead
CE Prim Sch SP5 ....153 E3
Alderholt Rd BA12 ....210 B1
Alderney Cl 6 SN4 ....48 A2
Alders The SP2 ....145 A3

Alderton Rd
  Grittleton SN14 ....54 D5
  Luckington SN14 ....53 D6
Alderton Way BA14 ....105 D5
Aldrin Cl 7 SP10 ....193 D2
Aldworth Dr 3 SP1 ....146 C5
Alexander Fields SN1 ....181 F1
Alexander Keiller Mus*
SN8 ....167 B1
Alexander Rd SN16 ....27 F4
Alexander Terr SN13 ....77 A1
Alexandra Cl SP2 ....145 C3
Alexandra Rd
  Fordingbridge SP6 ....210 D1
  Frome BA11 ....110 A4
  1 Swindon SN1 ....50 C7
Alexandra Terr SN8 ....213 D3
Alfred Gdns 6 SP10 ....193 D1
Alfred St Swindon SN1 ....50 C7
  Westbury BA13 ....109 A4
Alfred's Castle* RG17 ....164 B5
Alfred's Twr* BA10 ....122 F3
All Cannings CE Prim Sch
SN10 ....180 F8
All Saints CE Prim Sch
  Farley SP5 ....154 E8
  Whiteparish SP5 ....161 D3
All Saints Cl 2 BA13 ....109 F8
All Saints St 6 SN10 ....187 E7
All Saints VA Prim Sch
SP4 ....190 A3
Allen Rd Corsham SN13 ....84 C8
  Trowbridge BA14 ....105 B7
Allen Wr Dr SN6 ....210 D2
Allington Way SN14 ....133 C2
Allengrove La SN14 ....39 C3
Alley The
  Bishopstone SN6 ....205 E4
  Woodgreen SP6 ....211 A4
Allington Bath SN4 ....109 A8
Allington Tk SP4 ....198 E4
Allington Way
  Amesbury SP4 ....217 D2
  2 Chippenham SN14 ....70 A1
Alma Pl SN8 ....213 D3
Alma Rd SN8 ....170 A7
Alma St BA14 ....105 E8
Alma Terr SN11 ....81 B3
Almond Gr BA14 ....105 B5
Alnwick SN5 ....49 B4
Aloeric Prim Sch SN12 ....94 A3
Alpine Cl 6 SN5 ....48 F5
Alton Barnes White Horse*
SN8 ....173 C2
Alton Cl SN2 ....35 C5
Alton Rd SN8 ....181 F8
Altona Gdns 17 SP10 ....193 D2
Alum Cl BA14 ....105 E7
Alvescot Rd SN3 ....50 D5
Alveston Cl SN5 ....49 D6
Amber Ct SN1 ....50 D7
Amberley Cl Calne SN11 ....81 A4
  Swindon SN25 ....35 C4
Ambrose House Con &
Management Ctr SN1 ....50 B6
Ambrose Rd SN1 ....50 C7
American Mus In Britain*
BA2 ....90 A5
Amersham Rd SN3 ....51 B3
Amesbury Bsns Pk
SP4 ....217 D5
Amesbury By-Pass
SP4 ....217 B5
Amesbury CE Jun Sch
SP4 ....217 B4
Amesbury Cty Inf Sch
SP4 ....217 B4
Amesbury Rd
  Allington SP4 ....217 F4
  Amport SP11 ....192 E1
  Newton Tony SP4 ....199 A3
  Shrewton SP3 ....196 E6
Amesbury Sports Ctr
SP4 ....217 C4
Amity Dr SN8 ....175 D6
Amouracre BA14 ....105 F8
Ancaster Cl BA14 ....101 A1
Anchor Rd SN11 ....81 C2
Ancona Cl 12 SN5 ....49 A7
Andefaras Rd 6 SP10 ....193 D2
Anderson Cl SN3 ....51 D3
Anderson Rd SP1 ....146 C4
Andover La SP11 ....192 B4
Andover Rd
  Amport SP11 ....192 E1
  Chirton SN10 ....180 F3
  Fyfield SP11 ....192 D3
  Upavon SN9 ....181 F1
Andrew St SN1 ....50 A5
Andrew Cl 4 SP4 ....198 B7
Andrews Cl SN14 ....78 B7
Andrews Way SP1 ....151 F5
Angel La Hindon SP3 ....200 A3
  Mere BA12 ....139 A5
  27 Shaftesbury SP7 ....202 C2
Angela Cl SN8 ....213 D3
Angelica Cl 2 SN5 ....34 D4
Angler Rd
  Salisbury SP1 ....145 C3
  Swindon SN5 ....49 C6
Anglesey Cl 5 SN5 ....49 C6
Anglesey Mead SN15 ....79 A6
Angrove Cotts SN16 ....43 D4
Angus Cl SN5 ....49 B7
Anise Cl 4 SN4 ....23 D4
Anne Cres 24 SP4 ....198 B7
Annett's La RG17 ....176 F4

Annetts Cl SP4 ....217 C4
Anson Ave SN9 ....182 B2
Anson Gr SN12 ....94 C1
Anson Pl SN14 ....56 C7
Anstey Rd SN15 ....79 A4
Ansty Hill BA12 ....195 A6
Ansty Wlk SN2 ....35 B6
Anthony Cl SN16 ....25 C1
Anthony Rd SN4 ....64 A7
Anton La SP11 ....193 E4
Antrobus Rd SP4 ....217 B3
Apollo Cl SN25 ....34 B7
Apollo Rd SN15 ....59 E3
Apostle Way SP1 ....146 C5
Appleford Sch SP4 ....196 E7
Appleshaw Way
  Perham Down SP11 ....191 F3
  Salisbury SP1 ....146 D5
Appletree Cl SP5 ....211 C8
Appletree Rd SP5 ....211 C8
Applewood Cl SN14 ....78 B8
Applewood Ct SN6 ....49 D5
Apsley Cl BA14 ....102 B2
Aragon Cl SP4 ....217 C4
Aragon Ct SN3 ....51 A4
Arc Theatre The 8 SN1 ....105 A6
Arcade The 8 SN1 ....50 C6
Archer Cl SN2 ....35 F5
Archers Ct SP2 ....146 A2
Archers The SN6 ....22 F5
Arches La SN16 ....27 F2
Arcot Rd SP9 ....216 B3
Arden Cl SN12 ....94 C5
Argosy Rd SN16 ....49 A7
Argyle Cl SN13 ....70 C3
Argyle St SN12 ....93 D1
Ark The SN10 ....214 A3
Arkwright Rd SN25 ....35 D6
Arley Cl SN25 ....35 A5
Arlington Cl SN3 ....35 F5
Armitage Sq 4 SP4 ....197 E6
Armoury Rd 5 SP2 ....202 C2
Armstrong Rd BA11 ....110 B5
Armstrong Rise 10
  SP10 ....193 D2
Armstrong St 2 SN1 ....50 C7
Arn View
  Cold Harbour BA12 ....112 F1
  2 Warminster BA12 ....117 A8
Arney Cl SN13 ....84 E8
Arnfield Moor SN3 ....51 E2
Arnhem Cross SN15 ....60 B2
Arnold Rd BA14 ....104 E3
Arnolds Mead SN13 ....76 F2
Arran Cl 5 SN4 ....48 A2
Arran Way SN6 ....22 F7
Arras Cl BA14 ....105 A3
Arthur Bennett Ct SN1 ....50 A5
Artis Ave SN4 ....64 B7
Arun Rd SN25 ....34 F3
Arun Way 6 SO51 ....212 F6
Arundel Cl
  Chippenham SN14 ....78 A7
  Swindon SN3 ....51 B8
Arundell Cl BA13 ....109 B4
Ascham Rd SN5 ....49 A5
Ascot Cl SN14 ....78 A5
Ascott Cl SN25 ....34 F7
Ash Cl Lyneham SN15 ....60 B2
  4 Shaftesbury SP7 ....202 D2
  Swindon SN5 ....34 A6
  Tidworth SP9 ....216 E7
Ash Cres SP1 ....146 C5
Ash Dr BA14 ....105 C3
Ash Gdns SN13 ....36 E4
Ash Gr 1 Melksham SN12 ....94 A2
  Swindon SN1 ....75 A5
Ash Tree La SP7 ....206 B7
Ash Wlk
  Upton Lovell BA12 ....194 E4
  Warminster BA12 ....117 A7
Ashburn Pl SP6 ....210 D1
Ashburnham Cl 7 SN5 ....49 A4
Ashbury Ave SN3 ....51 B7
Ashbury Hill SN6 ....164 A7
Ashbury with Compton
  Beauchamp Prim Sch
  SN6 ....164 A8
Ashcroft Cotts SN8 ....169 B1
Ashdown Dr SN12 ....94 D6
Ashdown Pk* RG17 ....164 C5
Ashdown Terr SP7 ....216 D5
Ashdown Way SN2 ....34 C4
Ashe Cl SN15 ....70 D1
Ashe Cres SN15 ....70 D1
Ashen Copse Rd SN4 ....63 F7
Ashes La Freshford BA2 ....99 A4
  Kington Langley SN15 ....70 E7
Ashfield Rd
  Chippenham SN15 ....70 D1
  Salisbury SP2 ....145 D2
Ashford Cl 11 SP6 ....210 C1
Ashford Rd
  Fordingbridge SP6 ....210 C1
  Swindon SN1 ....50 B4
Ashford Trad Est SP2 ....145 E1
Ashgrove BA12 ....139 A4
Ashie Cl SN3 ....51 D3
Ashkirk Cl SN3 ....50 E6
Ashlade Firs Rd SN8 ....175 C6
Ashleigh Cl SN13 ....84 B8
Ashleigh Gr BA14 ....105 C3
Ashley Cl
  Atworth/Whitley SN12 ....85 D1

Ashley Cl continued
  Bradford-on-Avon BA15 ....100 B8
  Swindon SN3 ....50 F6
Ashley Coombe BA12 ....117 A4
Ashley Dro SN8 ....185 A4
Ashley Piece SN8 ....170 C2
Ashley Pl BA12 ....116 F4
Ashley Rd Bath BA1 ....82 C2
  Bradford-on-Avon BA15 ....91 B1
  Salisbury SP2 ....145 F2
Ashley Wlk SP4 ....217 D2
Ashleycross SP6 ....211 D1
Ashmead BA14 ....105 D6
Ashmead Ct BA14 ....105 D7
Ashmore Bottom
DT11 ....206 E1
Ashmore Cl
  Swindon SN3 ....51 C6
  Whiteparish SP5 ....161 D4
Ashmore La
  West Dean SP5 ....155 E2
  Whiteparish SP5 ....161 D6
Ashton Cl SN25 ....34 C7
Ashton Keynes CE Prim Sch
SN6 ....17 E7
Ashton Rd
  Ashton Keynes SN16 ....17 E7
  Siddington GL7 ....6 D8
  Trowbridge BA14 ....102 A2
Ashton Rise 2 BA14 ....102 A2
Ashton St BA14 ....105 E8
Ashtree Rd BA11 ....110 A7
Ashwell Cl SN3 ....50 F5
Ashwicke Rd SN14 ....74 B3
Ashwood Rd SN13 ....76 A1
Ashworth Rd SN5 ....49 E6
Askerton Cl 5 SN5 ....48 F8
Askew Cl 3 SN5 ....48 F5
Aspen Cl Colerne SN14 ....74 F6
  Trowbridge BA14 ....102 A8
  Wootton Bassett SN4 ....47 E3
Assheton Ct SP9 ....216 D7
Assisi Rd SP1 ....146 A4
Astley Cl SN9 ....215 C5
Aston Cl SN9 ....215 C5
Aston Mead SP1 ....146 C4
Astor Cres SP1 ....192 A5
Atbara Cl SN25 ....35 A3
Atcherly Rd SN1 ....166 A1
Athelstan Mus* SN16 ....28 A3
Athelstan Rd SN16 ....27 F4
Athena Ave SN2 ....35 E1
Athenaeum Ctr 2 BA12 ....117 B7
Atherton Cl 13 BA14 ....178 B2
Atherton Cres 16 RG17 ....177 B7
Atherton Pl 14 RG17 ....165 A2
Atherton Rd 11 RG17 ....177 B7
Athlone Cl 2 SP11 ....193 E4
Atholl Ct 5 SP4 ....193 E2
Attlee Cres SN2 ....35 E3
Attwood Rd SP1 ....146 C4
Atwell-Wilson Motor Mus*
SN11 ....89 D7
Atworth Cl SN2 ....35 B6
Atworth La SN13 ....84 E4
Atworth Prim Sch SN12 ....92 E8
Atyeo Cl BA13 ....112 B8
Atyeo Cl BA13 ....112 B8
Aubrey Rise 6 SN16 ....28 A5
Auckland Rd 3 SP4 ....198 F7
Auden Cl SN25 ....34 F5
Audley Cl BA14 ....105 A8
Audley Gate BA13 ....108 E2
Audley Rd SN14 ....78 C8
Augusta Cl SN25 ....34 C7
Augustine Way 9 SP10 ....193 C2
Austen Cres SN3 ....51 D4
Australian Ave SP2 ....145 D2
Avebury CE Prim Sch
SN8 ....173 B8
Avebury Cl Calne SN11 ....81 A3
  Westbury BA13 ....108 F4
Avebury Manor & Gdns*
SN8 ....167 B1
Avebury Rd
  Chippenham SN14 ....78 A6
  Swindon SN2 ....35 B5
Avebury Stone Circles*
SN8 ....167 C1
Avenell Rd 8 SN4 ....163 A6
Avening St SN2 ....35 D1
Avenla Rd SN4 ....34 D4
Avenue La Fleche
SN15 ....78 D6
Avenue Rd Frome BA11 ....110 A4
  Swindon SN1 ....50 C4
  Trowbridge BA14 ....105 B8
Avenue Sch BA12 ....117 B7
Avenue The*
  Amesbury SP4 ....197 E5
  Cherhill SN11 ....166 E2
  Claverton BA2 ....90 A4
  Durnford SP4 ....131 D1
  10 Durrington/Bulford
  SP4 ....198 B7
  Porton SP4 ....133 D6
  Salisbury SP1 ....146 B4
  South Tedworth SP9 ....216 C4
  Stanton Fitzwarren SN6 ....22 B7
  Tangley SP11 ....193 D5
  Tisbury SP3 ....203 E8
  Warminster BA12 ....117 A7
  Westbury BA13 ....109 A3
  Wilton SP2 ....144 B1
  Woodford SP2 ....145 A8
Avil's La SN14 ....56 F6

Avocet Cl SN3 ....51 E6
Avon App SP4 ....146 A3
Avon Bldgs SP4 ....217 A3
Avon Cl
  Bradford-on-Avon BA15 ....100 E5
  Calne SN11 ....81 A3
Avon Ct BA1 ....82 A4
Avon Dr SP5 ....153 E2
Avon Mead SN15 ....78 F8
Avon Meadow 1 SP6 ....210 D1
Avon Meadow SP5 ....211 A8
Avon Meadows SP4 ....131 C5
Avon Mid Sch SP2 ....145 D4
Avon Mills SN16 ....28 B2
Avon Pl Sh Ctr SN12 ....94 A4
Avon Rd Devizes SN10 ....179 C8
  2 Durrington/Bulford
  SP4 ....198 B7
  Malmesbury SN16 ....27 F4
  Melksham SN12 ....94 A6
  Tidworth SP9 ....216 C5
  Warminster BA12 ....117 A5
Avon Reach SN15 ....78 D7
Avon Rise SN14 ....39 E4
Avon Sq SN9 ....181 F3
Avon Terr
  Devizes SN10 ....214 A4
  Salisbury SP2 ....145 F2
Avon Valley Nature Reserve*
SP1 ....145 F3
Avon View SP1 ....210 F1
Avon Way BA14 ....101 D3
Avoncliff Sta BA15 ....99 E5
Avondale Sch SP4 ....217 D6
Avondown Rd SP4 ....198 B7
Avonfield BA14 ....101 F8
Avonfield Ave BA15 ....100 E5
Avonleaze Rd SN9 ....215 D5
Avonmead SN25 ....34 F6
Avonside Enterprise Pk
SN12 ....94 A5
Avonstoke Cl 3 SP4 ....217 B2
Avonvale Rd BA14 ....101 D2
Avonweir La SN15 ....57 F3
Avro Way SN12 ....94 C4
Awdry Ave SN12 ....94 C4
Awdry Cl
  Chippenham SN15 ....77 F7
  Heddington SN11 ....89 A2
Awdry Rd SN10 ....214 B3
Axbridge Cl SN3 ....51 A5
Axe & Cleaver La
BA14 ....105 C4
Axis Bsns Ctr SN5 ....49 D5
Aylesbury St SN1 ....50 C7
Ayleswade Rd SP2 ....152 A6
Aymer Pl SN3 ....51 C5
Ayr Cl SN14 ....77 F5
Ayrshire Cl
  Salisbury SP2 ....145 B8
  Swindon SN5 ....49 B7
Azalea Cl SN11 ....81 C1
Azalea Dr
  Trowbridge BA14 ....105 A4
  Warminster BA14 ....116 F7
Azelin Ct SN3 ....36 B3

B

Babington Pk 9 SN5 ....48 F5
Back La
  9 Aldbourne SN8 ....170 A6
  Bishop St Andrew SN26 ....21 B3
  Calne Without SN11 ....88 B4
  Cherhill SN11 ....166 E2
  Chitterne BA12 ....195 D7
  Great Bedwyn SN8 ....176 B3
  Great Hinton BA14 ....178 A3
  Maiden Bradley with Yarnfield
  BA12 ....118 F2
  Marlborough SN8 ....213 D3
  Penton Grafton SP11 ....193 A2
  Ramsbury SN8 ....170 B2
  Sixpenny Handley SP5 ....208 A4
  Tilshead SP3 ....188 B3
  Vernhams Dean SP11 ....185 C3
Back Rd Calne SN11 ....81 B2
  Chitterne BA12 ....195 D7
Back St
  Ashton Keynes SN6 ....17 E7
  East Garston RG17 ....171 E7
  Trowbridge BA14 ....101 C3
Bader Pk 16 SN12 ....178 B8
Badger Cl
  Devizes SN10 ....214 B2
  2 Wootton Bassett SN4 ....47 F2
Badgers Brook SN4 ....64 A5
Badgers Cl 3 SN4 ....163 B6
Badminton House*
GL9 ....38 F2
Badminton Pk* GL9 ....38 F3
Bagbury La SN5 ....33 B3
Bagbury Rd BA12 ....194 F4
Baghdad Rd 2 SP4 ....198 F7
Bailey's Barn BA15 ....100 E5
Bailey's Mead SN4 ....48 A3
Baileys Barn BA15 ....100 D5
Baileys Farm Gdns SN4 ....51 A6
Baileys Way SN4 ....64 B2
Bailiffe Piece SN6 ....8 D1
Bainbridge Cl 2 SN5 ....49 A4
Bainton Cl BA15 ....100 D7
Baird Cl SN5 ....49 A6
Bakehouse Cl SN15 ....96 B7
Bakers Cnr SN13 ....84 E4
Bakers Ct SN3 ....36 B3

Bakers Field SN15 ....60 A3
Bakers Rd SN4 ....64 B5
Balden Cl SN4 ....63 F6
Baldwin Cl SN4 ....65 D4
Bale Cl 6 SN5 ....48 F5
Ball Rd SN9 ....215 D4
Ballands Castle* BA9 ...137 A2
Balmoor Cl BA12 ....139 B3
Balmoral Cl
  Chippenham SN14 ....77 F7
  Swindon SN3 ....51 A3
Balmoral Rd
  Salisbury SP1 ....146 B4
  Trowbridge BA14 ....105 B5
Bampton Gr SN3 ....50 E6
Banbury Cl SN3 ....50 F3
Bancroft BA15 ....100 D7
Bancroft Cl SN5 ....48 F6
Bank St SN12 ....94 A4
Bank The SN14 ....75 C3
Bankfoot Cl 3 SN5 ......49 B7
Banks The SN15 ....59 E4
Bankside SN4 ....49 F4
Bankwaters Rd SN13 ......34 B8
Bannerdown Cl BA1 ....82 B4
Bannerdown Dr BA1 ....82 A4
Bannerdown Rd BA1 ....82 C5
Banwell Ave SN3 ....51 A5
Barbaras Rd SN13 ....84 D8
Barbel Cl SN11 ....81 B5
Barber's La SP5 ....151 C1
Barberry SP3 ....201 A3
Barbury Castle*
  SN4 ....168 B7
Barbury Cl SN25 ....34 F3
Barcelona Cres SN4 ......64 A7
Barcete Cl SN25 ....34 D7
Bardsey Cl 5 SN4 ....47 F2
Barford La SP5 ....159 C1
Barford St Martin CE Fst Sch
  SP3 ....143 A3
Bargates SN13 ....83 D6
Barken Rd
  4 Chippenham SN14 ....78 A1
  Chippenham SN14 ......78 A8
Barkstead Cl 3 SN5 ....49 B4
Barley Cl
  Malmesbury SN16 ....28 A2
  Warminster BA12 ......117 C5
Barley Hill La SN10 ....179 A7
Barlow Cl SN25 ....35 A8
Barn Cl
  Chippenham SN14 ......78 A8
  Corsham SN13 ....76 E1
Barn End SN14 ....74 A8
Barn Glebe BA14 ....101 E1
Barn Hill SP3 ....201 A3
Barn Moor Cl SN3 ....51 E3
Barn Owl Rd SN14 ....70 B2
Barn Piece SN4 ....83 D6
  Bradford-on-Avon BA15 .100 D4
Barn St SN8 ....213 D3
Barnack Cl BA14 ....101 A1
Barnard Cl SN3 ....51 B7
Barnard St 1 SP1 ....152 B8
Barncroft SP11 ....192 E3
Barnes Cl BA14 ....105 A7
Barnes Gn SN15 ....45 F6
Barnes Rd SN14 ....139 A5
Barnes Rd SN14 ....70 B2
Barnes Wallis Cl
  9 Amesbury SP4 ......217 E3
  Melksham Without BA14 .178 B8
Barnetts Hill SN13 ......83 F7
Barnfield Cl SN2 ....49 E7
Barnfield Rd SN2 ....49 E7
Barnfield Way BA1 ....82 B4
Barnstaple Cl SN3 ....51 B5
Barnum Ct SN2 ....50 A7
Baroda Rd SP4 ....216 A4
Baron Cl Lyneham SN15 ..59 C4
  4 Swindon SN3 ....36 B3
Barons Mead SN4 ....78 A8
Barra Cl SN6 ....22 E6
Barracks SN14 ....74 F4
Barrett La SN15 ....57 D2
Barrett Way SN4 ....64 B6
Barrington Cl SN3 ....51 D3
Barrington Rd SP1 .....146 C3
Barrow Cl SN8 ....213 F3
Barrow Gn SN15 ....70 E2
Barrow La BA9 ....136 B5
Barrow St La
  Mere BA12 ....139 F3
  West Knoyle BA12 ....140 A4
Barrow Water La BA9 ...136 A5
Barrowby Gate SN3 ......36 A4
Barrows La SP5 ....212 B7
Barry Glen Cl SN2 ....35 E1
Barry St SN1 ....79 F2
Barters La SP7 ....206 D8
Bartlett Cl 11 BA11 ...110 C6
Bartlett Rd SP1 ....146 B4
Bartletts SN10 ....179 C1
Bartletts Mead BA14 ....178 A4
Bartletts The SN14 .....53 D8
Barton Cl 12 SP1 ......193 C2
Barton Farm Ctry Pk*
  BA15 ....100 A5
Barton Hill 22 SP7 ....202 C2
Barton Hill House Sch
  SP7 ....202 C2
Barton La SN12 ....139 A5
Barton Lodge BA14 .....105 A6
Barton Orch BA15 ......100 C6
Barton Rd SN25 ....34 E3

Barton Way SN16 ....42 E4
Bartons Rd 20 SP6 .....210 D1
Bartons The 21 SP6 ....210 D1
Basepoint Bsns Ctr
  SN5 ....49 C8
Basil Cl SN2 ....34 D4
Basil Hill Rd SN13 ......84 C7
Basingstoke Cl 5 SN5 ...49 A4
Basset Down SN3 ....51 E7
Bassett Rd OX12 ....165 F8
Bassetts Pasture
  BA15 ....100 D4
Bassetts The SN13 ....83 D6
Batch The BA2 ....98 E1
Bath Acad of Art SN13 ..77 A2
Bath Rd Atworth SN12 ...93 B8
  Atworth/Whitley SN12 ..93 A8
  Box SN13 ....83 A6
  Bradford-on-Avon BA15 .91 C1
  Chippenham Without
    SN14 ....77 F5
  Colerne SN14 ....74 F3
  Corsham SN13 ....77 B4
  Crickdale SN6 ....19 D8
  Devizes SN10 ....179 C8
  Frome BA11 ....110 A6
  Hungerford RG17 .....176 F7
  Marlborough SN8 .....213 B2
  Melksham SN12 ....94 A5
  Melksham Without SN12 .93 E7
  Preshute SN8 ....174 C7
  Seend SN12 ....95 C1
  Swindon SN1 ....50 C4
  Upton Scudamore SN12 .112 D2
  Warminster BA12 .....112 D1
  Westonbirt with Lasborough
    GL8 ....25 D8
  Wootton Bassett SN4 ..47 C1
Bathampton St SN1 ....50 A6
Bathford CE VC Sch
  BA1 ....82 C2
Bathford Hill BA1 ....82 B2
Bathurst Rd SN1 ....50 D6
Batt's La SN8 ....183 F7
Batten Rd SP5 ....211 A8
Battens The 3 SN14 .....64 A7
Battlesbury Barracks
  BA12 ....117 E6
Battlesbury Rd BA12 ...117 E2
Battlewell SN5 ....33 A3
Baverstock La SP3 .....142 B5
Bawdsey Rd 4 SP4 ......217 D2
Baxter Cl SN25 ....35 A7
Bay Cl SN11 ....89 C8
Bay Tree Cl SN2 ....35 C2
Baydon Cl Swindon SN25 .34 F3
  Trowbridge BA14 .....105 C5
Baydon Gr SN11 ....81 B4
Baydon Rd
  Aldbourne SN8 ....164 B1
  Great Shefford RG17 ..171 E4
  Lambourn RG17 ....171 A6
Baydon St Nicholas CE Prim
  Sch SN8 ....164 C1
Baydons La SN15 ....78 E6
Bayleaf Ave SN2 ....34 D4
Bayliffes Cl SN15 ......79 A7
Baynton Way BA13 ......186 D8
Bayntun Cl
  Bromham SN15 ....96 A1
  Devizes SN10 ....214 C1
Baywater SN8 ....213 E4
Bazaar Rd SP9 ....216 B5
Beacon Cl
  Amesbury SP4 ....217 C4
  8 Swindon SN1 ......49 F4
Beacon Cl SP4 ....217 C4
Beacon Hill Rd 7 SP4 ..198 F7
Beacon View BA11 ......116 D6
Beaconsfield Way
  BA11 ....110 B7
Beale Cl SN14 ....78 B7
Beale Ct SN14 ....78 A7
Beale's Barton BA14 ...101 F8
Beales Cl SN11 ....50 B7
Beales Farm Rd 15
  RG17 ....165 A1
Beamish Cl 2 SN11 ....166 A1
Beanacre Old Manor*
  SN12 ....94 A8
Beanacre Rd
  Melksham SN12 ....94 A7
  Melksham Without SN12 .86 A6
Beanlands The SN4 .....163 A6
Bear Cl BA15 ....100 B7
Beard Ct SP11 ....192 E6
Bearfield Bldgs BA15 ..100 C8
Bearfield La RG17 .....171 A4
Bearwater RG17 ....177 B7
Beatrice Rd SP1 ....146 A4
Beatrice St SN2 ....50 B7
Beatrice Way BA14 .....105 E8
Beatty Ct SN3 ....50 A4
Beauchamp Cl 1 SP4 ...217 D3
Beauclerc St SN10 .....179 D8
Beaufort Cl 12 SN14 ...178 B8
Beaufort Gn SN3 ....51 B5
Beaufort Rd SN4 ....64 A7
Beaufoy Cl 9 SP7 .....202 D2
Beaulieu Cl SN5 ....49 C4
Beaulieu Rd 2 SP4 ....217 C2
Beaumaris Rd SN5 ....49 B5
Beaumont Rd SN3 ....50 E6
Beaumont Way SP4 ......217 D2
Beaven Cl SN15 ....78 F4

Beavens Ct BA12 ....117 B7
Beck Cl SN25 ....35 A3
Becket Way SP1 ....146 D1
Beckett Pl BA13 ....108 F1
Beckett St 14 SP3 .....203 E8
Beckett's La SP3 ......201 A3
Beckford Cl
  Tisbury SP3 ....200 D1
  Warminster BA12 .....117 B6
Beckhampton (Long
  Barrow)* SN8 ....173 A8
Beckhampton Rd SN8 ....173 B8
Beckhampton St SN1 .....50 C6
Beddington St SN1 ......79 F3
Beddoe Cl BA15 ....100 E4
Bede Dr 7 SP10 ....193 C2
Bedford Cl 2 SP6 .....210 D2
Bedford Rd
  6 Salisbury SP2 ....145 E2
  5 Swindon SN3 ....50 F6
Bedwin St SP1 ....146 B1
Bedwyn Cl SN2 ....35 C3
Bedwyn Dyke* SN8 ......176 C3
Bedwyn Sta SN8 ....176 B3
Bedwyn Stone Mus*
  SN8 ....176 B2
Beech Ave
  Melksham SN12 ....94 A3
  Swindon SN2 ....35 A2
  Warminster BA12 .....116 F6
Beech Cl Andover SP11 .193 B1
  Porton SP4 ....133 D6
Beech Dr SN5 ....34 A2
Beech Dr 5 Highworth SN6 .22 F5
  Trowbridge BA14 .....105 B6
Beech Grange SP5 ......212 C5
Beech Hanger SP4 .....199 C5
Beech Hill Rd SP9 .....216 F7
Beech Lea
  Broad Blunsdon SN26 ..21 C1
  Meysey Hampton GL7 ...1 A4
Beech Rd Colerne SN14 ..75 A5
  Corsham SN13 ....83 E7
Beech Sq 12 RG17 .....177 B6
Beech Wlk SN4 ....131 C1
Beech Wood 13 SN10 ...179 F1
Beechcroft Cl SP3 .....193 D1
Beechcroft Inf Sch
  SN25 ....35 E4
Beechcroft Rd
  Salisbury SP1 ....146 D1
  Swindon SN2 ....35 E4
Beeches Cl SN25 ....148 C3
Beeches La SN15 ....59 A5
Beeches The
  Bradford-on-Avon BA15 .101 A7
  Coombe Bissett SN5 ..156 F7
  Lydiard Millicent SN5 ..33 B1
  Melksham Without SN12 .93 C7
  Trowbridge BA14 .....101 F2
  Warminster BA12 ......117 B6
  4 West Wellow SO51 .212 F6
Beechfield SP4 ....199 B3
Beechfield Dr SN10 ....214 E5
Beechfield Rd SN13 .....76 E1
Beechgrove BA12 ....117 B8
Beechwood 8 SP10 .....210 C1
Beechwood Ave BA11 ...110 A6
Beehive Cl 1 SN5 ......49 A8
Begle Cl SN25 ....34 B7
Belcombe Ct* BA15 ....100 B6
Belcombe Rd BA15 .....100 B6
Belfast Mead SN15 ......60 C2
Belfry Dr SN14 ....41 E1
Belgrave Sq SN9 ......216 E6
Belgrave St SN1 ....50 D5
Bell Cl BA12 ....116 F5
Bell Gdns SN14 ....70 A8
Bell Hill Seend SN12 ...178 E4
  Warminster BA12 .....117 B6
Bell La Inkpen RG17 ...177 E2
  Lechlade GL7 ....2 C3
  Liddington SN4 ....163 A4
  Sutton Benger SN15 ..57 D2
Bell Piece SN15 ....57 D2
Bell St SP3 ....197 F2
Bellamy La
  4 Ludgershall SP11 ..192 B5
  Salisbury SP1 ....202 C2
Bellamy La SP1 ....152 B8
Belle Vue Rd
  Salisbury SP1 ....146 A1
  Swindon SN1 ....50 D4
Bellefield Cres BA14 ..105 A8
Belle Dr SN14 ....41 C3
Bellingham La SN6 ......2 A2
Bellot Dr
  2 Corsham SN13 ....76 E1
  Corsham SN13 ....84 E8
Bellott Dr SN13 ....84 E8
Bells La BA12 ....137 F7
Bellver SN5 ....49 B5
Belmont Cl
  10 Shaftesbury SP7 ..202 C1
  Swindon SN3 ....36 A4
Belmont Cres SN1 ....50 A3
Belmont Sch SP2 ....146 B1
Belsay SN5 ....49 B5
Belthane Pl SN12 ....93 C8
Belvedere Rd SN3 ....51 A3
Bembridge Cl SN3 ....51 B4

Bemerton St Johns CE Fst
  Sch SP2 ....145 C2
Ben La SP5 ....157 F2
Bence's La SN13 ....77 A2
Bendy Bow SN16 ....15 F7
Benin Rd SP11 ....191 F3
Bennett Cl SP5 ....211 C2
Bennett Hill Cl 3 SN4 ..47 F7
Bentham Cl SN5 ....49 D6
Bentham La SN5 ....33 A8
Bentley Cl SN1 ....51 A6
Bentley Dr BA14 ....81 C2
Bentley Way SP5 ....149 D5
Benwell Cl SN5 ....49 D6
Beranburh Field SN4 ....64 E2
Berenger Cl SN1 ....50 D5
Beresford Cl BA14 .....101 C4
Bergamot Cl SN8 ......174 C7
Bergman Cl SN25 ....35 B6
Berhills La SN10 ....95 F2
Bericot La SN4 ....65 E6
Berkeley Cl
  Melksham SN12 ....94 A2
  South Cerney GL7 ......5 F6
Berkeley Lawns SN3 .....50 F3
Berkeley Rd
  Trowbridge BA14 .....105 A8
  Wroughton SN4 ....64 B7
Berkeley Cl 2 SN14 ....78 A7
Berkley CE Fst Sch
  BA11 ....111 A7
Berkley Cross BA11 ...110 F6
Berkley La BA11 ....110 D8
Berkley Rd BA11 ......110 A5
Berkshire Dr SN5 ....49 A7
Berkshire Rd SP2 .....151 E7
Bermerton Heath & Barnards
  Folly Nature Reserve*
  SP2 ....145 C2
Berrington Rd SN3 ......51 A3
Berry Cl 4 SN9 ....190 A3
Berry Rd BA13 ....186 D8
Berry Wood La SP7 ....203 A3
Berrycroft
  Ashbury SN6 ....164 A7
  Mildenhall SN8 ......175 B8
Berryfield Cl SN12 .....93 F1
Berryfield La SN12 .....93 F1
Berryfield Pk SN12 .....93 F1
Berryfield Rd BA15 ....100 D8
Bertha's Field GL9 .....24 B4
Berton Cl SN26 ....21 C2
Berwick St James SP3 ..196 F2
  Stapleford SP3 ....129 E7
Besomer Dro SP5 ......211 D6
Bess Rd SN5 ....48 F4
Bessemer Cl SN2 ....35 A1
Bessemer Rd E SN2 .....35 A1
Bessemer Rd W SN2 .....34 F1
Best's La BA14 ....194 A5
Bethel Rd SN11 ....81 B4
Betjeman Ave SN4 ....47 E3
Betjeman Ave SN4 .....213 A2
Betony Cl SN25 ....34 E5
Bettertons Cl GL7 ......1 F7
Bevan Cl SN2 ....35 F3
Beverley SN5 ....49 C4
Beverley Cl SN12 ....94 C1
Beverley Cres SN9 ....182 B2
Beverley Hills Mobile Home
  Pk SP4 ....217 D3
Beverley Way SN14 .....178 B8
Beversbrook La SN11 ...81 B5
Beverstone Gr SN3 ......50 F4
Bevil SN5 ....49 A3
Bevisbury Hill Fort*
  SP11 ....185 A1
Bewley Cl SN3 ....51 C3
Bewley Ct* SN15 ......106 B6
Bewley La SN15 ....106 B6
Beyer Rd 5 SP4 ....217 D2
Bibury Rd SN3 ....50 E5
Bicton Rd SN25 ....34 C5
Biddel Springs SN6 ....23 B6
Bidden La BA12 ....195 D6
Biddesden La SP11 ....192 C5
Biddestone La SN14 ....68 E3
Biddestone Manor*
  SN14 ....76 F7
Biddulph Rd SP4 ......198 A2
Bideford Cl SN3 ....51 B5
Bidge La RG17 ....165 A2
Bilbo rough Dr 2 SN3 ..50 F5
Bilbury Rings* BA12 ...201 F7
Bill Turpin Ct SN3 .....51 B4
Bimport SP7 ....202 B1
Bincknoll Castle* SN4 ..62 F3
Bindon Cl SN5 ....49 A5
Bingham Rd
  Durrington SP4 ......197 E2
  Salisbury SP1 ....146 C4
Binknoll La SN4 ....62 F3
Birch Gdns BA14 ....102 B2
Birch Gr SN10 ....214 C5
Birch Gr Bower Hill SN12 ..94 C1
  Chippenham SN15 ......70 E1
Birch St SN1 ....50 B4
Birch Wlk 4 BA11 .....110 B7
Birchenleaze BA14 .....105 C3
Birches The SN3 ....51 B2
Birchill La BA11 ......110 A5
Birchwood Cl SN12 ....178 E8
Birchwood Dr 4 SP4 ...198 C2
Birchwood Rd SN3 ......36 A2

Birdbrook Rd SN2 ....35 E5
Birdcombe Rd 1 SN6 ....49 C5
Birds Marsh SN15 ....70 E2
Bishop Rd SN11 ....81 B4
Bishop Wordsworths Sch
  SP1 ....152 A8
Bishop's Palace* SP1 ..152 A7
Bishop's Wlk SP1 ......152 A8
Bishopdale Cl 2 SN5 ...34 A1
Bishopdown Rd SP1 ....146 B3
Bishops Cannings CE Pri Sch
  SN10 ....172 B3
Bishops Cl
  Chippenham SN15 ......78 F4
  Mere BA12 ....139 A6
  Tidworth SP9 ....216 D4
Bishops Dr SP2 ....151 F6
Bishops Mead SP1 .....146 B4
Bishopsfield 6 SN6 ....19 D8
Bishopstone CE Prim Sch
  SN6 ....163 E6
Bishopstone Hollow
  SP5 ....205 E3
Bishopstrow Rd BA12 ..117 E4
Bisley SN16 ....29 A6
Bisley Cl SN3 ....51 A5
Biss Cl BA12 ....112 F4
Biss Meadow BA14 .....105 A8
Bitham Brook Prim Sch
  BA13 ....109 B4
Bitham La Ham RG17 ...177 A3
  Westbury BA13 ....109 A3
Bitham Mill BA13 .....109 B3
Bitham Pk BA13 ....109 B4
Bittern Rd SN3 ....51 E6
Black Bridge Rd SN15 ..78 F8
Black Dog Hill
  Calne Without SN11 ....80 D2
  Chapmanslade BA13 ...111 E6
Black Horse La
  Westbury BA13 ....108 D1
  Winterbourne SP4 ....146 F8
Black La
  Pitton & Farley SP5 ..148 C4
  Redlynch SP5 ....211 E6
Blackbarn Rd SN4 .....134 B5
Blackberry La
  Potterne SN10 ....179 D5
  Winsley BA15 ....90 C1
Blackboard La SN10 ....80 D8
Blackboard La SN14 ...180 B4
Blackcross SN4 ....78 F6
Blackcross Rd SP4 ....217 C2
Blackdown 10 BA12 ...117 A8
Blackford La SN14 .....10 C4
Blackfriars Way SP1 ..152 B8
Blackhall Rd SO51 ....212 F3
Blacklands Crossroads
  SN11 ....99 E6
Blackman Gdns SN3 ....50 D3
Blackman's La 4 SN8 ..183 D8
Blackmoor Copse Nature
  Reserve* 155 A7
Blackmore La SN8 .....192 A7
Blackmore Rd
  Melksham SN12 ....94 C4
  3 Shaftesbury SP7 ..202 D2
Blackstone Ave SN15 ...54 C1
Blackthorn Cl SN14 ....47 E4
Blackthorn Mews SN15 ..75 F5
Blackthorn Way BA14 ..101 D4
Blackworth SN6 ....22 F8
Blagdon Wlk BA11 .....110 C7
Blagrove Ind Est SN1 ..49 A2
Blair Rd BA14 ....105 B7
Blake Cres SN3 ....36 C2
Blake Ct SN14 ....41 F1
Blakehill Farm Nature
  Reserve* SN6 ....19 A3
Blakeney Ave SN3 ....51 B7
Blakesley Cl 3 SN3 ....50 F4
Blakey Rd SP1 ....152 C8
Blandford Alley SN6 ...23 A6
Blandford Cl SN3 ....51 B6
Blandford Rd SP1 .....150 F1
Blaygrove Ind Est SN1 .49 A2
Bleak St BA9 ....137 C3
Blease Cl BA14 ....101 D4
Bleke St SP7 ....202 C2
Blendon Dr SP10 ......193 C1
Blenheim Pk
  21 Bowerhill SN12 ...178 B8
  21 Bowerhill SN12 ...178 B8
Blenheim Rd SN4 ....64 A7
Blenheim Cl BA12 .....116 F7
Bletchley Cl 1 SN3 ....51 B4
Blicks Cl SN14 ....28 B4
Blicks Cl SN14 ....41 F1
Blind La Ansty SP3 ....203 F5
  Berwick St John SP7 .207 B8
  Southwick BA14 ......104 F2
Blissford Rd SP6 ......210 F1
Blissmore La 8 SP11 ..192 B5
Bloody Shard Gate
  DT11 ....207 A1
Bloomsbury Cl 2 SN5 ..49 B4
Blounts Ct SN10 ......179 D5
Blue Boar Row SP1 ....146 A1
Bluebell Cl SN14 ......70 B3
Bluebell Gr SN11 ......81 B5

Blunsdon Abbey SN25 34 F8
Blunsdon Rd SN25 34 F4
Blunsdon Sta SN5 33 F8
Blyth Way SP1 146 D4
BMI Ridgeway Hospl
SN4 64 C6
Boar St BA12 139 A5
Boatman Cl SN25 34 A7
Bobbin La BA15 99 F4
Bobbin Pk BA15 99 F3
Bockhampton Rd
RG17 165 A1
Bockhampton Village*
RG17 165 B1
Bodiam Dr SN5 49 D4
Bodiam Dr N [4] SN5 49 D5
Bodiam Dr S [3] SN5 49 D4
Bodman Cl SN15 78 F4
Bodmin Cl SN3 51 A6
Bodyhorse Hill SN4 163 C6
Bohemia La SP5 211 D6
Bokerley Ditch* SP6 209 A5
Bokerley Junc SP5 208 E6
Boldrewood SN3 51 D3
Bolehyde Manor*
SN14 69 E4
Boleyn Cl SN5 49 A6
Bolingbroke Cl SN5 47 F6
Bolingbroke Rd SN2 34 F2
Bolland's Hill SN12 178 D8
Bonaker Cl SP4 133 D6
Bond St
Durrington/Bulford SP4 198 E6
Trowbridge BA14 105 C7
Bond St Bldgs BA14 105 C7
Boness Rd SN4 64 A7
Bonham La BA12 137 E7
Bonner Cl [10] SN5 48 F5
Bonners Cl SN16 28 A5
Bonnewe Rise SP4 217 D3
Boothmead SN14 78 B8
Borage Cl SN2 34 D5
Border Cl SN25 34 C5
Bore Hill BA12 116 F4
Boreham Cl BA12 117 C6
Boreham Field BA12 117 D6
Boreham Rd BA12 117 E5
Borgate Sch & Sixth Form Ctr
The SP6 210 E2
Borkum Cl [8] SP10 193 D2
Borough Fields SN4 47 D2
Borough Parade Sh Ctr
SN15 78 D7
Borough The SP5 211 A8
Boscombe Down Airfield
SP4 198 E3
Boscombe Rd
Amesbury SP4 217 C3
Swindon SN25 34 E4
Bosham Cl [6] SN5 49 B4
Boswell Rd BA15 99 F3
Bosworth Rd SN5 49 A5
Botany SN6 22 E5
Bothwell Rd SN3 50 F7
Botisdone Cl SP11 185 C3
Botley Copse SN5 34 A2
Bottlebush La BH21 208 E1
Bottom La
Ogbourne St George
SN8 169 A5
[1] West Wellow SO51 212 F6
Bouchers Way SP2 152 A5
Boulton Cl BA13 108 E1
Boundary Ave BA11 110 B5
Boundary Cl
Lyneham SN15 59 C3
Swindon SN2 35 F6
Boundary Rd
Chippenham SN15 78 F8
Salisbury SP1 146 E2
Boundary Wlk BA14 105 C4
Bourbon Cl BA12 117 B5
Bourne Ave SP1 146 C2
Bourne Cl Porton SP4 133 D6
[1] Salisbury SP1 152 D8
Warminster BA12 117 A5
[3] West Wellow SO51 212 F6
Bourne Gdns SP4 133 D6
Bourne Hill SP1 146 B1
Bourne La [6] SP9 199 D8
Bourne Lake Pk SN6 18 E6
Bourne Pk* SP11 193 F6
Bourne Rd Swindon SN2 34 F2
Tidworth SP9 216 D6
Bourne Ret Pk SP1 152 D7
Bourne Rise SN8 183 E1
Bourne Vale RG17 177 B7
Bourne Valley Cl SP4 133 E5
Bourne View SP4 199 A1
Bourne Way SP1 152 D7
Bourton Ave SN3 36 B2
Bourton La SN10 172 C3
Bouverie Ave
Salisbury SP2 152 A6
Swindon SN3 50 D3
Bouverie Ave S SP2 151 F5
Bouverie Cl SP2 151 F6
Bouverie Dr [17] SN10 179 F1
Bouverie Pk SN14 56 B5
Boveridge House Sch
BH21 209 B1
Bow Ct SN1 50 C4
Bow Wow GL7 7 A7
Bowd's La SN15 60 A6
Bowden Cres SN12 94 C6
Bowden Pk* SN15 87 B5
Bowdich Cl SP4 198 C7
Bower Gdns SP1 152 C8
Bower Hill Rd SP1 146 C2
Bower Rd SN8 175 D5
Bowerhill La SN12 94 E1
Bowerhill Prim Sch
SN12 94 C1
Bowers Hill SP5 211 D8
Bowers La SP11 185 B4
Bowes Lyon Ct SP2 145 D3
Bowldown Rd GL8 25 F8
Bowles Rd SN25 35 A5
Bowleymead SN3 51 D5
Bowling Gn La
Pentridge SP5 208 D5
Swindon SN1 50 C3
Bowls Barrow (Long
Barrow)* BA12 186 E1
Bowman Cl [5] SN3 36 B3
Bowman Ct SN4 47 C1
Bowmans Ct SN12 94 C6
Bowood Cl SN11 79 F3
Bowood House & Gdns*
SN11 88 C8
Bowood Rd SN1 50 B4
Box CE Prim Sch SN13 83 C6
Box Dr SN8 213 D8
Box Highlands Prim Sch
SN13 84 B8
Box Hill Box SN13 76 A1
Corsham SN13 83 F7
Box Rd BA1 82 C3
Box View SN14 75 B2
Boxbush Rd GL7 7 A7
Boxfields Rd SN13 83 F7
Boydell Cl SN5 49 B8
Boyle Ave [4] SN11 166 A1
Boyne's La DT11 206 B1
Boyton Manor* BA12 194 E2
Bozley Hill SP7 206 A8
Brabant Way [4] BA13 108 E1
Bracken Cl SP5 153 D3
Brackenbury [8] SP10 193 C1
Brackenbury Rd SP4 197 E7
Brackland SN10 180 A2
Bradbury Cl SN15 79 A5
Bradene Cl [3] SN4 47 E2
Bradenham Rd SN5 49 A5
Bradenstoke Abbey*
SN15 59 B3
Bradfield Cl BA12 117 D5
Bradford Rd
Atworth SN12 92 E7
Bathford BA1 82 B2
Box SN13 83 F3
Broughton Gifford SN12 93 F4
Corsham SN13 76 C1
Holt BA14 101 D8
Melksham SN12 94 A5
Rode BA11 103 F1
Swindon SN1 50 C4
Trowbridge BA14 101 B1
Winsley BA15 99 D6
Bradford-on-Avon Com
Hospl BA15 100 D8
Bradford-on-Avon Mus*
BA15 100 D6
Bradford-on-Avon Sta
BA15 100 C6
Bradford-on-Avon
Swimming Pool
BA15 100 C6
Bradley Cl Holt BA14 101 F8
Warminster BA12 116 E4
Bradley La Holt BA14 92 F1
Maiden Bradley with Yarnfield
BA12 118 C3
Bradley Mound*
BA12 118 F2
Bradley Pk* BA12 118 F1
Bradley Rd
Southwick BA14 105 B2
Swindon SN2 35 D4
Trowbridge BA14 105 C5
Warminster BA12 116 E4
Bradon Forest Sch SN5 33 B3
Bradwell Cl [2] SP10 193 C2
Bradwell Moor SN3 51 D2
Braemar Cl SN3 50 F3
Braemar Rise SP1 146 B4
Braemor Rd SN11 81 A4
Braemore CE Prim Sch
SP6 210 E4
Braithwaite Way [3]
BA11 110 C6
Brake Mead SN15 78 F7
Brakspear Dr SN13 76 E1
Bramble Cl SN2 35 E1
Bramble Dr
Chippenham SN15 79 A4
Westbury BA13 108 F5
Bramble Rd SN2 35 E1
Brambles The
Hinton Charterhouse BA2 98 E1
Salisbury SP1 146 C2
Trowbridge BA14 101 D2
Bramdean Cl [6] SN25 34 F6
Bramley Cl
Pewsey SN9 215 D6
[4] Warminster BA12 116 F7
Bramley Dr BA11 110 C6
Bramley Hill BA12 138 F5
Bramley La BA14 105 D7
Bramley Way SP4 217 C3
Bramleys The SP5 161 D3
Brampton Ct [8] SN12 178 B8
Bramptons The SN5 49 B7
Bramshaw Telegraph*
SP6 211 F3
Bramwell Cl SN2 35 E6
Brancaster Ave [1] SP10 193 C2
Branch Rd BA2 98 F2
Branders [4] SN6 19 D8
Brandon Cl SN5 49 A5
Branksome Rd SN25 34 E3
Branscombe Dr SN4 47 E1
Bransdown Hill
Easton Grey SN16 26 A3
Sherston SN16 25 F2
Brassknocker Hill BA2 90 A1
Bratch La SP3 201 F2
Bratton Ave SN10 214 C2
Bratton Camp* BA13 186 A6
Bratton Cl SN2 35 B5
Bratton Prim Sch
BA13 186 B7
Bratton Rd
West Ashton BA14 106 B4
Westbury BA13 109 C4
Bray St SN8 173 A8
Braybrooke Cl [2] SN5 48 F8
Braydon Ct SN2 35 C5
Braydon La SN6 18 F4
Breach Cl SP8 137 E2
Breach La Chute SP11 192 E8
[1] Shaftesbury SP7 202 B1
Southwick BA14 105 A3
Wootton Bassett SN4 61 B5
Breach The SN10 214 B2
Bread St BA12 116 F5
Bream Cl Calne SN11 81 A5
Melksham SN12 94 D6
Breamore Countryside Mus*
SP6 210 E5
Breamore House*
SP6 210 E6
Breamore Rd SP5 210 F7
Brecon Cl
Melksham SN12 94 D4
Swindon SN3 50 E2
Bremen Gdns [21] SP10 193 D2
Bremeridge Cl BA13 109 B3
Bremeridge Rd BA13 109 B3
Bremhill Cl SN2 35 C4
Bremhill View SN11 81 A4
Bremilham Rd SN16 27 F4
Bremilham Rise SN16 27 E3
Brendon Wlk SN3 51 B6
Breton Rd BA13 108 F2
Brettingham Gate SN3 64 F8
Brewer Mead SN15 78 F4
Brewers La SN11 81 C1
Brewery St SN6 23 A5
Brewery Wlk BA14 101 D1
Briar Cl Frome BA11 110 B7
Westbury BA13 108 F4
Briar Fields SN1 50 E7
Briar Leaze SN11 166 B3
Briars Cl SN4 47 E3
Briarswood Ct SN3 51 D3
Briary Rd GL7 2 C6
Brick Hill SN15 95 D6
Brick La Salisbury SP2 145 C2
Trowbridge BA14 101 D3
Brickham Rd [1] SN10 214 D5
Brickley La SN10 214 D2
Bricksteed Ave SN10 214 C3
Brickworth La SP5 160 E4
Brickyard La SP8 137 E1
Bridewell La SP7 202 A6
Bridewell Sq SN10 214 B3
Bridewell St SN8 213 C2
Bridge Ave BA14 105 A8
Bridge Ct BA13 108 E4
Bridge End Rd SN3 35 F1
Bridge Rd SP5 205 E4
Bridge St Bourton SP8 137 E2
Bradford-on-Avon BA15 100 D6
Fordingbridge SP6 210 D1
[26] Hungerford RG17 177 B7
Marlborough SN8 213 A2
Salisbury SP2 152 A8
Swindon SN1 50 B6
[3] Trowbridge BA14 105 D7
Bridge The SN15 78 D7
Bridgeman Cl SN3 36 B2
Bridgemead Cl SN5 49 D7
Bridgemead Ret Pk
SN5 49 E5
Bridgewater Cl SN2 50 A7
Bridlewood Prim Sch
SN25 34 F7
Bridport Rd SN3 51 B4
Brier Ct SP2 145 C4
Briery Cl SN3 36 A4
Bright Cl [3] SN15 78 F5
Bright St SN2 50 D8
Brighton Way SN14 77 F6
Brimble Hill SN4 64 D5
Brimble Hill Specl Sch
SN3 51 B5
Brimhill Rise BA13 111 D4
Brind Cl SN3 51 E6
Brind Rd SP4 197 F7
Brindley Cl SN2 34 E1
Brington Rd SN3 51 B8
Brinkworth Cl SN14 77 F7
Brinkworth Earl Danby's CE
Prim Sch SN15 45 E5
Brinkworth House Bsns &
Events Ctr SN15 45 C6
Brinkworth Rd SN15 45 C3
Brinscombe La [6] SP7 202 D1
Brionne Way [13] SP7 202 D2
Brisbane Gdns [7] SP4 198 F6
Bristol Rd
Chippenham SN14 78 C8
Chippenham Without
SN14 69 E2
Luckington SN14 39 D3
Bristol St
[3] Malmesbury SN16 28 A3
Swindon SN1 50 A6
Britannia Ave SN9 182 B2
Britannia Cres SN15 60 B2
Britannia Pl SN1 50 D4
Britannia Trade Pk SN3 35 F3
Britford CE Prim Sch
SP5 152 D5
Britford La SP2 152 B6
Britford La W [1] SP2 152 A6
British Row BA14 101 C1
Britmore La SP7 202 F4
Brittain Cl SN14 77 F7
Britten Rd SN25 34 E7
Brittox The SN10 214 B3
Brixham Ave SN3 50 E5
Broad Chalke CE Prim Sch
SP5 205 C4
Broad Hinton (Hackpen)
White Horse* SN4 167 E5
Broad Hinton CE Prim Sch
SN4 167 C7
Broad St Swindon SN1 50 C7
Trowbridge BA14 101 C1
Broad Stones BA15 90 E7
Broad Town CE Prim Sch
SN4 62 B1
Broad Town White Horse*
SN4 62 D1
Broadacres SN4 62 B2
Broadbury Banks*
SN9 181 B2
Broadcloth E La BA14 105 E7
Broadcloth La BA14 105 E7
Broadfield Rd SP4 133 D3
Broadfields SN9 215 B4
Broadlands Cl SP1 146 B4
Broadleas Cl SN10 214 A2
Broadleas Cres SN10 214 A2
Broadleas Gdns*
SN10 214 A1
Broadleas Pk SN10 214 A1
Broadleas Rd SN10 214 A2
Broadleaze
Down Ampney GL7 8 E8
Seagry SN15 57 D6
Broadley Pk BA14 105 D3
Broadmead
Corsham SN13 85 B7
Trowbridge BA14 101 A1
Broadmead La BA12 116 E1
Broadmead Wlk SN3 51 B7
Broadmoor Rd SN3 36 D7
Broadstone SN13 85 B7
Broadtown La
Broad Town SN4 62 B3
Wootton Bassett SN4 61 F5
Broadway
Market Lavington SN10 179 D2
Warminster BA12 116 E5
Broadway Cl GL7 10 D7
Broadway E BA13 108 D6
Broadway La GL7 7 A5
Broadway N BA13 108 C7
Broadway The SN25 35 A3
Broadwood Ave SN13 84 B8
Broadwood Cl [1] BA12 117 A8
Brockley Rise SN2 36 A5
Brocks Orch [8] SP3 196 E6
Broken Cross
Calne SN11 81 B3
Laverstock SP4 146 F6
Brokerswood Ctry Pk*
BA13 107 F6
Brokerswood Rd
BA14 105 A1
Bromley Cl [2] SN3 50 E6
Bronte Cl [2] SN3 51 D4
Brook Cl [16] SP3 203 E8
Brook Dr SN13 85 B7
Brook Dro BA13 108 C4
Brook Field Prim Sch
Sn5 49 A8
Brook Hill
Donhead St Andrew SP7 203 B2
Sherston SN16 40 C8
Brook La
Westbury BA13 108 D4
Woodgreen SP6 211 A4
Brook Rd BA14 101 B1
Brook St
Chippenham SN14 78 B8
Fovant SP3 204 E7
Great Bedwyn SN8 176 C3
Warminster BA12 116 E5
Brook Way SN11 81 C3
Brookdene SN25 34 E4
Brooke Cres SN2 34 C5
Brookfield SN6 22 F7
Brookfield Rise SN12 85 D1
Brookfields SO51 212 F6
Brooklands SN15 45 E5
Brooklands Ave SN2 34 F1
Brookleaze SN13 84 E5
Brooklime Cl [1] SN2 34 D4
Brookmead BA14 105 A3
Brooks Cl SN2 35 E5
Brooksby Way SN3 51 B8
Brookside
Crudwell SN16 14 E6
Hullavington SN14 41 F2
Brookside Cl BA1 82 A5
Brookwell Cl SN14 70 C2
Broomcroft Rd SN9 215 C5
Broome Manor La SN3 50 F2
Broomfield SN15 70 D2
Broomground BA15 99 E7
Broomhill SP5 212 C5
Brotherton Cl SN15 78 F5
Broughton Grange [6]
SN3 50 F4
Broughton Rd [2] BA14 105 C5
Brouncker's Well*
BA12 186 F5
Brow The SN25 34 E4
Brown St
[3] Salisbury SP1 146 B1
Salisbury SP1 152 B8
Trowbridge BA14 105 D7
Brown's Folly* BA1 82 C1
Brown's La SN8 176 B3
Browning Cl [1] SN3 36 B3
Brownings The SN13 83 D5
Brownleaze La SN10 179 D6
Browns La Alton SN8 173 C1
Damerham SP6 209 E3
Broxburn Rd BA12 116 D6
Bruce St SN2 49 F7
Bruddel Gr SN3 50 E2
Bruges Cl SN15 78 F7
Brunel Cl SN13 76 F1
Brunel Ct SN15 78 B6
Brunel Ctr The SN1 50 B6
Brunel Rd SP2 145 D1
Brunel Way Box SN13 83 D6
Frome BA11 110 C7
Brunkard's La SN9 215 D5
Brunswick St SN1 50 C4
Brushy Bush La SP5 207 F3
Bruton Wlk SN3 51 A4
Bruyn Rd SP6 210 E1
Bryans Cl Rd SN11 81 B3
Bryanston Way SN3 51 C6
Bryant Rd SN25 34 C5
Brydes Rd [21] SP11 192 A5
Brympton Cl [5] SP6 210 C1
Brynards Hill SN4 47 E1
Bryony Way SN2 34 D4
Bryworth La GL7 2 A6
Buckhurst Cres SN3 51 A6
Buckingham Rd
Chippenham SN15 79 A5
Swindon SN3 51 A3
Buckland Cl SN3 51 A6
Buckleaze Cl BA14 105 D5
Buckleaze La SN9 215 C5
Bucklebury Cl SN3 36 A1
Buckthorn Dr SN2 34 D4
Budbury Circ BA15 100 C7
Budbury Cl BA15 100 C7
Budbury Pl BA15 100 C7
Budbury Ridge BA15 100 C7
Budbury Tyning BA15 100 C7
Bude Rd SN5 49 F6
Budge La BA11 114 A8
Buettell Way SN16 27 F5
Buie Cl SN5 34 B2
Bulbridge Rd SP2 144 B1
Bulford CE Prim Sch
SP4 217 E8
Bulford Droveway
SP4 198 D7
Bulford Hill SP4 217 C8
Bulford Rd Bulford SP4 217 F8
Durrington/Bulford SP4 198 B7
Shipton Bellinger SP9 199 C8
South Tedworth SP9 216 A4
Bull La BA12 116 F2
Bull Pit BA15 100 D6
Bulldog La SN10 180 C3
Buller St SN2 35 D1
Bullfinch Cl SN3 51 D6
Bullock's Horn La
Charlton SN16 29 D7
Hankerton SN16 15 D1
Bulls La Box SN13 83 D6
Broad Chalke SP5 205 B4
Bulpit La RG17 177 B6
Bulpits Hill SP11 185 C3
Bumper's Batch BA2 98 A8
Bumpers Fram Ind Est
SN14 70 A1
Bumpers Way SN14 70 A1
Bunce Rd SN3 36 A2
Bungalows The SN2 35 C2
Bunnies La SN10 96 D2
Bunns La BA11 114 A2
Bunny La SP5 162 C4
Buntings The SN3 51 D7
Bupton Village*
SN11 166 D7
Burbage Prim Sch
SN8 183 D8
Burbage Rd
Easton SN9 183 A8
Milton Lilbourne SN9 182 F7
Swindon SN2 35 C6
Burbage Wharf* SN8 175 C2
Burcombe La SP2 144 B2
Burcot Cl SN25 34 C7
Burden Cl SN3 36 C1
Burderop Cl
[1] Trowbridge BA14 105 D5
Wroughton SN4 64 B8
Burderop Pk* SN4 64 F5
Burdett St [4] SN8 170 B2
Burford Ave
Salisbury SP2 152 B6
Swindon SN3 50 E5
Burford La SP2 152 B6

Burford Rd SP2 . . . . .152 B6
Burford St GL7 . . . . .2 C4
Burford's 2 RG17 . . . . . . .171 E7
Burgate Fields SN1 . . . . . .210 D2
Burgess Cl SN3 . . . . .36 A1
Burgess Gn SP1 . . . . .146 C4
Burghley Cl SN13 . . . . .51 A6
Burlands Rd SN12 . . . . .78 E6
Burleaze SN15 . . . . .78 C5
Burn Rd SN13 . . . . .76 E1
Burnet Cl
  Melksham SN12 . . . . .94 B2
  Swindon SN2 . . . . .34 D5
Burnet Way SP1 . . . . .146 D4
Burnett Rd BA14 . . . . .105 D6
Burnham Rd
  5 Fordingbridge SP6 . . .210 D2
  Swindon SN1 . . . . .51 B6
Burnhams Cl **1** SP10 . . .193 E2
Burnivale SN1 . . . . .28 A3
Burns Way SN2 . . . . .35 E4
Burnston Cl SN12 . . . . .94 D5
Burr La SN8 . . . . .176 F1
Burroughs Dro **2** SN3 . .183 D8
Burton Cl SN3 . . . . .36 A1
Burton Farm Cl SN14 . . . . .53 B3
Burton Hill SN16 . . . . .28 B2
Burton Hill Sch SN16 . . . . .28 A1
Burton Rd GL9 . . . . .52 F6
Burtons La SN13 . . . . .80 B2
Burwood Cl **7** SN4 . . . . .217 E3
Bury Camp (Hill Fort)*
  .67 B1
Bury Fields SN5 . . . . .33 D1
Bury Hill (Settlement)*
  .18 B1
Bury La BA13 . . . . .186 B7
Bury Mead BA12 . . . . .195 A2
Burycroft SN4 . . . . .163 A6
Burytown La SN26 . . . . . . .21 C2
Buscot Cl SN25 . . . . .34 E7
Buscot Old Parsonage*
  SN7 . . . . .2 C2
Bush Barrow* SP4 . . . . . .197 D4
Bush Farm Bison Ctr*
  BA12 . . . . .140 B3
Bustlers Hill SN16 . . . . .40 D8
Bute Cl SN6 . . . . .22 F7
Butleigh Rd SN25 . . . . .34 E7
Butler Cl SP2 . . . . .152 B6
Butler's Field GL7 . . . . .2 C5
Butler's Gdns BA11 . . . . . .110 A4
Butlers Cl SN16 . . . . .25 C1
Butt Cl SP11 . . . . .192 A6
Butt La SP5 . . . . .205 E4
Butt St SP11 . . . . .192 A5
Butt's La SP5 . . . . .90 F7
Butter Furlong Rd
  SP5 . . . . .154 C3
Buttercup Cl SN14 . . . . .70 B3
Butterfield Dr **2** SN4 . . .217 D3
Butterfly World* SN1 . . . . .48 F1
Buttermere SN3 . . . . .51 E3
Butterworth St SN1 . . . . . . .50 A5
Buttons Yd BA12 . . . . .117 B7
Butts (Tumuli) The*
  SP6 . . . . .211 E2
Butts Cl SN14 . . . . .76 E7
Butts Hill SN3 . . . . .129 E7
Butts La
  Kilmington BA12 . . . . .123 E6
  Steeple Ashton BA14 . . . .178 A3
Butts Mead **3** SP7 . . . .202 D1
Butts Rd Chiseldown SN4 . . .65 D5
  Salisbury SP1 . . . . .146 A2
Butts Terr SP2 . . . . .146 A2
Butts The
  Aldbourne SN8 . . . . .170 A6
  Biddestone SN14 . . . . .76 D7
  Bratton BA13 . . . . .186 B7
  Chippenham SN15 . . . . . . .78 E6
  Crudwell SN16 . . . . .14 E6
  Lydiard Millicent SN5 . . . . .48 C8
  Potterne SN10 . . . . .179 D5
  Shaftesbury SP7 . . . . .202 B2
  Shrewton SP3 . . . . .196 E7
  Steeple Ashton BA14 . . . .178 A3
  Westbury BA13 . . . . .109 A2
By Brook Valley CE Prim Sch
  SN14 . . . . .68 F5
Bydemill Gdns SN6 . . . . . . .22 E5
Byfield Way SN1 . . . . .51 B8
Byrd Cl **10** SN5 . . . . .48 F5
Byre Cl SN6 . . . . .19 D7
Byron Ave SN4 . . . . .47 F2
Byron Cl **11** SN11 . . . . .192 A5
Byron Ct SN3 . . . . .36 E5
Byron Rd SN10 . . . . .214 B1
Byron St **3** SN1 . . . . .50 C5
Bythebrook SN14 . . . . .70 B1
Bythesea Rd BA14 . . . . . . .105 C8
Byways Cl **4** SP1 . . . . . .152 C8

C

Cabot Dr SN5 . . . . .48 F6
Cabul Rd SP9 . . . . .216 B5
Cadby Cl BA14 . . . . .105 F8
Cadd La BA12 . . . . .138 F5
Cadley Cl SN2 . . . . .35 D2
Cadley Clay Shooting Gd
  SN8 . . . . .175 A5
Cadley Rd SN8 . . . . .183 E1
Cadnam Cres SP4 . . . . . . .217 F2
Caen Hill SN10 . . . . .179 C8
Caen Hill Gdns SN10 . . . . .179 C8

Caen Hill Locks*
  SN10 . . . . .179 C8
Caen View SN1 . . . . .49 E4
Caerleon Dr **4** SP10 . . .193 E2
Caesar Rd SP10 . . . . .193 E2
Caesar's Camp (Fort)*
  DT11 . . . . .206 F2
Cagney Dr SN25 . . . . .35 A5
Caird Lawns SN10 . . . . . . .214 C2
Cairndow Way SN2 . . . . . . .35 E5
Calcutt St SN6 . . . . .19 E8
Calder Cl SN3 . . . . .36 B2
Callaghan Cl **2** SN3 . . . .36 B2
Callas Hill SN4 . . . . .163 B5
Callas Rise **7** SN4 . . . .163 B5
Callenders SN5 . . . . .49 E5
Callow Croft **8** SN8 . . .183 D8
Callows Cross SN15 . . . . . .46 C6
Calne Heritage Ctr*
  SN11 . . . . .81 B2
Calne Rd SN15 . . . . .60 A1
Calstock Rd SN25 . . . . .34 B6
Calvert Rd SN3 . . . . .50 C6
Calves La SP7 . . . . .202 A2
Camargue Rd BA13 . . . . . .108 E1
Cambria Bridge Rd
  SN1 . . . . .50 A5
Cambria Pl SN1 . . . . .50 A5
Cambridge Cl SN3 . . . . .50 D4
Cambridge Rd SP1 . . . . . .146 B3
Camden Cl SN5 . . . . .49 A5
Camellia Dr BA12 . . . . .116 E7
Camelot Ct **25** SP10 . . .193 E2
Campbell Rd SN3 . . . . .36 A1
Camilla Cl SN4 . . . . .36 A1
Camomile Dr **28** SP11 . .192 A5
Campbell Rd SP1 . . . . .146 B2
Campden Rd SN3 . . . . .50 E5
Campion Cl Calne SN11 . . .81 B5
  Westbury BA13 . . . . .109 A5
Campion Dr
  Melksham SN12 . . . . .94 C2
  Trowbridge BA14 . . . . . . .105 D6
Campion Gate SN15 . . . . . . .48 F7
Camton Rd SN5 . . . . .48 F7
Canada Cl SN4 . . . . .163 A6
Canada Rise SN51 . . . . . . .212 F5
Canadian Ave SN2 . . . . . . .145 D2
Canal Cl Calne SN11 . . . . . .81 A2
  Wilcot SN8 . . . . .182 A8
Canal La SN5 . . . . .153 E2
Canal Rd
  Chippenham SN15 . . . . . . .78 F5
  Trowbridge BA14 . . . . . . .101 D3
Canal Rd Ind Est
  BA14 . . . . .101 D3
Canal Way SN10 . . . . .214 E6
Canal Wlk
  Hungerford RG17 . . . . . . .177 B7
  Swindon SN1 . . . . .50 B6
Canalside SN5 . . . . .153 E2
Canberra Dr SP4 . . . . .198 F6
Candown Rd SP3 . . . . .188 B2
Canford Cl SN3 . . . . .51 C6
Cann Hill SP7 . . . . .206 A7
Canney Cl SN4 . . . . .65 D4
Cannimore Cl BA12 . . . . . .116 E5
Cannimore Rd BA12 . . . . .116 D5
Cannon Sq SN12 . . . . .94 A4
Cannon St SN1 . . . . .50 D4
Cannwood La BA10 . . . . . .122 D8
Canons Cl
  Tidworth SP9 . . . . .216 D4
  Warminster BA12 . . . . . . .117 C5
Canons Ct SN12 . . . . .94 A4
Cantax Hill SN15 . . . . .86 C6
Cantelo Cl SN3 . . . . .34 F7
Canterbury Cl
  10 Amesbury SP4 . . . . .217 D3
  Swindon SN3 . . . . .50 F3
Canterbury St SN14 . . . . . . .78 C8
Cantors Way SN16 . . . . . . .17 C2
Capesthorne Dr SN25 . . . . .34 E6
Capitol Cl SN3 . . . . .36 D1
Capps La BA13 . . . . .109 E7
Caprice Cl **1** SN5 . . . . . .49 A7
Caradon Way SN1 . . . . . . .145 F4
Caradon Wlk SN3 . . . . .34 C7
Caraway Dr SN2 . . . . .34 C4
Carders Cnr **7** BA14 . . .105 D7
Cardigan Cl SN3 . . . . .50 E4
Cardigan Rd SN8 . . . . .213 C3
Cardwell Cl **1** SN3 . . . . .50 F7
Carey Cl SN5 . . . . .49 A5
Carfax Cl SN14 . . . . .78 A7
Carfax St SN1 . . . . .50 C5
Carisbrook Rd SN12 . . . . . .94 B2
Carisbrook Terr SN4 . . . . . .65 C3
Carisbrooke Cres
  BA14 . . . . .101 E5
Carleton Pl SN4 . . . . .217 A4
Carlisle Ave SN3 . . . . .50 D3
Carlton Cl **3** SN3 . . . . . .217 D3
Carlton Gate SN3 . . . . .50 F1
Carlton Row BA14 . . . . . . .105 D6
Carman Cl SN3 . . . . .36 B3
Carmel Wlk SN3 . . . . .50 F5
Carmelite Way SN12 . . . . .152 B7
Carnarvon Cl SN14 . . . . . . .78 A7
Carp Rd SN11 . . . . .81 A5
Carpenter Cl **5** SN15 . . .78 F7
Carpenter Dr SN4 . . . . . . .217 D4
Carpenter's Cl SN11 . . . . . .81 C5
Carpenters Cl SN16 . . . . . . .25 D1
Carpenters La
  4 Bratton BA13 . . . . . .186 B7

Carpenters La continued
  Swindon SN1 . . . . .50 D8
Carr St SN1 . . . . .50 B6
Carrick Cl SN15 . . . . .79 A8
Carrion Pond Dro
  SP2 . . . . .151 D7
Carroll Cl SN1 . . . . .51 D4
Carronbridge Rd SN5 . . . . .49 B6
Carshalton Rd SN3 . . . . . . .51 B3
Carstairs Ave SN3 . . . . .51 A3
Carter Cl SN25 . . . . .35 C6
Carter's Cl SP6 . . . . .211 C6
Cartway SN10 . . . . .180 E4
Cartwright Dr SN5 . . . . .49 B8
Carvers Hill SN8 . . . . .176 E1
Cary Cl SN5 . . . . .79 A4
Casley La BA11 . . . . .107 C7
Caspian Gdns SN3 . . . . . . .108 F1
Cassini Dr SN25 . . . . .34 B7
Casson Rd SN3 . . . . .36 A2
Castell Cl BA14 . . . . .106 B8
Casterbridge La **3**
  SP1 . . . . .192 F1
Casterley Camp*
  SN9 . . . . .189 D8
Castilian Mews **1** BA12 .195 A7
Castle Barrow* BA12 . . . .195 A7
Castle Combe Motor Racing
  Circuit* SN14 . . . . .68 C6
Castle Combe Motte &
  Baileys* SN14 . . . . .67 F8
Castle Cl SP11 . . . . .192 A6
Castle Dore SN5 . . . . .49 A5
Castle Grounds SN10 . . . . .214 A3
Castle Hill (Fort)*
  SN26 . . . . .21 D3
Castle Hill Cl **9** SP7 . . .202 B2
Castle Hill Cres BA12 . . . . .139 A6
Castle Hill Rd SP11 . . . . . .192 B5
Castle Keep
  Salisbury SP1 . . . . .145 E4
  4 Wilton SP2 . . . . .144 D3
Castle La Alderbury SP5 . . .153 E1
  Devizes SN10 . . . . .214 A3
  Marlborough SN8 . . . . . . .213 A3
Castle Meadow SP5 . . . . . .211 A8
Castle Pl Sh Ctr BA14 . . . .105 D8
Castle Prim Sch SP11 . . . .192 B5
  Devizes SN10 . . . . .214 A3
  3 Great Bedwyn SN8 . . .176 B3
Castle St
  Aldbourne SN8 . . . . .170 A6
  Calne SN11 . . . . .81 B2
  1 Ludgershall SP11 . . . .192 A5
  Mere BA12 . . . . .138 F5
  Salisbury SP1 . . . . .146 A2
  Trowbridge BA14 . . . . . . .105 D8
Castle View
  West Tisbury SP3 . . . . . . .203 B8
  Westbury BA13 . . . . .109 A4
Castle View Cl SN4 . . . . . . .65 E4
Castle View Rd
  Chiseldown SN4 . . . . .65 C4
  Swindon SN3 . . . . .36 C1
Castle Wlk SN1 . . . . .81 A2
Castle Woods **2** SP5 . . .211 C7
Castledown Foundation Sch
  SP11 . . . . .191 F5
Castlefield Cl **3** SN5 . . . .49 C6
Castlefields SN11 . . . . .81 C3
Castlehaven Cl SN15 . . . . . .79 A5
Castleton Rd SN5 . . . . .49 A7
Castley Rd BA14 . . . . .102 A2
Catalina Ct **17** SN12 . . . .178 B8
Cathedral Cl SP1 . . . . .152 B8
Catherine Cres
  Dinton SP3 . . . . .201 E2
  Swindon SP5 . . . . .210 F8
Catherine St SP1 . . . . .152 A8
Catherine Ford La
  Dinton SP3 . . . . .201 E1
  Fovant SP3 . . . . .204 E8
Catherine St
  Salisbury SP1 . . . . .152 B8
  5 Swindon SN1 . . . . . . .50 B6
Catherine Way BA11 . . . . . .82 A5
Catherine Wayte Cl
  SN25 . . . . .34 F4
Catherine Wayte Prim Sch
  SN25 . . . . .34 F4
Catmint Cl SN1 . . . . .51 C5
Cator Rd **8** SP4 . . . . . . .197 E7
Cats Hill La SP7 . . . . .203 A1
Catterick Cl **7** SN14 . . . .77 F6
Caulfield Rd SN2 . . . . .50 B8
Causeway Cl SN15 . . . . .78 E7
Causeway The
  Bishops Cannings SN10 . . . .45 D6
  Broad Chalke SP5 . . . . . .205 B4
  Chippenham SN15 . . . . . . .78 E7
  The Common SP5 . . . . . . .149 C7
  11 Trowbridge SP3 . . . .203 E8
Cavendish Rd BA14 . . . . . .104 F6
Cavendish Sq SN3 . . . . .51 A4
Caversham Cl SN9 . . . . .50 F5
Cawte Cl SN5 . . . . .49 A8
Caxton Cl
  2 Andover SP10 . . . . . .193 C1
  2 Swindon SN3 . . . . . . .51 A4
Caxton Rd BA11 . . . . .110 A3
Cayenne Pk SN7 . . . . .34 C4
Cecil Ave SP2 . . . . .145 C3
Cecil Rd SN3 . . . . .51 A6
Cecil Terr SP2 . . . . .145 D1

Cedar Cl Melksham SN12 . . .94 A3
  Salisbury SP2 . . . . .145 B4
  Worton SN10 . . . . .179 B4
Cedar Gr
  Chippenham SN15 . . . . . . .70 E1
  Trowbridge BA14 . . . . . . .105 B6
Cedars Cl SN2 . . . . .35 A2
Celandine Way SN14 . . . . . .70 B2
Central Ave SN26 . . . . .100 F7
Central Cl SP1 . . . . .192 A5
Central Trad Est SN3 . . . . . .50 D3
Centre The SP4 . . . . .217 A4
Centurion Cl
  Chippenham SN15 . . . . . . .79 A5
  1 Salisbury SP1 . . . . . .145 D2
Cerney Mews **3** SN3 . . . .51 C8
Cerney Wick La GL7 . . . . . . .7 D5
Chaddenwick Hill
  BA12 . . . . .140 B7
Chadwick Cl **22** SN12 . . .178 B8
Chaffeymoor Hill SP8 . . . .137 B1
Chaffinch Rd BA11 . . . . . . .110 B6
Chaffinch Dr **2** BA14 . . .105 B8
Chafyn Gr Sch SP1 . . . . . .146 C2
Chain Dro
  South Newton SP3 . . . . . .130 B6
  Stapleford SP3 . . . . .129 F7
Chain Hill SP3 . . . . .129 E7
Chain La BA12 . . . . .117 C6
Chalcot La
  Chapmanslade BA13 . . . . .111 F5
  Upton Scudamore BA13 . . .112 A6
Chalet Specl Sch The
  SN3 . . . . .51 D3
Chalfield Cres SN12 . . . . . .94 C5
Chalfont Cl BA14 . . . . .105 A8
Chalford Ave SN3 . . . . .51 B7
Chalgrove Field SN5 . . . . . .49 A3
Chalk Down SP4 . . . . .216 E7
Chalk Hill **3** SP3 . . . . . .196 F6
Chalk Pyt Rd SP5 . . . . .205 B4
Chalk's Cl **1** SP5 . . . . . .211 C8
Chalkcroft La SP11 . . . . . .193 A2
Challis Cl **5** SP11 . . . . . .192 B5
Chalvedon Gn SN3 . . . . .51 A5
Chamberlain Rd
  Chippenham Without
    . . . . .77 F7
  Swindon SN3 . . . . .50 A8
Chambers Ave SN3 . . . . . . .217 C2
Chambon Cl SN16 . . . . .17 C2
Champneys Rd **6** BA11 .110 A7
Chancel Way GL7 . . . . .2 C4
Chancellor Cl SN5 . . . . .48 F6
Chancery Cl **8** SN2 . . . .145 E2
Chancery La BA12 . . . . . . .117 C6
Chandler Cl SN3 . . . . .50 D5
Chandler Way **3** SN15 . . .78 F4
Chandler's La **1** SN8 . . .170 A7
Chandlers Cl SN10 . . . . . . .180 E8
Chandos Cl
  All Cannings SN10 . . . . . .180 F8
  Bishops Cannings SN10 . . .172 B2
Chandos Cl SN5 . . . . .49 A6
Chanterelle Pk BA15 . . . . .100 D5
Chantry Gdns BA14 . . . . . .105 B6
Chantry La Chute SP11 . . . .184 C2
  Swindon SN2 . . . . .213 D2
Chantry Mead **18** RG17 .177 B7
Chantry Mews BA12 . . . . . .117 A7
Chantry The* SP2 . . . . . . .144 C1
  Wilton SP2 . . . . .144 C1
Chants La **5** SP3 . . . . . .196 E6
Chapel Cl GL7 . . . . .10 D6
Chapel Cnr SN14 . . . . .41 F1
Chapel Ct **7** RG17 . . . . .177 B7
Chapel Hill
  Broad Blunsdon SN26 . . . . .21 B2
  Lacock SN15 . . . . .86 C6
Chapel La
  Acton Turville GL9 . . . . . . .53 A6
  Andover SP11 . . . . .193 E3
  Bishopstone SP5 . . . . .205 E4
  Box SN13 . . . . .83 D5
  Broad Town SN4 . . . . .167 B8
  Chippenham SN15 . . . . . . .78 E7
  Collingbourne Kingston
    SN8 . . . . .183 D2
  Corsham SN13 . . . . .84 E4
  Downton SP5 . . . . .159 B5
  Hankerton SN16 . . . . .15 C2
  12 Lambourn RG17 . . . .165 A2
  5 Ludgershall SP11 . . . .192 A5
  Melksham Without SN12 . . .86 A1
  Minety SN16 . . . . .17 A2
  Nomansland SP5 . . . . . . .212 C4
  Pen Selwood BA9 . . . . . . .137 C3
  Redlynch SP5 . . . . .211 D8
  1 Shrewton SP3 . . . . . .196 E6
  South Marston SN3 . . . . . . .36 E5
  Stapleford SP3 . . . . .129 E7
  Upavon SN9 . . . . .181 F2
  5 Wanborough SN4 . . . .163 B6
  Wingfield BA14 . . . . .104 B6
  Woodborough SN9 . . . . . .181 C7
  Zennor BA12 . . . . .137 D5
Chapel Mews SN3 . . . . .36 E5
Chapel Orch **6** SN3 . . . .163 B6
Chapel Path SN14 . . . . .70 A7
Chapel Pl **1** SP2 . . . . . .146 A1
Chapel Rd
  Asbury SN6 . . . . .164 A2
  Heytesbury BA12 . . . . . . .194 C5
  Kempsford GL7 . . . . .10 D7

Chapel Rise SN12 . . . . .92 E8
Chapel St
  Horningsham BA12 . . . . . .119 A7
  Swindon SN2 . . . . .50 D8
  Warminster BA12 . . . . . . .116 F5
Chaplin Wlk GL9 . . . . .24 B3
Chaplins Pl **3** SN4 . . . . .217 B3
Chapmanslade CE Prim Sch
  BA13 . . . . .111 C4
Charcoal Burners Rd
  SN8 . . . . .175 B4
Charcroft Hill BA10 . . . . . .122 A5
Charfield Cl SN3 . . . . .51 C5
Charbury Cl SN25 . . . . .34 E3
Charles Garrett Cl **35**
  SP7 . . . . .202 C2
Charles McPherson Gdns
  SN3 . . . . .51 C5
Charles Rd SP4 . . . . .198 B7
Charles St
  Corsham SN13 . . . . .76 F2
  2 Salisbury SP2 . . . . . .145 F1
  Trowbridge BA14 . . . . . . .101 C1
Charlham La GL7 . . . . .2 C3
Charlieu Ave SN11 . . . . .89 C8
Charlock Path SN25 . . . . . . .34 E5
Charlotte Ct SN14 . . . . . . .101 D1
Charlotte Mews SN3 . . . . . .50 D4
Charlotte Sq SN3 . . . . .101 D1
Charlotte St BA14 . . . . .101 D1
Charlton Cl SN2 . . . . .35 D5
Charlton Hill BA13 . . . . . . .186 D8
Charlton La SP7 . . . . .202 F1
Charlton Pk* SN16 . . . . . . .28 E7
Charlton Rd SN16 . . . . .28 E5
Charlwood Rd SN13 . . . . . . .84 F8
Charminster Cl SN3 . . . . . . .51 C6
Charnham La RG17 . . . . . . .177 B8
Charnham Pk RG17 . . . . . .177 B8
Charnham Pk Ind Est
  RG17 . . . . .177 B8
Charnwood Dr **9** SP6 . . .210 D2
Charnwood Rd
  Swindon SN2 . . . . .145 E1
  Trowbridge BA14 . . . . . . .101 A1
Charter Cl **3** SN10 . . . . .214 D5
Charter Prim Sch SN15 . . . .78 F6
Charter Rd SN15 . . . . .78 D7
Charterhouse Dr **4**
  SN10 . . . . .110 C7
Chartley La SN5 . . . . .49 A5
Chartwell Pl SP3 . . . . .196 E6
Chartwell Rd SN25 . . . . . . .34 A1
Chase Cres SP5 . . . . .207 E4
Chase Wood SN5 . . . . .34 A2
Chatham Cl SP1 . . . . .145 F4
Chatham Ct BA12 . . . . .117 B7
Chatsworth Rd SN25 . . . . . .34 A1
Chaucer Ave **8** SP10 . . .193 C1
Chaucer Cl SN4 . . . . .47 E3
Chaveywell Ct SN11 . . . . . . .81 B2
Cheapside BA12 . . . . .195 A4
Cheddar Cl BA11 . . . . .110 C7
Cheddar Rd SN25 . . . . .34 E3
Chedworth Gdns SN3 . . . . .51 A5
Cheese Mkt **1** SP1 . . . . .146 A1
Cheese Wharf* SN7 . . . . . . .2 F1
Chelmsford Rd SN5 . . . . . . .49 C7
Cheltenham Dr SN14 . . . . . .78 A5
Cheltenham St SN1 . . . . . . .50 B7
Chelwood Cl SN14 . . . . .78 A5
Chelworth House SN16 . . . .4 B1
Chelworth Rd SN6 . . . . .19 B6
Chemical Rd BA13 . . . . . . .108 C6
Cheney Manor Ind Est
  SN2 . . . . .34 E1
Cheney Manor Rd SN2 . . . .34 F2
Chepston Pl BA14 . . . . . . .100 F1
Chepstow Cl
  4 Chippenham SN14 . . . .78 A1
  Swindon SN5 . . . . .49 C3
Cheraton Cl SN3 . . . . .51 B7
Cherbury Wlk SN3 . . . . .51 A6
Cherhill CE Prim Sch
  SN11 . . . . .166 B1
Cherhill Cl SN25 . . . . .34 E3
Cherhill White Horse*
  SN11 . . . . .172 C8
Cherrington Field
  SN10 . . . . .180 F4
Cherry Cl Pewsey SN9 . . . .215 D5
  2 Lambourn RG17 . . . .165 A2
Cherry Gdns BA14 . . . . . . .102 A3
Cherry Gdns SN14 . . . . . . .78 A5
Cherry Gr **2** RG17 . . . . .177 B7
Cherry Orch
  Codford St Peter BA12 . . .195 A2
  Highworth SN6 . . . . .23 A5
  Marlborough SN8 . . . . . . .213 E2
Cherry Orch E **3** SN3 . . .51 E7
Cherry Orch La
  Cann SP7 . . . . .202 A1
  Luckington SN14 . . . . .53 C5
  Salisbury SP2 . . . . .145 D1
Cherry Orch N SN3 . . . . . . .51 E7
Cherry Orch W SN3 . . . . . . .51 E7
Cherry Rd SN14 . . . . .75 A5
Cherry Tree Ave SN9 . . . . .216 E4
Cherry Tree Cl SN11 . . . . . .81 B4
Cherry Tree Gr SN2 . . . . . . .35 C3
Cherry Tree Rd SN6 . . . . . . .19 D8
Cherry Tree Way **2**
  SP4 . . . . .217 C3
Chervil Cl **3** SN2 . . . . . . .34 C4
Chesford Cl SN3 . . . . .51 A3

Cheshire Cl
2 Bower Hill SN12 ......178 B8
Salisbury SP2 ....145 C4
Chester St SN1 ....50 B6
Chester Way SN14 .....78 A5
Chesterfield Cl
3 Amesbury SP4 ....217 E3
Swindon SN5 ....49 C6
Chesters The SN5 .....49 C6
Chestnut Ave
Netheravon SP4 ....190 A2
Swindon SN2 ....35 C3
Tidworth SP9 ....216 D7
Chestnut Cl
Down Ampney GL7 ....8 D7
Frome BA11 ....110 B7
Rowde SN10 ....96 D2
Salisbury SP1 ....146 D3
Chestnut Dr SN10 .....178 E5
Chestnut Gr
Trowbridge BA14 ......105 B5
Westwood BA15 ....99 F4
Chestnut Grange SN13 ..76 D1
Chestnut La RG17 .....165 C2
Chestnut Mews SN12 ...94 A4
Chestnut Rd
Chippenham SN14 ....78 B8
Sutton Benger SN15 ....72 D7
Chestnut Springs SN5 ..33 D1
Chestnut Wlk 11 RG17 ..178 B6
Chetcombe Rd BA12 ....139 B6
Chevalier Cl 8 SN5 ....48 F8
Cheverell Ave SP1 ....146 C3
Cheverell Cl BA14 ....105 D5
Cheverell Gn Rd SN10 .179 C2
Cheverell Rd
Cheverell Parva SN10 ..179 C1
West Lavington SN10 ..187 D8
Cheviot Cl Swindon SN5 ..49 A6
Trowbridge BA14 ......105 E7
Cheyral Cl SN14 ....70 B2
Cheyney Wlk BA13 .....109 B4
Chichester Cl SP2 ....152 B6
Chichester Pk BA13 ...109 A4
Chick's La SN8 ....183 E1
Chickerell Rd SN3 .....51 A6
Chicksgrove Rd SP3 ...203 F8
Chicory Cl SN2 ....34 C3
Child St 1 RG17 ....165 A1
Chilmark Rd
Tisbury SP3 ....200 F1
Trowbridge BA14 ......101 A1
Chilmark/Fonthill Bishop Pri
Sch SP3 ....201 B3
Chiltern Cl
Melksham SN12 ....94 C4
9 Warminster BA12 ....117 A8
Chilton Foliat CE Prim Sch
RG17 ....171 A2
Chilton Gdns SN25 .....34 F3
Chilton Way RG17 .....177 B7
Chilvester Hill SN11 ...80 E2
Chilworth Cl SN25 .....34 E6
Chine Rd SP4 ....131 C7
Chippenham Com Hospl
SN15 ....78 C6
Chippenham La SN14 ...77 B7
Chippenham Mus & Heritage
Ctr* SN15 ....78 E7
Chippenham Rd
Lyneham & Bradenstoke
SN15 ....59 E3
Marshfield SN14 ....14 A8
Chippenham Sta SN15 ..78 E8
Chipper La SP1 ....146 A1
Chirton CE Prim Sch
SN10 ....180 F4
Chirton Pl 8 BA14 ....105 D6
Chisbury Camp* SN8 ...176 C4
Chisbury La SN8 ......176 C5
Chiselbury Gr SP2 ....152 A6
Chiseldon Cl SN4 ......65 D4
Chiseldon Prim Sch
SN4 ....65 E4
Chitham Cl SN10 ......187 C8
Chitterne Rd
Codford BA12 ....195 B3
Shrewton SP3 ....196 B6
Chittoe Heath SN15 ...88 A2
Chivers Rd
Chippenham SN15 ......78 E5
Devizes SN10 ....214 D3
Chives Way SN2 ....34 D4
Chobham Cl SN2 ....36 A5
Cholderton Rare Breeds
Farm* SP4 ....199 A5
Cholderton Rd
Amport SP4 ....199 D3
Quarley SP4 ....199 F5
Chopping Knife La
SN8 ....175 A7
Choristers Sq 1 SP1 ..152 A8
Choulston Cl SP4 .....190 B3
Christ the King RC Prim Sch
SP4 ....58 A2
Christchurch CE Prim Sch
BA15 ....100 B8
Christchurch Terr
BA12 ....116 F5
Christian Malford CE Prim
Sch SN15 ....58 A2
Christie Cl SN3 ....51 D4
Christie Miller Rd SP2 .145 E2

Christie Miller Sports Ctr
SN12 ....94 B1
Christin Ct BA14 ......105 A8
Christopher Cl 2 SP2 .151 F5
Christopher Dr SN15 ...79 A4
Christy's Gdns 10 SP7 .202 C2
Christy's La 8 SP7 ....202 C2
Chubb Cl SN16 ....28 A5
Chudleigh SN5 ....49 B4
Chur St SP4 ....198 E6
Church Acre
Bradford-on-Avon BA15 .100 C7
Seagry SN15 ....57 F6
Church Bottom SP4 ...131 A5
Church Cl Bath BA1 ...82 B2
Bourton SP8 ....137 D1
10 Lambourn RG17 ....165 A2
Church Farm La
South Marston SN3 ....36 E4
Woodborough SN9 .....181 D7
Church Farm Mews
SN15 ....60 A2
Church Fields BA14 ...105 A5
Church Furlong SP3 ...129 E2
Church Hatch 1 SP5 ...211 B8
Church Hill
Bromham SN15 ....95 F7
Donhead St Mary SP7 ..203 A3
Limpley Stoke BA2 .....99 B5
Nettleton SN14 ....53 B3
Redlynch SP5 ....211 D7
Shaftesbury SP7 ......202 B2
West Overton SN4 ....173 F7
Wroughton SN4 ....63 F5
Church Hill Rise SN15 ..96 A7
Church La
Amesbury SP4 ....217 A3
Bishopstone SP5 ......150 A1
Bishopstone SN6 .....163 E6
Box SN13 ....83 C5
Bratton BA13 ....186 B7
Britford SP5 ....152 E5
Brokenborough SN16 ...22 F6
Buttermere SN8 ......185 C7
Codford St Peter BA12 .195 B2
5 Cricklade SN6 ......19 D8
Damerham SP6 ....209 F2
Dauntsey SN15 ....44 E1
Donhead SP7 ....159 A5
Durrington/Bulford SP4 .217 D8
East Kennet SN8 .....173 D6
Fovant SP3 ....204 D8
Great Somerton SN15 ...44 E1
Hankerton SN16 ....15 C2
Hawkesbury GL9 ....38 E5
Kington Langley SN15 ...70 E6
Limpley Stoke BA2 .....99 A5
6 Ludgershall SP11 ...192 A5
Lyneham SN15 ....60 A2
Marshfield SN14 ....74 A8
Melchet Park & Plaitford
SO51 ....212 E7
Melksham SN12 ....94 C6
Mildenhall SN8 ....175 A8
Norton SN16 ....41 D5
Ogbourne St Andrew
SN8 ....168 E3
Pitton & Farley SP5 ...148 C4
Rushall SN9 ....181 E2
Salisbury SP2 ....145 C2
2 Shaftesbury SP7 ....202 C1
Sherfield English SO51 .162 F3
Sherrington BA12 .....194 F2
Sopworth SN14 ....24 D1
6 Tisbury SP3 ....203 E8
8 Wootton Bassett SN4 ..47 F3
Stanton St Quintin SN14 .56 B5
Tidworth SP9 ....216 D4
Trowbridge BA14 ......105 A5
Vernhams Dean SP11 ...185 B4
West Lavington SN10 ..187 E8
Westbury BA13 ....108 E1
Wingfield BA14 ....104 C6
Church Mdws 1 SN9 ...199 D8
Church Piece SP7 .....57 D2
Church Pk SN15 ....59 C3
Church Pl
Lydiard Millicent SN5 ..33 C1
Swindon SN1 ....50 A6
Church Rails SP3 .....141 B1
Church Rd
Biddestone SN14 ....76 E7
Bratton BA13 ....186 B6
Calne Without SN11 ....80 A2
Cheverell Magna SN10 .179 B1
Christian Malford SN15 .58 B7
Derry Hill/Studley SN11 .79 F2
Froxfield SN8 ....171 A1
Ham SN8 ....177 A1
Heddington SN11 ....89 B1
Hilmarton SN11 ....73 F3
Idmiston SP4 ....133 F8
Keevil BA14 ....4 F7
Kilmington BA12 ......123 E5
Kington Langley SN15 ...70 E6
Liddington SN4 ....163 A4
Luckington SN14 ....39 E4
Milston SP4 ....198 C8
Norleaze BA13 ....109 A1
Pitton & Farley SP5 ...154 E7
St Paul Malmesbury Without
SN16 ....43 A3
Salisbury SP1 ....146 A3
Sherston GL8 ....25 B5
Silton GL8 ....138 A1
Stanton St Bernard SN8 .172 F7
Swindon SN1 ....50 D4
Wanborough SN4 ......163 A5
Woodborough SN9 .....181 D7

Church Rise SN13 .....84 E5
Church Row SN4 ......163 D6
Church St
Amesbury SP4 ....217 A3
Atworth SN12 ....92 D8
Bath BA1 ....82 B2
Berwick St John SP7 ..203 E1
Bower Chalke SP5 ....205 A2
Bradford-on-Avon BA15 .100 C6
Calne SN11 ....81 B2
Chiseldown SN4 ....65 D4
Collingbourne Ducis SN8 .191 E8
Corsham SN13 ....77 A2
Durrington/Bulford SP4 .198 B7
Great Bedwyn SN8 ....176 B2
Grimstead SP5 ....154 C2
Horningsham BA12 ....119 B7
Hungerford RG17 .....177 B7
Keevil BA14 ....4 F7
Lacock SN15 ....86 D6
Little Bedwyn SN8 ...176 D5
Longbridge Deverill
BA12 ....120 F7
Maiden Bradley with Yarnfield
BA12 ....118 E2
Market Lavington SN10 .179 F1
Melksham SN12 ....94 A4
Mere BA12 ....139 A5
Pewsey SN9 ....215 D4
Purton SN5 ....33 C4
Sennington BA14 .....102 F6
Sherston SN16 ....25 C1
Southwick BA14 ......104 F3
Swindon SN3 ....36 B3
Tisbury SP3 ....203 E8
Trowbridge BA14 .....101 D1
Warminster BA12 .....116 F7
West Lavington SN10 ..187 E7
Westbury BA13 ....109 A3
Winterbourne Stoke SP3 .196 F3
Wootton Bassett SN4 ...47 C2
Wylye BA12 ....201 E8
Church St Cl 15 SP3 ...203 E8
Church Tk SP3 ....137 D1
Church View
Castle Eaton SN6 .....10 B4
Chippenham SN14 ......70 C2
Church Way
Hungerford RG17 .....177 B7
7 Swindon SN3 ....36 B3
Church Wlk
Ashton Keynes SN6 .....6 E1
Bishopstone SN6 .....163 E6
Devizes SN10 ....214 C3
Melksham SN12 ....94 A4
Motcombe SP7 ....202 A4
Redlynch SP5 ....211 E7
Swindon SN5 ....35 E3
Church Wlk N SN25 ....34 F3
Church Wlk S SN25 ....34 F3
Churchacre SN6 ......148 C4
Churchfield SN25 .....34 F3
Churchfields BA15 ....91 E6
Churchfields Ind Est
SP2 ....145 E1
Churchfields Sch SN3 ..50 F5
Churchill Ave
Broad Blunsdon SN26 ...21 C2
Durrington/Bulford SP4 .217 D8
Melksham SN12 ....94 A4
Churchill Cl Calne SN11 .81 C1
9 Tisbury SP3 ....203 E8
8 Wootton Bassett SN4 ...47 F3
Churchill Ct SP2 .....144 D3
Churchill Est SP3 ....203 E8
Churchill Way E SP1 ..146 B1
Churchill Way N SP1 ..146 B1
Churchill Way S SP1 ..152 B7
Churchill Way W
Charlton SP10 ....193 C1
Salisbury SP2 ....146 A1
Churchlands SP4 ......35 A1
Churchward Ave SN2 ...35 A1
Churchward Dr BA11 ..110 C7
Churchway SN26 ......21 C2
Churn Cl GL7 ....6 F7
Chute Cswy SP11 .....184 E2
Circle The SN2 ....35 C2
Cirencester Rd
Fairford GL7 ....1 F6
Latton GL7 ....7 E8
Cirencester Way SN2 ...50 D8
City Cnr SN4 ....163 C6
City The SN12 ....94 A5
Clack La SP6 ....210 B3
Clanfield Rd SN3 ......51 B5
Clap La SP5 ....207 B4
Clardon La SN5 ....33 C6
Clare Wlk SN5 ....49 B4
Clarence Cl 5 SP11 ...192 A5
Clarence Rd
Chippenham SN14 ......77 F7
Trowbridge BA14 .....105 F8
Clarendon Ave SN10 ..214 D4
Clarendon Cl SP9 .....216 D7
Clarendon Dr SP4 .....217 A2
Clarendon Jun & Inf Sch
SP9 ....216 D7
Clarendon La 1 SN1 ...50 A5
Clarendon Pal* SP5 ...147 C1
Clarendon Rd
Aldebury SP5 ....153 D3
Clarendon Park SP5 ..152 F6

Clarendon Rd continued
Grimstead SP5 ....154 A4
Salisbury SP1 ....146 C1
Trowbridge BA14 .....105 E8
Clarendon Sch The
BA14 ....105 C6
Claridge Cl 3 SN8 ....170 A6
Clark Ave SN11 ....81 C5
Clark's Gdns 29 RG17 .177 B7
Clark's Pl 3 BA11 ....110 C6
Clarke Dr SN5 ....49 B8
Clarke's La SP11 .....193 A7
Clarkes Leaze SN14 ...68 F6
Clary Rd SN2 ....34 D5
Classics The 16 RG17 .165 A1
Clattinger Farm Nature
Reserve* SN16 ....16 E7
Claudius Cl 10 SP10 ..193 E2
Claverton Pumping Sta*
BA1 ....90 C5
Clay Cl SN5 ....49 B7
Clay St
Little Somerford SN15 ..44 C6
Longbridge Deverill
BA12 ....116 E1
Whiteparish SP5 ......161 C3
Clay The SN5 ....180 A1
Clayfurlong Gr GL7 ....4 F8
Clayhill Copse SN5 ...34 A2
Clays Cl SN2 ....35 E3
Clays The SN10 ......179 F1
Clayton Rd SP4 ......217 E8
Clearbury Ring* SP5 ..158 C5
Clearwood BA13 ......111 F8
Clearwood View BA13 .111 D4
Cleasby Cl SN5 ....49 D6
Cleavers The 8 SN8 ..183 D8
Cleaves Ave SN10 ....179 A4
Cleeve Lawns SN3 .....50 F3
Cleeve The
Corsham SN13 ....85 A8
Westwood BA15 ....99 F3
Cleevedale Rd BA13 ...85 A8
Cleeves Cl SN5 ....49 A6
Cleeves The SP3 .....143 B3
Clement's La BA12 ...139 B4
Clementine Rd SN25 ...34 B7
Clevedon Cl SN3 ......51 A6
Cleveland Gdns BA11 .101 E2
Cleveland Way BA11 ..108 E2
Cleverton Ct SN2 .....35 C5
Cley Hill (Hill Fort)*
BA12 ....116 A6
Cley View 5 BA12 ....116 E6
Cleyhill Gdns BA13 ...111 D5
Cliff Rd SN16 ....40 C8
Cliffe Dr BA2 ....99 A6
Cliffords SN6 ....19 D7
Clift Ave SN6 ....70 E1
Clift Cl SN13 ....84 A8
Clifton Cl SN14 ......78 B8
Clifton Rd SP2 ....145 F2
Clifton St SN1 ....50 A4
Clifts Bldgs BA11 ...110 A4
Clink Farm Ct 6 BA11 .110 C6
Clink Rd BA11 ....110 C6
Clinton Cl SN5 ....49 B7
Clipsham Rise BA14 ..104 F1
Clivey BA13 ....107 E1
Cloatley Manor* SN16 .15 D2
Cloatley Mdws Nature
Reserve* SN16 ......15 C2
Cloatley Rd SN16 ....15 C2
Cloche Way SN2 ......35 E3
Clockhouse SN14 .....77 F7
Cloford Cl BA14 .....101 A1
Cloister Gdn* SN16 ...28 A3
Close Cl BA14 ....105 A5
Close La Marston SN10 .179 A3
Rowde SN10 ....96 D2
Close The
Bulkington SN10 .....178 E5
Chippenham SN14 ....77 D8
Corsham SN13 ....85 C6
Kington St Michael SN14 .70 A8
Laverstock SP4 ......146 D8
Lechlade GL7 ....2 C5
Lydiard Millicent SN5 ..33 B3
4 Redlynch SP5 ......211 D8
Salisbury SP1 ....152 A8
Tangley SP11 ....193 C5
Warminster BA12 ....117 A7
Cloth Yd 1 BA14 .....105 E7
Close La BA14 ....105 E7
Cloudberry Rd SN25 ...34 D5
Clough La SP5 ....149 B1
Clouts Wood SN5 .....34 A2
Clouts Wood Nature
Reserve* SN4 ....63 F4
Clover Cl SN12 ....94 C3
Clover Dean SP4 ......58 A4
Clover Gdns 8 SP11 ..192 A5
Clover Pk SN2 ....34 C4
Cloverlands SN25 ....34 D4
Club La SN9 ....216 C4
Club Rd 1 SN8 ......198 F7
Clump Way SP4 ......217 A5
Clydesdale Cl
5 Swindon SN5 ....49 A7
Trowbridge BA14 .....105 D7
Clydesdale Dr SN13 ...83 D5
Coach Barton BA14 ..102 F6
Coach Hill SP11 .....192 E6
Coach Ho Mews SP4 ..217 B3
Coach Rd
Bradford-on-Avon BA15 .100 C6
Westbury BA13 ....109 B5

Coalpit Rd BA1 ....82 A4
Coalway La BA11 .....110 C7
Coate Rd SN8 ....173 B1
Coate Wr Ctry Pk*
SN3 ....51 A1
Coate Wr Nature Reserve*
SN3 ....51 B1
Cob Pl BA13 ....108 F1
Cobbett Cl SN25 .....35 A7
Cobbett Pl BA12 .....116 F6
Cobbett Rise BA12 ...117 A8
Cobden Rd SN2 ....50 A8
Cobley Cl SP5 ....208 D6
Cock Hall La BA14 ...101 A1
Cock Rd
Horningsham BA12 ....118 F8
Rowde SN10 ....95 F2
Cock-a-Troop La SN8 .175 B8
Cockleberry La SN15 ..70 F1
Cockleberry Rd SN15 .178 F3
Cocks Cl 5 SP4 ......197 E7
Coda La
BA12 ....195 B3
Codford Circ or Wilsbury
Ring* BA12 ....195 C3
Codford Rd BA12 .....195 C4
Codford Rising Sun (Hill
Figure)* BA12 ....195 C2
Coker's La BA12 .....123 F7
Colbert Ps SN25 .....36 C3
Colborne Cl SN15 ....79 B5
Colbourne St SN1 ....50 D7
Colchester Cl SN5 ...49 D4
Cold Harbour BA14 ..217 B3
Cold Harbour La SN8 .213 E4
Coldharbour La SP2 ..217 E3
Coldharbour Rd RG17 .177 B6
Cole Cl 2 Andover SP10 .193 E2
Swindon SN3 ....51 D6
Cole's La SP7 ....202 A1
Colebrook Jun & Inf Sch
SN3 ....51 C8
Colebrook Rd SN3 ....36 B1
Coleridge Cl
Warminster BA12 ....116 D6
Wootton Bassett SN4 ..47 E3
Coleridge Rd SN25 ...34 F6
Colerne Airfield SN14 .74 E3
Colerne CE Prim Sch
SN14 ....75 B3
Colerne Pk* SN14 ....75 F6
Coles's La SP5 ......212 A7
Colesway Coll SO51 ..212 F5
College Cl SN15 .....78 F8
College Fields SN8 ..213 C2
College Gdns SN13 ..105 D3
College Gr 1 SN4 ...163 A6
College Rd
1 Durrington/Bulford
SN8 ....198 B7
Swindon SN1 ....33 C4
Trowbridge BA14 .....105 B6
College St
Salisbury SP1 ....146 B1
Swindon SN1 ....50 C6
College Way 4 RG17 ..171 E7
Collen Cl 1 SN4 ....47 E3
Collett Ave SN2 .....35 A1
Collett Pl SN6 ......19 C8
Collett Way 8 BA11 ..110 C7
Collingbourne CE Prim Sch
SN8 ....191 E8
Collingbourne Cl 2
BA14 ....105 D5
Collingsmead SN3 ...51 E7
Collingwood Wlk 4
SP10 ....193 F1
Collins Cl 15 SP10 ..193 D2
Collins Cl SN3 ......216 C8
Collins La SN5 ......33 C5
Colman Pk SN25 .....35 A4
Coln Cres SN25 .....35 A4
Colquhoun Rd 2 SN8 .198 A6
Colston Cl SN3 ......51 A4
Colston Rd SN10 ....214 A4
Coltsfoot Cl SP4 ....217 C3
Column Rd SN8 ......175 E3
Combe La
Bratton BA13 ....186 B7
Hilmarton SN11 ....73 F6
Combe View
10 Hungerford RG17 ..177 B6
Yatton Keynell SN14 ..68 F5
Comet Ave SN9 ......182 B2
Comet Cl SN15 ....60 B2
Cofdbury La BA14 ...105 E7
Trowbridge BA14 .....105 E6
Commerce Bsns Ctr
BA13 ....108 E7
Commercial Rd
Devizes SN10 ....214 A4
Swindon SN1 ....50 B5
Common Dro DT11 ...207 B3
Common Hill
Cricklade SN6 ....19 B7
Great Hinton BA14 ...102 F2
Steeple Ashton BA14 .106 F8
Common Platt SN5 ...34 A2
Common Rd
St Paul Malmesbury Without
SN16 ....27 C2
Sixpenny Handley SP5 .207 F4
Whiteparish SP5 ......161 E1
Common Slip SN15 ...78 E7
Common The
Bromham SN15 ....95 E6
Holt BA14 ....92 F1
Kington Langley SN15 ...70 E6

Common The continued
Marlborough SN8 . . . . .213 D4
Minety SN16 . . . . .17 C1
Shrewton SP3 . . . . .49 C5
The Common SP5 . . . . .149 D6
Commonweal Rd SN1 . . .50 B3
Commonweal Sch The
SN1 . . . . .50 B3
Commonwood La SN16 . .40 D5
Compton Abbas Airfield
SP5 . . . . .206 C5
Compton Cl
4 Swindon SN3 . . . . . . .51 C4
Trowbridge BA14 . . . . .101 E4
Compton Gdns BA11 . . .110 C7
Compton Pk* SP3 . . . . .142 C1
Compton Rd
Hilmarton SN11 . . . . .73 F3
Tidworth SP9 . . . . .216 D6
Compton's Dr SO51 . . . .212 E7
Conan Doyle Wlk SN3 . .51 E4
Concord Wlk SN3 . . . . . .51 A5
Conference Cl 1 BA12 . .116 F7
Congreve Rd 4 SP4 . . .197 E7
Conholt Hill SP11 . . . . .185 A2
Conholt La SP11 . . . . . .185 B2
Conholt Pk* SP11 . . . . .184 F1
Conifer Crest 16 SN16 . .183 D8
Conifers The SN2 . . . . . .17 A2
Coniger the (Tumuli)*
SP3 . . . . .196 F5
Conigre BA14 . . . . .101 C1
Conigre Cl SN12 . . . . . . .94 A3
Conigre Hill BA15 . . . . .100 C7
Conigre Mead Nature
Reserve* SN12 . . . . . . .94 A4
Conisborough SN5 . . . . .49 C5
Coniston Cl 5 SP4 . . . .217 E3
Coniston Rd
Chippenham SN14 . . . . . .77 F6
Trowbridge BA14 . . . . .101 E2
Connaught Rd SP9 . . . .216 D6
Conrad Cl SN3 . . . . .51 D4
Consciences La SN10 . .214 A7
Constable Rd SN2 . . . . . .35 E2
Constable Way SP2 . . . .151 E7
Constantine Sq 20 SP10 .193 E2
Convent The* BA12 . . . .123 B2
Conway Cres SN12 . . . . .94 B2
Conway Rd
Chippenham SN14 . . . . . .78 A7
Swindon SN3 . . . . .51 C3
Conyers Cl 5 SN5 . . . . .48 F4
Cookham Rd SN25 . . . . .34 C7
Cooks Cl
Hullavington SN14 . . . . . .56 D6
Salisbury SP2 . . . . .145 B5
Seend SN12 . . . . .178 E8
Cooks La SO51 . . . . . . .162 F7
Coombe Barn La
BA12 . . . . .124 D5
Coombe Bissett CE Prim Sch
SP5 . . . . .150 F1
Coombe Cl SN4 . . . . . . .64 C5
Coombe La
Atworth SN12 . . . . .92 C7
Enford SN9 . . . . .190 C6
Coombe Rd
Salisbury SP2 . . . . .151 F5
Swindon SN25 . . . . .34 F3
Coombe St BA9 . . . . . . .137 D3
Coombe View SN4 . . . . .194 D3
Cooper Fields SN25 . . . .35 A5
Coopers Cl
Amesbury SP4 . . . . .217 B4
7 Malmesbury SN16 . . .28 A5
Coopers Ct SN9 . . . . . .215 B5
Cop Croft SN11 . . . . . . .81 B3
Copheap La BA12 . . . . .117 B7
Copheap Rise BA12 . . . .117 B7
Copper Beeches SN6 . . .22 F5
Coppice Cl Swindon SN2 .34 D3
Warminster BA12 . . . . .117 A7
Coppice La BA15 . . . . . .100 D7
Coppice St SN16 . . . . . . .15 E8
Coppice St SP7 . . . . . . .202 C5
Copse Ave SN1 . . . . .50 E8
Copse Dro SN8 . . . . . . .169 B5
Copse The
Alderbury SP5 . . . . .153 D2
Frome BA11 . . . . .110 B6
Copyhold 2 SN8 . . . . . .176 B3
Corbin Rd BA14 . . . . . .101 F1
Corby Ave SN3 . . . . .50 E3
Corfe Cl SN25 . . . . .35 A4
Corfe La BA14 . . . . .81 A4
Corfe Rd Melksham SN12 .94 B3
Swindon SN5 . . . . .49 B4
Coriander Way SN4 . . . .34 D5
Corinthian Cl 14 SP10 . .193 E2
Corn Gastons SN16 . . . .27 E3
Cornbrash Rise BA14 . . .102 A1
Corner Gd BA12 . . . . . .117 E5
Corner La SP7 . . . . .202 B5
Cornfield Rd SN10 . . . . .214 D3
Cornflower Cl SN11 . . . . .81 C5
Cornflower Rd SN25 . . . .34 C5
Cornflower Way
8 Ludgershall SP11 . . .192 A5
Melksham SN12 . . . . . . .94 B3
Cornmarket BA12 . . . . .117 B7
Cornmarsh Way SN3 . . .51 E2
Cornpits La SP6 . . . . . .209 E2
Cornwall Ave SN2 . . . . . .35 A1
Cornwall Cres SN12 . . . .94 C4
Cornwall Rd SP1 . . . . . .146 A3
Cornwell Cres SN10 . . . .214 A2

Coronation Cl
Christian Malford SN15 . . .58 A1
Donhead St Mary SP7 . . .203 A1
2 Pewsey SN9 . . . . . . .215 C5
Sutton Benger SN15 . . . . .57 F1
Coronation Dr SP7 . . . .203 A1
Coronation Rd
Atworth/Whitley SN12 . . .92 E8
Durrington/Bulford SP4 . .198 B7
Frome BA11 . . . . .110 B5
3 Ludgershall SP11 . . .192 A5
Melksham SN12 . . . . . . .94 B3
Salisbury SP2 . . . . .145 D3
Tidworth SP9 . . . . .216 C8
Wroughton SN4 . . . . .64 A6
Coronation Sq SN2 . . . .144 F3
Coronation St
Fairford GL7 . . . . .1 F7
4 Trowbridge BA14 . . .105 D7
Corporation St SN1 . . . . .50 C7
Corral Cl SN5 . . . . .34 A1
Corry The 1 SP3 . . . . .203 E8
Corsham Ct* SN13 . . . . .77 A2
Corsham Media Pk
SN13 . . . . .84 C6
Corsham Pk* SN13 . . . . .77 B2
Corsham Prim Sch
SN13 . . . . .77 B1
Corsham Rd
Atworth/Whitley SN12 . . .85 D1
Lacock SN13 . . . . .85 F8
Swindon SN2 . . . . .35 C5
Corsham Regis Prim Sch
SN13 . . . . .76 F2
Corsham Sch The SN13 .76 F1
Corsham Sports Club
SN13 . . . . .77 A1
Corsley CE Prim Sch
BA12 . . . . .111 D2
Corton (Long Barrow)*
BA12 . . . . .194 D3
Corton Cres SN5 . . . . . . .49 B6
Cory Way BA13 . . . . . . .108 E7
Coster View 5 SN8 . . . .176 B3
Coster's La SP5 . . . . . . .205 A2
Cote La BA12 . . . . .123 E4
Cotley Pl 4 BA12 . . . . .194 C5
Cotswold Cl Calne SN11 .81 D2
Melksham SN12 . . . . . . .94 C4
Cotswold Dr SN3 . . . . . .51 B6
Cotswold Wr Pk* SN6 . . .6 F7
Cotswold Wr Pk Gateway
Ctr* GL7 . . . . .7 E6
Cottage Mews 18 SP6 . .210 F1
Cottars Cl 3 SN3 . . . . . .36 B3
Cottington Cl SN4 . . . . . .64 B7
Cottle Mead SN13 . . . . . .84 E8
Cottles La BA15 . . . . . . .99 F6
Cotton House Gdns
BA12 . . . . .117 B7
Cottrell Cl RG17 . . . . . .177 C7
Couch La SN10 . . . . . . .214 A4
Coulston Hollow BA13 .186 F8
Coulston Rd SN13 . . . . . .77 A3
Council Houses The
SN15 . . . . .44 A4
Countess Rd SP4 . . . . .217 A4
County Bsns Pk SN1 . . . .50 F8
County Rd SN1 . . . . .50 D7
County Way BA14 . . . . .101 E1
Court Farm Cl 8 SP4 . .190 A4
Court Farm Cl 1 SN4 . .190 A3
Court Gdns Bath BA1 . . .82 A3
Stanton St Quintin SN14 . .56 B4
Court Hill
Damerham SP6 . . . . . . .209 F2
Potterne SN10 . . . . .179 C5
Court La Bathford BA1 . . .82 B1
Bratton BA13 . . . . .186 B7
Corsley BA12 . . . . .111 B1
Edington BA13 . . . . .186 D8
Court St Sherston SN16 . .25 C1
Tisbury SP3 . . . . .203 E8
Trowbridge BA14 . . . . .105 D8
Court St Cl SP3 . . . . . . .203 E8
Courtenay Rd SN3 . . . . .51 A6
Courts Gdns The*
BA14 . . . . .101 E8
Courtsknap Ct 7 SN1 . . .50 A5
Courtwood Cl 3 SP1 . . .152 C8
Coventry Cl SN4 . . . . . . .64 B7
Covingham Dr SN3 . . . . .51 C1
Covingham Pk Jun & Inf Sch
SN3 . . . . .51 C1
Covingham Sq SN3 . . . . .51 C1
Cow Dro SP5 . . . . .201 B4
Cow La Kimpton SP11 . . .192 B2
Laverstock SP1 . . . . . . .146 C1
Cow St SN5 . . . . .19 B1
Cowbridge Cres SN4 . . .28 C1
Cowdrey Cl SN5 . . . . . . .49 B4
Cowleaze Cres SN4 . . . . .63 F6
Cowleaze La BA13 . . . . .186 D8
Cowleaze Wlk SN2 . . . . .35 E4
Cowley Way SN15 . . . . . .57 D1
Cowley Wlk SN3 . . . . . . .51 B6
Cowslip Gr SN11 . . . . . . .81 B5
Cowslip Way SN4 . . . . . .70 B3
Cox's Hill
Ashton Keynes SN6 . . . . . .6 E2
Calne SN11 . . . . .81 B2
Cox's La SN8 . . . . .176 F1
Coxhill La SN10 . . . . . .179 D5
Coxstalls SN4 . . . . .47 D2
Crab La BA12 . . . . .138 A7
Crab Mill La SN5 . . . . . . .28 E1
Crabtree Copse SN5 . . . .34 A2
Crampton Rd SN3 . . . . . .51 A7

Cranborne Chase SN2 . . .34 C4
Cranborne Rd 1 SP7 . . .202 C2
Cranbury Cl SP5 . . . . . .211 A7
Crandon Lea BA14 . . . . .92 F1
Crane Furlong SN6 . . . . .23 A7
Crane St SP1 . . . . .152 A8
Cranebridge Rd SP2 . . .152 A8
Cranesbill Cl SN10 . . . .214 D5
Cranesbill Rd SN10 . . . .214 D5
Cranmore Ave SN3 . . . . .51 A3
Cranmore Ct BA14 . . . .101 A1
Cranwell Cl 8 SN14 . . . .78 A6
Cratchcroft La BA14 . . .178 A6
Crate La SP7 . . . . .202 C7
Craven Rd RG17 . . . . . .177 D3
Crawford Cl SN5 . . . . . . .49 A4
Crawlboys La SP11 . . . .192 B6
Crawley Ave SN2 . . . . . . .36 B1
Crawley Cres BA14 . . . .105 A8
Craybourne Rd SN12 . . .94 C6
Crays The SN12 . . . . . . .94 C6
Crench Comm Airfield
SN8 . . . . .174 E4
Crescent Rd
Durrington/Bulford SP4 . .217 D7
Melksham SN12 . . . . . . .94 C6
Crescent The
Bromham SN15 . . . . .96 C7
Calne SN11 . . . . .89 F8
Chiseldown SN4 . . . . .65 C3
6 Durrington/Bulford
SP4 . . . . .198 F7
Pewsey SN9 . . . . .215 B4
Swindon SN5 . . . . .33 F2
Westbury BA13 . . . . . . .109 A3
Wilton SP2 . . . . .144 B2
Cresswell Dr BA14 . . . .102 B2
Cresswell La SN15 . . . . .44 B8
Crestmount Dr SN3 . . . .145 C3
Creswells SN13 . . . . .84 F8
Cricketts La SN15 . . . . . .78 F5
Cricklade Leisure Ctr
SN6 . . . . .19 C8
Cricklade Mus* SN6 . . . .19 C8
Cricklade Rd
Highworth SN6 . . . . .22 F5
Purton SN5 . . . . .19 B8
Swindon SN25 . . . . .35 D1
Cricklade St SN1 . . . . . . .50 D5
Crieff Cl SN3 . . . . .51 B6
Crispin Cl 6 SN3 . . . . . .36 B3
Crockerton CE Prim Sch
BA12 . . . . .116 D2
Crockford Rd SP5 . . . . .154 B2
Croft Cl SN6 . . . . .8 C4
Croft Hts SP5 . . . . .161 D3
Croft La SN4 . . . . .8 C4
Croft Rd
6 Hungerford RG17 . . .177 B7
Swindon SN1 . . . . .50 C1
Croft Sports Hall SN1 . . .50 D3
Croft The
Bishopstone SP5 . . . . . .205 E5
Broad Hinton SN4 . . . . .167 D7
Milston SP4 . . . . .198 C8
Newton Tony SN4 . . . . .199 B3
Trowbridge BA14 . . . . .105 C6
Urchfont SN10 . . . . .180 A1
Crofton Beam Engines*
SN8 . . . . .176 A1
Crofton Rd SN6 . . . . .176 A1
Crombey St SN1 . . . . . . .50 B5
Cromer Ct SN3 . . . . .51 D3
Cromhall La SN14 . . . . . .69 A7
Crompton Rd SN25 . . . . .35 D6
Cromwell Rd SN13 . . . . .49 B3
Cromwell Rd SN10 . . . .214 D2
Crook Hill SP5 . . . . .204 A1
Crooked Cnr SN8 . . . . . .170 A6
Crookhays SP7 . . . . .202 C2
Crooks La SN10 . . . . . . .180 C4
Crookwood La SN10 . . .179 F4
Crosby Wlk SN3 . . . . . . .51 A3
Crosbys 8 SN8 . . . . . . .183 D8
Croscombe Gdns
BA11 . . . . .110 D6
Cross Hayes La SN16 . . .28 A3
Cross Keys Chequer 5
SP1 . . . . .146 B1
Cross Keys Rd SN13 . . . .77 A3
Cross La SN8 . . . . .213 D3
Cross St Swindon SN1 . . .50 C5
Trowbridge BA14 . . . . .101 D1
Cross The
Bishopstone SP5 . . . . . .205 E4
Mere BA12 . . . . .139 A5
21 Tisbury SP3 . . . . . .203 E8
Cross Tree Cres GL7 . . . .10 C7
Crossing La SN15 . . . . . .71 B3
Crossways SN4 . . . . .46 D6
Crossways Ave SN25 . . .35 C3
Crosswood Rd SN3 . . . . .51 A3
Crouchston Dro SP5 . . .205 A2
Crouchston Hollow
SP5 . . . . .205 A4
Crowdys Hill Specl Sch
SN3 . . . . .35 D2
Crowe Hill BA2 . . . . .99 B6
Crowe La BA2 . . . . .99 B5
Crowle Rd 11 RG17 . . . .165 A1
Crown Cl
Chippenham SN15 . . . . . .79 A5
Salisbury SP1 . . . . .145 D3
Crown Cl 4 SP11 . . . . . .192 A5
Crown Mews 30 RG17 . .177 B7
Crown Way SP10 . . . . . .193 F1
Crowood La SN8 . . . . . .170 B2

Crudwell CE Prim Sch
SN16 . . . . .14 F6
Crudwell La
Crudwell SN16 . . . . .14 B6
Long Newton GL8 . . . . . .13 D6
Crudwell Way SN25 . . . .35 C6
Crusades The 8 SP4 . . .146 C5
Cruse Cl SN14 . . . . .77 F8
Cuckoo La BA11 . . . . . . .110 A8
Cuckoo Pen Cl SN8 . . . .183 D3
Cuckoo's Mead SN3 . . . .51 E6
Cues La SN6 . . . . .163 E7
Cuffs La SP3 . . . . .203 E8
Cullerne Rd SN3 . . . . . . .36 C1
Cullerns The SN6 . . . . . .23 A6
Culver Rd BA15 . . . . . . .100 E5
Culver St 7 SP1 . . . . . .152 B8
Culvermead Cl SN8 . . . .176 A1
Culverwell Rd SN14 . . . .78 A7
Cumberland Rd SN3 . . . .50 E6
Cunetio Rd SN3 . . . . .51 C8
Cunnage La BA12 . . . . .139 F1
Cunningham Rd SN14 . . .78 A6
Curlcroft Rd SN13 . . . . . .84 D7
Curlew Dr SN14 . . . . .70 A2
Curnicks The SN4 . . . . . .65 C4
Cursus The*
Amesbury SP4 . . . . .197 D6
Lechlade GL7 . . . . .2 C5
Curtis Orch SN12 . . . . . .93 B4
Curtis St SN1 . . . . .50 B5
Curzon Cl SN11 . . . . .81 A3
Curzon St SN11 . . . . .81 A3
Cusance Way BA14 . . . .102 A1
Cuthwine Pl GL7 . . . . .2 C5
Cutting Hill RG17 . . . . .177 A2
Cuttle La SN14 . . . . .76 E8
Cuttle Cl SN15 . . . . .46 A7
Cuxhaven Way 10 SP10 .193 E2
Cvnieto Roman Town*
SN8 . . . . .175 B8
Cygnet Dr SN4 . . . . .217 C8
Cygnet Way BA14 . . . . .101 D5
Cygney Way RG17 . . . . .177 B8
Cyppa Ct SN15 . . . . .78 E6
Cypress Gr SN2 . . . . .35 A3
Cypress Way 7 BA11 . . .110 C7
Cypress Wlk SN14 . . . . . .74 F6
Cyprus Terr SN4 . . . . . .214 A4

D

Dacre Cl 13 SP10 . . . . .193 C2
Dacre Rd SN3 . . . . .51 A6
Dairy Mdw La SP1 . . . . .152 D7
Dairy Rd
Barford St Martin SP3 . .143 A4
Chiseldon SN4 . . . . .64 F4
Daisy Cl Melksham SN12 . .94 C3
Swindon SN2 . . . . .34 C3
Dales Cl SN25 . . . . .35 A7
Dales Rd BA13 . . . . .108 E2
Dalewood Rise SP1 . . . .146 E2
Dallas Ave SN13 . . . . . . .51 B7
Dallas Rd SN13 . . . . .78 C8
Dalwood Cl 3 SN3 . . . . .51 A3
Damask Way BA12 . . . .117 A5
Dammas Bsns Ctr SN1 . .50 D4
Dammas La SN1 . . . . . . .50 D4
Damy Gn SN13 . . . . .84 E5
Dando Dr SN8 . . . . .213 B2
Dane Cl BA15 . . . . .99 F2
Dane Rd SN4 . . . . .49 A6
Danegeld Cl 8 SP10 . . . .193 E2
Danes Cl SN15 . . . . .79 A5
Danestone Cl SN5 . . . . . .48 F7
Daniel Cl 9 SN1 . . . . . . .49 F4
Daniel's Well* SN16 . . . .28 A3
Daniell Crest BA12 . . . .116 F6
Danvers Mead SN15 . . . .79 A4
Danvers Rd BA13 . . . . . .109 B4
Darby Cl SN2 . . . . .34 E1
Darcey Cl SN5 . . . . .49 B6
Darcy Cl SN15 . . . . .78 F8
Darius Way SN25 . . . . . .35 A6
Dark La Berkley BA11 . . .110 E8
Castle Combe SN14 . . . . .68 B7
Grafton SN8 . . . . .175 F1
Kintbury RG17 . . . . .177 D8
Limpley Stoke BA2 . . . . . .99 B5
Malmesbury SN16 . . . . . .27 F3
Mere BA12 . . . . .139 A5
Dark La 4 SN8 . . . . . . .183 D8
Dark La B SN4 . . . . .178 A3
Darnley Cl SN3 . . . . .50 F3
Darrell Rd SP4 . . . . .217 C4
Dart Ave SN25 . . . . .34 F5
Dartmoor 7 SN1 . . . . . . .49 F4
Dartmoor Rd 2 BA13 . . .108 E1
Darwin Cl
4 Durrington/Bulford
SP4 . . . . .198 F6
Swindon SN3 . . . . .51 B7
Dasna Rd SP9 . . . . .216 B5
Daunch Cl SP9 . . . . .216 B7
Dauntsey La SP11 . . . . .192 E1
Dauntsey Pk* SN15 . . . . .44 C2
Dauntsey Rd SN15 . . . . .44 C2
Dauntseys Aided Prim Sch
SN10 . . . . .187 D8
Dauntseys Sch
Market Lavington SN10 . .179 E1
West Lavington SN10 . . .187 D8

Dave Watkins Ct SN2 . . .35 F3
Davenham Cl SN3 . . . . . .51 A3
Davenwood SN2 . . . . . . .35 F4
David Stoddart Gdns
SN2 . . . . .35 B1
David's Gdn SP5 . . . . . .148 C3
Davies Cl SN14 . . . . . . .213 A2
Davies Dr SN10 . . . . . . .214 E6
Davis Pl SN1 . . . . .50 B6
Daw Rd 11 SN10 . . . . . .179 F1
Dawbeney Dr SP4 . . . . .217 D3
Dawlish Rd SN3 . . . . .51 B5
Dawneys The SN16 . . . . .14 E6
Day Ho La SN3 . . . . .51 C2
Day St SN3 . . . . .36 A1
Day's La SN15 . . . . .56 D2
Days Ct SN16 . . . . .14 E6
De Havilland Pl 4 SN12 .178 A8
De Montfort Gr 8 RG17 .177 B6
De Vaux Pl SP1 . . . . . . .152 A7
Deacon Rd SP11 . . . . . .192 B2
Deacon St SN1 . . . . .50 B5
Dean Cl Frome BA11 . . . .110 C6
Melksham SN12 . . . . . . .94 C6
Dean La Fovant SP3 . . . .204 D7
Sixpenny Handley SP5 . .207 F6
Whiteparish SP5 . . . . . .161 D4
Dean La Dro SP5 . . . . . .207 F4
Dean Rd SP5 . . . . .155 B3
Dean St SN1 . . . . .49 F5
Dean Sta SP5 . . . . .155 F3
Deans Cl SN9 . . . . .216 D4
Deansfield SN6 . . . . .19 D7
Deansway SN5 . . . . .70 D2
Deben Cres SN25 . . . . . .34 F5
Deburgh St SN2 . . . . .49 F6
Deep La BA12 . . . . .111 D2
Deer Pk* SN8 . . . . .175 E2
Deerhurst Way 1 SN5 . . .49 D4
Delamere Dr SN3 . . . . . . .36 A4
Delamere Rd BA14 . . . .101 D2
Dell The SP11 . . . . .185 B3
Delta Bsns Pk SN5 . . . . .49 D6
Delta Office Pk SN5 . . . . .49 B5
Denbeck Wood SN5 . . . . .49 B6
Denbigh Cl SN3 . . . . .50 E3
Dene The Hindon SP3 . .200 B3
Warminster BA12 . . . . .117 E6
Deneb Dr SN25 . . . . .34 B7
Denes Ave BA12 . . . . . .139 A6
Denford La RG17 . . . . . .177 D8
Denholme Rd SN3 . . . . . .51 A3
Denison Rise SN1 . . . . .146 C3
Dennis La SP7 . . . . .203 B1
Derby Cl
Chippenham SN15 . . . . . .78 F5
Lambourn RG17 . . . . . .165 A1
Derby Ct SN3 . . . . .50 E6
Derriads Gn SN14 . . . . . .78 A7
Derriads La 3 SN14 . . . .77 F6
Derriads CE Prim Sch
SN11 . . . . .80 A2
Derry Pk SN16 . . . . .17 C2
Derry The SN8 . . . . .17 F8
Derwent Dr SN2 . . . . . . .35 F4
Desboroughs SN5 . . . . . .49 A3
Deva Cl SN3 . . . . .51 C2
Devenish Nature Reserve*
SN2 . . . . .131 D2
Deverell Cl BA15 . . . . . .100 E4
Devereux Cl 8 SN15 . . . .48 F5
Devereux Rd SP4 . . . . . .217 B3
Deverill Rd
Sutton Veny BA12 . . . . .117 C1
Warminster BA12 . . . . .116 F4
Devils Bed & Bolster The*
BA11 . . . . .107 A8
Devizes Castle* SN10 . .214 A3
Devizes Com Hospl
SN10 . . . . .214 B4
Devizes Leisure Ctr
SN10 . . . . .214 B3
Devizes Rd Box SN13 . . .83 E4
Bromham SN15 . . . . .88 B4
Caline Without SN11 . . . .87 F2
Charlton SN9 . . . . .181 D2
Derry Hill/Studley SN11 . .79 F1
Hilperton BA14 . . . . . . .102 C3
Potterne SN10 . . . . .179 D6
Poulshot SN10 . . . . .179 B7
Rowde SN10 . . . . .96 F2
Salisbury SP2 . . . . .145 E2
Swindon SN1 . . . . .50 D4
Trowbridge BA14 . . . . .102 E2
Wroughton SN4 . . . . .64 B6
Devizes Sch SN10 . . . . .214 C3
Devizes Sports Club
SN10 . . . . .214 C4
Devizes White Horse*
SN10 . . . . .97 F5
Devon Cl 5 SN14 . . . . . . .77 F8
Devon Dr BA13 . . . . .109 A5
Devon Rd SN2 . . . . .35 B1
Upavon Down SN9 . . . . .182 B2
Devonshire Pl SN12 . . . .94 C5
Devonshire Rd SP1 . . . .146 A3
Dewell Mews SN1 . . . . . .50 D3
Dewey La SN4 . . . . .65 C4
Deweys La SP11 . . . . . .192 A5
Dexter Cl SN5 . . . . .49 B7
Dial Cl SN12 . . . . .178 E8
Dianmer Cl SN4 . . . . .47 F5
Dickens Ave SN13 . . . . . .76 F2

Dickens Cl SN3 . . . . .51 D3
Dickenson Rd SN25 . . . . .34 C5
Dicketts Rd SN13 . . . . .85 A7
Dickson Rd SN15 . . . . .60 A1
Dickson Way 2 SN15 . . .78 F5
Diddledown Rd 8 SP4 . .217 C2
Dilton Cl BA13 . . . . .112 B6
Dilton Marsh CE Prim Sch
BA13 . . . . .112 B8
Dilton Marsh Sta
BA13 . . . . .108 C1
Dinah's Hollow SP7 . . . .206 B7
Dingle The 3 SN4 . . . . .163 A6
Dinmore Rd SN25 . . . . . . .34 F6
Dinton CE Fst Sch
SP3 . . . . .201 F2
Dinton Rd Fovant SP3 . .204 E8
Wylye BA12 . . . . .201 E8
Dione Cres SN25 . . . . .34 B7
Discover Salisbury (Medieval
Hall)* SP1 . . . . .152 A8
Distillery Mdws Nature
Reserve* SN16 . . . . .31 B7
Divinity Cl 2 SN4 . . . . . .163 B6
Dixon St SN1 . . . . .50 B5
Dixon Way SN11 . . . . .81 B4
Dobbin Cl SN3 . . . . .51 E7
Dobson Cl SN25 . . . . .35 A8
Dockle Way SN2 . . . . .35 F4
Doctors Hill SN13 . . . . . . .83 B5
Doctors Pl 8 SP3 . . . . . .203 E8
Dodford La SN15 . . . . .58 D6
Dodgson Cl SP6 . . . . .211 A4
Dog Kennel La BA13 . . .109 A1
Dog La SP7 . . . . .203 E1
Dog Trap La SN16 . . . . . . .16 E1
Doggetts La BA13 . . . . . .109 A4
Dogridge SN5 . . . . .33 A3
Dolphin Ind Est SP1 . . .152 D7
Dolphin St SP1 . . . . .152 B8
Don Cl SN25 . . . . .35 A4
Donaldson Rd SP1 . . . . .146 A2
Doncaster Cl SN14 . . . . . . .77 F5
Doncombe Hill SN14 . . . .74 E7
Doncombe La SN14 . . . . . .75 A6
Donhead Hollow SP7 . . .206 E8
Donnington Gr SN3 . . . . .50 F4
Dorcan Bsns Village
SN3 .51 E6
Dorcan Ind Est SN3 . . . . .51 E5
Dorcan Tech Coll SN3 . . .51 D6
Dorcan Way SN3 . . . . .51 A8
Dorchester Rd SN3 . . . . . .50 F3
Dores Cl SN2 . . . . .35 E3
Dores Rd SN3 . . . . .35 D3
Doris Archer Ct SN2 . . . . .35 B2
Dormers The SN6 . . . . .23 A6
Dorney Cl BA13 . . . . .108 F1
Dorney Rd SN25 . . . . .34 C8
Dorset Cl SP4 . . . . .217 E8
Dorset Cres SN11 . . . . . . .94 C3
Dorset Dr BA13 . . . . .109 A5
Dorset Gn SN4 . . . . .34 F2
Dorset Rd SP1 . . . . .146 B3
Double Hedges SP4 . . . .217 E7
Douglas Dr SN6 . . . . .19 D8
Doughty's La BA12 . . . . .195 A2
Douglas Brown's Wlk 6
SP4 . . . . .197 E6
Douglas Haig Rd SP1 . .146 A3
Douglas Rd 5 SN2 . . . . . .50 F6
Doulting Cl SN11 . . . . . . .110 D7
Dovecote Cl 3 BA14 . . .105 B8
Dovecote Dr SN13 . . . . . .76 F2
Dover St
Chippenham SN14 . . . . . .78 C7
Swindon SN1 . . . . .50 C5
Dovers La BA1 . . . . .82 C2
Dovers Pk BA1 . . . . .82 C2
Dovers Cl SN5 . . . . .161 C3
Dovetrees SN3 . . . . .51 D7
Doveys Terr SN15 . . . . . . .70 E7
Dowding Ave SN13 . . . . . .84 B8
Dowding Dr 5 SN11 . . .166 A1
Dowding Way SN12 . . . . .94 C1
Dowding St SN1 . . . . .50 C5
Downland Rd
Calne SN11 . . . . .81 A2
Swindon SN2 . . . . .34 D4
Downland Sch SN10 . . .214 B1
Downland Way 12 SP4 . .198 B3
Downlands 1 RG17 . . . .171 E7
Downlands Cl SP1 . . . . .211 A7
Downlands The 2 BA14 .117 B7
Downleaze 7 SP4 . . . . . .198 B2
Downs Cl
Bradford-on-Avon BA15 . .100 B7
Devizes SN10 . . . . .214 A3
Lambourn RG17 . . . . . . .171 C8
Downs La SN8 . . . . .185 B8

Downs Rd SN4 . . . . .65 E4
Downs The SN8 . . . . .170 A5
Downs View
Bradford-on-Avon BA15 . .100 B7
Highworth SN6 . . . . .23 A6
Warminster BA12 . . . . . .117 C6
Wootton Bassett SN4 . . . . .47 D1
Downs View Rd SN3 . . . . .50 F2
Downside Cl BA12 . . . . . .139 A6
Downside Pk BA14 . . . . .101 E2
Downslands Rd SN10 . .214 B1
Downsmead SN8 . . . . . . .164 B1
Downsview BA13 . . . . . . .186 C7
Downsview Rd BA13 . . .109 A4
Downsview Way SP11 . .191 F3
Downsway SP1 . . . . .146 B4
Downton Bus Ctr SP5 . .211 A8
Downton CE Prim Sch
SP5 . . . . .211 A8
Downton Hill SP5 . . . . . .211 C8
Downton L Ctr SP5 . . . . .210 F8
Downton Meml Gdns*
SP5 . . . . .211 A8
Downton Rd
Salisbury SP2 . . . . .152 B5
Swindon SN2 . . . . .35 B5
Downton Sch SP5 . . . . . .211 A8
Downview Rd SP6 . . . . . .209 B6
Downwood Cl 7 SP6 . .210 C7
Doyle Cl SN15 . . . . .34 C5
Dr Behr Ct SN2 . . . . .35 B2
Dragon La SN9 . . . . .181 F6
Drain Hill RG17 . . . . .165 A2
Drake Cl SP1 . . . . .146 C5
Drake Cres SN14 . . . . .77 F6
Drake St SN1 . . . . .193 F1
Drake's Way SN3 . . . . .50 E6
Drakes Ave SN10 . . . . . . .214 C2
Drakes Mdw Bsns Pk
SN3 .50 E7
Drakes Way Bsns Ctr
SN3 .51 A7
Draycot Fitz Payne*
SN9 . . . . .179 E1
Draycott Rd SN4 . . . . .65 C3
Draycott Cl SN3 . . . . .51 A7
Drew St SN2 . . . . .49 E7
Drew's Pond La SN10 . .214 B1
Drewitts La SN10 . . . . . .180 E8
Drifton Hill SN14 . . . . .66 E7
Drive The
Melchet Park & Plaitford
SO51 . . . . .162 C1
Swindon SN3 . . . . .51 B7
Drove Cl SP5 . . . . .150 F2
Drove La
Coombe Bissett SP5 . . . .150 F3
Market Lavington SN10 . .179 F1
Steeple Ashton BA14 . . .178 A2
Drove Prim Sch SN1 . . . . .50 D5
Drove Rd SN1 . . . . .50 D5
Drove The
Amesbury SP4 . . . . .217 B4
Hawkeridge BA13 . . . . . .108 D7
Droves The SP5 . . . . .207 E4
Druley Hill BA10 . . . . . . .123 B7
Drury Cl SN5 . . . . .47 F6
Drury La SN5 . . . . .175 D4
Dry Hill BA12 . . . . .116 E2
Dryden Cl SP2 . . . . .152 B5
Dryden St SN1 . . . . .50 B5
Drynham La BA14 . . . . . .105 D5
Drynham Pk BA14 . . . . . .105 D6
Duchess Way SN2 . . . . . . .35 D5
Duck La
Barford St Martin SP3 . . .143 B3
Laverstock SP1 . . . . .152 E8
Salisbury SP1 . . . . .146 D2
Duck Pool La BA14 . . . . .107 B6
Duck St
Berwick St James SP3 . . .196 F2
Ebbesborne Wake SP5 . .204 C3
Potterne SN10 . . . . .179 D5
Steeple Langford SP3 . . .128 D7
Sutton Veny BA12 . . . . . .194 A4
Tisbury SP3 . . . . .203 E8
West Lavington SN10 . . .187 E8
Duck's Nest (Long Barrow)*
SP6 . . . . .209 F7
Ducks Meadow SN8 . . . .213 D2
Dudley Ave SP6 . . . . .210 D2
Dudley Rd SN3 . . . . .50 F6
Dudmore Rd SN3 . . . . .50 D6
Duke St SN11 . . . . .101 D1
Duke's La BA12 . . . . .118 A1
Duke's Way SP4 . . . . .217 E8
Dukes Cl SN2 . . . . .35 E5
Dulverton Ave SN3 . . . . . .51 A5
Dumbarton Terr 2 SN1 . .50 C5
Dummer La SN11 . . . . . . .184 E1
Dummer Way SN15 . . . . . .79 A5
Dunbar Rd SN4 . . . . .64 A7
Dunbeath Ct SN4 . . . . . . .64 A7
Dunbeath Rd SN4 . . . . . . .35 E1
Duncan St SN11 . . . . .81 B5
Duncan's Cl SP11 . . . . . .192 D1
Dunch La SN12 . . . . .93 F7
Dundas Aqueduct*
. . . . .90 B2
Dundas Cl SN10 . . . . .179 C8
Dunford Cl BA14 . . . . . . .105 D6
Dunhills La SP11 . . . . . . .193 F4
Dunkirk Hill
Devizes SN10 . . . . .179 D8
Rowde SN10 . . . . .97 A1
Dunley Cl SN25 . . . . .34 D7
Dunley Way SN14 . . . . . . .78 A1
Dunn's La SP8 . . . . .138 A1

Dunnet Cl SN11 . . . . .81 B4
Dunnington Rd SN4 . . . . .61 D8
Dunns La SN14 . . . . .68 B8
Dunraven Cl SN3 . . . . .59 F4
Dunsford Cl SN1 . . . . .49 F4
Dunspit La DT11 . . . . . . .207 B1
Dunstable Cnr SP5 . . . . .148 E7
Dunstan's Dro SP5 . . . . .185 E1
Dunster Cl SN3 . . . . .50 E3
Dunvant Rd SN25 . . . . . . .34 C7
Dunwich Dr SN5 . . . . .34 A4
Dunworth Rise 6 SP3 . .203 E8
Durham St SN1 . . . . .50 C5
Durlett Rd SN10 . . . . .95 F2
Durley Pk SN13 . . . . .84 D6
Durnford Rd SN2 . . . . .35 C1
Durrington All Saints CE Inf
SP4 . . . . .198 C7
Durrington CE Jun Sch
SP4 . . . . .198 B6
Durrington Swimming &
Fitness Ctr SP4 . . . . . . .198 C7
Durrington Walls*
SP4 . . . . .217 A8
Durrington Wlk SN2 . . . . .35 C5
Dursden La SN9 . . . . .215 E6
Dursley Rd
Heywood BA13 . . . . .108 F8
North Bradley BA13 . . . .105 E1
Dutts BA13 . . . . .108 B1
Duxford CE I SN12 . . . .178 B8
Dyehouse La SN10 . . . . .214 A4
Dyer La BA12 . . . . .201 E8
Dyer's Cl SN15 . . . . .79 A6
Dyke Mews SN4 . . . . .65 D4
Dymocks La BA12 . . . . . .121 F8
Dymott Sq BA14 . . . . . . .102 A3

E

Eagle Cl SN3 . . . . .51 E7
Eagle Field SP2 . . . . .145 D4
Earl Cl SN5 . . . . .48 F7
Earl's Rise SP4 . . . . .133 A1
Earls Cl SN16 . . . . .15 E8
Earls Ct Rd SN4 . . . . .217 B3
Earlsputs La SP5 . . . . . . .208 E4
East Dunley Cotts SN14 . .40 E1
East End BA12 . . . . .117 B6
East End Ave BA12 . . . . .117 B6
East End La SN15 . . . . . . .44 D5
East Gomeldon Rd
SP4 . . . . .133 E4
East Kennett (Long
Barrow)* SN8 . . . . .173 D5
East La SN12 . . . . .93 B3
East Portway SP10 . . . . . .193 C1
East Sands SN8 . . . . .183 D8
East St Bourton SP8 . . . .137 E1
Hindon SP3 . . . . .200 A4
Lacock SN15 . . . . .86 D6
Salisbury SP2 . . . . .145 F1
10 Swindon SN1 . . . . . . .50 B6
Warminster BA12 . . . . . .117 B6
East Town Rd BA14 . . . .106 D3
East Woodlands Rd
BA11 . . . . .114 A7
East Yewstock Cres
SN15 . . . . .70 C1
Eastbourne Gdns
BA14 . . . . .101 E1
Eastbourne Rd SN14 . . .101 E1
Eastbury Shute RG17 . .171 C5
Eastbury Way SN25 . . . . .34 E7
Eastcott Comm SN10 . .180 A2
Eastcott Hill 5 SN1 . . . .50 C5
Eastcott Rd SN1 . . . . .50 C5
Eastcourt SN8 . . . . .183 D8
Eastcourt Rd SN8 . . . . . .183 D8
Eastern Ave
Chippenham SN15 . . . . . .78 F8
Swindon SN3 . . . . .50 E6
Easterton La SN9 . . . . . .215 D4
Eastfield
Ashton Keynes SN6 . . . . . .6 F1
2 Littleton Panell SN10 .187 E8
Easthill BA11 . . . . .118 A4
Eastleaze Rd SN5 . . . . . . .49 C6
Eastleigh Cl 4 BA11 . . .110 A7
Eastleigh Rd SN3 . . . . .51 A5
Eastman Cl SP5 . . . . .211 B7
Eastmere SN3 . . . . .51 E3
Easton Comm Hill
SP5 . . . . .149 E6
Easton Hollow SP5 . . . . .207 B7
Easton La SN14 . . . . .77 F3
Easton Royal Prim Sch
SP5 . . . . .183 A7
Easton Sq SN16 . . . . .25 D1
Easton Town SN16 . . . . . .25 D1
Eastover Cl SN11 . . . . .81 A3
Eastrop SN6 . . . . .23 B5
Eastrop Inf Sch SN6 . . . . .23 A5
Eastview Rd BA14 . . . . . .105 A7
Eastville Rd SN25 . . . . . . .35 C3
Eastwell Rd SN10 . . . . . .179 D5
Eastwood SO51 . . . . .162 E1
Eastwood Ave SN4 . . . . . .47 E1
Eaton Cl 13 SP1 . . . . .51 A4
Eaton Wood SN5 . . . . .34 A2
Ebbesborne Hollow
SP5 . . . . .204 D2
Ebble Cl SP6 . . . . .210 B1
Ebble Cres BA12 . . . . . . .117 A5
Ebor Cl SN25 . . . . .34 F7
Ebor Gdns SN11 . . . . .89 C8

Ebor Paddock SN11 . . . . .89 C8
Eccleston Cl SN3 . . . . .51 B3
Echo Lodge Mdws Nature
Reserve* SN15 . . . . .46 E7
Ecklington SN3 . . . . .51 C5
Edale Moor SN3 . . . . .51 E3
Eddington Hill RG17 . . .177 C8
Edelweiss Cl 20 SP11 . .192 A5
Eden Gr SN12 . . . . .85 D1
Eden Pk Cl BA1 . . . . .82 A4
Eden Pk Dr BA1 . . . . .82 A4
Eden Vale Rd BA13 . . . . .108 F3
Edencroft SN6 . . . . .23 B8
Edgam Pl SP2 . . . . .144 F3
Edgar Cl 6 SP10 . . . . . . .193 E2
Edgar Row Cl 1 SN4 . . . .64 A6
Edgecorner La SN14 . . . . .53 A3
Edgehill SN5 . . . . .49 B3
Edgeware Rd SN1 . . . . . . .50 C6
Edgeworth Rd 4 SN5 . . .49 B7
Edinburgh Rd SN11 . . . . .81 F1
Edinburgh St SN2 . . . . . . .35 D1
Edinburgh Way SN13 . . .84 A7
Edington Cl SN5 . . . . .49 B5
Edington Priory*
BA13 . . . . .186 C8
Edington Rd BA14 . . . . . .178 A3
Edison Bsns Pk SN3 . . . .51 D5
Edison Rd
Salisbury SP2 . . . . .151 E8
Swindon SN3 . . . . .51 D5
Edmund St SN1 . . . . .50 C5
Edric's Gn SP4 . . . . .199 C5
Edrich Sq SP10 . . . . .193 E1
Edridge Cl SN15 . . . . .78 F5
Edridge Pl 4 SN13 . . . . . .76 E1
Edward Rd SN10 . . . . . . .214 B2
Edward Richardson & Phyllis
Amey Nature Reserve*
GL6 .2 C6
Edward St BA13 . . . . .109 A3
Edwards Hill 12 RG17 . .165 A1
Edwards Meadow
SN8 . . . . .213 B3
Edwards Rd SP4 . . . . .217 B3
Egerton Cl SN3 . . . . .51 B7
Eider Ave SN15 . . . . .60 A1
Elbe Way SN10 . . . . .193 D2
Elborough Rd SN2 . . . . . .34 D4
Elcombe Ave 4 SN4 . . . .64 A6
Elcombe Cl BA14 . . . . . . .105 C5
Elcombe Gdns SN10 . . .214 A4
Elcombe La SP5 . . . . .204 B2
Elcot Cl SN8 . . . . .213 F3
Elcot La SN8 . . . . .213 F3
Elcot Orch SN8 . . . . .175 A8
Elden Rd SP9 . . . . .191 D5
Eldene Dr SN3 . . . . .51 C4
Eldene Prim Sch SN3 . . . .51 D4
Elder Cl SN2 . . . . .34 C3
Eldrene Ct SN3 . . . . .51 C4
Eleanor Cl 16 SP1 . . . . .192 A5
Elgar Cl SN25 . . . . .34 E7
Elgin Dr SN2 . . . . .35 E1
Eliot Cl SN3 . . . . .51 D3
Elizabeth Cl
3 Downton SP5 . . . . . . .210 F8
Melksham Without SN12 . .93 F1
Elizabeth Gdns GL7 . . . . .1 A5
Elizabeth Pl 5 SN1 . . . . . .79 A4
Elizabeth Rd
16 Durrington/Bulford
SP4 . . . . .198 B7
Wilton SP2 . . . . .144 B5
Elizabeth Sq 2 SP4 . . . .216 E7
Elley Gn SN13 . . . . .84 E6
Ellingdon Rd SN4 . . . . . . .63 F7
Elliott Cl SN10 . . . . .214 B1
Elliott Gn SP4 . . . . .133 C3
Elliott Pl BA14 . . . . .101 A1
Elm Cl Bower Hill SN12 . .94 C1
Calne SN11 . . . . .89 C8
6 Ludgershall SP11 . . . .192 B5
Lyneham SN15 . . . . .60 B2
Motcombe SP7 . . . . .202 A5
Pitton & Farley SP5 . . . .148 C4
Rowde SN10 . . . . .96 D1
Salisbury SP1 . . . . .146 D3
Trowbridge BA14 . . . . . .105 C3
Wootton Bassett SN4 . . . . .47 E4
Elm Ct SN10 . . . . .214 B1
Elm Gr Corsham SN13 . . .76 E1
Swindon SN2 . . . . .35 A2
Salisbury SP1 . . . . .146 D3
Swindon SN2 . . . . .49 A8
Elm Gr Pl SP1 . . . . .146 D3
Elm Gr Rd SP1 . . . . .146 D3
Elm Hayes SN13 . . . . .85 A7
Elm Hill BA12 . . . . .113 C1
Elm Leigh BA11 . . . . .110 C6
Elm Pk SN4 . . . . .47 D1
Elm Rd Colerne SN14 . . . .75 A6
Swindon SN2 . . . . .35 A2
Elm Tree Cl SN10 . . . . . .214 D2
Elm Tree Gdns SN10 . . .214 D2
Elm View GL7 . . . . .5 F4
Elmdale Cl BA14 . . . . . . .105 A7
Elmdale Rd BA14 . . . . . .105 A7
Elmer Cl SN16 . . . . .28 A5
Elmfield BA13 . . . . .100 C7
Elmfield Cl 7 SP5 . . . . . .211 C7
Elmina Rd SN1 . . . . .50 C7
Elmore SN3 . . . . .51 A4
Elms Cl SN5 . . . . .210 B1
Elms Cross Dr SN13 . . . .85 A6
Elms The
Bradford-on-Avon BA15 . .100 B8
Highworth SN6 . . . . .22 F5

Elms The continued
Holt BA14 . . . . .92 E1
Swindon SN1 . . . . .48 F8
Elmswood Cl SN2 . . . . . . .35 E5
Elmwood SN5 . . . . .70 E2
Elmwood Ave 6 SP6 . . .210 C1
Elsham Way SN25 . . . . . . .35 A5
Elston La SP3 . . . . .196 F2
Elstree Way
Haydon Wick SN25 . . . . . .34 F6
Swindon SN3 . . . . .35 A7
Ely Cl SN5 . . . . .49 C4
Embankment SN1 . . . . . . .50 D3
Embry Cl 3 SN11 . . . . . .166 A1
Emden Rd 18 SP10 . . . .193 D2
Emerson Cl SN3 . . . . .51 B3
Emery Gate SN15 . . . . . . .78 E7
Emery La SN15 . . . . .78 E7
Emlyn Sq SN1 . . . . .50 B6
Emmanuel Cl SN25 . . . . .35 A4
Emmaus Sch BA14 . . . . .101 D5
Emmett Hill Mdws Nature
Reserve* SN16 . . . . .31 B7
Emms La 10 BA13 . . . . .186 B7
Empire Rd SP2 . . . . .145 C2
Empress Way SP11 . . . . .192 A5
Emwell St BA12 . . . . .117 A7
Endless St SP1 . . . . .146 A1
Enford Ave SN2 . . . . .35 C6
Enford Hill SN9 . . . . .189 F6
Engineer Rd BA13 . . . . . .108 C6
Englefield SN4 . . . . .47 E1
Enham La SP10 . . . . .193 E3
Eningen View SN11 . . . . .81 B1
Ensor Cl SN25 . . . . .35 A8
Epping Cl BA12 . . . . .117 A8
Epping Dr SN3 . . . . .94 C6
Epsom Cl SN4 . . . . .77 F6
Epsom Rd BA14 . . . . .105 C4
Erin Ct 2 SN1 . . . . .50 A5
Eriskay Gdns SN3 . . . . . .108 F2
Erleigh Dr SN15 . . . . .78 C7
Erlestoke Way SN25 . . . . .35 C6
Ermin Cl SN8 . . . . .170 C8
Ermin St 1 Baydon SN8 .164 C1
Baydon SN8 . . . . .170 C8
Blunsdon St Andrew SN26 . .20 F2
Swindon SN3 . . . . .35 F4
Ernie La SP4 . . . . .81 C4
Ernle Rd SN11 . . . . .81 C4
Erskine Barracks SP2 . .144 F4
Escott Cl 4 SN15 . . . . . . .78 F4
Eshton Wlk SN3 . . . . .51 A3
Esmead SN15 . . . . .78 F8
Espringham Pl SP2 . . . . .144 B4
Essex Pl 8 RG17 . . . . . . .165 A2
Essex Sq SP2 . . . . .151 D4
Essex Wlk SN3 . . . . .50 F6
Estate Yd The SN12 . . . .172 B3
Estcourt Cres SN10 . . . .214 B4
Estcourt Rd SP1 . . . . . . .146 B3
Estcourt St SN10 . . . . . .214 B3
Estcourt Terr SN10 . . . .214 B5
Eston Medieval Village of*
SN14 . . . . .69 D8
Ethelbert Dr 4 SP10 . . .193 C2
Ethelred Pl SN13 . . . . .76 E1
Ethendun 8 BA13 . . . . . .186 B7
Euclid St SN1 . . . . .50 C6
Euro Way SN1 . . . . .48 F3
Europa & Brittania Pk
SN3 .51 A8
Evans Cl SN15 . . . . .70 E1
Eveleigh Rd SN4 . . . . .47 E2
Evelyn St SN1 . . . . .50 D3
Even Swindon Inf Sch
SN2 .49 F7
Even Swindon Jun Sch
SN2 .49 F7
Eveque Ct SP2 . . . . .144 F3
Evergreen Way SP4 . . . .217 C2
Evergreens Cl SN3 . . . . . .36 C7
Everland Rd 18 RG17 . .177 B7
Everland Rd Ind Est
RG17 . . . . .177 C2
Everleigh Barrows*
SN9 . . . . .182 E3
Everleigh Cl BA14 . . . . . .105 D5
Everleigh Rd
Collingbourne Ducis
SN8 . . . . .191 B8
Pewsey SN9 . . . . .215 C3
Swindon SN3 . . . . .35 C5
Eworth Cl SN5 . . . . .48 F5
Exbury Cl 2 SN25 . . . . . .35 C6
Exe Cl SN25 . . . . .35 A4
Exeter Cl SN14 . . . . .77 F6
Exeter House Specl Sch
SP1 . . . . .146 B2
Exeter St Salisbury SP1 .152 B7
Swindon SN1 . . . . .50 B4
Exmoor Cl 1 BA14 . . . . .105 D5
Exmoor Rd 6 BA13 . . . .108 E1
Exmouth St SN1 . . . . .50 A5
Eyles Rd SN10 . . . . .214 B1
Eyres Dr SP5 . . . . .153 E2
Eyres Way SP1 . . . . .152 C7

F

Factory Hill SP8 . . . . .137 F2
Factory La BA12 . . . . .116 F6
Fair Mile
Collingbourne Kingston
SN8 . . . . .183 F1
Grafton SN8 . . . . .184 A1
Fair View Rd SP2 . . . . . . .144 E5

Fairdown Ave BA13 .....109 B3
Fairfax Cl
  Amesbury SP4 ....217 A4
  Swindon SN3 ....50 F7
Fairfield **11** Cricklade SN6 ..19 D8
  4 Great Bedwyn SN8 ...176 B3
  Rode BA11 ....103 F1
  Wootton Bassett SN4 ....47 E3
Fairfield Cl
  Frome BA11 ....110 A7
  Marshfield SN14 ....74 A8
Fairfield Meadows
  BA14 ....104 C3
Fairfield Rd
  Salisbury SP1 ....146 A4
  Warminster BA12 ......117 B7
Fairfields **21** BA12 ......177 B7
Fairfoot Cl SN14 ....78 A7
Fairford Airfield GL7 ...1 E1
Fairford Cres SN25 .....35 C3
Fairground The **2** SP11 .192 F1
Fairhaven BA13 ....108 D1
Fairholme Way SN2 ....35 F4
Fairlane SP7 ....202 C1
Fairlawn SN3 ....51 D3
Fairleigh Rise SN15 ....70 F7
Fairview Colerne SN14 ..75 C6
  Swindon SN1 ....50 B5
Fairview Rd
  1 Andover SP11 ....192 F1
  Hungerford RG17 ......177 B2
  Salisbury SP1 ....146 C1
Fairway Calne SN11 .....89 C8
  Melksham SN12 ....94 C5
Fairway The SN10 .....214 A1
Fairways Amport SP11 ..192 E1
  Dilton Marsh BA13 ....108 D1
Fairwood Cl BA14 .....102 A2
Fairwood Rd
  Dilton Marsh BA13 ....108 C3
  North Bradley BA13 ...107 F5
Falcon Rd SN11 ....81 D3
Falcon Way SN12 ......94 D1
Falconer Mews SN25 ...35 B6
Falconscroft SN3 ......51 C8
Falconsway SP2 ....152 A5
Falconwood Cl **8** SP6 ..210 C1
Falkner Cl SN4 ....64 A7
Falkner Cl SN8 ....213 B3
Fallow Field Cl SN14 ..70 B2
Falmouth Gr SN3 ......50 E4
Fanshaw Way SN12 ...117 A5
Fanstones Rd SN3 .....51 C4
Fantley La SP8 ....138 B1
Far View Rd SP3 ......196 F7
Faraday Pk SN3 ....51 E5
Faraday Rd
  Salisbury SP2 ....145 C1
  Swindon SN3 ....51 E5
Fareham Cl SN3 ....51 B5
Farfield La SN6 ....19 E4
Fargo Cl SP4 ....198 A6
Fargo Rd SP4 ....217 A7
Farington Rd **2** SN1 ...50 B6
Farleigh Ave
  Melksham SN12 ....94 B3
  Trowbridge BA14 .....105 A7
Farleigh Castle* BA2 ..103 E8
Farleigh Cl
  1 Chippenham SN14 ...77 F6
  Westbury BA13 ....108 F4
Farleigh Coll SN3 .....103 C6
Farleigh Cres SN3 .....50 E7
Farleigh Pk* BA2 .....103 D8
Farleigh Rd BA12 .....103 A5
Farleigh Rise BA1 .....82 D1
Farley Cl BA11 ....110 C6
Farley Rd SP1 ....146 C1
Farm La Aldbourne SN8 .170 A6
  Great Bedwyn SN8 ....176 B3
  Salisbury SP1 ....145 E1
Farman Cl SN3 ....51 C4
Farmer Cl SN15 ....70 E1
Farmer Cres SN25 .....35 C6
Farmer Giles Farmstead*
  SP3 ....201 C3
Farmhouse Cl SN14 ....78 A4
Farmhouse Dr SN15 ....78 A4
Farnborough Rd SN3 ...51 B3
Farne Way SN4 ....48 A2
Farnsby St SN1 ....50 B6
Farrar Dr SN8 ....213 A2
Farrells Field SN4 .....68 F4
Farrfield SP2 ....35 C4
Farriers Cl SN1 ....50 E8
Farriers Field SN9 ....181 F2
Farthing Row BA11 ...103 E1
Faulkner Sq RG17 .....177 C7
Faverole Way SN4 ....102 A2
Fayre Gdns GL7 ....1 C6
Feather Wood SN6 .....49 D5
Featherbed La SN6 ...163 F7
Ferne Way SN6 ....48 E4
Fergusson Rd SN10 ...214 D1
Fermoy BA11 ....110 B6
Ferndale Jun & Inf Sch
  SN2 ....35 F3
Ferndale Rd SN2 ......49 F8
Ferne Hollow SP5 ....207 A8
Ferne Wall Cnr SP7 ...203 B1

Ferney Way SP5 ......207 C4
Fernham Rd SN25 .....34 E3
Ferozeshah Rd SN10 ..214 E6
Ferrers Dr SN5 ....48 F4
Ferris Gr SN12 ....94 C4
Ferris Mead BA12 ....117 A6
Festival Ave SP2 .....145 C3
Feversham Rd SP1 ....146 B3
Fiddington Clay SN10 .179 F1
Fiddington Hill SN10 ..180 A1
Fiddle The SN6 ....19 C7
Field Barn La SP3 ....201 F3
Field Cl South Cerney GL7 ..7 A7
  Westbury BA13 ......109 A4
Field La BA9 ....137 B3
Field La SN1 ....50 A3
Field View
  Chippenham SN15 .....78 D7
  Enford SN9 ....190 A6
Field Way BA14 ......104 F6
Fieldfare SN3 ....51 D7
Fieldins BA15 ....99 E7
Fields The Mere BA12 .139 B4
  Swindon SN3 ....36 A1
Fieldside SN10 ....187 E8
Figgins La SN8 ....213 D2
Figsbury Rd SP4 .....133 B1
Figsbury Ridge SP4 ...44 E3
Figsbury Ring* SP4 ...147 D8
Filands SN15 ....78 D8
Finchale Rd SN25 .....34 C7
Finchdale SN3 ....51 D8
Finches La
  2 Baydon SN8 ......164 C1
  Baydon SN8 ....170 C8
Finchley Rd SP2 .....145 E2
Finkley Rd SN11 .....193 F2
Finnis Rd **3** SP4 ....217 C3
Fir Gn La SN8 ....183 D8
Fir Gr SN11 ....89 D8
Fir Rd SN14 ....74 F6
Fir Tree Cl SN2 ......35 A2
Fire Brigade Mus*
  SN10 ....179 C5
Firecrest View **3** SN3 ..51 E6
Firs Cl SN15 ....148 C2
Firs Hill Way SN10 ...179 E5
Firs Rd Alderbury SP5 .153 E2
  Firsdown SP5 ....148 B7
Firs The
  Chippenham SN14 ......78 A6
  Inkpen RG17 ....177 F3
  Limpley Stoke BA2 ....99 A5
First Broad Dr
  Barford St Martin SP3 .201 A1
  Wilton SP2 ....144 A7
First La SN12 ....85 C1
Firth Cl SN25 ....35 A3
Fish Row SP1 ....152 A8
Fishers Brook BA11 ..110 A5
Fisherton Island SP2 ..145 F1
Fisherton Manor Mid Sch
  SP2 ....145 E1
Fisherton St **2** SP1 ..145 F1
Fison Wlk SN3 ....146 D4
Fitwell Rd SP1 ....146 D4
Fitzmaurice Cl
  Bradford-on-Avon BA15 .100 E4
  Calne Without SN11 ....79 F2
  Swindon SN3 ....51 D7
Fitzmaurice Pl BA15 ..100 D5
Fitzmaurice Prim Sch
  BA15 ....100 D5
Fitzroy Rd SN1 ....50 C2
Five Ash La BA12 ....117 C2
Five Rivers Leisure Ctr
  SP1 ....145 F3
Five Stiles Rd SN8 ...213 F2
Five Thorn La SN15 ..164 B1
Fiveways Cl SN8 .....164 B1
Fladbury Cl SN5 .....205 E4
Flashett The SP5 .....149 D6
Flaxfields End **16** SP6 .210 D1
Flayburn Rd SN25 ....34 C7
Fleece Cotts **2** BA14 .105 E7
Fleet Rd SN15 ....78 D8
Fleet St SN1 ....50 B6
Fleetwood Cl SN3 ....84 E6
Fleetwood Rise SN12 .93 A8
Fleming Cl SP11 .....192 A5
Fleming Way SN1 ....50 B6
Flensburg Cl **20** SP10 .193 D2
Flers Ct BA12 ....117 A6
Fleur De Lys Dr SP4 ..105 A4
Flint Cl SN11 ....49 C4
Flint La SP11 ....193 A4
Flintjack Pl **2** RG17 ..165 A1
Flisteridge Rd SN16 ..16 C3
Flit Croft **4** SP4 ....217 C2
Flood The SP5 ....149 B7
Florence Ct **21** SP10 .193 E2
Florence St SN2 ......50 B8
Flower La
  Amesbury SP4 ....217 A3
  Melchet Park & Plaitford
  SO51 ....212 F7
Flowers Mead **6** BA13 .186 B7
Flowers Yd SN15 .....78 C7
Folkestone Cl SP11 ..193 C1
Folkestone Ct SN14 ...78 A6
Folkestone Rd
  Salisbury SP2 ....151 F6
  Swindon SN1 ....50 A4
Folly Barrow* DT11 ..206 B2
Folly Cl Highworth SN6 ..23 A7
  Salisbury SP1 ....151 F5
Folly Cres SN6 ....23 A7

Folly Dr SN6 ....23 A7
Folly La Alderbury SP5 ..153 C3
  Melksham Without SN12 ..93 B8
  Salisbury SP2 ....145 D3
  Warminster BA12 .....116 B5
Folly La E SN15 ......86 C5
Folly La W SN15 .....86 B5
Folly Rd Inkpen RG17 ..177 F3
  Lambourn SN8 ....164 F1
  Roundway SN10 .....214 C7
Folly The SN15 ....44 A2
Folly View SP2 ......144 B5
Folly Way SN6 ....23 A7
Follyfield
  Bradford-on-Avon BA15 ..100 D4
  Hankerton SN16 ......15 B2
Fonthill Wlk SN3 .....50 E5
Foot's Hill Cann SP7 ..206 A7
Footshill BA12 ....117 C2
Ford St SN1 ....50 A5
Fordbrook Bsns Ctr
  SN9 ....215 C6
Fordingbridge Hospl
  SP6 ....210 D2
Fordingbridge Jun & Inf Sch
  SP6 ....210 D2
Fordson Rd SN10 ....214 D1
Fore St Ashton Keynes SN6 ..6 F1
  Trowbridge BA14 ....101 D1
  Warminster BA12 ....116 E5
  Westbury BA13 ......109 A4
  Wylye BA12 ....201 E8
Foreminster Ct BA12 .116 F5
Forest & Sandridge CE Prim
  Sch SN12 ....94 F5
Forest Dale Rd SN8 ..176 B3
Forest Dr SP9 ....216 E7
Forest Hill SN8 ......176 B3
Forest La
  Chippenham SN15 .....78 E3
  Chute SP11 ....192 D8
  Melksham Without SN12 ..86 F2
Forest Rd
  Bramshaw SP5 ......212 B3
  7 Frome BA11 ......110 B7
  Horningsham BA12 ..118 D8
  Melksham SN12 ......94 B5
  Redlynch SP6 ....211 D6
  Wooton Rivers SN8 ..174 F2
Forest Rd Cnr BA12 ..118 E7
Forest Wlk BA13 ....111 C4
Forester Cl **5** SN3 ...50 D7
Foresters Pk Rd SN12 .94 C4
Forge Cl
  Milton Lilbourne SN9 .182 E7
  South Newton SP2 ...130 B1
Forge Fields SN5 ....48 D8
Forge La
  West Overton SN8 ...173 F7
  Zennor BA12 ....137 F3
Forge The
  Hungerford RG17 ....177 C7
  Lower Stanton St Quinton
  SN14 ....30 D6
Forman St SN11 .....81 C3
Forres Sandle Manor Sch
  SP6 ....210 C1
Forrester Gn SN14 ...75 B3
Forster Cl SN3 ....51 E7
Fortis Hill SP7 ......203 C3
Fortune Way SN15 ...78 F5
Fortunes Field SN4 ..167 C2
Forty Acres Rd SN14 .31 C3
Forty The SN6 ....19 D7
Forum Cl SN3 ....51 C8
Fosbury Hill Fort*
  SP3 ....185 A3
Foss Way SN14 ......74 E5
Fosse Cl SN2 ....49 F6
Fosse Cotts SN16 ....27 A6
Fosse La BA1 ....82 A4
Fosseway Cl SN14 ....75 B3
Foster Rd BA11 ......110 A3
Fosters Bushes **2** SP4 .217 A3
Fotherby Cres SP1 ...146 C4
Foundry La SN15 .....70 E1
Foundry Rd
  3 Malmesbury SN16 ..28 A4
  2 Redlynch SP5 .....211 C8
Fountain Mead **8** SP7 .202 C2
Four Acre Cl SN6 ....18 A8
Fourmile Hill SN4 ...132 B3
Fovant Cl SN5 ....34 A1
Fovant Regimental Badges*
  SP3 ....204 F7
Fowey SN25 ....49 A3
Fowler's Hill SP1 ....152 C8
Fowler's Rd SP1 .....152 B8
Fowlers La SN8 ......173 B8
Fox Brook SN4 ......47 F2
Fox Cl SN14 ....70 B1
Fox Croft Wlk SN14 ..78 F4
Fox Talbot Mus* SN15 ..86 D5
Fox Wood SN5 ....49 D5
Foxbridge SN3 ......51 D7
Foxbury Cl RG17 .....165 A1
Foxcote Gdns **2** BA11 ..110 C7
Foxcott SN6 ....23 A7
Foxcote Cl SP10 .....193 C1
Foxcote Gdns SP10 ...193 C1
Foxglove Cl SN12 ....94 C3
Foxglove Dr BA14 ...105 E6
Foxglove Rd SN25 ....34 D5
Foxglove Way SN11 ..81 B5
Foxgrove SN14 ......70 A2
Foxhall Cl SN25 .....34 C7
Foxleaze SN6 ....8 C1

Foxcs Cl SN2 ....35 E4
Foxley Cnr SN10 ....180 D4
Foxley Fields SN10 ..180 C4
Foxley Rd Norton SN16 ..41 E8
  St Paul Malmesbury Without
  SN16 ....27 D2
Foxtail Gdns SP10 ...192 A5
Foyle Rd SP7 ....202 B1
Foyle Rd SP11 ......192 C2
Foyle's Mead BA12 ..201 E8
Frampton Cl SN5 .....49 B6
Frampton Ct SN14 ...105 A6
Francis Rd **10** SN10 ..179 F1
Francis St BA14 .....101 C1
Francis Way SP2 ....152 A5
Francomes SN25 .....35 A6
Francomes Field **17**
  RG17 ....165 A1
Frank Warman Ct **8** SN3 ..36 B3
Frankenbury* SP6 ...210 F2
Frankland Rd SN1 ....48 E3
Frankton Gdns **2** SN3 ..36 B2
Fraser Cl SN3 ....51 B7
Frederick Taylor Ct
  BA12 ....116 F4
Fredericks Ave SN14 ..77 F7
Fredericks Way SN14 .93 F8
Free's Ave SN8 ......213 B5
Freegrove Dr SN15 ...73 F8
Freegrove Rd SN15 ..73 F8
Freemans Cl **4** RG17 .177 B7
Freesia Cl **2** BA12 ..116 E7
Freestone Way SN15 .73 D6
Fremantle Rd SP1 ...191 F4
French Mill La SP7 ..202 C1
French Mill Rise **16** SP7 ..202 C1
Frensham Way SN5 ..215 D6
Fresden Village* SN6 ..23 C4
Freshbrook Prim Sch
  SN5 ....49 A3
Freshford CE Prim Sch
  BA2 ....99 B5
Freshford La BA2 ....99 A4
Freshford Sta BA2 ...99 C5
Friar's Orch **4** SP1 ..152 B8
Friars Cl BA13 ....112 C8
Friars The SN4 ......94 C6
Friary Cl SN3 ....50 D7
Friary La SP1 ....152 B7
Friary The SP1 ......152 B8
Fricker's La SP3 .....200 F3
Friday La SN9 ....181 D3
Friday St SN15 ......58 C3
Fridays Ham La SN6 ..7 B3
Friesian Cl SN5 .....49 A7
Friesland Cl SN5 ....49 A7
Friggle St BA11 .....110 D1
Frilford Dr SN3 ......36 A1
Frith Copse SN5 .....34 A2
Frittillary Mews SN1 .50 D6
Frobisher Dr SN3 ....51 E6
Frog La Avebury SN8 .173 B8
  Chilmark SP3 ....201 A3
  Great Bedwyn SN8 ..176 C3
  Great Somerford SN15 ..44 B3
  Hullavington SN14 ....41 F1
  Longbridge Deverill
  BA12 ....121 A6
  Motcombe SP7 ......202 B4
  West Overton SN8 ...173 F7
Frogmore Rd BA13 ..108 F5
Frogwell Cl SN14 .....77 F8
Frogwell Pk SN14 ....78 A8
Frogwell Prim Sch
  SN14 ....78 A7
Frome Com Coll BA11 .110 A7
Frome Leisure Ctr
  BA11 ....110 A7
Frome Rd
  Bradford-on-Avon BA15 ..100 C5
  Maiden Bradley with Yarnfield
  BA12 ....118 F3
  Southwick BA14 .....104 F3
  Swindon SN25 ....34 F4
  Trowbridge BA14 ....105 C2
  Westwood BA15 .....100 C3
  Wingfield BA14 ......104 C6
Frome Sta BA11 .....110 D4
Frome Valley Rd BA12 ..118 E3
Front Horse Hill La
  SP7 ....203 A1
Front St RG17 ....171 E7
Fruitfields Cl SN10 ..214 B1
Fry Cl **2** SN1 ......49 F4
Fry Sq SP10 ....193 C1
Fryern Ct Rd SP6 ...210 D3
Fugglestone SP2 ....144 F3
Fulford Rd BA14 .....101 C2
Fuller Ave SN13 ......84 E8
Fuller Cl SN2 ....35 F5
Fullers Ave SN8 .....191 D8
Fullers Way **4** SN13 ..84 A8
Fullers Wlk SN6 .....19 D8
Fulmar Cl SN11 ......81 A5
Fulney Cl BA14 ......101 F2
Furlong Cl Rowde SN10 ..96 E1
  Swindon SN25 ....34 F4
Furlong Gdns SN8 ...191 E8
Furlong Way SP9 ....216 F7
Furnax La BA12 .....112 F1
Furnham Cl SN3 .....36 B3
Furze Cl SN9 ....34 A2
Furze Hill SN9 ......182 F2
Furze Hill La SN10 ..179 D7

Fai – Gey **229**

Furzehill SN13 ......84 F8
Furzley La SO51 ....212 F3
Furzley Rd SO51 ....212 F2
Fussells Lodge (Long
  Barrow)* SP5 ....147 D5
Fyfield Ave SN4 .....35 C5
Fyfield Cl **2** SP1 ...146 D5
Fyfield Down National Nature
  Reserve* SN8 ....167 F1
Fyfield La SP11 .....192 D1
Fyfield Rd SP11 .....192 E1
Fyfield Way SP11 ...191 F3
Fynamore Com Prim Sch
  SN11 ....81 A4
Fyne Cl **3** SN5 ....34 B2

G

Gable Cl SN2 ....35 B6
Gables Cl SN10 .....214 D2
Gabriel Cl **4** BA11 ..110 C6
Gains La SN10 ......214 A4
Gainsborough Ave SN4 ..47 F3
Gainsborough Ct **2** SP2 ..145 C3
Gainsborough Ct **1**
  SP10 ....193 D1
Gainsborough Rise
  BA14 ....105 A6
Gainsborough Way
  SN5 ....49 A3
Gairlock Cl SN5 .....34 B2
Gaisford Chase SN10 .179 B4
Galatea Cl SN2 ......49 A7
Gales Cl SN15 ....73 F8
Gales Gd SN8 ....213 E3
Gallery at Handel House*
  SN10 ....214 B3
Galley La SN8 ....176 C3
Galloway Cl **1** SN5 ..49 A7
Galloway Cl **1** SN5 ..34 C5
Gallows Barrow* SP4 .190 B3
Gallows Leap SN11 ..81 A5
Galsworthy Cl SN3 ...51 D4
Galton Way SN2 .....49 A3
Gambia St SN1 ......50 D6
Gamekeepers Cl SN25 ..34 F7
Gantlettdene SN3 ...51 E6
Ganton Way SN2 ....35 E1
Garden The SN2 .....49 A7
Garden Trading Est
  SN10 ....214 C5
Gardeners Gn **2** SP9 ..199 C8
Gardens The
  Rushall SN9 ....181 E3
  Heddington SN11 .....89 B1
  Swindon SN25 ....35 A3
  Upavon SN9 ....181 F2
Garendon Ct **2** SP10 ..210 D1
Garfield Cl SN3 .....51 C3
Garlings The **6** SN8 ..170 A6
Garrard Way SN3 ....51 A8
Garraways **6** SN4 ..47 F2
Garsdon Mill SN16 ...28 F5
Garsington Dr SN25 ..34 C7
Garston BA11 ....110 A4
Garston La **3** BA11 ..110 A4
Garstons The BA1 ...82 D2
Garth Cl SN14 ....70 B1
Gartons Rd SN5 .....48 F7
Gas La Cricklade SN6 ..19 D8
  Salisbury SP2 ....145 F1
Gascelyn Cl SN14 ....78 A7
Gascoigne's La SP7 ..202 C1
Gason Hill Rd SP9 ..216 C8
Gasper St BA12 .....137 C6
Gassons Rd GL7 .....2 C5
Gassons Way GL7 ....2 C4
Gaston La SN16 ......40 C8
Gaston's Rd SN14 ...78 C8
Gastons Rd SN16 ....27 F3
Gaters La SN4 ......133 A2
Gatehouse Cl SN5 ...48 F5
Gauntlet Rd SN25 ...217 B4
Gaveller Rd SN25 ...34 C7
Gawaine Cl **3** SN15 ..193 E2
Gawthorne Dr SP2 ..151 F6
Gay's Pl SN2 ....35 E4
Gaynor Cl SN25 .....35 A6
Gaza Rd SP4 ....198 F7
Geneville Rise **3** SP4 ..217 C3
Genoa Ct **10** SP10 ..193 E2
Gentle St BA11 ......119 C7
George Cl SN11 ......89 A1
George Gay Gdns **7** SN3 ..50 F4
George Ln SN13 .....83 D6
George St (South) **6**
  SP2 ....145 F1
George St
  Salisbury SP2 ....145 F1
  Swindon SN1 ....50 A6
  Trowbridge BA14 ....101 D1
  Warminster BA12 ....117 A7
George VI Ct SN3 ....84 F8
George VI Rd SP9 ...216 C8
George Ward Sch The
  SN12 ....93 F6
Gerard Wlk SN5 .....49 A6
Germain's La SN14 ...76 A8
Geys Hill BA12 ......115 A7

Giant's Cave (Long Barrow)*
SN14 ....39 C2
Giant's Chair The
(Tumulus)* SN14 ....53 E1
Gibbs Cl **2** Salisbury SP1 .146 C5
Swindon SN1 ....51 E7
Westbury BA13 ....109 E8
Gibbs La SN14 ....55 F8
Gibbs Leaze BA14 ....102 A1
Gibson Cl SN12 ....94 C1
Gifford Rd SN3 ....36 B3
Giffords The BA14 ....102 A4
Gigant St Salisbury SP1 ..152 B8
Swallowcliffe SP3 ....204 A6
Gilbert Way SP1 ....146 C4
Gilbert's Gn **3** SP9 ....199 D8
Gilberts Piece SN8 ....183 E1
Giles Ave **1** SN6 ....19 D7
Giles La SO51 ....212 E2
Giles La End St SP5 ....212 E2
Gilling Way SN3 ....51 D6
Gillingham Adult Ed Ctr
SP7 ....202 B3
Gilman Cl SN25 ....35 A8
Giotto Cl SN25 ....34 B7
Gipsy La
Chippenham SN15 ....78 D6
Frome BA11 ....110 B7
Holt BA14 ....92 F2
Marlborough RG17 ....177 C8
Swindon SN2 ....50 E8
Warminster BA12 ....117 B5
Gladstone Rd
Chippenham SN15 ....78 D7
Trowbridge BA14 ....105 B7
Gladys Plumley Gdns
SN2 ....50 C8
Glass's La SP3 ....204 D7
Glebe Cl
7 Fairley Farm SP5 ....148 C4
Pitton & Farley SP5 ....148 C4
Glebe Field BA12 ....117 A6
Glebe Gdns SP7 ....202 A4
Glebe La Kemble GL7 ....4 F7
Landford SP5 ....212 C6
Glebe Pl RG17 ....171 A1
Glebe Rd
2 Durrington/Bulford
SP4 ....198 B7
Trowbridge BA14 ....105 A7
Wootton Bassett SN4 ....47 D1
Glebe The
All Cannings SN10 ....180 F8
Calne SN11 ....81 C3
Freshford BA3 ....99 B4
Hinton Charterhouse BA2 ....98 D2
Glebe Way SN13 ....76 E1
Glebelands **3** BA12 ....194 C5
Glendale Cres SN1 ....152 D8
Gleneagle Rd SN4 ....198 C7
Gleneagles Cl SN1 ....78 F7
Glenfield Cl SP5 ....149 D6
Glenmore Rd
Haydon Wick SN25 ....34 C5
Salisbury SP1 ....146 C3
Glenside SN12 ....94 C6
Glenville Cl SN4 ....61 E8
Glenwood Cl SN1 ....50 C2
Glevum Cl SN3 ....33 C5
Glevum Rd SN3 ....36 C1
Globe St SN1 ....50 C4
Gloucester Cl **3** SN14 ....78 A6
Gloucester Rd
Calne Without SN11 ....81 F1
8 Malmesbury SN16 ....28 A3
Trowbridge BA14 ....105 B7
Gloucester Sq SN12 ....94 C4
Gloucester St SN1 ....50 B7
Gloucester Wlk BA13 ....109 A4
Glover Rd SP4 ....197 F7
Glyn Pl SP7 ....206 B8
Glyndebourne Cl SP2 ....145 C2
Goatacre La SN11 ....73 F7
Goddard Ave SN1 ....50 B4
Goddard Cl **1** SN9 ....215 C5
Goddard Pk Prim Sch
SN1 ....51 A4
Goddard Rd SN9 ....215 C5
Goddards La SN8 ....170 A6
Godley Rd SP2 ....152 A6
Godolphin Cl SP5 ....49 A3
Godolphin Prep Sch
SP1 ....146 C1
Godolphin Sch The
SP1 ....152 C8
Godwin Cl SN1 ....50 C4
Godwin Rd SN3 ....36 B3
Godwins Cl SN12 ....84 E1
Gogg's La SN15 ....211 D7
Gold Hill **3** SP7 ....202 C1
Gold View SN5 ....48 F5
Goldcrest Wlk SN3 ....51 F7
Golden Cross SP6 ....211 E4
Golding Ave SN8 ....213 A2
Goldney Ave SN14 ....78 C7
Goldsborough Cl SN5 ....49 B6
Gomeldon Medieval Village
of* SP4 ....133 C5
Gomeldon Prim Sch
SP4 ....133 C4
Gomeldon Rd SP4 ....133 D5
Gooch Cl BA11 ....110 D6
Gooch St SN1 ....50 C7
Goodbody Rd **1** SP4 ....198 A6

Goodes Hill SN13 ....85 D3
Goodings La RG17 ....171 D6
Goodwin Cl BA12 ....117 E8
Goodwood Cl BA14 ....105 E4
Goodwood Way **3** SN14 ....77 F5
Godwyns G **5** SP9 ....199 C8
Goor La SN8 ....164 B2
Goose Gn RG17 ....165 A2
Goose St Marston SN10 ....179 A3
Southwick BA14 ....105 A2
Gooselands
Crudwell SN16 ....14 D5
Westbury BA13 ....108 F2
Gordon Gdns **4** SN1 ....50 C6
Gordon Rd **5** SN1 ....50 C6
Gore Cl SN25 ....34 F6
Gore Cross SN10 ....187 E5
Gore La BA13 ....111 B4
Gore Rd SP4 ....197 E7
Gores La SN9 ....181 C5
Gorringe Rd SP2 ....145 D1
Gorse Hill Inf Sch SN2 ....35 D1
Gorse Hill Jun Sch
SN2 ....35 D1
Gosditch
Ashton Keynes SN6 ....17 E8
Latton SN6 ....8 C4
Goughs Way SN4 ....47 E2
Gould Cl **1** SP11 ....192 A5
Goulding Cl **3** SN3 ....36 B2
Gower Cl Swindon SN2 ....35 F2
4 Swindon SN5 ....48 F5
Gower Rd **10** SP7 ....202 D2
Grace Cl SP2 ....145 B5
Grace La SN4 ....211 A4
Graemar La SO51 ....162 E1
Grafton CE Prim Sch
SN8 ....183 F7
Grafton Rd SN8 ....183 F7
Grafton Rd
Burbage SN8 ....183 D7
Swindon SN2 ....35 C5
Graham St SN1 ....50 D7
Grailey Cl SN3 ....51 C4
Gramp's Hill OX12 ....165 F7
Gramshaw Rd **2** SP2 ....145 D2
Granary Cl
East Grafton SN8 ....183 F7
4 Swindon SN5 ....48 F8
Granary Rd **6** SN8 ....176 B3
Grand Ave **1** SN8 ....175 E3
Grand Trunk Rd SP9 ....216 B4
Grandison Cl SN1 ....50 C3
Grange Cl
Atworth/Whitley SN12 ....85 D1
Fyfield SP11 ....192 D1
Highworth SN6 ....23 A5
Grange Com Inf Sch
SN3 ....36 B3
Grange Dr SN3 ....36 B3
Grange Gdns SN1 ....146 C2
Grange Jun Sch SN3 ....36 B2
Grange Pk Way SN5 ....48 F5
Grange Rd BA11 ....110 A7
Grange View BA15 ....100 E7
Granham Cl SN15 ....78 F4
Granham Cl SN8 ....213 D1
Granham Hill SN8 ....213 D1
Grans Barrow (Long
Barrow)* SP6 ....209 E6
Grantham Cl SN3 ....49 B3
Granthams The **4**
RG17 ....165 A2
Grantley Cl SN3 ....51 A3
Grants Rd SN9 ....190 A6
Granville Gdns **28** SP7 ....202 C2
Granville Rd BA14 ....94 A6
Granville St SN1 ....50 C6
Grasmere
Bower Hill SN12 ....94 D1
Swindon SN3 ....51 E3
Trowbridge BA14 ....101 E2
Grasmere Cl **1** SP2 ....151 F6
Graspan Rd **12** SP11 ....192 B5
Grateley Rd SP4 ....199 C5
Gravel Cl SP5 ....211 A8
Gravel The BA14 ....92 E1
Greaveney Sq SN10 ....193 E1
Grays Cl **3** SP2 ....202 A4
Grays Leaze BA14 ....105 C2
Graythwaite Cl **3** SN25 ......34 F6
Great Barn* SN4 ....167 B1
Great Bedwyn CE Prim Sch
SN8 ....176 B4
Great Chalfield Manor*
BA14 ....92 D3
Great Croft SP5 ....148 C7
Great Dro SP4 ....132 F1
Great Ground **15** SP7 ......202 D2
Great Hill SN4 ....163 B8
Great La SP7 ....202 C1
Great Lodge Cpe SN8 ....175 B5
Great Parks BA14 ....92 F1
Great Roc Rd BA13 ....108 E3
Great Western Ave
SP3 ....200 B1
Great Western Hospl The
SN3 ....51 D1
Great Western Way
SN5 ....48 F3
Great Wethers* SN8 ....174 A7
Great Wishford CE Fst Sch
SP2 ....130 A4
Greater La BA13 ....186 C8

Greatwoods BA12 ....186 C8
Green Acres **18** SN8 ....170 B2
Green Beeches SN12 ....93 D8
Green Cl
East Grafton SN8 ....183 F7
Holt BA14 ....101 F8
Whiteparish SP5 ....161 D4
Green Dro Fovant SP3 ....204 B8
Grimstead SP5 ....154 B4
Pewsey SN9 ....215 D3
Smannell SP11 ....193 E5
Green Farm Rise SN8 ....176 D7
Green Gate Rd SN10 ....180 D4
Green La Ashmore SP5 ....206 E4
Cheverell Magna SN10 ....179 C1
Codford BA12 ....195 A3
Colerne SN14 ....75 A3
Deanend SP5 ....207 E4
Devizes SN10 ....214 B1
Downton SP5 ....211 A8
Downton SP5 ....211 B1
Fordingbridge SP6 ....211 A8
Hinton Charterhouse BA2 ....98 E1
Laverstock SP4 ....146 D8
Rockbourne SP6 ....210 C3
Steeple Ashton BA14 ....102 C1
Sherston SN16 ....25 C1
Southwick BA14 ....104 D2
Trowbridge BA14 ....105 E8
Westbury BA13 ....99 E6
Green La Hospl SN10 ....214 B1
Green La Wood Nature
Reserve* BA14 ....106 C8
Green Mdw Ave SN25 ....34 F4
Green Pk La SN1 ....107 A6
Green Rd Codford BA12 ....195 A3
Corsham SN13 ....85 B4
Swindon SN3 ....35 E3
Green Ride BA12 ....123 E5
Green St SN8 ....167 C1
Green Terr SN1 ....101 C2
Green The
Alderbury SP5 ....153 C3
Biddestone SN14 ....76 E8
Brokenborough SN16 ....27 D7
Calne SN11 ....81 B2
Cheverell Magna SN10 ....179 C2
Dauntsey SN15 ....59 A8
Fairford GL7 ....1 F7
Highworth SN6 ....22 F5
7 Liddington SN4 ....163 A4
Lyneham & Bradenstoke
SN15 ....60 A4
Marlborough SN8 ....213 E3
Oaksey SN16 ....15 F7
Pitton & Farley SP5 ....148 C3
Salisbury SP1 ....146 B1
Upper Woodford SP4 ....131 D7
Whiteparish SP5 ....161 D4
Green Valley Ave SN25 ....34 F4
Greenacres
Dilton Marsh BA13 ....112 A8
Warminster BA12 ....210 F8
Greenacres Way SN11 ....80 F4
Green's Ct **3** SP1 ....152 B8
Green's La SN4 ....64 B5
Greenaway **4** SN4 ....163 A5
Greenbridge Ind Est
SN3 ....51 A7
Greenbridge Rd SN3 ....51 A7
Greenbridge Ret Pk
SN3 ....51 A7
Greencroft St SP1 ....146 B1
Greencroft The **6** SP1 ......146 B1
Greendown Com Sch
SN3 ....48 F5
Greenfield Rd SN10 ....214 C1
Greenfields
Grimstead SP5 ....154 C2
Smannell SP11 ....193 E4
South Marston SN3 ....36 E5
Greenham Wlk SN3 ....51 B6
Greenhill
Sutton Veny BA12 ....117 F1
Westwells SN13 ....84 D7
Greenhill Gdns
Sutton Veny BA12 ....117 F1
Trowbridge BA14 ....102 A4
Greenhill Rd SN2 ....34 E2
Greenhouse Rd SN10 ....180 F8
Greenland Cl SN12 ....92 E8
Greenland View BA15 ....100 D6
Greenlands **1** BA12 ....194 C5
Greenlands **20** SP9 ....198 B7
Greenlands Rd SN2 ....35 E3
Greenlane Cl SN4 ....64 B4
Greenmeadow Prim Sch
SN25 ....35 A4
Greens Cl SN14 ....41 F1
Greens La SN14 ....172 A8
Greens Meade **6** SP5 ....211 C7
Greenslade CI SN25 ....34 F7
Greentrees Prim Sch
SP1 ....146 C5
Greenway SN4 ....60 F2
Greenway Ave SN15 ....70 D1
Greenway CI SN3 ....51 B7
Greenway Ct SN15 ....70 D2
Greenway La SN15 ....73 F8
Greenway Gdns
Chippenham SN15 ....70 D1
Trowbridge BA14 ....101 E3
Greenway Pk SN15 ....70 D1
Greenway Rd SN8 ....169 B1
Greenways RG17 ....165 A1

Greenwich Cl SN25 ....35 A5
Greenwood Ave SP1 ....146 D1
Greenwood Rd SN2 ....94 A3
Gregory Cl SN15 ....57 C1
Grenadier Cl **2** BA12 ....116 F7
Gresham Cl SN3 ....50 F6
Grey Wethers or Sarsen
Stones* SN8 ....167 F2
Grey's Cnr BA9 ....136 A5
Greyfriars Cl SP1 ....152 B7
Greyhound La **1** SP2 ....146 A4
Greystones SN15 ....96 B8
Greywethers Ave SP3 ....50 E3
Grierson Cl SN1 ....81 B3
Griffin Alley **6** SN16 ....28 A3
Griffins Ct **3** SP2 ....146 A1
Griffiths Cl SN3 ....36 B1
Grimstead Beeches*
SP5 ....160 D7
Grimstead Rd SP5 ....153 F1
Grindal Dr SN5 ....48 F5
Grittleton House Sch
SN14 ....54 E4
Grocyn Cl SN14 ....75 B3
Grosmont Dr SN5 ....149 C6
Grosvenor close SP9 ....216 E6
Grosvenor Cl
Shaftesbury SP7 ....202 C2
Swindon SN1 ....50 A4
Ground Cnr SN11 ....81 D8
Groundwell SN25 ....35 C6
Groundwell Ind Est
SN25 ....35 D5
Groundwell Rd SN1 ....50 D5
Grove Hill SN6 ....23 A7
Grove La
Kington St Michael SN14 ....69 F8
Yatton Keynell SN14 ....69 A6
Grove Leaze BA15 ....100 B6
Grove Orch SN6 ....22 F7
Grove Prim Sch BA14 ....105 B5
Grove Rd Corsham SN13 ....77 A1
2 Market Lavington SN10 179 F1
Sherston SN16 ....40 C8
Grove The
Codford St Peter BA12 ....195 A2
Crudwell SN16 ....4 C1
Penton Mewsey SP11 ....193 A2
Warminster BA12 ....117 B8
Grovelands Ave SN1 ....50 C3
Grovelands Way BA12 ....116 E7
Groveley Rd SP3 ....143 B3
Grovely Castle* SP3 ....128 F4
Grovely Cl SN5 ....34 A1
Grovely Rd SP3 ....128 F4
Grovely View SP2 ....144 B1
Groves St SN2 ....49 F6
Groves The SN3 ....51 D3
Grundys SN3 ....51 D3
Gryphon Cl BA13 ....108 E3
Guilder La SP1 ....152 B8
Guildford Ave SN3 ....50 F3
Guildhall Sq **8** SP1 ....152 A8
Gullet The SN13 ....83 F7
Gulliver's La BA14 ....178 A4
Gundry Cl
Chippenham SN15 ....78 F5
Devizes SN10 ....214 C4
Gunner St SP4 ....198 E6
Gunsite Rd SN8 ....173 C6
Gunville Hill SP5 ....149 E6
Gunville Rd SP5 ....149 D6
Guppy St SN2 ....49 F7
Gurston Meadow SP5 ....205 A4
Gurston Rd SP5 ....205 A4
Guthrie Cl Inf Sch
SN1 ....81 C4
Guthrie Cl SN1 ....81 C4
Guyers La SN13 ....76 D2
Gwyns Piece **14** RG17 ......165 A2

H

Ha'penny Bridge* GL7 ....2 C3
Habrel's Cl SN15 ....78 F6
Hackett Cl SN11 ....35 E4
Hackleton Rise SN3 ....51 B8
Hackney Way BA13 ....108 F3
Hackpen Cl SN4 ....64 B7
Hackthorne Rd SP4 ....198 B7
Haddon Cl **14** SN5 ....48 F5
Haddons Cl SN16 ....27 E2
Haden Rd **6** BA14 ....105 D7
Hadleigh Cl SN5 ....49 C6
Hadleigh Rise SP4 ....36 A5
Hadrian Rd **8** SP10 ....193 E2
Hadrians Cl
Salisbury SP2 ....145 C1
Swindon SN3 ....51 C8
Haig Cl SN3 ....35 E4
Haig Rd SP4 ....217 F6
Haimes La **10** SP7 ....202 C2
Hale House* SN4 ....211 A5
Hale La SP6 ....211 B5
Hale Prim Sch SP6 ....211 A6
Hale Rd SP6 ....211 B5
Hales Castle* BA11 ....114 D5
Hales Rd **6** SN4 ....64 B4
Hale High Down SP5 ....207 B3
Half Mile Mile RG17 ....171 A5
Halfpenny La SP4 ....206 E4
Halfpenny Row SP4 ....103 E1
Halfway Cl BA14 ....101 F2
Halfway Firs SN13 ....76 C1
Halfway La SN14 ....170 C2
Halifax Cl SN3 ....64 A7

Halifax Rd SN12 ....94 C1
Hall Cl SN4 ....64 A6
Hallam Moor SN3 ....51 E2
Hallsfield SN6 ....8 D1
Hallum Cl SP1 ....146 D4
Halton Rd SP11 ....191 F4
Halve The BA14 ....101 D1
Ham Cl SN8 ....183 D3
Ham Hill Nature Reserve*
SN8 ....185 B8
Ham La Biddestone SN14 ....76 C8
Kempsford GL7 ....10 E6
South Cerney GL7 ....6 F6
Ham Rd Ham RG17 ....177 A2
Liddington SN4 ....163 A5
Ham The
Durrington/Bulford SP4 ....198 C7
Kington St Michael SN14 ....70 A8
9 Market Lavington SN10 179 F1
Westbury BA13 ....108 C5
Hambidge La GL7 ....2 C1
Hamble Cl SP10 ....193 F1
Hamble Rd SN25 ....34 C4
Hambleton Ave SN10 ....214 C6
Hamblin Meadow
RG17 ....177 C8
Hamilton Cl
Amesbury SP4 ....217 E3
Swindon SN3 ....50 F7
Hamilton Dr
Chippenham SN14 ....77 F5
2 Market Lavington SN10 179 F1
Hamilton Pk **3** SP5 ....211 B8
Hamilton Rd SP1 ....146 A2
Hamlet Ct SN15 ....70 D1
Hamlet Gdns SP11 ....193 E3
Hamlet The SN15 ....78 F3
Hammer St BA10 ....122 C7
Hammond Way BA14 ....101 D4
Hammonds SN6 ....19 E8
Hampshire Cl
Durrington/Bulford SP4 ....217 E8
7 Swindon SN5 ....49 A7
Hampshire Gdns
BA13 ....109 A4
Hampshire Pl SN12 ....94 B5
Hampsley Rd SN13 ....89 C1
Hampstead Way SN25 ....34 F7
Hampton Cl SN12 ....94 C1
Hampton Ct **3** SN9 ....215 C5
Hampton Dr SN5 ....48 F5
Hamptworth Rd SP5 ....211 F6
Hamshill Ditches*
SP3 ....143 B7
Hamworthy Rd SN3 ....51 C6
Hanbury Rd SN3 ....51 A4
Hancock Cl SN15 ....79 A5
Handel St SN2 ....50 C8
Handley Sq **5** SN3 ....204 D3
Hanging Bushes La
SP11 ....193 A1
Hanging Langford Camp*
SP3 ....201 F2
Hanging Stone* SN9 ....181 B7
Hangman's Stone*
RG17 ....164 F4
Hankerton Priory SN16 ....15 B6
Hankerton Rd SN16 ....16 C2
Hanks Cl SN16 ....28 A5
Hannington La SN6 ....36 B6
Hanover Cl BA14 ....101 E4
Hanover Ct SN3 ....51 D7
Harbour Cl SN15 ....34 F3
Harcourt Mews **5** BA11 ..110 A4
Harcourt Rd SN2 ....50 A6
Harcourt Terr SP2 ....151 E4
Hardenhuish Ave SN15 ....70 C3
Hardenhuish La SN14 ....70 B3
Hardenhuish Pk*
SN14 ....70 C1
Hardens Cl SN15 ....79 A5
Hardens Mead SN15 ....79 A4
Hardhams Rise SN13 ....84 F8
Hardie St SN3 ....36 A1
Harding St **8** SN1 ....50 B6
Hardwick Cl SN25 ....35 A5
Hardyfair Cl **5** SP11 ....192 F1
Hare Cl SN2 ....34 F3
Hare Knapp BA15 ....100 B6
Hare St Bremhill SN15 ....72 C5
Pewsey SN9 ....182 A2
Hare Warren Cl SP2 ....144 C1
Harebell Cl SN25 ....34 D5
Harefield Cres SP4 ....190 A3
Harepit Way* SN13 ....172 F4
Hares Patch SN14 ....69 F6
Haresdown Hill GL7 ....3 F1
Harford Cl **3** SN15 ....78 F1
Harford St **4** BA14 ....105 E4
Hargreaves Rd
Swindon SN3 ....35 D4
Trowbridge BA14 ....101 E2
Harlech Cl SN5 ....49 B6
Harlestone Rd SN3 ....51 A3
Harmony Pl **8** BA14 ....105 D7
Harnham CE Jun Sch
SP2 ....151 F7
Harnham Inf Sch SP2 ....151 F6
Harnham Rd SP2 ....151 F7
Harnham Trad Est
SP2 ....151 D2
Harnish Way SN14 ....70 B3
Harnwood Rd SP2 ....151 F6
Harper Rd SP2 ....145 D2
Harper's La SN16 ....28 A3
Harptree Cl SN5 ....49 A4
Harriers The SN3 ....51 C8

Harrington Dr 4 SP4 . . .198 E6
Harrington Wlk SN3 . . .51 A7
Harris Cl 5 RG17 . . .165 A2
Harris La SN9 . . .183 A7
Harris Rd
  Ashton Keynes SN6 . . .7 A1
  Calne SN11 . . .81 C5
  Swindon SN2 . . .35 A2
Harrow Cl SN3 . . .36 A1
Harrow La SN5 . . .60 B2
Harrow Way SP11 . . .193 B1
Harrow Way Com Prim Sch
  SP10 . . .193 C1
Harroway La SP11 . . .193 B1
Hartfield SN10 . . .214 A2
Hartham La SN13 . . .76 E5
Harthill Dro SP5 . . .211 D7
Hartington Rd
  Salisbury SP2 . . .145 E2
  Swindon SN25 . . .34 C7
Hartland Cl SN3 . . .51 A5
Hartley Way SN1 . . .146 B4
Hartmoor Cl SN10 . . .214 A2
Hartmoor Rd SN10 . . .214 A2
Harts La SN14 . . .76 E8
Hartsthorn Cl SN2 . . .34 D3
Harvard Cl
  10 Bower Hill SN12 . . .178 B8
  1 Salisbury SP2 . . .151 F5
Harvest La SP5 . . .205 F4
Harvester Cl 7 SN5 . . .48 F8
Harvey Gr SN2 . . .34 F2
Hastings Ave SN9 . . .182 B2
Hastings Cl SN9 . . .182 B2
Hastings Dr SN15 . . .60 B2
Hastings Rd SN3 . . .85 A8
Hatch La SP3 . . .203 C8
Hatch Rd SN3 . . .36 B4
Hatchbury La SP11 . . .185 C3
Hatcher's Cres SN26 . . .22 A2
Hatches La SP1 . . .152 D7
Hatchet Cl SN5 . . .211 C6
Hatchet Hill SN4 . . .163 D6
Hatchet La SP11 . . .193 B5
Hatfield Cl SN25 . . .34 E6
Hatfields SN10 . . .181 A5
Hathaway Cl SP5 . . .145 F4
Hathaway Rd SN2 . . .35 E5
Hathaway Ret Pk SN3 . . .35 E4
Hatherden CE Prim Sch
  SP11 . . .193 C5
Hatherell Rd SN15 . . .78 F4
Hatherhall Cl SN3 . . .36 C2
Hatherleigh Cl SN3 . . .51 B6
Hatherley Rd SN3 . . .51 B6
Hathersage Moor SN3 . . .51 E2
Hattem Pl 2 SP10 . . .193 D2
Hatton Gr SN3 . . .50 F6
Hatton Way SN3 . . .76 E1
Havard Way 2 SP4 . . .217 D2
Havelock Sq SN1 . . .50 B5
Havelock St
  Swindon SN1 . . .50 B5
  Trowbridge BA14 . . .105 C7
Haven Cl SN3 . . .51 B8
Havering La SN9 . . .182 E7
Havisham Dr SN5 . . .34 D6
Hawcroft BA12 . . .92 E1
Hawfinch Cl SN3 . . .51 E5
Hawk's Worth Cl 6
  BA11 . . .110 C7
Hawker Rd SN3 . . .51 C4
Hawkeridge Pk BA13 . . .108 E2
Hawkeridge Rd BA13 . . .105 E2
Hawkesdene 4 SP7 . . .202 C1
Hawkesdene La SP7 . . .202 C2
Hawkins Cl SN5 . . .78 F5
Hawkins Meadow SN8 . . .213 B2
Hawkins St 16 SN8 . . .170 A6
Hawkins St SN2 . . .50 A7
Hawksridge 4 SP2 . . .152 A5
Hawkstreet SN15 . . .96 B6
Hawkswood SN3 . . .51 D8
Hawksworth Trad Est
  SN2 . . .50 A8
Hawksworth Way SN2 . . .50 A7
Hawthorn Ave SN2 . . .35 C2
Hawthorn Cl
  Pewsey SN9 . . .215 D5
  1 Salisbury SP2 . . .145 F1
  2 Shaftesbury SP7 . . .202 D2
Hawthorn Gr BA14 . . .105 C5
Hawthorn Rd
  Chippenham SN15 . . .70 C1
  Frome BA11 . . .110 A6
  Tidworth SP9 . . .216 D7
Hay La SN5 . . .48 F6
Hay St SN14 . . .74 A8
Haydock Cl 4 SN14 . . .77 F5
Haydon Cl SN25 . . .34 E5
Haydon Ct Dr SN25 . . .34 E5
Haydon End La SN25 . . .34 D6
Haydon St SN1 . . .50 C7
Haydon View Rd SN25 . . .35 C3
Haydon Wick Prim Sch
  SN25 . . .34 E4
Haydonleigh Dr SN25 . . .34 E4
Haydonleigh Prim Sch
  SN25 . . .34 E4
Haydown Leas SP11 . . .185 C3
Haye's La GL9 . . .24 C6
Hayes Cl BA14 . . .101 E3
Hayes Knoll Sta SN5 . . .33 C6
Hayesdown Fst Sch
  BA11 . . .110 B5
Hayfield SN14 . . .70 A2
Hayfield Ct RG17 . . .171 C7
Haygrove Cl BA12 . . .116 D6

Hayle Rd SN5 . . .49 F6
Haynes Cl SN3 . . .51 C4
Haynes Rd BA13 . . .109 A3
Haywain 4 SN4 . . .217 B3
Haywain Cl SN25 . . .35 C6
Hayward Cl
  Chippenham SN15 . . .78 F5
  Swindon SN25 . . .35 A6
Hayward Pl BA13 . . .108 F5
Haywards Pl SN10 . . .179 F2
Hazel Cl
  Marlborough SN8 . . .175 A7
  Salisbury SP2 . . .145 B3
Hazel Copse 2 SN14 . . .77 F6
Hazel End SN4 . . .47 L1
Hazel Cl Calne SN11 . . .81 B1
  Swindon SN2 . . .35 C3
  Trowbridge BA14 . . .105 B5
Hazel Way SN14 . . .75 A5
Hazelbury Cres SN3 . . .51 C7
Hazelbury Hill SN13 . . .83 D6
Hazelbury Manor Gdns*
  SN13 . . .83 F5
Hazeldon La SN14 . . .203 D6
Hazelwood Rd SN12 . . .94 A3
Hazlemere Cl SN14 . . .51 B4
Hazzard's Hill BA12 . . .139 B5
Headington Hts SN11 . . .89 B1
Headlands Gr SN3 . . .35 E3
Headlands Sch SN2 . . .35 D3
Headquarters Rd
  8 Durrington/Bulford
  SP4 . . .198 F6
  Westbury BA13 . . .108 C6
Heale Gdn* SP4 . . .131 D5
Heale Cl BA12 . . .115 B8
Heath La
  Buttermere SN8 . . .185 C7
  Great Somerford SN15 . . .43 D2
Heath Sq 1 SP4 . . .197 E6
Heath View Dr SP2 . . .145 C3
Heath Way SN11 . . .81 B8
Heathcote Rd SN12 . . .94 C5
Heather Ave SN12 . . .94 C4
Heather Cl BA13 . . .108 F4
Heather Shaw BA14 . . .105 E8
Heather Way SN11 . . .81 C1
Heathfield SN15 . . .70 E2
Heathfields Way 2 SP7 . . .202 C2
Heathlands The BA12 . . .116 F5
Heathway BA12 . . .115 C8
Heaton Cl SN3 . . .35 A6
Heaven's Gate* BA12 . . .115 C1
Hebden Rd BA15 . . .99 F3
Heddington CE Prim Sch
  SN11 . . .89 B1
Heddington Cl
  Swindon SN2 . . .35 B5
  Trowbridge BA14 . . .105 C5
Hedge Row SN4 . . .163 A6
Hedges The 4 SN4 . . .163 A6
Hedgesparrow La SN3 . . .83 F8
Heights The SN1 . . .50 A4
Helena Rd SN3 . . .34 C8
Helena Terr 7 SP1 . . .146 B1
Helmdon Rd BA14 . . .101 A1
Helmsdale SN25 . . .34 F4
Helmsdale Wlk SN5 . . .51 A4
Helps Well Rd BA14 . . .102 B2
Helston Rd SN3 . . .51 A5
Henderson Cl BA14 . . .105 B7
Hendon Pl SN12 . . .94 E1
Henfords Marsh BA12 . . .117 B4
Hengest Cl 5 SP10 . . .193 C2
Henley Dr SN3 . . .23 A7
Henley La SN13 . . .83 C4
Henman Cl
  Devizes SN10 . . .214 B4
  Swindon SN25 . . .35 A5
Henry St 9 Swindon SN1 . . .50 B6
Henset Village* SN8 . . .175 E7
Hepworth Rd 5 SN25 . . .34 F6
Herbert Rd
  3 Redlynch SP5 . . .211 C7
  Salisbury SP2 . . .145 C3
Hercules Way 1 SN12 . . .178 B8
Herd St SN8 . . .213 D4
Hereford Cl SN14 . . .78 A5
Hereford Lawns SN3 . . .50 F8
Herepath SN8 . . .167 C1
Herman Miller Ind Est
Hermitage La SN4 . . .35 E3
Hermsham St SP7 . . .203 C4
Heron Cl SN11 . . .81 D3
Heron Way SN14 . . .77 F6
Heron Wlk 12 SN4 . . .198 C7
Heronbridge Cl 2 SN5 . . .49 C7
Herongate RG17 . . .177 B8
Herons Cl BA12 . . .115 F8
Heronscroft BA12 . . .117 D5
Heronslade BA12 . . .117 D5
Heronswood SP2 . . .152 A5
Herschell Cl SN25 . . .34 B7
Hertford Cl
  1 Fordingbridge SP6 . . .210 D2
  4 Swindon SN3 . . .50 F6
Hesketh Cres SN1 . . .50 D3

Hewitt Cl Swindon SN3 . . .51 C4
  Trowbridge BA14 . . .105 E7
Hewlett Cl SN15 . . .79 A5
Hexham Cl
  4 Chippenham SN14 . . .77 F6
  Swindon SN5 . . .49 B5
Heyford Cl 8 SP4 . . .217 E3
Heytesbury CE Prim Sch
  BA12 . . .194 C5
Heytsbury Gdns 4 SN5 . . .48 F4
Heywood CE SN4 . . .35 B5
Heywood Prep Sch
  SN13 . . .77 A2
Hicks Cl SN4 . . .64 A6
Hidcot Ct SN25 . . .34 E7
High Clear Down Nature
  Reserve* SN8 . . .169 D7
High La SP5 . . .205 B4
High Lawn SN10 . . .179 D8
High Mead SN4 . . .47 F2
High Rd
  Ashton Keynes SN6 . . .6 F1
  Bishopstone SP5 . . .205 E4
  Britford SP5 . . .152 D4
High St Alderbury SP5 . . .153 C3
  Amesbury SP4 . . .217 A3
  Ansty SP3 . . .203 F6
  Ashbury SN6 . . .164 A7
  Ashmore SP5 . . .206 E4
  Avebury SN8 . . .173 B8
  Badminton GL9 . . .38 E2
  Bath BA1 . . .82 D2
  Berwick St James SP3 . . .196 F2
  Bishopstone SN6 . . .163 E6
  Box SN13 . . .83 C5
  Broad Blunsdon SN26 . . .21 B1
  Bromham SN15 . . .96 A7
  Bulford SP4 . . .217 D8
  Burbage SN8 . . .175 C1
  Calne SN11 . . .81 B3
  Chapmanslade BA13 . . .111 B4
  Cherwell Magna SN10 . . .179 C1
  Chippenham SN15 . . .78 D7
  Chiseldown SN4 . . .65 D4
  Codford BA12 . . .195 A2
  Colerne SN14 . . .75 B3
  Collingbourne Ducis SN8 . . .191 E8
  Compton Chamberlayne
  SP3 . . .205 A8
  Corsham SN13 . . .77 A1
  Cricklade SN6 . . .19 E8
  Damerham SP6 . . .209 F3
  Dauntsey SN15 . . .59 B2
  Durrington/Bulford SP4 . . .198 B7
  Erlestoke SN10 . . .187 A8
  Figheldean SN4 . . .190 B1
  24 Fordingbridge SP6 . . .210 D1
  Fovant SP3 . . .204 E7
  Great Bedwyn SN8 . . .176 B3
  Heytesbury BA12 . . .194 C5
  Highworth SN6 . . .23 A5
  Hindon SP3 . . .200 A4
  Hinton Charterhouse BA2 . . .98 E1
  Hungerford RG17 . . .177 B7
  Idmiston SP4 . . .133 D5
  Kempsford GL7 . . .10 C7
  Lacock SN15 . . .86 D5
  Lambourn RG17 . . .164 F3
  Lechlade GL7 . . .2 C4
  Limpley Stoke BA2 . . .99 B5
  Little Bedwyn SN8 . . .176 D4
  Littleton Panell SN10 . . .187 D8
  9 Ludgershall SP11 . . .192 A5
  Maiden Bradley with Yarnfield
  BA12 . . .118 E3
  Malmesbury SN16 . . .28 A3
  Market Lavington SN10 . . .179 F1
  Marlborough SN8 . . .213 A1
  Melksham SN12 . . .94 A4
  Meysey Hampton GL7 . . .1 A5
  Netheravon SP4 . . .190 A3
  Ogbourne St George
  SN8 . . .168 F5
  Pewsey SN9 . . .215 D5
  Pitton & Farley SP5 . . .148 C3
  Porton SP4 . . .133 D6
  Purton SN5 . . .33 B4
  Ramsbury SN8 . . .170 B2
  Rode BA11 . . .103 F1
  Rowde SN10 . . .96 D2
  Salisbury SP1 . . .152 A8
  Seend SN12 . . .178 E8
  Semington BA14 . . .102 F6
  18 Shaftesbury SP7 . . .202 C1
  Shipton Bellinger SP9 . . .199 D8
  Shrewton SP3 . . .196 E7
  Sixpenny Handley SP5 . . .208 A4
  South Cerney GL7 . . .6 F6
  Steeple Ashton BA14 . . .178 A3
  Stourton with Gasper
  BA12 . . .123 F1
  Sutton Benger SN15 . . .57 C2
  Sutton Veny BA12 . . .117 F1
  Swindon SN25 . . .34 E4
  Swindon SN3 . . .50 D4
  Tilshead SP3 . . .188 B2
  Tisbury SP3 . . .203 E8
  Upavon SN9 . . .181 F2
  Urchfont SN10 . . .180 C4
  Wanborough SN4 . . .163 B6
  Warminster BA12 . . .117 A7
  West Lavington SN10 . . .179 D1
  Winterbourne Stoke SP3 . . .190 F4
  Woodgreen SP6 . . .211 A4
  Wootton Bassett SN4 . . .47 D1

High St continued
  Worton SN10 . . .179 B4
  Wroughton SN4 . . .64 A5
  Wylye BA12 . . .201 E8
  Zeale SP8 . . .137 F3
High St Brow SN8 . . .169 A6
High View Cl SP3 . . .203 E7
Highbury Ave SP2 . . .145 E2
Highbury Cl 2 SP2 . . .145 E2
Highbury Pk SP2 . . .117 C6
Highbury Rd
  SP2 . . .145 E2
Highclere Ave SN3 . . .50 F4
Highden Way SN6 . . .35 A7
Higher Barn Cl SP7 . . .206 B7
Higher Blandford Rd 2
  SP7 . . .202 D1
Higher Mere Pk*
  BA12 . . .202 A8
Highfield SN15 . . .96 C7
Highfield Cl SP4 . . .102 F5
Highfield Cres SP5 . . .149 B6
Highfield Rd Salisbury SP2 . . .145 E2
  Salisbury SP2 . . .145 E2
Highfield Rise 1 SP3 . . .196 F6
Highgate Cottage SN4 . . .46 F5
Highgrove Cl SN11 . . .81 D2
Highland Cl 8 SN5 . . .49 A7
Highland View SP2 . . .130 A2
Highlands SN10 . . .179 D5
Highlands Cl SN13 . . .84 A8
Highlands Rd SP2 . . .152 A6
Highlands Way SN6 . . .161 D4
Highmoor Copse SN5 . . .34 A1
Highnam Cl SN3 . . .36 A1
Highridge Cl SN5 . . .33 A3
Highway Comm SN1 . . .166 B6
Highway La SN13 . . .158 F5
Highwood Cl 3 SN2 . . .34 D4
Highworth Ind Est SN6 . . .23 A7
Highworth Rd
  Highworth SN6 . . .22 D1
  Shrivenham SN6 . . .23 E1
  South Marston SN3 . . .36 E6
Highworth Recn Ctr
  SN6 . . .22 F5
Highworth Warneford Sch
  SN6 . . .23 A5
Hilary Cl SN5 . . .35 C4
Hilbourne Cl BA12 . . .117 B7
Hillcote Hospl SP1 . . .145 C3
Hillcrest Colerne SN14 . . .75 C6
  Malmesbury SN16 . . .28 B2
Hillcroft SN11 . . .81 C2
Hilldrop Cl SN8 . . .170 B2
Hilldrop Rd
  Lamborn RG17 . . .171 A6
  Ramsbury SN8 . . .169 F3
Hilliers Yd SN8 . . .213 D3
Hillingdon Rd SN3 . . .51 B4
Hillmead Dr SN5 . . .34 B1
Hillocks The SN4 . . .60 B5
Hillside Leigh SN6 . . .18 C5
  Nettleton SN14 . . .53 A4
Hillside Ave SN1 . . .50 A4
Hillside Cl
  Heddington SN11 . . .89 B1
  West Tytherley SP5 . . .155 F2
Hillside Dr SN4 . . .133 C3
Hillside Pk BA13 . . .109 B3
Hillside Rd
  4 Hungerford RG17 . . .177 B6
  South Newton SP2 . . .130 B2
Hillside Way SN26 . . .21 A1
Hilltop Cl 2 SP3 . . .196 F6
Hilltop Way SN1 . . .146 A5
Hillview SP5 . . .204 C3
Hillwell SN1 . . .217 B4
Hillwood Cl BA14 . . .101 A1
Hillwood La BA12 . . .116 F5
Hillworth Gdns SN10 . . .214 A3
Hillworth Rd 18 SN10 . . .214 A3
Hillyard Cl SN3 . . .48 F4
Hilmarton Ave 1 SN2 . . .35 C5

Hilmarton Prim Sch
  SN11 . . .166 A6
Hilperton CE Prim Sch
  BA14 . . .102 A3
Hilperton Dr BA14 . . .102 A2
Hilperton Rd BA14 . . .101 E1
Hinde's Meadow SP3 . . .196 F7
Hindon La SP3 . . .200 D1
Hindon Rd
  Chilmark SP3 . . .201 B3
  East Knoyle SP3 . . .141 C2
  Kingston Deverill BA12 . . .126 D7
Hinkson Cl SN25 . . .34 F8
Hinton Hill
  Bishopstone SN4 . . .163 D6
  Hinton Charterhouse BA2 . . .98 A1
Hinton Ho* BA2 . . .98 E1
Hinton La BA14 . . .178 A5
Hinton Priory* SP3 . . .98 F3
Hinton Springs SN6 . . .163 D6
Hinton St . . .50 B8
Hitchings Skilling SN14 . . .75 B3
Hither Cl SN14 . . .78 A8
Hither Spring SN13 . . .84 F8
Hither Way SN15 . . .86 D5
Hoadley Gn SN1 . . .146 D4
Hobbes Cl SN16 . . .27 F4
Hobbs Hill BA14 . . .178 B5
Hobbs Wlk SN13 . . .77 A1
Hobhouse Cl BA15 . . .100 E4
Hobley Dr SN3 . . .36 A3
Hocketts Cl SN15 . . .66 B6
Hodds Hill SN5 . . .34 B2
Hodge La SN16 . . .27 F4
Hodges Barn Gdns*
  GL8 . . .26 F8
Hodson Rd SN4 . . .65 C4
Hoggington La BA14 . . .104 D4
Hoggs La SN5 . . .33 A4
Holben Cl 8 SN5 . . .49 A5
Holbein Ct SN5 . . .49 A5
Holbein Field 12 SN5 . . .49 A5
Holbein Mews 6 SN5 . . .49 A5
Holbein Pl SN5 . . .49 A5
Holbein Sq 10 SN5 . . .49 A4
Holbein Wlk 9 SN5 . . .49 A4
Holborn Hill OX12 . . .165 E8
Holbrook La SN15 . . .105 D6
Holbrook Prim Sch
  BA14 . . .105 D6
Holbrook Vale SN12 . . .93 F1
Holbrook Way SN1 . . .50 B6
Holcombe La BA2 . . .82 A1
Holdcroft Cl SN26 . . .21 C2
Holden Cres SN25 . . .35 A6
Holden Garson Rd
  SN3 . . .35 B6
Holders Rd SN4 . . .217 C4
Holford Cres GL7 . . .10 E6
Holinshed Pl 4 SN5 . . .49 B6
Holinshed Mews 3 SN5 . . .49 A5
Holland Cl SN15 . . .79 A4
Holland Dr 11 SN10 . . .193 D2
Holliday Cl SN25 . . .35 A6
Hollies La BA1 . . .82 A6
Hollies Moor SN3 . . .51 D2
Hollis Gdns SN14 . . .39 A3
Hollis Way BA14 . . .104 F3
Hollow La SN14 . . .184 A7
Hollow The
  Bratton BA13 . . .186 A7
  Chirton SN10 . . .180 F4
  Corsley BA12 . . .111 B1
  Dilton Marsh BA13 . . .112 C8
  Shrewton SP3 . . .196 E7
  Sixpenny Handley SP5 . . .208 A4
  Steeple Langford SP3 . . .128 C5
Hollow Way SN3 . . .51 D8
Holloway 6 Salisbury SP1 . . .152 B8
  Swindon SN3 . . .36 C1
Holloway Hill SN14 . . .66 E8
Holloway La SN3 . . .141 B1
Hollows Cl SP2 . . .151 F6
Hollows The SN2 . . .144 B4
Holly Cl Calne SN11 . . .81 C1
  Pewsey SN9 . . .215 D6
  Swindon SN2 . . .35 A2
Holly Ct BA11 . . .110 B7
Holly Dr SN14 . . .75 A5
Hollybush Cl
  Acton Turville GL9 . . .53 A6
  Chippenham Without
  SN14 . . .70 A2
  Winsley BA15 . . .99 E2
Hollybush La SN9 . . .215 D6
Hollybush Rd BA12 . . .117 A8
Holmbury Cl BA11 . . .110 C6
Holme La BA13 . . .186 B7
Holmeleaze BA14 . . .178 A4
Holmes Cl SN15 . . .78 F4
Holmfield 1 SN16 . . .187 E8
Holmleigh SN25 . . .34 E4
Holmoak Ct SN3 . . .51 D2
Holt La Tangley SP11 . . .193 B8
  Teffont SP3 . . .201 C1
Holt Rd
  Bradford-on-Avon BA15 . . .100 E6
  Witham Friary BA11 . . .123 B1
Holt VC Prim Sch BA14 . . .92 F1
Holy Family Cath Prim Sch
  SN3 . . .51 B6
Holy Rood Church* SN3 . . .50 E4
Holy Rood Cath Inf Sch
  SN1 . . .50 C5

Holy Rood Cath Jun Sch
SN3 ....50 D5
Holy Trinity CE Prim Sch
Calne SN11 ....81 C1
Cheverell Magna SN10 .....187 B8
Holyrood Cl BA14 ....105 B5
Trowbridge BA14 ....105 D7
Home Cl Chiseldown SN4 ...65 C4
Trowbridge BA14 ....105 D7
Home Farm Cl
Heddington SN11 ....89 B1
Mildenhall SN8 ....175 B8
Steeple Ashton BA14 ......178 A3
Home Farm Gdns 10
SP10 ....193 C2
Home Farm Rd SP2 ....144 C1
Home Fields SN14 ....68 F5
Home Gd Cricklade SN6 ....19 C8
Wootton Bassett SN4 ....48 A2
Homefarm SN6 ....22 F6
Homefield Mere BA12 .....138 F5
Motcombe SP7 ....202 C2
Wootton Bassett SN4 ....47 E2
Homefield Way RG17 .....177 B7
Homefields
Longbridge Deverill
BA12 ....120 F6
Marlborough SN8 ....213 F2
Homelands The 1
BA12 ....116 E5
Homes Mead SN13 ....76 D1
Homington Rd
Britford SP5 ....151 D3
Coombe Bissett SP5 ......157 B8
Honey Garston SN11 ....81 C3
Honey Hill 2 RG17 ....165 A2
Honey Knob Hill SN14 .....55 F1
Honey La Norton SN16 .....41 E6
Westbury BA13 ....112 D8
Honeybone Wlk SN3 ....51 E7
Honeybrook Cl SN14 ....78 B8
Honeybunch Cnr SN8 ....164 C6
Honeyfields 10 RG17 ....177 B7
Honeylight View 3 SN25 ..35 A6
Honeymans Cl BA14 ......105 F8
Honeymead SN11 ....81 C3
Honeysuckle Cl
Calne Without SN11 ....80 F4
Chippenham Without
SN14 ....70 B3
Swindon SN25 ....34 D5
4 Trowbridge BA14 ....105 D7
Honiton Rd SN3 ....51 B5
Hook Cl SN5 ....34 A1
Hook St Hook SN4 ....47 F4
Swindon SN5 ....48 F4
Hooks Hill SN5 ....33 C4
Hooks La SN10 ....179 A7
Hookwood La SP11 ....192 E8
Hoopers Pl SN1 ....50 D4
Hop Gdns The SP5 ....161 C3
Hopgood Cl SN10 ....214 F6
Hopkinson Way SP10 .....193 B1
Hops Cl SP3 ....201 A3
Hopton Cl SN5 ....49 B3
Hopton Pk Ind Est
SN10 ....214 E7
Hopton Rd SN10 ....214 D6
Horace St SN2 ....49 F7
Horcott Rd Fairford GL7 ....1 F6
Roughmoor SN5 ....34 B2
Horder Mews SN3 ....50 D4
Horham Cres SN3 ....51 A4
Horn's La SN14 ....167 B8
Hornbeam Cl 1 BA11 ....110 C6
Hornbeam Cres SN12 ......94 A3
Hornbury Cl SN2 ....35 B2
Hornbury Cl SN16 ....17 A2
Hornbury Hill SN16 ....17 A2
Hornchurch Rd 20 SN12 .178 B8
Horne Rd SP4 ....199 B6
Horningsham Prim Sch
BA12 ....119 B2
Hornsey Gdns SN2 ....36 A5
Horse Barrow* SN4 ....133 D3
Horse Fair La SN6 ....19 E8
Horse Rd BA14 ....101 F4
Horse Shoe La SP3 ....142 C3
Horsebrook Pk SN11 ....81 B2
Horsebrook The SN11 ......81 C2
Horsefair La SN10 ....59 C3
Horsell Cl 2 SN4 ....47 E2
Horseponds 8 SP7 ....202 B2
Horsepool SN5 ....96 B8
Horseshoe Cres SN5 ....34 A1
Horseshoe La SP11 ....193 F8
Horton Ave SN10 ....214 E6
Horton Cl BA15 ....100 E4
Horton Rd
Bishops Cannings SN10 ..172 B2
Devizes SN10 ....214 F7
Swindon SN2 ....35 E6
Hospital Rd BA13 ....109 A2
Hossil La SN6 ....30 E6
Houldsworth Ave
BA12 ....117 D8
Howard Cl SN3 ....50 F6
Howard-Vyse Rd SP4 ....197 F7
Howgare Rd SP5 ....205 B2
Hreod Parkway Sch
SN2 ....34 E3
Hubble View SN5 ....34 B6
Hubert Hamilton Rd
SP4 ....198 E6

Huddleston Cl SN2 ....50 D8
Hudson Rd
Amesbury SP4 ....217 C4
Malmesbury SN16 ....27 F4
Salisbury SP1 ....145 F3
Hudson Way SN25 ....35 A5
Hudswell La SN13 ....84 C8
Hughes Cl SN8 ....213 A2
Hughes St SN2 ....49 F7
Hugo Dr SN25 ....35 A6
Hulbert Cl SN13 ....76 E1
Hullavington Airfield
SN14 ....56 A7
Hullavington CE Prim Sch
SN14 ....41 F1
Hulse Rd SP1 ....146 A2
Humber La SN9 ....216 B4
Humphrey's La 3 RG17 ..171 E7
Hungerdown La SN14 ......78 A6
Hungerdown Ave BA14 ...105 A7
Hungerford City Prim Sch
RG17 ....177 B7
Hungerford Hill
Great Shefford RG17 .....171 F4
Lambourn RG17 ....165 A1
Hungerford La
Andover SP10 ....193 E3
Chute SP11 ....185 A1
Kintbury RG17 ....177 F6
Tangley SP11 ....193 A8
Hungerford Leisure Ctr
RG17 ....177 B6
Hungerford Rd
Buttermere SN8 ....185 B7
Calne SN11 ....81 B4
Chippenham SN15 ....70 D1
Grafton SN8 ....184 A7
Hungerford RG17 ....177 C7
Hungerford Sta RG17 ....177 C7
Hunsdon Cl SN3 ....51 A6
Hunt Cl The BA14 ....102 F5
Hunt St SN1 ....50 C5
Huntenhull La BA13 ......111 D4
Hunter's Gr SN2 ....35 B1
Hunters Chase BA11 .....108 F2
Hunters Mead SP7 ....202 A5
Hunters Meadow SN4 .....68 F5
Huntingdon Pl BA15 .....100 C7
Huntingdon Rise
BA15 ....100 C7
Huntingdon St BA15 .....100 C8
Huntingdon Way SN14 ....78 A6
Huntley Cl SN3 ....50 F7
Hunts Hill SN26 ....21 B2
Hunts Mead SN15 ....96 A7
Hunts Mill Rd SN4 ....61 A8
Hunts Rise SN3 ....36 C7
Huntsland SN4 ....47 F2
Hurdcott La SP4 ....146 F8
Hurley Cl 5 SP4 ....217 D3
Hurricane Rd SN12 ....94 C1
Hurst Cres SN2 ....35 C3
Hurst's La SN9 ....181 C7
Huxley Cl GL7 ....7 A7
Hyam Cotts SN2 ....27 C4
Hyde La
Marlborough SN8 ....213 C3
Purton SN5 ....33 C4
Hyde Rd Swindon SN25 ...35 D6
Trowbridge BA14 ....101 C2
Hyde The SN1 ....33 D4
Hylder Cl SN2 ....34 D4
Hyson Cres 6 SP11 ......192 B5
Hysopp Cl SN2 ....34 C4
Hythe Rd SN1 ....50 B5

Icknield Sch SP10 ....193 F1
Icknield Way
Andover SP10 ....193 E2
Bishopstone SN6 ....163 E6
Icomb Cl SN5 ....49 C4
Idlebush Barrow*
SN7 ....164 E7
Idmiston CE Prim Sch
SP4 ....133 G6
Idmiston Rd SP4 ....133 E6
Idovers Dr SN5 ....49 C4
Idstone Hill SN6 ....163 F7
Idstone Rd SN6 ....164 A7
Iffley Rd SN2 ....49 F8
Ilford Fields SN3 ....99 E3
Ilford Hill BA15 ....99 F2
Ilford La BA15 ....99 D3
Ilford Manor* BA15 ....99 E3
Iles Ct SN11 ....73 F7
Ilkeston Rd SN25 ....34 C7
Ilynton Ave SP5 ....148 C2
Imber Ave
Amesbury SP4 ....217 D2
Warminster BA12 ....117 C7
Imber Pl SP3 ....188 B3
Imber Rd Bratton BA13 ..186 C6
10 Shaftesbury SP7 ......202 D2
Warminster BA12 ....117 D8
Imber Wlk SN2 ....34 D4
Imberwood Cl BA12 ......117 C7
Imly Cl BA12 ....117 F1
India Ave SP2 ....145 C2
Indigo Gdns BA13 ....108 F3
Indigo La BA13 ....108 F3
Ingles Edge RG17 ....177 E2
Inglesham Cl BA14 ....105 C5
Inglesham Rd SN2 ....35 C4
Inglesham Village* SN6 ...2 B1
Inglewood Rd RG17 ......177 E5

Ingram Pl BA13 ....108 F4
Ingram Rd BA13 ....94 D5
Ingram St SN16 ....28 A3
Inkpen Prim Sch
RG17 ....177 E3
Inkpen Rd RG17 ....177 C5
Inlands Cl SN9 ....215 C5
Inmarsh La SN14 ....178 E7
Inmead BA13 ....186 C8
Innox Mill Cl BA14 ....101 B3
Innox Rd BA14 ....101 B1
Intercity Trad Est SN12 ...94 A5
Inverary Rd SN4 ....64 A7
Ipswich St SN2 ....50 C8
Ironstone Cl SN25 ....34 E7
Irston Way 4 SN5 ....49 B4
Irving Way SN8 ....213 C2
Isbury Rd SN8 ....213 E2
Isis Cl Calne SN11 ....81 A4
Swindon SN25 ....35 A3
Island The SN10 ....214 B3
Islandsmead SN3 ....51 C6
Islay Cres SN4 ....22 F6
Isles Rd 6 SN8 ....170 B2
Islington SN8 ....101 D1
Islington St SN1 ....50 C6
Itchen Cl 2 SO51 ....212 F6
Ivies The SN9 ....181 F5
Ivy Fields SN13 ....77 A2
Ivy La
Broad Blunsdon SN26 .....21 B2
Chippenham SN15 ....178 D7
South Wraxall BA15 ....91 E5
Ivy La SN15 ....178 D8
Ivy Mead BA12 ....139 B5
Ivy Rd SN15 ....178 D7
Ivy Rd Ind Est SN15 ......78 D7
Ivy St SP1 ....152 B8
Ivy Terr BA15 ....100 D7
Ixworth Cl 10 SN5 ....49 A7

Jack Paul Cl BA12 ....139 A6
Jack Thorne Cl SN5 ....34 A2
Jack's Hedge Cnr
BH21 ....208 F2
Jackaments Barn GL7 ....4 B6
Jackson's La SN15 ....70 D5
Jackson Cl SN10 ....214 C2
Jacob's Barrow* SP5 .....211 E4
Jacobs Wlk SN3 ....51 D4
Jagdalik Rd SP9 ....216 C4
Jaggard View SN4 ....217 C3
Jaggards La SN13 ....84 D5
James Cl SN15 ....79 A4
James Rd SP4 ....217 C4
James St Salisbury SP2 .145 F1
Trowbridge BA14 ....101 D2
James Watt Cl SN2 ....50 A7
James's Hill BA10 ....122 A7
Jamrud Rd SP9 ....216 B5
Jarvis St SN9 ....181 F2
Jasmine Cl Calne SN11 ....81 B3
Chippenham SN14 ....70 A1
Swindon SN2 ....34 D4
Jasmine Way BA14 ....105 E7
Javelin Cl 6 SN4 ....217 D3
Jay Cl BA11 ....110 B6
Jeanneau Cl 24 SP7 .....202 C2
Jefferies Ave SN2 ....35 D2
Jefferies Cl SN8 ....213 B2
Jellicoe Ct SP10 ....193 F1
Jenkins St BA14 ....101 C1
Jenner Cl SN4 ....163 A6
Jennings St SN2 ....49 F6
Jerram Gall The*
SP1 ....152 B8
Jersey My SN5 ....49 B8
Jervis Ct 8 SP10 ....193 F1
Jewel Cl 4 SN5 ....33 F5
Jewell Cl SP1 ....146 D4
Joanna Cl 4 SP5 ....210 F8
Jobbers La SP3 ....203 E7
Jockey La SN15 ....96 A7
John Alder Cl SN4 ....65 C3
John Aubrey Cl SN14 ......68 F6
John Bentley Sch
Calne SN11 ....81 B1
Calne SN11 ....89 B8
John Betjeman Cl 1
SN16 ....28 A5
John French Way SP4 ...217 E8
John Gay Rd 5 SP4 ......217 B3
John Herring Cres SN3 ....36 A1
John Ivie Ctr Pru SP1 ...152 B7
John O'Gaunt Com Tech Coll
RG17 ....177 B6
John of Gaunt Rd GL7 ....10 D6
John of Gaunt Sch The
BA14 ....105 B8
John Rennie Cl
Bradford-on-Avon BA15 .100 E4
Devizes SN10 ....214 A2
John Rumble Cl SN10 ...214 C3
John St SN1 ....50 C5
Johnson Way SN11 ....192 A5
Joiner La SN1 ....35 C5
Jole Cl SN2 ....35 E5
Joles La BA11 ....110 F1
Jolliffe St 8 SN1 ....50 A5
Jones's Mill Nature Reserve*
SN9 ....215 D1
Jones Hill BA15 ....100 C5
Jordan Cl SN15 ....78 F5
Joseph St 5 SN1 ....50 A5
Joule Rd 3 SP10 ....193 B1

Joyce Cl SN25 ....35 A6
Jubb's La SN5 ....169 A5
Jubilee Cl
Bermerton Heath SP2 ...145 C3
2 Sandleheath SP6 ......210 C1
Westbury BA13 ....109 A3
Jubilee Ct
North Tidworth SP9 ....216 D7
3 Salisbury SP2 ....145 F2
Jubilee Gdns GL7 ....6 F7
Jubilee Hill SP4 ....197 F1
Jubilee Rd
Devizes SN10 ....214 D3
Sandleheath SP6 ....210 C1
Swindon SN3 ....34 D3
Juggler's La SN11 ....146 C2
Juliana Cl 3 SN5 ....49 A7
Jump Farm SN10 ....214 D3
Jump Farm Rd SN10 .....214 C3
Junction Rd
Alderbury SP5 ....153 E3
Bradford-on-Avon BA15 .100 D6
Devizes SN10 ....214 D3
Juniper Cl SN3 ....51 B8
Juniper Dr SN11 ....146 A5
Juniper Rd SP5 ....148 C7
Juno Way SN11 ....49 F4
Jutland Cres 3 SP10 .....193 D2

Kandahar SN8 ....170 A7
Kandy Rd 3 SP4 ....198 E6
Karachi Cl SP9 ....216 C2
Karslake Cl 6 SN3 ....51 C4
Kashmir Rd 1 SP4 ....198 E6
Katherine House Gall*
SN8 ....213 E2
Katherine's Wlk GL7 ....2 D4
Katifer La SN16 ....28 A3
Keates Cl BA14 ....101 D1
Keats Cl SN4 ....47 F3
Keats Cres SN2 ....102 F8
Keble Cl Lechlade GL7 .....2 D5
Swindon SN3 ....51 C7
Keels SN6 ....8 C1
Keevil Airfield BA14 ......178 C4
Keevil Ave SN11 ....81 A3
Keevil CE Prim Sch
BA14 ....178 B5
Kelham Cl 8 SN3 ....50 F4
Kelham Gdns SN8 ....213 E3
Kellsborough Rd SN4 ......63 F7
Kelly Gdns SN25 ....34 F6
Kelmscot Rd SN25 ....35 C3
Kelsey Rd SP1 ....146 B1
Kelso Ct 3 SN1 ....78 A5
Kelston Rd SN8 ....176 C4
Kelvin Rd SN3 ....51 A7
Kemble Bsns Pk GL7 ....4 A3
Kemble Dr SN2 ....35 C2
Kemble Sta GL7 ....4 F8
Kembles Cl SN16 ....28 C2
Kembrey Bsns Pk SN2 ....35 D2
Kembrey St SN2 ....35 D2
Kemerton Wlk SN3 ....51 A3
Kemmel Rd SP11 ....191 F4
Kemp Cl SN3 ....214 C3
Kemp's La BA11 ....110 F7
Kempsfield SN10 ....214 C1
Kempton Pk Ct 10 SN14 ..77 F6
Ken Savage Cl SN3 ....51 A6
Kendal SN5 ....49 B4
Kendrick Cl Ind Est SP9 ..49 B8
Kenilworth Cl SN11 ....94 B3
Kenilworth Gdns SN12 ....94 B3
Kenilworth Lawns SN3 ....50 F3
Kennedy Ave SN12 ....85 D1
Kennedy Dr SN3 ....51 D4
Kennedy Meadow
RG17 ....177 B6
Kennet Ave 6 SN2 ....36 B2
Kennet Dr 6 SN3 ....38 E2
Kennet & Avon Canal Mus
The* SN10 ....214 B4
Kennet Ave SN25 ....35 B3
Kennet Cl
Melksham SN12 ....94 A6
Warminster BA12 ....117 A5
Kennet Ct RG17 ....177 C5
Kennet Gdns BA15 ....100 D5
Kennet Mews SN3 ....213 D3
Kennet Pl SN8 ....213 E3
Kennet Rd
Devizes SN10 ....214 D3
South Tedworth SP9 .....216 E6
Wroughton SN4 ....49 A7
Kennet Way
Hungerford RG17 ....177 B8
Trowbridge BA14 ....101 D3
Kennett Valley CE Prim Sch
SN8 ....173 D8
Kensington Cl BA14 .....101 D2
Kensington Fields
BA14 ....104 F7
Kensington Rd 1 SP2 ...145 F2
Kensington Way SN14 ....77 F7
Kent Cl SN14 ....78 A6
Kent Rd Salisbury SP2 ...151 E6
Swindon SN1 ....50 B4
Kenton Cl SN3 ....51 A3
Kenton Dr BA14 ....101 F1
Kents Hill SP3 ....201 A3
Kenwin Cl SN3 ....36 B2
Kenwood Cl SN3 ....214 C3
Kerby Ave SP4 ....190 B3
Kerrs Way SN4 ....64 A6

Kerry Cl
Derry Hill/Studley SN11 ...79 F2
Swindon SN5 ....49 A7
Kershaw Rd SN3 ....51 C4
Kestrel Dr SN3 ....51 E6
Keswick Rd SN3 ....51 B3
Kettle La BA14 ....106 A2
Ketton Cl BA14 ....101 A3
Kew Dr 4 BA14 ....105 A7
Kewlake La SO51 ....212 F8
Keynes Ctry Pk* GL7 ....6 B5
Keyneston Rd SN3 ....50 F5
Keynsham Wlk SN3 ....51 B6
Kibblewhite Cl SN5 ....33 B3
Kickdom Cl SP4 ....217 D2
Kidston Way SN13 ....84 A6
Kiel Dr SP10 ....193 D2
Kilben Cl SN5 ....48 F7
Kilda Rd SN6 ....22 F6
Kill Barrow (Long Barrow)*
BA12 ....187 A7
Kiln Cl Alderbury SP5 ....153 F1
Devizes SN10 ....214 D2
Kiln La Redlynch SP5 ....211 D6
Swindon SN2 ....34 F1
Kilns The SN11 ....81 C4
Kilsby Dr SN3 ....51 E5
Kilsyth Cl SN5 ....49 B5
Kilverts Cl SN14 ....78 A7
Kimberley Rd SN3 ....51 A4
Kimbolton Cl 8 SN5 ....49 A4
Kimmeridge Cl SN3 ....51 C6
Kimpton Thruxton & Fyfield
CE Prim Sch SP11 ......192 C1
King Alfred Cl SN9 ....215 D5
King Alfred St SN15 ....78 C8
King Alfred Way BA15 .....99 D2
King Alfred's CE Mid Sch
SP7 ....202 D2
King Alfred's Way
SP7 ....202 C2
King Arthur's Way
SP10 ....193 C2
King Barrow*
Bishopstrow BA12 ....117 F5
Winterbourne Stoke
SP4 ....197 C2
King Charles Rd SN5 ......49 B4
King Henry Dr
Chippenham SN15 ....79 A4
Swindon SN5 ....48 F4
King John St SN1 ....50 D4
King John's House*
SP5 ....207 B4
King La BA12 ....116 E5
King Oak* SN8 ....175 C6
King St Melksham SN12 ..94 A3
3 Swindon SN1 ....50 B6
Warminster BA12 ....116 E5
Wilton SP2 ....144 D4
King William St SN1 ....50 C4
King William St CE Prim Sch
SN1 ....50 C4
King's House* SP1 ....152 A7
King's La SP3 ....203 F5
King's Rd SP1 ....146 A2
King's Wall SN16 ....28 A2
Kingdom Ave BA13 ....108 C5
Kingdown Com Sch
BA12 ....117 D6
Kingfisher Cl SP2 ....152 A5
Kingfisher Dr
Bower Hill SN15 ....94 D1
Devizes SN10 ....214 E5
7 Durrington/Bulford
SP4 ....198 C2
Swindon SN3 ....51 D7
Westbury BA13 ....109 A4
Kingfishers 2 SP9 ....199 D8
Kingham Cl SN14 ....78 C7
Kings Ave
Chippenham Without
SN14 ....77 B2
Corsham SN13 ....76 F2
Highworth SN6 ....23 A5
Kings Ct 5 BA12 ....116 E6
Kings Dr SN8 ....175 C6
Kings Gate SN4 ....47 E2
Kings Gdns BA14 ....101 E5
Kings Hill 18 SP7 ....202 C2
Kings Lodge Prim Sch
SN15 ....79 A5
Kings Meadow SN16 .....14 D5
Kings Orch BA14 ....116 E5
Kings Paddock SP5 ......149 A5
Kings Rd
Easterton SN10 ....180 A3
Enham Alamein SP11 ....193 E4
Market Lavington SN10 .179 F2
Kings Rise BA12 ....116 E6
Kingsborough Ct SN8 .....13 D8
Kingsbourne Cl SP9 .....133 B3
Kingsbury Cl SN12 ....94 A3
Kingsbury Sq 3 SP2 .....144 D3
Kingsbury St
Calne SN11 ....81 B2
Marlborough SN8 ....213 D3
Kingscote Cl 11 SN5 ......48 F8
Kingsdown Gr RG17 ....82 F2
Kingsdown Ind Est SN2 ..36 A6
Kingsdown La SN25 ....35 B5
Kingsdown Rd
Stratton St Margaret SN2 .36 A6
Swindon SN2 ....37 A5
3 Trowbridge BA14 .....105 C6
Kingsdown Sch SN2 ......35 F5
Kingsettle Hill BA10 .....122 C6

Kingsfield BA15 ....100 D7
Kingsfield Grange Rd
  BA15 ....100 E7
Kingsford CI SP5 ....211 C7
Kingshill Rd SN1 ....50 A4
Kingsland Rd SP2 ....145 F2
Kingsley Ave SN4 ....47 E3
Kingsley Gdns SN10 ....214 C3
Kingsley PI BA14 ....100 F1
Kingsley Rd
  Chippenham SN14 ....78 B6
  Devizes SN10 ....214 C3
Kingsley Way SN2 ....35 D5
Kingsman La 15 SP7 ....202 C1
Kingsmanor Wharf
  SN10 ....214 D5
Kingsmead Lechlade GL7 ....2 C5
Stratford SP2 ....130 A3
Kingsmead House
  SN15 ....44 A5
Kingsmead Mill* SN15 ..43 F6
Kingsthorpe Gr SN3 ....51 C8
Kingston CI SN16 ....43 F8
Kingston Ave BA15 ....100 C6
Kingston La BA12 ....118 F2
Kingston PI SO51 ....212 F4
Kingston Rd
  Bradford-on-Avon BA15 ..100 D6
  Shalbourne SN8 ....176 F1
  Swindon SN3 ....51 A4
Kingsway Preshute SN8 ..168 B1
  Wilton SP2 ....144 E5
Kingsway CI 11 SN3 ....50 F4
Kingswood
  Trowbridge BA14 ....104 F6
  Wroughton SN4 ....64 A5
Kingswood Ave SN5 ....50 A5
Kington La SN14 ....43 A4
Kington St Michael CE Prim
  Sch SN14 ....70 A8
Kingway View SN16 ....42 E4
Kintbury Rd RG17 ....177 F3
Kipling Gdns SN2 ....35 E4
Kirby CI SN3 ....51 D5
Kirby Rd SN13 ....76 E1
Kirkee Rd SP9 ....216 C5
Kirkstall CI SN5 ....49 C4
Kirktonhill Rd SN5 ....49 D6
Kishorn CI 5 SN5 ....34 B2
Kitchen Barrow*
  SN10 ....172 E3
Kitchener Rd SN4 ....217 B4
Kitchener St SN2 ....50 C8
Kite Hill SN4 ....163 A5
Kite's Nest La SP8 ....137 E2
Kitefield 2 SN6 ....19 D8
Kivel Ct SP2 ....146 A2
Kiwi Prim Sch SP4 ....198 E6
Kiwi Rd 6 SP4 ....198 F7
Kiwi The* SN4 ....198 E6
Knap Barrow (Long
  Barrow)* SP6 ....209 D8
Knap Hill (Causewayed
  Enclosure)* SN8 ...173 E2
Knap La SP3 ....200 F2
Knap The BA14 ....102 A3
Knapp CI SN2 ....35 A2
Knapp Hill SN15 ....205 A4
  Great Bedwyn SN8 ....176 B3
  7 Shaftesbury SP7 ...202 B2
Knapps The BA14 ....102 F5
Knighton Barrow (Long
  Barrow)* SP4 ....197 F3
Knighton Rd SP5 ....205 C4
Knights CI
  11 Chippenham SN15 ...78 F4
  West Overton SN8 ...173 F6
Knights Enham Prim Sch
  SP10 ....193 E2
Knightsbridge Rd
  SP11 ....193 F4
Knockdown Rd SN16 ..25 C1
Knoll CI OX12 ....165 F8
Knoll The
  12 Aldbourne SN8 ..170 A6
  Kempsford GL7 ....10 D7
  Westbury BA13 ....109 B4
Knolton Wlk SN3 ....51 A4
Knook Barrow (Long
  Barrow)* BA12 ....194 F7
Knook Castle* BA12 ...195 A7
Knook Manor* BA12 ...194 D5
Knowlands SN6 ....23 A7
Knowle The SN3 ....84 F8
Knowledge Hill 2 SN8 ..170 B2
Knowsley Rd SN3 ....51 A4
Kohat CI SP9 ....216 B7
Kyneton Way SN14 ....70 A8

L

La Retraite Swan SP1 ..146 B2
Labour-in-Vain Hill
  SN11 ....172 A8
Laburnam Dr SN4 ....47 E3
Laburnum CI 3 BA11 ..110 B7
Laburnum Dr SN12 ....94 A3
Laburnum Gr BA14 ....105 B6
Laburnum Rd SN2 ....35 C3
Lacemakers Rd SN16 ..28 A5
Lackham Cir SN14 ....78 B6
Lackham Ctry Pk*
  SN15 ....78 F1
Lacock Abbey* SN15 ..86 D5

Lacock CE Prim Sch
  SN15 ....86 D5
Lacock Gdns BA14 ....102 B2
Lacock Pottery* SN15 ..86 D6
Lacock Rd
  Corsham SN13 ....85 D8
  Swindon SN2 ....35 C4
Ladbrook La SN13 ....77 C1
Ladds La SN15 ....78 E7
Lady Coventry Rd SN15 ..78 F7
Lady Diana Ct 18 SP11 ..192 A5
Lady Down View 6 SP3 ..203 E8
Lady Godley CI SP9 ...216 C5
Lady Jane Wlk 22 SP11 ..192 A5
Lady La SN25 ....21 B1
Lady Margaret Hungerford
  Almshouse* SN13 ....177 C1
Lady Mead SN6 ....19 D8
Ladydown SN11 ....81 B4
Ladyfield Rd SN14 ....78 B7
Ladysmith SP4 ....133 D3
Ladysmith Rd
  Chiseldon SN4 ....65 D1
  Salisbury SP2 ....145 D3
Ladywood 13 SN10 ..179 F1
Laggar The SN13 ....77 A2
Lagos St 3 SN1 ....50 C7
Lagpond La SP3 ....204 B7
Lahore CI SP9 ....216 C7
Lahore Rd SP9 ....216 C5
Laines Head SN14 ....70 C2
Lainesmead Prim Sch
  SN3 ....50 E5
Lainey's CI SN8 ....213 D4
Lake Group (Tumuli)*
  SP4 ....197 D3
Lake House* SP4 ....197 F1
Lake View SN11 ....89 D8
Lakeside Fairford GL7 ....1 F6
  South Cerney SN3 ....50 E3
Lakeside CI SP10 ....193 C1
Lamb Ale Gn SN4 ....105 D6
Lambdown App SP11 ..191 F3
Lambert CI SN4 ....105 D6
Lambert CI BA14 ....104 F6
Lamora CI 12 SN5 ....48 F8
Lampeter SP SN25 ....34 C6
Lamplighters Wlk
  BA14 ....105 C7
Lanac Rd SN1 ....36 A1
Lancaster CI 6 RG17 ..177 B6
Lancaster Mews SN5 ...36 C5
Lancaster Rd
  Bower Hill SN12 ....94 B1
  Kempsford GL7 ....10 C6
  Wroughton SN4 ....64 A6
Lancaster Sq
  Hungerford RG17 ....177 B6
  Lyneham SN15 ....60 A2
Landale CI 3 SP11 ..193 E4
Landford CE Prim Sch
  SP5 ....212 C6
Landor Rd SP25 ....34 F8
Lane The SN4 ....163 C7
Lane-side 9 SP7 ....202 C2
Lane's CI SP4 ....217 C4
Lanes End SN3 ....85 D5
Lanes End Hill BA12 ..115 A8
Lanfear CI SP4 ....217 C4
Langdale Dr SN5 ....36 B1
Langet GL7 ....50 E6
Langford Gr SN3 ....50 E6
Langford La SP5 ....160 A3
Langford Rd
  Great Wishford SP2 ..129 F4
  Trowbridge BA14 ....101 C2
Langfords La 8 SP7 ..202 B1
Langham Pl BA11 ....103 F1
Langholm Ave BA12 ..116 C6
Langholm CI BA12 ....116 D6
Langley Fitzurse CE Prim
  Sch SN15 ....70 E6
Langley Gdn SP6 ....210 E2
Langley Pk SN15 ....51 C6
Langley Rd
  Chippenham SN15 ....70 E6
  Swindon SN3 ....34 B1
  Trowbridge BA14 ....105 C3
Langley Wood National
  Nature Reserve*
  SP5 ....211 F7
Langport CI 5 SN5 ....49 B4
Langstone Way SN5 ....49 C6
Lanham's CI SN3 ....109 A2
Lanhill (Long Barrow)*
  SN14 ....69 B2
Lanhill View SN14 ....70 A2
Lanhydrock CI 9 SN5 ...49 A4
Lansbury Dr SN2 ....35 F4
Lansdown CI
  Melksham SN12 ....94 D6
  Trowbridge BA14 ....105 B7
Lansdown Gr SN15 ....70 D1
Lansdown Rd SN1 ....50 B4

Lansdowne CI SN11 ....81 A4
Lansdowne Cres SN11 ..79 F2
Lansdowne Terr SN10 ..214 A3
Lapwing CI 1 SN4 ....51 E6
Lapwing Cres SN4 ....70 E2
Larch CI SN12 ....94 C5
Larch Gr BA14 ....105 B6
Larch Rd SN14 ....74 F6
Larch Row SP6 ....210 F1
Larchfield CI BA11 ....110 B7
Larchmore CI SN25 ....35 A3
Lark CI SP9 ....216 D7
Lark Down BA14 ....101 E1
Larkham Rise SN4 ....64 A6
Larkhill Prim Sch SP4 ..197 E2
Larkhill Rd SP4 ....198 B7
Larkrise SP BA14 ....101 E1
Larkrise 3 SN13 ....51 C8
Larkspur BA14 ....101 E1
Larmer Tree Gdns*
  SP5 ....207 B3
Late Broads BA15 ....99 D7
Latimer Gdns SN14 ....41 E1
Latton CI SN2 ....35 B6
Laughton Way SN25 ....35 A6
Launcelot CI 22 SP10 ..193 E2
Laundry La 6 SP7 ....202 B1
Laura PI SN13 ....83 F7
Laurel CI BA11 ....110 B7
Laurel Dr Colerne SN14 ..74 F6
  Marlborough SN8 ....213 F2
Laurel Gr BA14 ....105 C6
Laurels The
  Hungerford RG17 ....177 C8
  Melksham Without SN12 ..86 A1
  Westwood BA15 ....99 F3
Lavender CI SN12 ....192 A5
  Melksham SN12 ....94 C3
  5 Trowbridge BA14 ..105 F7
Lavender Dr SN11 ....110 B7
Lavender Dr SN11 ....81 B1
Laverstock Pk SN1 ....146 D1
Laverstock Pk W SP1 ..146 C1
Laverstock Rd SP1 ....146 C1
Laverton CI 1 BA13 ..109 A3
Laverton Gn 3 BA13 ..108 F1
Laverton Rd BA13 ....108 F1
Lavington CI 10 SN8 ..183 D8
Lavington Comp Sch
  SN10 ....179 E1
Lavington Hill SN10 ..187 F8
Lavington La SN10 ....187 E8
Lawn Farm CI SN9 ....182 E7
Lawn The SN4 ....50 F2
Lawns The SN4 ....47 D2
Lawrence CI
  4 Amesbury SP4 ....217 C3
  Devizes SN10 ....214 C1
  Swindon SN3 ....51 C4
Lawrence Mead 3 SN8 ..170 B2
Lawrence Rd SP4 ....197 F7
Lawson Rd 8 SP4 ....198 A6
Lawton CI SN3 ....51 A3
Layton La SP7 ....202 C1
Le Marchant CI SN12 ..214 D5
Lea & Garsdon CE Prim Sch
  SN16 ....28 F2
Lea CI SN25 ....35 A7
Lea House SN16 ....28 D1
Leaden Hall Sch SP1 ..152 A7
Leafield Ind Est SN13 ..84 E6
Leafield PI BA14 ....104 E6
Leafield Rd SN13 ....84 E6
Leafield Way SN13 ....84 E6
Leafy La SN13 ....76 A1
Leamington Gr SN3 ....50 F2
Leap Gate
  Hilperton BA14 ....102 A1
  Trowbridge BA14 ....106 A8
Leatler CI SP3 ....204 D8
Leaze Rd
  Marlborough SN8 ....213 C4
  Melksham SN12 ....94 A2
Leaze The
  Ashton Keynes SN6 ......6 F1
  Durrington/Bulford SP4 ..217 E8
  South Cerney GL7 ......7 E1
Lechlade Rd Buscot SN7 ....2 D2
  Inglesham SN6 ....12 A6
Ledge Hill SN10 ....179 E2
Ledger Hill CI SP4 ....217 D8
Lee Cres SN15 ....57 C1
Lees CI SP2 ....145 F2
Legate CI SN15 ....79 B5
Leicester St SN1 ....50 D6
Leigh CI SN13 ....108 E1
Leigh La BA13 ....202 E8
Leigh Pk Rd BA15 ....100 D8
Leigh Rd
  Bradford-on-Avon BA15 ..91 A1
  Holt BA14 ....92 C1
  Swindon SN2 ....35 D3
  Westbury BA13 ....108 F1
Leighton Ave BA13 ....50 F4
Leighton Gn BA13 ....109 A2
Leighton Pk N 4 BA13 ..108 F1
Leighton Pk N 4 BA13 ..108 F1
Leighton Pk W 2 BA13 ..108 F1
Leland CI 5 SN16 ....28 A5
Lena CI 20 SP11 ....192 A5
Lennards The GL7 ......7 A1
Lennox Dr SP2 ....145 B3
Lenta Bsns Ctr SN1 ....50 B6
Lenton CI SN14 ....77 F7

Leonard Cheshire CI 4
  SP4 ....217 D2
Lesley Anne Skeete Ct
  SN3 ....51 B4
Leslie CI SN5 ....49 A4
Leslie Rise BA15 ....99 F3
Lethbridge Prim Sch
  SN1 ....50 C3
Lethbridge Rd SN1 ....50 C3
Letterage Rd SN5 ....34 A2
Levell Ct 12 SP11 ....192 A5
Leven SN5 ....49 A3
Leversedge Rd 2 BA11 ..110 A7
Leverton Gate SN3 ....50 F1
Leverton La RG17 ....171 B1
Lewington Mews 14
  RG17 ....177 B6
Lewis CI SN25 ....34 F6
Lewisham Castle*
  SN8 ....169 C4
Lewisham St SN25 ....34 F3
Ley The SN13 ....83 D5
Leylands Rd SN13 ....76 B1
Leys Hill BA11 ....110 A6
Leys La BA11 ....110 A6
Leystone CI BA11 ....110 A6
Lichen CI 3 SN2 ....34 D4
Lickhill Rd SN11 ....81 A4
Lidbury Camp* SN9 ..190 C8
Liddiards Gn SN8 ....168 F5
Liddington Castle (Fort)*
  SN4 ....163 A2
Liddington St SN2 ....35 C3
Liddington Way BA14 ..105 D5
Liden Dr SN3 ....51 D4
Liden Prim Sch SN3 ....51 D3
Lienbrook 8 SN4 ....163 A4
Light CI SN13 ....77 A2
Light's La SN5 ....153 C2
Lightfoot Rd SP4 ....197 F7
Lightning Rd 1 SP4 ..217 D2
Liguiel CI 9 RG17 ..177 B6
Lilac Ct SN2 ....35 B2
Lilac Gr BA14 ....105 B5
Lilac Way SN11 ....81 B1
Lilian Lock Gdns SN2 ..35 C5
Lillywhite Cres 1 SP10 ..193 E2
Lily Wlk 11 SP4 ....198 C7
Lime Ave Badminton GL9 ..38 C1
  Melksham SN12 ....94 A1
Lime CI Colerne SN14 ....75 A5
  Frome BA11 ....110 B7
  Lyneham & Bradenstoke
  SN15 ....60 C2
  Pewsey SN9 ....215 D6
Lime Kiln SN4 ....47 D3
Lime Kiln Sports Ctr
  SN4 ....47 D3
Lime Kiln Way SP2 ..152 A5
Lime Tree CI SN11 ....81 A3
Lime Trees SN15 ....58 A2
Limekiln Rd SP11 ....192 E6
Limes Ave SN2 ....35 B3
Limes PI SN6 ......8 C4
Limes Rd GL7 ......7 A6
Limes The
  Badminton GL9 ....38 E2
  Motcombe SP7 ....202 A4
  Porton SP4 ....133 C6
Limpley Stoke Rd BA15 ..99 D6
Lincoln Gn SN12 ....94 C7
Lincoln Gr SN12 ....94 C7
Lincoln St SN1 ....50 C6
Linden CI Calne SN11 ..81 B2
  Colerne SN14 ....75 A6
  Ludgershall SP11 ....192 B5
  Salisbury SP1 ....146 D1
  Wootton Bassett SN4 ..47 E3
Linden Cres BA15 ....100 A3
Linden Gr 2 SN12 ....94 A2
Linden Lea GL7 ......8 E8
Linden Pk SP7 ....202 D1
Linden PI BA11 ....101 B1
Linden Way SN5 ....34 A2
Lindford Rd SP1 ....146 D5
Lindisfarne 1 SN4 ....48 A2
Lindsay CI SN3 ....50 F3
Lindlar CI 15 SP7 ....202 C2
Lindley CI SP9 ....216 D6
Lineacre CI SN5 ....48 F4
Lingen CI 12 SP10 ....193 D2
Lingfield CI 6 SN14 ......77 F5
Link La BA15 ....83 A1
Link Leisure Ctr SN5 ..49 B5
Link Rd SP11 ....108 E7
Link Way SP1 ....146 C3
Links The Corsham SN13 ..84 E7
  Pewsey SN9 ....215 B4
Linley CI SN1 ....50 D3
Linley Rd SN26 ....21 C2
Linnet Way BA11 ....110 B6
Linnetsdene
  6 Salisbury SP2 ....152 A5
  Swindon SN3 ....51 C8
Linslade SN2 ....50 A7
Linslade St SN2 ....50 A7
Linsvale CI BA11 ....110 C5
Linsvale Dr BA11 ....110 C5
Lipgate SN10 ....180 F8
Liskeard Way SN5 ....49 A5
Lisle CI SP4 ....49 A5
Lismore Rd SN6 ....22 C6
Lister Gr BA15 ....99 F3
Lister Rd SN4 ....64 B7
Litchfield CI 11 SP10 ..193 C2
Little Anne St SN2 ....35 A1

Little Badminton La
  SN16 ....38 F2
Little Britox SN10 ....214 A3
Little Challows SN14 ....76 D7
Little Clarendon*
  SP3 ....201 F2
Little Comm BA14 ....105 D3
Little Content La 17
  SP7 ....202 C2
Little Ct La BA13 ....186 D8
Little Down SN14 ....78 B7
Little Dro SP6 ....211 A4
Little Englands SN15 ....78 E6
Little Hill BA12 ....116 E2
Little Ingleburn SN16 ....28 A2
Little Island SN9 ....215 B5
Little London
  Heytesbury BA12 ....194 C5
  Swindon BA12 ....50 D4
Little Mead SN8 ....176 F1
Little Parks BA14 ....92 F1
Little Pk CI SN15 ....59 F1
Little Rose La SN26 ....20 F5
Little Sands SN14 ....68 F5
Little Woodbury*
  SP5 ....152 B4
Little Woodfalls Dr
  SP5 ....211 C6
Littlecote CI 3 SN5 ....49 D5
Littlecote Rd
  Chippenham SN14 ....78 A6
  Froxfield SN8 ....178 C5
Littlecote Roman Villa*
  RG17 ....170 D1
Littledown SP7 ....202 C2
Littlefield La SP5 ....208 A4
Littlejohn Ave SN12 ....94 C6
Littlemead SN13 ....83 B5
Littlemill La SP6 ....209 F3
Littleton Drew La GL9 ....53 A6
Littleworth La SN12 ......85 C2
Livery Rd
  West Dean SP5 ....155 F3
  Winterslow SP5 ....149 B4
Livia CI 16 SP10 ....193 E2
Lock's Hill BA11 ....110 A3
Lock's La SP2 ....145 A3
Lockeridge CI SN3 ....193 E8
Lockeridge La SN8 ....174 B7
Locking CI SN12 ....178 B8
Locks Cross SN13 ....84 E5
Locks La SN5 ....33 B5
Locks The SN10 ....179 D8
Locksgreen Cres 1 SN2 ..34 F3
Lockside 1 SN15 ....78 F5
Lockswell CI SN14 ....79 A4
Loddon Way SN15 ....100 C5
Loder's La SP3 ....204 A5
Lodersfield GL7 ......2 C4
Lodge CI SN11 ....81 A3
Lodge Dr BA14 ....105 F8
Lodge Dro SP5 ....211 C6
Lodge Hill BA14 ....110 C5
Lodge La SP11 ....192 E6
Lodge Rd
  Chippenham SN15 ....79 A5
  Horningsham BA12 ....119 A8
Lodowicks SN11 ....80 D7
Logan CI 1 SN3 ....50 E6
Lomond CI SN13 ....34 B2
London La SN5 ....17 C1
London Rd
  Amesbury SP4 ....217 B4
  Bishops Cannings SN10 ..214 E6
  Box SN13 ....83 D7
  Calne SN11 ....81 B2
  Chippenham SN15 ....78 F6
  Marlborough SN8 ....213 D2
  Salisbury SP1 ....146 C3
  Shrewton SP3 ....196 F7
London Rd E BA1 ....82 A3
London Ride SN8 ....176 A5
London St SN1 ....50 B6
Londonderry Gdns
  SP4 ....198 E7
Long Acre SN5 ....33 B3
Long Barrow Rd SN11 ..81 A3
Long Bottom SP11 ....192 D6
Long CI
  Chippenham SN15 ....78 F6
  Downton SP5 ....211 A8
Long CI Ave SN13 ....76 B1
Long CI W SP1 ....211 A8
Long Cross
  Bramshaw SO43 ....212 C2
  Shaftesbury SP7 ....202 B2
Long Dro Burbage SN8 ..183 D8
  Grimstead SP5 ....154 B4
Long Harry SN8 ....213 E2
Long Hedge RG17 ....165 B1
Long Hill BA12 ....138 C5
Long Hollow BA13 ....186 D7
Long La Bourton SP8 ....137 B1
  Cann SP7 ....206 A8
Long Leaze La SN12 ....94 C3
Long Ridings SN14 ....70 C2
Long River Rd BA13 ....109 D2
Long Row SN6 ....10 B4
Long St SN10 ....214 B3
Long Steeple La SP5 ..210 C6
Long Stones* SN8 ....173 A4

Longbarrow Cross Roads
SP4 ....**197** C4
Longcombe Dr BA12 ....**115** E3
Longcroft Ave SN10 ....**214** C3
Longcroft Cres SN10 ...**214** C3
Longcroft Rd SN10 ......**214** C3
Longfellow Cl SN25 ......**35** A8
Longfellow Cres SN4 ....**47** F3
Longfield Cl 3 SP4 ......**198** B7
Longfield Rd BA14 ......**105** D7
Longfields SN13 ....**173** B8
Longfields Wlk SN10 ...**214** C6
Longford Castle*
SP5 ....**153** A2
Longford Pk* SP5 ....**152** E2
Longford Rd SN10 ....**94** A2
Longhill Dr 1 SP2 ....**152** B3
Longland SP2 ....**145** E1
Longlands Cl BA13 ....**186** C3
Longleat Gdns SN2 ......**35** C4
Longleat House*
BA12 ....**114** F3
Longleat Safari Pk*
BA12 ....**115** B4
Longleaze SN4 ....**47** E3
Longleaze Prim Sch
SN4 ....**47** E3
Longleys Cl SN10 ....**214** E2
Longmead SP7 ....**202** C2
Longmeadow Prim Sch
BA14 ....**105** E7
Longsplatt SN13 ....**83** D3
Longstock Cl SN5 ....**49** B6
Longstone Rd SN14 ....**70** A1
Longthorpe Cl SN5 ....**49** D4
Longworth Dr SN25 ......**34** B7
Lonsdale Cl SN26 ....**21** C2
Lonsdale Gdns SN12 .....**94** A2
Loop Rd SN4 ....**173** A7
Lopcombe Cnr SP4 ......**135** D3
Lopes Way BA13 ....**108** F4
Lord's La SN15 ....**59** F5
Lord's Mead SN14 ....**78** A8
Lords Croft SP4 ....**217** B4
Lordsmead Rd BA12 .....**139** B4
Lorne St SN1 ....**50** A5
Lottage Rd SN8 ....**170** A7
Lottage Way 2 SN8 ......**170** A7
Lotts The SN4 ....**17** F8
Loughborough Cl 1 SN5 **48** F4
Louviers Way SN1 ....**51** C2
Lovage Way BA12 ....**139** B6
Love La Box SN13 ....**83** F7
Salisbury SP1 ....**152** B8
4 Shaftesbury SP7 ....**202** B1
Woodgreen SP6 ....**211** A4
Loveage Cl 6 SN2 ....**34** D4
Lovel's La SN8 ....**170** B3
Lovel Rd BA12 ....**194** E3
Lovell Cl SN3 ....**51** D7
Lover's La SN16 ....**28** A4
Loveridge Cl
5 Andover SP10 ....**193** E2
Swindon SN2 ....**35** E6
Low La BA14 ....**104** C7
Lovett Gn SP1 ....**146** C4
Low La SN11 ....**81** D2
Low Rd SN10 ....**179** C1
Lowa Cl SP9 ....**216** C6
Lowa Rd SP9 ....**216** B6
Lowbourne SN12 ....**94** B4
Lowbourne Jun Sch
SN12 ....**94** B5
Lowbourne Rd
SN12 ....**94** B5
Lowden SN15 ....**78** C7
Lowden Ave SN14 ....**78** C7
Lowden Hill SN15 ....**78** C7
Lower Alma St BA14 ....**105** E8
Lower Backway 7 SP3 ..**196** E6
Lower Bartons 30 SN6 .**210** D1
Britford SP5 ....**152** C5
Coombe Bissett SP5 ....**151** C1
Downton SP5 ....**159** B4
Edington BA13 ....**186** C8
Erlestoke BA13 ....**178** F2
Netheravon SP4 ....**190** A3
Odstock SP5 ....**152** B4
Salisbury SP2 ....**144** F2
Lower S Rd SP5 ....**207** C4
Lower Stoke
Limpley Stoke BA2 ....**99** A6

Lower Stoke *continued*
Monkton Combe BA2 ....**90** A1
Lower Westbury Rd
BA13 ....**109** E5
Lower Wharf SN10 ......**214** A4
Lower Woodrow SN12 ...**86** F1
Lowes Cl 2 SN5 ....**34** B2
Lowmead BA14 ....**101** E1
Loxley Cl SN12 ....**94** B6
Loxley Wlk SN3 ....**51** B3
Loyalty St SN14 ....**78** C8
Lubeck Dr 22 SP10 ......**193** D2
Lucerne Cl
10 Swindon SN5 ....**48** F8
Wootton Bassett SN4 ....**47** D4
Lucewood La SN5 ....**154** C7
Luckett Way SN11 ....**81** C4
Luckington Com Sch
SN14 ....**39** E5
Luckington Ct* SN14 .....**39** F5
Lucknam Pk* SN14 ....**75** B6
Luddesdown Rd SN5 .....**49** C4
Ludgershall Castle*
SP11 ....**192** A6
Ludgershall Rd
Collingbourne Ducis SN8 ..**191** E8
4 Swindon SN5 ....**49** F4
Tidworth SP9 ....**216** C8
Ludgershall Sports Club
SP11 ....**192** A5
Ludlow Cl
Chippenham SN15 ....**79** A5
10 Frome BA11 ....**110** C6
Swindon SN3 ....**50** F4
Warminster BA12 ....**116** F4
Westbury BA13 ....**108** F4
Ludmead Rd SN14 ....**85** A8
Ludwell Hill SP7 ....**203** A1
Ludwell Prim Sch
SP7 ....**203** A1
Lugbury (Long Barrow)*
SN14 ....**53** E2
Lukas Cl SN25 ....**34** F7
Luke St SP7 ....**203** E1
Lulworth Rd SN25 ....**34** F3
Lumley Cl 2 Swindon SN5 **49** A4
Lumley Wlk 8 SP4 ......**217** D3
Luxfield Rd BA12 ....**116** E7
Lyall Cl SN25 ....**34** F8
Lyburn Rd SP5 ....**212** A5
Lyddon Way SN25 ....**34** F8
Lydford Cl 4 SN5 ....**49** A8
Lydiard Fields Bsns Pk
SN5 ....**48** E3
Lydiard Millicent CE Prim
Sch SN5 ....**48** B8
Lydiard Pk* SN5 ....**48** E6
Lydiard Way BA14 ....**105** D5
Lye The SN12 ....**178** D8
Lyes Gr BA13 ....**108** E8
Lyme Ave BA12 ....**116** F6
Lyme Way SN25 ....**35** A5
Lymers The SN11 ....**166** E2
Lynch Cl SN3 ....**139** B5
Lynch Field The 8 SN4 ...**163** A5
Lynch Rd 4 RG17 ....**165** A2
Lynch The SN4 ....**176** F1
Lynchet Cl 7 SN10 ......**179** F1
Lynchets Rd SP4 ....**217** B3
Lynchfield Rd 7 SP4 ....**217** B3
Lynden Cl SN8 ....**184** A7
Lyndhurst Cres SN3 ....**51** A6
Lyndhurst Rd
Amesbury SP4 ....**217** C3
Landford SP5 ....**212** C6
Lyneham Cl SN2 ....**35** B6
Lyneham Jun & Infants Sch
SN15 ....**60** B2
Lyneham Way BA14 .....**105** F8
Lynmouth Rd SN5 ....**49** F4
Lynn Farm Cotts SN12 ...**86** C6
Lynt Rd SN6 ....**12** A5
Lynton Rd SN12 ....**34** E1
Lynwood Gr SN2 ....**34** D3
Lynwood Rd BA14 ....**101** A1
Lyons Wlk 13 SP7 ....**202** C1
Lypiatt SN13 ....**84** F6
Lypiatt Mead SN13 ....**85** A8
Lypiatt Prim Sch SN13 ...**84** F6
Lypiatt Rd SN13 ....**85** A7
Lysander Rd
Bower Hill SN12 ....**94** B1
Laverstock SN4 ....**146** C8
Melksham Without SN12 ..**178** B8
Lysley Cl SN15 ....**79** A5
Lyster Rd SP6 ....**210** E1
Lytchett Way SN11 ....**51** C6
Lytham Cl SN15 ....**78** F7**

M

MacAdam Way SP10 ....**193** B1
MacCullum Rd SP11 .....**193** E4
MacKenzie Cl 1 SN3 .....**51** D4
Mackintosh Davidson Wood
Nature Reserve*
BA12 ....**140** D3
MacKlin Cl 21 RG17 .....**177** B7
MacKlin Rd SP2 ....**145** E2
MacNeice Dr SN8 ....**213** A2
Maddington 2 SP3 ....**196** E6
Maddle Rd RG17 ....**164** E4
Maddocks Hill 4 BA12 .**116** E5
Maddocks Rd BA14 .....**101** D4

Magdalen La BA14 ......**104** B7
Magdalen Rd SN4 ....**64** A6
Magdalene La 7 SP7 ...**202** C1
Magic Rdbt SN1 ....**50** E6
Magister Rd SN12 ....**94** D1
Magnolia Cl 1 BA11 ...**110** C6
Magnolia Ct SN2 ....**35** B2
Magnolia Rise
Calne SN11 ....**81** B1
Trowbridge BA14 ....**105** E7
Magnon Rd BA15 ....**100** B7
Magpie La SN3 ....**51** B6
Magpie Mews SN10 .....**214** B3
Maidavale SN20 ....**34** D6
Maiden La SN11 ....**166** B1
Maidencroft Cotts GL7 ...**1** A8
Maidstone Rd SN1 ....**50** B4
Main Rd Amesbury SP4 .**217** D2
Cherhill SN11 ....**166** B1
Christian Malford SN15 ...**58** E5
Ogbourne St Andrew
SN8 ....**213** D8
Sutton Benger SN15 ....**57** F2
Main St
Great Hinton BA14 ....**178** A6
Westbury BA13 ....**108** C6
Main St E BA13 ....**108** C6
Maitland Cl SN15 ....**79** A4
Maitland Rd SN3 ....**51** A7
Majestic Cl 4 SN5 ....**49** A7
Maldwyn Cl 9 SN5 ....**48** F8
Mall The
South Tedworth SP9 ....**216** A4
Swindon SN1 ....**50** B3
Mallard Ave SN15 ....**70** C1
Mallard Cl
2 Bower Hill SN12 ....**178** B8
Calne SN11 ....**81** D2
Salisbury SP2 ....**151** F7
Westbury BA13 ....**109** B4
Mallards The 20 SP3 ...**203** E8
Mallow Cl 2 Swindon SN2 ...**34** B4
5 Trowbridge BA14 ......**105** D6
Malmesbury Abbey*
SN16 ....**28** A3
Malmesbury CE Prim Sch
SN16 ....**28** A2
Malmesbury Com Hospl
SN16 ....**28** B1
Malmesbury House*
SP1 ....**152** A8
Malmesbury Ind Est
SN16 ....**28** A4
Malmesbury Rd
Chippenham SN15 ....**70** C1
Leigh SN5 ....**17** E3
Malmesbury Sch SN16 .....**27** E3
Malmesbury Swimming Pool
SN16 ....**27** E4
Malmpit Hill BA12 ....**193** F4
Malt House La SN13 ....**83** B2
Malt Shovel La RG17 ...**164** F2
Malthouse Cl
Ashbury SN6 ....**164** A8
Broad Blunsdon SN26 ....**21** C2
Malthouse La
Chute SP11 ....**192** E8
4 Salisbury SP2 ....**146** A1
Maltings The
Malmesbury SN16 ....**28** A3
Salisbury SP2 ....**145** F1
Warminster BA12 ....**116** F6
Wootton Bassett SN4 ....**47** D1
Yatton Keynell SN14 ....**68** F6
Malvern Cl
Melksham SN12 ....**94** D4
7 Warminster BA12 ......**117** A8
Malvern Rd SN2 ....**35** C1
Malvern Way SN4 ....**133** D6
Mampitts La SP7 ....**202** D1
Manchester Rd SN1 ....**50** C7
Mand Wood BA14 ....**101** F8
Manley Cl BA14 ....**101** C1
Manning Cl 8 SP1 ....**146** C5
Mannington La SN5 ....**49** F9
Mannington Pk SN2 ....**49** F7
Mannington Ret Pk
SN1 ....**49** E4
Manor Bridge Ct SP9 ..**216** D7
Manor Cl
Broad Blunsdon SN26 ....**21** C2
Figheldean SP4 ....**190** D1
Semington BA14 ....**102** F5
Sherston SN16 ....**25** C1
3 Shipton Bellinger SP9 .**199** D8
Wroughton SN4 ....**64** B7
Manor Copse SP11 ......**193** E3
Manor Cotts SN14 ....**24** D1
Manor Cres SN2 ....**215** C4
Manor Ct SN9 ....**215** C4
Manor Dr BA1 ....**82** A3
Manor Farm Cl SN8 ....**205** C4
Manor Farm Ct SN8 ....**173** D6
Manor Farm Dr SN15 ....**57** C2
Manor Farm La
Great Wishford SP2 ....**129** F4
Patney SN10 ....**180** F5
Manor Farm Rd
Salisbury SP1 ....**146** C1
Trowbridge BA14 ....**101** B2
Manor Fields 5 BA13 ...**186** B7
Manor Gdns
Swindon SN2 ....**34** F1

Manor Gdns *continued*
Warminster BA12 ....**117** A7
Manor Ho SN14 ....**68** E5
Manor House*
Manor La Baydon SN8 ..**170** C8
Broad Hinton SN4 ....**167** C7
Manor Orch SN6 ....**19** E8
Manor Pk
Froxfield SN8 ....**176** D6
Great Somerford SN15 .....**44** A2
South Marston SN3 ....**36** E4
Manor Rd
Chippenham SN14 ....**78** A8
Corsham SN13 ....**76** F2
7 Great Bedwyn SN8 ....**176** B3
Mere BA12 ....**138** F7
Salisbury SP1 ....**146** C1
Swindon SN1 ....**49** F5
Trowbridge BA14 ....**105** A6
Upton Lovell BA12 ....**194** E3
Manor The*
Keevil BA14 ....**178** A4
Longbridge Deverill
BA12 ....**120** F5
Manor View SN10 ....**28** F2
Mansion House Mews
SN13 ....**77** A1
Mantles La BA12 ....**194** C5
Manton Cl
Marlborough SN8 ....**213** A1
Trowbridge BA14 ....**105** C6
Manton Dro SN8 ....**174** C6
Manton Hollow SN8 .....**213** A2
Manton Rd SN8 ....**174** C7
Manton Way SN8 ....**213** A2
Maple Cl Caine SN11 ......**81** B1
Melksham SN12 ....**94** C3
Pewsey SN9 ....**215** D6
5 Shaftesbury SP7 ....**202** C2
Maple Cres
7 Ludgershall SP11 ......**192** B5
Wilton SP2 ....**144** F3
Maple Ct 8 BA11 ....**110** A7
Maple Dr Firsdown SP5 .**148** C7
Wootton Bassett SN4 ....**47** E4
Trowbridge BA14 ....**105** C6
Maple Gr
Chippenham SN15 ....**70** D2
3 Durrington/Bulford
SP4 ....**198** B7
Maplecroft 3 SP2 ....**152** A5
Mapperton Hill SP8 .....**138** E1
Maranatha Christian Sch
SN6 ....**22** E1
Marbrean Cl 4 SP6 ......**210** C1
March Cl SN25 ....**35** A6
Marchment Cl SP2 ....**144** F4
Marden Henge* SN9 ....**181** B5
Marden Rd SN12 ....**178** B8
Marden Wlk 2 BA14 ....**105** D6
Margaret Leckie Ct 5
SN3 ....**50** F6
Margaret Stancomb Infants'
Sch BA14 ....**101** C1
Margha Rd SP9 ....**216** C6
Marie Ave 8 SP5 ....**210** F8
Marigold Cl
Melksham SN12 ....**94** C3
Swindon SN2 ....**34** D4
Marina Dr BA14 ....**101** D4
Marina Rd
20 Durrington/Bulford
SP4 ....**198** B7
Salisbury SP1 ....**152** C7
Marine Cl SN4 ....**64** B7
Mariner Rd SN25 ....**34** B7
Maristow St BA13 ....**109** A3
Marjoram Cl SN2 ....**34** D5
Markan Rd SP4 ....**133** F7
Markenfield 2 SN5 ....**49** D4
Market Hill SN11 ....**81** B3
Market Lavington Mus*
SN10 ....**179** F1
Market Pl Box SN13 ....**83** D6
Chippenham SN15 ....**78** E7
Colerne SN14 ....**74** F5
Lechlade GL7 ....**2** C4
16 Market Lavington SN10 **179** F1
Marshfield SN14 ....**74** A8
Pewsey SN9 ....**215** C5
Warminster BA12 ....**117** A7
2 Westbury BA13 ....**109** A3
Market Pl The SN10 .....**214** A4
Market Sq The SN3 ....**50** D4
Market St
Bradford-on-Avon BA15 ..**100** D7
4 Malmesbury SN16 ......**28** A3
Swindon SN1 ....**50** B6
Trowbridge BA14 ....**105** D8
Markham Pl SN4 ....**50** F7
Markham Rd SN3 ....**64** A5
Marl La SP6 ....**210** D1
Marlborough Bsns Pk
SN8 ....**213** B1
Marlborough Coll
SN8 ....**213** C2
Marlborough Craft Ctr*
SN8 ....**213** D2
Marlborough La SN14 ...**78** C7
Marlborough Leisure Ctr
SN8 ....**213** C2
Marlborough Rd
3 Aldbourne SN8 ....**170** A6
Bulford SP4 ....**198** E6

Marlborough Rd *continued*
Burbage SN8 ....**175** C1
Chiseldon SN3 ....**51** C2
Collingbourne Ducis SN8 .**183** E8
Everleigh SN8 ....**183** A1
Liddington SN4 ....**51** E1
Pewsey SN9 ....**215** B6
Salisbury SP1 ....**146** A2
Swindon SN3 ....**50** D3
Wootton Bassett SN4 ....**61** E7
Wroughton SN4 ....**64** B6
Marlborough St 1 SN5 ...**50** A5
Marlborough White Horse*
SN8 ....**213** C1
Marlowe Ave SN3 ....**50** F7
Marlowe Way SN4 ....**47** F2
Marney Rd SN5 ....**49** A5
Marsh Farm La SN4 ....**50** F7
Marsh La
Breamore SP6 ....**210** E4
Cherhill SN11 ....**166** A1
Coombe Bissett SP5 ....**150** F2
Hungerford RG17 ....**177** A7
Nettleton SN14 ....**53** C4
Pen Selwood BA9 ....**137** A4
Rowde SN10 ....**96** D2
Salisbury SP2 ....**145** F1
Marsh Rd Berkley BA11 .**107** C1
Rode BA11 ....**103** F2
Trowbridge BA14 ....**101** E5
Marsh St BA12 ....**117** A5
Marsh The SN4 ....**51** F3
Marshall Rd
Roundway SN10 ....**214** D1
Swindon SN5 ....**49** B8
Marshfield St SN14 ....**78** C7
Marshfield VC CE Prim Sch
SN14 ....**74** B8
Marshfield Way SN3 ......**36** A2
Marshgate SN1 ....**50** A4
Marshmead La SP4 ......**101** F4
Marshmead Cl SP5 ......**152** F6
Marshwood SP3 ....**201** E3
Marsland Rd SN2 ....**35** D2
Marston Ave SN2 ....**35** D2
Marston Rd BA14 ....**105** B8
Martha's La 6 SP10 ......**193** D2
Marti Cl SN12 ....**94** C4
Martigny Rd SN12 ....**94** B3
Martin Cres SP9 ....**216** C6
Martin Crest 2 BA12 ....**116** E5
Martin Dro End SP6 .....**209** F4
Martin Way SN11 ....**81** D3
Martin's Cl SN8 ....**213** E3
Martin's St 4 SP7 ....**202** C1
Martinbushes Rd SP4 ..**198** A7
Martinfield SN3 ....**51** D2
Martingale Rd SN8 ......**183** D2
Martingate SN13 ....**77** A1
Martins Cl
Chippenham SN15 ....**79** A8
2 Salisbury SP3 ....**152** A5
Steeple Ashton BA14 ......**178** C4
Martins Croft SN14 ....**75** B3
Martins Rd BA14 ....**178** C4
Martins Rd SN4 ....**178** C5
Martins Rise SP5 ....**161** C4
Martinsell Gn SN9 ....**215** D5
Martinsell Hill (Fort)*
SN8 ....**174** D2
Marytsham Rd SP4 ....**217** D2
Martlet Cl SN12 ....**94** D1
Martor Ind Est SN14 .....**64** A2
Marvins Ct SN3 ....**188** B2
Mary Barters La SP3 ...**204** E8
Maryland Cl SP2 ....**145** B5
Masefield Cl SN2 ....**47** F3
Masefield Ave SN3 ....**51** F4
Masefield Rd BA12 ......**116** A6
Maskelyne Way SN4 ......**63** F6
Mason Rd SN25 ....**35** B6
Masons La SN15 ....**100** D7
Masons The SN5 ....**33** A3
Masons Way SN13 ....**76** D3
Massey Cl SN15 ....**78** E5
Massey Rd SN10 ....**214** B4
Massinger Wlk SN3 ....**50** F6
Matford Hill SN15 ....**79** A8
Matilda Way SN10 ....**214** B4
Matley Moor SN3 ....**51** E4
Matravers Ct BA13 ......**108** F3
Matravers Sch BA13 ....**108** F8
Matravers Rd SN5 ....**49** B8
Matrons Cots SP5 ....**153** F1
Matthews Cl SN10 ....**214** C4
Maud Cl SN10 ....**214** D4
Maud Heath Ct SN15 .....**78** E8
Maud Heath Prim Sch
SN15 ....**72** A2
Maud Heath's Cswy
Chippenham SN15 ....**70** D1
Langley Burrell Without
SN15 ....**71** B3
Maud Heath's Mon*
SN11 ....**80** C8
Maud Heath's Stone*
SN11 ....**80** C8
Maulton Cl SN4 ....**101** D8
Maunders Dr BA14 ......**101** D4
Maundrell Cl SN10 ....**96** D2
Maundrell Rd SN11 ....**81** C6
Maunsell Way SN4 ....**64** B7
Maur Cl SN15 ....**78** F7
Maurys La SO51 ....**212** F6
Maxcroft La BA14 ....**101** E5
Maxey Cl SN5 ....**49** B6

Maxwell St SN1 ....50 A6
May Cl SN2 ....35 C1
May La SP5 ....204 D3
May Tree Rd ☑ SP10 ...193 C1
May's La SN4 ....65 D4
Mayenne Pl SN10 ......179 C8
Mayfair Rd SP1 ....146 D1
Mayfield ☑ SN4 ....163 A5
Mayfield Ave Ind. Pk
SP11 ....192 E1
Mayfield Cl
☑ Shipton Bellinger SP9 .199 C8
Swindon SN3 ....51 B7
Mayfield Rd ☑ SP6 ...210 C1
Mayfly Cl ☑ SP6 ......210 D1
Mayfly Rd SN25 ......184 A7
Mayo Cl SN13 ....76 E2
Mays Firs SP6 ....211 D5
Maytree Cl ☑ BA11 ...110 B7
McArthur Glen Designer
Outlet Village SN2 ....50 A6
McKie Rd ☑ SP4 .....217 D2
McNeill Rd SP4 ......198 A7
Mead Pk SN12 ....84 F1
Mead Prim Sch The
BA14 ....102 B1
Mead The
Ashton Keynes SN6 .....17 F8
Warminster BA12 ......117 A7
Westbury BA13 ....109 A5
Winsley BA15 ....99 E7
Mead Way SN5 ....34 B2
Meade Rd ☑ SP11 ....192 B5
Meadens La SP5 ......151 A1
Meadlands ☑ 76 E1
Meadow Ave ☑ SP6 ...210 D1
Meadow Cl
Chippenham SN14 ......78 A7
☑ Fordingbridge SP6 ...210 D1
Yatton Keynell SN14 ...68 F6
Meadow Ct
☑ Fordingbridge SP6 ..210 D1
Whiteparish SP5 ......161 E4
Meadow Dr SN10 ......214 C3
Meadow Pk BA1 ....82 B3
Meadow Rd (South) ☑
SP2 ....145 F1
Meadow Rd
Durrington/Bulford SP4 .217 E8
Melksham SN12 ....94 C7
☑ Salisbury SP2 .....145 F1
Swindon SN2 ....49 E7
Meadow Springs SN5 ...48 B8
Meadow View
☑ Fittleton SP4 .....190 A4
Kempsford GL7 ....10 C7
Meadow Way
Chiseldon SN4 ....65 E7
South Cerney GL7 ....6 F7
Meadow Well SN8 ....183 C8
Meadowcroft SN2 ......35 F3
Meadowfield BA15 ...100 B6
Meadows The
Bourton SP8 ....137 E2
Lydiard Tregoze SN5 ...47 F5
Salisbury SP1 ....152 D8
Meadowsweet Cl ☑
SN25 ....34 E5
Meadowsweet Dr SN11 ..80 F3
Meads Rd SP4 ....198 B7
Meads The SN14 ....53 B3
Meadway
☑ Shrewton SP3 ......196 F6
Wingfield BA14 ....105 A8
Meares Dr SN5 ....49 B8
Mears Rd ☑ SP4 .....198 A6
Medbourne SN4 ....163 A3
Medbourne Rd SN4 ...163 A4
Medbourne Sp SN10 ...50 C6
Medgbury Rd SN1 .....50 C6
Medieval Hall* SP1 ..152 C8
Medina Way SN2 ....35 F4
Medlar Ct SN2 ....35 B2
Medway SN25 ....34 F4
Medway Rd SN25 ......34 F4
Meerut Rd SP9 ....216 C6
Melbourne Cl SN3 .....50 F3
Melbourne Gdns ☑ SP4 .198 A6
Melbourne St BA11 ...186 B7
Melbury Abbas Mill*
SP7 ....206 A7
Melbury Down* SP5 ..206 A7
Melbury St SP7 ......206 B6
Melbury Way ☑ SP7 ..202 D2
Melchet Cl SO51 .....162 D1
Melford Wlk SN3 ......51 C7
Melfort Cl SN3 ....34 B2
Meliot Rise ☑ SP10 ..193 E2
Melksham Blue Pool
SN12 ....94 A4
Melksham Cl SN2 ......35 B6
Melksham Com Hospl
SN12 ....94 B3
Melksham La SN12 .....93 C4
Melksham Rd
Chippenham SN15 ......78 B5
Holt SN12 ....93 A2
Lacock SN15 ....86 D5
Melksham Sta SN12 ...94 A6
Mellow Gd SN25 ....34 E5
Melrose Ave BA12 ...116 E6
Melrose Cl
☑ Swindon SN3 ....49 C6
☑ Warminster BA12 ..116 E6
Melsome Rd SN15 .....59 F1

Melton Rd BA14 ......101 C2
Melville Cl ☑ SN3 ....50 F6
Melvin Cl SP1 ....146 D1
Mendip Cl
☑ Frome BA11 ....110 A7
Melksham SN12 ....94 C4
Swindon SN25 ....35 C3
☑ Warminster BA12 ..117 A8
Mendip Dr BA11 .....110 A7
Menham Cl SN2 ....35 D2
Merchants House The*
SN8 ....213 D3
Mercia Ave SP10 .....193 C2
Mere Ave SN14 ....41 F1
Mere Castle* BA12 ..138 F6
Mere Cl BA12 ....139 A5
Mere Sch BA12 ....139 B5
Meridien Wlk SN3 .....51 B4
Meridian Wlk BA14 ..105 A8
Merifield SN14 ....77 A1
Merino Way SN8 ......173 B8
Merlin Cl ☑ SP10 ....193 E2
Merlin Way
Bower Hill SN12 ....94 B1
Stratton St Margaret SN3 .51 D8
Swindon SN3 ....36 D1
Merrifield Rd SP4 ...146 C6
Merrivale Gr SN3 ......50 E5
Mersey Ct SP10 ......193 F1
Merton Ave SN3 ....35 D4
Merton Cl ☑ SP6 ....210 D2
Merton St ☑ SN1 .....50 C6
Mervyn Webb Pl SN2 ..50 D8
Mesh Pond SP5 ......210 F8
Methuen Ave SN12 ....94 B6
Methuen Dr BA15 ....100 E4
Methuen Dr ☑ SP1 ..152 C8
Methuen Pk ☑ SN14 ..77 F5
Methuen Way SN13 ....76 F2
Mews The
Highworth SN6 ....23 A6
☑ Lydiard Millicent SN5 .48 D8
Warminster BA12 ....117 A7
Meyrick Ave SP2 ....152 A5
Meysey Cl GL7 ....1 A5
Michael Pym's Rd SN16 .28 A3
Middle Field Cl SN10 .214 C3
Middle Gd Cricklade SN6 .19 C8
Fovant SP3 ....204 D8
Wootton Bassett SN4 ..48 A2
Middle La
Atworth/Whitley SN12 ..85 D1
Cherhill SN11 ....166 B1
Martin SP6 ....209 A7
Trowbridge BA14 .....105 D3
Middle St SP2 ....151 E7
Middle Stoke BA2 .....99 A6
Middleleaze Dr SN5 ...48 F8
Middlemass Gn SN9 ..215 D5
Middleton SN11 ......149 B7
Middleton Cl
Swindon SN3 ....50 F6
☑ Warminster BA12 ..116 E6
Middleton Medieval Village
of* BA12 ....194 A7
Middleton Rd
Salisbury SP1 ....145 F2
The Common SP5 .....149 B7
Middletons Cl RG17 ...177 B7
Middlewick La SN13 ..76 D3
Midford Hill BA2 ......98 C4
Midford La BA2 ....98 E7
Midford Rd BA2 ....98 B7
Midhurst Ave SN3 .....51 B5
Midlands Ind Est The
BA14 ....92 E1
Midlands The BA14 ...92 E1
Midwinter Cl SN5 .....34 B2
Midwinter Gdns SN3 ..36 A2
Milbourne La SN16 ...28 C4
Milbourne Pk SN16 ...28 C4
Mildenhall Way SN10 .35 B6
Mildmay Cl ☑ SN5 ....48 F5
Mile Dr SN14 ....44 E1
Miles's La SP5 ......161 E5
Milestone Way SN15 ..70 C2
Milford Hill SP1 .....152 B8
Milford Hollow ☑ SP1 .152 C8
Milford Ind Est ☑ SP1 .152 C8
Milford Manor Gdns
SP1 ....152 B8
Milford Mill Rd SP1 ..152 D8
Milford Pk SP1 ......152 C8
Milford St
Salisbury SP1 ....152 B8
Swindon SN1 ....50 C6
Mill Cl Devizes SN10 .214 C1
Longbridge Deverill
BA12 ....120 F6
South Cerney GL7 ......7 A7
Winterbourne SN4 .....64 B6
Wroughton SN4 ....64 B6
Mill Cl ☑ SN6 ....210 D1
Mill Dro SN10 ....183 C1
Mill Head SN10 ......179 A4
Mill Hill Ave SP9 ....216 C8
Mill Hollow La SP7 ..206 A7
Mill La Bishopstone SP5 .150 A1
Bourton SP8 ....137 E2
Box SN13 ....83 C7
Bradford-on-Avon BA15 .100 D6
Broughton Gifford SN12 .93 C3
Cherhill SN11 ....166 B1
Chilmark SP3 ....200 F2
Fairford GL7 ....1 F1

Mill La continued
Fovant SP3 ....204 D8
Heytesbury BA12 ....194 C5
Lambourn RG17 ......165 B1
Lechlade GL7 ....2 E4
Little Somerford SN15 .43 F5
Malmesbury SN16 .....28 A3
Melbury Abbas SP7 ..206 A7
Mere BA12 ....139 B5
Monkton Combe BA2 ..98 E8
Poulshot SN10 ....179 A5
Ramsbury SN8 ....170 B2
St Paul Malmesbury Without
SN16 ....42 E5
Salisbury SP1 ....145 E5
Selwood BA11 ....114 F8
Shaftesbury SN8 ....176 F2
Stanton Fitzwarren SN6 .22 A2
Swindon SN1 ....50 A3
The Common SP5 .....149 E6
West Lavington SN10 .187 E8
Whiteparish BA13 ....112 D8
Winterbourne Monkton
SN16 ....167 C3
Winterslow SP5 .....149 D7
Zeale SP8 ....137 F2
Mill La Devizes SN10 .214 C1
Netheravon SP4 .....190 A4
Potterne SN10 ......179 D3
Salisbury SP1 ....145 F1
Worton SN10 ....179 A4
Mill Rise SP8 ....137 E2
Mill Sch The SN10 ...179 C6
Mill St Calne SN11 ....81 B2
Fontmell Magna SP7 .206 A3
Heytesbury BA12 ....194 C5
Trowbridge BA14 ....105 D8
Mill Stream App SP2 .146 A1
Milland Cl SN25 ......35 B6
Millard Cl ☑ SN15 ...78 F4
Millbourn Cl SP1 .....99 D7
Millbrook ☑ SP1 ....146 B2
Millbrook La SP7 ....141 C1
Millbuck Cl SN11 .....35 E1
Millennium Visitor Ctr*
GL7 ....6 B4
Millennium Way SP2 .152 B5
Miller Cl Chirton SN10 .180 F4
Salisbury SP1 ....145 F1
Swindon SN5 ....48 F8
Miller's La DT11 ....207 D1
Millfield SP11 ....165 A1
Millgreen Rd ☑ SP4 .217 C2
Millhand Villas BA14 .105 E7
Millington Dr ☑ BA14 .105 A7
Mills Rd SN4 ....94 C4
Mills Way SN4 ......217 D4
Milne Cres ☑ SP4 ...197 E6
Milne Rd SP4 ....198 E6
Milston Ave SN2 ......35 C5
Milston Down (Long
Barrows)* SP4 ......190 E1
Milston Dro SP4 ....190 E1
Milston Rd Bulford SP4 .198 C7
Durrington/Bulford SP4 .217 D8
Milston View ☑ SP4 .198 C7
Milton Ave
☑ Andover SP10 .....193 C1
Melksham SN12 ....94 B4
Milton Pl GL7 ....1 F6
Milton Rd
Amesbury SP4 ....217 E2
Pewsey SN9 ....215 C5
Salisbury SP1 ....152 B6
Swindon SN1 ....50 B6
Milton St GL7 ....1 F6
Milton's Way SN4 .....47 C1
Milverton Ct SN3 .....51 A5
Minden Cl ☑ SP10 ...193 D2
Minety CE Prim Sch
SN16 ....11 B2
Minety La SN16 ....16 A7
Minety Rd SN2 ....35 B5
Minnow Cl SN25 ......34 A7
Minories Rd SP4 ....216 E6
Minster CE Prim Sch
BA12 ....117 A5
Minster Cl SN25 ......34 F7
Minster St
☑ Salisbury SP1 ....146 A1
Wilton SP2 ....144 D3
Minster View BA12 ..117 A5
Minster Way SN14 ....78 A5
Mint Cl SN2 ....34 C3
Minton Distribution Pk
SP4 ....217 C4
Minty's Top SN15 .....96 A7
Mir Cres SN4 ....34 B7
Mitchell Cl ☑ SP10 ..193 C1
Mitchell Rd SP12 ....178 B8
Mitchell Rd SP2 ....151 D8
Mitchells Cl ☑ SP5 ..210 C7
Mizmaze* SP6 ....210 D7
Moat Rd BA13 ....108 D6
Moberly Rd SP1 .....146 B3
Moffat Rise SN16 .....28 A5
Moggs La SP11 ......172 A8
Mompesson Ho* SP2 .152 A8
Monastery Rd BA3 ..186 C8
Monet Cl SN25 ....34 A7
Moneyer Rd ☑ SP10 .193 D2
Monk's La SN11 ....85 B6
Monkley La BA14 ....104 C1
Monks Cl SP9 ....216 C7
Monks Pk Gdns SN13 .85 B5
Monks Way SN15 ......79 A1
Monkton Cl SN3 ......51 B4

Monkton Dro BH21 ..208 D1
Monkton Farleigh & S
Wraxall CE VC Prim Sch
BA15 ....90 E7
Monkton Hill SN15 ...78 D7
Monkton House* SN12 .93 C1
Monkton Rd SN15 ....78 F7
Monkton Pk Prim Sch
SN15 ....78 E7
Monmouth Cl ☑ SN3 .50 F6
Monmouth Dr BA11 ..110 B5
Monmouth Rd SP3 ..203 D8
Mons Ave SN4 ....198 E6
Mons La SN15 ....86 D8
Montagu Cl SN2 ......49 F7
Montague Cl SN15 ....79 A7
Montague Pl BA14 ..102 A1
Montague Pl SN12 ...94 C5
Montague Rd SP2 ...151 D7
Monteagle Cl SN5 ....49 A4
Montgomery Ave SN2 .35 B2
Montgomery Gdns
SP2 ....145 E2
Montgomery Rd SP1 .193 E3
Montrose Cl SN2 ......34 E2
Monument Hill SN10 .214 C1
Monxton Cl ☑ SP1 ..146 D5
Moody's Hill SP5 ....155 E2
Moon Cl SN14 ....75 B3
Moonrakers SN10 ...214 D5
Moor Barton SN13 ...84 D6
Moor Hill SN3 ....204 D8
Moor La
Charlton Heath SN16 ..29 D6
Whiteparish SP5 ....161 A1
Moor Pk SN13 ....84 C8
Moore's Pl SN8 ....64 C8
Moore's Rd ☑ SP4 ..177 B7
Moores Yd BA14 ....104 C6
Moorgate GL7 ....2 B4
Moorhen Cl
Swindon SN3 ....51 E5
Trowbridge BA14 ....101 D4
Moorings The SN1 ....50 A5
Moorlands SN15 ......70 E2
Moorlands The SN10 .214 A2
Moormead Rd SN4 ....64 B6
Moors Cl SN15 ....70 C5
Moot (Motte & Bailey) The*
SP5 ....211 B8
Downton SP5 ....211 B7
Moot Gdns SP5 ......211 A7
Moot La SP5 ....211 A7
Mopes La SN5 ....33 D2
Mora Rd SN2 ....35 E1
Moredon Inf Sch SN2 .34 D2
Moredon Jun Sch SN2 .34 E2
Moredon Pk SN2 ......34 F3
Moredon Rd SN25 ....34 F3
Moresby Cl SN5 ....49 C6
Moreton Cl BA13 ....108 E2
Morgan's La
Pentridge SP5 ....208 E5
Winterbourne SP4 ...133 A2
Morgans Rise Rd ☑
SP5 ....211 C8
Morgans Vale & Woodfalls
CE Prim Sch SP5 ....211 C8
Morgans Vale Rd SP5 .211 C7
Morie Cl SN5 ....34 B1
Morley Field SP1 ...117 C7
Morley Pl ☑ RG17 ..177 B7
Morley St SN1 ....50 C5
Morrice La Bath BA1 ..82 B3
Morris Rd SN8 ......213 B2
Morris St SN2 ....49 F7
Morrison St SN2 ......49 F7
Morse Cl SN15 ....78 E4
Morse St SN1 ....50 B5
Mortimer Cl SN5 ......61 D8
Mortimer St BA14 ..105 C7
Moss Mead SN14 .....77 F8
Motcombe CE VA Prim Sch
SP7 ....202 A4
Motcombe Grange Sch
SP7 ....202 A5
Motcombe Rd SP7 ..202 B3
Moulton Dr BA15 ...100 D4
Mount Carmel Rd
SP11 ....199 F3
Mount Hts SP5 ......211 C8
Mount Pl
Barford St Martin SP3 .143 B4
Warminster BA12 ...117 A5
Mount Pleasant
Atworth SN12 ....85 A1
Atworth/Whitley SN12 .93 A8
Bradford-on-Avon BA15 .100 D7
Chippenham SN14 .....70 A1
Lechlade GL7 ....2 C4
South Newton SP2 ..130 A4
Mountain Wood BA2 ..82 B2
Mountford Manor Prim Sch
SN3 ....50 F6
Mountings The SN4 ..64 B8
Mountpleasant SP4 ..203 D8
Mountsfield BA14 ...110 A2
Moxhams ☑ SP6 .....210 D1
Moyle Pk SN14 ......102 A1
Moyne Cl SN10 ......179 D8
Moyne Gdns ☑ SP4 .217 D3
Mud La SN5 ....32 F2
Muddyford Rd SP6 ..211 C8
Muirfield SN25 ....34 D7

Mulberry Cl SN14 .....70 B1
Mulberry Ct
Frome BA11 ....110 B7
Sixpenny Handley SP5 .208 B4
Mulberry Gr SN2 .....35 A2
Mulcaster Ave SN5 ...48 F5
Mulling Cl SN14 ......75 A3
Mundy Ave SN3 ....51 C4
Munks Cl ☑ SP2 ....151 E7
Munnings Ct ☑ SP10 .193 C1
Munro Cl SN3 ....50 E6
Murdock Rd SN3 ......51 E6
Murray Rd BA14 ....101 D2
Murray Wlk SN12 .....94 B5
Murrayfield SN15 .....70 E1
Muscott Cl ☑ SP9 ..199 C8
Muscovey Cl SN15 ....60 A2
Mustons La ☑ SP7 ..202 C2
Mycroft Rd SN25 .....34 C6
Myrfield Rd ☑ SP1 ..146 D5
Myrtle Ave SN2 .....116 F6
Myrtle Gdns SN2 .....35 C2
Mythern Meadow
BA15 ....100 E5

N

Nadder Cl ☑ SP3 ...203 E8
Nadder La SP7 ......144 F2
Nadder Rd SP9 .....216 D6
Nadder Terr SP2 ....144 C2
Naini Tal Rd SP9 ...216 C6
Namtwich SN5 ....49 A3
Napier Cl SN2 ....50 A7
Napier Cres SP1 ....146 D1
Napier Wlk SP10 ....193 F1
Napiers ☑ SN8 .....176 B3
Narrow Wine St BA14 .105 D8
Nash Cl SN25 ....35 A8
Nash Rd SN8 ....173 A8
National Monuments Records
Ctr* SN2 ....50 A7
Naughton Ave SN10 .214 E6
Naunton Rd SN3 .....51 A6
Neal Cl ☑ SP4 .....101 E4
Neale's Barrow* SP2 .150 A6
Neeld Cl SN14 ....68 F6
Neeld Cres SN14 .....78 B8
Neigh Bridge Ctry Pk*
GL7 ....5 F2
Nell Hill SN6 ....22 A7
Nelson Cl ☑ SP4 ...198 F6
Nelson Rd SP2 ......146 A2
Nelson St SN1 ....49 F5
Nelson Wlk SP10 ....193 F1
Nepaul Rd SP9 ......216 C7
Ness Cl ☑ SN5 ....34 B2
Nestings The BA14 ..105 A5
Neston Cres SN13 ....84 E6
Neston Pk* SN13 ....84 E5
Netheravon Cl SP1 ..146 B3
Netheravon Rd
Durrington SP4 ....198 B7
Figheldean SP4 .....190 B1
Salisbury SP1 ....145 E3
Nethercote Hill SN15 .86 D6
Netherhampton Rd
Netherhampton SP2 ..150 F8
Quidhampton SP2 ...144 F1
Netherhampton SN3 ..84 D6
Netherstreet SN15 ...96 D6
Netherton Cl SN3 ....51 B4
Netherton House*
SP11 ....185 F4
Nett Rd SP3 ....196 F6
Nettlebed Nursery SP7 .202 C2
Nettlecombe ☑ SP7 ..202 D2
Nettlemead La BA12 .201 F8
Nettleton Rd SN14 ...53 B3
Netton St SP5 ......205 E4
Neville Cl SP1 ......146 C4
Neville Terr SN15 .....57 D1
Nevis Cl SN5 ....34 B2
New Bottom Rd SP4 .145 E7
New Bridge Cl ☑ SN1 .50 C7
New Bridge Rd SP1 ..152 A7
New Bridge Sq ☑ SN1 .50 C7
New Broughton Rd
SN12 ....94 A5
New Canal SP1 ......152 A8
New Cl Bourton SP8 .137 E2
West Knoyle BA12 ...140 E7
New Cl Cty Prim Sch
BA12 ....117 B6
New Coll SN5 ....50 C5
New Coll Wlk SN3 ....50 C5
New Cres SP11 .....192 A5
New Cut BA12 ......139 A6
New Dro SP11 ......192 A5
New Haig Rd ☑ SP4 .198 E6
New Hall Hospl SP5 ..158 F8
New Harnham Rd SP2 .152 A6
New Hayward Gardens
RG17 ....171 C2
New House La SP11 ..192 E4
New King Barrows*
SP4 ....197 F5
New Lane Ct SP11 ..202 D1
New Lawns SN12 .....94 B4
New Pk Rd SN10 ....214 B4

New Pk St SN10 ....214 A4
New Rd Bath BA1 ....82 C2
Bradford-on-Avon BA15 ..100 E7
Bromham SN15 ....96 A5
Calne Without SN11 ....79 F3
Chippenham SN15 ....78 D7
Chiseldon SN4 ....65 D3
Codford BA12 ....195 A3
Donhead St Andrew SP7 ..203 B4
22 Durrington/Bulford
SP4 ....198 B7
East Knoyle SP3 ....141 B3
Erlestoke BA13 ....179 A2
Kilmington BA12 ....123 D6
Landford SP5 ....212 D5
Limpley Stoke BA2 ....99 B5
Maiden Bradley with Yarnfield
BA11 ....123 D8
Marlborough SN8 ....213 D3
Melksham Without SN12 ...94 E7
Purton SN5 ....33 C5
Rockbourne SP6 ....210 A5
2 Shaftesbury SP7 ....202 B2
1 Trowbridge BA14 ....105 A7
Wootton Bassett SN4 ......47 D1
Zeale SP8 ....138 A3
New Severalls The
SN9 ....182 E7
New St
16 Market Lavington SN10 .179 F1
Salisbury SP1 ....152 A8
Winterbourne Stoke SP3 ..196 F3
New Terr BA14 ....101 C7
New Town La SN6 ....163 E6
New Ward Rd SP4 ....198 E7
New Zealand Ave SP2 ....145 D2
Newall Tuck Rd SN15 .....78 F7
Newark CI SN5 ....49 B3
Newbourne Gdns SN14 .....56 D6
Newburgh PI SN6 ....22 F6
Newburn Cres SN1 ....49 F5
Newbury Ave SN1 ....80 F4
Newbury Dr
Chippenham SN14 ....77 F5
Swindon SN5 ....49 B3
Newbury Rd
Andover SP10 ....193 E2
Lambourn RG17 ....165 A4
Newbury St RG17 ....165 A1
Newby Acre SN8 ....213 D4
Newby CI 4 SN10 ....187 E8
Newcastle St SN1 ....50 D6
Newcombe Dr SN2 ....50 A7
Newcombe Trad Est
SN2 ....50 B7
Newcroft CI SN11 ....81 B4
Newcroft Rd SN11 ....81 B4
Newhall St SN1 ....50 B5
Newhurst Pk BA14 ....102 A2
Newland Rd SN25 ....35 A3
Newlands CI SN15 ....70 E7
Newlands Rd SN13 ....77 A1
Newleaze
Steeple Ashton BA14 .....178 A4
Trowbridge BA14 ....101 F4
Newleaze Pk SN12 ....93 B4
Newman Rd SN10 ....214 C1
Newmans Way SP4 ....217 E2
Newmarket Ave BA14 .....105 E4
Newmarket CI 4 SN14 ....77 F6
Newmeadow Copse
SN5 ....34 A1
Newopaul Way BA12 ......116 B9
Newport BA12 ....117 A7
Newport St SN1 ....50 D3
Newstead CI 11 SN25 ....34 F6
Newth's La SN5 ....19 D2
Newton Abbot CI 6
SN14 ....50 C4
Newton Barrow* SP2 ....130 E3
Newton CI SN5 ....161 C3
Newton La SP5 ....161 B3
Newton Rd SP2 ....145 D1
Newton Tony CE Prim Sch
SP4 ....199 B3
Newton Way SN2 ....35 C4
Newtown
Bradford-on-Avon BA15 ..100 C6
Heytesbury BA12 ....194 C5
Hullavington SN14 ....41 F1
Trowbridge BA14 ....105 C8
Westbury BA13 ....109 C3
Newtown Com Prim Sch
BA14 ....105 C8
Newtown Rd SN8 ....170 C2
Nicolson CI 18 SP4 ......217 E3
Niebull CI SN16 ....28 A5
Nightingale Ave BA11 ....110 B6
Nightingale CI 8 SO51 ..212 F6
Nightingale Dr BA13 .....109 B4
Nightingale La
South Marston SN3 ....36 F4
Tisbury SP3 ....203 C6
Nightingale Rd BA14 ....105 A8
Nightingale Wlk SP2 ....145 C2
Nightwood Copse 3
SN5 ....34 A1
Nindum Rd SN3 ....36 C1
Nine Acre Dr SN13 ....76 D1
Nine Rd SN4 ....168 E8
Noade St SP5 ....206 E4
Noble St SN16 ....40 C8
Nolan CI SN25 ....34 F8
Nolands Rd SN11 ....166 D2

Nomansland & Hamptworth
CE Prim Sch SP5 ....212 B4
Norcliffe Rd SN3 ....51 B4
Nore Marsh Rd SN4 ......47 E1
Noredown Way SN4 ....47 E1
Noremarsh Jun Sch
SN4 ....47 E1
Norfolk CI 1 SN3 ....50 F6
Norfolk Rd SP2 ....151 E7
Norley La SN11 ....80 C3
Norman CI SN15 ....79 A4
Norman Rd SN2 ....35 C1
Normandy Way 14 SP6 ..210 D1
Norney Rd BA13 ....179 A4
Norridge View 4 BA12 ..116 E7
Norrington La SN12 ......93 C6
Norrington Manor*
SP5 ....204 A2
Norris CI SN4 ....65 C3
Norris Rd BA14 ....102 B3
North Bank Rise SN4 .....47 F2
North Bradley CE Prim Sch
BA14 ....105 D2
North Charford Crossing
SP6 ....210 F6
North Charford Dro
SP6 ....210 C8
North Comm La SP5 .....212 B7
North Cote SN11 ....81 A4
North End SN11 ....81 A4
North End Gdns SN16 ...25 C1
North Farm CT RG17 ....165 B2
North La SN5 ....212 C4
North Leaze CI SN2 .....34 F3
North Mdw National Nature
Reserve* SN6 ....8 C1
North Mdw Rd SN6 ....8 C1
North Rd
Amesbury SP4 ....217 E2
Ashmore SP5 ....206 E5
Mere BA12 ....139 A6
North Row BA12 ....117 A7
North St
Broad Chalke SP5 ....205 B4
Calne SN11 ....81 B4
Mere BA12 ....139 A5
Pewsey SN9 ....215 A5
Salisbury SP2 ....145 F1
Swindon SN1 ....50 C5
Wilton SP2 ....144 D3
North Standen Rd
RG17 ....177 A6
North Star Ave SN2 ......50 B8
North Star Ind Est SN2 ..50 B7
North View
Berwick St James SP3 ...196 F2
Highworth SN6 ....22 F5
North View Hts RG17 ...177 C7
North View PI SN8 .....213 D4
North View Rd SN13 ....84 A8
North Way Calne SN11 ....81 A4
Trowbridge BA14 ....105 A7
North Wlk SP1 ....152 A8
Northacre Ind Est
BA13 ....108 D5
Northampton St SN1 ....50 C5
Northbourne Rd SN25 ...35 A7
Northbrook SN10 ....179 F1
Northbrook CI 1 SN10 ..179 F1
Northbrook Rd SN12 ....93 F7
Northcote Cres 7 BA11 .110 A7
Northcroft Rd 1 SN13 ..76 B1
Northern CI GL7 ....10 E6
Northen Terr
Durrington SP4 ....197 F7
Larkhill SP4 ....198 A7
Northern Rd SN2 ....35 A1
Northfield BA12 ....99 F7
Northfield La SN14 ......66 A2
Northfield Way SN3 .....51 B7
Northfields
Bulkington SN10 ....178 E5
Calne SN11 ....81 A4
1 Lambourn RG17 ......165 A2
Northgate Gdns SN10 ...214 A4
Northgate St SN10 ......214 A4
Northlands Ind Est
BA12 ....117 B7
Northleaze SN13 ....76 D1
Northleigh BA15 ....91 E1
Northmoor La GL7 ....6 F8
Northside SP4 ....146 D8
Northview 20 RG17 .....177 B7
Northview Prim Sch
SN6 ....23 A7
Northway SP4 ....134 B7
Northwood SN15 ....70 E2
Norton Dr SP4 ....146 D6
Norton Gr SN3 ....50 D5
Norton Rd BA12 ....117 F1
Norwood Castle (site of)*
SN16 ....9 F7
Norwood CI 3 SN3 ......51 D4
Notton House Sch
SN15 ....86 B8
Noyes CI
Chippenham SN14 ....77 F8
Haydon Wick SN2 ....34 C5
Nuffield CI SN3 ....49 A8
Nunns Pk SP5 ....161 D4
Nunton Dro SP5 ....152 D1
Nurseries The
Christian Malford SN15 ..58 A2
Swindon SN1 ....50 A5
Nursery CI
4 Amesbury SP4 ....217 B3
Atworth/Whitley SN12 ...92 E8
Trowbridge BA14 ....102 A3

Nursery CI continued
Wroughton SN4 ....64 A5
Nursery Gdns
Corsham SN13 ....85 A8
Mere BA12 ....139 A5
Nursery Rd
Colerne SN14 ....75 A3
Salisbury SP2 ....145 E1
Nursery The SN16 ....27 F6
Nursteed CI SN10 ....214 D2
Nursteed Com Prim Sch
SN10 ....214 E3
Nursteed Pk SN10 ......214 C2
Nursteed Rd SN10 ......214 C2
Nursteed Rd Ind Est
SN10 ....214 C1
Nutbane La SP11 ....193 A4
Nuthatch CI 4 SN3 .....51 E6
Nutley Ct 8 SN8 ....183 D8
Nutmeg CI 7 SN2 ....34 D4
Nyland Rd SN3 ....51 C7
Nyland Sch SN3 ....51 B7
Nythe Cty Prim Sch
SN3 ....51 B8
Nythe Rd SN3 ....36 B1

O

O'Donnell CI SN15 ....70 E1
Oak Ash Gn SP2 ....144 C2
Oak CI
Bishops Cannings SN10 ..172 B2
Pitton & Farley SP5 .....154 E7
South Newton SP2 ......130 B2
Tidworth SP9 ....216 E7
Oak Dr Alderbury SP5 ..153 D2
Highworth SN6 ....22 F5
Trowbridge BA14 ....105 C3
Oak Gdns SN3 ....36 A4
Oak Hill SN8 ....176 E6
Oak La Easterton SN10 ..179 F2
Figheldean SP4 ....190 B2
Mere BA12 ....139 B4
Oak Lodge CI SN14 .....78 C8
Oak PI SP4 ....217 C4
Oak Rd
Chippenham Without
SN14 ....77 F6
Colerne SN14 ....74 F5
Down Ampney GL7 ....8 E6
Oak St GL7 ....2 C4
Oak Tree Ave SN2 ....35 D3
Oak Tree Dros PR4 SN3 .36 C7
Oak Tree CI BA14 ......101 B1
Oak Tree Sch
SN3 ....51 A4
Oakapple CI 4 SN4 ....163 B6
Oakbournes The 5 SP1 ..146 C5
Oakes CI 8 RG17 ......177 B7
Oakes La GL9 ....52 B5
Oakford La SN14 ....74 B2
Oakford Wlk SN3 ....51 A6
Oakham CI SN5 ....49 C5
Oakhurst Way SN25 ....34 F7
Oakie CI SN25 ....35 A5
Oaklands SN15 ....70 D2
Oaklands CI 12 SP6 ...210 D1
Oaklea La SP5 ....153 E2
Oakleaze SN16 ....17 B2
Oakleigh Dr SP5 ....212 C5
Oakley Flats GL7 ......116 F7
Oakley La DT11 ....207 D2
Oaks The
Chippenham SN15 ....70 D2
Kemble GL7 ....4 F7
Warminster BA12 ....117 A8
Oaksey Rd Minety SN16 ..16 C4
Swindon SN2 ....35 C4
Oakwood Dr SN12 ......94 B4
Oakwood Gr SP5 ......153 D3
Oakwood Rd SN5 ....49 C7
Oamaru Way SN4 ......210 D3
Oare Hill SN8 ....174 B2
Oare Prim Sch SN8 .....174 B2
Oasis Leisure Ctr SN2 ..50 B7
Oasthouse CI 8 SN5 ....49 A8
Oate Hill SN15 ....78 F6
Oatfields BA14 ....101 D4
Oathill La GL7 ....3 B8
Oathills SN13 ....84 F8
Oatmeal Row 6 SP1 ....152 A8
Obelisk Terr 6 BA12 ...116 F7
Oberon Way SN3 ....35 A5
Ocotal Way SN1 ....50 D8
Odcroft CI SN15 ....79 A7
Oddford Vale 17 SP3 ...203 E8
Odstock Prim Sch
SP5 ....152 B1
Odstock Rd
Britford SP2 ....152 C6
Swindon SP2 ....35 C6
Ogbourne SN14 ....75 B3
Ogbourne St George & St
Andrew Prim Sch SN8 ..168 F5
Ogbury Camp* SP4 .....198 A1
Ogilvie Sq SN11 ....81 C3
Okebourne Pk SN6 .....51 C3
Okeford CT SN4 ....51 C7
Okus Gr SP2 ....51 A6
Okus Rd SN1 ....49 F3
Okus Trad Est SN1 .....49 F4
Olaf CI 18 SP10 ....193 E2
Old Alexander Rd SN16 ..27 F4
Old Bakery CI SN16 ....28 F2
Old Barn GL8 ....3 C5
Old Batch The BA15 ...100 B8

Old Beasants SN8 ......174 A6
Old Blandford Rd SP2 ..151 F6
Old Boundary Rd 5
SP7 ....202 C1
Old Brickyard Rd SP6 ..210 B1
Old Broughton Rd
SN12 ....94 A5
Old Cann Sch SP7 .....202 D1
Old Castle Rd SP1 .....146 A5
Old Chapel CI SP5 .....153 D3
Old Chase Rd SN8 .....169 A4
Old Coach Rd
Durrington/Bulford SP4 ..217 D8
North Wraxall SN14 .....67 D2
Shipton Bellinger SP11 ..191 F1
Old Common Way 18 SN11 .192 A5
Old Ct SN4 ....47 D1
Old Dairy CI SP2 ....145 C3
Old Dairy Ct SN12 ......94 C5
Old Dairy The SP5 ......152 D1
Old Derry Hill SN15 .....79 D2
Old Ditton Rd BA13 ...112 E7
Old Down Rd GL9 ....52 C8
Old English Dr 2 SP10 .193 D2
Old Forge CI SN5 ....45 E6
Old Granary La SP4 ....217 B3
Old Hardenhuish La
SN14 ....70 B1
Old Hayward La RG17 ..171 B1
Old Hollow BA12 ......139 B6
Old Hospl Rd SN9 .....215 B6
Old King Barrows*
SP4 ....197 F5
Old Malmesbury Rd
SN4 ....47 E4
Old Malthouse La SP4 ..147 B7
Old Manor Hospl SP2 ..145 E1
Old Manor House*
BA12 ....194 A4
Old Mdws Wlk SP2 ....151 E7
Old Midford Rd BA2 ....98 A7
Old Mill La SN3 ....50 D3
Old Orch The SN16 .....28 A6
Old Post Office La 5
SP4 ....190 A3
Old Pound Ct SP8 .....137 D1
Old Rd Alderbury SP5 ..153 C3
Chippenham SN15 ....78 D8
Derry Hill/Studley SN11 ..80 B2
Old Rly CI 1 SN16 ......28 A4
Old Ropeworks The*
SN8 ....213 C2
Old Sarum* SP1 ....145 F6
Old Sarum Barracks
SP4 ....146 C8
Old Sarum Bsns Pk
SP4 ....146 C8
Old Sarum Pk SP4 .....146 D8
Old Sawmills The
RG17 ....177 F3
Old Sch Cl SN16 ....96 C7
Old Sch Ct SN13 ....51 B6
Old Sch Yd SN13 ....85 A8
Old Severalls The SN9 ..182 E7
Old Shaft Rd SN13 .....84 C7
Old Shaftesbury Dro
SP2 ....150 A6
Old Shaftesbury Dro
SP2 ....151 D5
Old Shaw La SN5 ....48 F8
Old Sodom La SN15 ....59 B8
Old St SP2 ....152 A6
Old Sta Yd The 14 RG17 .165 A1
Old Track BA2 ....98 F7
Old Vicarage La GL7 ...4 F7
Old Vineries The 10
SP6 ....210 C1
Old Ward Rd 8 SP4 ....198 E6
Old Wardour Castle*
SN11 ....203 D5
Oldbury Castle (Hill Fort)*
SN11 ....172 C8
Oldbury Prior SN11 ....81 C1
Oldbury Way SN11 .....81 A3
Oldenburgh Rd 8 BA13 .108 E1
Oldfield Pk SN10 ....108 E3
Oldfield Rd
Salisbury SP1 ....146 C5
Westbury BA13 ....108 E4
Oldford Hill BA11 ......110 A8
Oldhat Barrow* SN9 ...183 A3
Oldlands Wlk SN3 ......51 A3
Olive Gr SN2 ....35 B3
Olivemead La SN15 ....45 C1
Oliver Ave SN13 ....76 F2
Oliver CI SN5 ....48 F6
Oliver Tomkins Jun & Inf Sch
SN5 ....49 B5
Oliver's Castle (Fort)*
SN10 ....97 C6
Oliver's La 5 SN16 ......28 A3
Olivers CI SN11 ....166 B1
Olivers Hill SN11 ....166 B1
Olivier CI SP2 ....145 C5
Olivier Rd Swindon SN25 .35 B6
Wilton SP2 ....144 B5
Olympia The SN8 ......168 E3
Olympiad L Ctr* SN15 ..78 E8
Omdurman St SN2 .....35 B1
Orange CI SN6 ....23 A6
Orangery The RG17 ...177 C8
Orbital Sh Pk SN25 ....34 E6
Orchard CI Calne SN11 ..81 C2
Devizes SN10 ....214 B1
12 Fordingbridge SP6 ..210 D1
Lechlade GL7 ....2 B4
5 Ramsbury SN8 ......170 B2
2 Wanborough SN4 ....163 A6

Orchard CI continued
Warminster BA12 ....117 B8
West Ashton BA14 .....106 B4
Westbury BA13 ....112 C8
Westwood BA15 ....99 F3
Orchard Cres SN14 .....78 B7
Orchard Ct
Bratton BA13 ....186 A7
St Paul Malmesbury Without
SN16 ....28 A2
Orchard Dr BA14 ......104 E2
Orchard End SP4 ......217 D8
Orchard Gdns
Melksham SN12 ....94 A3
Purton SN5 ....33 A3
Orchard Gr
Bromham SN15 ....96 D7
Swindon SN2 ....35 D3
Orchard Mead 3 SN4 ..48 A2
Orchard Pk CI 8 RG17 .177 B6
Orchard Pl SN10 ....187 E8
Orchard Rd
Chippenham SN14 ......78 B7
Corsham SN13 ....77 A2
Marlborough SN8 ......213 E2
Redlynch SP5 ....211 C8
Salisbury SP2 ....145 D2
Trowbridge BA14 ......105 D7
Westbury BA13 ....109 A3
Orchard The
Chirton SN10 ....180 F4
Kington St Michael SN14 ..70 A8
Limpley Stoke BA2 .....99 C5
Semington BA14 ......102 F6
Sixpenny Handley SP5 ..208 B4
Upton Scudamore BA12 ..112 F4
Orchard Way
Amesbury SP4 ....217 C3
Longbridge Deverill
BA12 ....116 E1
Trowbridge BA14 ......105 C3
Orchid CI SN25 ....35 C3
Orchid Dr 30 SP11 ....192 A5
Ordnance Rd SP9 .....216 D6
Orford Rd SP4 ....217 D2
Orkney CI SN5 ....49 B7
Orlando CI 4 SN5 ......48 F5
Orpington Way BA14 ..102 B1
Orrin CI SN5 ....34 B1
Orwell CI
Malmesbury SN16 ......28 A5
Swindon SN25 ....35 A5
Osborne Rd BA14 .....101 E3
Osborne St SN2 ....50 B8
Oslings La BA1 ....82 B2
Osmund CI SN10 ......214 D3
Osmund Rd SN10 ......214 D2
Osprey CI
Bower Hill SN12 ....94 D1
Swindon SN3 ....51 E6
Osterley Rd SN25 ......34 E6
Otter Way SN4 ....47 F2
Overbrook SN3 ....51 C3
Overhouse Dr 12 SP3 ..203 E8
Overton Gdns SN1 .....36 B2
Overtown Hill SN4 .....64 C5
Overway La SP7 ....203 B2
Owen CI SN10 ....214 D3
Owl CI SN3 ....51 E6
Owlets The SN3 ....51 E6
Owlswood 9 SP2 ......152 A5
Ox Dro
Berwick St John SP5 ..207 B7
Bishopstone SP5 ......205 F2
Bower Chalke SP5 .....208 A8
Kimpton SP11 ....192 A1
Teffont SP3 ....201 C5
Ox Row 4 SP1 ....152 A8
Oxencroft 8 SP7 ......202 C2
Oxford Brooks Univ
SN2 ....50 A8
Oxford Rd Calne SN11 ..81 B3
Swindon SN3 ....36 A1
Upavon Down SN9 ....182 B2
Oxford St
Aldbourne SN8 ....170 A6
Hungerford RG17 .....177 C8
Lambourn RG17 ....165 A1
Malmesbury SN16 ......28 A3
Marlborough SN8 ......213 D3
Ramsbury SN8 ....170 B2
Swindon SN1 ....50 B6
Oxon PI SN6 ....163 E6
Oxyard BA12 ....195 B2

P

Pack Hill SN4 ....51 F2
Pack Horse La BA2 ......98 A7
Packhorse Bridge*
SN15 ....86 E5
Packhorse La SN5 ....33 E8
Packington CI SN5 ......49 B7
Packway The
Durrington SP4 ....197 A7
Shrewton SP3 ....196 F7
Paddington Dr SN5 ....49 E5
Paddock CI Enford SN9 ..190 A6
Great Somerford SN15 ..44 A2
4 Shaftesbury SP7 ....202 D1
Sixpenny Handley SP5 ..208 A3
Swindon SN25 ....34 E5
Winterbourne SP4 .....133 B2
Paddock End SN14 .....70 A7
Paddock La
Chilmark SP3 ....200 F2
Corsham SN13 ....84 D6

Paddock The
Highworth SN6 ....23 A5
Market Lavington SN10 ...180 A1
8 Tisbury SP3 ....203 E8
Paddock Way SP1 ....146 E2
Paddock Wood 16 SP4 .198 B7
Paddocks The
10 Aldbourne SN8 ......170 A6
Chippenham SN15 ....78 E6
Mere BA12 ....139 A5
14 Ramsbury SN8 .....170 B2
5 Swindon SN3 ....36 A2
Padfield Gdns SN12 ...93 F1
Padstow Rd SN5 ......49 F5
Page Cl Calne SN11 .....81 C3
Chippenham SN14 ....78 A7
Paget Cl SP9 ....216 B8
Pagnell La SN10 .....179 D1
Pains Way 3 SP4 .....217 C2
Painters Mead BA14 ...102 A2
Pakenham Rd SN5 .....51 B4
Palairet Cl BA15 .....100 D4
Palestine Rd SP11 ....199 F3
Palm Rd SN14 ....75 A5
Palmer Dr BA15 ......100 D8
Palmer Rd
Swindon SP2 ....145 E2
Trowbridge BA14 .....101 D2
Palmer St SN14 ......78 C7
Palmers Way 11 SN4 ..163 A6
Palmerston Meadow
SN9 ....190 A6
Pampas Ct 1 BA12 ...116 E6
Pans La SN10 ....214 B2
Panters Rd SP2 ......204 C8
Pantiles The 12 SP6 ..210 C1
Parade The
Marlborough SN8 ......213 D3
Swindon SN1 ....50 C6
Paradise La BA12 ....116 E1
Parham La SN10 .....179 E2
Parham View 7 SN5 ...48 F5
Parhams Ct SN4 ......47 E1
Park Terr SP7 ....203 B1
Park Ave
Chippenham SN14 ......78 B8
Corsham SN13 ....84 A8
Highworth SN6 ....23 A5
Park Cl Calne SN11 ...81 C2
Malmesbury SN16 ......27 F4
Salisbury SP1 ....146 A4
Trowbridge BA14 .....105 D3
Park Dr SP3 ....201 B3
Park End SN6 ....17 F8
Park Field SN10 .....214 C5
Park La
Castle Combe SN14 ....68 A7
Cherhill SN11 ....166 C1
Chippenham SN15 ......78 D8
Corsham SN13 ....76 D1
Great Somerford SN15 ..44 A2
Heytesbury BA12 .....194 D5
Heywood BA13 ....109 C7
Lea & Cleverton SN16 ..29 D3
Lydiard Millicent SN5 ..48 E4
Malmesbury SN16 ......27 E5
North Wraxall SN14 ...68 A2
Odstock SN5 ....152 D4
Salisbury SP1 ....146 A3
Sutton Benger SN15 ...57 D2
Swindon SN1 ....50 A6
West Dean SP5 ......149 F1
Park Mead SN16 ......27 F4
Park Pl SN6 ....6 F1
Park Rd
Fordingbridge SP6 ....210 D1
Malmesbury SN16 ......27 F4
Market Lavington SN10 .179 E1
Rushall SN9 ....181 F3
Salisbury SP1 ....146 D2
Tidworth SP9 ....216 D5
Tisbury SP3 ....203 E8
Trowbridge BA14 .....105 D8
Westbury BA13 ....112 B8
Park Springs SN5 ....49 C5
Park St Charlton SN16 ..29 A6
Heytesbury BA12 .....194 C5
Hungerford RG17 .....177 B7
Salisbury SP1 ....146 B2
Swindon SN3 ....36 C2
Trowbridge BA14 .....105 C7
Park Terr SN15 ......78 C8
Park The
Erlestoke SN10 ....179 A1
8 Lamborn RG17 .....165 A2
Park View
Chirton SN10 ....180 F4
Devizes SN10 ....179 D8
Park View Dr
Lydiard Millicent SN5 ..48 D8
1 Westbury BA13 .....108 F1
Park Way RG17 ......177 B6
Parkers La SN15 .....70 D6
Parkhouse Cnr SP4 ...199 D6
Parkhouse Rd SP9 ...199 C8
Parkland Way SN4 ...133 D6
Parklands
Malmesbury SN16 ......27 E4
Trowbridge BA14 .....101 D2
Parklands Cl SN16 ...27 E4
Parklands Rd SN1 ....50 A1
Parklands The SN14 ..55 E8
Parkside
Chippenham SN15 ......78 D8
Swindon SN3 ....36 A3
Parkstone Wlk SN3 ...51 B3

Parkwater Rd SP5 ....161 E1
Parliament Row SN16 .28 A2
Parliament St SN14 ..78 B7
Parr Cl SN5 ....49 A6
Parsley Cl SN2 ......34 D5
Parsonage Cl
51 Fordingbridge SP6 ..210 D1
Salisbury SP1 ....145 E5
Parsonage Down National
Nature Reserve*
...........196 D5
Parsonage Gn SP2 ...151 E6
Parsonage Hill SP5 ..154 D7
Parsonage La
Charlton Musgrove BA9 ..136 C2
Hungerford RG17 .....177 B7
9 Lambourn RG17 ....166 A1
20 Market Lavington SN10 .179 F1
Parsonage Pk Dr 3
SP6 ....210 D1
Parsonage Pl 9 RG17 .165 A2
Parsonage Rd
Amesbury SP4 ....217 B3
Swindon SN1 ....36 A3
Trowbridge BA14 .....102 A1
Parsonage The SP5 ..208 B4
Parsonage Vale SN8 .183 D2
Parsonage Way SN15 ..70 F1
Parsons Cl SP4 ......133 D5
Parsons Gn 4 SP3 ...196 E6
Parsons La BA12 ....116 E2
Parsons Pool 19 SP7 .202 C2
Parsons Way SN4 ....47 E1
Partridge Cl
Chippenham SN14 ......70 B2
Corsham SN13 ....76 E1
Swindon SN3 ....51 E6
Partridge Hill SP5 ..212 E6
Partridge Way SP4 ..146 C8
Passmore Cl SN3 ....51 E7
Pasture Cl SN2 ......49 E7
Pastures The BA15 ...99 A8
Pat-yat GL7 ....4 B5
Patchway SN4 ....78 B8
Patchway The SN10 ..214 D3
Pathfinder Way
Bemerton SN12 ......94 C2
8 Swindon SN25 .....34 B7
Patney Rd SN10 .....180 F5
Paul St SN13 ....76 A1
Paul's Dene Cres SP1 .146 A5
Paul's Dene Rd SP1 .146 A5
Paulet Cl 3 SN5 .....49 A4
Pauls Croft SN6 .....78 C6
Pavely Cl SN15 .....78 C6
Pavely Gdns BA14 ...102 A1
Paven Cl SN5 ....33 A4
Pavenhill SN5 ....33 A4
Paxcroft Prim Sch
...........101 F1
Paxcroft Way SP1 ...105 F8
Paxmans Rd BA14 ...108 E5
Payne Cl SN15 ......78 E4
Payne's Hill 2 SP1 ..152 B8
Peacock Cl SN8 .....173 E6
Peak The SN5 ......33 B3
Peaks Down SN12 ...94 D1
Pealsham Gdns 6 SP6 .210 D1
Pear Ash La BA9 ....137 C4
Pear Tree Cl SN5 ....212 C5
Pear Tree La SN10 ..187 B8
Pear Tree Orch 2 BA13 .186 B7
Pearce Cl SN2 ......35 B6
Pearce Way SP1 ....146 D5
Pearl Rd SN5 ....49 A7
Peartree Cl
Atworth/Whitley SN12 ..85 C1
Purton SN5 ....33 C5
7 West Wellow SO51 ..212 F6
Peatmoor Com Prim Sch
...........35 A2
Peatmoor Way SN5 ..34 A1
Peel Cir SN13 ......84 D8
Peel Cl SN12 ....94 A3
Pegasus Way SN12 ..94 C1
Pelch La SN12 ......178 D8
Pembridge Rd SP6 ...210 E1
Pembroke Cl 1 BA14 .105 D6
Pembroke Ct SN2 ...34 E1
Pembroke Gdns SN25 .34 E3
Pembroke Pk Fst Sch
...........145 C3

Penny Hill SN8 .....191 E8
Penny La
Chippenham SN15 ......78 F4
Swindon SN3 ....50 F7
Penny Royal Cl SN11 .80 F3
Penny's Cl 3 SP6 ....210 D1
Penny's Cres 4 SP6 .210 D2
Penny's La
Pitton & Farley SP5 ..154 E7
Wilton SP2 ....144 D3
Pennycress Cl SN25 ..34 E4
Pennycress Dr SN12 ..94 D1
Pennyfarthing St SP1 .146 B1
Pennys La SP6 ......210 D2
Penrose Wlk SN3 ....51 A5
Pensbroudcill SP2 ...145 C3
Pensford Way BA11 ..110 D6
Penton La SP11 .....193 A3
Penton Lodge Sch
SP11 ....193 B2
Pentridge Cl SN3 ...51 C7
Pentylands Cl SN6 ..222 F7
Penzance Dr SN5 ....49 F5
Pepper Pl BA12 ....117 D7
Pepperace La BA14 ..101 F1
Pepperbox Hill SN5 ..22 E6
Pepperbox Rise SP5 .153 E2
Pepperbox The* SP5 .160 C6
Peppercombe Wood Nature
Reserve* SN10 ......180 A4
Peppercorn Orch
BA14 ....178 A6
Percheron Cl 11 SN5 .49 A7
Percheron Pl BA14 ...105 A7
Percy St SN2 ....49 F7
Peregrine Cl SN3 ....51 D8
Perham Cres 1 SP1 ..192 B5
Periwinkle Cl SN2 ...34 C3
Perrinsfield GL7 ......2 D6
Perriwinkle Cl BA14 .116 D6
Perry's La Seend SN12 .178 D8
Wroughton SN4 ......64 A6
Perth Rd SP11 .....191 F4
Peshawar Cl SP9 ...216 B7
Peter Furkins Ct SN1 .50 A5
Peters Finger Rd SP5 .152 E7
Petersfield Rd SN3 ..51 B4
Peto Gdn The* BA15 ..99 C2
Petter Cl SN4 ......64 B7
Petticoat La
Redlynch SP5 ....211 D8
Westbury BA13 ....112 C8
Pettridge La BA14 ...139 A5
Petty La SN11 ......79 F3
Pevensey Way SN5 ..49 C5
Pew Hill SN15 ......70 E2
Pewsey Downs National
Nature Reserve*
SN8 ....173 C2
Pewsey Prim Sch SN9 .215 B5
Pewsey Rd
Marlborough SN8 .....213 D2
Rushall SN9 ....181 D2
Pewsey Sports Ctr &
Swimming Pool SN9 .215 B5
Pewsey Sta SN9 ....215 B5
Pewsey Vale Sch SN9 .215 B5
Pewsey White Horse*
SN9 ....215 E1
Pewsham Lock SN15 ..78 E5
Pewsham Rd SN5 ....35 D5
Pewsham Way SN15 ..78 D5
Pheasant Bsns Pk SN14 .78 B5
Pheasant Cl
8 Chippenham Without
SN14 ....77 F6
Swindon SN3 ....51 E5
Pheasantry The GL7 ..8 F2
Philip Cl SN12 ......94 C6
Philip Ct SP2 ......145 D3
Philip Rd
4 Durrington/Bulford
SP4 ....198 B7
Wilton SP2 ....144 B5
Philipps House & Dinton Pk*
SP3 ....201 E2
Philip Cl SN10 .....214 C4
Phillips Cl SN14 ....77 F7
Phillips La
Salisbury SN1 ....145 E6
Swindon SN1 ....50 A4
Phillips Way BA14 ...108 E4
Phipps Cl BA13 ....108 F4
Phoebe Way SN25 ...34 F7
Phoenix Rise BA13 ..108 E3
Phoenix Sq SN10 ...215 C4
Picket Cl SP6 ......210 D1
Picket Cnr SP11 ....211 F3
Picket Post Gate
BA12 ....116 A4
Picketleaze SN14 ....78 A7
Pickford Way SN25 ..35 B6
Pickwick SN13 ......76 F2
Pickwick Cl SN13 ...76 F2
Picquet The 12 BA13 .186 B7
Picton Cl SN13 .....49 A7
Picton Rd SN13 .....76 F1
Pig La
Bishops Cannings SN10 .172 C1
Hullavington SN6 ....43 C7
Pigeon House La SN3 .36 A3
Pigott Cl 4 SP4 ....190 A4
Pigtrough La SP7 ...203 B4
Pike Cnr SN10 ......180 C7
Pikefield Cres SN16 ..29 A6
Pilgrim Cl SN5 .....49 A7

Pilgrims Mead SP1 ..146 C5
Pill Hill SP5 ....161 C4
Pilots View SP4 ....217 D3
Pilton Cl SN5 ....49 A8
Pimperleaze Rd BA12 .139 C7
Pinckneys Way 18 SP4 .198 B7
Pine Cl Corsham SN13 ..76 A1
Landford SP5 ....212 C5
12 Melksham SN12 ....94 A3
Pine Ct 3 BA11 .....110 B7
Pine Wlk
Amesbury SP4 ....217 D3
Trowbridge BA14 .....105 C3
Pinehurst Inf Sch SN2 ..35 B2
Pinehurst Jun Sch SN2 .35 B2
Pinehurst Rd SN2 ....35 C3
Pinehurst Sports Ctr
SN2 ....35 B3
Pines Rd SN10 ......214 C2
Pines The SN5 ......211 A1
Pinetree Rise SN2 ....35 B3
Pinetum Cl SN10 ....214 A2
Pineview Cl SP5 ....211 C6
Pinewood Way
Colerne SN14 ....74 F7
Salisbury SP2 ....145 B4
Pinewoods Cl SP2 ...145 B4
Pinfield La SN15 ....78 F4
Pinhills SN11 ....81 A2
Pink La SN16 ....29 E5
Pinkney Pk* SN16 ....25 F1
Pinnegar Way SN3 ..51 E6
Pinnocks Pl SN2 ....35 F4
Pintail Ct SN15 .....60 B1
Pintail Way BA13 ...109 A4
Pioneer Cl 3 SN5 ....49 A7
Pipehouse La BA2 ...98 F4
Pipers Cl SN4 ......61 D8
Pipers Way SN1 ....50 C1
Pipitdene SN3 ......51 D7
Piplar Gd BA11 .....100 D4
Pippin The SN11 ....81 B3
Pippins The 3 BA12 .116 F7
Pipsmore Rd
5 Chippenham SN14 ..70 A1
Chippenham SN14 ....78 A8
Pir Wlk SP4 ....199 C4
Pitchens End SN4 ...167 C7
Pitchens The SN4 ...64 B5
Pitman Ave BA14 ...105 B6
Pitman Ct BA14 ....105 B6
Pitton CE Prim Sch
SP5 ....148 B3
Pitton Rd SP5 ......154 D8
Pitts Croft SN13 ....84 E5
Pitts La
Bishopstone SP5 .....205 F4
Chitterne BA12 ......195 D2
Sedgehill & Semley SP7 .202 B7
Pittsfield SN6 ......19 D7
Pix Mead Gdns 1 SP7 .202 D1
Place Rd SN12 ......94 A3
Plane Tree Cl SN2 ..85 C1
Planks The SN3 ....50 D4
Plantation Rd
Chippenham SN14 ....78 C8
Tidworth SP9 ....216 D5
Wellow SO51 ....212 F4
Plantation The SP5 ..149 A5
Plants Gn BA12 ....117 B6
Plassey Rd SP9 ....216 C7
Platford St SN11 ...81 B2
Platt Cl RG17 ......177 C6
Platt La RG17 ......170 E7
Plattes Cl SN5 .....49 B8
Play Cl SN5 ....33 C4
Player Ct 8 SP6 ....210 D2
Playhouse Salisbury*
...........146 A1
Pleydell Rd SN1 ....50 C2
Pleydells 3 SN6 .....19 D8
Plough La
Kington Langley SN15 .70 C5
Marston SN10 ....179 A3
Plum La SN10 ......180 E4
Plume of Feathers La
SN8 ....213 E3
Plummer Cl SN14 ...64 A6
Plumpton Cl SN14 ..77 F6
Plymouth St SN1 ....50 D4
Poachers Way SN25 ..34 F7
Pockeredge Dr SN13 ..84 E7
Pockeridge Rd SN13 ..84 E7
Poinder Gn SP5 ....149 A5
Polaris Way SN2 ...34 A4
Polden Rd 1 SP1 ....152 C7
Polebarn Rd BA14 ...105 D8
Pollen Gn SP4 .....190 B2
Pollen La SN4 ......167 C8
Poltondale SN3 .....51 D7
Pomeroy La BA14 ...104 B6
Pond Cl SN5 ....49 F5
Pond La SN5 ....33 C1
Ponting St SN1 .....50 D7
Ponting's Cl SN26 ..21 C2
Pool Gastons Rd SN16 .27 E4
Pool Kn SN13 ......84 E6
Poole Keynes House
GL7 ....3 A8
Poole Rd SN5 ......34 E3
Poores Rd 17 SP4 ..198 B7
Pope Cl SN15 ......78 E5
Popham Ct SN15 ....78 F5
Poplar Ave SN14 ...105 B4
Poplar Tree La BA14 .104 A8
Poplar Way
Colerne SN14 ....75 A5
Salisbury SP1 ....146 C5

Poplars The
Chippenham SN14 ......70 A1
Fovant SP3 ....204 D8
Trowbridge BA14 ....105 A5
Popplechurch Dr 5 SN3 .51 E7
Poppy Cl SN11 .....80 F4
Porchester Cl 8 SP10 .193 C2
Port Down RG17 ....177 C7
Port Hill SN8 ......213 D5
Port Regis Sch SP7* .202 A3
Port Way BA13 .....186 A6
Portal Ave SN13 ....84 B8
Portal Rd SN13 .....70 C1
Portal Pl SN15 .....60 A1
Portal Rd SN2 .....35 A2
Porte Marsh Ind Est
SN11 ....81 C5
Porte Marsh Rd SN11 .81 C5
Portfield Rd SP5 ...150 A4
Portland Ave
Bretford SN3 ....151 F5
Swindon SN1 ....50 A4
Portland Way SN11 ..81 C2
Portman Rd SN12 ...94 A6
Portnell's La SP8 ...137 F4
Portway SN1 ....50 D6
Portway
Chippenham SN14 .....78 B6
Frome BA11 ....110 A4
Warminster BA12 ....117 A7
Winterbourne SP4 ...133 A3
Portway Ind Est SP10 .193 B1
Portway La BA12 ...117 A8
Portway Rd BA13 ...117 A8
Portwell 3 SN6 .....19 D7
Post Office La
Broad Hinton SN4 ...167 C2
Corsham SN13 ....77 A1
Post Office Rd
Chippenham SN15 .....78 A8
Poston Way BA15 ...99 D7
Pot La BA11 ....110 F8
Potley La SN13 ....84 E7
Potterdown Rd 3 SN3 .51 E7
Potterne CE Prim Sch
SN10 ....179 D5
Potterne Rd SN10 ...214 A1
Potters Way SP1 ...152 E8
Pottery La RG17 ...177 E3
Pottle St BA12 .....119 A6
Pottows Field SN11 ..166 B1
Poulsen Cl BA12 ...116 D7
Poulshot Rd SN10 ...179 A5
Poulton SN5 ....100 D5
Poulton Cl BA13 ...100 C5
Poulton La SN13 ...50 C8
Pound Cl Lyneham SN15 .60 A3
Semington BA14 .....102 F6
Pound Farm Cl SN14 .101 E4
Pound Hill
Melchet Park & Plaitford
SO51 ....212 F7
St Paul Malmesbury Without
SN16 ....43 A3
Pound La
Bradford-on-Avon BA15 .100 C5
Damerham SP6 ....209 E3
Melchet Park & Plaitford
SO51 ....212 F7
Semington BA14 .....102 E6
Shaftesbury SP7 ....202 D2
Swindon SN3 ....35 B2
Wilcot SN8 ....174 B2
Pound Mead SN13 ...84 F8
Pound Piece
Ashbury SN6 ....164 A8
5 Hungerford RG17 ..177 B7
Pound Pill SN13 ....77 A1
Pound Row BA12 ...116 F6
Pound St
Ebbesborne Wake SP5 .204 D3
Warminster BA12 ....116 F6
Pound The
Bromham SN15 ......96 B7
Mere BA12 ....139 A4
Powells Way GL8 ...25 B8
Power Rd SP4 ......217 B2
Pownall Rd SN4 ....198 A6
Poynder Pl SN11 ...166 A6
Poynder Rd SN11 ...76 E1
Poynings Way SN5 ..48 F4
Prescombe Down National
Nature Reserve*
SP5 ....204 C4
Preshute La SN8 ...213 B2
Preshute Parochial Prim Sch
SN8 ....213 A1
Prestbury Dr SN4 ..64 A6
Prestly Wood 3 SN13 .76 E1
Pretoria Rd 16 SP11 .192 B5
Priddy Cl SP1 .....110 C7
Priestley Gr SN11 ..81 C2
Priestley Prim Sch
SN11 ....81 C2
Priestly Wood Rd 6
SN13 ....76 E1
Primrose Cl Calne SN11 .80 D5
Swindon SN2 ....34 D5
Primrose Dr SN12 ..94 C4

Primrose Hill
Tockenham SN4 ....60 D6
Wilton SP2 ....144 D4
Primrose La
Manningford SN9 ....181 F6
Redlynch SP5 ....211 C7
Primrose Rd
2 Ludgershall SP11 ....192 A5
Salisbury SP2 ....146 B4
Primrose Way SN14 ....70 B2
Primrose Wlk 1 BA12 ..116 E7
Prince Charles Ct 14
SP11 ....192 A5
Prince Charles Dr
SN11 ....81 C3
Princecroft La 3 BA12 ..116 E6
Princecroft Prim Sch
BA12 ....116 E6
Princes Cl SP5 ....211 D8
Princes Hill SP5 ......211 D8
Princes St 4 SN1 ......50 C5
Princess Anne Rd 9
BA11 ....110 A4
Princess Gdns
Trowbridge BA14 ....101 E4
Warminster BA12 ......117 D6
Princess Margaret Hospl
SN3 ....51 D1
Princess Mary Gdns 19
SP11 ....192 A5
Prior Pk Prep Sch SN6 ..19 E7
Prior's Hill SN4 ....64 B5
Priorsfield SN8 ....213 E2
Priory Ave RG17 ......177 B6
Priory Cl Alderbury SP5 .153 F2
 Bradford-on-Avon BA15 .100 C7
 5 Hungerford RG17 ....177 B6
 6 Shrewton SP3 ....196 E6
 Wilton SP2 ....144 C2
Priory Gn SN6 ....23 A6
Priory New Rd SN13 ....76 F2
Priory Pk BA15 ....100 D7
Priory Pl 1 RG17 ......177 B6
Priory Rd
 Hungerford RG17 ......177 B6
 Swindon SN3 ....51 A4
Priory Sq 5 SP7 ....146 A1
Priory St SN13 ....76 F2
Pritchard Cl SN2 ....35 F5
Private Rd BA11 ....123 C8
Prixar La SP11 ....192 D2
Pro Logis Pk SN3 ......36 C6
Proby Pl BA14 ....102 A1
Professions Cnr SP5 ...206 D6
Prospect Box SN13 .....83 B4
 Corsham SN13 ....85 A7
Prospect Hill SN13 .....50 C5
Prospect Pl
 Bathford BA1 ....82 D2
 Mere BA12 ....138 F5
 Swindon SN1 ....50 C4
 Trowbridge BA14 ......101 D1
Prospect Rd SP2 ....146 B4
Prospect Sq 3 BA13 ...109 A3
Proud Cl SN5 ....33 B3
Providence La SN13 .....76 F1
Providence Terr SN15 ...78 D7
Provis Mead SN15 ......79 A4
Provost St 23 SP6 .....210 D1
Pub La SN10 ....180 F8
Puck Well Nature Reserve*
 BA12 ....140 C4
Pucklands SN10 ....180 E5
Puddleslosh La SP6 ....210 C2
Pullman Dr* SP2 ....145 B3
Pulsar Rd SN25 ....34 B7
Pump La Bathford BA1 ...82 B1
 Long Newnton GL8 .....13 C4
Purbeck Cl SN3 ....51 C7
Purbeck Pl* SN11 ....81 D2
Purleigh Rd SN13 ......76 E1
Purley Ave SN3 ....51 B3
Purley Cl SN4 ....51 F1
Purley Way SO51 ......212 E6
Purlpit SN12 ....85 A1
Purlyn Acre SN8 ......213 D4
Purslane Cl SN2 ....34 C3
Purton Mus* SN5 ......33 C4
Purton Rd SN2 ....34 C3
Purvis Cl 4 SP4 ....217 E3
Pyatts Cnr BA14 ......178 C4
Pye La SN4 ....167 A8

Q

Quadrangle The SN15 ...78 C6
Quakers Wlk SN11 .....73 F7
Quantock Cl
 Melksham Without SN12 .94 D4
 8 Warminster BA12 ...117 A8
Quarr Barton SN11 .....81 B3
Quarries The SN1 ......50 C3
Quarry Cl BA2 ....99 D6
Quarry Cres SN6 ......22 F6
Quarry Fields Ind Est
 BA12 ....138 E5
Quarry Hill SN13 ....83 E6
Quarry La Colerne SN14 .75 B3
 Melbury Abbas SP7 ....206 A7
Quarry Mews SN1 .....50 C3
Quarry Rd SN1 ....50 C4
Quarrybrook Cl SN3 ....36 E5
Quarrydale Cl* SN3 .....81 B2

Quartermaster Rd
 BA13 ....108 D6
Quarterway La BA14 ...101 E1
Quawey Rd SP5 ....211 D7
Quebec Rd SN4 ....168 E8
Queen Alexandra Rd
 SP2 ....145 D3
Queen Elizabeth Dr
 SN2 ....34 C4
Queen Manor Rd
 Clarendon Park SP5 ...147 B1
 Laverstock SP5 ....152 E8
Queen Mary Rd SP2 ...145 D3
Queen Oak* SN6 ......175 C4
Queen St Hale SP6 .....211 B5
 Salisbury SP1 ....146 A1
 Swindon SN1 ....50 B6
 Wilton SP2 ....144 D4
Queen's Barrow*
 BA12 ....201 A7
Queen's Dr SN3 ....50 E6
Queen's Rd
 Devizes SN10 ....214 A2
 Westbury BA13 ....108 E3
 Wootton Bassett SN4 ..47 E2
Queenborough SN5 .....49 C4
Queens Ave
 Corsham SN13 ....76 F3
 Highworth SN6 ....23 A6
Queens Chase BA12 ...117 A8
Queens Cl
 27 Ludgershall SP11 ..192 A5
 Sutton Benger SN15 ...57 D2
Queens Club Gdns
 BA14 ....105 A8
Queens Cres SN14 .....78 A6
Queens Cres Sch SN14 .78 A6
Queens Dr SN3 ....51 B2
Queens Gdns
 Hannington SN6 ....21 F8
 Mere BA12 ....139 B6
 Salisbury SP1 ....146 B2
 7 Tisbury SP3 ....203 E8
 Trowbridge BA14 .....101 C2
Queens Sq SN15 ....78 F6
Queens Way SN8 ......213 F2
Queensberry Rd
 Amesbury SP4 ....217 C4
 Salisbury SP1 ....146 A3
Queensfield SN2 ....35 D5
Queensway
 Andover SP10 ....193 F1
 Melksham SN12 ....94 C4
 2 Netheravon SP4 ....190 A3
 Warminster BA12 .....117 D6
Queintin Rd SN1 ....50 D3
Quemerford Calne SN11 .81 C1
 Calne Without SN11 ...89 D8
Quidham St SP5 ......204 F2
Quilling Cl BA14 ......105 C7

R

Rabley Wood View
 SN8 ....213 E4
Radcliffe Rd SP2 ......152 A6
Radcot Cl SN5 ....34 A1
Radley Bottom
 Hungerford Newton
 RG17 ....171 D2
 Kintbury RG17 ......177 F7
Radley Cl SN3 ....51 C7
Radnor Cl SN10 ......214 C2
Radnor Pk SN16 ....42 E4
Radnor Pl 3 SN12 .....94 A2
Radnor Rd SN1 ....146 A3
Radnor St SN1 ....50 A5
Radstock Ave SN3 .....51 B6
Radway Rd SN3 ....35 F3
Raffin La SN9 ....215 C4
Raggett St SN1 ....50 C5
Raglan Cl SN3 ....50 E2
Ragleth Gr BA14 ......101 E2
Railway Village Mus*
 SN1 ....50 B5
Rainer Cl SN3 ....36 B3
Raleigh Ave SN3 ....50 F6
Raleigh Cres SP4 .....217 E3
Rambler Cl BA14 ......105 A1
Ramblers Mead SP11 ..193 A2
Rambridge Cres SP2 ...145 B5
Ramleaze Dr
 Salisbury SP2 ....145 C5
 Swindon SN5 ....49 A7
Rampart Rd SP1 ......146 B1
Ramsbury Ave SN2 .....35 B6
Ramsbury Dr RG17 ....177 C7
Ramsbury Manor*
 SN8 ....169 F1
Ramsbury Prim Sch
 SN8 ....170 B2
Ramsbury Terr RG17 ..177 C7
Ramsbury Wlk BA14 ..105 D6
Ramscliff SN10 ....187 F7
Ramscombe La BA1 ....82 A6
Ramsden Rd SN1 ....48 F3
Ramsthorn Cl SN2 .....34 D4
Randall Cres SN13 .....49 A8
Randall Cl SN13 ....76 D1
Randall's Croft Rd
 SP2 ....144 B2
Randolph Cl SN10 .....50 F5
Rank The BA14 ......105 C3

Rannoch Cl 4 SN5 .....34 B2
Ransome Ct SN5 ....49 B8
Raspberry La 8 SP7 ...202 C1
Ratcliff's Gdn 6 SP7 ..202 D1
Ratcoombe Rd SN5 .....34 A2
Ratfyn Barrow* SP4 ...217 B4
Ratfyn Rd SP4 ....217 B4
Raven Cl SP9 ....216 D6
Ravenglass Rd SN5 ....49 C6
Ravenhurst SN16 ......14 E6
Ravens Wlk SN4 ....48 A2
Ravenscroft
 7 Salisbury SP2 ......152 A5
 Swindon SN3 ....51 C8
Ravenscroft Gdns
 BA14 ....101 F1
Ravensroost Wood & Mdws
 Nature Reserve*
 SN16 ....31 A5
Rawlence Rd
 Salisbury SP2 ....145 B3
 Wilton SP2 ....144 C2
Rawlings Cl SN3 ....36 E4
Rawlings Ct SP11 .....192 A5
Rawlingswell La SN8 ..213 E3
Rawlins Rd SN9 ......215 C5
Rawlinson Rd SN4 .....198 E6
Rawston Cl SN3 ....51 C6
Ray Cl Chippenham SN15 .78 F5
 Swindon SN25 ....35 A4
Raybrook Cres SN2 ....49 E6
Rayfield Gr SN2 ....50 B8
Read St SN1 ....50 A5
Reading St 4 SN1 ......50 B6
Recreation Rd
 10 Durrington/Bulford
 SP4 ....198 B7
 Ludgershall SN11 .....192 A5
Rectory Cl Alton SN8 ..181 C8
 Stanton St Quintin SN14 .56 B4
 11 Warminster BA12 ..117 A8
Rectory Hill SP5 ....155 F3
Rectory La
 Alderbury SP5 ....153 E2
 Breamore SP6 ....210 E5
 Charlton Musgrove BA9 .136 B1
 Cricklade SN6 ....19 E8
 Letcombe Bassett OX12 .165 F8
 Rectory Pl 2 SP11 ...192 F1
Rectory Rd
 Alderbury SP5 ....153 E2
 Salisbury SP2 ....151 F8
 Sutton Mandeville SP3 .204 C7
Rectory Wood Sch SN8 .170 A6
Reculver Way 4 SP10 ..193 C2
Red Cross House*
 SN10 ....214 B4
Red Gables Cl SN3 .....33 A3
Red La Mildenhall SN8 .169 B2
 Sixpenny Handley SP5 .208 A3
Red Lion La SN6 ......19 E8
Red Pit BA13 ....112 A8
Red Post La SP11 .....192 F1
Red Way The BA12 ...115 F3
Redbridge Cl 1 SN1 ....49 F4
Redcap Gdns SN5 .....49 A7
Redcliffe St SN2 ....49 F6
Redenham Dr SP11 ...192 E4
Redford Cl* SP1 ......146 D3
Redgrave Cl BA14 .....105 D6
Redhill Cl SN11 ....79 F2
Redhills SN4 ....62 B1
Redhorn Gdns SN10 ..214 B2
Redhouse Way SN25 ...34 F7
Redland SN14 ....78 B8
Redland La BA13 ......108 F2
Redland Prim Sch
 SN14 ....78 B8
Redlands 8 BA13 .....186 B7
Redlands Cl SN6 ......19 D8
Redlynch CE Prim Sch
 SP5 ....211 E6
Redlynch Cl SN2 ....35 C5
Redman Rd SN11 ......81 C6
Redmans La SP7 .....206 A4
Redposts Dr SN2 ......49 F4
Redruth Cl SN3 ....51 B5
Redstocks La SN12 ....95 A4
Redwing Ave SN14 ....70 B2
Redwood Way SN14 ...75 A5
Reed Wlk 10 SP4 .....198 C7
Reeds SN6 ....19 C8
Reeds Cnr SN8 ....213 F2
Reeds Farm Rd SN16 ..28 A4
Reeds Gd SN8 ....213 F3
Reeves Cl 2 SN3 ......51 C4
Reeves Rd SN10 .....214 D1
Regent Cir SN1 ....50 C5
Regent Pl
 1 Hungerford RG17 ..177 B7
 Swindon SN1 ....50 C6
Regent St 6 SN1 ......50 C6
Regents Pl
 Bradford-on-Avon BA15 .100 D5
 Studley Green BA14 ..104 F6
Reid's Piece SN5 ....33 B3
Reith Way 2 SP10 ....193 B1
Rendall's Barn GL7 ....4 E5
Rendells Ct SN10 .....214 B3
Renoir Cl SN25 ....35 A8
Restrop Rd SN5 ....33 A3
Restrop View SN5 .....33 A4
Retinagham Way SN14 .36 A1
Reto Gr BA15 ....99 F3
Retreat The
 Frome BA11 ....110 B4
 Highworth SN6 ....22 F6
Revell St* SN2 ....35 E4

Reynolds Ct 4 SP10 ...193 D1
Reynolds Way SN25 ....35 A8
Rhine Cl SN1 ....49 F4
Rhuddlan SN5 ....49 B4
Ricardo Rd SN15 ......78 D8
Richard Jefferies Mus*
 SN3 ....51 E2
Richard Webb Mews
 SN1 ....50 B3
Richards Cl SN4 ....47 F1
Richards Way SN2 ....151 E7
Richborough Dr 3
 SP10 ....193 C2
Richmond Cl 2 SN14 ..105 A7
Richmond Cres SP9 ...216 E6
Richmond Rd SN4 .....51 F7
Richmond St SN6 .....6 F1
Richmond Rd
 Calne Without SN11 ...81 A4
 2 Salisbury SP2 ......145 F2
Rickbarton 2 SN10 ...187 E7
Rickfield BA13 ....100 B6
Rickworth Pl BA12 ...195 A3
Riddle Gn SN4 ....49 A8
Ridge Nether Moor
 SN3 ....51 D2
Ridge The
 Broad Blunsdon SN26 ..21 B2
 Redlynch SP5 ....211 C7
Ridge Way SP7 ....202 C3
Ridgemead SN11 ....81 B4
Ridgeway SP3 ....201 A3
Ridgeway Cl SN2 ......34 F2
Ridgeway Rd BA12 ...117 B6
Ridgeway La SN15 ....44 E1
Ridgeway Rd
 Salisbury SP2 ....146 B2
 Swindon SN2 ....35 E5
Ridgeway Sch The SN4 .64 B7
Ridgeway The
 Chiseldon SN4 ....65 D2
 Crudwell SN16 ....14 E6
 Liddington SN4 ......163 A2
 Warminster BA12 .....117 B6
Ridgmount 6 SN4 ....198 B7
Ridings Mead SN14 ....70 C2
Ridings The SN14 .....70 A8
Rigsby's La SN6 ....16 F5
Ringsbury Camp* SN5 ..32 E2
Ringsbury Cl SN5 ......32 F3
Ringwood Ave 5 SP4 ..217 C3
Ringwood Cl SN3 ......51 B6
Ringwood Rd 27 SP6 ..210 D1
Rinsdale Cl SN5 ....34 B1
Ripley Cl SN1 ....50 C4
Ripon Cl SN14 ....78 A5
Ripon Way SN3 ....51 A3
Ripple Field SN5 ....49 B4
Rise The SN11 ....89 C8
Risingham Mead SN5 ..49 C5
Rivar Rd SN8 ....176 F1
Rivenhall Rd SN5 .....49 C5
River Par SN15 ....78 D8
River Pk SN8 ....213 D2
River Ray Ind Est SN2 ..49 E7
River St
 Chippenham SN15 .....78 E7
 Pewsey SN9 ....215 C5
River Way
 6 Durrington/Bulford
 SP4 ....198 C7
 South Cerney GL7 ....6 F7
 Trowbridge BA14 .....101 C1
Riverbourne Rd
 Laverstock SN4 ......146 D1
 Salisbury SP1 ....152 D8
Riverdale Cl
 9 Fordingbridge SP6 .210 D1
 Swindon SN1 ....50 C2
Riverdale Wlk SN1 .....50 C2
Rivergate SN1 ....49 C8
Rivermead SP4 ....133 F8
Rivermead Dr SN5 .....49 C7
Rivermead Ind Est SN5 .49 C7
Rivers Reach 6 BA11 ..110 A4
Rivers Way SN6 ....22 F6
Riverside Calne SN11 ..89 D8
 Wilton SP2 ....144 D3
Riverside Cl
 Salisbury SP1 ....146 D2
 South Newton SP2 ....130 A4
Riverside Dr
 Chippenham SN15 .....79 A8
 Melksham SN12 ....94 A6
Riverside Pk SN15 .....44 A2
Riverside Pl SN15 ....210 E1
Riverside Rd SP3 .....146 D2
Riverside Terr SP3 ...129 E7
Roach's La GL9 ....38 C1
Road Hill Box SN13 ....82 E8
 Colerne SN14 ....74 D1
Robbers' Stone*
 SN10 ....187 E6
Robbins Ridge SP4 ...217 C2
Robert Franklin Way
 GL7 ....7 A7
Robert Le King Prim Sch
 SN1 ....50 A5
Roberts Cl SN4 ....64 B5
Roberts of Kandahar Rd
 BA12 ....113 F1
Roberts Rd
 North Tidworth SP11 ..192 A5
 Salisbury SP2 ....145 D3
Robin Cl BA12 ....117 C6
Robin Hill La SP4 .....217 C8
Robin Hood's Ball*
 SP4 ....189 C1

Robin Hood's Bower*
 BA12 ....117 B1
Robinia Cl SN9 ....215 D5
Robins Cl
 Chippenham SN14 .....70 B2
 Wootton Bassett SN4 ..48 A2
Robins Hill RG17 .....177 F3
Robinsgreen SN3 ......51 D7
Robinson Cl SN3 ....51 D6
Rochdale Ave SN11 ....81 B4
Roche Cl SN3 ....51 D4
Roche Ct* SP5 ....135 E1
Rochelle Ct 10 SN10 ..179 F1
Rocher Cl BA13 ......108 F3
Rochester Cl 5 SN5 ....49 A5
Rochford Cl SN5 ......49 A5
Rock La BA12 ....117 D6
Rock Rd BA14 ....105 B7
Rockbourne La SP6 ...209 F3
Rockbourne Mus*
 SP6 ....210 A4
Rockbourne Roman Villa*
 SP6 ....210 A4
Rockdown Ct SN2 .....35 D4
Rocker Bench SN6 ...163 E6
Rockfel Rd RG17 .....165 A1
Rockfield SN14 ....75 B3
Rockley Rd SN8 ......213 C7
Rockmoor La SP11 ...185 C5
Rodbourne Cheney Prim Sch
 SN25 ....35 A3
Rodbourne House
 SN16 ....43 B4
Rodbourne Rd
 St Paul Malmesbury Without
 SN16 ....42 F4
 Swindon SN2 ....49 F7
Rodden Manor*
 BA11 ....110 D4
Rodden Rd BA11 .....110 A5
Roddenbury Cl BA11 ..110 B5
Roddenbury View
 BA12 ....115 A8
Rode Bridge* BA11 ...103 E1
Rode Hill BA11 ......103 F1
Rode Tropical Bird Gdns*
 BA11 ....103 D2
Rodney Ct SP10 .....193 F1
Rodsleigh BA14 ......104 F6
Rodway 16 SN4 ......163 A6
Rodwell Cl 3 SN3 .....51 A4
Rodwell Pk BA14 ....101 E2
Roebuck Cl SN4 ....47 F2
Roger Penny Way
 SP6 ....211 C3
Rogers Cl
 Quidhampton SP2 ....145 A3
 Swindon SN3 ....51 A7
Rogers Meadow SN8 ..213 D5
Rogers's La RG17 .....171 D7
Rolleston St 1 SN1 ....50 C5
Rollestone Rd SP3 ...196 E6
Rollestone St 1 SP1 ..146 B1
Roman Cres SN1 ......50 B3
Roman Meadow SN5 ..211 A8
Roman Rd SP2 ....145 D2
Roman Way
 Andover SP10 ....193 E2
 Chippenham SN15 .....79 B5
 Highworth SN6 ....22 F5
 Lechlade GL7 ....2 D5
 15 Market Lavington SN10 .179 F1
Roman Way Prim Sch
 SN1 ....193 E2
Romer Rd SP2 ....152 A6
Romney Way SN5 .....49 A6
Romsey Rd
 Amesbury SP4 ....217 D2
 Whiteparish SP5 .....162 B3
Romsey St SN2 ....49 F6
Ron Golding Cl SN16 ...28 A5
Rook St BA12 ....139 A4
Rookery Cottages SP5 .155 F4
Rookery La Ansty SP3 .203 F6
 Breamore SP6 ....210 D5
 Swallowcliffe SP3 ....204 A6
Rookery Meadow SN8 ..174 A2
Rookes La SN10 ......179 C5
Rookes La SN10 ......110 E6
Rooks Nest Cl SN15 ...78 F4
Rookwood Gdns 9 SP6 .210 C1
Rope Wlk SN12 ....94 B3
Rope Yd SN4 ....47 D1
Rosary The SN4 ....47 D1
Rose St SN2 ....49 F7
Rosebery St SN1 ......50 D7
Rosebrock Gdns SN12 ..94 C3
Rosedale Gdns BA14 ..101 A1
Rosedale Rd SN3 ......51 B4
Rosefield Way BA13 ..108 F4
Rosehill Cl SN15 ....59 D3
Roseland Ave SN10 ..214 C3
Rosemary Cl Calne SN11 .80 F4
 Laverstock SP1 ......146 D1
 Swindon SN2 ....34 D3
Rosemary La
 Freshford BA2 ....99 B4
 2 Salisbury SP1 ......152 A8
Rosenheim Rise 1
 BA13 ....186 B7
Rosetta Cl SN25 ......34 B7
Rosewood Ct SN3 .....51 D3
Ross Gdns SN3 ....51 A4
Ross Rd SN6 ....19 C7
Rossett Gdns BA14 ...105 A8
Rothe Rise BA13 .....108 F1
Rother Cl SN25 ....34 F5

Rotherstone SN10 214 A4
Rotten Row SN4 163 A6
Rougemont Cl SP1 146 B1
Rough St SN13 84 F5
Roughmoor Way SN5 34 A1
Round Barrow Cl SN14 75 B3
Round Hill
25 Fordingbridge SP6 210 D1
West Kington SN14 67 A7
Round House SN11 81 D1
Roundaway La SP11 193 A5
Roundhills Mead SN6 23 B6
Roundpond SN12 93 F6
Roundponds SN12 93 F6
Roundstone Prep Sch BA14 105 E8
Roundstone St BA14 101 D1
Roundway Cl SN11 89 B1
Roundway Down SN5 49 B3
Roundway Gdns SN10 214 B6
Roundway Ind Est SN10 214 C5
Roundway Pk SN10 214 C5
Roundwood View SN15 58 A3
Rovers Farm & Visitor Ctr* SN6 37 B6
Roves La SN6 23 B1
Row La SN12 178 C7
Row The SP5 211 C8
Rowan Cl Colerne SN14 75 A5
5 Durrington/Bulford SP4 198 B7
Salisbury SP2 145 B4
Rowan Ct Frome BA11 110 B7
Melksham SN12 94 A3
Rowan Dr SN4 47 E1
Rowan Rd SN2 35 A3
Rowans The SN16 27 F4
Rowbarrow SP2 152 B5
Rowbarrow Cl SP2 152 B5
Rowde CE Prim Sch SN10 96 E2
Rowde Ct Rd SN10 96 D1
Rowdeford Sch SN10 96 D3
Rowden Hill SN15 78 C6
Rowden La
Bradford-on-Avon BA15 100 D4
Chippenham SN15 78 C5
Rowden Rd SN15 78 C6
Rowe Mead SN15 78 E5
Rowe's Hill BA12 119 C8
Rowland Hill Cl SN3 51 E4
Rowlands Cl BA1 82 B2
Rowley Medieval Village of* BA15 99 F1
Rowley Pl SN12 94 B4
Rowton Heath Way SN5 49 A4
Royal Cescent The SP9 216 D7
Royal Cl SN15 78 D6
Royal Cres SP9 216 D7
Royal Field Cl SN14 55 E8
Royal Oak Cl SN15 78 F6
Royce Cl 5 SP10 193 B1
Royston Rd SN3 51 A4
Rubens Cl SN25 34 F8
Ruckley Gdns SN3 36 B2
Rudge Hill BA11 107 D5
Rudge La
Beckington BA11 107 B6
Wilcot SN8 174 B1
Rudge Rd BA11 107 B2
Rumble Dene SN15 78 E5
Rune Dr 4 SP10 193 D2
Rushall CE Prim Sch SN9 181 E3
Rushall Cl SN2 35 B5
Rushall Dro SN9 181 D1
Rushall Rd SN9 181 F3
Rushcroft Cl SN16 28 F1
Rushey La BA15 91 F3
Rushmead La SN14 66 A3
Rushmere Path SN25 34 E5
Rushmore Pk* SP5 207 C5
Rushton Rd SN3 51 A3
Rushy Platt Ind Est SN5 49 E4
Rushy Platt Nature Reserve* SN1 49 F4
Ruskin Ave
Melksham SN12 94 B4
Swindon SN2 35 F3
Ruskin Dr
Warminster BA12 116 D6
Wootton Bassett SN4 47 F3
Ruskin Jun Sch SN2 35 F4
Russell Mill La SN10 179 D1
Russell Rd SP2 145 E2
Russell St SP2 144 D3
Russell Wlk SN3 50 E6
Russet Ct BA12 116 F7
Russley Cl SN5 33 F1
Russley Pk* SN8 164 A3
Rusty La SN12 178 E8
Rutland Cl SN12 94 C3
Rutland Cres BA14 105 C6
Rutland Rd 1 SN3 50 F5
Rutts La 3 SN10 187 E7
Ruxley Cl SN4 47 D1
Ryan Ave SN14 78 A7
Ryan Cl SN5 34 B2
Rybury Camp (Hill Fort)* SN10 173 A2
Rycote Cl SN5 49 A6
Rydal Cl SN25 34 F5
Rye Cl SN5 49 A7
Ryeland Way BA14 105 E7
Ryeleaze SN10 179 D5
Rylands Way SN4 47 E2
Ryles La SN8 174 B6
Ryon Cl 11 SP10 193 E2

S

Sack Hill BA12 113 F1
Sackville Cl SN3 50 F7
Saddleback Cl SN11 81 C2
Saddleback La SN10 179 E5
Saddleback Rd SN5 49 A7
Saddlers Mead SP2 144 C3
Saddlers Way SN8 183 D7
Sadler Wlk SN3 50 F5
Sadlers Mead SN15 78 E8
Sadlers Rd RG17 177 C3
Saffron Cl 2 Swindon SN2 34 E3
Wootton Bassett SN4 47 E4
Saffron Meadows SN11 80 F3
Sage Cl SN2 34 D5
St Albans Cl
Salisbury SP1 146 D5
Swindon SN2 49 E7
St Aldhelm Rd BA15 100 E5
St Aldhelms Rd SN16 27 F4
St Alphege Gdns 7 SP10 193 D1
St Ambrose Cl SN3 51 D6
St Andrew CE Prim Sch SN26 21 C1
St Andrew's Cl
Wilton SP2 144 B2
Wooton Rivers SN8 174 F1
St Andrew's Rd
Melksham SN12 94 C5
Salisbury SP2 145 C2
South Newton SP2 130 B2
St Andrews SP1 146 D2
St Andrews CE Prim Sch SP1 146 E3
St Andrews Cl SN4 64 B7
St Andrews Gn SN3 51 E7
St Andrews Rd
Tidworth SP9 216 C6
Warminster BA12 116 D6
St Ann Pl SP1 152 B8
St Ann St SP1 152 B8
St Annes Cl SP4 217 C4
St Arild's Rd GL9 24 B4
St Athan Cl BA14 178 B8
St Augustine's Rd 5 BA14 105 B8
St Augustines Cath Coll BA14 105 B8
St Austell Way SN5 49 F6
St Barnabas CE Prim Sch SN10 179 F1
St Bartholomew's St SP7 203 B4
St Bartholomews CE Prim Sch SN4 47 E2
St Bedes Cl 5 SP1 146 D5
St Birinus Gdns SP10 193 D2
St Birinus Rd 4 SP5 211 C7
St Birstan Gdns 9 SP10 193 D1
St Brendans Cl SP1 146 C5
St Catherines Cl SN11 81 C4
St Catherines RC Prim Sch SN2 35 F5
St Christophers Cl 4 SP1 146 D5
St Clair Rd SP2 152 B6
St Clements Ct SN3 51 A4
St Clements Way SP1 146 C5
St David's Way SN8 213 D3
St Davids Cl SP1 146 D5
St Dennis Rd 7 SN16 28 A3
St Dunstan CE Prim Sch SN11 81 C4
St Dunstan Cl SN11 81 B5
St Edith's Cl SP2 144 C1
St Edith's Marsh SN15 96 D5
St Edmund RC Prim Sch SN11 81 C5
St Edmund's Church St 2 SP1 146 B1
St Edmunds CE Girls Sch SP1 146 E3
St Edwards 12 SP7 202 C2
St Edwards Meadow SP4 133 B2
St Edwards Sch SO51 162 B2
St Francis Ave SN15 78 C6
St Francis CE VA Prim Sch SN25 34 C5
St Francis Rd SP1 146 A4
St Francis Sch SN9 215 B6
St George's Cl
Ogbourne St George SN8 169 A5
Warminster BA12 117 E5
St George's Rd
Salisbury SP2 151 D7
Semington BA14 102 E5
11 Shaftesbury SP7 202 C1
St Georges CE Prim Sch BA14 102 E6
St Georges CE Sch SP8 137 E1
St Georges Hospl BA14 102 E5
St Georges Pl BA14 102 E5
St Georges RC Prim Sch BA12 117 D5
St Georges Rd
35 Fordingbridge SP6 210 D1
Tidworth SP9 216 C6
St Giles Cl SN16 29 A2
St Gregory's Ave SP2 145 D2
St Helens View SN1 49 F4
St Ives Ct SN3 51 B7
St James SN15 59 A7
St James Cl SN2 35 D5
St James Gdns SN10 214 B4
St James St 7 SP11 192 A5
St James's Cl SP1 146 D5
St James's St SP7 202 B1
St John CE Fst Sch SP3 203 D8
St John Rd SN4 64 A6
St John's Cl
Donhead St Mary SP7 203 A1
Marlborough SN8 213 D4
2 Salisbury SP1 152 D8
St John's Cres BA14 104 F6
St John's Ct SP2 144 C3
St John's Hill 7 SP7 202 B1
St John's Priory Pk GL7 2 E3
St John's Rd
Frome BA11 110 B5
Warminster BA12 117 C5
St John's St
Devizes SN10 214 A3
Lechlade GL7 2 C4
Malmesbury SN16 28 B2
Salisbury SP1 152 B8
St Johns Alley SN10 214 A3
St Johns Cath Prim Sch BA14 105 B8
St Johns CE Prim Sch BA12 117 C6
St Johns Churchyard SN10 214 A3
St Johns Cl
Pewsey SN9 215 D5
19 Tisbury SP3 203 E8
St Johns Ct SN10 214 A3
St Johns Sch & Com Coll SN8 213 D1
St Johns Sch (Lower) SN8 175 A8
St Joseph's Cath Sch SN3 50 E7
St Joseph's Dr SN15 78 C6
St Josephs Cath Sch SP1 146 E3
St Josephs Cl SP1 146 C4
St Josephs RC Comp Lower Sch SN3 50 E7
St Josephs RC Prim Sch
Dunkirk SN10 179 D8
Malmesbury SN16 28 B3
St Judes Cl SP1 146 D4
St Just Cl SP4 199 B3
St Katharines CE Prim Sch SN8 175 E3
St Katherine Gn 2 SN3 51 E7
St Katherines SN4 167 C6
St Laurence CE Prim Sch GL7 2 D3
St Laurence Rd BA15 100 E5
St Laurence Sch BA15 100 C7
St Lawrence Cl SP1 145 E5
St Lawrence Cres 6 SP7 202 C2
St Lawrence Rd GL7 2 C4
St Lawrence Sq 8 RG17 177 B7
St Leonard's SN16 16 D3
St Leonard's Church* BA12 194 A4
St Leonard's Cl SP4 217 D8
St Leonards Cl SN16 16 D3
St Lukes Cl 8 SP1 146 D5
St Lukes Dr SN15 78 C6
St Lukes Sch SN2 35 D5
St Margaret's Cl 2 SP1 152 C8
St Margaret's Gdns SN12 94 C5
St Margaret's Gn 1 SN3 36 B2
St Margaret's Hill BA15 100 D6
St Margaret's Mead SN8 213 F2
St Margaret's Pl BA15 100 D6
St Margaret's Rd SN1 50 D3
St Margaret's St BA15 100 D6
St Margaret's Villas BA15 100 D6
St Margarets Cl SN11 81 A4
St Margarets Gdns SN15 78 C6
St Margarets Hospl SN3 36 B4
St Margarets Ret Pk SN4 36 D2
St Mark's Ave SP1 146 B3
St Mark's Rd SP1 146 B2
St Marks CE Jun Sch SP1 146 B3
St Martin's Chapel* SN8 176 C4
St Martin's Church St 5 SP1 152 B8
St Martin's Cl SP3 143 A4
St Martins SN8 213 E3
St Martins CE Prim Sch SP1 152 C8
St Martins Cl SP3 143 A4
St Mary St SN15 78 E7
St Mary's BA14 178 A3
St Mary's Church (remains of)* SP7 206 A5
St Mary's Cl
Chitterne BA12 195 D6
Dinton SP3 201 E2
Kempsford GL7 10 E6
Lyneham SN15 59 C3
Potterne SN10 179 D5
Redlynch SP5 211 D7
Sixpenny Handley SP5 208 A4
Trowbridge BA14 101 E4
Wilton SP2 144 C1
Wylye BA12 201 E8
St Mary's Controlled Inf Sch SN8 213 E2
St Mary's Gdns BA14 101 E4
St Mary's La 2 SN16 28 A3
St Mary's Pl SN15 78 D8
St Mary's Rd
Dinton SP3 201 E2
Frome BA11 110 B5
12 Market Lavington SN10 179 F1
Salisbury SP2 151 F7
St Mary's St 1 SN16 28 A3
St Marys Cath Prim Sch SN2 35 A1
St Marys CE Prim Sch
Broughton Gifford SN12 93 B3
Purton SN5 33 C4
Steeple Ashton BA14 178 A3
St Marys Field GL7 1 A5
St Marys Gdns SN10 214 B4
St Marys Gr SN2 35 B1
St Marys La
Dilton Marsh BA13 108 B1
Westbury BA13 112 C8
St Marys RC Prim Sch SN15 78 C6
St Marys Sch
Calne SN11 81 B3
Coombe SP7 202 E1
St Matthews Cl
Rowde SN10 96 D2
6 Salisbury SP1 146 D5
St Mellion Cl SN15 78 F7
St Michael's Ave SN6 22 E6
St Michael's Cl
8 Aldbourne SN8 170 A6
Brinkworth SN15 45 E6
3 Lambourn RG17 165 A1
Trowbridge BA14 102 A3
Wilton SP2 144 B1
St Michael's Rd
Melksham SN12 94 A3
Salisbury SP2 145 C4
St Michael's Way SP9 216 E7
St Michaels CE Controlled Prim Sch SN12 94 B4
St Michaels CE Prim Sch SP4 190 B2
St Michaels Cl
Lyneham & Bradenstoke SN15 59 F4
Tidworth SP9 216 C5
St Michaels Prim Sch SN8 170 A6
St Nicholas CE VC Prim Sch SN15 96 A7
St Nicholas Cl
Calne SN11 81 C4
11 Ludgershall SP11 192 B5
Trowbridge BA14 105 D3
Wilton SP2 144 B1
Winsley BA15 99 D7
St Nicholas Sch SN14 70 C2
St Nicholas' Rd SP1 152 A7
St Osmund's Cl SP1 146 A5
St Osmunds RC Prim Sch SP1 152 A7
St Patricks Ave SP9 216 B5
St Patricks RC Prim Sch SN13 77 A1
St Paul St SN15 78 D8
St Paul's Dr SN3 51 E6
St Paul's Rd SP2 145 F1
St Paul's St SN2 35 C1
St Pauls Prim Sch SN15 70 D2
St Peter's Church* SP3 127 D4
St Peter's Cl
Wilton SP2 144 B2
Winterbourne Stoke SP3 196 F3
St Peter's Pump* BA12 123 C3
St Peters CE Prim Sch
Appleshaw SP11 192 E4
Chippenham SN14 78 A8
Dunkirk SN10 179 D8
St Peters Cl
Chippenham SN15 78 C6
5 Shipton Bellinger SP9 199 D8
St Peters Jun Sch SN8 213 E3
St Peters Rd SP1 146 C5
St Philip's Rd SN2 35 E3
St Rumbold's Rd 9 SP7 202 C1
St Sampsons CE Jun Sch SN6 19 D8
St Sampsons Inf Sch SN6 19 D8
St Stephen's Pl BA14 105 D8
St Swithin Way 8 SP10 193 D1
St Teresa's Dr SN15 78 C7
St Teresas Cl 7 SP1 146 C5
St Thomas a' Becket CE Prim Sch SP3 188 B3
St Thomas Cl 14 SP10 193 D2
St Thomas' Rd BA14 101 D1
St Thomas's Sq SP1 146 A1
St Thomas's Way SP1 146 C5
St Ursula's Cl 9 SP1 146 D5
Saintes Cl 1 SP1 146 D5
Salamander Ct SP9 216 D7
Salcombe Gr SN3 50 E5
Salisbury & S Wiltshire Mus & Stonehenge Gall* SP1 152 A7
Salisbury Arts Ctr* SP1 146 B1
Salisbury Bsns Pk SP1 152 D7
Salisbury Cath* SP1 152 A8
Salisbury Cath Sch SP1 152 A7
Salisbury Cl 1 SN14 78 A6
Salisbury Coll SP1 152 B8
Salisbury District Hospl SP5 152 B3
Salisbury Hill SN8 213 E1
Salisbury Hollow BA13 186 D8
Salisbury Mus & Stonehenge Gallery* SP1 152 A7
Salisbury Racecourse SP2 150 E5
Salisbury Rd
Amesbury SP4 217 B3
Breamore SP6 210 F5
Chilmark SP3 201 A4
Downton SP5 211 A8
Fordingbridge SP6 210 E1
Hungerford RG17 177 B6
Marlborough SN8 213 E2
Netheravon SP4 190 A3
Pewsey SN9 215 C3
Plaitford/Landford SO51 212 E6
14 Shaftesbury SP7 202 C1
Shipton Bellinger SP9 199 D7
9 Shrewton SP3 196 E6
South Tedworth SP9 216 C3
Steeple Langford SP3 128 C8
Wilton SP2 144 E3
Salisbury Rd Ind Est SN9 215 B3
Salisbury Sch of English SP1 152 B8
Salisbury St
Amesbury SP4 217 A3
Devizes SN10 179 D8
26 Fordingbridge SP6 210 D1
Mere BA12 139 A5
3 Shaftesbury SP7 202 C1
Swindon SN1 50 D7
Salisbury Sta SP2 145 F1
Salisbury Swimming Baths SP1 146 B2
Sally In the Wood BA1 90 C6
Sally Kings La 5 SP7 202 B2
Salmons Leap SN11 81 A5
Salt La Salisbury SP1 146 B1
Winterbourne SP4 133 C3
Salt Spring Dr SN4 47 C1
Salt Way Prim Sch SN5 49 A7
Saltash Rd SN5 49 F5
Salter Cl BA14 105 E7
Saltersford La SN14 78 A5
Saltram Cl SN3 51 C6
Salzgitter Dr SN25 35 A8
Sambourne CE Prim Sch BA12 116 F6
Sambourne Chase BA12 117 A7
Sambourne Gdns BA12 117 A6
Sambourne Rd
Minety SN5 17 D2
Warminster BA12 117 A6
Sambre Rd SN4 65 D1
Sams La SN26 21 C1
Sanctuary The* SN8 173 D6
Sand Hole La
6 Westbury BA13 108 F1
Westbury BA13 112 E8
Sand St BA12 121 A6
Sandacre Rd
1 Swindon SN5 34 A1
3 Swindon SN5 48 F8
Sandalwood Rd 1 BA13 108 E1
Sand's La SN10 96 D2
Sanden Cl RG17 177 B7
Sanders Rd BA14 101 C2
Sandes Cl SN15 78 C7
Sandfield
Littleton Panell SN10 187 E8
Sutton Veny BA12 194 A5
Sandford Pk BA14 104 F7
Sandgate SN3 36 B1
Sandhills Rd SP3 142 A4
Sandle Copse SP6 210 B1
Sandlea Cl SN14 68 F5
Sandleaze SN10 179 C4
Sandleheath Rd SP6 210 A1
Sandown Ave SN3 50 E3
Sandown Ctr BA14 105 E4
Sandown Dr SN14 77 F6
Sandown Pl 7 SP2 145 F1
Sandpiper Bridge SN3 51 E7
Sandpiper Gdns SN14 70 A2
Sandpit Hill SP3 141 A2
Sandpit Rd SN11 81 D4

Sandpits La
Sherston SN16 . . . . .25 C1
Steeple Ashton BA14 . . . . . . .106 E6
Sandridge Comm SN12 . .94 D5
Sandridge Hill 95 A6
Sandridge La SN15 . . . . . . .95 C7
Sandridge Pk* SN12 . . . . . .95 B4
Sandridge Rd SN12 . . . . . .94 B5
Sandringham Rd
Swindon SN3 . . . . .50 F3
Trowbridge BA14 . . . . .105 B5
Sandringhams The
SP5 . . . . .153 E1
Sandroyd Sch SP5 . . . . . . .207 C5
Sands Cl SN10 . . . . .96 D1
Sands The SN9 . . . . .181 C7
Sands' La SP7 . . . . .203 C3
Sandstone Rd SN25 . . . . . .34 F2
Sandwood Cl SN5 . . . . . . .34 B2
Sandy La
Edington BA13 . . . . .186 C7
Redlynch SP5 . . . . .211 D8
Swindon SN1 . . . . .50 B4
Sandy Lea Ave 5 SN13 . .76 B1
Sandy Leaze BA15 . . . . . .100 C6
Sandy Ridge SN11 . . . . . . .81 C1
Sanford St 3 SN1 . . . . . . .50 C6
Sangster Ave SN14 . . . . . .94 B4
Sarsen Cl SN1 . . . . .49 F4
Sarson La SP11 . . . . .192 E1
Sarum Ave SN12 . . . . .94 B2
Sarum Cl Salisbury SP2 . .145 E3
Shipton Bellinger SP9 . . . . . .199 C8
Sarum Dr SN10 . . . . .214 C2
Sarum Gdns BA13 . . . . . .109 A4
Sarum Rd SN14 . . . . .78 A6
Sarum St Pauls CE Prim Sch
SP2 . . . . .145 F2
Sarum Way Calne SN11 . . .81 A3
2 Hungerford RG17 . . . . . . .177 B6
Sassoon Cl BA12 . . . . .116 D6
Saunders Gr SN13 . . . . . . .76 D1
Saunders Meadow
SN8 . . . . .183 E1
Savernake Ave SN12 . . . . .94 C6
Savernake Cl 4 BA12 . . . .117 A8
Savernake Cres SN8 . . . . .213 F2
Savernake Ct SN8 . . . . . . .213 E2
Savernake Hospl SN8 . . . .175 A7
Savernake Rd
Burbage SN8 . . . . .175 D1
Corsham SN13 . . . . .84 D8
Savernake St SN1 . . . . .50 B5
Savill Cres SN14 . . . . .63 F7
Sawpit Dr SN8 . . . . .175 C5
Sawpit Hill BA12 . . . . .140 B4
Sawyer Cl SN25 . . . . .35 B6
Sawyers Cl SN16 . . . . .17 A2
Sawyers Cres SN3 . . . . . . .76 D1
Sawyers Hill SN16 . . . . . . .17 A2
Saxby Rd SN15 . . . . .70 E1
Saxifrage Bank SN12 . . . . .94 C3
Saxon Cl Cricklade SN6 . . .19 D7
14 Market Lavington SN10 . .179 F1
Sherston SN16 . . . . .25 C1
Trowbridge BA13 . . . . .109 A4
Saxon Ct
North Tidworth SP9 . . . . .216 D7
Swindon SN3 . . . . .50 D4
Saxon Dr BA14 . . . . .101 E4
Saxon Leas SP5 . . . . .149 C6
Saxon Meadow SP5 . . . . .211 A8
Saxon Mill SN4 . . . . .65 D5
Saxon Rd SP2 . . . . .151 F6
Saxon Rise SN8 . . . . .183 E1
Saxon Spur 10 SP7 . . . . . .202 C2
Saxon St SN14 . . . . .78 B8
Saxon Way
Andover SP10 . . . . .193 D2
Winsley BA15 . . . . .99 F7
Saxonhurst 4 SP5 . . . . . .211 B8
Saxons Acre BA12 . . . . . .116 D6
Saxton Wlk SN5 . . . . .49 B8
Scallows La SO51 . . . . . . .212 F7
Scamell's Rd SP2 . . . . . . .146 A2
Scarborough Rd SN2 . . . . .49 F8
Scarlet Cl SN25 . . . . .34 F7
Scholard's La 16 SN8 . . . .170 B2
School Cl
Chiseldown SN4 . . . . .65 E4
Keevil BA14 . . . . .178 C5
St Paul Malmesbury Without
SN16 . . . . .28 A1
Vernhams Dean SP11 . . . . . .185 C3
School Dr 25 SP4 . . . . . . .198 B7
School Hill
Alderbury SP5 . . . . .153 C2
Brinkworth SN15 . . . . .45 E5
School La
All Cannings SN10 . . . . .180 A8
1 Amesbury SP4 . . . . .217 B3
Badminton GL9 . . . . .38 E2
Bromham SN15 . . . . .96 A7
Castle Combe SN14 . . . . .68 A7
Castle Eaton SN6 . . . . .10 B4
East Garston RG17 . . . . .171 E8
Grittleton SN14 . . . . .54 E5
Hindon SP3 . . . . .200 B3
Lea SN16 . . . . .29 A2
Little Bedwyn SN8 . . . . .176 C5
Marlborough SN8 . . . . .213 A2
Meysey Hampton GL7 . . . . . . .1 A4
South Cerney GL7 . . . . .6 F6
Staverton BA14 . . . . .101 D5
Westbury BA13 . . . . .108 E1

School La continued
Wroughton SN4 . . . . .64 A6
School Rd Calne SN11 . . . .81 A4
1 Durrington/Bulford
SP4 . . . . .198 C7
Kemble GL7 . . . . .4 F7
Nomansland SP5 . . . . .212 C4
Redlynch SP5 . . . . .211 E6
Seend SN12 . . . . .178 D8
School Wlk SN14 . . . . .78 A7
Scotby Ave SN3 . . . . .50 E2
Scotchel Gn SN9 . . . . . . .215 D5
Scotchel La SN9 . . . . .215 D5
Scotland Hill SN15 . . . . . .57 A5
Scotland La
Beckington BA11 . . . . .107 C4
Landford SP5 . . . . .212 B8
Scotland Rd SN12 . . . . . . .94 A6
Scotney Cres 2 SN25 . . . .34 F6
Scots La SP1 . . . . .146 A1
Scott Cl SN8 . . . . .183 C8
Scott's Hill SP7 . . . . .203 C4
Scotts Cl SN11 . . . . .89 B2
Scratchbury Camp*
BA12 . . . . .194 B7
Scrubbity Barrows*
SP5 . . . . .207 E4
Seaford Cl SN5 . . . . .49 A6
Seagrim Rd SP4 . . . . .144 C2
Seagry CE Prim Sch
SN15 . . . . .57 D6
Seagry Ct SN4 . . . . .35 B5
Seagry Hill SN15 . . . . .57 D3
Seagry Rd
Hullavington SN14 . . . . .56 D6
Sutton Benger SN15 . . . . .57 D2
Seaton Cl SN25 . . . . .34 F5
Second Broad Dr SP3 . . .128 C2
Sedgebrook SN3 . . . . .51 D2
Sedgefield Gdns SN10 . . .214 B4
Sedgefield Way SN14 . . . .77 F6
Seend CE Prim Sch
SN12 . . . . .178 D8
Seend Hill SN12 . . . . .178 F8
Sefton Way SN25 . . . . .34 C7
Selby Cres SN5 . . . . .49 B4
Seldon Cl 4 SN3 . . . . .50 E6
Selions Cl SN14 . . . . .70 B2
Selwood Anglican/Methodist
Mid Sch BA11 . . . . .110 B6
Selwood Cres 1 BA11 . . .110 A7
Semington Rd
Berryfield SN12 . . . . .94 A1
Melksham Without SN12 . . . .178 A8
Semley Ceva Prim Sch
SP7 . . . . .202 F5
Semley Wlk SN2 . . . . .35 C4
Senior Dr SP2 . . . . .152 A5
Sergeant Rogers Way
SN10 . . . . .214 E7
Seth Ward Dr SP1 . . . . . .146 D4
Seven Barrows*
Lambourn RG17 . . . . .165 A5
South Tedworth SP9 . . . . . . .191 B3
Seven Fields Nature
Reserve* SN25 . . . . .35 B5
Seven Fields Prim Sch
SN25 . . . . .35 B4
Sevenfields SN6 . . . . .23 A7
Severn Ave SN25 . . . . .35 A4
Severn Cl SN11 . . . . .81 A5
Severn Rd SN12 . . . . .94 A6
Seymour Ct BA14 . . . . . . .101 C1
Seymour Rd
Chippenham SN15 . . . . .78 F8
Swindon SN3 . . . . .50 F6
Trowbridge BA14 . . . . .101 C2
Seymours Ct* BA11 . . . . .107 A6
Shackleton Cl SN12 . . . . . .94 D1
Shackleton Rd SN10 . . . . .214 D2
Shackleton Sq SN10 . . . . .193 F2
Shady Bower SP1 . . . . . . .152 C8
Shady Bower Cl SP1 . . . . .152 C8
Shaftesbury Ave SN3 . . . .51 B4
Shaftesbury Ct BA14 . . . .105 A6
Shaftesbury Dro SP21 . . .151 E5
Shaftesbury Leisure Ctr
SP7 . . . . .202 C1
Shaftesbury Mus*
SP7 . . . . .202 C1
Shaftesbury Prim Sch
SP7 . . . . .202 D1
Shaftesbury Rd
Barford St Martin SP3 . . . . . .143 B3
Mere BA12 . . . . .139 A5
Motcombe SP7 . . . . .202 A3
Wilton SP2 . . . . .144 B3
Shaftesbury Sch SP7 . . . .202 C1
Shaftesbury St 16 SP6 . . .210 D1
Shails La
Melksham Without SN12 . . . .178 A8
Trowbridge BA14 . . . . .101 C1
Shakespeare Ave
SP10 . . . . .193 C1
Shakespeare Dr SN8 . . . .213 C3
Shakespeare Path SN3 . . .35 F3
Shakespeare Rd
Salisbury SP1 . . . . .145 F4
Wootton Bassett SN4 . . . . . . .47 F3
Shalbourne CE Prim Sch
SN8 . . . . .176 F2
Shalbourne Rd
Hungerford RG17 . . . . .177 A7
Swindon SN2 . . . . .35 B5
Shalford La BA9 . . . . .136 A3
Shallow Wagon La
BA13 . . . . .108 F6
Shallowbrooks La SN14 . .39 F8
Shallows The SP6 . . . . . . .210 F4

Shambles The BA15 . . . . .100 D7
Shanklin Rd SN2 . . . . .34 E4
Shaplands 4 SN3 . . . . .36 A2
Shapwick Cl SN3 . . . . .51 C7
Sharcott Dro SN9 . . . . . . .215 A4
Share La SP3 . . . . .203 C6
Sharp Cl SN5 . . . . .49 B7
Sharpley Cl SP6 . . . . .210 D2
Sharratt Ave 4 SP1 . . . . .146 C5
Shave La BA10 . . . . .122 A4
Shaw CE Prim Sch
SN12 . . . . .93 D8
Shaw Hill
Collingbourne Ducis SN8 . . . .191 E7
Melksham Without SN12 . . . . .93 D7
Swindon SN5 . . . . .49 B7
Shaw Ridge Leisure Pk*
SN5 .49 B6
Shaw Ridge Prim Sch
SN5 .49 B7
Shaw Village* SN8 . . . . .173 F4
Shawgrove SN8 . . . . .176 B3
Shear Cross BA12 . . . . . . .116 E1
Shearman St BA14 . . . . . .105 D7
Shearwater Way SN13 . . . .84 D7
Shearwood Rd SN5 . . . . . .34 A1
Sheasby Cl SP5 . . . . .208 A3
Sheen Cl Salisbury SP2 . . .145 A4
Swindon SN3 . . . . .36 E2
Sheep Fair Way 1
RG17 . . . . .165 A1
Sheep St Devizes SN10 . . .214 B3
Highworth SN6 . . . . .23 A5
Sheepbridge Rd SP4 . . . .198 E7
Sheepcote Barton 3
BA14 . . . . .105 E7
Sheepdrove Rd RG17 . . . .165 B2
Sheepridge SN8 . . . . .168 E3
Sheepscroft SN14 . . . . .70 B2
Sheepwash La BA12 . . . . .201 E8
Sheerwold Cl SN3 . . . . . . .36 A3
Sheffield La SN13 . . . . .76 D1
Sheldon Manor & Gdns*
SN14 . . . . .78 A8
Sheldon Rd SN13 . . . . .78 B7
Sheldon Sch SN14 . . . . . . .70 B1
Shelfinch SN5 . . . . .51 C8
Shelley Ave 2 SN14 . . . . .47 F3
Shelley Dr SP1 . . . . .145 F4
Shelley Gdns SN12 . . . . . . .94 B4
Shelley St SN1 . . . . .50 B5
Shelley Way BA12 . . . . . . .116 D6
Shelly's Wlk GL7 . . . . .2 D4
Shenton Cl SN3 . . . . .36 B3
Shepherd Spring Jun & Inf
Sch 30 SP10 . . . . .193 E2
Shepherd's La
Donhead St Andrew SP7 . . . .203 B2
Selwood BA11 . . . . .114 D6
Shepherds Breach 1
SN4 .47 E2
Shepherds Cl
Coombe Bissett SP5 . . . . . . .151 A1
Odstock SP5 . . . . .152 A1
Shepherds Mead
BA13 . . . . .112 A8
Shepherds Rise SP11 . . . .185 C3
Sheppard Cl SN15 . . . . . . .78 F5
Sheppard St SN1 . . . . .50 B7
Sheppards Rise SN15 . . . .46 B7
Shepperton Way SN25 . . . .34 F6
Sherborne Pl SN3 . . . . .51 D3
Sherborne St GL7 . . . . .2 C4
Sherfield SP4 . . . . .133 A2
Sherfield English La
SO51 . . . . .212 F7
Sherfield English Rd
SP5 . . . . .212 E6
Sherfields SN5 . . . . .47 E1
Sherford Rd SN25 . . . . .34 E4
Sheridan Dr SN4 . . . . .47 F3
Sheringham Ct SN3 . . . . . .51 D3
Sherington Mead SN15 . . .79 B4
Sherrington La BA12 . . . . .195 A2
Sherrington Mead
SN15 . . . . .79 B4
Sherston Ave SN2 . . . . .35 C5
Sherston Rd
Brokenborough SN16 . . . . . . .27 C4
Luckington SN14 . . . . .39 E5
Sherwood Ave SN12 . . . . . .94 C6
Sherwood Cl 3 BA12 . . . .117 A8
Sherwood Rd SN3 . . . . .51 B4
Shetland Cl
Swindon SN5 . . . . .49 B7
Westbury BA13 . . . . .108 D2
Shetland Gdns SN5 . . . . . .49 A7
Shipley Dr SN25 . . . . .34 F6
Shipton Bellinger Prim Sch
SP9 . . . . .199 C8
Shipton Gr SN3 . . . . .50 E5
Shiptons La SN15 . . . . .43 F2
Shire Cl SN5 . . . . .49 A7
Shire Ct 8 SP1 . . . . .152 B8
Shire Hill SN14 . . . . .66 A7
Shire Way BA13 . . . . .108 D2
Shires Sh Ctr The
BA14 . . . . .105 C8
Shirley Cl SN3 . . . . .50 F7
Shockerwick La BA1 . . . . . .82 A5
Shoddesden La SP11 . . . .192 B4
Shoemaker La SN15 . . . . . .45 F6
Shop La Badminton GL9 . . .38 E2

Shop La continued
Wingfield BA14 . . . . .104 C6
Shore Pl BA14 . . . . .100 F1
Shoreland Cl BA13 . . . . . .108 F3
Short Dro SN4 . . . . .65 F7
Short La Andover SP11 . . .193 B1
Barford St Martin SP3 . . . . . .143 A4
Short River Rd BA13 . . . .109 D2
Short St
Ludgershall SP11 . . . . .192 A5
Melksham SN12 . . . . .94 C6
Shortlands SP2 . . . . .144 B3
Shorts Gn La SP7 . . . . . . .202 A4
Shoscombe Gdns 3
BA11 . . . . .110 C2
Shrapnel Rd 1 SP4 . . . . .197 E7
Shrewsbury Rd SN3 . . . . . .50 F6
Shrewton CE Prim Sch
SP3 . . . . .196 E7
Shrewton Cl BA14 . . . . . . .105 D6
Shrewton Rd BA12 . . . . . .195 E6
Shrewton Wlk SN25 . . . . . .35 C1
Shrivenham Rd
Highworth SN6 . . . . .23 B4
Swindon SN1 . . . . .50 D3
Swindon SN3 . . . . .36 E2
Shropshire Cl
Salisbury SP2 . . . . .145 C5
1 Swindon SN5 . . . . .49 B7
Shurnhold SN12 . . . . .93 F5
Shute End Rd SP5 . . . . . . .153 B4
Shutts La SP5 . . . . .153 A1
Sidbury Circular Rd
SP9 . . . . .216 B7
Sidbury Hill Ave SP9 . . . .216 C8
Sidings The 2 SP5 . . . . . .211 B8
Sidmouth Par SN10 . . . . . .214 B4
Sidney Cl Swindon SN5 . . . .48 F4
3 Swindon SN3 . . . . .50 E6
Sidney St SP2 . . . . .145 F1
Sidney Wood Ct SN4 . . . . .35 D7
Signal St SP4 . . . . .198 E6
Signal Way SN1 . . . . .50 D3
Silbury Cl
Chippenham SN14 . . . . .78 A6
Westbury BA13 . . . . .108 F4
Silbury Hill* SN1 . . . . . . .173 C7
Silbury Mews SN25 . . . . . .34 E3
Silbury Rd SN11 . . . . .81 B5
Silchester Way SN5 . . . . . .49 C6
Sillen La SP6 . . . . .209 B6
Sillington La SN10 . . . . . .179 B7
Silton Rd Swindon SN3 . . . .76 D1
Silton Rd SP9 . . . . .137 F2
Silver Barrow* SP9 . . . . .188 D2
Silver Birch Rd BA14 . . . .105 B5
Silver Cl SN16 . . . . .17 B2
Silver La BA11 . . . . .114 C6
Silver Meadows BA14 . . . .105 A5
Silver St Alderbury SP5 . . .153 B2
Bradford-on-Avon BA15 . . . .100 D6
Calne SN11 . . . . .81 B1
Calne Without SN11 . . . . .89 B8
Colerne SN14 . . . . .75 B3
Corsham SN13 . . . . .85 C6
Kington Langley SN15 . . . . . . .70 F7
Malmesbury SN16 . . . . .28 A3
Minety SN16 . . . . .14 C2
Potterne SN10 . . . . .179 D5
Salisbury SP1 . . . . .152 A8
Sherston SN16 . . . . .40 C8
South Cerney GL7 . . . . .6 F7
South Marston SN3 . . . . .36 E4
Trowbridge BA14 . . . . .105 D8
Warminster BA12 . . . . .117 A7
Westbury BA13 . . . . .112 C8
Wilton SP2 . . . . .144 D3
Silver St La
Bromham SN15 . . . . .87 D1
Trowbridge BA14 . . . . .105 B6
Silver Wood SP5 . . . . .153 C3
Silverless St SN8 . . . . .213 D3
Silverton Rd SN3 . . . . .51 B6
Silverwood Dr SP1 . . . . . .146 D2
Simmance Way SP4 . . . . .217 C3
Simnel Cl SN5 . . . . .48 F5
Simonds Rd 4 7 SP11 . . .192 A5
Six Acre La
Shalbourne RG17 . . . . .176 F3
West Knoyle BA12 . . . . .140 A4
Sixpenny Handley Fst Sch
SP5 . . . . .208 A4
Skew Bridge Cl SN4 . . . . . .64 A6
Skew Bridge Rd SP2 . . . .145 D2
Skew Rd SP2 . . . . .145 B2
Skinner's Cl SN6 . . . . .22 F7
Skye Cl SN6 . . . . .22 F7
Slab La SP5 . . . . .211 C7
Slade Dr SN3 . . . . .36 B1
Slade La SN14 . . . . .81 C3
Sladesbrook BA15 . . . . . . .100 E8
Slag La BA13 . . . . .108 F5
Slate Way SN5 . . . . .148 B3
Slater Rd SP4 . . . . .215 C5
Slaughterford Rd SN14 . . .68 C1
Sleight La SN10 . . . . .179 F6
Sleight La SN10 . . . . .214 E1
Slessor Rd
Lyneham SN15 . . . . .60 A1
Lyneham & Bradenstoke
SN15 . . . . .166 A8
Sling Orch SP3 . . . . .204 E7
Sling Rd SP4 . . . . .198 E7
Slipway The SN4 . . . . .101 D4
Slodbrook La SP8 . . . . . . .138 D1
Slowgrove Cl BA14 . . . . . .105 F8

Small St SN10 . . . . .180 F4
Smallbrook Gdns
BA14 . . . . .101 D5
Smallbrook La BA12 . . . . .117 D5
Smallbrook Mdws Nature
Reserve* BA12 . . . . .117 C5
Smallbrook Rd BA12 . . . . .117 B5
Smannell Rd SP11 . . . . . .193 F2
Smay Down La SN8 . . . . .184 E6
Smeaton Rd
1 Andover SP10 . . . . .193 B1
Salisbury SP2 . . . . .145 E1
Smitan Brook SN3 . . . . .51 D6
Smith St SN14 . . . . .78 B2
Smitham Bridge Rd
RG17 . . . . .177 B7
Smith's Hill SP7 . . . . .165 F7
Smithfield St 2 SP4 . . . . .217 B3
Smiths Cl SN9 . . . . .215 B5
Smithy Yd SN13 . . . . .77 A2
Smithy La SN9 . . . . .181 C6
Smithys La SN8 . . . . .183 C8
Snail-Creep Hanging*
SP3 . . . . .200 D7
Snails' La SN10 . . . . .214 A3
Snap Village* SN8 . . . . . .169 C7
Snapgorse BA13 . . . . .109 A3
Snappers Cl SN4 . . . . .64 B5
Snarlton La SN12 . . . . .94 D5
Snoddington Rd
Fyfield SP11 . . . . .192 D1
Shipton Bellinger SP9 . . . . . .199 E7
Snow Hill Dinton SP3 . . . .201 F2
1 Swindon SN4 . . . . .65 D4
Snowberry La SN12 . . . . . .94 C3
Snowdon Pl SN2 . . . . .35 E4
Snowdrop Cl SN25 . . . . . . .34 D5
Snowshill Cl SN25 . . . . . . .34 F5
Snowswick La SN7 . . . . . . .12 E7
Snuff St SN10 . . . . .214 A4
Soake's Sq SP11 . . . . .193 F2
Sock's La BA10 . . . . .122 A7
Sodom La SN15 . . . . .59 C7
Soldier's Ring* SP6 . . . . .209 C7
Solstice Pk Bsns Park
SP4 . . . . .217 D4
Solstice Rise SP4 . . . . . . .217 B3
Somerdale Cl 6 SN5 . . . . .49 C6
Somerford Cl SN2 . . . . .35 C4
Somerford Lakes Reserve*
GL7 . . . . .5 D2
Somerfords Walter Powell CE
Prim Sch 1 RG17 . . . . . .177 B7
Somerleyton Ct SN10 . . . .187 D8
Somerset Cl 1 RG17 . . . .177 B7
Somerset Cres BA13 . . . . .109 A5
Somerset Rd
Salisbury SP1 . . . . .146 B3
1 Swindon SN3 . . . . .51 A5
Somerset Way BA14 . . . . .105 A5
Somerton Gdns BA11 . . . .110 C2
Somerville Ct 2 SP10 . . . .193 F1
Somerville Rd SN3 . . . . . . .50 F6
Somme Rd SP11 . . . . .191 F4
Sopwith Pk 2 SP10 . . . . . .193 C1
Sopworth Rd SN14 . . . . . . .39 C5
Sorley Cl SN8 . . . . .213 B3
Sorrel Cl Melksham SN12 . .94 B3
Trowbridge BA14 . . . . .105 A5
Wootton Bassett SN4 . . . . . . .47 E4
Sorrel Dr SN14 . . . . .70 B3
Sound Copse SN5 . . . . .34 B2
Souter Ave BA12 . . . . .116 E5
South Bank SN8 . . . . .174 F2
South Charford Dro
SP6 . . . . .210 D6
South Cliffe Rd 6 SN3 . . .179 F1
South Cross La SN10 . . . . .179 C3
South Dr SN3 . . . . .36 C4
South Hills Sch SP2 . . . . .150 D8
South La Downton SP5 . . . .211 A8
Nomansland SP5 . . . . .212 C4
South Marston CE Prim Sch
SN3 .36 E4
South Marston Park
SN3 .36 B4
South Mdw La SN5 . . . . . . .19 F3
South Mill Cl SP4 . . . . . . .217 B2
South Mill Rd SP4 . . . . . . .217 B2
South Pk* SP11 . . . . .192 B4
South Pl Calne SN11 . . . . . .81 B2
Corsham SN13 . . . . .77 A1
South St
Aldbourne SN8 . . . . .170 A6
Avebury SN8 . . . . .173 B8
Broad Chalke SP5 . . . . .205 B4
Corsham SN13 . . . . .77 A1
Great Wishford SP2 . . . . . . .130 A3
8 Salisbury SP2 . . . . .145 F1
Swindon SN1 . . . . .50 C4
Warminster BA12 . . . . .116 E5
Wilton SP2 . . . . .144 C1
South Ugford Medieval
Village of* SP2 . . . . .144 A2
South View RG17 . . . . .177 B7
South View Pl SN8 . . . . . . .213 C3
South View SN8 . . . . .213 C3
South Way
Alderbury SP5 . . . . .153 C2
Trowbridge BA14 . . . . .105 D7
South Western Rd
SP2 . . . . .145 F1
South Wilts Gram Sch
SP1 . . . . .146 A3
Southampton Rd
Alderbury SP5 . . . . .153 C2

Southampton St SN1 ....50 D6
Southay BA13 ....186 B7
Southbank Gdns RG17 .165 B1
Southbank Glen SN4 ....47 F2
Southbourne Way
SP4 ....133 D6
Southbrook BA12 ....139 C4
Southbrook Gdns
BA12 ....139 B4
Southbrook La SN3 .....178 B1
Southcot Rd SN10 ......93 F6
Southcott St SN2 ....35 B1
Southbroom Inf Sch
SN10 ....214 C2
Southbroom Jun Sch
SN10 ....214 C2
Southbroom Rd SN10 .214 B3
Southcott Dr BA13 ......111 D4
Southcroft Rd 3 SN13 ..76 E1
Southdown 3 SN4 ......163 A5
Southernwood Dr SN2 ..34 C4
Southerwicks SN13 .....84 F8
Southey Cl SN25 ....34 F8
Southfield
4 Aldbourne SN8 ......170 A6
Southwick BA14 ....104 F2
West Overton SN8 .....173 F6
Southfield Jun Sch
SN6 ....23 A5
Southfields BA11 ....110 A3
Southgate SN10 ....214 B2
Southgate Cl SN10 ....214 B2
Southleigh BA15 ....100 C5
Southleigh View BA12 ..117 C5
Southmead SN14 ....78 B6
Southmill Hill SP4 ......217 B1
Southside
Laverstock SP4 ....146 D8
Shipton Moyne GL8 .....26 E7
Southview Rd BA14 ....105 D6
Southville Rd BA15 .....100 E5
Southward La SN8 .....170 A6
Southwark Cl SN9 ......216 E6
Southway SP4 ....134 B7
Southway Rd BA15 .....100 D4
Southwell Cl 2 SN14 ...78 A5
Southwick Ave SN4 ....35 B5
Southwick CE Prim Sch
BA14 ....104 F3
Southwick Ctry Pk*
BA14 ....104 F5
Southwick Rd BA14 ....105 C2
Southwold Cl SN25 .....34 A6
Southwood Rd BA14 ...105 F8
Sovereign Cl SP2 ....145 F1
Soyuz Cres SN25 ....34 B7
Spa Cl SN6 ....23 B6
Spa Ct SN12 ....94 B3
Spa Rd SN12 ....94 B3
Spackman La SN13 .....84 E8
Spanbourn Ave SN14 ..78 D7
Sparcells Dr SN5 ....34 B2
Speedwell Cl
Melksham SN12 ....94 C2
1 Swindon SN25 ......34 E5
3 Trowbridge BA14 ...105 D4
Spencer Cl
Melksham SN12 ....94 A6
Swindon SN5 ....48 F7
Spencers Orch
Bradford-on-Avon BA15 .100 D5
Wroughton SN4 ....64 B6
Spenser Cl SN3 ....51 A7
Spereholt SN5 ....49 D4
Spey Ct SP10 ....193 F1
Spiders Island SP5 .....153 F2
Spiers Piece BA14 ......178 B3
Spin Hill SN10 ....179 E1
Spindle Tree Ct SN2 ...35 B2
Spouts La SO51 ....212 F7
Spracklands SP3 ....201 F2
Sprats Barn Cres SN4 ..47 D3
Spratsgate La GL7 .....6 B4
Spray Leaze 10 SP11 ..192 B5
Spray Rd RG17 ....177 C2
Spring Gdns Lechlade GL7 ..2 C4
Swindon SN1 ....50 C6
Spring La SN13 ....84 C7
Spring Meadow SN8 ...191 D4
Spring Meadows
BA14 ....105 A5
Spring Rd BA11 ....110 A6

Spring The 6 SN10 ....187 E8
Spring Tining SN13 ....76 F1
Springers Cl SN10 .....214 D4
Springfield BA15 ....100 E6
Springfield Bldgs SN15 ..78 D8
Springfield Cl
Corsham SN13 ....84 A8
7 Shaftesbury SP7 ...202 C2
Trowbridge BA14 ......101 E2
Springfield Cres
15 Redlynch SP5 ......211 C7
Wootton Bassett SN4 ..47 D2
Springfield Dr SN11 ...81 A3
Springfield Gdns SN12 ..85 C1
Springfield Pk
18 Tisbury SP3 ....203 E8
Trowbridge BA14 ......101 E1
Springfield Rd
Rowde SN10 ....96 D1
Swindon SN1 ....50 C3
Westbury BA13 ....108 F2
Springfield Sports Ctr
SN13 ....76 F1
Springfields Sch SN11 ..81 A3
Springhead BA12 ......194 A4
Springhill Cl 8 SN5 ....49 C5
Spur Way SN4 ....35 E3
Square The Calne SN11 ..81 B3
Mere BA12 ....139 A5
Pewsey SN9 ....215 C5
Swindon SN3 ....50 D4
Squarey Cl SP5 ....211 A7
Squires Copse SN5 .....34 A1
Squires Hill Cl
4 Wootton Bassett SN4 ..47 F2
7 Wootton Bassett SN4 ..48 A2
Squirrel Cres 1 SN4 ...47 F2
Squirrel's Cnr BH21 ...208 D1
Stables Rd SP9 ....216 C4
Stacey's La SN4 ....163 B5
Stafford St SN1 ....50 B5
Stag Hill RG17 ....171 A1
Stainers Mead SP7 ....202 A5
Stallard St BA14 ....105 C8
Stalls The BA12 ....139 A5
Stancombe Pk SN5 ....49 D5
Stancombe Pk 1 SN5 ..49 D5
Standen Way SN25 .....35 A7
Standings 6 SN5 ......49 A8
Stanford Rd SN25 .....34 C7
Stanier Cl BA11 ....110 D6
Stanier Rd SN11 ....81 C6
Stanier St SN1 ....50 B5
Stanley Cl 9 SN4 ......163 B6
Stanley Honey Ct 7 SN3 ..50 F6
Stanley Little Rd SP2 ..145 B3
Stanley St SN1 ....50 B5
Stanley Terr SN10 .....214 B2
Stanmore St SN1 ......50 A5
Stansfield Cl 5 SN4 ...49 D4
Stanton Cl BA14 ....101 A6
Stanton Ctry Pk* SN6 ..36 B8
Stanton La SN14 ....56 A1
Stanton Pk Farm* SN6 ..36 B8
Stanton Pk Nature Reserve*
SN6 ....36 B8
Stanton St Quintin Prim Sch
SN14 ....56 A1
Stanway Cl 9 SN4 .....51 A4
Stapleford Castle Ring &
Bailey* SP3 ....129 D8
Stapleford Cl SN15 ....78 E4
Stapleford Way SN11 ..81 A3
Staples Hill BA2 ....99 C3
Stapleton Cl SN6 ......22 F5
Star La SN14 ....74 D8
Star The BA14 ....101 E7
Stardust Cres SN25 ...34 B7
Staring Cl 6 SN5 ......48 F8
Station App
4 Frome BA11 ....110 A4
Melksham SN12 ....94 A6
Minety SN16 ....17 C2
Swindon SN1 ....50 D3
Westbury BA13 ....108 E4
Station Hill SN15 ......78 D8
Station Ind Est SN1 ...50 B6
Station Rd
Ashbury SN6 ....164 A8
Badminton GL9 ....38 F1
Calne SN11 ....81 B2
Chiseldown SN4 ....66 B6
Christian Malford SN15 ..58 A2
Codford BA12 ....194 F3
Corsham SN13 ....77 A1
Dauntsey SN15 ....174 A3
East Garston RG17 ....171 E7
Great Wishford SP2 ...129 F3
Highworth SN6 ....92 E1
Holt BA14 ....92 E1
19 Lambourn RG17 ...177 B7
Kemble GL7 ....4 F7
10 Lambourn RG17 ...165 A1
Lechlade GL7 ....2 C4
Limpley Stoke BA2 ....99 C5
Minety SN16 ....17 C1
Purton SN5 ....33 C5
Sandleheath SP6 ....33 A1
Sedgehill & Semley SP7 ..202 D5
Swindon SN1 ....50 B7
Tidworth SP9 ....216 D5
Warminster BA12 ......117 B7

Station Rd *continued*
Westbury BA13 ....108 E5
Wootton Bassett SN4 ..47 D1
Station Terr 4 SP2 .....145 F1
Station Way BA14 .....105 C8
Staverton CE Prim Sch
BA14 ....101 C6
Staverton Way 2 SN2 ..35 C6
Stavordale Priory*
BA9 ....136 D5
Steadings The
Salisbury SP4 ....146 D6
Wootton Bassett SN4 ..47 F1
Steam Mus of the Great
Western Rly* SN2 .....50 A6
Stedham Wlk SN6 ......51 B4
Steel's La BA9 ....137 A3
Steele Cl SN10 ....214 D4
Steels Dro SP6 ....211 A4
Steels La SN5 ....209 F2
Steep Hollow SP3 .....201 E3
Steep St BA12 ....139 A5
Steepe Way SN8 ....175 C1
Steeple Langford CE Fst Sch
SP8 ....128 C8
Stenbury Cl SN25 .....35 A7
Stenness Cl SN5 ....34 C2
Stephen Martin Gdns 7
SP6 ....210 D1
Stephens Cl 1 SP2 ....151 E7
Stephens Rd SN3 ......36 A1
Stephens Way BA12 ..116 F8
Stephenson Dr BA11 ..110 C6
Stephenson Rd
Salisbury SP2 ....145 E1
Swindon SN25 ....35 C7
The Ham BA13 ....108 D5
Steplake La SN10 .....212 F8
Steplake Rd SO51 ....212 F8
Sterling Cl BA11 ....110 C6
Stert Valley La SN10 ..180 A6
Stevenson Rd SN2 .....35 B4
Stewart Cl
Chippenham SN15 .....78 F4
Swindon SN3 ....35 B6
Steway La BA1 ....82 B6
Stickleback Rd SN11 ..81 B6
Still Man Cl BA14 .....101 E8
Stirling Cl
3 Bower Hill SN12 ...178 B8
Wroughton SN4 ....64 A7
Stirling Rd
Market Lavington SN10 ..180 A1
South Marston Park SN3 ..36 C6
Stirling Way BA11 .....110 C6
Stobberts Pl 4 SN10 ..179 F1
Stobberts Rd 3 SN10 ..179 F1
Stock La
Aldbourne SN8 ....169 D4
Landford SP5 ....212 C7
Stock's Cross SO43 ...212 D2
Stockbridge Copse
SN5 ....34 A2
Stockham Cl SN6 ......19 E8
Stockley Hollow SN11 ..89 C6
Stockley Rd SN11 .....89 C6
Stockley Rd SN11 .....89 D3
Stockport Rd SP4 .....217 D1
Stocks Bridge La SP5 ..151 A1
Stockton Earthworks*
BA12 ....201 A6
Stockton House*
BA12 ....195 B1
Stockton Rd SN2 ......35 C4
Stockwell Rd SN10 ...214 C4
Stockwood Cl SP1 ....146 C3
Stockwood Rd SN14 ..78 B6
Stoke Comm La SN5 ..19 A2
Stoke Common Mdws Nature
Reserve* SN6 ....18 E1
Stoke Mead BA2 ......98 F7
Stokehill BA14 ....106 A8
Stokes Rd SN13 ....85 A8
Stokes' Croft SN11 ....81 B4
Stokesay Dr SN5 ......49 C4
Stonar Sch SN12 ......92 B8
Stone (site of King's Elm)*
SP3 ....142 B1
Stone Ave* SN8 ....173 C8
Stone Cl SP5 ....149 C6
Stone La
Lydiard Millicent SN5 ..33 E1
Sutton Benger SN15 ..175 D8
Stonebridge Cl SN8 ...213 F3
Stonebridge Dr BA11 ..110 B7
Stonecrop Way SN2 ...35 E4
Stonefield Dr SN6 .....23 A5
Stonehenge* SN7 .....218 C1
Stonehenge Cursus*
SP4 ....197 C6
Stonehenge Rd SN9 ..198 A4
Stonehenge Sch The
SP4 ....217 B4
Stonehill Barn GL8 ....3 C6
Stonehill Gn SN5 ......49 D6
Stonehill La GL8 ....3 C6
Stonelea Cl SN14 .....78 A8
Stoneleigh Rise BA14 ..110 A6
Stoneover La
Lydiard Tregoze SN4 ..48 A3
Wootton Bassett SN4 ..47 F2
Stones La SN6 ....22 F6
Stonewall Terr BA11 ..110 A3
Stoney Bridge BA12 ..140 D5
Stoney Cross 20 SP11 ..192 A5
Stony Gutter BA14 ...102 D1

Stony La
Damerham SP6 ....209 E2
Lambourn RG17 ....171 B6
Stonybeck Cl SN5 .....49 D6
Stop St SP3 ....200 C2
Stoppers Hill SN15 ...46 B7
Stops Hill SP3 ....200 B3
Stormore BA13 ....111 F8
Storridge Rd BA13 ....108 C6
Stour Cl 8 SO51 ......212 F6
Stour Wlk SN25 ....35 B4
Stourhead House & Gdns*
BA12 ....123 F1
Stourton House Flower Gdn*
BA12 ....123 E3
Stourton La BA12 .....123 E3
Stourton Pk BA14 .....102 B3
Stowell Pk* SN8 ......182 A8
Straight La Dean SP5 ..207 E3
Lambourn RG17 ....171 C6
Strangford La SN8 ....181 B3
Steeple Ashton BA14 ..178 A3
Stranks Cl SN6 ....23 A4
Stratford Cl SN5 ......49 D5
Stratford Rd SN1 ......146 A3
Stratford Sub Castle CE Prim
Sch SP1 ....145 D5
Stratford Tony Rd
SP5 ....150 C2
Stratton Orch 1 SN3 ..36 A2
Stratton Rd & Marshgate Ind
Est SN1 ....50 F8
Stratton Rd
Pewsey SN9 ....215 C4
Swindon SN1 ....50 F8
Strattons Wlk SN12 ...94 B4
Strawberry Hill SN10 ..187 E2
Strawberry La GL7 ....1 A4
Street La
Brewham BA10 ....122 A4
Sedgehill & Semley SP7 ..202 C6
Street The
All Cannings SN10 ....172 F1
Alvediston SP5 ....204 B2
Bishops Cannings SN10 ..172 B1
Brinkworth SN15 ......45 F6
Broughton Gifford SN12 ..93 B4
Castle Combe SN14 ...68 A7
Castle Eaton SN6 .....10 B4
Charlton SN16 ....29 B6
Cherhill SN11 ....166 B1
Chilmark SP3 ....201 A3
Chirton SN10 ....180 F4
Crudwell SN16 ....14 E3
Didmarton GL9 ....24 C3
East Knoyle SP3 ......141 C1
Holt BA14 ....101 D8
Hullavington SN14 ...41 F1
Kilmington BA12 ......123 F4
Latton SN6 ....8 F4
Lea SN16 ....22 E7
Liddington SN4 ....163 A4
Little Somerford SN15 ..44 C5
Luckington SN14 .....39 E4
Lydiard Millicent SN5 ..48 D8
Marden SN10 ....181 A4
Marston Maisey SN6 ..9 D6
Milton Lilbourne SN9 ..182 E7
Motcombe SP7 ....202 A5
Nettleton SN14 ....53 B4
Oaksey SN16 ....15 F5
Pitton & Farley SP5 ..154 E7
Shipton Moyne GL8 ..26 E8
Swindon SN25 ....34 E3
West Knoyle SP3 ......140 D5
Winterslow SP5 ....149 A5
Yatton Keynell SN14 ..68 F6
Stroma Way SN6 ......22 E7
Strongrove Hill RG17 ..177 A7
Strongs Cl BA14 ......178 C4
Stroud La SN10 ....179 F5
Stroud's Hill SN4 .....65 D4
Stuart Cl 2 Swindon SN3 ..50 F6
Stuart Gn BA12 ....117 A6
Stuart Rd SP9 ....193 D1
Stubbs La SN14 ....70 A7
Stubhampton Bottom
DT11 ....206 C3
Stubsmead SN3 ....51 C5
Stuckton Rd SP6 .....210 D3
Studio Theatre* SP2 ..146 A2
Studland Hill BA12 ...51 B3
Studland Pk BA13 ....108 E5
Studley Gn Prim Sch
BA14 ....105 A6
Studley Hill SN11 .....80 A4
Studley La SN11 ....80 A3
Studley Rise BA14 ....105 A6
Sturford La BA12 .....115 A8
Styles Ave BA11 ....110 C4
Styles Cl BA11 ....110 B4
Styles Hill BA11 ......110 C4
Styles Pk BA11 ....110 C4
Styles The SP5 ....205 F4
Sudeley Dr GL7 ....2 C4
Sudeley Way SN5 .....48 F5
Suffolk Cl SN14 ....78 A8
Suffolk Pl GL7 ....8 D7
Suffolk Rd
Salisbury SP2 ....151 E6
5 Westbury Leigh BA13 ..108 C1
Suffolk St SN2 ....50 C6
Summer Down Wlk
BA14 ....105 C5

Summer La
Castle Combe SN14 ...53 F3
Monkton Combe BA2 ..98 D8
Summer Rd BA13 .....108 F4
Summerdown Ct
BA13 ....109 A4
Summerhouse Rd SN4 ..63 F7
Summerleaze BA14 ...105 A6
Summerlock App 2
SP2 ....146 A1
Summers La SN4 .....167 C7
Summers St SN2 ......49 F7
Sumsions Dr SN3 .....76 D1
Sun La BA13 ....108 C3
Sunderland Cl 11 SN12 ..178 B8
Sunningdale Cl SN15 ..78 F7
Sunningdale Rd SN25 ..35 C4
Sunnyhill SN6 ....191 D8
Sunnyhill Rd SN1 .....174 C1
Sunnyhill Rd SP1 .....146 A4
Sunnyside SN10 ......187 E8
Sunnyside Ave SN1 ..50 A4
Surrendell Cottage
SN14 ....55 B8
Surrey Pl BA14 ....105 B7
Surrey Rd SN2 ....35 A1
Sussex Rd SP2 ....151 E6
Sussex Sq SN3 ....50 E6
Sutherland Cresent
SN14 ....70 B3
Sutherland Cl 5 SP10 ..193 D1
Suthmere Dr SN8 ....183 D8
Sutton Benger CE Prim Sch
SN15 ....57 D2
Sutton Bottom SP3 ..141 B5
Sutton Hill
Sherrington BA12 .....195 A4
Sutton Mandeville SP3 ..204 C7
Sutton La
Langley Burrell Without
SN15 ....71 C5
Sutton Benger SN15 ..57 D1
Sutton Pk SN26 ....21 C1
Sutton Rd Fovant SP3 ..204 D7
Kington Langley SN15 ..70 F7
Swindon SN3 ....51 C4
Sutton Veny CE Prim Sch
BA12 ....194 A4
Suvla La 6 SP4 ....198 E6
Swaddon St SN11 ....81 B4
Swallet House SN15 ..58 B5
Swallow Cl
Tidworth SP9 ....216 D6
2 Warminster BA12 ..116 E5
Swallow Dr
Frome BA11 ....110 B6
1 Trowbridge BA14 ..105 B8
Swallowdale SN3 .....51 D7
Swallowfield Ave SN3 ..50 F5
Swallowmead 1 SP2 ..152 A5
Swallows Mead 9 SN4 ..48 A2
Swan Barton SN16 ...40 C8
Swan Cl
3 Durrington/Bulford
SP4 ....198 C7
Lechlade GL7 ....2 C4
Salisbury SP2 ....152 A6
Swan Dr BA14 ....101 D5
Swan La SN6 ....17 F5
Swan Meadow SN9 ..215 D3
Swan Rd Corsham SN13 ..76 E1
Pewsey SN9 ....215 C4
Swanage Wlk SN3 ....50 E3
Swan's Bottom 7 SN8 ..170 B2
Swan's Cl 3 SN8 .....170 B2
Swanborough Cl 6 SN15 ..78 F4
Swanborough Tump*
SN9 ....181 F6
Swanbrook SN3 ....51 D8
Swangate RG17 ....177 B8
Swansfield GL7 ....2 D6
Swattons Cl SN4 .....217 E8
Swayne Cl 6 SN15 ...78 F5
Swayne Rd SP2 ....145 A5
Swaynes Cl 1 SP1 ....146 B2
Sweet Briar Rd SN12 ..94 C3
Sweetmans Rd SP7 ..202 C2
Swift Ave SN25 ....35 A7
Swift Mead BA12 .....116 E5
Swiftdown 5 SP2 .....152 A5
Swillbrook Lakes Nature
Reserve* SN16 ....16 F8
Swinburne Pl SN4 ....47 E3
Swindon & Cricklade Rly*
SN25 ....33 F8
Swindon Arts Ctr*
SN1 ....50 C4
Swindon Coll
Marlborough SN8 .....213 D3
Swindon SN5 ....49 B6
Swindon SN1 ....50 C4
Swindon SN2 ....50 B8
Swindon Mus & Art Gall*
SN1 ....50 D4
Swindon Rd
Cricklade SN6 ....19 F7
Highworth SN6 ....92 F3
Hilmarton SN11 ....73 F3
Kington Langley SN15 ..70 F5
Lydiard Tregoze SN4 ..48 C2
Swindon SN16 ....36 A1
Wootton Bassett SN4 ..47 F3
Wroughton SN4 ....64 C2
Swindon St SN6 ....23 A5
Swindon Sta SN2 .....50 B7

Swindon Town Football Club
 SN1 ....50 D7
Swinley Dr SN5 ....34 A1
Sword Gdns 5 SN1 ....49 F4
Swynford Cl GL7 ....10 D6
Sycamore Cl
 Lyneham & Bradenstoke
 SN15 ....60 C2
 North Tidworth SP9 ......216 E6
 Sixpenny Handley SP5 ...208 A4
Sycamore Dr
 6 Frome BA11 ....110 B7
 Salisbury SP1 ....146 C5
Sycamore Gr
 Swindon SN2 ....35 C2
 Trowbridge BA14 ....105 C5
 Westbury BA13 ....108 F3
Sydnalls La SN3 ....115 D6
Symonds SN5 ....49 B3
Syon Cl Corsham SN13 ....84 E8
 4 Swindon SN5 ....34 F6
Syringa Ct SP2 ....145 C1
Sywell Rd SN3 ....51 C8

T

Tadpole La
 Blunsdon St Andrew SN25 .34 C8
 Purton SN5 ....33 F8
Talavera Rd SN4 ....168 E8
Talbot Cl
 Melksham SN12 ....94 D5
 Salisbury SP1 ....146 C4
Talbot Rd SN4 ....105 A7
Talboys (Medieval Hall
 House)* SN14 ....178 B4
Tallis Wlk SN5 ....49 A5
Tallow La 5 SN4 ....163 A6
Tamar Cl SN25 ....35 A4
Tamar Rd SN12 ....94 A6
Tamesis Dr GL7 ....4 F7
Tam La SN8 ....33 A4
Tamarisk Cl SN11 ....81 C1
Tangmere Cl DB SN12 .....178 B8
Tank La SP5 ....205 B4
Tankard La 12 SN8 ....170 B2
Tankey's Cl 6 BA11 ....112 A7
Tanner Cl SN15 ....78 F5
Tanners Cl
 Winterbourne SP4 ....133 A1
 Wootton Bassett SN4 .....47 D2
Tanners Field SP4 ....217 D3
Tanners Hill SN16 ....40 C8
Tanners La
 Sandleheath SP6 ....210 A1
 Shrewton SP3 ....196 E7
 Winterbourne SP4 ....133 A1
Tansley Moor SN3 ....51 E3
Tanyard La 6 SP2 ....202 B1
Taplow Wlk SN3 ....51 A4
Taramah Gdns II SP3 .....203 E8
Targetts Mead SP3 ....203 E8
Tarka Cl SN25 ....34 F7
Tarragon Cl SN2 ....34 C4
Tarrant's Hill 24 RG17 ....177 B7
Tarters The SN16 ....40 D8
Tascroft BA12 ....116 B5
Tawny Owl Cl SN3 ....51 C8
Taylor Cres SN4 ....36 A4
Taylors Gn SN8 ....174 A7
Taylors La SN8 ....168 B1
Taylors View BA14 ....101 D1
Teal Ave SN15 ....60 A1
Teal Cl BA13 ....109 B4
Tealgate RG17 ....177 B8
Tealsbrook SN4 ....51 D7
Teapot St BA12 ....201 E8
Teasel Cl Devizes SN10 ...124 E2
 28 Ludgershall SP11 .....192 A5
Teasels The BA12 ....116 F6
Techno Ind Est SN2 ....35 E1
Tedder Ave SN13 ....84 A8
Tees Cl SN3 ....35 B2
Tees Cl SN25 ....35 A4
Teeswater Cl SN5 ....49 A6
Teffont Field Bldgs*
 SP3 ....201 D4
Teffont Manor* SP3 ....201 D2
Telford Rd SP2 ....151 E8
Telford Way SN1 ....49 E4
Tellcroft Cl SN13 ....84 F8
Tellings Orch SN16 ....16 D3
Tempest Rd 9 SP4 ....217 D3
Templar's Firs SN4 ....61 E8
Temple St SN1 ....50 C5
Ten Acres SP7 ....202 C2
Tenby Cl SN3 ....50 F3
Tennis Cnr Dro BA11 ....107 D2
Tennyson Cl BA12 ....116 E6
Tennyson Rd SN4 ....47 F3
Tennyson St SN1 ....50 B5
Tenzing Gdns SN25 ....35 C3
Tern Cl SN11 ....81 D2
Terncliff SN3 ....51 A3
Tetbury Hill SN16 ....27 F6
Tetbury La SN16 ....14 D6

Tetbury Rd SN16 ....25 D2
Tethering Dro SP6 ....211 C6
Tewkesbury Way
 Lydiard Millicent SN5 .....48 E7
 Swindon SN5 ....49 A6
Thackeray Cl SN3 ....51 D4
Thackeray Cres SN12 ....94 B4
Thames Ave SN25 ....34 E5
Thames Cl BA12 ....117 A5
Thames Cres SN12 ....94 A6
Thames La SN6 ....19 E8
Thames St SN7 ....2 C3
Thames View
 Ashton Keynes SN6 ....17 F8
 Ewen GL7 ....5 C8
Thamesdown Dr
 Haydon Wick SN25 ....34 B7
 Swindon SN25 ....35 A7
Thatcham Cl SN11 ....81 A4
Thatchers The SN25 ....35 C7
Theatre Sq SN1 ....50 C6
Thestfield Dr BA14 ....101 D4
Thetford Way SN25 ....34 C5
Thicketts Rd SN8 ....169 C1
Thickwood La SN14 ....75 C6
Thirsk Cl SN14 ....78 A5
Thistlebarrow Rd SN1 ......146 A4
Thistledown 6 SN4 ....163 A6
Thomas Byron Rd
 SN10 ....214 C1
Thomas Ct SN11 ....81 C1
Thomas Hardy Dr 8
 SP7 ....202 D2
Thomas Mead SN15 ....78 E5
Thomas St SN2 ....49 F7
Thomas Wyatt Rd
 SN10 ....214 B1
Thompson Cl SP2 ....151 E5
Thompsons Hill SN16 ....40 C7
Thomson Way SN8 ....213 B2
Thorley Cl SN25 ....35 A6
Thornbank SN12 ....94 A3
Thornbridge Ave SN3 ....51 A4
Thornbury Rd SN25 ....35 A5
Thorne Cl SN25 ....150 F1
Thorne Rd
 2 Netheravon SP4 ....190 A4
 Swindon SN3 ....51 C4
Thorneydown Rd SP4 .....133 E1
Thornford Dr SN5 ....49 C5
Thornhill Dr SN25 ....35 A8
Thornhill Ind Est SN2 ....35 E1
Thornhill Rd BA12 ....116 D5
Thorns The SN8 ....213 D5
Thornton Cres SP4 ....144 F4
Threadgill Way 6 SP9 .....199 C8
Three Barrows* SN8 ....164 B3
Three Cuppes La 4
 SP1 ....146 B1
Three Horseshoes Wlk 3
 BA12 ....117 A2
Three Oak Hill Dr
 SN8 ....175 D4
Three Shire Stones*
 SN14 ....74 D1
Three Sisters Rd 1
 SN4 ....163 B6
Thresher Dr SN25 ....35 C6
Thrushel Cl SN25 ....34 E4
Thruxton Motor Racing
 Circuit* SP11 ....192 C1
Thurlestone Rd SN3 ....50 E5
Thurlow Cl IO SP4 ....217 E3
Thursday St SN3 ....34 D6
Thyme Cl SN2 ....34 C3
Tibb's Meadow SP11 ....192 D8
Tiberius Rd 24 SP10 ....193 E2
Tidcombe (Long Barrow)*
 SN8 ....184 D4
Tidling Cnr SN16 ....16 C5
Tidworth Cl 3 SN1 ....49 F4
Tidworth Coll SP9 ....216 D3
Tidworth Leisure Ctr
 SP9 ....216 D6
Tidworth Oval* SP9 ....216 C5
Tidworth Rd
 Bulford SP4 ....199 A7
 Collingbourne Ducis
 SN8 ....191 D7
 Ludgershall SP11 ....191 F5
 Milston SP4 ....191 B1
 Porton SP4 ....133 E7
Tilia Wlk BA10 ....122 A5
Tilley's La SN3 ....36 A2
Tilshead Wlk SN2 ....35 B5
Timandra Cl 1 SN25 ....35 A4
Timber St SN15 ....78 E7
Timberley La SP5 ....211 E7
Timbrell St BA14 ....101 D1
Timbrells The GL7 ....5 C8
Timor Rd BA13 ....108 E2
Tin Pit SN8 ....213 E4
Tinhead Rd BA13 ....186 C8
Tinings The SN3 ....79 A8
Tinkers Field SN4 ....47 D2
Tinkers Mead SN9 ....215 D4
Tinneys Cl SP5 ....211 C6
Tintagel Cl
 18 Andover SP10 ....193 E2
 Swindon SN5 ....49 B4
Tintern Rd SN10 ....214 B1
Tisbury & District Sports Ctr
 SP3 ....203 D8
Tisbury Cl 1 SN2 ....50 C6
Tisbury Rd SP3 ....204 D8
Tisbury Row SP3 ....203 F8
Tisbury Sta SP3 ....203 E7

Tismeads Cres SN1 ....50 C2
Titan Barrow BA1 ....82 C2
Titchfield Cl 5 SN5 ....48 F5
Tithe Barn Cres SN1 ....49 F3
Tittymouse La SP11 ....192 F1
Tiverton Rd SN2 ....35 C1
Tobruk Cl 5 SP11 ....193 E4
Tobruk Rd SN11 ....191 F3
Tobys Ct 22 SP7 ....202 C2
Tockenham Cnr SN4 ....60 D6
Tockenham Way SN3 ....35 B6
Toghill Cres SN13 ....76 B1
Tokes La SP7 ....202 E6
Toll Down Way SN14 ....53 A4
Tollard Rd SN13 ....51 C6
Tollgate Cl SP4 ....217 A5
Tollgate Rd SP7 ....202 C3
Tollgate Rd
 Andover SP10 ....193 C1
 Salisbury SP1 ....152 B8
Tombs Rd SP4 ....198 A6
Toothill Prim Sch SN5 .....49 C4
Top La
 Atworth/Whitley SN12 .....85 C1
 Stourton with Gasper
 BA12 ....137 D7
Top Rd GL7 ....10 C7
Top St SN15 ....44 A2
Toppers Cl SN25 ....35 A3
Tormarton Rd
 Acton Turville GL9 ....52 E6
 Marshfield SN14 ....66 A2
Tornio Cl SN10 ....214 D4
Torr Cl SN14 ....70 B2
Torridge Cl SN25 ....34 F4
Torrington Ct SN3 ....51 A5
Torun Way SN25 ....34 D6
Tottenham Ho* SN8 ....175 F2
Tottenham Pk* SN8 ....175 F3
Totterdown Cl 3 SN3 ....51 E7
Totterdown La GL7 ....1 F3
Tucla La SN14 ....75 B3
Totworth Rd SN3 ....34 C8
Touchorne La SP3 ....141 A4
Tournament Rd SP2 ....145 C3
Tout Hill SP7 ....202 B2
Tovey Cl 3 SP10 ....193 F1
Tovey Rd SN2 ....35 B2
Tow Barrow (Long Barrow)*
 SN8 ....184 B4
Towcester Cl SN14 ....77 F5
Towcester Pl 1 SN14 ......77 F5
Towcester Rd
 Nether Stowey SN14 .....105 E4
 Swindon SN3 ....51 C8
Towell Rd 5 SP4 ....198 A6
Tower Cl Andover SP10 ...193 E2
 Trowbridge BA14 ....105 A7
Tower Hill
 Dilton Marsh BA13 ....112 D7
 Iwerne Minster DT11 ....206 A1
Tower Mews SP1 ....146 B2
Tower Rd
 Melksham SN12 ....94 C5
 Stourton with Gasper
 BA12 ....122 F3
Tower View SN11 ....90 C2
Town Bridge
 Bradford-on-Avon*
 BA15 ....100 C6
Town Cl SN14 ....69 F8
Town Farm Pl SP5 ....208 B4
Town Gdns* SN1 ....50 C4
Town Mill SN8 ....213 D2
Town Path SP2 ....151 E7
Townfield IO SN8 ....170 B2
Townsend
 Chitterne BA12 ....195 D7
 Britton & Farleigh SP5 ...148 C4
Townsend Cl BA12 ....138 C4
Townsend La SP6 ....209 A6
Townsend Pl SN14 ....77 F8
Towpath Rd BA14 ....101 D4
Tracy Cl SN25 ....35 A6
Trafalgar Ho* SP5 ....159 D4
Trajan Rd SN2 ....36 C1
Transfer Bridges Ind Est
 SN2 ....50 D8
Travellers Rest SN15 ....49 E2
Tree Tops Cl SN15 ....59 C3
Tregantle Wlk SN4 ....51 B6
Tregoze Prim Sch SN5 .....49 A6
Tregoze Way SN5 ....48 F6
Trenchard Ave
 Box SN13 ....84 A8
 Calne Without SN11 ....81 F1
 6 Corsham SN13 ....76 B1
 Winterbourne SP4 ....133 C2
Trenchard Cl 6 SN14 ....78 A6
Trenchard Rd
 Lyneham SN15 ....60 A1
 Stanton Fitzwarren SN6 ...22 B2
Trent Cres SN12 ....94 A6
Trent Rd SN25 ....35 A4
Trentham Cl SN3 ....51 A6
Trevithick Cl 3 BA11 ....110 C6
Triangle The SN6 ....19 D8
Trimm's Dro SP6 ....211 A4
Trimnells SN14 ....75 B3
Trinity Cl SN3 ....35 A2
Trinity Pk SN1 ....81 C1
Trinity Rise SP11 ....193 A2
Trinity St SP1 ....152 B8
Tropenell Cl 2 BA15 ....76 E1
Trout La SN13 ....84 B7
Trow Brinkworth SN15 .....59 F8

Trow La continued
 Maiden Bradley with Yarnfield
 BA12 ....118 E4
Trowbridge Com Hospl
 BA14 ....101 D2
Trowbridge Lodge Pk
 BA14 ....105 A6
Trowbridge Mus*
 BA14 ....105 D8
Trowbridge Parochial Jun
 Sch BA14 ....101 E2
Trowbridge Rd
 Bradford-on-Avon BA15 .100 E5
 Bratton BA13 ....186 A8
 Seend SN12 ....178 C7
 Southwick BA14 ....102 A2
 Westbury BA13 ....109 B5
Trowbridge Sports Ctr
 BA14 ....105 B6
Trowbridge Sta BA14 ......105 C8
Trowbridge Rd
 Trumann Cl SN3 ....51 C4
 Truro Wlk SN14 ....77 F6
 Tryhorn Dr SP1 ....146 E5
Tryon Cl SN3 ....51 D2
Tubbs Farm Cl 6 RG17 ...165 A1
Tucker Cl 6 SP4 ....217 C2
Tuckers La SN15 ....59 A3
Tuckmill Rd GL7 ....10 E6
Tudor Cl SN30 ....36 B1
Tudor Dr BA14 ....101 E4
Tudor Rd SN14 ....41 A5
Tudor Wlk SN3 ....50 C6
Tugela Rd SN15 ....70 E1
Tuggy's La BA2 ....98 E1
Tulip Tree Cl SN2 ....35 C2
Tulse Hill Zeale BA12 ......138 A4
 Zennor BA12 ....137 F3
Tumlins SN10 ....180 F8
Tunball La SN8 ....184 F4
Tuners La SN16 ....14 E6
Tunnel Hill SP5 ....153 C2
Tupman Rd SN3 ....36 E2
Turf Ho La SN11 ....72 D1
Turin Ct 17 SP10 ....193 E2
Turl St SN1 ....50 C6
Turnball SN4 ....65 D4
Turnberry Cl SN15 ....78 F7
Turner Cl 2 SP1 ....151 E7
Turner Ct SN1 ....50 A5
Turnham Gdns SN1 ....49 A4
Turnpike 4 SN8 ....170 A6
Turnpike Rd
 Blunsdon St Andrew SN26 .35 C8
 Highworth SN6 ....23 A6
Turnpike The
 Chippenham SN15 ....79 B5
 East Knoyle SP3 ....202 D8
Turpin Way SN14 ....77 F7
Tutton Hill SN14 ....75 B3
Twatley Cotts SN16 ....27 C4
Tweed Cl SN25 ....34 F4
Twickenham Way SN3 ......70 E1
Twineham Gdns SP5 ....153 F2
Twineham Rd SN25 ....34 C8
Twyford Cl SN3 ....51 B6
Twynham Cl SP5 ....211 A7
Twynnoy Cl SN25 ....35 B5
Tyburn Cl SN3 ....49 B5
Tydeman St SN2 ....35 D1
Tye Gdns SN4 ....48 F5
Tylees Cl SN10 ....214 B3
Tylers Cl SP1 ....151 D7
Tyndales Meadow
 SP3 ....201 F2
Tyneham Rd SN3 ....51 B6
Tyning Cl 1 BA14 ....105 A7
Tyning Rd SN11 ....81 C1
Tyning Rd
 Bathampton BA2 ....82 A2
 Winsley BA15 ....99 B4
Tyning The BA2 ....99 B4
Tynings The
 Biddestone SN14 ....76 D7
 Westbury BA13 ....76 B7
Tynings Way BA15 ....99 F3
Tyrone Ave SP4 ....198 E7
Tytherington Rd BA12 ....194 C5
Tytherley Rd SP5 ....149 E6

U

Ullswater Cl SN3 ....51 E3
Ulysses Rd SN25 ....34 C4
Umbers Hill 2 SP7 ....202 B1
Underdown Cl 12 SN4 .....163 A6
Underhill Mere BA12 ....138 E5
 Pen Selwood BA9 ....138 D2
Underwood Dr SP4 ....217 D2
Union Rd
 Chippenham SN15 ....78 D5
 Tisbury SP3 ....203 D7
Union Row SN1 ....50 B6
Union St Melksham SN12 ..94 A4
 Swindon SN1 ....50 B6
 Trowbridge BA14 ....101 D1
Unity St SN14 ....101 D1
University of Bath in Swindon
 (Oakfield Campus)
 SN3 ....36 A2
Upavon Airfield SN9 ....182 B1
Upavon Ct SN2 ....35 C5
Upavon Prim Sch SN9 .....182 A1

Upcott SN6 ....8 C4
Upfield SN3 ....51 D3
Upham Rd SN3 ....50 E5
Upham Village* SN8 ....169 C8
Upland Rise BA13 ....109 B2
Upland Way SN3 ....51 D3
Uplands 28 RG17 ....177 B7
Uplands Cl BA2 ....99 C6
Uplands Specl Sch SN2 ...35 C4
Uplands The BA12 ....117 C7
Upnor Cl SP11 ....191 F4
Upper Avon Sch SP4 ....198 C7
Upper Backway SP3 ....196 F7
Upper Broad St SN1 ....101 C1
Upper Church Fields
 SN8 ....213 A1
Upper Dro SP10 ....193 C1
Upper Eddington
 RG17 ....177 C8
Upper Folly SP2 ....146 B4
Upper Garston La 8
 BA13 ....186 B7
Upper Isbury SN8 ....213 E2
Upper La SN13 ....84 B7
Upper Lambourn Rd
 RG17 ....165 A3
Upper Ley SN3 ....183 D5
Upper Marsh La BA12 .....117 A5
Upper Marsh Rd BA12 ....117 A5
Upper Noremarsh SN4 .....47 F1
Upper North Rd SP5 ....207 C5
Upper Pavenhill SN5 ....32 F4
Upper Potley SN13 ....84 E7
Upper Regents Pk
 SN5 ....100 D6
Upper St SP7 ....151 D7
Upper Waterhay Nature
 Reserve* SN6 ....18 D7
Upper Wr St BA12 ....139 B5
Uppington La SP3 ....129 E8
Upton Cl Swindon SN25 ...34 F5
 8 Warminster BA12 ......116 E7
Upton Great Barrow*
 BA12 ....194 F6
Urchront CE Prim Sch
 SN10 ....180 B4
Urchront Manor Coll
 SN10 ....180 B3
Urchront Way SN2 ....35 C4
Utah Cl SN1 ....49 F4
Utterson View SN15 ....78 C7
Uxbridge Rd SN5 ....49 A4

V

Vale Leaze SN15 ....44 C5
Vale Rd Pewsey SN9 ....215 B5
 Redlynch SP5 ....211 C7
Vale View SN4 ....47 D1
Vale View Rd SP2 ....130 B2
Valens Terr SN13 ....83 E6
Valentia Cl IE SN12 ....178 B8
Valiant Cl 9 SN4 ....178 B8
Valletta Gdns SN14 ....50 A6
Valley Cl SN1 ....211 C7
Valley Rd BA13 ....76 E1
Valley The SN2 ....145 C5
Valley View SN11 ....81 A2
Valley Way SN14 ....75 C6
Valleyside SN1 ....50 A4
Van Diemen's Cl SN8 .....213 E2
Vanbrugh Gate SN3 ....50 F1
Vanessa Ave SN1 ....146 D1
Vastern Wharf SN4 ....61 A7
Vasterne Cl SN4 ....33 B5
Vega Cl SN25 ....35 A4
Velley Hill SN13 ....85 C5
Venice Ct SP11 ....193 F2
Venn The 11 SP7 ....202 C2
Ventnor Cl SN2 ....34 E4
Ventry Cl 3 SP1 ....146 B2
Ventry The 4 SP1 ....146 B2
Verden Way 19 SP10 ......193 E2
Verney Cl SN3 ....51 D6
Vernham Dean Gullum's Prim
 Sch SP11 ....185 C3
Vernon Cl 3 SP4 ....217 E3
Verona Rd SP1 ....145 F4
Verulam Cl SN3 ....51 D8
Verwood Cl SN3 ....51 B4
Vespasian Cl SN3 ....51 B4
Vespasian Rd IE SP10 ....193 E2
Vicarage Cl Calne SN11 ...81 B3
 Marlborough SN8 ....213 E3
Vicarage Gdns 3 SN15 ....57 F6
Vicarage La
 Charlton SN16 ....29 B7
 Colerne SN14 ....75 C3
 Easterton SN10 ....179 F2
 Hankerton SN16 ....15 B5
 Highworth SN6 ....23 B2
 Steeple Ashton BA14 ....178 A3
 Upavon SN9 ....181 F2
Vicarage Mews SN13 ......116 F7
Vicarage Pk 1 SP5 ....211 C7
Vicarage Rd
 Salisbury SP1 ....211 E7
 Swindon SN2 ....34 F1
 Tisbury SP3 ....203 E8
Vice La SN13 ....212 E2
Victoria Cl
 Lyneham SN11 ....73 E8
 Swindon SN2 ....144 C4
Victoria Cross Rd SN4 ......63 F7
Victoria Cl SP1 ....146 A3
Victoria Dr SN15 ....60 B1

Victoria Gdns
14 Sandleheath SP6 . . . . . . .210 C1
Trowbridge BA14 . . . . .101 E2
Victoria Hospl SN1 . . . . . . .50 B4
Victoria Pk SN10 . . . . .187 B8
Victoria Rd
Devizes SN10 . . . . .214 B4
Frome BA11 . . . . .110 A4
Salisbury SP1 . . . . .146 A2
Sandleheath SP6 . . . . .210 C1
Swindon SN1 . . . . .50 C5
Trowbridge BA14 . . . . .101 E3
Victoria St SP7 . . . . .202 C2
Victoria Terr SN11 . . . . .81 B3
Victory Rd BA13 . . . . .108 C6
Vigo Inf Sch SP10 . . . . .193 F1
Viking Cl SN25 . . . . .34 F7
Viking Way
Andover SP10 . . . . .193 E2
Salisbury SP2 . . . . .152 B5
**Village Mus the Castle
Combe** * SN14 . . . . .68 A7
Village St SN8 . . . . .173 D1
Villiers Cl
Chippenham SN15 . . . . .78 F7
Lydiard Tregoze SN5 . . . . . . .48 F7
Vimoutiers Ct 12 SP6 . . . . . .210 D1
Vimy Cres 8 SN4 . . . . .198 E6
Vincent Cl SN12 . . . . .94 C4
Vincients Rd SN14 . . . . .69 F1
**Vincients Wood Nature
Reserve** * SN14 . . . . .77 F7
Viner's La GL9 . . . . .53 B5
Virginia Cl 1 SP4 . . . . .217 E3
Virginia Dr BA12 . . . . .116 E7
Viscount Way SN3 . . . . .36 C6
Vockins Cl SP9 . . . . .216 C8
Volpe Cl SN5 . . . . .48 F4
Volta Rd SN1 . . . . .50 C6
Vorda Rd SN6 . . . . .23 A7
Vowley View SN4 . . . . .47 F1
Voyager Dr SN25 . . . . .34 B7

W

Wade Hill SN6 . . . . .22 F5
Wadswick La SN13 . . . . .84 B3
Waggoner Cl SN25 . . . . .35 B6
Wagtail Cl SN3 . . . . .51 C8
Waiblingen Way SN10 . . . .214 A4
Wain-a-Long Rd SP1 . . . . .146 C1
Wains Way SN4 . . . . .47 E2
Wainwright Cl 3 SN1 . . . . . .51 D4
Wainwright Dr 5 BA11 . . . .110 C7
Waite Meads Cl SN5 . . . . . . .33 C4
Wakefield Cl
Kempsford GL7 . . . . .10 E6
Swindon SN5 . . . . .49 A4
Walbury Hill (Fort) *
RG17 . . . . .185 F8
Walcot Rd SN3 . . . . .50 E5
Walden Lodge Cl
SN10 . . . . .214 B2
Waldron Cl 8 SN3 . . . . .51 C4
Waleran Cl SP5 . . . . .153 E2
Walker Rd BA11 . . . . .110 A3
Walker's La 3 RG17 . . . . . .165 A2
Wallbridge BA11 . . . . .110 A4
Wallbridge Ave 2 BA11 . .110 A4
Wallbridge Mdws 1
BA11 . . . . .110 A4
Wallbridge Mills BA11 . . .110 A4
Waller Rd SN10 . . . . .214 E7
Wallingford Cl SN5 . . . . . . .49 C3
Wallingtons Rd RG17 . . . . .177 F4
Wallis Dr SN3 . . . . .35 A8
Wallsworth Rd 4 SN3 . . . . . .51 A4
Walmesley Chase
BA14 . . . . .102 A1
Walnut Cl
3 Netheravon SP4 . . . . . . .190 A4
Pewsey SN9 . . . . .215 D5
Rowde SN10 . . . . .96 D1
Sutton Veny BA12 . . . . . . .121 F8
Walnut Dr SN14 . . . . .74 F6
Walnut Gr BA14 . . . . .105 B6
Walnut Rd BA12 . . . . .139 B4
Walnut Tree Cl SN3 . . . . . . .36 B2
Walnut Tree Gdns SN5 . . . .48 D8
Walnut Trees Hill SN6 . . . .164 A8
Walnut Wlk 1 SN10 . . . . . .179 C8
Walronds Cl SN4 . . . . .170 C8
Walsingham Rd SN3 . . . . . . .50 F6
Walter Cl SN5 . . . . .49 A6
Walter Sutton Cl SN11 . . . . .80 F3
Walton Cl 3 SN3 . . . . .50 F4
Walwayne Ct Prim Sch
BA14 . . . . .102 A1
Walwayne Field SN2 . . . . . .36 A5
Walworth Rd SP10 . . . . . . .193 F1
Wanborough Prim Sch
SN4 . . . . .163 A6
Wanborough Rd
Swindon SN3 . . . . .36 C1
Swindon SN3 . . . . .51 F6
Wansdyke * SN11 . . . . . . .172 C5
Wansdyke Cty Prim Sch
SN10 . . . . .214 B1
Wansdyke Dr SN11 . . . . .81 A3
Wansdyke Rd SN8 . . . . . . .176 B4
Wansdyke St SN1 . . . . .50 C4
Wantage Rd SN4 . . . . .64 C5
Wantage Rd 8 RG17 . . . . .177 B6
War Meml Ave 8 RG17 . . .177 B6
Waram Cl RG17 . . . . .177 C8

Warbeck Gate 11 SN5 . . . . .48 F5
Warbler Cl 1 BA14 . . . . . . .105 B8
Warburton Cl BA14 . . . . . . .105 A6
Ward Cl SN3 . . . . .51 A4
Wardour Cl SN3 . . . . .51 A4
Wardour Ct SN3 . . . . .60 A2
Wardour Pl 4 SN12 . . . . .94 A2
Wardour RC Prim Sch
SP3 . . . . .203 C6
Wardour Rd 4 SN4 . . . . .78 A6
Wardrobe Mus * SP1 . . . .152 A8
Wareham Cl SN4 . . . . .49 B5
Wareleigh Dr BA1 . . . . .82 A3
Warleigh La BA1 . . . . .82 B1
Warmer's Inn La SN16 . . . . .27 D8
Warminster Ave 2 SN2 . . . .35 C5
Warminster Coll BA12 . . . .117 A7
Warminster Com Hospl
BA12 . . . . .117 A7
**Warminster Dewey
Musuem** * BA12 . . . . .117 B7
Warminster Prep Sch
BA12 . . . . .116 F7
Warminster Rd
Claverton BA2 . . . . .90 B4
Frome BA11 . . . . .110 B4
Westbury BA13 . . . . .108 F1
Wilton SP2 . . . . .144 D5
Warminster Sch BA12 . . . .117 C6
Warminster Sports Ctr
BA12 . . . . .117 D6
Warminster Sta BA12 . . . .117 A6
Warneage Gn 2 SN4 . . . . .163 A5
Warneford Cl 4 SN5 . . . . . . .49 D4
Warner Cl 2 SN3 . . . . .36 B3
Warren Cres SN11 . . . . .81 C4
Warren Rd BA14 . . . . .101 D5
Warrener Cl SN25 . . . . .35 B7
Warrens La SP5 . . . . .159 A4
Warwick Cl
Chippenham SN14 . . . . .77 F5
Salisbury SP1 . . . . .145 F3
Warwick Cres SN14 . . . . . . .24 A4
Warwick Rd SN1 . . . . .50 C5
Washbourne Rd SN4 . . . . . . .47 E1
Washern Cl SP2 . . . . .144 C1
Washers Pit * DT11 . . . . . .206 D3
Washington Rd BA13 . . . . .108 C6
Washmeres SN14 . . . . .75 B2
Waspool La GL7 . . . . .6 D8
Wason Rd 5 SP4 . . . . .197 E6
Wastfield SN13 . . . . .84 F8
Water Ditchampton
SP2 . . . . .144 C4
Water Field SN5 . . . . .49 A4
Water Furlongs 2 SN6 . . . . .19 D7
Water La
Castle Combe SN14 . . . . . . .68 A7
Enford SN9 . . . . .190 B6
Horningsham BA12 . . . . . . .119 A8
Salisbury SP2 . . . . .152 A8
Water Meadows SN16 . . . . .28 A2
Water St
Berwick St John SP7 . . . . . .203 E1
Durrington/Bulford SP4 . . . .217 D8
Mere BA12 . . . . .139 B5
Upton Lovell BA12 . . . . . . .194 A5
Watercrook Mews 2
SN5 . . . . .49 D5
Waterdown Cl 2 SN2 . . . . . .34 C4
Waterford Beck BA14 . . . . .104 F6
Watergate La SP4 . . . . .217 C2
Watergates SN13 . . . . .75 C3
Waterhouse La BA2 . . . . . . .98 F8
Waterloo Rd SP1 . . . . .152 C7
Watermead SN3 . . . . .36 C2
Watermeadow La
BA12 . . . . .195 C1
Watermint Way SN10 . . . . . .80 F4
Waters Bank Rd SN13 . . . . .108 A5
Waters Edge SN15 . . . . .78 E5
Waters Rd SP1 . . . . .146 A4
Waterside Pk Ind Est
SN1 . . . . .49 E8
Waterside Way SN3 . . . . . . .51 A1
Watersmeet Rd SP2 . . . . . .152 A4
Waterworks Rd BA14 . . . . .105 B7
Watery La
Donhead St Mary SP7 . . . . .203 A3
Shaftesbury SP7 . . . . .202 C1
Sutton Veny BA12 . . . . . . .117 F4
Watling Cl SN2 . . . . .49 E6
Watson Rd SP4 . . . . .197 E2
Watt Cl 4 SP10 . . . . .193 C1
Watt Rd SP2 . . . . .151 D8
Watt's Way 2 SN10 . . . . . .179 F1
Watts La SN14 . . . . .41 F1
Wavell Rd
Salisbury SP2 . . . . .152 A4
Swindon SN2 . . . . .35 B2
Tidworth SP9 . . . . .216 B8
Waverley Cl
7 Fordingbridge SP6 . . . . .210 D2
Frome BA11 . . . . .110 C6
Waverley Ct SN13 . . . . .85 A8
Waverley Gdns SN12 . . . . . . .94 A3
Waverley Rd
Fordingbridge SP6 . . . . . . .210 D2
Swindon SN3 . . . . .36 C1
Waylands Cricklade SN6 . . . .7 F1
Devizes SN10 . . . . .214 D3
Wayne Cl SN25 . . . . .35 A4
Wayside Cl
Frome BA11 . . . . .110 C6
Kington Langley SN15 . . . . . .70 E7
Swindon SN2 . . . . .35 F4
Weaveland Rd 2 SP3 . . . . .203 E8
Weavern Ct SN14 . . . . .76 A5
Weavern La SN13 . . . . .76 A5

Weavers Cl 3 SN16 . . . . . . .28 A5
Weavers Crofts SN12 . . . . . .94 A5
Weavers Dr BA14 . . . . .105 D7
Weavers La RG17 . . . . .177 E3
Weavers Mead SN10 . . . . . .179 C1
Weavers The SN3 . . . . .50 D4
Webb Cl SN15 . . . . .78 E5
Webbers Ct BA14 . . . . .105 A6
Webbington Rd SN15 . . . . . .78 E5
Webbs Ct SN15 . . . . .60 A3
Webbs Way
Burbage SN8 . . . . .183 D8
Malmesbury SN16 . . . . .28 A5
Webbs Wood SN5 . . . . .34 A2
Wedgewood Cl SN2 . . . . . . .50 A7
Wedmore Ave SN15 . . . . . . .70 C1
Wedmore Cl BA11 . . . . .110 C7
Weedon Rd SN3 . . . . .51 B8
Weeke Cl SN15 . . . . .210 F8
Weir Hayes 7 SN13 . . . . . . .76 B1
Weir La SN14 . . . . .74 A8
Weir The BA13 . . . . .186 C8
Weirside Ave SN4 . . . . .64 B6
Welbeck Cl SN3 . . . . .50 E5
Welcombe Ave SN3 . . . . . . .51 A5
Well Cl SN3 . . . . .70 C1
Well Cl SN4 . . . . .65 D4
Well House Cl SN3 . . . . . . .210 B6
Well La Godshill SP6 . . . . . .211 A1
Hawkesbury GL9 . . . . .38 C5
4 Shaftesbury SP7 . . . . . . .202 B2
Wele Sley Cl 18 SN12 . . . .178 B8
Weller Rd SN13 . . . . .76 F2
Wellhead Dro BA13 . . . . . . .109 A1
Wellhead La BA13 . . . . .109 A1
Wellington Dr
Bishops Cannings SN10 . . . .214 F7
Bower Hill SN12 . . . . .94 C1
Wellington Pl SN14 . . . . . . .55 F8
Wellington Rd
5 Durrington/Bulford
SP4 . . . . .198 F7
South Marston SN3 . . . . . . .36 C6
Wellington Sq SN12 . . . . . . .94 C1
Wellington St SN1 . . . . .50 C7
Wellington Way SP1 . . . . . .145 D3
Wellow Dr BA11 . . . . .110 C6
Wellow La BA2 . . . . .98 D1
Wellow Wood Rd
SO51 . . . . .212 F8
Wells Cl
Chippenham SN14 . . . . .78 A5
Durrington SP4 . . . . .198 A6
Wells St SN1 . . . . .50 C6
Welsh Way GL7 . . . . .1 D8
Welton Rd SN5 . . . . .49 A4
Wembley St SN2 . . . . .49 F8
Wenhill Hts SN11 . . . . .81 B2
Wenhill La SN11 . . . . .81 A1
Wensleydale Cl SN5 . . . . . . .49 A6
Wentworth Cl SN15 . . . . . . .78 F7
Wentworth Pk 1 SN5 . . . . . .49 A4
Were Cl 8 BA12 . . . . .116 E7
Werg SN8 . . . . .175 B8
Wesley Cl BA14 . . . . .104 E2
Wesley La BA14 . . . . .105 C7
Wesley St SN1 . . . . .50 C4
Wessex Cl Calne SN11 . . . .81 C3
2 Hungerford RG17 . . . . . .177 B7
Semington BA14 . . . . .94 B3
Wessex Ct BA12 . . . . .117 C6
Wessex Pl 2 RG17 . . . . . . .177 B7
Wessex Rd
Chippenham SN14 . . . . .78 B8
Salisbury SP1 . . . . .146 C1
Wilton SP2 . . . . .144 C1
Wessex Way SN6 . . . . .23 B7
Wessex Wlk BA13 . . . . .109 A4
Wessington Cl SN11 . . . . . . .81 C1
Wessington Ct SN11 . . . . . . .81 C1
Wessington Pk SN11 . . . . . . .81 C1
West Allcourt GL7 . . . . .2 C4
West Ashton CE Prim Sch
BA14 . . . . .105 E8
West Ashton Rd BA14 . . . . .105 E8
West Bourton Rd SP8 . . . . .137 E1
West Cepen Way
Chippenham SN14 . . . . .70 B3
Chippenham Without . . . . . .
. . . . .77 F5
West Ditch La BA14 . . . . . .106 E4
West End
Bishops Cannings SN10 . . . .172 B3
Melksham SN12 . . . . .94 A3
Westbury BA13 . . . . .109 A3
West End La
Bishopstone SN6 . . . . .163 E6
Donhead St Andrew SP7 . . .203 B2
West End Rd
Salisbury SP2 . . . . .145 E2
Swindon SN3 . . . . .36 A1
West Ennox La SN13 . . . . . .84 A6
West Hay Gr GL7 . . . . .4 F7
West Highland Rd
SN25 . . . . .34 B7
West Hill
Broad Blunsdon SN26 . . . . . .21 B2
Melksham Without SN12 . . . .93 F3
West Kennett Long Barrow *
SN8 . . . . .173 C6
West La Kemble GL7 . . . . . . .1 C3
Melbury Abbas SP7 . . . . . . .206 A7
West Manton SN8 . . . . .174 C7
West Mill La SN6 . . . . .8 C1
West Par BA12 . . . . .116 F6

West Pk
Appleshaw SP11 . . . . .192 E3
Rockbourne SP6 . . . . .210 A3
West Pk Dr SP6 . . . . .209 F3
West Pk La SP6 . . . . .209 F3
West Pk Rd SN13 . . . . .76 E1
West Portway SP10 . . . . . . .193 C1
West St Aldbourne SN8 . . . .170 A6
Barford St Martin SP3 . . . . .143 A4
Castle Combe SN14 . . . . . . .68 A7
22 Fordingbridge SP6 . . . . .210 D1
Great Somerford SN15 . . . . .43 F2
Great Wishford SP2 . . . . . .129 F4
Lacock SN15 . . . . .86 D5
4 Malmesbury SN16 . . . . . .28 A4
Salisbury SP2 . . . . .145 F1
Trowbridge BA14 . . . . .105 C8
Warminster BA12 . . . . .116 E6
Wilton SP2 . . . . .144 C3
West St Pl BA12 . . . . .116 E6
West Swindon Sh Ctr
SN5 . . . . .49 B5
West View
Everleigh SN8 . . . . .191 A8
Swindon SN3 . . . . .51 B7
West View Cres SN10 . . . . .214 A3
West View Rd BA1 . . . . .82 A3
West Way GL7 . . . . .2 C5
West Wilts Trading Est
BA13 . . . . .108 C7
West Wiltshire Craft Ctr *
BA13 . . . . .108 D6
West Wlk SP1 . . . . .152 A7
Westbourne Cl SP1 . . . . . . .152 C8
Westbourne Gdns 6
BA14 . . . . .105 B8
Westbourne Rd
Trowbridge BA14 . . . . .105 B8
Westbury BA13 . . . . .109 A3
Westbrook Cl
Chippenham SN14 . . . . .78 A7
3 Hungerford RG17 . . . . . .177 B7
Westbrook Grn SN15 . . . . . .95 E8
Westbrook Rd
Bromham SN15 . . . . .88 A1
Swindon SN2 . . . . .35 A1
Westbury CE Jun Sch
BA13 . . . . .108 F3
Westbury Com Hospl
BA13 . . . . .109 A2
Westbury Ind Est
BA13 . . . . .108 E1
Westbury Leigh BA13 . . . . .108 E1
Westbury Leigh CE Prim Sch
BA13 . . . . .108 E1
Westbury Pk SN4 . . . . .47 D1
Westbury Rd
Bratton BA13 . . . . .186 A7
Cheverell Magna SN10 . . . .179 C1
Heywood BA13 . . . . .109 E6
North Bradley BA14 . . . . . .105 A4
Swindon SN2 . . . . .35 B5
Warminster BA12 . . . . .113 A2
Westbury Sta BA13 . . . . . .108 E5
Westbury View SN12 . . . . . .94 C4
Westbury Visitor Ctr *
BA13 . . . . .109 A3
Westbury White Horse *
BA13 . . . . .186 E7
Westcombe La BA12 . . . . . .195 E1
Westcott Cl 9 BA11 . . . . . .110 C6
Westcott Pl SN1 . . . . .50 A5
Westcott St SN1 . . . . .50 A5
Westcroft SN14 . . . . .78 A5
Westcroft St SN14 . . . . .50 A5
Westerham Wlk SN11 . . . . . .81 C2
Westerleigh Cl SN14 . . . . . .78 B6
**Western Downland CE Prim
Sch** SP6 . . . . .210 A5
Western Downland Prim Sch
SP6 . . . . .209 F2
Western Way
Melksham SN12 . . . . .93 F3
Salisbury SP2 . . . . .145 B3
Westfield BA15 . . . . .100 B7
Westfield Chase 18 SN8 . . .170 A6
Westfield Cl
14 Durrington/Bulford
SP4 . . . . .198 B7
Laverstock SP1 . . . . .146 D2
Trowbridge BA14 . . . . .105 A6
Westfield Est BA14 . . . . . . .137 F4
Westfield Rd SN2 . . . . .34 D4
Westfield Way SN2 . . . . .34 D4
Westgrove 17 SP6 . . . . . . .210 D1
Westhill Cl SN6 . . . . .22 F5
Westlake Pl SN15 . . . . .57 D1
Westland Cl 3 SN4 . . . . . . .217 D3
Westlands 2 BA12 . . . . . . .194 C5
Westlands La SN12 . . . . .89 F2
Westlea Campus SN5 . . . . . .49 C5
Westlea Dr SN5 . . . . .49 C5
Westlea Prim Sch SN5 . . . . .49 A5
Westlecot Rd SN1 . . . . .50 B3
Westleigh BA12 . . . . .116 F6
Westmead Dr SN5 . . . . .49 D7
Westmead Cres BA14 . . . . .105 A4
Westmead La SN15 . . . . . . .78 D7
Westmead Terr SN15 . . . . . .78 D7
Westminster Gdns
SN14 . . . . .78 B7
Westminster Meml Hospl
SP7 . . . . .202 B1
Westminster Rd
Salisbury SP2 . . . . .145 F2

Westminster Rd continued
Swindon SN5 . . . . .49 B4
Westmorland Rd SN1 . . . . . .50 D5
Weston Cl 1 SP11 . . . . . . .193 E4
Weston La SP5 . . . . .149 B5
Westonbirt Arboretum *
GL8 . . . . .25 B8
Westonbirt Sch GL8 . . . . . .25 E8
Westpoint Bsns Pk
SN14 . . . . .70 A1
Westrop SN6 . . . . .22 F6
Westrop Prim Sch SN6 . . . .22 F6
Westside SP4 . . . . .199 A2
Westview Orch BA2 . . . . . . .99 B5
Westwells SN13 . . . . .84 B7
Westwells Rd SN13 . . . . . . .84 B7
Westwood Manor House *
BA15 . . . . .100 A3
Westwood Rd
Corsham SN13 . . . . .84 B8
Salisbury SP2 . . . . .145 B4
Swindon SN2 . . . . .35 C6
Wingfield BA15 . . . . .100 D2
Westwood St Thomas Sch
SP2 . . . . .145 A4
**Westwood with Iford Prim
Sch** BA15 . . . . .99 F3
Westwoods BA1 . . . . .82 B3
Wet La BA12 . . . . .139 D2
Wet Pits La SN8 . . . . .168 E3
Wetherby Cl 1 SN14 . . . . . .78 A5
Wexland Ave SP4 . . . . .189 F3
Wey Cl SN25 . . . . .35 A4
Weyhill Cl SN3 . . . . .51 B5
Weyhill Gdns 7 SP11 . . . . .192 F1
Weyhill Rd SP11 . . . . .193 A1
Weymouth St BA12 . . . . . . .117 A6
Whaddon La
Hilperton BA14 . . . . .102 B5
Trowbridge BA14 . . . . .102 A3
Whalley Cres SN4 . . . . .63 F6
Wharf Cl SN12 . . . . .94 B3
Wharf La Kempsford GL7 . .214 A4
Lechlade GL7 . . . . .2 D3
Wharf Rd SN4 . . . . .49 C1
Wharf St SN10 . . . . .214 A4
Wharf St SN13 . . . . .83 D6
Wharf Theatre & Ctr The
SN12 . . . . .94 B3
Warnings The GL7 . . . . .10 D6
Whatcombe Brow
SP3 . . . . .196 D8
Whatleys Cl SN10 . . . . .179 A4
Whatleys Orch SN6 . . . . . .163 E6
Wheatlands SN25 . . . . .34 E4
Wheatsheaf La SN16 . . . . . .16 A8
Wheeler Ave SN2 . . . . .51 E4
Wheeler Cl SN3 . . . . .25 B5
Wheelwright's Cl SP5 . . . . .208 A4
Whelford Rd GL7 . . . . .10 F2
Whilestone Way SN3 . . . . . .36 C1
Whinyates Rd 2 SP4 . . . . .197 E7
Whitbeck Rd SN10 . . . . . . .179 C8
Whitbourne Ave SN3 . . . . . .51 C5
Whitbred Cl 2 SN5 . . . . . . .49 B7
Whitbred Rd SN13 . . . . . . .145 C5
Whitby Gr SN2 . . . . .35 C3
Whitchers Meadow
SN6 . . . . .153 D4
Whitcombe Cl SN15 . . . . . . .73 F8
**White Barrow (Long
Barrow)** * SP3 . . . . .188 B1
White Beam Cl SN2 . . . . . . .35 B2
White Castle SN5 . . . . .49 A3
White Cliff * BA13 . . . . . . .186 B6
White Edge Moor SN2 . . . . .51 D2
White Ennox La SN13 . . . . . .83 F7
White Farm La SN8 . . . . . . .185 C2
White Hart La 12 SP7 . . . . .202 C1
White Hill
Bishopstone SN4 . . . . .163 D5
Pitton & Farley SP5 . . . . . . .148 C3
White Horse Bsns Pk
BA14 . . . . .105 D6
White Horse Cl BA14 . . . . .105 D6
White Horse Dr 8
BA11 . . . . .110 C6
White Horse Rd
Cricklade SN6 . . . . .19 D8
Swindon SN3 . . . . .36 A1
White Horse Sports Ctr
SN11 . . . . .81 C1
White Horse Way
Calne SN11 . . . . .81 B1
Westbury BA13 . . . . .109 A3
White Lion Pk SN16 . . . . . . .27 E4
White Pit La SP7 . . . . .206 B6
White Rd Mere BA12 . . . . . .139 B6
Savernake SN8 . . . . .175 A6
White Row Hill BA14 . . . . . .105 A4
White Sheet Castle *
BA12 . . . . .124 E1
**White Sheet Hill Nature
Reserve** * BA12 . . . . .124 E2
White Sheet La BA12 . . . . .124 C1
White Shute RG17 . . . . . . .171 A8
White St
Easterton SN10 . . . . .180 A1
Horningsham BA12 . . . . . . .119 B3
22 Market Lavington SN10 .179 F1
White Way
Broad Town SN4 . . . . .167 A4

White Way continued
Pitton & Farley SP5 ....148 C3
White's Hill SN8 ....169 F2
Whitebridge Rd SP1 ..196 D1
Whitecroft BA13 ....112 C8
Whitefriars La SN6 ......6 E3
Whitefield Cl SN1 ....82 B4
Whitefield Cres SN5 .....34 A1
Whitefriars La SN6 ......6 E3
Whitefriars Rd **1** SP1 ..152 B7
Whitegates SN4 ....48 A5
Whitehead St SN1 ....50 B5
Whiteheads La BA15 ....100 D7
Whitehill SN15 ....100 D7
Whitehill La SN4 ....47 B2
Whitehill Way SN5 ....48 F3
Whitehorn Cl SN4 ....47 E4
Whitehorn Dr SP5 ....212 C5
Whitehouse La GL8 ......26 B8
Whitehouse Rd SN2 .....50 B8
Whiteland Rise BA13 ...109 B2
Whitelands SN3 ....36 A1
Whitelands La BA14 ....106 F4
Whitelocks Piece
RG17 ....171 A1
Whiteman St SN2 ....50 C8
Whitemarsh BA12 ....139 B4
Whiterow Pk BA14 ......105 A6
Whites Cnr SN2 ....85 D1
Whitesbury Rd SP5 .....152 B1
Whitesheet CE Prim Sch
BA12 ....138 A4
Whitesheets Prim Sch
BA12 ....138 A4
Whiteshoot SP5 ....211 D6
Whiteshoot Hill SP5 ....211 D6
Whitestone Rd BA11 ...110 B6
Whitfield Cl BA12 ....117 C7
Whitgift Cl SN5 ....48 F6
Whitley Rd **14** SN8 .....170 A6
Whitlock Rise SP5 ......205 F5
Whitmarsh Cl **7** SP4 ..190 A4
Whitmore Cl SN1 ....148 C3
Whitney St SN1 ....50 C5
Whitsbury Rd SP6 ......210 D2
Whittington Rd SN5 ....49 C6
Whittle Ave SN11 ....166 A1
Whittle Cl SN14 ....78 A7
Whittle Rd
 Andover SP10 ....193 B3
 Salisbury SP2 ....145 D1
Whittonditch Rd SN8 ..170 C2
Whitworth Rd SN2 ......35 C3
Wichelstok Cl SN1 ......50 C5
Wick La Devizes SN10 ..214 B1
 Downton SP5 ....210 E8
 Lacock SN15 ....85 F4
 Manningford SN9 ......181 F5
 Wanborough SN4 ......51 F6
Wick Rd SN16 ....16 A4
Wickdown Ave SN25 ...34 F3
Wicker Hill BA14 ....101 C1
Wickfield SN10 ....214 B2
Wicks Cl SN15 ....34 E5
Wicks Dr SN15 ....78 F5
Wickwater La GL7 ......7 C4
Widbrook Meadow
BA14 ....105 A8
Widbrook View BA15 ..100 E5
Widhill La SN26 ....21 A1
Wigmore Ave SN3 ......50 F3
Wilcot Ave SN2 ....35 D5
Wilcot Cl
 Amesbury SP4 ....217 D2
 Trowbridge BA14 ......105 C6
Wilcot Rd SN9 ....215 B5
Wilcox Cl SN2 ....35 C2
Wild Acre **9** SN4 ....163 A6
Wildern Sq SN3 ....36 A4
Wilderness The BA15 ..100 C7
Wildmoorway La GL7 ..7 B7
Wiley Terr SP2 ....144 D4
Wilkins Cl SN2 ....35 F5
William Cl SP1 ....146 D1
William Rd SN10 ....214 D1
William Robbins Ct
SN25 ....34 F3
William St Calne SN11 ..81 C4
 Swindon SN1 ....50 A5
William Stumpes Cl **7**
SN16 ....28 A5
Williams Gr SN13 ......85 A8
Williamson Cl **3** SP11 ..192 A5
Willis Cl
 5 Chippenham SN15 ..78 F4
 Great Bedwyn SN8 ....176 C3
Willis Way SN5 ....33 B3
Willoughby Cl BA13 ...108 D6
Willoughby Rd SP4 ....197 E6
Willow Ave **5** SP6 ....210 D1
Willow Cl
 Laverstock SP1 ....146 D2
 Melksham SN12 ....94 A3
Willow Cres
 Broughton Gifford SN12 ..93 A5
 Warminster BA12 ......117 C5
Willow Dr
 Devizes SN10 ....214 E5
 4 Durrington SP4 ....198 B7
Willow Gr
 Chippenham SN15 .....70 E2
 Trowbridge BA14 ......105 B5
 Westbury BA13 ....108 A3
Willow View SN4 ....105 C3
Willow View Cl SN16 ...27 F4

Willow Way SP7 ....202 A4
Willow Wlk SN4 ....64 B6
Willowbank SN14 ....70 A1
Willowbrook SN15 .....33 C4
Willowbrook End SN15 ..37 C2
Willowherb Cl SN25 ...34 E5
Willows Ave SN2 ....35 C3
Willows The Calne SN11 ..39 E8
 Highworth SN6 ....23 A5
 Swindon SN5 ....34 A2
Wills Ave SN1 ....50 E8
Wilman Way SP2 ....151 F5
Wilsford Group (Tumuli)*
SP4 ....197 D2
Wilsford St SP2 ....197 D2
Wilson Rd Larkhill SP4 ..197 E6
 Swindon SN25 ....34 F6
Wilson Sq BA12 ....117 C7
Wilton Carpet Factory*
SP2 ....144 D4
Wilton CE Fst Sch
SP2 ....144 B4
Wilton CE Mid Sch
SP2 ....144 B4
Wilton Dr BA14 ....105 D6
Wilton Ho* SP2 ....144 D2
Wilton Pk* SP2 ....144 D1
Wilton Rd
 Barford St Martin SP3 ..143 C3
 East Grafton SN8 ......183 E4
 Quidhampton SP2 ....144 F3
 Salisbury SP2 ....201 F8
Wilton Sh Village SP2 ..144 E3
Wilton Windmill*
SN8 ....184 B8
Wilton Wlk SN2 ....35 C6
Wiltshire Ave SN2 .....50 A8
Wiltshire Cl
 Bulford SP4 ....217 F8
 3 Hungerford RG17 ..177 B7
Wiltshire Coll
 Calne SN11 ....81 B2
 Chippenham SN15 ....78 E8
 Chippenham SN15 ....78 E1
 Devizes SN10 ....214 B3
 Malmesbury SN16 ....28 A3
 Melksham SN12 ....94 A5
 Trowbridge BA14 ......105 C8
 Trowbridge BA14 ......105 C8
 Warminster BA12 .....117 A5
Wiltshire Cres SN12 ..94 C4
Wiltshire Dr **4** BA14 ..105 D6
Wiltshire Gall The*
SP1 ....145 F1
Wiltshire Heritage Mus*
SN10 ....214 A3
Wiltshire Music Ctr
BA15 ....100 B8
Wiltshire Rd SP2 ....151 E8
Wiltshire Way BA13 ...109 A4
Wimpole Cl SN3 ....51 B4
Win Gn View **7** SP7 ..202 D2
Winchester
 Amesbury SP4 ....217 D2
 2 Chippenham SN14 ..78 A6
 North Bradley BA14 ..105 C2
 Swindon SN3 ....36 B1
Winchester St SP1 ....146 B1
Windene Bsns Pk
SP7 ....202 C3
Wincombe La SP7 ......202 D2
Wincombe Pk* SP7 ....202 C3
Windbrook Meadow
SN2 ....36 A4
Windermere SN3 ....51 D3
Windermere Rd BA14 ..101 E2
Windflower Rd SN25 ..34 E5
Winding Way SP4 ......145 B3
Windlass Way SN5 .....78 E5
Windlesham Rd SP1 ..146 B4
Windmill Cl
 3 Aldbourne SN8 ....170 A7
 Alderbury SP5 ....153 E2
 4 Shaftesbury SP7 ..202 C2
Windmill Hill (Causewayed
Enclosure)* SN4 .....167 A2
Windmill Hill Bsns Pk
SN5 ....48 F3
Windmill Hill Prim Sch
SN5 ....49 A3
Windmill La
 Hurstbourne Tarrant
 SP11 ....193 F8
 Winterbourne SP4 ....133 B4
Windmill Piece SN4 ...65 D4
Windmill Rd GL7 ....4 F8
Windmill Tump (Long
Barrow)* GL7 ....3 A7
Windrush SN6 ....22 C7
Windrush Rd SN25 ....35 A3
Windsor Ave SN12 ....94 B3
Windsor Cl
 Chippenham SN14 ....78 A6
 Lydiard Tregoze SN4 ..47 F6
Windsor Cres BA11 ...110 A5
Windsor Dr
 Devizes SN10 ....214 D3
 1 Trowbridge BA14 ..105 B5
 Westbury BA13 ....109 B4
Windsor Mews **8** SP4 ..198 B7
Windsor Rd
 Calne Without SN11 ..81 C1
 9 Durrington/Bulford
 SP4 ....198 B7
 North Bradley BA14 ..105 E4
 9 Salisbury SP1 ....145 F1
 Swindon SN3 ....50 F2

Windsor St **10** SP2 .....145 F1
Windwhistle Cnr SP7 ..202 E2
Windwhistle La
 Alderbury SP5 ....160 B7
 Grimstead SP5 ....154 B1
Windwhistle Way SP5 ..153 F2
Wine St
 Bradford-on-Avon BA15 ..100 C6
 Devizes SN10 ....214 B3
Wing Rd SP4 ....198 E6
Wingate Par SN2 ....35 A2
Wingfield SN2 ....36 A5
Wingfield Ave SN2 ....35 C6
Wingfield CE Prim Sch
BA14 ....104 C6
Wingfield Rd BA14 ....105 A2
Winifred St SN1 ....50 D3
Winkelbury Hill (Hill Fort)*
SP7 ....207 C8
Winkins La SN15 ....44 A2
Winkworth Cottage
SN16 ....29 C2
Winlaw CE Prim Sch
SN16 ....29 C2
Winscombe Ct BA11 ..110 B5
Winsley CE Prim Sch
BA15 ....99 E1
Winsley Cl SN3 ....53 C4
Winsley Hill BA2 ....99 B6
Winsley Rd BA15 ......100 B7
Winstanley Cl **8** SN5 ..49 A4
Winston Rd SN12 ......93 F1
Winter Gn SN1 ....50 C4
Winterbourne Earls CE Prim
Sch SP4 ....133 A1
Winterbourne Stoke Group
(Tumuli)* SP4 ....197 C4
Winterslow CE Prim Sch
SP5 ....149 B6
Winterslow Rd
 Idmiston SP4 ....198 C1
 Porton SP4 ....133 D6
 Swindon SN3 ....35 B5
 2 Trowbridge BA14 ..105 A3
Winton Cl SP9 ....216 D4
Winton Rd SN3 ....36 A4
Winwick Rd SN5 ....49 B4
Wirr The SP3 ....128 D7
Wirral Way SN25 ....34 C4
Wise Cl SN2 ....35 E3
Wise La SP5 ....141 A2
Wiseman Cl **2** SN1 ...51 E6
Wishart Way SN15 ....34 C4
Wishford Rd SP2 ....144 B5
Witan Cl **8** SP1 ....193 E2
Witchcombe La SN10 ..179 B1
Witch Cl SN10 ....180 B3
Witfield Cl SN5 ....33 B5
Witham Way SP2 ......35 F4
Witherington Rd
 Alderbury SP5 ....153 C2
 Downton SP5 ....159 C7
Witherington Ring (Field
System)* SP5 ....159 D7
Withers The **8** SN4 ..164 A3
Withies The SN8 ....175 D1
Withy Bed SN4 ....61 C1
Withy Cl
 Trowbridge BA14 ......105 A8
 Wootton Bassett SN4 ..47 D3
 6 Bradford La RG17 ..177 F5
Withymead Rd SN14 ..74 A8
Witt Rd SP5 ....149 D5
Wittenham View **7** SP4 ..217 C2
Wittensford La SO51 ..212 F1
Witts La SN5 ....33 B5
Wivenhoe Ct **7** BA11 ..110 C4
Woburn Cl
 Swindon SN25 ....34 F6
 Trowbridge BA14 ......105 A4
Wolferton Dr SP1 .....146 D5
Wolfhall Rd SN8 ....183 D8
Wolsely Ave SN3 ......51 A4
Wolverton Cl SN14 ....77 F6
Wood H Dr SN2 ....17 F6
Wood La
 Brinkworth SN15 ......46 D7
 Chapmanslade BA13 ..111 A4
 Chippenham SN15 ....78 E6
 Fonthill Gifford SP3 ..200 C2
 Lydiard Millicent SN5 ..32 A1
 Nettleton SN14 ....47 C8
 Purton SN5 ....31 E1
 Sherston GL8 ....25 B5
Wood Rd SP4 ....198 A6
Wood St Calne SN11 ..81 B3
 Clyffe Pypard SN4 ....61 D1
 Swindon SN1 ....50 D4
 Wootton Bassett SN4 ..47 D2
Woodborough CE Aided Prim
Sch SN9 ....181 D4
Woodborough Cl
BA14 ....105 D5
Woodborough Rd
 Beechingstoke SN9 ..181 B6
 Corsham SN13 ....85 B7
 Pewsey SN9 ....215 A5
Woodbury RG17 ....165 B1
Woodbury Cl SP3 .....49 A8
Woodbury Gdns SP2 ..152 A5
Woodchester SN5 .....49 C5
Woodcock Cl SP9 .....216 D6
Woodcock Gdns BA12 ..117 C6
Woodcock Ind Est
BA12 ....117 C7
Woodcock La BA12 ...117 B8
Woodcock Pk BA12 ...117 C6
Woodcock Rd BA12 ...117 C6
Woodcombe SN12 ....94 C6

Woodcote Rd SN8 ....185 B8
Woodcutters Mews
SN25 ....35 C6
Woodfern SP6 ....210 F1
Woodfolds SN16 ....15 F7
Woodford Cl **3** SN2 ..35 C6
Woodford Valley CE Prim Sch
SP4 ....131 C5
Woodhayes Rd BA11 ..110 C6
Woodhenge* SP4 .....217 A7
Woodhill Ave SN11 ...81 C3
Woodhill Dr SN4 ....166 E7
Woodhill Rise SN11 ..81 C4
Woodhill Village*
SN4 ....166 D8
Woodhouse Castle (rems
of)* BA12 ....114 E1
Woodhouse Gdns
BA14 ....102 B2
Woodhouse Rd **3** SN3 ..50 F5
Woodland Dr SP9 .....216 B6
Woodland Heritage Ctr The*
BA13 ....107 F5
Woodland Ind Est
BA11 ....108 F2
Woodland Pk SN11 ...81 B2
Woodland Rd
 Patney SN10 ....180 F5
 2 Warminster BA12 ..116 E6
Woodland View
 Westbury BA13 ....112 B8
 Swindon SN4 ....50 B1
Woodland Way
 Devizes SN10 ....214 A1
 Salisbury SP1 ....146 E2
Woodlands SN13 ......76 E2
Woodlands Bglws SN14 ..78 B7
Woodlands Dr SP7 ....203 E1
Woodlands Manor*
BA12 ....139 A3
Woodlands Prim Sch
SP2 ....145 B4
Woodlands Rd
 Chippenham SN14 ....78 C8
 Mere BA12 ....43 D7
 Mildenhall SN8 ....169 A1
 Pewsey SN9 ....215 D4
Woodlands Rd Ind Est
BA12 ....139 B4
Woodlands The BA12 ..113 A1
Woodlea SN14 ....75 C6
Woodlea Grange SP5 ..213 E1
Woodling Cres SP6 ..210 F1
Woodman Mead **5**
BA12 ....116 F7
Woodmarsh BA14 ....105 D4
Woodpecker Mews
SN14 ....70 B2
Woodroffe Sq SN11 ..81 C2
Woodrow Rd SN12 ...94 D7
Woodrow Rd SN12 ...94 C6
Woods Cl SN16 ....29 F6
Woodsage Way SN11 ..80 F3
Woods's La SP3 ....200 F2
Woodshaw Mead **8** SN4 ..48 A2
Woodside Ave SN3 ...50 E5
Woodside Rd
 Salisbury SP1 ....145 C3
 South Marston SN3 ..36 C7
Woodsman Rd SN5 ...35 B6
Woodstock Gdns SN12 ..94 B3
Woodstock Rd SP1 ...146 B2
Woodvill Rd SP1 ......146 D4
Woodway Cotts GL9 ..24 E5
Woolands La **1** SP7 ..202 B2
Woolcott La SP8 ......137 D1
Wooley Dr BA15 ....100 E7
Woolford Grange **2** SN4 ..48 A2
Woollaton Cl SN5 .....49 A5
Woolley Cl BA15 ......100 E7
Woolley Cl BA15 ......100 E7
Woolley St BA15 ......100 E6
Woolley Terr BA15 ...100 E6
Woolmer Dro SN8 ....168 F6
Woolpack Meadows
BA14 ....105 C4
Wootton Bassett Inf Sch
SN4 ....47 C1
Wootton Bassett Mus*
SN4 ....47 D1
Wootton Bassett Rd
SN5 ....49 E5
Wootton Bassett Sch
SN4 ....47 D3
Wor Barrow (Long Barrow)*
SP5 ....208 C4
Worcester Lodge*
GL9 ....24 A3
Wordsworth Cl **1** SN4 ..47 F3
Wordsworth Dr SN2 ..35 F3
Wordsworth Rd SP1 ..146 B2
Worksley Dr SN5 ......49 A4
Worsted Cl SN4 ....105 E7
Wortheys Cl SN16 ....28 A5
Worton & Marston Prim Sch
SN10 ....179 B4
Worton Rd SN10 ......179 D4
Wouldham Cl SP11 ...191 F4
Wren Cl Frome BA11 ..110 B7
 3 Warminster BA12 ..116 E5
Wren Ct BA14 ....105 B8
Wrenscroft SP2 ....152 A5
Wrenswood SN3 ......51 D8
Wroughton Airfield
SN4 ....63 F2

Wroughton Inf Sch
SN4 ....64 A6
Wroughton Jun Sch
SN4 ....64 A7
Wroughton Science
Museum* SN3 ....64 B1
Wych Elm Rd BA11 ...110 C6
Wychurch Rd **4** SN16 ..28 A5
Wyck Village* SP3 ....203 E7
Wycombe Cl SN1 ......79 F2
Wycombe La SN10 ...172 F1
Wye Rd BA14 ....101 E4
Wyld Ct SN25 ....34 E8
Wyle Down National Nature
Reserve* BA12 ....201 E7
Wylye Cl Swindon SN25 ..34 F4
 Warminster BA12 ....116 F5
Wylye Rd
 Steeple Langford SP3 ..128 B7
 Tidworth SP9 ....216 D7
 Warminster BA12 .....117 A5
 Wylye BA12 ....201 F8
Wyncies The SN6 .....163 E6
Wynd The SN11 ....81 B4
Wyndham Cl SN5 .....79 A8
Wyndham La SN4 ....199 A2
Wyndham Pk SP1 ....146 B2
Wyndham Pk Inf Sch
SP1 ....146 B3
Wyndham Rd
 Salisbury SP1 ....146 A2
 Swindon SN2 ....50 A7
Wyndham Terr SP1 ..146 B2
Wynford Rd BA11 .....110 B6
Wynndale Cl SN3 .....36 A4
Wynsome St BA14 ...104 F3
Wynwards Rd SN25 ..35 A5
Wythburn Rd BA11 ..110 C5
Wyver Coll SN8 ....213 E1
Wyvern Ave SN11 ....81 C3
Wyvern Cl SN1 ....50 C3
Wyvern Coll SP1 ......146 E3
Wyvern Rd
 Bowerhill SN12 ....94 D1
 Durrington/Bulford SP4 ..198 B7
Wyvern Theatre & Arts Ctr*
SN1 ....50 C6
Wyvern Wlk BA13 ....108 E3
Wyville Rd BA11 ....110 C5

Y

Yard Ct BA12 ....117 B6
Yard La SN15 ....96 D7
Yard's La SN9 ....181 C5
Yardley Cl SN2 ....34 F2
Yarmley La SP5 ....149 B6
Yarmouth Cl SN5 .....49 B4
Yarnbrook Rd
 Steeple Ashton BA14 ..102 E1
 West Ashton BA14 ...105 F2
Yarnbury Castle (Fort)*
BA12 ....196 B3
Yarnton Cl SN3 ....49 A8
Yarrow Cl SN2 ....34 C3
Yatton Rd SN14 ....68 E1
Yeatmans Cl **6** SP7 ..202 B2
Yeatmans La **3** SP7 ..202 B2
Yeats Cl SN25 ....35 A8
Yellow Way Rd BA11 ..118 A5
Yellowhammer Cl SN3 ..51 C5
Yeoman Cl
 5 Market Lavington SN10 ..179 F1
 Swindon SN5 ....49 A7
Yeoman Way BA14 ...105 C2
Yeovil Cl SN3 ....51 B9
Yerbury St **1** BA14 ..105 E8
Yew Tree Cl Calne SN11 ..81 A3
 Chirton SN10 ....180 F4
 The Common SP5 ....149 B6
Yew Tree Gdns SN3 ..36 E4
Yew Tree La SN4 .....167 C7
Yews The BA12 ....139 A6
Yewstock Cres W SN15 ..70 C1
Yewtree Cl **8** SP4 ...198 C7
Yiewsley Cres SN3 ...36 B2
Yockney Cl SN13 .....76 E1
Yonder Way **7** SN4 ..163 A6
York Bldgs BA14 .....101 D1
York Cl
 Chippenham SN14 ...78 A6
 Corsham SN13 ....76 F2
York Dro SP5 ....212 C4
York La SN4 ....46 A7
York Rd
 7 Hungerford RG17 ..177 B6
 Lyneham SN15 ....60 B2
 Salisbury SP2 ....145 F1
 Stapleford SP3 ....197 B1
 Swindon SN1 ....50 D6
 Upavon Down SN9 ..182 B3
Youngs Paddock SP5 ..149 C6
Yule Hill SP3 ....203 F6

Z

Zakopane Rd SN25 ..34 D6
Zander Rd SN1 ....81 B5
Zeals Gn Dr BA12 ...138 A4
Zeals Rise BA12 ......137 F4
Zig Zag Hill SP7 ......206 C5
Zion Rd SP1 ....199 F3
Zouch Ave SP9 ....216 C2
Zouch Cl SP9 ....216 C2
Zouch Farm Rd SP9 ..216 C2
Zouch Prim Sch SP9 ..216 B6

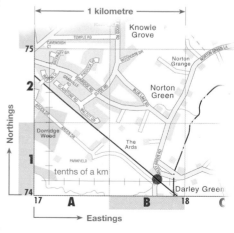

NG NH NJ NK
NM NN NO NP
NR NS NT NU
NX NY NZ
SC SD SE TA
SH SJ SK TF TG
SM SN SO SP TL TM
SR SS ST SU TQ TR
SW SX SY SZ TV

Using the Ordnance Survey National Grid

Any feature in this atlas can be given a unique reference to help you find the same feature on other Ordnance Survey maps of the area, or to help someone else locate you if they do not have a Street Atlas.

The grid squares in this atlas match the Ordnance Survey National Grid and are at 500 metre intervals. The small figures at the bottom and sides of every other grid line are the National Grid kilometre values (**00** to **99** km) and are repeated across the country every 100 km (see left).

To give a unique National Grid reference you need to locate where in the country you are. The country is divided into 100 km squares with each square given a unique two-letter reference. Use the administrative map to determine in which 100 km square a particular page of this atlas falls.

The bold letters and numbers between each grid line (**A** to **F**, **1** to **8**) are for use within a specific Street Atlas only, and when used with the page number, are a convenient way of referencing these grid squares.

Example The railway bridge over DARLEY GREEN RD in grid square B1

Step 1: Identify the two-letter reference, in this example the page is in **SP**

Step 2: Identify the 1 km square in which the railway bridge falls. Use the figures in the southwest corner of this square: Eastings **17**, Northings **74**. This gives a unique reference: **SP 17 74**, accurate to 1 km.

Step 3: To give a more precise reference accurate to 100 m you need to estimate how many tenths along and how many tenths up this 1 km square the feature is (to help with this the 1 km square is divided into four 500 m squares). This makes the bridge about **8** tenths along and about **1** tenth up from the southwest corner.

This gives a unique reference: **SP 178 741**, accurate to 100 m.

Eastings (read from left to right along the bottom) come before Northings (read from bottom to top). If you have trouble remembering say to yourself "Along the hall, THEN up the stairs"!

PHILIP'S MAPS
the Gold Standard for drivers

◆ **Philip's street atlases cover every county in England, Wales, Northern Ireland and much of Scotland**

◆ Every named street is shown, including alleys, lanes and walkways

◆ Thousands of additional features marked: stations, public buildings, car parks, places of interest

◆ Route-planning maps to get you close to your destination

◆ Postcodes on the maps and in the index

◆ Widely used by the emergency services, transport companies and local authorities

BEST BUY • BEST BUY **Auto EXPRESS** *BEST BUY • BEST BUY*

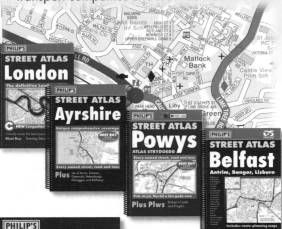

PHILIP'S NAVIGATOR Britain
'The ultimate in UK mapping'
The Sunday Times

For national mapping, choose **Philip's Navigator Britain** the most detailed road atlas available of England, Wales and Scotland. Hailed by Auto Express as 'the ultimate road atlas', the atlas shows every road and lane in Britain.

Street atlases currently available

England
Bedfordshire and Luton
Berkshire
Birmingham and West Midlands
Bristol and Bath
Buckinghamshire and Milton Keynes
Cambridgeshire and Peterborough
Cheshire
Cornwall
Cumbria
Derbyshire
Devon
Dorset
County Durham and Teesside
Essex
North Essex
South Essex
Gloucestershire and Bristol
Hampshire
North Hampshire
South Hampshire
Herefordshire Monmouthshire
Hertfordshire
Isle of Wight
Kent
East Kent
West Kent
Lancashire
Leicestershire and Rutland
Lincolnshire
Liverpool and Merseyside
London
Greater Manchester
Norfolk
Northamptonshire
Northumberland
Nottinghamshire
Oxfordshire
Shropshire
Somerset
Staffordshire
Suffolk
Surrey
East Sussex
West Sussex
Tyne and Wear
Warwickshire and Coventry
Wiltshire and Swindon
Worcestershire
East Yorkshire Northern Lincolnshire
North Yorkshire
South Yorkshire
West Yorkshire

Wales
Anglesey, Conwy and Gwynedd
Cardiff, Swansea and The Valleys
Carmarthenshire, Pembrokeshire and Swansea
Ceredigion and South Gwynedd
Denbighshire, Flintshire, Wrexham
Herefordshire Monmouthshire
Powys

Scotland
Aberdeenshire
Ayrshire
Dumfries and Galloway
Edinburgh and East Central Scotland
Fife and Tayside
Glasgow and West Central Scotland
Inverness and Moray
Lanarkshire
Scottish Borders

Northern Ireland
County Antrim and County Londonderry
County Armagh and County Down
Belfast
County Tyrone and County Fermanagh

How to order
Philip's maps and atlases are available from bookshops, motorway services and petrol stations. You can order dire from the publisher by phoning **0207 531 8473** or online at **www.philips-maps.co.uk**
For bulk orders only, e-mail philips@philips-maps.co.uk